PROFESSIONAL RESPONSIBILITY

PROBLEMS, CASES, AND MATERIALS

Fourth Edition

■ ■ ■

By

James R. Devine

Associate Dean and Professor of Law
University of Missouri–Columbia
[Deceased]

William B. Fisch

Professor of Law Emeritus
University of Missouri–Columbia

Stephen D. Easton

Dean and Professor of Law
University of Wyoming College of Law

AMERICAN CASEBOOK SERIES®

WEST®
A Thomson Reuters business

Mat #40787423

COPYRIGHT © 1985, 1995 WEST PUBLISHING CO.
© 2004 West, a Thomson business
© 2013 Thomson Reuters

    610 Opperman Drive
    St. Paul, MN 55123
    1–800–313–9378

Printed in the United States of America

ISBN: 978–0–314–90885–8

In memory of Jim Devine,
a great lawyer, teacher, scholar,
colleague, friend, husband, and father.
Law students, lawyers, and their clients
lost a great friend with his departure.

William B. Fisch and Stephen D. Easton

PREFACE TO THE FOURTH EDITION

It is with a heavy heart, but a renewed sense of purpose, that we present this new edition. Both the heavy heart and the renewed sense of purpose result from the loss of our dear friend, Jim Devine, shortly after we started work on this edition.

Jim loved lawyers and lawyering, and his interest in Professional Responsibility stemmed from an intense fascination with the realities of legal practice and the many ethical issues lawyers and judges inevitably face. He believed in the high standards that the organized profession seeks to articulate and to which most lawyers try their best to adhere, and saw the teaching of Professional Responsibility as a crucial opportunity to help future attorneys not only learn primary values but also begin to understand the concrete and sometimes counterintuitive complexities of the rules they will be expected to follow.

Joining the University of Missouri law faculty in 1980 following several years of successful practice in New Jersey, Jim immediately put his passion and experience—which included service on the ethics committee of his county bar—to work in teaching a section of Professional Responsibility and in helping to develop problem-oriented teaching materials. He was a man of many passions, including Civil Procedure, Sports Law, and sports in general (swimming in particular), but much of his academic zeal was reserved for this field. This casebook, which began in the 1970s as a set of handout problems for Fisch's use in the course, would not have grown to a more complete package of teaching materials and then to full fruition as a published coursebook without his dedication to the subject, to his students, and to the practice of law. Particularly in subsequent editions, he took the lead in planning and organizing our efforts.

Missing our leader, completion of the Fourth Edition has taken a bit longer than we hoped and planned, but we have had the advantage of Jim's many suggestions as well his full revised draft of Chapter 2.

This edition is a bit longer than the Third Edition, which was neither as long as the first, nor as short as the second. It continues our purpose of introducing students to the law of lawyering, with a focus on the practical but also an eye to the theoretical underpinnings behind the Model Rules. It remains our view that professional responsibility involves not only the Model Rules, the assorted state versions of these rules, the RESTATEMENT OF THE LAW GOVERNING LAWYERS, statutes, cases, and advisory opinions, but also concepts of morality, ethics, etiquette, competence, and education. Discussion of all is encouraged throughout the book.

Reflecting the work of the ABA's Ethics 2000 Commission, this edition focuses primarily on the ABA Model Rules of Professional Conduct adopted after 2002, including those adopted in the summer, 2003, in response to the federal Sarbanes–Oxley Act. It reflects the changes to the Model Rules enacted by the ABA after the previous edition, especially the changes allowing possible curing of conflicts of interest from an attorney's previous work at another firm via notice and screening. It also reflects the 2007 revision to the ABA Model Code of Judicial Conduct, another new development since the publication of the Third Edition. While there are never any certainties when multiple authors are involved, we believe the book references virtually all of the current Model Rules of Professional Conduct as well as almost all of the Code of Judicial Conduct.

As in prior editions, however, the rules need context. As a result, students are introduced to rules, the RESTATEMENT, cases, advisory opinions, statutes, constitutional provisions, and other materials by problem situations that lawyers might face. Each problem is followed by readings and notes designed to help students solve the questions following the problems. Some of the notes raise further, related issues. In this edition, notes are generally titled and numbered for ease of reference.

Chapter 1, *Pervasive Issues*, attempts to provide context to all of the material. The first problem raises issues of personal morality as well as questions about the adversary system, etiquette between lawyers, and professional responsibility. The readings are selected to provide a definition of "ethics" for all of the material that follows. The readings in this chapter can often be used later in the semester for philosophical foundation to some of the more difficult rules.

Chapter 2, *The Legal Profession and the Practice of Law*, considers the legal profession as an institution, its relation to the various branches of government, and the processes of admission and discipline.

Chapter 3, *The Attorney–Client Relationship*, examines how lawyers attract clients through advertising and solicitation, the several ways in which the attorney-client relationship is established, the mutual rights and obligations of the parties (including malpractice and the fee relationship), and termination of the relationship.

Chapters 4 and 5, *Confidentiality* and *Conflicts of Interest*, deal with two of the most important dimensions of the lawyer's duty of loyalty to the client. The duty of confidentiality protects against voluntary disclosure of information acquired by the lawyer during the representation. Conflict of interest rules focus on the avoidance of situations creating competing loyalties for the lawyer to the potential detriment of a particular client. The conflict of interest chapter contains analogous material regarding judicial disqualification and recusal.

Chapter 6, *Particular Lawyer Roles and Responsibilities*, discusses problems specific to certain roles of the lawyer, many of which bring into play additional rules or procedures governing the lawyer's conduct. The role of advocate, for example, involves the relationship between Federal Rule of Civil Procedure 11 and ethics rules relating to "frivolous claims." The roles of both prosecutor and criminal defense attorney often involve specific constitutional rights, as well as rules of ethics. Included in the concerns of any advocate, and timely in today's legal world, are the constitutional and ethical issues of fair trial and free press. The chapter also reviews roles outside traditional advocacy in litigation, including the lawyer as counselor, advisor, evaluator, and participant in alternative dispute resolution. This chapter explores the lawyer as judge, focusing primarily on judicial elections and trial conduct, then concludes with a brief consideration of the lawyer as human being.

As in prior editions, each problem is followed by one or more references to the Model Rules of Professional Conduct and/or the Code of Judicial Conduct. Because the states seem to be somewhat slower in adopting new versions of the Judicial Code than in implementing ABA-proposed changes to the Model Rules, we have adopted the practice of referencing the previous (pre–2007) version of the Judicial Code. As in the Third Edition, we have also included references to the American Law Institute's RESTATEMENT (SECOND) OF THE LAW GOVERNING LAWYERS.

In editing materials cited in the text, we used the following conventions. First, when quoting, we have generally followed the format found in the material being quoted, with occasional minor formatting changes to keep the readings relatively consistent. Other modifications of the original material are indicated by [bracketed phrases or letters]. Where the only modification is deletion of material in the original, we have inserted three asterisks, i.e., * * *. A [bracketed phrase or letter] or * * * may, therefore, indicate a deletion of any length. Absent unusual circumstances, you will not see * * * next to a [bracketed phrase or letter], because the latter indicates a change, possibly including a deletion of material. We have not inserted * * * when the only deletion from the original is a footnote, because it is assumed that most footnotes are not included in this text. When a footnote found in the original is included in this text, we have retained the number from the original. When we added a footnote, we used small letters (i.e., a, b, c, etc.). In many instances, when a principal case or article cites a state-specific or outdated version of a Model Rule (or of another provision), we have made a [bracketed] change to the citation, to cite the latest version.

This book is primarily designed for a three credit hour course in Professional Responsibility or Legal Ethics. We believe that the entire book can be covered in such a course, though we admit that this goal requires the instructor and the students to pick up the pace in certain areas. In a two credit hour course, Chapters 1–5 can comfortably be covered, with some pruning, probably in Chapter 2 (Unauthorized Practice?) or Chapter 3. In a four credit hour course, instructors can add state cases, statutes, and variations to the current rules for a very comfortable course.

WILLIAM B. FISCH
STEPHEN D. EASTON

August 2012

ACKNOWLEDGMENTS

As was the case with the first three editions, we salute our consumers. We are indebted to our students at the University of Missouri–Columbia and the University of Wyoming. Not only have they let us know which problems and questions work and which do not, but they have also given us specific and very helpful editorial suggestions that have avoided many errors and caused many improvements. Particularly in working drafts of this edition, our students have been marvelous at pointing out our errors.

A number of people helped in preparation of this book, and we are grateful to each of them. Several research assistants read, commented on, and did citation checking on these materials. No law students should be required to read as much professional responsibility material as have Mike Gleason, Jason Johnson, Jennifer Kirk, Rocio Ocano, Katie Osten, David Singleton, Sean Smith, and Nora Wheeler. Vonnie Jenkin, Lisa Nunley, and especially Christine Michel of the University of Wyoming College of Law contributed many hours of service to the creation of this edition. The incomparable Marivern Easton added her usual sharp proofreading eye, as well as repeated efforts to talk one of the authors off the inevitable ledge of casebook authorship.

We wish to express our appreciation for permission to reprint all or portions of the following copyrighted materials:

The following material from the **American Bar Association**. Reprinted by permission. Copies of ABA *Model Rules of Professional Conduct* are available from Service Center, American Bar Association, 321 North Clark Street, Chicago, IL 60654, 1–800–285–2211:

  ABA Commission on Billable Hours, Report (2001–2002)

  ABA Model Rules of Professional Conduct, Rule 7.2(b) Comment [6]

  ABA Standards for Imposing Lawyer Sanctions, Standard 4.1 (1986)

  Commission on Evaluation of Professional Standards, Proposed Model Rules of Professional Conduct, Rules 8.1 (Discussion Draft 1980)

  Committee on Ethics and Professional Responsibility, Formal Opinions 92–362, 93–379, 97–409, 06–439, and 09–455.

American Law Institute, RESTATEMENT (THIRD) OF THE LAW GOVERNING LAWYERS, §§ 35 (Comment e).

James J. Alfini, *Settlement Ethics and Lawyering in ADR Proceedings: A Proposal to Revise Rule 4.1*, 19 Northern Illinois Law Review 255 (1999).

Robert H. Aronson, *Professional Responsibility: Education and Enforcement*, 51 Washington Law Review 273 (1976). Reprinted with the permission of the Fred B. Rothman Company.

Barbara Allen Babcock, *Defending the Guilty*, 32 Cleveland State Law Review 175 (1983–1984).

William C. Becker, *The Client Retention Agreement—The Engagement Letter*, 23 Akron Law Review 323 (1990).

Ryan Brett Bell and Paula Odysseos, *Sex Drugs and Court TV? How America's Increasing Interest in Trial Publicity Impacts our Lawyers and the Legal System*, 15 Georgetown Journal of Legal Ethics 653 (2002). Reprinted with permission of the publisher, Georgetown Journal of Legal Ethics © 2002.

Alberto Bernabe–Riefkohl, *Silence is Golden: The * * * Rules on Attorney Extrajudicial Speech*, 13 Loyola University Chicago Law Journal 323 (2002).

Gabriel J. Chin, *Making* Padilla *Practical: Defense Counsel and Collateral Consequences at Guilty Plea*, 54 Howard Law Journal 675 (2011).

Collin Croft, *Reconceptualizing American Legal Professionalism: A Proposal for Deliberative Moral Community*, 67 New York University Law Review 1256 (1992).

Morris Dees, *Remember Me to My Clients*, April, 1990 TRIAL. Reprinted with permission of TRIAL (April, 1990). Copyright American Association for Justice, formerly Association of Trial Lawyers of America (ATLA®).

James R. Devine, *Minnesota's Togstad Decision: Expanding the Ethical Responsibility of All Lawyers*, 38 Journal of the Missouri Bar 40 (1982).

Stephen D. Easton, *My Last Lecture: Unsolicited Advice for Future (and Current) Lawyers*, 56 South Carolina Law Review 229 (2004).

Stephen Gillers, Regulation of Lawyers: Problems of Law and Ethics (4th ed. 1995). Copyright Little, Brown and Company and Stephen Gillers.

David E. Johnson, Jr., Trust and Business Accounting for Attorneys (1986 & 2006). Copyright David E. Johnson.

John Lande & Forrest S. Mosten, *Before You Take a Collaborative Law Case: What the Ethical Rules Say About Conflicts of Interest, Client Screening, and Informed Consent*, Family Advocate, Fall 2010, at 31.

Robert P. Lawry, *Cross-Examining the Truthful Witness: The Ideal Within the Central Moral Tradition of Lawyering*, 100 Dickinson Law Review 563 (1996).

Norman Lefstein, *Client Perjury in Criminal Cases: Still in Search of an Answer*, 1 Georgetown Journal of Legal Ethics 521 (1988). Reprinted with the permission of the publisher. Copyright © 1988 by Georgetown University and Norman Lefstein.

Scott R. Peppet, *The (New) Ethics of Collaborative Law*, Dispute Resolution Magazine, Winter 2008, at 23.

Deborah Rhode, Professional Responsibility: Ethics by the Pervasive Method (1994). Copyright Little, Brown and Company and Deborah L. Rhode.

Thomas L. Shaffer, *The Unique, Novel, and Unsound Adversary Ethic*, 41 Vanderbilt Law Review 697 (1988). Copyright Vanderbilt Law Review.

Marjorie P. Slaughter, *Lawyers and the Media: The Right to Speak Versus the Duty to Remain Silent*, 11 Georgetown Journal of Legal Ethics 89 (1997). Reprinted with permission of the publisher, Georgetown Journal of Legal Ethics © 1997.

William H. Simon, *Ethical Discretion in Lawyering*, 101 Harvard Law Review 1083 (1993). Copyright © 1993 by the Harvard Law Review Association.

Antone G. Singsen, III, *Competition in Personal Legal Services*, 2 Georgetown Journal of Legal Ethics 21 (1988). Reprinted with the permission of the publisher, Georgetown Journal of Legal Ethics © 1988.

Timothy P. Terrell & James H. Wildman, *Rethinking "Professionalism,"* 41 Emory Law Journal 403 (1992). Copyright Emory Law Journal, James H. Wildman, Timothy P. Terrell.

Richard Wasserstrom, *Lawyers as Professionals: Some Moral Issues*, 5 Human Rights 1 (1975).

8 Wigmore on Evidence sec. 2292 (McNaughton rev. ed. 1961). Copyright © Little, Brown and Company.

Charles W. Wolfram, Modern Legal Ethics § 4.1 at 146–47 (West, 1986). Reprinted with permission of West Publishing Company.

WILLIAM B. FISCH

STEPHEN D. EASTON

September, 2012

SUMMARY OF CONTENTS

TABLE OF CONTENTS

―――――

TABLE OF CASES

The principal cases are in bold type. Cases cited or discussed in the text are in roman type. References are to pages. Cases cited in principal cases and within other quoted materials are not included.

TABLE OF MODEL RULES OF PROFESSIONAL CONDUCT

TABLE OF CODE OF JUDICIAL CONDUCT

TABLE OF RESTATEMENT (THIRD) OF THE LAW GOVERNING LAWYERS

TABLE OF ABA STANDARDS AND FORMAL OPINIONS

PROFESSIONAL RESPONSIBILITY
PROBLEMS, CASES, AND MATERIALS

Fourth Edition

CHAPTER 1

PERVASIVE ISSUES

■ ■ ■

INTRODUCTION

The readings and notes in this chapter reflect persistent questions about the profession we have chosen. They are questions which are of particular concern to law students wanting to know just what sort of calling they are taking up. Law school courses all too frequently gloss over them, perhaps because no clear answers are at hand or because the respectability of the entire enterprise seems to be in question. These questions will, however, be central to this course. No endorsement of particular answers is intended, nor even a claim that generally applicable answers to all of the questions can be given. Our modest aim, without pretense of completeness, is rather to legitimize the questions, and to provide an entry into the rather substantial, and growing, body of critical literature about the legal profession.

We introduce these readings, as we do each section of the book, with a problem designed to illustrate a practical setting in which the issues are raised. This first problem raises issues similar to that of the principal case that follows.

The readings in this chapter will introduce you to the legal profession and the Model Rules of Professional Conduct that govern it. They will also introduce you to some of the philosophical underpinnings for the Model Rules. Many of the issues raised in this chapter will recur in the same or slightly different form in subsequent chapters. They therefore form something of a theme to the course.

PROBLEM

You represent the defendant employer in an employment discrimination suit brought in state court by Joseph Salina, his wife Sara, and his son James, each of whom is employed by the defendant. They claim that the defendant denied them promotions, raises, and preferred job assignments because of their Hispanic ancestry. The judge granted your motion to dismiss for failure to state a claim. The judge made his decision solely on the basis of a novel interpretation of the applicable statute, an interpretation you had not argued and which is probably inconsistent with a prior decision of the state supreme court. Counsel for the Salinas makes clear his intention to appeal, and you are persuaded that the trial judge's rationale will not stand, though you remain persuaded that your theory for your motion to dismiss is still arguable. Shortly thereafter you learn that Joseph Salina died of natural causes.

Counsel for the Salinas now files his notice of appeal, with four days to spare in the appeal period. You see immediately that the notice of appeal carries the caption "Joseph Salina, et al.," and that the body of the notice simply refers to "the plaintiffs." You are aware that the state court of appeals, relying on a state supreme court interpretation of the applicable procedural rules, will treat this failure to name each party individually as jurisdictional with respect to the unnamed parties and will dismiss the appeal as to those parties on its own motion, but not until after the appeal period has expired. You explain the error to your client on the day that you receive the notice, including the fact that for the next four days the Salinas' counsel can amend the notice to correct the error. You advise your client that there is a good chance that the appeal would be successful on the merits, so that you would have to go to trial on the wife's and son's claims. Your client looks at you with a frown and says: "I know you lawyers stick together and all that, but don't even think about talking to the other guy! We'll just see how smart he is!"

QUESTION

What, if anything, should you do? After answering this question to yourself now, before you have read any law in this area, please continue to consider this question as you review the materials below. Do these materials help you decide what to do?

RULE REFERENCES

Model Rules of Professional Conduct [hereinafter "Model Rules"] Preamble, Scope, and Rules 1.0 and 1.2

SPRUNG v. NEGWER MATERIALS, INC.

Supreme Court of Missouri, En Banc, 1989.
775 S.W.2d 97.

[On December 27, 1984, attorney Godfrey Padberg filed a civil suit for damages on behalf of plaintiff Melvin James Sprung, Jr. for damages Sprung sustained when a cart that was rented from the Defendant tipped over, dumping drywall on him. The defendant was served with the summons and complaint on January 11, 1985 and delivered them to its insurance company, which sent them on to the Kortenhof and Ely law firm. A lawyer at Kortenhof and Ely had prepared an entry of appearance and request for extension of time to answer. Unfortunately, a secretary at the law firm sent all of the documents to the insurance company and none to the court. The law firm had in place several systems for checking on pending actions, but none of them alerted the firm to the fact that no pleadings had actually been filed in the action.

On February 28, 1985, after receiving no responsive pleading or motion, the plaintiff's attorney moved for entry of default and obtained a proof hearing date of March 11, 1985. On March 11, plaintiff's attorney put on evidence of plaintiff's damages and plaintiff was awarded judgment against defendant in the amount of $1,500,000. Under Missouri procedure as it existed at the time, this judgment would likely have been set aside if defendant's attorney had filed a motion by April 11, 1985.

Defendant's attorney, who was unaware that no responsive pleading had been filed with the court, prepared an answer and requests for discovery on March 23, 1985 and mailed a copy to plaintiff's counsel.

The response of plaintiff's counsel to this motion is taken from a dissenting opinion:

> I called him [Sprung, plaintiff] to tell him that within the 30 day period there had been an answer filed and he asked me what that meant and I said, "I don't really know what they mean by this, but there is an attorney now who thinks that it's still a lawsuit," and that's what I told him.
>
> Q So it appeared to you that Mr. Ely was filing an answer and had no realization that there had already been a default judgment?
>
> A That's correct.
>
> Q And you passed that information on to Mr. Sprung?
>
> A Right.
>
> Kortenhof and Ely ... may have been responsible for the default.... But I said you know, "I could talk to him about it and find out if they're involved. If they're involved, they'll file a motion to set it aside." I said, "If the insurance company's involved and they're not involved, they're still going to file a motion to set it aside," and that was basically it and he said, "Well, what will that mean to me?" I said, "There's a chance you can lose your verdict (sic)," and he said, "Don't do it."

Plaintiff's counsel did not do anything and later further testified:

> So after the 30 day period I waited until 10 more days, which would be the normal appeal time and sometime after that, maybe the 41st, 42nd, depending on what day of the week it was, I don't recall, I called Ben on the phone and said, "Ben, I'd like to come down and see you," and he said, "Okay." And I came on downstairs and talked to him.

After defendant's attorney learned that a final judgment had been entered, the attorney filed, on defendant's behalf, two motions to set aside the default judgment. The trial court granted one of the motions, but that decision was reversed on appeal. In *Sprung v. Negwer Materials, Inc.*, 727 S.W.2d 883 (Mo. 1987) (en banc) (*Sprung I*), the Missouri Supreme Court affirmed the denial of the motions to set aside the default judgment, but remanded the case for an evidentiary hearing on whether the actions of plaintiff's counsel would support a separate action in equity to set aside the final judgment by default. Following that hearing, the trial court denied relief to the defendant. That denial was then appealed.

This case (*Sprung II*) was finally decided with one principal opinion, three concurring opinions, and three dissenting opinions. Presented here is a portion of the principal opinion and one of the dissenting opinions from *Sprung I*, one of the concurring opinions in *Sprung II*, and one of the dissenting opinions in *Sprung II*.]

BILLINGS, JUDGE * * *

In its first point, appellant claims the trial court erred in refusing to set aside the default judgment on equitable grounds. In order for one to prevail in setting aside a default judgment on equitable grounds, he must show a meritorious defense, good reason or excuse for the default and that no injustice will accrue to the party who obtained the default judgment as a result of setting aside the judgment. [The court found that both the law firm and the insurance company had safeguards in place to prevent matters like this one from being ignored, but that all of these systems apparently failed in this case.]

The law is well-settled that the neglect of a defendant's attorney or his insurer which results in a default judgment is imputable to the defendant. * * *

A lawyer is charged during the progress of a cause with the duty, and in fact presumed, to know what is going on in his case. * * * He must vigilantly follow the progress of a case in which he is involved. * * * And, although the law favors a trial on the merits, such a generalization must be carefully applied to the facts of each case in the interest of justice; for, the law defends with equal vigor the integrity of the legal process and procedural rules and, thus, does not sanction the disregard thereof. * * *

In its second point, appellant claims the failure of respondent's attorney to advise appellant's attorney that a default judgment had been entered until after its entry provides a basis for setting aside the judgment.

[The court affirmed prior holdings refusing to recognize a duty of the respondent to notify the appellant of the entry of default in the underlying action.]

In *Friedman v. The Caring Group, Inc.*, 750 S.W.2d 102, 103–04 (Mo.Ct.App. 1988), the issue of the conduct of a plaintiff's attorney as to the entry of a default judgment was squarely before the appellate court. The court refused to hold that the failure of plaintiff's attorney to notify defendant's attorney, who had entered his appearance in the case but [had] not filed an answer, that plaintiff's attorney intended to take a default judgment provided a basis for setting aside the judgment. In the present case, respondent's attorney did not know that appellant was represented by an attorney until after the default judgment was entered. The Court concludes plaintiff's attorney had no duty to inform the defendant or its attorney that a judgment had been entered. * * *

The judgment of the trial court [refusing to set aside the judgment of $1,500,000] is affirmed.

[CONCURRING AND DISSENTING OPINIONS]

[DONNELLY, J., dissenting from *Sprung I*, 727 S.W.2d at 893–94]

Given the holding in *Bates and [Van] O'Steen v. State Bar of Arizona*, 433 U.S. 350, 97 S.Ct. 2691, 53 L.Ed.2d 810 (1977) [the first case granting First Amendment protection to advertising by lawyers], it may border on the ridiculous to speak of the practice of law as a profession and not a business.

However, being somewhat old-fashioned, I must express the view that a lawyer does not inevitably violate his obligation to seek the lawful objectives of his client when he treats opposing counsel with courtesy and consideration. * * *

In this case, attorney for plaintiff took a default judgment in the amount of $1,500,000 on March 11, 1985. He was on notice of facts indicating the neglect of opposing counsel on March 29, 1985, when discovery motions were filed but was instructed by his client "to protect his judgment." On April 22, 1985, after time had run under [the procedural rule], he advised opposing counsel of the default judgment. On May 3, 1985, motions to set aside the default judgment were filed. * * * The trial court, in its discretion set aside the default judgment and, in my view, corrected what must be considered a miscarriage of justice. * * *

If I may conclude with a personal observation:

Judges at times become so enamored of jargon in codes of "professional" responsibility that they forget what it was like to practice law. Here, the attorney for plaintiff was directed by his client to conceal the taking of the default judgment from his brother lawyer. What was he to do in such circumstance? Should he have invited the wrath of his client and risked a claim of malpractice? Had he acted as a professional and not as a hired representative who did solely the bidding of his client, would/could this Court have protected him?

Of course, the equity due *the parties*, not the attorneys, is at issue here. And it was plaintiff Sprung who insisted on concealment and gained the advantage. In my view, equity demands that we * * * require the parties to resolve their controversy by a trial on the merits.

I respectfully dissent.

[BLACKMAR, C.J., dissenting in *Sprung II*, 775 S.W.2d at 106–13]

Plaintiff's counsel's own testimony shows that he was perfectly well aware of what had happened when he received communications from defendant's counsel on March 23 and March 29, 1985. He knew that counsel was proceeding with the defense of the case, on the mistaken assumption that it was properly pending, and that the extension papers must not have reached him or the courthouse. He knew that if defense counsel were alerted, the default judgment would probably be set aside as of course. * * * He also knew that if the situation remained the same until April 10 had passed, the default would be infinitely more difficult to set aside. Knowing these circumstances, he deliberately refrained from answering his mail, or even from acknowledging the communication. His conduct should shock all right-thinking lawyers.

The Court should not hesitate to say that this kind of conduct is unacceptable in our profession. The processing of civil litigation requires that lawyers deal with each other in accordance with the highest standards of trust and candor. The two communications called for a response within a reasonable time, which in the setting of this case means "without delay." Perhaps counsel did not have a duty to tell his opponent in so many words that he had taken a default, but at the very least he could dictate a letter saying, "we have no record of your firm's involvement in the case."

I accept the proposition that a lawyer has a duty to advance his client's interest by all honorable means, and would reject any suggestion that "professional courtesy" should prevail over the lawyer's duty to his client. I would like to be remembered as a lawyer who went all out for his clients. But I would stop short of taking advantage of a mistake known to me. Nor would I sanction a situation in which the Court permits other lawyers to get away with conduct which I consider the legal equivalent of fraud. * * * This Court, in the last analysis, sets the standards which Missouri lawyers must observe. It should not allow this plaintiff and his attorney to profit from deceptive conduct or deceptive silence.

In one of the earliest treatises on legal ethics the late Judge George Sharswood, sometime Chief Justice of Pennsylvania, speaks as follows:

> Let [the reader] shun most carefully the reputation of a **sharp** practitioner. Let him be liberal to the slips and oversights of his opponent whenever he can do so, and in plain cases not shelter himself behind the instructions of his client. The client has no right to require him to be illiberal—and he should throw up his brief sooner than do what revolts against his own sense of what is demanded by honor and propriety.

Sharswood, *An Essay on Professional Ethics*, 73–74 (6th Ed. 1930).

We should require lawyers to comply with this standard, not only as a matter of professional courtesy, but as a positive rule of law. Here there was a duty to reply to the correspondence, and, since there was a critical limit, to make some sort of response within that time limit. Lying in wait until the response was stripped of its meaning should not be countenanced. * * *

It is interesting to consider what plaintiff's counsel would have done if defense counsel had called him on the telephone seeking to arrange a time for depositions. I hardly think that he could properly have agreed on a date, without advising counsel that he had taken a default. * * * This example differs only in degree and not in kind from the actual situation before us.

It has been suggested, unfortunately, that plaintiff's counsel was justified in doing as he did because his client might have sued him for malpractice. We should certainly take this occasion to say so all can hear that communications between opposing counsel are a part of the normal practice of law, essential in the orderly handling of litigation, and that a lawyer cannot subject himself to malpractice liability by acting honorably toward his forensic opponents. * * *

I would vacate the default judgment and remand so that the case may proceed to trial.

[RENDLEN, J., concurring in *Sprung II*, 775 S.W.2d at 103]

When, during the course of this litigation, respondent's attorney received information indicating appellant was represented by counsel, he promptly communicated this fact to his client as required by [the Preamble to the Rules].

It was the attorney's responsibility as an *advisor* of his client in our adversary system to do what he did * * *.

He was, of course, more than an advisor—he was an advocate:

> As *advocate*, a lawyer zealously asserts the client's position under the rules of the *adversary system*.

[Preamble to the Rules] (Emphasis added.)

After communicating with the client and explaining the situation in explicit terms, they shared the decision as to the course of action to follow, all consistent with the provisions of Rule 1.2 * * * which indicates that, except in certain specified instances, an attorney shall abide by the client's decisions concerning the objectives of representation. Though in the case at bar we need not decide whether he was obligated absolutely to follow the client's direction, it is clear that plaintiff's counsel made a good faith, albeit difficult, decision which we cannot say was unethical. Assuming arguendo respondent's counsel had chosen to disregard his client's direction and the judgment had been vacated at his behest, or as a result of his conduct, clearly he would risk a charge of failing to comply with an obligation imposed by the Rules of Professional Conduct, to say nothing of malpractice claims by his client that could flow from the formidable choice he was required to make.

For these reasons too, I concur in the majority opinion of the Court.

A. FORMAL PROFESSIONAL RULES

Several of the opinions in *Sprung* mention either the Model Rules of Professional Conduct (the Model Rules) or the Model Code of Professional Responsibility (the Code). These are formal standards of conduct for lawyers, proposed at different times by the American Bar Association for adoption by state and federal lawyer disciplinary jurisdictions. The opinions of Judges Blackmar and Rendlen in particular seem to suggest such rules might be in conflict with what a lawyer should do under the circumstances of that case. The next excerpt offers a critical review of the development, purposes, and effects of those rules.

COLIN CROFT, RECONCEPTUALIZING AMERICAN LEGAL PROFESSIONALISM: A PROPOSAL FOR DELIBERATIVE MORAL COMMUNITY

67 New York University Law Review 1256 (1992).

* * * *The Evolution of Professional Codes of Conduct*

Frustrated republican-influenced practitioners[a] sought a universal code of conduct as early as the first quarter of the eighteenth century. Through most of the 1800s, however, informal sanctioning and socialization of local legal practice norms appeared to serve the ends sought by proponents of such a code, through enforcement by localized groups of practitioners and the apprenticeship system. By the early twentieth century, such methods increasingly were perceived as inadequate, as the bar underwent the transformation to organizational practice * * *. Drawing primarily upon the work of republican-minded lawyers like George Sharswood, and to a lesser extent David Hoffman, the ABA adopted its Canons of Professional Ethics (Canons) in 1908. Adoption by state bar associations and judicial decisions interpreting the Canons soon followed. By 1920, all but thirteen states and the District of Columbia had adopted the Canons in some form, and the ABA Committee on Professional Ethics and Grievances was beginning to receive requests for interpretation.

* * * The [Sharswood/Hoffman-influenced] Canons were, in voice, "fraternal admonitions"—norms issuing from an autonomous professional society. As such, they presumed widely understood and approved practice norms resting upon the traditional tenets of noblesse oblige—a conceptualization of legal practice as an elite craft, practiced independently, with a commitment to civic-political affairs. Although largely hortatory, the Canons did address proper ethical conduct in specific practice situations. * * *

Initially, the Canons functioned not as an enforceable legal code, but rather as collective "evidence" that certain assumed practice norms existed. This evidence was gradually transformed into an enforceable legal code by the creation of integrated state bars, increased disciplinary enforce-

---

a. ["Republican" is used here in its democracy, rather than political party, sense. Eds.]

ment with higher penalties enforced by courts, and an evolution of the Canons' general norms into more specific, binding legal rules through periodic interpretation. The increased issuance, and eventual publication, of formal and informal ethics opinions by the Standing Committee on Professional Ethics, * * * had the effect of clarifying and narrowing the general precepts set forth in the Canons. * * * Like a constitution, the Canons were interpreted as required, creating an organic and evolving body of norms to meet the changing needs and contexts of legal practice.

Ultimately, an increased need for clarification, as well as the uncertainty of what the Canons actually represented, convinced many members of the bar that the Canons were hopelessly outdated and outmoded; no longer were they assumed to stand as "evidence" of the professional norms that had been thought to exist at the time of the Canons' initial adoption. By 1965, an ABA Special Committee on Evaluation of Ethical Standards, created to study and report on the adequacy and effectiveness of the Canons, reported that "the existing Canons are in need of substantial revision." The Committee emphasized the need for "sharpening and clarification" of the Canons' standards to "facilitate more effective disciplinary action and . . . increase significantly the level of voluntary compliance." Rather than modify the existing Canons, however, the Committee decided that it was necessary to draft a new code. By 1968, a tentative draft had been produced, and after distribution to lawyers, judges, and scholars, a second draft was completed in 1969. On August 12, 1969, the ABA House of Delegates unanimously passed a final draft of the new code.

The new Model Code of Professional Responsibility (Model Code) was innovative in form, although substantively it broke little new ground, essentially restating the 1908 Canons and the numerous informal and formal ABA opinions interpreting them. However, the split from the Canons in voice and form was significant. Unlike the 1908 Canons and the Model Code's Canons and Ethical Considerations, which represented "fraternal understandings that memorialized a shared group discourse," the new Model Code's set of Disciplinary Rules "functioned as a statute defining the legal contours of a vocation whose practitioners were connected primarily by having been licensed to practice law." Thus, a step was made down the path of "legalization" of professional norms, articulated as narrow rules and prohibitions statutorily drawn.

Most states quickly adopted the Model Code, and federal courts recognized it as a set of enforceable legal standards in overseeing the conduct of federal litigators. However, motivated by an effort to augment the profession's image in the wake of Watergate, as well as to reinforce the primacy of the ABA as "lawgiver for the practice of law," in the summer of 1977 a new ABA Commission on Evaluation of Professional Standards was appointed to evaluate the still infant Model Code. Six years of discussion, debate, and drafting ensued, due in large part to the personal leadership of Committee Chair Robert J. Kutak of Omaha. After significant reversals and substantive changes from the early Kutak Commission drafts, in 1983 the ABA House of Delegates adopted the Model

Rules of Professional Conduct (Model Rules) which supplanted the Code after less than fourteen years of strained existence. * * *

In form, the Model Rules abandoned the three-tiered structure of the Model Code in favor of a restatement format, in which brief, straightforward Rules are augmented by explanatory Comments. Kutak succeeded in his purpose: simplified presentation of clear standards, and reconciliation of the profession's practice norms with the substantive law of agency, contract, and torts. The end result, however, raised the question of whether a professional code that merely followed existing legal mandates properly could be understood as a "code of ethics," and not merely as a glorified legal practice handbook.

In any event, the Model Rules represent a further step toward legalistic, rule-based professional standards in the law. Unlike the 1908 Canons or the 1969 Model Code's Canons and Ethical Considerations, the Model Rules largely "eschew descriptions of morals ... root(ing) out both the language and the discipline of ethical reasoning." As such, the Model Rules "are not ethics but instead (are) a set of regulatory mandates and prohibitions." The Model Rules supplant professional obligations with legal mandates, moving away from the profession's norms toward an uninspired scheme of bureaucratic regulation, intentionally established, rather than organically derived. * * *

NOTES ON PROFESSIONAL RULES

1. **Ethics 2000 Commission:** The ABA continues to review and revise its Model Rules, which have been adopted by the majority of American disciplinary authorities, but with a greater degree of variance in particular rules than was the case with the Model Code of Professional Responsibility. In 1997, the ABA appointed the "Ethics 2000 Commission" to study the Model Rules and propose amendments where appropriate. Most of the extensive recommendations of that body were adopted by the House of Delegates of the American Bar Association in February and August, 2002, took effect at the beginning of 2003, and serve as the basis for the current version of the Model Rules. As a cursory reading of the Model Rules reveals, some rules require certain lawyer conduct, while others permit conduct or allow exceptions to otherwise required conduct. The rules are both "partly obligatory and disciplinary and partly constitutive and descriptive in that they define a lawyer's professional role." Model Rules Scope ¶ [14]. Many states have revised their rules to incorporate some of the Ethics 2000 amendments, though the states almost always modify the Model Rules to some extent.

The Model Rules continue to evolve. The ABA has enacted a few additional amendments to the Model Rules since its adoption of the Ethics 2000 Commission proposals in 2002. In 2009, ABA President Carolyn B. Lamm created the ABA Commission on Ethics 20/20, which is tasked with reviewing the Model Rules in light of advancing technology and the globalization of legal practice. Many observers expect the Ethics 20/20 process to result in further amendment of the Model Rules. *See* Bruce A. Green, *ABA Ethics Reform from "MDP" to "20/20": Some Cautionary Reflections*, 2009 ABA J.Prof.Law. 1, at

2; James Podgers, *Stage Two: Ethics 20/20 Sharpens Its Ideas on Technology, Globalization*, ABA J., January 2011, at 62. The Commission's work, including discussion drafts and proposals, can be followed at www.abanet.org/ethics 2020.

2. **American Law Institute RESTATEMENT:** Shortly after the adoption of the Model Rules, in about 1985, the American Law Institute began work on the RESTATEMENT OF THE LAW GOVERNING LAWYERS. The RESTATEMENT, which was completed and published in 2000, provides guidance beyond the scope of the Model Rules, covering the formation of the lawyer-client relationship, civil liability of lawyers to clients and third parties, and attorney-client privilege in the law of evidence, among others. The RESTATEMENT draws not only on the texts of adopted rules but also on judicial decisions and other interpretations, and states the Institute's own position on issues where consensus is lacking in the various American jurisdictions. As a result, its provisions are sometimes slightly different from those in the Model Rules. *See* AMERICAN LAW INSTITUTE, RESTATEMENT (THIRD) OF THE LAW GOVERNING LAWYERS Foreword (2000) (hereinafter "RESTATEMENT"). The provisions of the RESTATEMENT are not binding on courts, although courts generally find the RESTATEMENT influential in dealing with lawyer conduct. *See Chem–Age Ind., Inc. v. Glover*, 2002 SD 122, ¶ 33, 652 N.W.2d 756, 770.

3. **Ethics Opinions:** Croft mentions publication of "formal and informal ethics opinions." In the United States, ethics opinions are published not only by the American Bar Association, mentioned by Croft, but also by state, county, and, in some cases, local bar associations. Additionally, some specialized bar associations, such as the patent bar, offer ethics opinions. Finally, many state disciplinary authorities will provide either formal or informal opinions to lawyers upon request. *See* Peter A. Joy, *Making Ethics Opinions Meaningful: Toward More Effective Regulation of Lawyers' Conduct*, 15 Geo.J. Legal Ethics 313, 320 (2002). Because many questions faced by lawyers do not have a specific answer within the formal rules of professional conduct, ethics opinions provide guidance to lawyers with ethical dilemmas. In addition, "lawyers acting in conformity with ethics opinions also receive explicit or customary protection from discipline in many jurisdictions." *See id.* at 330. While not even the opinions of ethics committees within the same disciplinary system are binding on courts, recent studies have found that "federal and state courts rely on published state and local * * * ethics opinions as a source of guidance with increasing frequency." *Id.* at 340.

4. Consider Model Rule 1.6 in relation to our problem. Is the information you learned—that the notice of appeal contains a potentially fatal clerical error, and that your client insists on taking advantage of it—"information relating to the representation" within the meaning of that Model Rule? If you agree that it almost certainly is, is there an exception within Model Rule 1.6 that authorizes you to reveal to your adversary the nature of the problem?

5. Next consider Model Rule 1.2(a). At this stage, you may assume that the "objectives of representation" include the remedies the client wants from the case. If the lawyer "shall abide by" the client's decision regarding the objectives, how would the lawyer ever be able to inform the other side about a procedural defect without the client's permission? If, instead, you assume that

whether or not to advise adversary counsel is an issue of the "means" whereby the client's objectives are accomplished, can the lawyer ever choose means that substantively disadvantage the client?

6.   If the decision to not tell the adversary, thereby allowing the client to win, relates to the objectives of the representation, and if you cannot reveal such information because there are no exceptions to confidentiality, is Chief Judge Blackmar, in *Sprung*, arguing that counsel should ignore the rules when he states: "[A] lawyer cannot subject himself to malpractice liability by acting honorably toward his forensic opponents"?

7.   How would not doing anything about the mistake square with your own conscience? What does it say about the relationship between you and your client if you simply accept his command? Would you accept such conduct from a nonlawyer layperson?

8.   Given your skills as an advocate, if you really wanted to, do you think you could talk your client into letting you do something about the error? Is that what the dissenting judges in *Sprung* want you to do?

The next reading may help in your consideration of these questions.

B.   CRITICISM OF THE LAWYER'S "TRADITIONAL" ROLE

The lawyer in *Sprung* acted in accordance with what many perceive to be the lawyer's "traditional" role, also called the "amoral" role, which is understood to require the lawyer to pursue the client's goals without regard to the personal morality of those goals. The next reading and the notes following it discuss this tradition.

RICHARD WASSERSTROM, LAWYERS AS PROFESSIONALS: SOME MORAL ISSUES
5 Human Rights 1 (1975).

In this paper I examine two moral criticisms of lawyers which, if well-founded, are fundamental. Neither is new but each appears to apply with particular force today. Both tend to be made by those not in the mainstream of the legal profession and to be rejected by those who are in it. Both in some sense concern the lawyer-client relationship.

The first criticism centers around the lawyer's stance toward the world at large. The accusation is that the lawyer-client relationship renders the lawyer at best systematically amoral and at worst more than occasionally immoral in his or her dealings with the rest of mankind.

The second criticism focuses upon the relationship between the lawyer and the client. Here the charge is that it is the lawyer-client relationship which is morally objectionable because it is a relationship in which the lawyer dominates and in which the lawyer typically, and perhaps inevitably, treats the client in both an impersonal and a paternalistic fashion.

To a considerable degree these two criticisms of lawyers derive, I believe, from the fact that the lawyer is a professional. And to the extent to which this is the case, the more generic problems I will be exploring are those of professionalism generally. But in some respects, the lawyer's situation is different from that of other professionals. The lawyer is vulnerable to some moral criticism that does not readily or as easily attach to any other professional. And this, too, is an issue that I shall be examining. * * *

Conventional wisdom has it that where the attorney-client relationship exists, the point of view of the attorney is properly different—and appreciably so—from that which would be appropriate in the absence of the attorney-client relationship. For where the attorney-client relationship exists, it is often appropriate and many times even obligatory for the attorney to do things that, all other things being equal, an ordinary person need not, and should not do. What is characteristic of this role of a lawyer is the lawyer's required indifference to a wide variety of ends and consequences that in other contexts would be of undeniable moral significance. Once a lawyer represents a client, the lawyer has a duty to make his or her expertise fully available in the realization of the end sought by the client, irrespective, for the most part, of the moral worth to which the end will be put or the character of the client who seeks to utilize it. Provided that the end sought is not illegal, the lawyer is, in essence, an amoral technician whose peculiar skills and knowledge in respect to the law are available to those with whom the relationship of client is established. The question, as I have indicated, is whether this particular and pervasive feature of professionalism is itself justifiable. * * *

Most clients come to lawyers to get the lawyers to help them do things that they could not easily do without the assistance provided by the lawyer's special competence. They wish, for instance, to dispose of their property in a certain way at death. They wish to contract for the purchase or sale of a house or a business. They wish to set up a corporation which will manufacture and market a new product. They wish to minimize their income taxes. And so on. In each case, they need the assistance of the professional, the lawyer, for he or she alone has the special skill which will make it possible for the client to achieve the desired result.

And in each case, the role-differentiated character of the lawyer's way of being tends to render irrelevant what would otherwise be morally relevant considerations. * * * Suppose a client can avoid the payment of taxes through a loophole only available to a few wealthy taxpayers. Should the lawyer refuse to tell the client of a loophole because the lawyer thinks it an unfair advantage for the rich? Suppose a client wants to start a corporation that will manufacture, distribute and promote a harmful but not illegal substance, e.g., cigarettes. Should the lawyer refuse to prepare the articles of incorporation for the corporation? In each case, the accepted view within the profession is that these matters are just of no concern to the lawyer *qua* lawyer. The lawyer need not of course agree to represent the client (and that is equally true for the unpopular client accused of a heinous crime), but there is nothing wrong with representing a client whose aims and purposes are quite immoral. And having agreed to do so, the lawyer is required to provide the best possible assistance, without regard to his or her disapproval of the objective that is sought.

The lesson, on this view, is clear. The job of the lawyer, so the argument typically concludes, is not to approve or disapprove of the character of his or her client, the cause for which the client seeks the lawyer's assistance, or the avenues provided by the law to achieve that which the client wants to accomplish. The lawyer's task is, instead, to provide that competence which the client lacks and the lawyer, as professional, possesses. In this way, the lawyer as professional comes to inhabit a simplified universe which is strikingly amoral—which regards as morally irrelevant any number of factors which nonprofessional citizens might take to be important, if not decisive, in their everyday lives. And the difficulty I have with all of this is that the arguments for such a way of life seem to be not quite so convincing to me as they do to many lawyers. I am, that is, at best uncertain that it is a good thing for lawyers to be so professional—for them to embrace so completely this role-differentiated way of approaching matters. * * *

To be sure, on occasion, a lawyer may find it uncomfortable to represent an extremely unpopular client. On occasion, too, a lawyer may feel ill at ease invoking a rule of law or practice which he or she thinks to be an unfair or undesirable one. Nonetheless, for most lawyers, most of the time, pursuing the interests of one's clients is an attractive and satisfying way to live in part just because the moral world of the lawyer is a simpler, less complicated, and less ambiguous world than the moral world of ordinary life. There is, I think, something quite seductive about being able to turn aside so many ostensibly difficult moral dilemmas and decisions with the reply: but that is not my concern; my job as a lawyer is not to judge the rights and wrong of the client or the cause; it is to defend as best I can my client's interests. For the ethical problems that can arise within this constricted point of view are, to say the least, typically neither momentous nor terribly vexing. Role-differentiated behavior is enticing and reassuring precisely because it does constrain and delimit an otherwise often intractable and confusing moral world. * * *

I do believe that the amoral behavior of the *criminal* defense lawyer is justifiable. But I think that jurisdiction depends at least as much upon the special needs of an accused as upon any more general defense of a lawyer's role-differentiated behavior. As a matter of fact I think it likely that many persons such as myself have been misled by the special features of the criminal case. Because a deprivation of liberty is so serious, because the prosecutorial resources of the state are so vast, and because, perhaps, of a serious skepticism about the rightness of punishment even where wrongdoing has occurred, it is easy to accept the view that it makes sense to charge the defense counsel with the job of making the best possible case for the accused—without regard, so to speak, for the merits. This coupled with the fact that it is an adversarial proceeding succeeds, I think, in justifying the amorality of the criminal defense counsel. But this does not, however, justify a comparable perspective on the part of lawyers generally. Once we leave the peculiar situation of the criminal defense lawyer, I think it quite likely that the role-differentiated amorality of the lawyer is almost certainly excessive and at times inappropriate. That is to say, this special case to one side, I am inclined to think that we might all be better served if lawyers were to see themselves less as subject to role-differentiated behavior and more as subject to the demands of the moral point of view. In this sense it may be that we need a good deal less rather than more professionalism in our society generally and among lawyers in particular.

Moreover, even if I am wrong about all this, four things do seem to me to be true and important.

First, all of the arguments that support the role-differentiated amorality of the lawyer on institutional grounds can succeed only if the enormous degree of trust and confidence in the institutions themselves is itself justified. If the institutions work well and fairly, there may be good sense to deferring important moral concerns and criticisms to another time and place, to the level of institutional criticism and assessment. But the less certain we are entitled to be of either the rightness or the self-corrective nature of the larger institutions of which the professional is a part, the less apparent it is that we should encourage the professional to avoid direct engagement with the moral issues as they arise. * * *

Second, it is clear that there are definite character traits that the professional such as the lawyer must take on if the system is to work. What is less clear is that they are admirable ones. Even if the role-differentiated amorality of the professional lawyer is justified by the virtues of the adversary system, this also means that the lawyer *qua* lawyer will be encouraged to be competitive rather than cooperative; aggressive rather than accommodating; ruthless rather than compassionate; and pragmatic rather than principled. This is, I think, part of the logic of the role-differentiated behavior of lawyers in particular, and to a lesser degree of professionals in general. * * *

Third, there is a special feature of the role-differentiated behavior of the lawyer that distinguishes it from the comparable behavior of other professionals. What I have in mind can be brought out through the following question: Why is it that it seems far less plausible to talk critically about the amorality of the doctor, for instance, who treats all patients irrespective of their moral character than it does to talk critically about the comparable amorality of the lawyer? Why is it that it seems so obviously sensible, simple and right for the doctor's behavior to be narrowly and rigidly role-differentiated, i.e., just to try to cure those who are ill? And why is it that at the very least it seems so complicated, uncertain, and troublesome to decide whether it is right for the lawyer's behavior to be similarly role-differentiated?

The answer, I think, is twofold. To begin with (and this I think is the less interesting point) it is, so to speak, intrinsically good to try to cure disease, but in no comparable way is it intrinsically good to try to win every lawsuit or help every client realize his or her objective. In addition (and this I take to be the truly interesting point), the lawyer's behavior is different in kind from the doctor's. The lawyer—and especially the lawyer as advocate—directly says and affirms things. The lawyer makes the case for the client. He or she tries to explain, persuade and convince others that the client's cause should prevail. The lawyer lives with and within a dilemma that is not shared by other professionals. If the lawyer actually believes everything that he or she asserts on behalf of the client, then it appears to be proper to regard the lawyer as in fact embracing and endorsing the points of view that he or she articulates. If the lawyer does not in fact believe what is urged by way of argument, if the lawyer is only playing a role, then it appears to be proper to tax the lawyer with hypocrisy and insincerity. To be sure, actors in a play take on roles and say things that the characters, not the actors, believe. But we know it is a play and that they are actors. The law courts are not, however, theaters, and the lawyers both talk about justice and they genuinely seek to persuade. The fact that the lawyer's words, thoughts, and convictions are, apparently, for sale and at the service of the client helps us, I think, to understand the peculiar hostility which is more than occasionally uniquely directed by lay persons toward lawyers. The verbal, role-differentiated behavior of the lawyer *qua* advocate puts the lawyer's integrity into question in a way that distinguishes the lawyer from the other professionals.

Fourth, and related closely to the three points just discussed, even if on balance the role-differentiated character of the lawyer's way of thinking and acting is ultimately deemed to be justifiable within the system on systemic instrumental grounds, it still remains the case that we do pay a social price for that way of thought and action. For to become and to be a professional, such as a lawyer, is to incorporate within oneself ways of behaving and ways of thinking that shape the whole person. It is especially hard, if not impossible, because of the nature of the professions, for one's professional way of thinking not to dominate one's entire adult life.
* * *

The role-differentiated behavior of the professional also lies at the heart of the second of the two moral issues I want to discuss, namely, the character of the interpersonal relationship that exists between the lawyer and the client. As I indicated at the outset, the charge that I want to examine here is that the relationship between the lawyer and the client is typically, if not inevitably, a morally defective one in which the client is not treated with the respect and dignity that he or she deserves.

[T]he lawyer can both be overly concerned with the interest of the client and at the same time fail to view the client as a whole person, entitled to be treated in certain ways.

One way to begin to explore the problem is to see that one pervasive, and I think necessary, feature of the relationship between any professional and client or patient is that it is in some sense a relationship of inequality. This relationship of inequality is intrinsic to the existence of professionalism. * * * To be sure, the client can often decide whether or not to enter into a relationship with a professional. And often, too, the client has the power to decide whether to terminate the relationship. But the significant thing I want to focus upon is that while the relationship exists, there are important respects in which the relationship cannot be a relationship between equals and must be one in which it is the professional who is in control. * * *

To begin with, there is the fact that one characteristic of professions is that the professional is the possessor of expert knowledge of a sort not readily or easily attainable by members of the community at large. Hence, in the most straightforward of all senses the client, typically, is dependent upon the professional's skill or knowledge because the client does not possess the same knowledge.

Moreover, virtually every profession has its own technical language, a private terminology which can only be fully understood by the members of the profession. The presence of such a language plays the dual role of creating and affirming the membership of the professionals within the profession and of preventing the client from fully discussing or understanding his or her concerns in the language of the profession.

These circumstances, together with others, produce the added consequence that the client is in a poor position effectively to evaluate how well or badly the professional performs. In the professions, the professional does not look primarily to the client to evaluate the professional's work. The assessment of ongoing professional competence is something that is largely a matter of self-assessment conducted by the practi[c]ing professional. Where external assessment does occur, it is carried out not by clients or patients but by other members of the profession, themselves. It is significant, and surely surprising to the outsider, to discover to what degree the professions are self-regulating. They control who shall be admitted to the professions and they determine (typically only if there has been a serious complaint) whether the members of the profession are performing in a minimally satisfactory way. This leads professionals to have a powerful motive to be far more concerned with the way they are viewed by their colleagues than with the way they are viewed by their clients. This means, too, that clients will necessarily lack the power to make effective evaluations and criticisms of the way the professional is responding to the client's needs.

[O]ne question that is raised is whether it is a proper and serious criticism of the professions that the relationship between the professional and the client is an inherently unequal one in this sense.

One possible response would be to reject the view that all relationships of inequality (in this sense of inequality) are in fact undesirable.

Such a response might claim, for example, that there is nothing at all wrong with inequality in relationships as long as the inequality is consensually imposed. Or, it may be argued, this kind of inequality is wholly unobjectionable because it is fitting, desired, or necessary in the circumstances. And, finally, it may be urged, whatever undesirability does attach to relationships by virtue of their lack of equality is outweighed by the benefits of role-differentiated relationships.

A third possible response * * * might begin by conceding, at least for purposes of argument, that some inequality may be inevitable in any professional-client relationship. It might concede, too, that a measure of this kind of inequality may even on occasion be desirable. But it sees the relationship between the professional and the client as typically flawed in a more fundamental way, as involving far more than the kind of relatively benign inequality delineated above. This criticism focuses upon the fact that the professional often, if not systematically, interacts with the client in both a manipulative and a paternalistic fashion. The point is not that the professional is merely dominant within the relationship. Rather, it is that from the professional's point of view the client is seen and responded to more like an object than a human being, and more like a child than an adult. The professional does not, in short, treat the client like a person; the professional does not accord the client the respect that he or she deserves. And these, it is claimed, are without question genuine moral defects in any meaningful human relationship. They are, moreover, defects that are capable of being eradicated once their cause is perceived and corrective action taken. The solution, so the argument goes, is to "deprofessionalize" the professions; not do away with the professions entirely, but weaken or eliminate those features of professionalism that produce these kinds of defective * * * interpersonal relationships. * * *

The issue seems to me difficult just because I do think that there are important and distinctive competencies that are at the heart of the legal profession. If there were not, the solution would be simple. If there were no such competencies—if, that is, lawyers didn't really help people any more than (so it is sometimes claimed) therapists do—then no significant social goods would be furthered by the maintenance of the legal profession. But, as I have said, my own view is that there are special competencies and that they are valuable. This makes it harder to determine what to preserve and what to shed. The question, as I see it, is how to weaken the bad consequences of the role-differentiated lawyer-client relationship without destroying the good that lawyers do.

Without developing the claim at all adequately in terms of scope or detail, I want finally to suggest the direction this might take. Desirable change could be brought about in part by a sustained effort to simplify legal language and to make the legal processes less mysterious and more directly available to lay persons. The way the law works now, it is very hard for lay persons either to understand it or to evaluate or solve legal problems * * * on their own. * * *

NOTES ON PROFESSIONAL MODELS AND CRITICISMS

1. **Wasserstrom and the Current Model Rules:** Wasserstrom's article was published in 1975, prior to the adoption of the current Model Rules. At the time, none of the provisions of the Model Code of Professional Responsibility directly addressed either of his criticisms. Consider these criticisms today in light of Model Rule 2.1. That rule permits the lawyer to advise clients about not only the legal, but also the moral, political, social, and economic consequences of client conduct. Does this allow the lawyer to add a "moral" component to an otherwise "amoral" activity? Also, consider again Model Rule 1.2(a)'s attempt to specifically delineate those decisions that belong specifically to the client. Is such a rule an attempted response to Wasserstrom's inequality criticism?

2. **Other Models of Lawyer Practice:** Wasserstrom criticizes the traditional attorney-client relationship from the client's perspective. In another article, the author criticizes the relationship from the perspective of the attorney within that relationship. In William H. Simon, *Ethical Discretion in Lawyering*, 101 Harv.L.Rev. 1083 (1988), the author suggests that two models currently describe the practice of most lawyers. The *"libertarian"* model is similar to Wasserstrom's first criticism. It favors procedure over substance. Under this model, it is entirely permissible for lawyers to assert defenses such as the statute of limitations or the statute of frauds to defeat otherwise legitimate claims. The second model seen by Simon is the *"regulatory"* model. Under this model, the lawyer's primary function is to assure enforcement of the substantive law. Simon prefers neither of these two models, because "under both approaches, the lawyer has little or no discretion to consider whether there might be legal reasons why a particular course of action should not be pursued or a particular claim not enforced, even though the course is legally permissible or the claim potentially enforceable." Instead, Simon suggests a third *"discretionary"* model.

> The lawyer should take those actions that, considering the relevant circumstances of the particular case, seem most likely to promote justice. This "seek justice" maxim suggests a kind of noncategorical judgment that might be called pragmatist, ad hoc, or dialectical, but that I will call discretionary. * * *

> There are two dimensions to the judgment that the discretionary approach requires of the lawyer. * * *

A. *Relative Merit*

Neither [the libertarian nor the regulatory] approaches adequately confronts a central fact about the legal system: [S]ome rights or interests are more important than others. [One example would be the constitutional law dichotomy between "fundamental" or "compelling" interests versus all others.] A legal system that recognizes some interests as more important than others should try to distribute legal resources in a way that protects the most important ones[,] because the practical value of some rights depends more on the relative than on the absolute amount of the citizen's enforcement resources. * * *

The proper standard requires not only a threshold judgment, but also a relative one. In deciding whether to commit herself to a client's claims and goals, a lawyer should assess their merits in relation to the merits of the claims and goals of others whom she might serve. The criteria the lawyer should employ in making this assessment are suggested by the bases of legal concern about the distribution of services: the extent to which the claims and goals are grounded in the law, the importance of the interests involved, and the extent to which the representation would contribute to the equalization of access to the legal system.

Of course, merit cannot be the only consideration to determine how the lawyer allocates her efforts. The lawyer's financial interests are also necessarily important. But the financial considerations that tacitly determine the distribution of legal services under the dominant approaches are substantially arbitrary in relation to the most basic goals of the legal system—those concerning legal merit. Lawyers can mitigate the tendency of the market to produce an inappropriate distribution of legal services by integrating considerations of relative merit into their decisions about whom to represent and how to do so. In making such judgments, lawyers will have to balance their legitimate financial concerns with their commitment to a just distribution of legal services. A lawyer who cannot refuse to assist a particular client without impairing her ability to earn a reasonable income may have to compromise her judgments of relative merit more than one who can say no without great financial sacrifice. * * *

B. Internal Merit

The second aspect of the lawyer's assessment of merit involves an attempt to reconcile the conflicting legal values implicated directly in the client's claim or goal. These conflicts usually arise in the form of the overlapping tensions between substance and procedure, purpose and form, and broad and narrow framing. * * *

Consider a well-known scenario involving two lawyers negotiating a personal injury case. The plaintiff is an indigent who has suffered severe injury as a result of the undisputed negligence of the defendant, but he may have negligently contributed to his own injury. During negotiation, the insurance company lawyer conducting the defense realizes that the plaintiff's lawyer is unaware that a recent statute abolishing the contributory negligence defense would apply retroactively to this case. The plaintiff's lawyer is negotiating under the assumption that there is a substantial probability that his client's negligence will entirely preclude recovery when in fact there is no such probability. The defense lawyer proceeds to conclude the negotiation without correcting the mistaken impression. * * *

The libertarian and regulatory approaches would resolve [this case] through categorical rules, of nondisclosure in the libertarian approach or disclosure in the regulatory approach. The discretionary approach requires a more complex judgment.

[In this case,] the critical concern for the defense lawyer should be whether the settlement likely to occur in the absence of disclosure would be fair (in the sense that it reasonably vindicates the merits of the relevant claims). On the facts given, it seems probable that the settlement would not be fair. * * *

The discretionary approach suggests that disciplinary rules should ideally be expressed as rebuttable presumptions—as instructions to behave a certain way unless circumstances indicate that the values relevant to the rule would not be served by doing so. The rules would be elaborated less by categorical specifications and more by discussions of the general values expressed in the rule and by examples, in the fashion of common law elaboration. Rules of this sort would leave a substantial range of autonomy to those subject to them, but discipline would be appropriate when someone failed to apply the rules in good faith or with minimal competence. * * *

Prof. Simon elaborates on this "seek justice" model in William H. Simon, The Practice of Justice: A Theory of Lawyers' Ethics (1998). Specifically on the hypothetical on negotiating a settlement of a tort claim involving contributory negligence, see William H. Simon, *Role Differentiation and Lawyers' Ethics: A Critique of Some Academic Perspectives*, 23 Geo.J. Legal Ethics 987 (2010).

For an extended defense of role-differentiated morality, combined with a critique of the "working ethical theory of lawyers" about legal ethics, see W. Bradley Wendel, Lawyers and Fidelity to Law (2010). Wendel characterizes lawyers' "standard conception" as involving three principles: partisanship (exclusive concern for the legal interest of clients), neutrality toward the ordinary morality of the client's objectives, and moral non-accountability to others for those objectives. *Id.* at 29. Wendel rejects the claims of "ordinary morality" as a primary basis for judging the professional behavior of lawyers, but argues that the overriding moral principle of lawyering should be "fidelity to law," defining his theme in his introduction:

> The theory of legal ethics I will set out here places fidelity to law, not pursuit of clients' interests, at the center of lawyers' obligations. Law deserves respect because of its capacity to underwrite a distinction between raw power and lawful power * * *. Citizens can appeal to legal entitlements, * * * and only indirectly to morality, because citizens accept for moral reasons the legitimacy of laws enacted through fair procedures. Unlike the dominant tradition in academic legal ethics, it is not an appeal directly to ordinary morality, justice, or the public interest.

Id. at 2. Wendel distinguishes his critique of the "standard conception" of the lawyer's role from that of Simon, among others, concluding that "when Simon talks about justice, he means to refer to substantive justice, quite apart from the legal merits of a party's position." *Id.* at 46. Among the numerous responses to this work, see William H. Simon, *Authoritarian Legal Ethics: Bradley Wendel and the Positivist Turn*, 90 Tex.L.Rev. 709 (2012); Stephen L. Pepper, *The Lawyer Knows More Than The Law*, 90 Tex.L.Rev. 691 (2012), and Alice Woolley, *To What Should Lawyers Be Faithful? A Review Essay of W. Bradley Wendel's Lawyers and Fidelity to Law*, ___ Crim.Just.Ethics ___

(2012) (working paper accessed at http://papers.ssrn.com/sol3/papers.cfm? abstract_id=2018449).

3. **Lawyer's Own Moral Standards:** Neither Wasserstrom nor Simon mention the issue, but what is the lawyer to do when the stated rules of the profession (*e.g.*, the Model Rules) require her to act against her own moral standards? Various approaches to "professional knavery" are critically examined in Gerald J. Postema, *Self–Image, Integrity, and Professional Responsibility*, in The Good Lawyer: Lawyers' Roles and Lawyers' Ethics 286 (David Luban ed., 1983). One might (i) declare lawyering to be an amoral enterprise, exempting it from all moral judgment; (ii) regard the profession as an activity requiring the lawyer to sacrifice moral integrity, and either make the sacrifice or look for another profession; (iii) integrate the essential moral imperatives of the profession into an overall conception of self, deal with the more distasteful professional duties as one does with other conflicts between moral claims that everyone faces, and accept responsibility for the resolution—which might involve withdrawal from the profession, if the conflict could not be resolved; or (iv) detach oneself from responsibility for the "professional knavery," and treat it either as wholly external to oneself or as a separate self, judged by separate rules. The "responsible person," argues Postema, should choose the third alternative, which he calls the "integration strategy." *Id.* at 290.

Other discussions of the problem are found in John J. Flynn, *Professional Ethics and the Lawyer's Duty to Self*, 1976 Wash.U.L.Q. 429, which argues that the role-morality of the profession is incomplete and must be balanced by the individual lawyer's self-conception, and Serena Stier, *Legal Ethics: The Integrity Thesis*, 52 Ohio St.L.J. 551 (1991), which finds ample room in the traditional conception for morally active lawyering. For a further argument that the professional role does not exempt the lawyer from personal moral responsibility, see Murray L. Schwartz, *The Professionalism and Accountability of Lawyers*, 66 Calif.L.Rev. 669 (1978). Reflections on the difficulty of resolving conflicts between moral and professional duty, together with moral support for the effort, are offered in Richard A. Matasar, *The Pain of Moral Lawyering*, 75 Iowa L.Rev. 975 (1990), and Julie A. Oseid & Stephen D. Easton, *The Trump Card: A Lawyer's Personal Conscience or Professional Duty?*, 10 Wyo.L.Rev. 415 (2010).

4. Consider the conduct of the lawyer in *Sprung* in light of both Wasserstrom's and Simon's critiques and apply your answers to our problem.

a. Is there any indication that the lawyer in *Sprung* did not discuss the moral, social, or economic consequences of the proposed action with the client? Is the lawyer's conduct simply "amoral"?

b. Is there any indication that the lawyer in *Sprung* attempted to use his advocacy skills to overcome the free will of the client in a way that made the relationship unequal?

c. Did the lawyer in *Sprung* consider the relative merits of the claim? He knew, for example, that worker compensation benefits to Sprung had been terminated. As a result, he spent a winter unable to pay for heat. He had multiple surgeries, spent two years in a body cast, and had steel rods attached to his spine with metal clips. When the lawyer asked Sprung about what to do, the lawyer indicated that Sprung could get an even bigger judgment with a jury, but also that the trial could go badly. The lawyer also explained that the opposing lawyers were his friends and that they would likely be sued for malpractice by their client if their mistake were not corrected. *See* Sylvia Johnson, Legal Ethics in the Eye of the Beholder: The *Sprung* Case (unpublished manuscript).

5. If none of Wasserstrom's or Simon's criticisms of the profession are applicable, why do the dissenting judges in *Sprung* criticize the lawyer? Part of the answer may lie in the nature of the adversary system, as intimated by Wasserstrom.

C. THE "ADVERSARY SYSTEM"

One of the underlying assumptions about the organizational framework within which most lawyers function is that it is an "adversary system." *Sprung* certainly reflects that system. Does either Wasserstrom or Simon fully consider its demands and expectations? Can it be argued that it is the "adversary system" itself that creates inequality between lawyer and client? Is it possible for Simon's discretion to be exercised within it? What indeed is this system, and how did it arise?

Consider these questions in connection with the next reading.

ROBERT H. ARONSON, PROFESSIONAL RESPONSIBILITY: EDUCATION AND ENFORCEMENT

51 Washington Law Review 273 (1976).

* * * *B. The System Model*

A system-oriented model of professional responsibility would define the lawyer's role in terms of the legal system's overall goals. The lawyer's primary function would be to serve those goals to the best of his or her ability regardless of personal ethics. The duty as a member of the legal profession to subordinate personal morality for the good of the system is not an adoption of the maxim "the end justifies the means." Rather, it calls for awareness of the fact that each ethical dilemma does not stand on its own as a discrete entity, unrelated to other parts of the system, and recognition that choosing the "best" or most ethical course of action in a given situation might have an adverse, "unethical" effect somewhere else in the system. * * *

Because the system model defines professional responsibility in individual cases in terms of a goal or guiding principle, it is essential that the Bar achieve consensus as to the overall goal of each subpart of our system of justice. The two most widely accepted goals of the system, each often dictating somewhat different behavior in different situations, are truth-oriented and adversary-oriented, with a subclass of the latter applying only to criminal justice: innocence-oriented. The following sections illustrate how each of these system models would operate, indicating the advantages and disadvantages of each. The final determination as to the most preferable is left to future consideration by the legal profession.

1. Truth-oriented model

Under this model the Anglo–American trial is seen as a process "within which man's capacity for impartial judgment can attain its fullest realization,"[55] and the function of the advocate is "to assist the trier of fact in making this impartial judgment."[56] On a practical level, extensive discovery procedures for civil litigation and the easing of barriers to pretrial discovery in criminal law aid in implementing the truth-oriented model. Partisan advocacy is appropriate only insofar as it aids in the correct adjudication of the facts; when it "misleads, distorts and obfuscates," it is unacceptable. For example, [Model Rule 3.3(a)(2)] obligates an attorney to disclose to the court mandatory precedent which he knows is directly contrary to his client's position and which is not cited by the opposing attorney. This provision is based on ABA Opinion 146, which interpreted former Canon 22 requiring an attorney to deal with the court with "candor and fairness." With respect to the duty to disclose adverse legal authority, then, an attorney is ethically required to subordinate the client's interests to the profession's interest in truth.

In addition to its intuitive appeal, the truth-oriented model permits the lawyer to subordinate the client's interest to a higher personal moral value. A lawyer is not forced to choose between what he or she personally believes to be moral and professional responsibility to the client:[62]

> He [the barrister] gives to his client the benefit of his learning, his talents, and his judgment, but he never forgets what he owes to himself and to others.... He has a prior and perpetual retainer on behalf of truth and justice. He is the professional representative but not the alter ego of his client.

[I]f our system were devoted to eliciting the truth above all other goals, professional responsibility would be both easy to teach and to enforce. If an attorney's actions for any reason hindered or distorted rather than aided and enlightened the search for truth, he would be remiss in his professional conduct. Yet in our system of adjudication, truth is often not the highest goal. Monroe Freedman has demonstrated that

---

55. *See Professional Responsibility: Report of the Joint Conference,* [44 A.B.A.J.] 1159, 1161 [(1958)].

56. [John T.] Noonan, [Jr.], *The Purposes of Advocacy and the Limits of Confidentiality,* 64 Mich.L.Rev. 1485, 1487 (1966). *See also* [David G.] Bress, *Standards of Conduct of the Prosecution and Defense Function: An Attorney's Viewpoint,* 5 Am.Crim.L.Q. 23, 24–25 (1966): "All lawyers must remember that the basic purpose of the trial is the determination of truth."

62. [Warren E.] Burger, *Standards of Conduct for Prosecution and Defense Personnel: A Judge's Viewpoint,* 5 Am.Crim.L.Q. 11, 15 (1966) (quoting an unidentified "great British barrister, later a judge"). *See also* [Henry S.] Drinker, *Some Remarks on Mr. Curtis' "The Ethics of Advocacy,"* 4 Stan.L.Rev. 349 (1952): "Of course no one could say that an occasion might not possibly arise when there was no alternative except the truth or a lie and when the consequences of the truth were such that the lawyer might be tempted to lie. This, however, would not make it right for him to do so." *Id.* at 350.

many of the accepted rules of our legal system often serve to hinder, rather than to further, the discovery of truth:[63]

> The lawyer is an officer of the court, participating in a search for truth. Yet no lawyer would consider that he had acted unethically in pleading the statute of frauds or the statute of limitations as a bar to a just claim. Similarly, no lawyer would consider it unethical to prevent the introduction of evidence such as a murder weapon seized in violation of the fourth amendment or a truthful but involuntary confession, or to defend a guilty man on grounds of denial of a speedy trial. *Such are permissible because there are policy considerations that at times justify frustrating the search for truth and the prosecution of a just claim.*

Justice, not truth, is the overriding goal of the American legal system, and "[j]ustice is something larger and more intimate than truth. Truth is only one of the ingredients of justice. Its whole is the satisfaction of those concerned."[64]

Even if it were possible to conduct legal proceedings in such a way that the truth always emerged, neither the profession nor the public would be satisfied unless the truth was obtained in a just manner. In fact, we have demonstrated a willingness to sacrifice some measure of truth in order to assure the litigants and the public that justice has been obtained as well as the truth discovered. In a criminal proceeding, probably the best means of eliciting the truth would be skillful interrogation of the accused. Yet the fifth amendment privilege against self-incrimination protects the accused from any questioning by law enforcement officers. Although the requirement that police obtain evidence of a crime independently of the accused has truth-serving components, the primary purposes for the privilege are humanitarian in nature and unavoidably interfere with the discovery of the truth. In sum, the existing legal system is designed to effectuate goals which sometimes take precedence over the search for absolute truth. * * *

2. *Adversary-oriented model*

Rather than requiring the judge to perform the functions of both investigator and arbitrator, the adversary system requires that each side investigate, introduce, and argue the evidence most favorable to its own side of a legal dispute:[77]

> The philosophy of adjudication that is expressed in "the adversary system" is, speaking generally, a philosophy that insists on keeping distinct the function of the advocate, on the one hand, from that of the judge, or of the judge from that of jury, on the other. The decision

---

63. [Monroe H.] Freedman, *Professional Responsibility of the Criminal Defense Lawyer: The Three Hardest Questions*, 64 Mich.L.Rev. 1469, 1482 (1966) (emphasis added).

64. [Charles P.] Curtis, *The Ethics of Advocacy*, 4 Stan.L.Rev. 3, 12 (1951).

77. [Lon L.] Fuller, *The Adversary System*, in Talks on American Law 30 (H[arold J]. Berman ed. 1961).

of the case is for the judge, or for the judge and jury. That decision must be as objective and as free from bias as it possibly can.

This method of presentation avoids the natural tendency to "judge too swiftly in terms of the familiar that which is not yet fully known."[78] No matter how great an effort one makes to remain neutral, past experience, subconscious biases, and preconceptions formed from preliminary investigation inevitably lead to prejudgment. Once a number of facts indicate guilt, for example, the virtually irresistible tendency is to find additional evidence substantiating the initial judgment. Contrary evidence or testimony is thereafter not as actively pursued. The adversary system recognizes this psychological tendency, but avoids its dysfunctional aspects by instructing each side of a dispute to form a bias and pursue all facts, testimony, legal precedents, and arguments in its favor, and attack all evidence and arguments for the opposing side. Through partisan advocacy, both sides are fully presented to a trier of fact.

A second function served by the adversary process of adjudication is not only to ensure that justice in fact *has* been done, but that it also *appears* to have been done. To the extent that trials take the place of self-help by wronged individuals; to the extent that rehabilitation of criminal offenders requires that those convicted believe themselves to have been tried fairly; and to the extent that the orderly functioning of government and protection against resort to violence require faith in the integrity of the legal system; it is essential that all sides in a controversy be seen to have been adequately represented. This function is aided, particularly with respect to the accused in a criminal trial, by providing a partisan advocate on either side of the controversy.

A third function of the adversary process in criminal cases, particularly related to its educative aspect of making justice apparent, is the preservation of the presumption of innocence. Professor Goldstein deems the presumption of innocence central to the accusatorial system:[81]

> An accusatorial system assumes a social equilibrium which is not lightly to be disturbed, and assigns great social value to keeping the state out of disputes, especially when stigma and sanction may follow. As a result, the person who charges another with crime cannot rely on his assertion alone to shift to the accused the obligation of proving his innocence. The accuser must, in the first instance, present reasonably persuasive evidence of guilt. It is in this sense that the presumption of innocence is at the heart of the accus[a]torial system. Until certain procedures and proofs are satisfied, the accused is to be treated by the

---

78. *Professional Responsibility: Report of the Joint Conference*, [44 A.B.A.J. 1159,] 1160 [(1958)].

81. [Abraham S.] Goldstein, *Reflections on Two Models: Inquisitorial Themes in American Criminal Procedure*, 26 Stan.L.Rev. 1009, 1017 (1974) (emphasis in original). Professor Goldstein notes: "Comparativists generally assume that inquisitorial systems are primarily concerned with enforcing criminal laws and are only incidentally concerned with the manner in which it is done." *Id.* at 1018.

legal system *as if* he is innocent and need lend no aid to those who would convict him.

The best way to accomplish this goal is by providing the accused a representative who does not act according to a personal opinion on the facts, but rather assumes innocence and acts as an advocate to promote that view.

In maintaining the adversary system and the presumption of innocence in the criminal justice system, each of the participants in the system functions properly only if he understands and is able to fulfill his role. It is in part due to the nature of the adversary system—that the attorney must remain firmly in role—that he may not express a personal belief as to the guilt or innocence of the client. Personal views should be irrelevant to proper performance of this role. Loyalty to the client, within the bounds of the law, must be paid absolute deference because the system can only function properly if a member of the legal profession argues the defendant's cause as forcefully and convincingly as possible. * * *

a. Equal adversaries alternative

Proper functioning of the adversary-oriented model requires that the advocates have equal weapons and "play according to the rules." [A]ssuring that the adversaries are, as nearly as possible, of equal ability in presenting their respective sides [is difficult]. The innate and developed capacities of attorneys can only be kept above a specified minimum level through Bar examination, continuing education programs, and effective assistance of counsel doctrines. The equality of their relative resources and bargaining positions, however, might be increased through statutory reform, case law, or possibly by varying ethical rules for the conduct of attorneys according to the nature of the client.

[I]t is clear that adoption of the adversary model necessarily implies a commitment to ensuring the equality of the adversaries. Without this commitment, indigent litigants will be no better off under a true adversary model than they are under the existing situation model. * * *

b. Innocence-oriented alternative

The innocence-oriented subclassification to the adversary system would go further in affording procedural protections to the accused in criminal cases. The adversary process is primarily concerned with pitting two adversaries against each other so that the trier of fact can weigh the issues presented and be better able to render a just and enlightened decision. The innocence-oriented model, on the other hand, is founded upon a series of philosophical and social policy premises which often render irrelevant the most accurate determination of truth in a particular case, even by the adversary method. It is more important that the presumption of innocence be preserved in terms of its inherent goals. * * *

An attorney therefore can find that it is his ethical duty, under the innocence-oriented view, to defend fully and enthusiastically an accused whom he believes to be guilty. He may hold judgment in abeyance until the trier of fact determines guilt or innocence, convince himself of his client's innocence simply by constant investigation and argument to prove that innocence, or treat the process as a game which, so long as he plays by the rules, it is his job to win.

If the innocence model is to serve as a viable instrument of criminal justice, however, its purpose and rationale must constantly be explained to the public to avoid the appearance of unethical conduct and misunderstanding of the lawyer's duty to his client.

NOTES ON THE ADVERSARY SYSTEM

1. One author suggests that the adversary system is more than just a "model," noting that in this country, "the phrase 'adversary system' is synonymous with the American system for the administration of justice—a system that was constitutionalized by the Framers * * *." As a result, "the adversary system represents far more than a simple model for resolving disputes. Rather, it consists of a core of basic rights that recognize and protect the dignity of the individual in a free society." Monroe H. Freedman, *Our Constitutionalized Adversary System*, 1 Chap.L.Rev. 57, at 57 (1998).

2. Other authors, however, disagree. Consider the following excerpt from Thomas L. Shaffer, *The Unique, Novel, and Unsound Adversary Ethic*, 41 Vand.L.Rev. 697 (1988):

> The dominant ethic in the American legal profession * * * is the adversary ethic. The adversary ethic, in the words of the late Justice Abe Fortas, claims that "[l]awyers are agents, not principals; and they should neither criticize nor tolerate criticism based upon the character of the client whom they represent or the cause that they prosecute or defend. They cannot and should not accept responsibility for the client's practices." This ethic is the principal—and often the only—reference point in professional discussions. Although it is embedded in our professional codes, our cases, and our law offices, this Article argues that the adversary ethic is unique, novel, and unsound. * * *

> The adversary ethic in America is a unique professional notion. It is a departure both from classical moral philosophy and from the American religious tradition. This lawyer's ethic is an instance of what Emile Durkheim called "the decentralization of the moral life"—a separate morality defined by lawyers for lawyers, described within their professional associations and manifested [by codes of ethics] in a closed understanding of the morals of practice. As my colleague Steven Hobbs has expressed it, the lawyers of America give themselves "a free pass out of the community's moral discussions." * * *

> The adversary ethic traces its origins from four events of significant concern to American lawyers, events that coincided with the emergence of the large commercial centers of the northeast—particularly in New York

City—as the dust cleared from the Civil War. The first of these events was a process of justification for lawyers who were representing the "robber barons" of the railroad, manufacturing, and financial industries. Michael Schudson's example is Daniel Drew, James Fisk, Jay Gould, and the Erie Railroad's fight against Commodore Vanderbilt and the New York Central Railroad. It was a late nineteenth century hostile take-over in which Vanderbilt was buying up Erie stock, and Drew, Fisk, and Gould, not interested in such delicacies as poison pills, white knights, or crown-jewel sales, met the competition by printing new stock.

Clients fled a jurisdiction in order to evade an injunction; clients frequently bribed legislators, and very possibly directed the commission of murder. Their lawyers included the distinguished David Dudley Field, law reformer, author of the Field code of procedure, brother of a Supreme Court justice, and advocate for the powerful. These lawyers represented their clients in the legislature and the courts. They continually frustrated the judicial process by meeting any injunction against their clients with a countermanding injunction from another judge. This tactic was possible because of the curious jurisdictional provisions of the procedural code drafted by Field. The most illustrious lawyers in New York City—Samuel Tilden, Thomas Shearman, and many other founders of the Bar Association of the City of New York—represented parties to such corporate wars in the 1870s.

The second event that contributed to the development of the adversary ethic was growth and strength for the practice of law in law firms. Although law firms in America date from the 1820s, they were not significant as professional associations until the 1870s. The third event was the founding of the first local and national bar associations. The fourth event was the appearance of the first codes of legal ethics. All four of these events provoked or occurred in response to a public and journalistic perception that America's leading lawyers were acting immorally.

The articulate laymen of that era—including, for example, Henry Adams, who was a social critic, novelist, and descendant of presidents, and Samuel Bowles, editor of the Springfield Republican—reacted publicly by expressing stern moral disapproval of the activities of the country's leading lawyers. These laymen argued that this behavior on the part of American lawyers was a betrayal of the personal public responsibility that Adams' ancestors had accepted as the burden of being American lawyers. "[P]ublic opinion," Adams said, "was silent or was disregarded."

This argument was based on the perception that the lawyers for the robber barons were refusing to cooperate with a public consideration of the common good. What was crucial, if republican[b] social ethics were to remain plausible, was the claim that Bowles, Adams, and editorials in the *New York Times* made about the relevance of the lawyers' behavior in the robber baron cases: the issue was not so much that the behavior was wrong, but that its rightness or wrongness was a matter of public concern. It was not intrusive for newspaper writers to question what

---

b. ["Republican" here refers to democracy-related values, not the party or the newspaper. Eds.]

lawyers did for clients because the community was within legitimate limits when it called upon lawyers to account for what they did for clients, and to do so publicly. The republicans' attempts at fraternal correction were, functionally, not so much condemnations as invitations to discuss the common good. The lawyers declined the invitations, not with the argument that what they and their clients talked about were not moral matters, but with the argument that they were private moral matters. * * *

The moral alarm sounded by Henry Adams was also alarm toward the secret power of corporate business. Alexis de Tocqueville feared the early beginnings of government by moneyed corporations in America. De Tocqueville's conception of American democracy was the basis of Adams' republican argument: corporations don't act; only people act. To take seriously the legal fiction that the corporation acts was to give up the moral argument. To behave as if lawyers for business corporations are not accountable for what the officers of their corporate clients do adds insulation to the denial of responsibility by corporate officers, as it extends the denial of responsibility by the legal profession.

Louis Auchincloss' character Henry Knox, a third-generation successor to the New York law-firm lawyers of the 1870s, remembered well the lessons of his professional grandfathers: "Your client wants you to do something grasping and selfish. But quite within the law", Knox said. "As a lawyer you're not his conscience, are you? You advise him that he can do it. So he does it and tells his victim: 'My lawyer made me!' You're satisfied, and so is he . . . . "

Bowles and Adams argued that a lawyer's work for his clients is public business. The lawyers responded by invoking the notion of individual rights—especially what a later generation has come to talk of as a right to privacy. Adams and Bowles argued that power should be exercised in such a way that the people can see it and contain it. The final issue for Adams and Bowles was public sovereignty. The lawyers' defense was autonomy and the sovereignty of the individual—every man is his own tyrant.

These were important arguments. They still are. It might be useful to ponder these arguments a bit and to notice how familiar use of words of moral and legal debate were used in them. The word "rights," for example shows up on the adversary ethic, robber baron side of the argument. David Dudley Field claimed that what he and his clients talked about and decided to do was not public business. He and his clients had a right to keep the legal decisions made in Field's law office from the public. Adams and the newspapermen claimed that Field's law practice was public business because corporate business and office decisions in aid of corporate business were matters of public concern. These republicans were not as interested in talking about the rights of the robber barons as they were in talking about the morals of the robber barons: the republicans insisted that a substantive, moral, public debate was a legitimate interest, as against the assertion of individual rights, privacy in lawyer-client relationships, and autonomy in deciding, within the councils of a business enterprise, what the business should do.

The word "rules" is also useful in understanding the adversary ethic argument. As it did in Field's day, the republican professional world still talks about character, disposition, virtue, and habit. The new rhetoric of adversary ethics talks of privacy—and privacy needs rules. * * * Rights lead to rules and, during these corporate lawyers' professional lives, the rules were gathered into codes, which were promulgated by bar associations and protected by (as well as protective of) law firms. * * *

Proponents of the adversary ethic have an affinity for words such as rights, rules, privacy, individualism, contract, independence, detachment, and self-government. Proponents of the republican argument have an affinity for words such as community, commonality, connection, context, relationship, response, influence, attachment, virtue, moral discourse, and common good. The recent professional history of lawyers—and the codification of that recent history in professional regulation—is the history of a movement toward rights and rules, and a movement away from moral discourse about the common good. Most of what we now call jurisprudence, and virtually all of what we think of as constitutional jurisprudence, embodies the rules-rights side of these verbal preferences. Republican political thought in America, including republican legal ethics, embodies the context-virtue side. * * *

The recent professional history of lawyers thus describes a novel moral world. At least it would have appeared novel to earlier generations of American lawyers and to generations elsewhere. Indeed, it appears strange to some of us in this generation. The adversary ethic description of law practice does not resemble the republican moral world that the earliest American lawyers thought they had forged from the Revolution: "religious in its roots and civic in its expression." The republicans insisted—as they still insist—that law is a profession of public responsibility. Henry Adams knew it. Samuel Bowles and the editorial writers at the *New York Times* had perceived it. * * *

The point of my argument is the conclusion—which I now invite you to make—that the adversary ethic is not, for all the official, pretentious support it receives, a settled matter. If history is persuasive, my invitation is to consider the argument that the adversary ethic is not only unique and novel but also unsound. It is still possible to ask an American lawyer: Does your practice make people better—not just your client, but other people in the community? I want to be able to revive classical social ethics and apply it to the legal profession. "When you embark on a public career," Socrates asked, "pray will you concern yourself with anything else than how we citizens can be made as good as possible?" The adversary ethic supposes that such a question is irrelevant. Whether the lawyer even makes her own client better is no one's business but her own. I am arguing that the adversary ethic is not as firmly in place as it thinks it is, and that has never made sense. * * *

3. Professor Aronson writes that the adversary system requires advocates on both sides to have "equal weapons and 'play according to the rules.' "

If you follow your client's advice in our problem, do both sides of the Salinas dispute have "equal weapons"? Did both sides in *Sprung*?

4. Whose interest would be served by your calling the opponent's attention to the error? That of the Salinas, that of their counsel, or that of the judicial system? Does that depend on the likely outcome of the appeal, and of a possible trial if the appeal is successful? Are these relevant *moral* considerations in the decision? When both sides do not have "equal weapons," judges must make decisions like those espoused by the dissenters in *Sprung*. As Judge Donnelly states: "Of course, the equity due the parties, not the attorneys, is at issue here." To look at the "equities," however, virtually requires the court to find that Sprung, or his lawyer, did something that would justify equitable intervention on behalf of the adversary. Is such conduct what the dissenting judges are seeking? And when judges look at the equities, are they performing a different function than that of the attorney? That is, when it comes to assessing the conduct of the parties, and their attorneys, are judges much more likely to be interested in a "truth-oriented" model than an "adversarial" one?

5. How you define "equality of representation" and whether that definition includes a notion of improving individual or community life will, in part, determine what reforms you think will be needed to achieve this ideal. As you formulate your definition in this course, you might ask: As to my definition of "equality of representation" (1) To what degree is the individual lawyer responsible for achieving this goal? (2) What problems might arise as a result of achieving this goal? (3) What are the alternatives? While you are developing that definition, remember the lesson from the Preamble to the Model Rules: "Virtually all difficult ethical problems arise from conflict between a lawyer's responsibilities to clients, to the legal system and to the lawyer's own interest in remaining an ethical person while earning a satisfactory living." Model Rules Preamble ¶ [9].

D. DEFINING "PROFESSIONALISM"

Several of the readings in this chapter have used the words "profession" and "professionalism" when dealing with lawyers. You have probably heard these words used in conjunction with or even interchangeably with "professional ethics" or "professional responsibility." In addition, the dissenting judges in *Sprung* seem to indicate that the lawyer acted unprofessionally, but we have not been able to pinpoint any deficiency in that lawyer's conduct under the Model Rules. The final readings in this chapter seek to provide a working definition of the term "professionalism" in a way that summarizes much of the earlier reading.

TIMOTHY P. TERRELL & JAMES H. WILDMAN, RETHINKING "PROFESSIONALISM"
41 Emory Law Journal 403 (1992).

Over the past few years, "professionalism" has been much on the minds of lawyers across the country. * * * "Professionalism" is now the accepted allusion to the Bar's ambitious struggle to reverse a troubling decline in the esteem in which lawyers are held—not only by the public but also, ironically, by lawyers themselves. Being a lawyer, particularly one engaged in private practice, seems suddenly an embarrassment rather than a source of pride. The Bar's response * * * has been predictably defensive and schizophrenic: members are usually reminded by their leaders that, as a group, lawyers really aren't as bad as people seem to think, but they are admonished nevertheless that the profession is threatened by a decline in common decency, attitudes, and standards. * * *

The perspective of this Essay is that the concept of professionalism has become confused and disjointed because it has been diagnosed too hastily. * * *

I. THE CHALLENGE OF PROFESSIONALISM

The Bar's quandary as it struggles to reinvigorate a sense of legal professionalism stems from two basic problems. The first is simply that we do not appreciate adequately the lofty goal we have set for ourselves—that is, determining what professionalism must entail if it is to have any real meaning in lawyers' lives. * * * The second problem is that we do not understand why the idea of professionalism is so elusive for us. If other professions can readily point with pride to a set of shared and lasting values, why do we have so much trouble doing so? * * *

A. Professionalism and "Tradition"

The debate over professionalism might be better understood if we put it in a new, but quite useful, perspective provided by the esteemed political theorist Jaroslav Pelikan. Professor Pelikan suggests that a society can assess its history in two very different ways: one he calls "tradition," the other "traditionalism." To summarize in very short form, Pelikan argues that a society's sense of "tradition" is a positive and useful social force. It is an appreciation of one's cultural heritage that provides a perspective from which to connect current circumstances to the past, and hence improve the understanding of both. By linking one generation to the next, this heritage embodies what Pelikan calls a "living faith of the dead." In contrast, "traditionalism" is "the dead faith of the living." It is a superficial and simplistic appreciation of one's heritage that provides no meaningful sense of perspective and judgment. It is a reverence of the past for its own sake—a nostalgia for the "good old days." It is empty of moral content, and therefore sadly pretentious.

Pelikan's distinction illuminates the dilemma we face concerning our understanding of the task of lawyering: our references to "professionalism" may be nothing more than a sentimental form of "traditionalism," a call for more civility and public respect simply because this is our impression of a happier past. If so, the effort amounts to little more than improving the profession's window dressing. No substance would lie behind it—no "living faith" begun by others that we feel responsible to continue and further. Legal "professionalism" would instead be a "dead faith" with no lasting, fundamental characteristics—a fad of the moment.

If instead "professionalism" is to refer to a true "professional tradition," lawyering must be capable of being uniquely defined by a set of essential, timeless principles that impose important restraints and create special expectations separating the attorney from others. Such a separation would in turn be a source of legitimate pride, not shame, in the services provided. * * *

II. The Bar's Changing "Tradition" * * *

C. Minimum Points of "Procedural" Agreement Concerning Professionalism * * *

We believe there are three * * * propositions that lie behind all discussions of professionalism * * *.

1. Universality

We would argue that all lawyers believe that, if "professionalism" exists, then it applies to all lawyers and all areas of the practice of law, not to some smaller group within the Bar. In other words, we do not believe that some areas of legal expertise, such as tax law or criminal defense work, are inherently unprofessional or unworthy just because of the nature of the work involved. * * * By the same token, law can be practiced with a sense of professionalism in big firms or small firms, in private practice or in government law offices, or whether a fee is being charged for the service or not.

2. Relevance

As a second point of * * * agreement, we believe all lawyers accept the idea that some set of special demands is made on them—which we now characterize as "ethics" and "professionalism"—even if their substance remains controversial. Despite moral diversity and competition, * * * we would all agree that there is some difference between "proper" and "improper" professional conduct, even if we are not sure where the line between the two should be drawn. * * *

3. Functions

Despite an inevitable focus on actions rather than attitudes, the demands of professionalism, whatever they may be in detail, serve two functions that can have an impact on attitudes. First, * * * professionalism would help the Bar attract people to the profession who already have the values we hope will continue within it. * * * Second, * * * professionalism would announce to all new entrants into the profession that the Bar's contemporary moral diversity and competitiveness, while consistent with the minimal standards of the [Model Rules], nevertheless have their limits. In other words, some aspirational, professional values would be expected to be held by each lawyer regardless of his or her personal proclivities or desires.

The central issue in the professionalism debate, then, becomes: What are those values or aspirations that we must all share? * * *

V.   THE ELEMENTS OF A PROFESSIONAL TRADITION: SIX VALUES * * *

The essence of professionalism is composed of six interrelated values. * * * All six must be combined together and given their proper weights to form the full meaning of the term. Blending them reveals, at a minimum, that professionalism is quite consistent with the hard work and long hours of any law practice, private or public.

A.   An Ethic of Excellence

Perhaps most central of all to professionalism is a dedication to excellence in the services rendered to a client. Little else matters if the job performed is second-rate or the client's interests have not been thoroughly considered. The client, of course, can be any recipient of legal services—a private or public entity, fee-paying or pro bono, individual or institution. All deserve the lawyer's appropriate attention and the full measure of the lawyer's expertise. And the services can be of any legal type—whenever the lawyer's knowledge of and judgment concerning the law and the legal system might be relevant to a client's interests. * * *

B.   An Ethic of Integrity: A Responsibility To Say "No"

At some point, the "excellence" of a lawyer's service to a client necessarily entails delivering advice that the client would rather not hear. As painful and economically dangerous as this may be in the short run, professionalism demands a recognition of the long-range good produced by forthright acknowledgment of the limits of the law.

This does not mean that lawyers have a responsibility to turn their backs on their clients and their interests in favor of some higher "good"; instead, it means more subtly that a professional attitude will help a lawyer bring the client's interests and the interests of the legal system closer together so that one need not be sacrificed so harshly to the other. But in certain instances, tough choices will be necessary: providing excellent service to a client does not include being the client's slave. Part of the service for which the client pays, and part of the concept of professionalism, is the value of professional independence.

C.   A Respect for the System and Rule of Law: A Responsibility To Say "Why"

This is the direct extension of the ethic of integrity: if we must sometimes say "no," we must also be able to say "why." We must believe that there is in fact some "long-range good" to which we can refer to justify our activities generally. That good is the basic integrity of our system of law * * *.

[O]ur respect for the rule of law in society should be an active one. * * * We must recognize that the social usefulness of the law, and in turn the esteem in which lawyers are held, depends ultimately on the respect the law receives from non-lawyers. But that objective can only be achieved if we lead by example. Only if lawyers take seriously their special responsibility to hold the law in respect themselves will others understand fully its importance to our culture. * * *

D. A Respect for Other Lawyers and Their Work

Based on the first three values we have discussed, we can now see that civility within the profession is not entirely a trivial matter. It does in fact have its place among our basic professional values. This is not because of the historic background of the Bar as a "gentlemen's club" in which etiquette would be expected, and it is not because a law degree in and of itself entitles anyone to special deference. Instead, civility should follow from the recognition of the lawyer's social function, not his or her social status. Because that function is based on the principle of the rule of law and its critical importance to our culture, our duty to that principle demands concomitantly that we respect the law's practitioners as well. This means not only that lawyers should treat each other with a certain courteousness in order to permit the legal system to function without unnecessary interference, but in addition it means that lawyers have a particular responsibility in conversations with their clients to avoid holding judges and other lawyers in disrepute. * * *

This does not mean that lawyers should stop criticizing each other, or that we should consider it unseemly for one lawyer to sue another for malpractice. To adopt these attitudes would be to limit professionalism to this one value, when in fact civility must be understood in its relation to several other principles, including quite fundamentally the lawyer's responsibility to his or her clients and their rights. * * *

E. A Commitment to Accountability

This value of respect within professionalism requires lawyers to recognize that their clients (and by extension, society as a whole) are entitled to understand the services that the lawyer renders, and moreover to have the sense that the fees charged for those services are fair. This accountability is the cornerstone of the professional independence lawyers enjoy: people generally accept the idea that lawyers need independence in order to provide their full value to society, but the public will continue to believe this only if lawyers respect the reciprocal social demand that they be accountable for their services. * * *

F. A Responsibility for Adequate Distribution of Legal Services

The final value we would include within the essence of professionalism is a lawyer's special responsibility to assist in the effort to distribute legal services widely in our society. This moral duty * * * follows from the importance of law to our culture. Because law pervades all significant social arrangements and institutions, legal services must be widely available to the citizenry, and the legal system should be functioning adequately on their behalf. [R]egardless of the government's proper role in this regard, lawyers have a special professional responsibility here as well. * * *

VI. CONCLUSION

Our list of fundamental professional values does not contain anything about the public popularity that lawyers may or may not enjoy. We believe any such concern with external perceptions is misplaced because it has the issue backwards. The principal purpose of professionalism is to generate and maintain a core sense of *self*-respect within lawyers individually and the Bar generally. The respect of the public can be achieved only *after* that internal effort has been successful.

NOTES ON TRADITION/TRADITIONALISM

1. In *Sprung*, Judge Blackmar writes that the lawyer's conduct "is unacceptable in our profession. * * * I would like to be remembered as a lawyer who went all out for his clients. But I would stop short of taking advantage of a mistake known to me." Are his statements looking at the "tradition" of being a lawyer? Or, are they yearning for "traditionalism"?

2. One lawyer many consider to represent the best "traditions" of the legal profession is Morris Dees, a former book publisher who is now the Chief Counsel and Co–Founder of the Southern Poverty Law Center. Dees represents clients in various civil rights activities. Consider his view of "professionalism" and "tradition" in Morris Dees, *Remember Me By My Clients, They Make My Life Worthwhile*, Trial, Apr. 1990, at 64, 65:

[A]bout a week before Christmas in 1985, my 16–year–old daughter, Ellie, and I were decorating the Christmas tree about 10:30 at night.

The guard inside my house ran to me and said, "Mr. Dees, the outer perimeter guard on the walkie-talkie said he spotted a white guy on the property in a paramilitary uniform with an AR–15 across his chest."

The guard asked us to go to the safe room the FBI had set up inside my house. The FBI had word that some people in the Aryan Nation in Coeur d'Alene, Idaho, were trying to kill me. That all stemmed from some cases I had been working on against the Ku Klux Klan in Alabama and other places.

Ellie and I went into this small room. She was afraid. She turned to me and said, "Daddy, why do you do this kind of work?" [That night,] I lay in bed thinking, "Why do I do this? How did I get messed up doing these kinds of cases and risking my family's lives?" * * *

In 1982, Vietnamese fishermen in Houston and the Galveston Bay area were being harassed by the Ku Klux Klan. The Klan burned a couple of Vietnamese fisherman's boats and threatened to blow more boats out of the bay if they went fishing on opening day, May 15, 1982.

I was asked to represent the fisherman to see whether I could stop the Klan from blowing boats out of the water. We filed suit 30 days before the shrimping season opened. * * *

When we started taking depositions, the Klan threatened our clients. One plaintiff, Nguyen Van Nam, the leader, said, "We've got to drop this lawsuit."

I said, "We can't. If you drop this case, then the Vietnamese earning a living at the 7–Elevens are going to have to pull out of there because the Klan's going to go after them next and then other Vietnamese businesses later. They won't stop."

"The council of elders told us to drop this case." (Each Vietnamese community has a council of old people to advise the community in these resettlement areas.)

"Let me talk to the elders," I said. I remember going into a Catholic church to speak to them—about 30 or 35 old men, fine-looking folks, who spoke very little English. I had an interpreter with me. * * *

I drew on every bit of the reserve I had to try to put the present problem in the simplest, easiest terms to understand. * * * So I told them that we have something called a Bill of Rights, something called a Constitution, and something called a Declaration of Independence that says all people are created equal.

"The Klan doesn't represent the American people. The Klan may be getting a lot of publicity, but don't back off. Stand up to them." I was saying this to refugees from Vietnam who had come to start a new life, who mistakenly thought they were being attacked because the American people as a whole—not just a fringe element—didn't want them here. And just about three-quarters of the way through the talk, they began to understand, and they began to clap lightly. Finally, the whole room broke out in applause. The interpreter told me the elders would continue the lawsuit.

The day that [the judge] issued the temporary restraining order—later made into a permanent injunction against the Klan, ordering them not even to appear before a Vietnamese in a Klan uniform—and on May 15 when the U.S. Marshals lined both sides of the Seabrook, Texas, pass into Galveston Bay as a Catholic priest blessed those shrimp boats, I felt proud indeed to be a lawyer. * * *

Another client comes to mind: Tommy Whisenhaut. He murdered at least three women. Tommy is a psychopathic killer.

I was appointed to represent him in 1976, three death sentences ago. We got two of them reversed.

I believe in insanity as a defense. An insane person is not responsible for the acts he commits. Richard Cohen and I intend to stick in there until the year [2010], if we have to for Tommy. But even my wife asks how I can represent this man who obviously raped and murdered these women.

God knows it's not the money. I don't get a penny for representing Tommy Whisenhaut. I can't even get the state to pay the $1,000 fee Alabama allows for indigent defendants in criminal cases. * * *

Then there was Beulah Mae Donald, whose son was lynched by the Klan. She's a courageous woman. She was the plaintiff in [a lawsuit I filed against seven Klansmen and the United Klans of America. In an earlier case, a "black man had killed a white police officer. A black man was tried for the crime. The Klan met and decided that if that black defendant got off for killing the officer, they were going 'to kill a nigger.' If a black could get away with killing a white, then whites should get away with killing a black. Such was their reasoning. There was a hung jury, 11 to 1 for acquittal. Two Klansmen picked Michael Donald, a 19–year–old college student, off the street that night and lynched him." After these Klansmen were arrested and convicted, suit was filed against the Klan for sponsoring the actions. Mrs. Donald was afraid to be the plaintiff, fearing that she and her family would be harassed. She, however,] agreed to go through with the case. It would be the first time she faced the men who had killed her son, but she wanted everyone to know that her son was not an evil person. She also wanted to find out who had been involved in the lynching—every last one of them.

She sat through that trial and heard our main witness, one of the lynchers who had decided he was going to testify for the plaintiff. His name was James Knowles.

Knowles told in graphic detail about picking Michael up from the street, about how he and another Klansman put the rope around Michael's neck after beating him senseless in the bushes at the edge of town. He told how one of them put his boot on Michael's face and pulled hard so the rope would choke him to death. He told how the boot left a print on the side of Michael's face. The mother listened quietly, occasionally crying.

During closing, Knowles asked me if he could say something to the jury. (He had heard the judge ask the other defendants if they wanted to say something at that time.) I said, "Sure, tell them anything you want to tell them."

Knowles stood before the jury and said, "Ladies and gentlemen, everything that Mr. Dees said happened, happened. We did everything he said, and I hope that you all can return a large verdict that will send a message not only to these Klansmen here but to Klansmen and people living all over the United States."

He then began to shake as he grasped the jury rail. His body shook with sobs. As he regained his composure, he turned to Mrs. Donald, and said, "Mrs. Donald, I hope you can forgive me for what I did to your son."

She looked at him in front of that jury and whispered, "Son, I've already forgiven you."

That was the most dramatic and moving moment I have had in a courtroom in almost 30 years of practice.

I thought to myself, here's a woman who has lost one of the most precious things in her life, her son, and she can look at the Klansman who killed him and say, "I forgive you." * * *

If we are ever going to change the attitudes of manufacturers who market unsafe products [and] of the white supremacists and skinheads who beat people over the head, we've first got to change their hearts and their minds.

I want to thank Mrs. Donald for teaching me that the way you do this is to start loving more than you hate. You have to be willing to forgive those who hurt you and have sincere concern for the welfare of those whose lives you affect. And I want to thank all my other clients. They represent what the law means to me.

3.   Now assume that in one of his cases, Dees discovered the attorneys for the Klan had not filed documents on time and, as a result, would likely be barred from pursuing their arguments. Assume Dees met with his clients, told them of the legal issues involved, and told them that if the Klan was unable to continue, they would likely win. Assume Dees also told his clients that if the Klan was allowed back in the case, the Klan might win, but that Dees believed his case was very strong. Assume the clients were able to determine that if they won in a shortened hearing without the Klan, they would not have to face the people who had harassed them for so many years. As a result, assume the clients told Dees to not let the Klan back into the case if that were at all possible. Finally, assume Dees went along with his clients' demand. Would Dees be upholding the "traditions" of the profession by taking judgment on behalf of his clients without letting the Klan back into the case?

CHAPTER 2

THE LEGAL PROFESSION AND
THE PRACTICE OF LAW

■ ■ ■

INTRODUCTION

Courts derive their authority from many sources. Some powers are conferred expressly by applicable constitutional provisions, and some are delegated to the courts by legislative enactment. In dealing with the practice of law, however, the courts have traditionally invoked powers claimed to be "inherent" in the judicial function. These inherent powers permit the courts to adopt rules to accomplish the necessary functions of the judicial branch. In the exercise of these inherent powers, the courts have not considered themselves limited to merely "procedural" regulation. The courts have long considered lawyers a part of the judicial system. The lawyer serves as a facilitator in assuring that the court system functions smoothly in resolving disputes.

In Chapter One, we noted the self-regulating function of professional organizations such as the American Bar Association (ABA) in promulgating codes of conduct and in interpreting these codes through advisory opinions. In this chapter, you will begin to see the profession of law not as an entirely independent agency, but as a part—or at least an extension—of the judicial branch of government. As such, most of what lawyers do is subject to rules adopted not by a legislature, but by a court. In Part A we examine the claim of courts to an inherent power to regulate the practice of law, which can result in exempting lawyers from statutes otherwise applicable to all citizens. Part B examines the problem of federalism in the practice of law, in particular the constraints imposed on state regulation by the federal constitution and statutes, as interpreted by the federal courts. Part C studies the licensing or "admission" process itself. In Part D we look at the lawyer's monopoly on the provision of legal services, which is sanctioned by the court's licensing authority and its power to prevent unlicensed persons from providing such services. Part E reviews the lawyer disciplinary process. Part F discusses the regulation of lawyers in law firms.

A. JUDICIAL REGULATION AND
THE DOCTRINE OF INHERENT POWER

PROBLEM

Several years ago, the state legislature adopted a new statute entitled "A Statute to Fix the Term of Public Officers Appointed to Serve as City Attorney in Cities with a Population of More than 10,000." This statute provides: "In every city with a population of more than 10,000, the city council shall appoint a city attorney who shall serve a three-year term, unless sooner removed by the council upon a showing of good cause for such removal." As a result of a change in the political winds during the past year, your city has something of a problem. For many years, the city council was controlled by Republicans. The Republican majority appointed and repeatedly reappointed Suzanne Davis, also a Republican, as city attorney. Davis' last appointment came on January 1, last year, just a few months before the Democrats won all vacant city council seats to gain control of the council by 6–1. Even after the Democratic victory, however, Suzanne Davis refused to leave her position, claiming that she was appointed by the prior Republican majority and still had two and a half years left in her appointment.

The majority has approached you about how to remove Davis. In looking through your professional conduct rules, you stumbled upon Rule 1.16. Your Supreme Court adopted this rule and made it applicable to all attorneys in your state. Rule 1.16 provides that "a lawyer shall not represent a client * * * if * * * the lawyer is discharged." Commentators and state court decisions interpret this rule as giving the client the right to discharge counsel at any time. Relying on this provision, the council's new majority votes to discharge Davis, who refuses to vacate her office. At their direction, you file suit against Davis seeking her ouster.

QUESTIONS

1.   Before reading any material in this section, based only on the knowledge you bring to this course, answer this question: Who will win this suit and why?

2.   Now, read the material following this problem and again answer the question: Who will win this suit and why? If you changed your answer, what was it about the reading that caused you to do so?

RULE REFERENCES

Model Rule 1.16(a)(3)

RESTATEMENT § 1

SUCCESSION OF WALLACE

Supreme Court of Louisiana, 1991.
574 So.2d 348.

DENNIS, JUSTICE

An attorney disciplinary rule of this court provides that an attorney representing a client in any matter is required to withdraw from employment if he is discharged by his client. Rules of Professional Conduct, Rule 1.16(a)(3). The state constitutional question presented by this case is whether the legislature by the enactment of La.R.S. 9:2448 may validly supersede or amend this court's attorney disciplinary rule to provide that an executor of an estate may discharge the attorney designated in the testator's will "only for just cause."

The testator, Charles Wrennon Wallace, died March 9, 1981 leaving a statutory will in which he appointed his wife, Ruth Pearl Brink Wallace, executrix of his estate, and Jacqueline Mae Goldberg, attorney to act for the executrix and the estate. Mrs. Wallace filed a petition to probate the will. Subsequently Mrs. Wallace filed a rule to show cause why La.R.S. 9:2448 should not be declared unconstitutional, as being in conflict with this court's rules adopted pursuant to its inherent judicial power, and why she should not be able to discharge the attorney designated in the testator's will and employ an attorney of her choice to assist her in administering the succession. The district court denied the executrix relief and the court of appeal refused to exercise its supervisory jurisdiction. We granted certiorari to decide whether the statute in question is unconstitutional because it conflicts with a valid rule of this court regulating the professional conduct of attorneys and their relationships with their clients and the courts.

1.   THIS COURT'S RESPONSIBILITY AND POWER

This court has exclusive and plenary power to define and regulate all facets of the practice of law, including the admission of attorneys to the bar, the professional responsibility and conduct of lawyers, the discipline, suspension and disbarment of lawyers, and the client-attorney relationship. * * * The sources of this power are this court's inherent judicial power emanating from the constitutional separation of powers, * * * the traditional inherent and essential function of attorneys as officers of the courts, * * * and this court's exclusive original jurisdiction of attorney disciplinary proceedings. * * * The standards governing the conduct of attorneys by rules of this court unquestionably have the force and effect of substantive law. * * *

Conversely, the legislature cannot enact laws defining or regulating the practice of law in any aspect without this court's approval or acquiescence because that power properly belongs to this court and is reserved for it by the constitutional separation of powers. * * * Accordingly, a legislative act purporting to regulate the practice of law has commendatory effect only until it is approved by this court as a provision in aid of its inherent judicial power. This court will ratify legislative acts that are useful or necessary to the exercise of its inherent judicial power, but it will strike down statutes which tend to impede or frustrate its authority. * * *

The people's constitutional reposition of power carries with it a mandate for the full and responsible use of that power. * * * Consequently, this court has not only the power but also the responsibility to regulate the practice of law in this state. * * * Accordingly, this court has not hesitated to meet its judicial responsibility for the use of the inherent judicial power and original attorney disciplinary jurisdiction vested in it by the constitution.[1]

In defining and regulating the client-attorney relationship this court has adopted a number of interrelated rules as part of the Code of Professional Responsibility. * * *

These rules are designed to give the client the right to control and direct the assertion and protection of his legal rights as fully as practicable, and to encourage and require an attorney to act with loyalty and in the best interest of his client. * * *

2. THE RULE OF THIS COURT

Rule 1.16(a)(3), the rule defining and regulating the client-attorney relationship most pertinent to the present case, provides unequivocally that "a lawyer ... shall withdraw from the representation of a client if ... the lawyer is discharged." The comment under the Rules of Professional Conduct Rule 1.16, explains that the rule means "[a] client has a right to discharge a lawyer at any time, *with or without cause*, subject to liability for payment for the lawyer's services." (Emphasis added). Moreover, this court has held that "Disciplinary Rule 2–110(B)(4) [the identical predecessor provision to Model Rule 1.16] recognizes the client's *absolute* right to discharge his attorney.... Thus an attorney can [not] force his continued representation of a client who wishes to discharge him...." *Scott v. Kemper Ins. Co.*, 377 So.2d 66, 69–70 (La. 1979) (Emphasis added) * * *.

4. THE STATUTE, THE CONFLICT, THE RESOLUTION

Following [an earlier series of cases and legislative enactments,] the legislature * * * enacted La.R.S. 9:2448. * * * The central, foundational

---

1. The wide range of rules adopted pursuant to this responsibility include adopting the Articles of Incorporation of the Louisiana State Bar Association as the "rules of this court" (Supreme Court of Louisiana Order Book March 12, 1941) (These rules include the Code of Professional Responsibility.); Re-establishing the requirements for admission to the bar (Rule 17); Vacating and repealing Article XV of the articles of Incorporation of the Louisiana State Bar Association and adopting new rules for lawyer disciplinary enforcement (Rule 19, § 1); Establishing one permanent statewide agency, the Disciplinary Board of the Louisiana State Bar Association, to administer the lawyer discipline and disability system (Rule 19, § 2); Requiring lawyers admitted to practice to pay an annual fee for costs of discipline and enforcement of rules (Rule 19, § 8); Establishing sanctions for attorney misconduct (Rule 19, § 10); Allowing for the limited participation of law students in trial work (Rule 20); Establishing the requirements for continuing legal education (Rule 30); and, Instituting a mandatory program governing the interest on lawyers' trust accounts (IOLTA) (Rule 1.15, Rules of Professional Conduct (as amended December 13, 1990)).

part of the statute is La.R.S. 9:2448(B)(2), which provides that an attorney designated by a testator in his will may be removed as such only for just cause. * * * This core element of the statute is in direct, irreconcilable conflict with Rule 1.16(a)(3), the disciplinary rule of this court providing that an attorney is required to withdraw from employment if he is discharged by his client with or without cause. Rule 1.16(a)(3) is an important element of the Code of Professional Responsibility giving the client the [absolute] right to fire a lawyer in whom he has lost faith or confidence. Consequently, we cannot ratify La.R.S. 9:2448 as being helpful or beneficial to the exercise of our inherent judicial power and responsibility. Instead of aiding our efforts to define and regulate the practice of law and the client-attorney relationship by adopting and enforcing Rule 1.16(a)(3), the statute tends to obstruct, impede and defeat our progress. Furthermore, to acknowledge the * * * rule, the constitutional power of this court to enact it and yet permit the legislative act to supplant the rule, would degrade this court, weaken the profession and impede the administration of justice. Accordingly, we refuse to approve La.R.S. 9:2448 and will strike it as being null and void. * * *

[There will] be judgment in favor of plaintiff declaring that, insofar as it conflicts with Rule 1.16(a)(3), LSA–R.S. 9:2448 is unconstitutional, null, void, and of no effect.

NOTES ON INHERENT POWER

1. The *Wallace* court refers to its power to regulate the practice of law as "emanating from the constitutional separation of powers, * * * the traditional inherent and essential function of attorneys as officers of the courts, * * * and this court's exclusive original jurisdiction of attorney disciplinary proceedings." The court's jurisdiction over disciplinary proceedings is specified in the state constitution Art. 5 § 5(B) (1999), without any reference to substantive powers of regulation.

2. **Other State Constitutional Provisions:** Some state constitutions make clear the state supreme court's regulatory power over lawyers, generally by a provision something like this: "The Supreme Court shall have the power to prescribe general rules governing admission to the bar and the practice of law." Other states have more generic provisions like Louisiana Art. 5 § 5(A): "The supreme court has general supervisory jurisdiction over all other courts." This type of provision might suggest that the court's inherent power to regulate lawyers would be limited to lawyers and cases actually appearing in court. However, the legal profession in the United States has traditionally been unitary—admission to practice before the courts includes the right to practice non-forensic law as well—and few state supreme courts have felt constrained to limit the scope of their "inherent power" to forensic matters only.

3. **Affirmative v. Negative "Inherent Power":** Charles W. Wolfram, in *Lawyer Turf and Lawyer Regulation–The Role of the Inherent–Powers Doctrine*, 12 U.Ark. Little Rock L.J. 1 (1989–1990), distinguishes between two "inherent power" claims. In the first, which he calls "affirmative," the court

claims regulatory power sufficient to allow the judicial system to function in the absence of constitutional provision or statute. The court is allowed to fill the void because the close historical ties between the courts and lawyers make it logical for the court to perform the regulatory function. The fact that many modern lawyers do not regularly appear in court does not dilute this claim of inherent power, in his view, because it is appropriate for judges and litigators who are experts in the special judicial setting to take a leadership role for the profession as a whole.

In the second claim, which Wolfram calls "negative," the court's inherent power is exclusive, and any regulation of lawyers adopted by the legislature or executive—whether or not it is inconsistent with a judicially adopted rule—is treated as invalid unless approved or ratified by the judiciary. In Wolfram's view, this use of inherent power goes beyond the normal understanding of "separation of powers," which would justify invalidating only such legislation as "effectively invades the province of a coordinate branch of government." Wolfram views the negative aspect of inherent power, given that the judges themselves are lawyers, as inappropriately preserving a lawyer monopoly over the process of lawyer regulation.

The RESTATEMENT, for which Professor Wolfram served as Reporter, takes no formal position on the scope of the inherent power claim, stating in § 1 simply that a lawyer admitted to the bar in any jurisdiction "is subject to applicable law governing such matters as professional discipline," and, in Comment *c* to that section, describing the exclusive power claim as the position of "some states" and as not made at all by the federal courts. The Reporter's Note to Comment *c*, however, characterizes the negative claim as "unpersuasive," citing *Wallace* among others as representing "extravagantly broad judicial claims of exclusive inherent powers to regulate lawyers" and attributing a strong view of the exclusive power of courts to the ABA, as expressed in the Model Rules of Professional Conduct Preamble ¶ 9 (now ¶ 10) and other Model Rules and recommendations.

4. **More Moderate State Claims:** A number of states have taken a more nuanced position, recognizing that not every legislative or executive act that affects attorneys necessarily infringes upon essential judicial prerogatives. *See* RESTATEMENT, § 1, Comment *c*, Reporter's Note (characterizing the judiciary's "essential activity" as "adjudicating disputes" and citing several state decisions as taking the "more persuasive" position that the power to regulate lawyers is to be shared "so long as this poses no threat to the continued vitality of the judicial branch"); *see also* Nathan M. Crystal, *Core Values: False and True*, 70 Fordham L.Rev. 747, 769–71 (2001) (finding support in court decisions in several states and the federal system for the proposition that exclusive power of courts to regulate lawyers is not a "core value" in American law). In California, for example, while the state supreme court struck down a statute authorizing corporations to appear in court through non-lawyer employees as inconsistent with settled judicial rule, *Merco Construction Engineers, Inc. v. Municipal Court*, 581 P.2d 636 (Cal. 1978), it sustained a statute requiring summary disbarment of a lawyer convicted of a felony involving fraud or deception committed in the course of practicing law and having a client as its victim, where the statute expressly acknowledged the primary authority of the courts and was not inconsistent with any

judicially-adopted rule, *In re Paguirigan*, 17 P.3d 758 (Cal. 2001). In another case, the California Supreme Court sustained a statute providing for appointment of some members of the State Bar Court Hearing Department (part of the attorney disciplinary structure, itself governed by statute) by the Governor and the legislature, where the Supreme Court retained full authority over qualifications for appointment, because the legislation was found to be supplementary to, and in aid of, the Court's "inherent authority as the final policy maker in this area." *Obrien v. Jones*, 999 P.2d 95, 101 (Cal. 2000).

5. **Inherent Power and Public Office:** At least one state supreme court has determined that its rules concerning a lawyer's duty to withdraw when discharged by her client are not intended to apply to lawyers who hold a public office, the terms of which are determined by constitution or statute. In *Coyle v. Board of Chosen Freeholders*, 787 A.2d 881 (N.J. 2002), a statute required every county to appoint a county attorney, with a three-year term subject to termination only for cause and not "for political reasons." Coyle was appointed by a 2–1 vote of the Board to a new term just before an election where one of the majority members was defeated and replaced by a member of the opposing party, giving it the majority. When the new majority discharged Coyle without cause and appointed a new attorney, Coyle sued for a declaration that the discharge was ineffective. The Board invoked Model Rule 1.16, which gives a client the right to discharge an attorney at any time, with or without cause. The court held that the Model Rule was not intended to apply to such situations, noting: (i) that it had previously been held by a New Jersey appellate court that an essentially identical provision of the Model Code of Professional Responsibility was inapplicable to a similar case involving the same statute, because the office was created for the benefit of the citizenry and not just the members of the Board; and (ii) that when it adopted the original Model Rules, the ABA acted on a commission report that cited the New Jersey appellate court's decision for the proposition that the general right of a client to discharge for any reason did not apply to statutorily created public offices where the term and right to discharge were governed by the statute, *see* ABA Commission on Evaluation of Professional Standards, Proposed Final Draft, Model Rules of Professional Conduct, Rule 1.16 *Legal Background* (May 30, 1981).

6. **Inherent Power and the Executive Branch:** Most inherent power cases, like *Wallace*, involve legislative pronouncements that affect the practice of law. The court's inherent power to regulate the practice of law also extends to the executive branch. In *Massameno v. Statewide Grievance Committee*, 663 A.2d 317 (Conn. 1995), a criminal defendant was charged with sexual abuse of his children. At the time, the defendant's wife was attempting to divorce the defendant and was represented by an attorney in that divorce proceeding. The prosecutor assigned to the criminal case interviewed the defendant's wife outside the presence of her attorney, and the wife's attorney alleged a violation of Model Rule 4.2. When the statewide lawyer disciplinary organization found probable cause to investigate the prosecutor's conduct, the prosecutor sought an injunction to prevent the disciplinary agency, an agent of the state supreme court, from investigating the conduct of a prosecutor, an officer of the executive branch. The court found that even though the prosecutor was an executive officer, it was the judicial branch that maintained the "obligation

and authority * * * to investigate and discipline prosecutors." 663 A.2d at 337. As a result, to the extent that the executive officer "is also an attorney licensed to practice law, that person's conduct is regulated by the judiciary." *Id.* at 338 (Berdon, J., concurring).

7. Once the court asserts exclusive power over the practice of law, either based on a reading of its constitutional authority or inherently, are any of the following types of rules inappropriate exercises of such power?

    a. Rules governing subjects on the bar examination, including passing scores on the Multistate Bar Examination, a statewide essay and performance examinations, and the Multistate Professional Responsibility Examination;

    b. Rules requiring newly admitted lawyers to attend an "introduction to law practice" series of lectures;

    c. Rules requiring lawyers to attend continuing legal education courses, including courses covering rules of ethics;

    d. Rules requiring lawyers to keep client funds in interest bearing trust accounts and to turn the interest over to a statewide agency that makes grants of the interest to poverty law programs;

    e. Rules requiring lawyers to volunteer a specific amount of time to *pro bono* activities;

    f. Rules requiring lawyers to abide by the ABA Model Rules;

    g. Rules relating to the organization and activities of a state bar association and requiring mandatory membership therein.

8. Assuming continued use of both the affirmative and negative aspects of the inherent powers doctrine by a state supreme court, neither the state's executive nor the state legislature could limit or control use, and possible abuse, of the power. At what point can the "supremacy" of federal law be used to interfere with Wolfram's perceived potential misuse of inherent power?

B. FEDERAL INTERVENTION IN STATE REGULATION

PROBLEM

As president of the National Organization for Minority Lawyers, Sheila Hinds has been active in defending the rights of minorities. When the state supreme court announced several years ago its opinion that there were too many lawyers in the state and that, starting five years in the future, only those with the twenty highest scores on the bar examination would be allowed admission to the bar, Hinds was furious. She believed this rule would discriminate against minority law students, many of whom had not received as strong an elementary and secondary education as other students. Because they started with inferior schooling, Hinds believed that some minority law students would not be able to make up enough ground to score high enough to gain admission. She held a press conference and called the court's ruling "a travesty" and the action of "a kangaroo court," then called the new rule "a legalized lynching" of minorities.

QUESTIONS

As you read the next case and early notes, consider the following questions:

(a) Assume that the state supreme court did adopt a new rule limiting membership in the bar to those who obtain the highest twenty scores on the bar examination, and that sufficient notice of this rule change has been published to eliminate any procedural due process or "takings" claim. Sheila Hinds represents graduating third year minority law students and claims that because the supreme court controls the admission to the bar, and because the court also defines the practice of law and appoints committees responsible for prosecuting actions against those alleged to be engaged in the unauthorized practice of law, the court is engaged in an illegal monopoly and a restraint of trade. Hinds files suit against the court in the United States District Court alleging antitrust violations. The court, through its attorneys, moves for summary judgment. What result? Why?

(b) Assume instead that it was the Board of Bar Examiners that adopted the new rule. The Board adopted the rule without specific direction from the court, although the members are all appointed by the court. Does your answer to question (a) change? If you need more facts, what facts do you need?

(c) Assume that before the summary judgment motion is heard in either case, Hinds is granted limited discovery and finds, in court internal records, a memo from the chair of the Board of Bar Examiners advising Board colleagues that the proposed rule would, based on past test scores, severely limit the likelihood that minorities will pass the examination. In addition, there are memos from three of the justices acknowledging this result and arguing in favor of the rule, in part because of that result. Hinds then amends her federal complaint to add a count against the justices for violating the civil rights of the minority law students under federal law. Will this claim be successful? If it is, can Hinds recover damages? Injunctive relief? Attorney's fees?

RULE REFERENCES

Model Rules 8.1, 5.4(a), and 5.5(b).

LAWLINE v. AMERICAN BAR ASSOCIATION

United States Court of Appeals, Seventh Circuit, 1992.
956 F.2d 1378.

CUMMINGS, CIRCUIT JUDGE

This case presents antitrust and constitutional challenges to two legal ethics rules recommended by the American Bar Association and adopted by the Illinois Supreme Court and the United States District Court for the Northern District of Illinois. The disciplinary rules at issue forbid lawyers from assisting laypersons in the unauthorized practice of law (the "unauthorized practice rule") and also forbid lawyers from entering into partnerships with non-lawyers if any of the activities of the partnership consist of the practice of law (the "partnership rule"). Specifically, plaintiffs challenge ethics rules 5.4(b) and 5.5([a]) contained in the ABA Model Rules of Professional Responsibility (the "Model Rules"). Model Rule 5.4(b) provides that "[a] lawyer shall not form a partnership with a nonlawyer if any of the activities of the partnership consist of the practice of law." Model Rule 5.5(b) states that "[a] lawyer shall not: assist a person who is not a member of the bar in the performance of activity that constitutes unauthorized practice of law." The Illinois Supreme Court and the Northern District of Illinois have adopted these rules verbatim. * * *

Plaintiffs contend that these two rules violate Sections 1 and 2 of the Sherman Antitrust Act (15 U.S.C. §§ 1 and 2). Plaintiffs also claim that the adoption of these two rules violates their constitutional right to due process and equal protection, as well as the rights secured them by the First Amendment. As a result of this alleged deprivation of rights, plaintiffs base part of their suit on the Civil Rights Act of 1871 (42 U.S.C. § 1983). They seek an award of money damages and a declaratory judgment that the contested rules are unconstitutional.

The district court dismissed plaintiffs' complaint * * * for failure to state a claim on which relief can be granted. * * * For the reasons discussed below, we affirm the judgment of the district court.

I.

[Plaintiff Lawline is] an unincorporated association of lawyers, paralegals and laypersons with its principal office in Chicago. [Another plaintiff is] Thomas Holstein, an Illinois lawyer who is the managing director and supervising attorney of Lawline * * *.

According to the plaintiffs, Holstein founded Lawline in 1978 to use law students, paralegals and lawyers to answer legal questions from the public without charge over the telephone and to assist them in representing themselves in routine legal matters. Lawline's other stated purposes are to refer members of the public without financial resources to agencies providing legal services and to refer them to young lawyers who charge reduced fees, thus creating a "prototype legal delivery system" subsidized by referral fees. In its ten years of existence, Lawline is said to have answered legal questions for more than 500,000 people, particularly in Illinois, Indiana and Wisconsin, and also nationally through a toll-free telephone number. * * *

The complaint names as defendants [among others] the American Bar Association ("ABA"), the Illinois State Bar Association ("ISBA"), the Chicago Bar Association ("CBA"), the Justices of the Illinois Supreme Court, the members of its Committee on Professional Responsibility, the members of its Attorney Registration and Disciplinary Commission

("ARDC"), * * * and five members of the executive committee of the [United States District Court for the Northern District of Illinois.]

The ABA House of Delegates [as well as the Illinois Supreme Court on recommendation from its Committee on Professional Responsibility and the Northern District] adopted Model Rule 5.4(b) and Rule 5.5([a]) * * *. Plaintiffs allege that the adoption of the two ethics rules at issue was the result of a conspiracy among the ABA House of Delegates, ISBA Delegates, and CBA Delegates to protect traditional law firms and restrain trade. In pursuance of the conspiracy the defendants allegedly agreed to have the three bar associations issue advisory ethics opinions prohibiting non-lawyers from owning financial interests in law firms and prohibiting lawyers from forming partnerships with non-lawyers if any of the activities of the partnership consist of the practice of law. * * *

In their pleadings, plaintiffs * * * assert that [the challenged rules] resulted from a conspiracy between the courts and the organized bar to monopolize the dissemination of legal advice in violation of the Sherman Act (Count I) and to deprive plaintiffs of their First Amendment rights to freedom of speech and association as well as their rights of due process and equal protection in violation of the 1871 Civil Rights Act (Count II). Count III sought a declaratory judgment that the Northern District and Illinois rules are unconstitutional on their face. * * *

II.

A. Sherman Act Immunity

[The trial court] held that all defendants were immune from federal antitrust liability so that Count I was dismissed. * * * We agree.

As to the three bar associations, *Eastern Railroad Presidents Conference v. Noerr Motor Freight, Inc.*, 365 U.S. 127, 81 S.Ct. 523, 5 L.Ed.2d 464 [(1961),] controls. The disciplinary rules at issue in this case were adopted by the Illinois Supreme Court and by the court below. It is because of their adoption by these two governmental bodies that plaintiffs are supposedly restrained from practicing law. As the Supreme Court held in *Noerr*, "[W]here a restraint upon trade or monopolization is the result of valid governmental action, as opposed to private action, no violation of the [Sherman] Act can be made out." 365 U.S. at 136, 81 S.Ct. at 529. It is immaterial that these rules were prompted by the defendant bar associations, because *Noerr* also decided that "the Sherman Act does not prohibit two or more persons from associating together in an attempt to persuade the legislature or the executive [here the judiciary acting in a legislative capacity] to take particular action with respect to the law that would produce a restraint or monopoly." * * * It is immaterial too that the bar associations encouraged the adoption of these rules because *Allied Tube & Conduit Corporation v. Indian Head, Inc.*, 486 U.S. 492, 499, 108 S.Ct. 1931, 1936, 100 L.Ed.2d 497 [(1988),] decided that "those urging the governmental action enjoy absolute immunity for the anticompetitive restraint."

The plaintiffs also challenge as anticompetitive certain ethical opinions promulgated by the defendant bar associations. However, this Court has held that "when a trade association provides information" (by giving its approval in that case, its disapproval in this case) "but does not constrain others to follow its recommendations, it does not violate the antitrust laws." *Schachar v. American Academy of Ophthalmology, Inc.*, 870 F.2d 397, 399 (7th Cir. 1989) (citing *Consolidated Metal Products, Inc. v. American Petroleum Institute*, 846 F.2d 284 (5th Cir. 1988)). This is so even where the organization at issue has a towering reputation. * * * Even if the Illinois State Bar Association had issued an opinion that it believed certain types of conduct to be violative of the Illinois Rules of Professional Conduct, that opinion could have no anti[-]competitive effect unless the Illinois State Supreme Court or the Northern District agreed with the ISBA's assessment. It is Illinois' and the Northern District's promulgation and enforcement of the challenged ethics rules and not private parties' interpretation of those rules that restrains competition. In sum, the three bar associations are immune from the alleged antitrust liability.

The district court also correctly held that the justices of the Illinois Supreme Court, the Attorney Registration and Disciplinary Commission, [and] the Executive Committee of the district court * * * are immune from antitrust liability. The Illinois Supreme Court and the ARDC are protected by the state-action doctrine enunciated in *Parker v. Brown*, 317 U.S. 341, 63 S.Ct. 307, 87 L.Ed. 315 [(1943)]. There the Supreme Court adopted a state-action immunity from the Sherman Act because its legislative history showed no congressional purpose to restrain state action or official action directed by a state. Here the Illinois Supreme Court was acting in a legislative capacity and therefore in the same position as a state legislature, so that the activities in question are exempt from Sherman Act liability. *Hoover v. Ronwin*, 466 U.S. 558, 568, 104 S.Ct. 1989, 1995, 80 L.Ed.2d 590 [(1984)]; *Bates v. State Bar of Arizona*, 433 U.S. 350, 360, 97 S.Ct. 2691, 2697, 53 L.Ed.2d 810 [(1977)]. The ARDC serves as an agent of the Illinois Supreme Court; consequently the members of the ARDC also enjoy antitrust immunity. *Bates*, 433 U.S. at 361, 97 S.Ct. at 2697; *Hoover*, 466 U.S. at 572–573, 104 S.Ct. at 1997.

Similarly, the Executive Committee of the district court is insulated from Sherman Act liability. The members of that committee consist of five federal district court judges who are responsible for supervising and disciplining attorneys practicing before them. Since they are serving as instrumentalities of the United States, this suit cannot be maintained against them. * * *

As the district judge held, Count I must be dismissed because all the defendants are immune from federal antitrust liability.

B. LIABILITY UNDER SECTION 1983 OF THE CIVIL RIGHTS ACT OF 1871

1. State Action

In Count II plaintiffs allege that defendants' adoption and enforcement of the disciplinary rules at issue contravene the First Amendment and the Due Process and Equal Protection clauses of the United States Constitution, thus violating Section 1983 of the 1871 Civil Rights Act. In order to establish a viable claim of deprivation of rights under Section 1983, plaintiffs must not only show that their constitutional rights were violated, they must also show that the defendants acted under color of state law. Here the three bar associations have not engaged in state action by formulating the disciplinary rules in question. *National Collegiate Athletic Association v. Tarkanian*, 488 U.S. 179, 194, 109 S.Ct. 454, 463, 102 L.Ed.2d 469 [(1988)] (holding that a state actor's voluntary decision to adopt a private association's rules did not transform the private association's rules into state rules nor did it transform the private actor into a state actor). In concluding that the private bar associations are not state actors for the purpose of Section 1983, this Court relies upon the fact that "the power to prescribe rules governing attorney conduct and to discipline attorneys for violating those rules, rests solely in [the Illinois Supreme Court]." *People ex rel. Brazen v. Finley*, 119 Ill.2d 485, 494, 116 Ill.Dec. 683, 687, 519 N.E.2d 898, 902 (1988). The Illinois Supreme Court has not only adopted its own disciplinary rules, but has also appointed an Attorney Registration and Disciplinary Commission not affiliated with the private bar associations to administer those rules. Similarly, the Northern District exercises exclusive power to regulate attorney conduct within its jurisdiction. * * *

Consequently, Count II is not viable against the three bar associations. Therefore it becomes necessary to see whether Count II states a claim against the Illinois Supreme Court, the ARDC and the Northern District's Executive Committee. As state actors performing acts in their legislative capacity, these defendants are immune from money damages. *Supreme Court of Virginia v. Consumers Union*, 446 U.S. 719, 731–737, 100 S.Ct. 1967, 1974–1977, 64 L.Ed.2d 641 [(1980)].

2. Constitutional Challenges

Due Process and Equal Protection

Plaintiffs also seek a declaratory judgment that the rules in question are unconstitutional as violative of the Due Process Clause and the Equal Protection Clause. Unless a governmental regulation draws a suspect classification or infringes on a fundamental right, the government need only show that its regulation is rationally related to a legitimate state interest. [T]he two rules in question meet this test because they are designed to safeguard the public, maintain the integrity of the profession, and protect the administration of justice from reproach * * *.

First Amendment

The plaintiffs also assert that both the unauthorized practice rule and the partnership rule violate their First Amendment rights in violation of Section 1983 of the Civil Rights Act. [The court concluded that simply because a trial court could apply the rule in the future in a way that could affect the First Amendment rights of a party did not render the rule facially invalid. Further, the court found that the two rules were not unconstitutionally vague and did not violate any associational freedoms of the plaintiffs.]

Since these two rules do not violate the Due Process and Equal Protection clauses or the First Amendment, Count II was properly dismissed. * * *

[The court also sustained the District Court's dismissal of Count III.]

Judgment of dismissal affirmed.

NOTES ON FEDERAL INTERVENTION

1. **Bar Associations:** The court dismisses this action against the ABA, the Illinois State Bar Association, and the Chicago Bar Association because, even though these associations may have adopted rules and may have issued "advisory" opinions, any action taken against the plaintiffs was taken by the court, not the bar. However, when the ABA directly adopted accreditation rules for law schools, as opposed to merely recommending rules of conduct for adoption by various courts that have regulatory authority over lawyers, the ABA recognized that it is a private actor that could be liable for potential antitrust violations. *See United States v. Am. Bar Ass'n*, 934 F.Supp. 435 (D.D.C. 1996). Beyond recommending rules of conduct and accreditation rules, what is the role of the organized bar?

2. Voluntary bar associations have existed in the Unites States since colonial times, the first reported organized bar being the "New York Bar Association," an association that attempted to control the admission of lawyers. As a formal organization, the "Association of the Bar of the City of New York" was formed in 1870. It was followed in 1878 by the ABA. *See* Frank P. Barker, *Progress in Bar Associations: The Trend Toward the All–Inclusive Bar*, 3 Mo.B.J. 52, 52–53 (1932). While these voluntary bar organizations proved useful, and continue today, lack of membership and resources prevented these organizations from aiding enforcement of ethics codes against non-member lawyers. As a result, in 1915 the American Judicature Society proposed that states incorporate bar associations through legislation. Such legislation could require membership of all lawyers who practiced in a state and would thus permit the bar association effectively to enforce the ethical obligation of lawyers. In 1921, North Dakota was the first state to incorporate its bar, followed by Idaho and Alabama (1923), New Mexico (1925), California (1927), Nevada (1928), Oklahoma (1929), and Utah and South Dakota (1931). Barker, *supra*.

Integration of the bar was also accomplished through legislation in Arizona, Washington, and North Carolina in 1933, Louisiana and Kentucky in 1934, Oregon and Michigan in 1935, Virginia in 1938, Texas in 1939, West Virginia in 1945, and Alaska in 1955. *Lathrop v. Donohue*, 367 U.S. 820, 826 n.3 (1961). In Wisconsin, compulsory membership in the state bar was first required by legislation, and later compelled by order of the state supreme court. *Id.* at 821–22. In Missouri, the failure of legislative attempts to incorporate the bar helped prompt the Supreme Court of Missouri to assert its inherent power and, by court rule, both incorporate the bar and require membership of practicing attorneys. *See* James R. Devine, *Lawyer Discipline in Missouri: Is a New Ethics Code Necessary?*, 46 Mo.L.Rev. 709, 730–33 (1981).

3. Mandatory bar membership creates First Amendment associational freedom problems. If the mandatory bar uses dues to finance certain activities—usually lobbying activities—is there an infringement of the First Amendment rights of those lawyers who object to the lobbying efforts? In *Keller v. State Bar of California*, 496 U.S. 1, 5 (1990), the Court discussed these problems in the context of the integrated State Bar of California, whose activities included " 'examining applicants for admission, formulating rules of professional conduct, disciplining members for misconduct, preventing unlawful practice of the law, and engaging in study and recommendation of changes in procedural law and improvement of the administration of justice.' " In addition, however, the state bar engaged in lobbying of the state legislature, filing of *amicus* briefs, and adopting resolutions on public issues. Among the lobbying efforts contested by the plaintiffs were efforts:

(1) prohibiting state and local agency employers from requiring employees to take polygraph tests;

(2) prohibiting possession of armor-piercing handgun ammunition;

(3) creating an unlimited right of action to sue anybody causing air pollution; and

(4) requesting Congress to refrain from enacting a guest-worker program or from permitting the importation of workers from other countries.

Id. at 15.

While the Court upheld a prior decision permitting state rules compelling membership in the bar and payment of bar dues as a prerequisite to the practice of law, it also imposed limits on the lobbying activities of the bar. The Court analogized the role of the bar to that of a union. A union has the right to compel all who receive the benefit of union representation—regardless of whether they are members of the union—to pay union dues. Similarly, those who wish to practice law can be compelled to support the bar's activities as "professional advisers to those ultimately charged with the regulation of the legal profession." The bar could not, however, compel dues to support "activities having political or ideological coloration * * *." Noting that the exact parameters of permissible activities are unclear, the Court wrote:

But the extreme ends of the spectrum are clear: Compulsory dues may not be expended to endorse or advance a gun control or nuclear weapons freeze initiative; at the other end of the spectrum petitioners have no valid constitutional objection to their compulsory dues being spent for activities connected with disciplining members of the Bar or proposing ethical codes for the profession.

Id. at 15–16.

Suppose the bar wanted to improve the public image of lawyers and engaged in a public relations campaign to improve that image. Can lawyers who do not want the overall image of lawyers improved successfully challenge this spending? No, according to the United States Court of Appeals for the Ninth Circuit. *Gardner v. State Bar of Nev.*, 284 F.3d 1040 (9th Cir. 2002).

4. Please determine if your state has a voluntary or mandatory bar association.

5. **"State Actor" Antitrust Immunity:** The *Lawline* court held that both the Executive Committee of the United States District Court and the Supreme Court of Illinois were acting in a legislative capacity when adopting rules and were therefore "state actors" immune from antitrust liability. This immunity results from the Supreme Court's interpretation of the antitrust laws in *Parker v. Brown*, 317 U.S. 341 (1943). Under that interpretation, Congress did not intend antitrust liability to attach to states when acting as such. When, however, the state or its agents are acting on behalf of the state, those "state actors" are generally subject to liability when they deny constitutional guarantees.

6. **"Judicial Immunity":** The *Lawline* court holds that even though the Supreme Court of Illinois, the U.S. District Court Executive Committee, and the Illinois Attorney Registration and Disciplinary Commission (ARDC) are state actors, they enjoy immunity as judicial bodies from liability in *damages suits* for violations of federal civil rights laws. Why? What is the benefit of judicial immunity? Why does that immunity extend beyond the actual judges to the bar committees appointed by them? Are members of all similarly situated supreme court committees likewise immune under all circumstances? Suppose, for example, that the ARDC decided for themselves that there were too many lawyers and they adopted the rule contained in the problem. In *Hoover v. Ronwin*, 466 U.S. 558 (1984), involving a judicial challenge to admissions rules adopted by a committee of the Arizona Supreme Court and discussed in *Lawline*, the Court discussed what is necessary for immunity to be applicable when legislation is adopted by someone or a group other than the legislature or the court:

> [I]n cases involving the anti[-]competitive conduct of a nonsovereign state representative[,] the Court has required a showing that the conduct is pursuant to a "clearly articulated and affirmatively expressed state policy" to replace competition with regulation. * * * The Court also has found the degree to which the state legislature or supreme court supervises its representative to be relevant to the inquiry.

Id. at 568–69.

Immunity for agents thus requires that they be (i) supervised and (ii) acting pursuant to a clearly articulated policy. In *Hoover*, the Court found both requirements met under the following circumstances:

> The [state] Supreme Court Rules specified the subjects to be tested, and the general qualifications required of applicants for the Bar. [The Rules] authorized the Committee to determine an appropriate "grading or scoring system" and * * * required the Committee to submit its grading formula to the Supreme Court * * *. After giving and grading the examination, the Committee's authority was limited to making recommendations to the Supreme Court. The court itself made the final decision to grant or deny admission to practice. Finally, [the Rules] provided for a detailed mandatory review procedure by which an aggrieved candidate could challenge the Committee's grading formula.

466 U.S. at 572–73. In dissent, Justices Stevens, White and Blackmun wanted greater supervision, indicating their belief that "the sovereign must *require* the restraint."

7. In *Goldfarb v. Virginia State Bar*, 421 U.S. 773 (1975), the Court did not find adequate supervision for immunity. There, the state bar adopted a "minimum fee schedule" that would prevent a lawyer from charging less than a certain amount for an enumerated service. The rule thus eliminated price competition for professional services. Without some rule or statute authorizing the action, the Court found that it could not "fairly be said that the State of Virginia through its Supreme Court Rules required the anti[-]competitive activities of either respondent." *Id.* at 790.

8. If judicial immunity prevents liability for damages to the court and its agents in *Lawline*, how did the court get to a substantive discussion of the request for declaratory judgment that the two rules violate due process, equal protection, and the First Amendment? Under *Supreme Court of Virginia v. Consumers Union of U.S., Inc.*, 446 U.S. 719 (1980), mentioned in the opinion, judicial immunity applies only to damages liability. When the federal civil rights claim seeks declarative or injunctive relief, the threat to judicial independence posed by damages liability is not present, so there is no need for judicial immunity. As a result, the *Lawline* court was required to decide the substantive issue before declining to issue a declaratory judgment.

9. **Procedural Bars to Federal Judicial Intervention–Abstention:** Return to the problem at the beginning of this section. Assume that when Hinds held her press conference, it was viewed by Arthur Albert, a member of the local bar ethics committee. After Hinds called the state supreme court "a kangaroo court" and made the other statements, Albert filed a complaint with the local committee questioning whether Hinds' comments constituted "conduct that is prejudicial to the administration of justice," thereby violating the state's version of Model Rule 8.4(d). The committee investigated this complaint and then filed a charge against Hinds. Instead of answering that charge, Hinds filed another suit in the federal court, alleging that enforcement of this rule against her would violate her federal First Amendment rights. The defendant, the local bar ethics committee, moved to dismiss this claim. While you now recognize that Hinds cannot file either a federal antitrust action or an action for damages against the court, what about her claim that enforcement of the rule against her in the disciplinary proceeding would violate her constitutional rights? Isn't that in the nature of a declaratory judgment? Should it be permitted? In *Middlesex County Ethics Comm. v. Garden State Bar Ass'n*, 457 U.S. 423, 432 (1982), the case upon which our problem is based, disciplinary proceedings were instituted against a New Jersey lawyer. Rather than assert a First Amendment defense in the state disciplinary proceeding, the lawyer instead filed a federal civil rights claim. The *Middlesex County* Court reviewed the decision in *Younger v. Harris*, 401 U.S. 37 (1971), which barred a federal court from enjoining an ongoing state criminal proceeding unless there was an exceptional and immediate danger of irreparable loss and held the doctrine applicable to state disciplinary proceedings if (1) the disciplinary proceeding "constitute[s] an ongoing state judicial proceeding," (2) the disciplinary proceeding involves "important state interests," and (3) constitutional challenges can be raised in the state proceeding.

10. **Procedural Bars to Federal Judicial Intervention—*"Rooker–Feldman"***: Return again to our problem. Assume that the federal court dismisses Hinds' suit and the ethics charge proceeds to a hearing before the local committee. At that hearing, Hinds presents her argument that enforcement of Model Rule 8.4(b) against her in this situation will violate her federal First Amendment rights. The committee hears this claim and denies it, finding instead that Hinds has violated the rule and is deserving of discipline. Hinds now files suit in the federal court, alleging that enforcement of the rule against her will violate her federal First Amendment rights. Will this claim survive a motion to dismiss?

In *Brown v. Florida Bar,* No. 2:08–cv–308–FtM–29SPC, 2009 WL 1513999 (M.D. Fla. May 29, 2009), the plaintiff attorney filed a federal lawsuit alleging that the Florida Supreme Court denied her federal constitutional rights during a disciplinary process. Despite the existence of this federal question, the federal court found that it had no jurisdiction:

> "The *Rooker–Feldman* doctrine [*Rooker v. Fidelity Trust Co.,* 263 U.S. 413, 44 S.Ct. 149, 68 L.Ed. 362 (1923); *District of Columbia Court of Appeals v. Feldman,* 460 U.S. 462, 103 S.Ct. 1303, 75 L.Ed.2d 206 (1983)] makes clear that federal district courts cannot review state court final judgments because that task is reserved for state appellate courts or, as a last resort, the United States Supreme Court." * * * This is a narrow doctrine, confined to "cases brought by state-court losers complaining of injuries caused by state-court judgments rendered before the district court proceedings commenced and inviting district court review and rejection of those judgments." * * * As in *Feldman,* Brown seeks to have a federal district court review and reject the judgment of the highest state court as to its application of bar rules and regulations to her conduct. A district court has no such authority. * * * Plaintiff's proper recourse to challenge the decision of the Florida Supreme Court was to file a writ of certiorari with the United [States] Supreme Court.

Id. at *6.

11. Look again at the problem, in light of federal abstention under *Younger* and the *"Rooker–Feldman* bar." If the disciplinary panel has jurisdiction to hear Hinds' constitutional challenge, and if she loses in that venue, when can she first present her federal claim to a federal court? Consider again the notion of federal court review of the inherent power of the state court to regulate the practice of law and its implications:

     a. The ABA and other federal, state, and local bar associations, which recommend rules to the states, are not liable in antitrust for merely recommending those rules.

     b. The state supreme court, and the agencies it supervises, are not liable for the monopolistic nature of those rules because they are state actors exempt from the antitrust rules.

     c. The state supreme court, and the agencies it supervises, are "state actors" but are liable for civil rights violations as such actors only in actions seeking declaratory and injunctive relief, not in actions seeking damages.

d. Even when a federal civil rights action against a state supreme court or an agency it supervises is permissible because it seeks injunctive relief, the action can be thwarted if the federal issue can be raised in a state disciplinary proceeding that is either then-pending or is filed thereafter.

e. When the federal civil rights issue is raised in the state proceeding and the state proceeding errs in applying the federal law, that error cannot be the subject of a subsequent parallel federal proceeding. Instead, the litigant must proceed through all appeals in state court and then petition for *certiorari* to the United States Supreme Court.

12. In the wake of several scandals involving large public companies in the late 1990s and early 2000s, Congress enacted the Sarbanes–Oxley Act, Pub.L.No. 107–204 (July 30, 2002), 15 U.S.C. § 7201, et seq., for the protection of investors in public companies. One section of the act requires the Securities and Exchange Commission to adopt rules of conduct for attorneys appearing before the commission. *See* 15 U.S.C. § 7245 (2006), *quoted in infra* section 4(B), Notes on Corrective Disclosure, note 1. To the extent rules adopted by the commission might conflict with Model Rule 1.13, which do you think will govern the conduct of a federal securities lawyer? Why? *See* Daniel R. Coquillette & Judith A. McMorrow, *Zacharias's Prophecy: The Federalization of Legal Ethics Through Legislative, Court, and Agency Regulation*, 48 San Diego L.Rev. 123, 133–34 (2011) (citing Sarbanes–Oxley and the resultant SEC regulation of attorneys as an example of the federalization of professional responsibility).

C. ADMISSION TO PRACTICE

PROBLEM

James Johnson recently graduated from the law school of Atlantic State University. As a student, Johnson had been found guilty of violation of the law school's "honor code" for plagiarizing a brief in a Legal Writing course. In addition, while attending a professional football game one Sunday, Johnson had consumed more beer than he had planned and ran onto the field during the game. He entered a guilty plea in municipal court to an ordinance violation. Johnson is also the president of a local "social" group called F.O.E., for "Friends Opposed to Europeans." The group and its literature spoke of their "hatred for people of all countries of Europe who opposed United States involvement in the activities of Middle Eastern countries."

QUESTION

The natural tendency is to assume that the state must prove that an offense was actually committed, if an offense could disqualify the student from membership in a state-controlled organization like the bar. Additionally, some tend to assume that minor or "youthful transgressions" will not prevent a person from joining a licensed profession. Are these assumptions correct? In reading this set of materials, determine if Johnson can be denied admission to the bar based on either the plagiarism or football game incident. Also, determine who must prove that Johnson does, or does not, have the requisite moral character to be a member of the bar.

RULE REFERENCES

Model Rule 8.1

IN RE WHITE

Supreme Court of Georgia, 2008.
656 S.E.2d 527.

PER CURIAM.

* * * Willie Jay White applied to sit for the Georgia Bar Exam. As part of the application process, White submitted a request for certification of fitness to practice law. * * *

In his application, White provided information, as required, regarding a one-year academic suspension for plagiarism resulting from an incident at the end of his second year of law school. The Board conducted an investigation, [and was concerned with] White's lack of candor during the fitness application process itself. * * *

A majority of the Board told White directly or by clear implication that they did not believe his account of how and why he had submitted a paper at the end of his second year of law school that was a virtually verbatim reproduction of sections of five previously published sources, none of which was cited in the paper. The Board gave White multiple opportunities to provide a fuller and more convincing explanation for his conduct, but he declined to do so. The Board voted tentatively to deny White certification of fitness to practice law.

White requested a formal hearing, and a hearing officer was appointed to review the matter. * * * White again failed to offer any credible explanation for his plagiarism. Despite the overwhelming evidence to the contrary, White was either unwilling or unable to admit that he deliberately took sections of five previously published works, typed them word-for-word into his computer, made minute changes in citations and wording, and then printed out the resulting 35–page paper with 211 footnotes and submitted it to his professor as his own work. The hearing officer submitted a written report [recommending denial of White's application.]

The applicant bears the burden of establishing that he or she is fit to practice law. Where the evidence for and against certification of fitness is in equipoise, the applicant has failed to carry this burden, and the Board must deny certification. * * * The decision whether, in light of the facts, an applicant is fit to practice law in Georgia rests ultimately with this Court.

[The court adopts the findings of the Board and the hearing officer.] From the time the plagiarism was first discovered through the application and investigation process by the Board and up to the present day, White has failed to offer a plausible explanation of his actions. As a result, he has never accepted full responsibility for what he did, and he has not yet been rehabilitated.

Our independent review of the record confirms not only the factual findings of the hearing officer and the Board, but also that White presently lacks the integrity, character, and moral fitness required for admission to the Georgia Bar. Accordingly, the Board properly denied his application for certification of fitness to practice law, and we affirm the Board's judgment.

NOTES ON ADMISSION TO THE BAR

1. In *Schware v. Board of Bar Examiners*, 353 U.S. 232, 239 (1957), the U.S. Supreme Court addressed the requirements of the due process clause of the 14th Amendment of the federal constitution as applied to a state's denial of admission to the bar on the ground of character, and in doing so held that while states could expect high standards of character and fitness, any inquiry about an applicant "must have a rational connection with the applicant's fitness or capacity to practice law." In a companion case, however, the Court also recognized that the phrase "good moral character" is a "vague qualification, which is easily adapted to fit personal views and predilections, [and is therefore potentially] a dangerous instrument for arbitrary and discriminatory denial" of a bar license. *Konigsberg v. State Bar*, 353 U.S. 252, 263 (1957).

2. **Character and Fitness:** Generally, graduation from an ABA approved law school and passage of your state's bar examination are the "black and white" parts of the bar admission process. Character and fitness inquiries are more "gray." *See* Richard L. Sloane, *Barbarian at the Gates: Revisiting the Case of Matthew F. Hale to Reaffirm that Character and Fitness Evaluations Appropriately Preclude Racists from the Practice of Law*, 15 Geo.J. Legal Ethics 397, 406 (2002). The standard's grayness, however, does not diminish its importance. "Requiring each applicant to satisfy the 'good moral character and general fitness to practice law' standard is thoroughly consistent with the notion of lawyers being officers of the court," and further recognizes "the interconnectedness between the legal community and non-legal society." *Id.* at 407–08. Most bar applicants denied admission because of character and fitness deficiencies fail "because of convictions for serious crimes or evidence that they cannot be trusted with clients' money or with the presumption of truthfulness in court." Lex Populi, *Making Law Safe for Bigots, Why Recent Bar Rejection of a Racist Is a Black-and-White Issue*, Conn.L.Trib., July 26, 1999, at 17. For example, in Illinois in 1999, of the 3,200 applicants who took the bar examination, only about 25 had their cases reviewed by inquiry panels dealing with character and fitness. Mark Schauerte, *Illinois Seeks to Deny a Law License to Vocal Racist*, St. Louis Post–Dispatch, Feb. 22, 1999, at A1, 1999 WLNR 953466.

3. **Prior Criminal Conviction(s):** What should a court do with applicants who are convicted of crimes prior to law school? Some states increase the burden of proof on such applicants. In *In re King*, 136 P.3d 878 (Ariz. 2006), the court considered a former sheriff's deputy applicant who pleaded

guilty in Texas to one count of attempted murder after an incident where he became upset at a bar and shot two men "several times at close range, emptying his fully loaded weapon and firing some bullets through the door." An initial seven-year prison sentence was later suspended, and King was placed on probation, during which he underwent "health counseling and group therapy." He ultimately went to law school and passed the Texas bar examination. He practiced in Texas for almost ten years without disciplinary issue and then applied to be admitted to the Arizona bar. In denying King's admission, the Arizona court held that applicants previously convicted of a "serious crime" must satisfy two elements. First, they must prove "complete rehabilitation" with the extent of that proof dependent on the seriousness of the prior crime. Second, the applicant must then prove "present good moral character."

4. **Pre–Graduation Application to the Bar:** In many states, students submit applications to the state bar prior to law school graduation. Subsequent to graduation, students are required to certify that no facts have changed since the original application. Similarly, many law schools impose upon students an affirmative duty to update their law school application when life's events necessitate change. Failing to update either the law school or the bar application can create serious consequences. In *Florida Board of Bar Examiners re Doe*, 770 So.2d 670, 672 (Fla. 2000), the applicant had a pending criminal battery charge at the time of a "no" answer to the law school application question: " 'Are there any criminal charges pending or expected to be brought against you?' " The applicant claimed an honest mistake because he believed the criminal matter was " 'about to be dismissed.' " The applicant also failed to advise the Board of Bar Examiners of a law school honor code charge and an academic dismissal. The applicant was denied admission. In *In re Strzempek*, 962 A.2d 988 (Md. 2008), an applicant filed a bar application and was subsequently arrested for driving while intoxicated and related charges prior to taking the actual bar examination. The applicant did not amend the bar application until nine months later after learning he passed the bar. He was denied admission.

5. **The Case of Sarah Baird:** Return to the problem at the beginning of this section: Assume the bar's character and fitness committee learns of Johnson's involvement with and leadership of F.O.E. Can Johnson's activities with this group serve as a basis for denying his admission? A leading case on this issue is *Baird v. State Bar*, 401 U.S. 1 (1971), where the Court considered the bar application of Sarah Baird, a 1967 graduate of Stanford Law School. Baird exhibited a character and fitness record without blemish, and there was no hint that she hid anything from examiners in her application for admission. She did, however, refuse to answer one question that asked if she had ever been a member of the Communist Party or any other organization " 'that advocates overthrow of the United States Government by force or violence.' " Because she refused to answer this question, her application was denied on character and fitness grounds. *Id.* at 4–5. On oral argument to the Supreme Court, Baird's attorney presented the following hypothetical to the Court: " 'Take the ardent, hard-core racist who in his mind disbelieves in the equal protection clause; he disbelieves in *Brown v. Board of Education*; and he believes in as many venal thoughts as he possibly can.' " Continuing the

hypothetical, Baird's lawyer argued: " 'That man has the right to practice law just as much as the person who has an abhorrent left-wing belief, because you judge a man by his conduct.' " Populi, *supra* note 2. Holding that a heavy burden rests with the state whenever it inquires into "an individual's beliefs," a plurality of the Supreme Court wrote: "[W]e hold that views and beliefs are immune from bar association inquisitions designed to lay a foundation for barring an applicant from the practice of law." 401 U.S. at 8. Baird received her law license.

6. **The Case of Matthew Hale:** Matthew Hale was the "pontifex maximus" of the World Church of the Creator, a "religion" whose main tenet was "that the white race was the supreme act of creation and that only whites are capable of further divine creativity." Michael A. Fletcher, *Behind the Hate: A Racist 'Church' Linked to Violent Plots and Murder*, Wash. Post, July 6, 1999, at A8. Hale graduated from law school and passed the bar exam. A hearing panel voted 2–1 not to admit Hale, so review by a five member panel was automatic. *See Hale v. Comm. on Character and Fitness*, No. 01 C 5065, 2002 WL 398524 (N.D.Ill. Mar. 13, 2002). The five member panel agreed with the majority of the three member panel and refused admission to Hale because, among other reasons, "Hale's belief in private-sector racial discrimination and his intent to privately discriminate were inconsistent with the letter and spirit of the Rules of Professional Conduct." *Hale v. Comm. on Character and Fitness, id.* at 2. The Supreme Court of Illinois rejected Hale's appeal. *Id.*; Aaron Chambers, *Court Rejects Racist Hale's Bid to Join Bar*, Chi. Daily L.Bull., Nov. 12, 1999, at 1. In a dissenting opinion, Justice Heiple pointed out that the hearing panel voted to deny Hale a license "without finding that [Hale] has engaged in any specific conduct." He argued that the court "should address whether it is appropriate" for the hearing panel to base its decision "on speculative predictions of future actionable misconduct." *In re Hale*, 723 N.E.2d 206, 206 (Ill. 1999) (Heiple, J., dissenting). If Hale's case is simply a speech case, how can it be distinguished from Sarah Baird's case? If *Hale* is not simply a speech case, what factors make it different?

7. **The Bar Examination Process and Disabilities:** Federal laws regulating accommodations for disabilities are applicable to the bar examination process.

a. In *Bartlett v. New York State Board of Law Examiners*, No. 93 CIV. 4986(SS), 2001 WL 930792 (S.D.N.Y. Aug. 15, 2001), the plaintiff suffered from dyslexia. Pursuant to the Americans with Disabilities Act and the Rehabilitation Act, she was awarded double-time spread out over four days, plus large print and a computer, to take the New York state bar. The court found that plaintiff was disabled in the major life function of reading and, as a result, was also disabled in the major life function of working.

b. In *Clark v. Virginia Board of Bar Examiners*, 880 F.Supp. 430, 433 (E.D.Va. 1995), the court held that Virginia's question relating to mental health ("Have you within the past five (5) years been treated or counse[l]ed for * * * mental, emotional or nervous disorders?") was overly broad under the Americans with Disabilities Act and needed to be revised to permissibly serve the bar examiners' purpose of protecting the public. In *In re Petition and Questionnaire for Admission to the Rhode Island Bar*, 683 A.2d 1333, 1337 (R.I. 1996), the court approved a mental health question that asked if the applicant was currently "suffering from any disorder that impairs your judgment or that would otherwise adversely affect your ability to practice law." In *Campbell v. Greisberger*, 865 F.Supp. 115, 121 (W.D.N.Y. 1994), *aff'd*, 80 F.3d 703 (2d Cir. 1996), the court noted that the bar examiners cannot deny admission based on a mental illness, but can inquire into any conduct allegedly caused by that mental illness. If that conduct is " 'incompatible with a lawyer's duties,' " the bar examiners can deny the application.

D. THE UNAUTHORIZED PRACTICE OF LAW

D(1) GENERALLY

PROBLEM

Grant Anthony graduated from a local college with a Bachelor of Arts in paralegal studies. He has opened an office and attracts clients for several different enterprises:

First, Grant sells "Divorce Kits," which include pre-printed forms that consumers can fill out and file in their local court in order to begin the process of obtaining an "uncontested" divorce. Contained within the "kit" are printed instructions for use of the forms. These instructions were not written by Grant, but came with the "kits" when he purchased them from a nationwide distributor.

Second, Grant has made a deal with Angela Hazendorf, a local lawyer who was one of Grant's instructors in college, whereby Grant will sell "Living Trust Kits" at seminars in which Angela Hazendorf is the featured speaker. Angela will discuss the legal problems associated with such instruments and then refer people to Grant, who will sell the kits and help the "client" assemble the necessary data and fill out the forms.

Third, Grant wants to be of service to local landlords, many of whom are partnerships and corporations and most of whom do not live in town, but live instead in one of the state's larger cities. Grant asked Angela Hazendorf to prepare forms for eviction actions. Grant then sold the forms to landlords, who filled them out to institute eviction proceedings against tenants. When an eviction matter came on for hearing in the local court, Grant appeared for the individual, partnership, or corporate landlord. For his appearance, Grant obtained from the landlord a statutory "power of attorney" that provided that Grant was "authorized to assert and prosecute before a court or administrative agency a claim, claim for relief, cause of action, counterclaim, or cross complaint" in the name of the principal.

QUESTIONS

Which, if any, of the activities described above constitute the unauthorized practice of law? As you read the next case and the first notes following it, ask: What is the real danger if "clients" are represented by "advisors" not authorized to practice law? Cynics have argued that "unauthorized practice" rules are simply "guild" provisions designed to keep intact the lawyer monopoly. Do you agree?

RULE REFERENCES

Model Rule 5.5(a)

RESTATEMENT § 4

UNITED STATES v. JOHNSON

United States Court of Appeals, Seventh Circuit, 2003.
327 F.3d 554.

BAUER, CIRCUIT JUDGE.

Hugh Wesley Robinson and National Legal Professional Associates ("NLPA") appeal a district court order imposing monetary sanctions after the court determined that Robinson and NLPA (together, "Appellants") were engaged in the unauthorized practice of law in the Southern District of Illinois. * * *

BACKGROUND

[NLPA is] an Ohio-based firm providing pretrial, sentencing, and post-conviction consulting services, and Robinson served as NLPA's Administrative Director and Director of Case Analysis and Research. In 1985, the Ohio Supreme Court permanently disbarred Robinson from the practice of law following a federal criminal conviction for mail fraud. Robinson is not licensed to practice law in any other jurisdiction. In order to market its paralegal services, NLPA routinely provided criminal defendants with literature explaining those services and the method by which a defendant's legal counsel might hire NLPA. Since NLPA was not a law firm, nor was Robinson (nor any of NLPA's consultants under his direction) a licensed attorney, NLPA's services could comprise only part of the client's defense team under the supervision of a licensed attorney. Though NLPA marketed itself directly to criminal defendants as potential clients, and clients or their families bore sole responsibility for paying NLPA's fees, only a defendant's attorney had the ultimate authority and discretion to hire NLPA.

[Willard Johnson, the named defendant in these proceedings, was being prosecuted on federal drug-trafficking charges. Johnson was represented by court-appointed counsel Philip J. Kavanaugh III.] Johnson contacted NLPA in early 2000 after learning of the organization from a fellow inmate at the St. Clair County Jail, and Robinson replied by letter containing a promotional brochure entitled, "Helpful tips you should know when you've been BUSTED!" Convinced of the necessity of Appellants' services to the success of his defense, Johnson insisted that Kavanaugh enlist NLPA's assistance. Relying on his own professional judgment, however, Kavanaugh declined to associate himself with Appellants, prompting Johnson's [filing of a] disciplinary complaint against Kavanaugh and Kavanaugh's subsequent motion to withdraw as Johnson's counsel. * * *

Chief Judge G. Patrick Murphy heard Kavanaugh's withdrawal motion. Prior to excusing Kavanaugh, the court inquired of, and Kavanaugh confirmed, Appellants' involvement in the case. Concerned that Appellants might have interfered with Kavanaugh's representation of Johnson, the court reacted as follows:

> Well I'll tell you. This is about—there is a group from Cincinnati, and frankly, I've had them before, and they're, at best, dimwits, and they give advice to these defendants, who, God bless them, don't know any better, and they muck up the cases, and they're never here when you need them, and I'm full of it, and I'm going to prepare the necessary orders, and I'm going to have whoever they are in Court for practicing law here in Illinois through the mail. I'm going to have them here, and they're going to be sitting right in front of me, and I'm going to have some questions of them.

[P]ursuant to the district court's inherent powers, Chief Judge Murphy filed an order to show cause why Appellants should not be held in contempt of court for engaging in the unauthorized practice of law and why the court should not issue a cease and desist order against their practicing law in the Southern District of Illinois. He further ordered Robinson to appear personally * * * and to bring with him a list of all cases in the Southern District of Illinois in which Appellants had advised criminal defendants or contacted incarcerated defendants. At the * * * hearing * * *, the district court heard evidence of Appellants' conduct in connection with Johnson's case and others * * *.

Ultimately, the district court did not hold Appellants in contempt, but it did determine that they had engaged in the unauthorized practice of law in cases other than Johnson's. Chief Judge Murphy reasoned that the practical effect of Appellants' unsolicited marketing activities targeting criminal defendants was to interfere with the attorney-client relationship. By making procedural and strategic recommendations to clients, Appellants indirectly pressured defense attorneys to pursue certain courses of legal action. An attorney who refused to comply with Appellants' legal advice risked losing the confidence (and, consequently, the employ) of his client. Chief Judge Murphy characterized the situation as one "where the NLPA is * * *" effectively hijacking the professional decision-making authority of defense counsel. [As a result,] Appellants' activities exceeded the scope of their permitted paralegal function and reached the level of practicing law.

[T]he district court [therefore] placed restrictions on Appellants' permitted paralegal activities [and entered a monetary sanction against them]. * * *[6]

Appellants contest the district court's finding that they engaged in the unauthorized practice of law and its imposition of the monetary sanction.

ANALYSIS

I. *Invocation of Inherent Powers*

Appellants challenge the district court's authority and jurisdiction, pursuant to its inherent powers, to determine that they engaged in the unauthorized practice of law and to impose sanctions therefor. * * *

Whether the district court properly invoked its inherent powers is a question of law reviewable de novo. * * * Key among the inherent powers incidental to all courts is the authority to "control admission to its bar and to discipline attorneys who appear before it[." There is no conflict between state provisions on unauthorized practice and the imposition of sanctions by the federal court within that state]. Finally, we find no fault with the district court's assumption of the roles of complainant, prosecutor, judge, and jury in reaching its determination that Appellants were engaged in the unauthorized practice of law, since the court's inherent authority includes the "power to conduct independent investigations in order to determine whether the court has been the victim of fraud or deceit." * * *

II. *Unauthorized Practice Finding*

Appellants also challenge the sufficiency of the evidence upon which the district court based its finding that they engaged in the unauthorized practice of law. The issue of whether Appellants engaged in the unauthorized practice of law requires us to examine, as a preliminary matter, what constitutes the practice of law.[10] In Illinois, the practice of law includes, at a minimum, representation provided in court proceedings along with any services rendered incident thereto, even if rendered out of court. * * * More generally, providing *any* advice or other service "requiring the use of any legal skill or knowledge, ... the legal effect of which, under the facts and conditions involved, must be carefully determined," amounts to

---

6. The order prohibited Appellants from (i) directly soliciting criminal defendants or their families; (ii) sending promotional materials to criminal defendants or their families; (iii) providing research or consulting services to any criminal defendant without an authentic and bona fide request from defense counsel; and (iv) supervising or purporting to supervise decisions of defense counsel. The order further required Appellants, prior to providing any services, (i) to obtain signed authorization from defense counsel and (ii) to disclose fully to the defendant and his family NLPA's limited role as a strictly paralegal service.

10. One commentator has aptly described the practice of law in the following general terms:

Decisions indicate that the practice of law generally includes not only the conduct of litigation and appearances in court, but also the preparation of pleadings and other papers incident to any action or special proceeding in any court or other judicial body; conveyancing, the preparation of all legal instruments of all kinds whereby a legal right is secured, the rendering of opinions as to the validity or invalidity or the title to real or personal property, the giving of any legal advice, and any action for others in any matter connected with the law.

Comment, *Unauthorized Practice of Law: Remedial Procedures,* 1 DePaul L.Rev. 108 (1952) (internal citation omitted).

practicing law. * * * Only under the direct supervision of a licensed attorney may certain of these functions be performed by a paralegal. Absent the imprimatur of meaningful attorney supervision, any legal advice or other legal service provided by a nonlawyer constitutes the unauthorized practice of law.

What the district court found problematic about Appellants' activities was not the performance of those permitted paralegal functions. The preparation of pretrial motions and other services offered by Appellants, including recommendations vis-a-vis litigation strategy, might have been permissible if performed at the request and under the direction of a lawyer. Rather, what troubled Chief Judge Murphy was the reality that Appellants operated without—and, in some cases, in contravention of— attorney oversight. Appellants' promotional literature alone, while not the only evidence upon which the district court relied, is a sufficient evidentiary basis for finding that Appellants' conduct improperly inverted the attorney-client-paralegal dynamic.[12] Once Appellants, through their aggressive marketing techniques, undermined a defendant's confidence in his or her counsel, and then exploited those doubts to make strategic recommendations to—and, in the words of the district court, "to foist their services upon"—both client and counsel, any appearance of attorney supervision became meaningless. The district court therefore properly determined that Appellants were engaged in the unauthorized practice of law.

III. *Imposition of Sanctions*

[The court found that the trial court abused its discretionary power by imposing a punitive sanction after finding that the defendants were not in contempt. The court thus affirmed the finding of unauthorized practice and reversed the $7,000 punitive sanction against Appellants.]

NOTES ON UNAUTHORIZED PRACTICE

1. **Unauthorized Practice Generally:** Do you agree that when clients are represented in legal proceedings by nonlawyers there is a "potential danger to the public"? Consider *Florida Bar v. Schramek*, 616 So.2d 979 (Fla. 1993). Schramek was a Florida resident, without any apparent training in the

---

12. The following passage from NLPA's promotional materials is illustrative:

A word of warning: If, after having reviewed this information, you are interested in having [NLPA] assist your counsel with your case, keep in mind that many attorneys become extremely paranoid when they know that their client is considering asking NLPA to become involved in working on the "defense team." [I]f your attorney appears reluctant to have NLPA become involved, or if he tells you he "knows everything" and that there is nothing NLPA could bring to your defense team, you need to give serious thought to his real motive for making such a statement.... Keep in mind, *this is your life* and you as the defendant have every right to have as much assistance from any source that you deem appropriate. [sic] Your attorney works for you, you do not work for him. Therefore, should you decide to have NLPA assist you, when you speak with your attorney about this matter, be firm in explaining to him that although you appreciate all that he is doing to try and help, you want to have NLPA involved in the case and that you, as his client, are instructing him to work with us.

(Emphasis in original).

law, who, with his wife, operated a business that sold "kits" for those seeking legal advice and served as the only directors of the "L.A.W. Clinic, Inc." In one incident, Schramek advised a litigant in matrimonial litigation that child support guidelines favored a reduction in child support. The litigant lost the reduction motion and had to pay the other party's attorney's fees. In two other matters, Schramek represented persons who sought a "living trust." In both cases, deeds prepared by Schramek proved defective. In each instance, harm was caused to the clients. In another matter, Schramek appeared before the Florida Supreme Court on behalf of a corporation charged with engaging in the unauthorized practice of law. In so doing, Schramek admitted that he also engaged in the unauthorized practice. Rather than strike his pleading, which the bar sought, the court allowed Schramek to appear to prevent a default by the party alleged to be involved in the unauthorized practice. As a result, however, of the court's failure to strike his pleadings in this Supreme Court case, Schramek claimed that the Supreme Court had therefore admitted him to the practice in Florida. The Supreme Court corrected this misapprehension: "By our ruling in [the earlier case], we in no way authorized Schramek to practice law in this state. * * * We expressly hold that Daniel E. Schramek is not now, nor has he ever been, authorized to practice law in the state of Florida." *Id.* at 986.

2. **"Practice of Law":** Should there be a uniform definition of the "practice of law" or should the issue be resolved case-by-case? As noted by the American Law Institute: "The definitions and tests employed by courts to delineate unauthorized practice by nonlawyers have been vague or conclusory, while jurisdictions have differed significantly in describing what constitutes unauthorized practice in particular areas." RESTATEMENT, § 4, Comment *c* (2000).

In 2002 the ABA appointed a Task Force to consider a model definition of the "Practice of Law," which circulated a discussion draft with the following definition: "The 'practice of law' is the application of legal principles and judgment with regard to the circumstances or objectives of a person that require the knowledge and skill of a person trained in the law." *ABA Group Floats Model Rule That Would Define Practice of Law*, 18 Laws.Man. on Prof. Conduct (ABA/BNA) 620, 621 (2002). After receiving extensive critical comment from interested parties, including Justice Department and Federal Trade Commission officials concerned with antitrust implications, the Task Force settled for a recommendation that each state adopt its own definition, which should "include the basic premise that the practice of law is the application of legal principles and judgment to the circumstances or objectives of another person or entity." ABA Task Force on the Model Definition of the Practice of Law, Report to the House of Delegates and Recommendation (2003).

3. **"Kits" and Forms:** When Grant, the nonlawyer in the problem, seeks to sell "Divorce Kits," what issues arise? In light of the first two notes above, is selling a "product," that is, a "Kit," the practice of law? When will consumers most likely be misled? When dealing with "kits" and some other services, the courts draw a distinction between selling the documents themselves and giving any advice concerning those documents. Merely selling a kit, filling in forms as directed by the client, or providing the client a manual that

details action the client should take in certain situations, are not considered the unauthorized practice of law. Advice, of any kind, is. *People v. Landlords Prof'l Servs.*, 264 Cal.Rptr. 548 (Ct.App. 1989); *see also Fla. Bar re Advisory Op.–Nonlawyer Preparation of Living Trusts*, 613 So.2d 426 (Fla. 1992) (the determination of need for a living trust, together with the independent assembly and drafting of forms, does constitute the practice of law, but gathering of information needed for living trusts does not); *N.J. State Bar Ass'n v. Divorce Ctr. of Atl. Cnty.*, 477 A.2d 415 (N.J.Super.Ct. Ch.Div. 1984) (sale of kits is not, but giving of advice in connection therewith is, the unauthorized practice).

4. **Law Students:** Assume, in our problem, that Grant was not a nonlawyer, but instead, a second year law student at your law school. What are the unauthorized practice implications when a litigant is represented by a law student? According to a Nebraska ethics opinion, it would be unauthorized practice for a law student to work on a "900" telephone line which is managed by a law firm and offers legal advice to the public. Neb. State Bar, Ethics Op. 94–2 (1991). In Pennsylvania, another opinion found it to be unauthorized practice for a third year law student to conduct depositions on behalf of a client by making objections, advising the client, and examining the client. Pa. Bar, Ethics Op. 91–137 (1991). However, a number of jurisdictions have court rules authorizing student practice under specified circumstances. Some, but by no means all, of these rules even allow the student to appear without a supervising attorney. *See, e.g., City of Seattle v. Ratliff*, 667 P.2d 630 (Wash. 1983) (allowing solo student appearance after a supervised appearance). Does your state have a student practice rule? What does it provide?

5. **Web–Based Advice:** Assume, in the problem, that Grant sought to sell his "Divorce Kits" via an internet site. Are there additional problems? Consider *Office of Disciplinary Counsel v. Palmer*, 761 N.E.2d 716, 718–20 (Ohio Bd.Unauth.Prac. 2001):

> David Palmer is Executive Director, Chairman, and sole active member of the Committee to Expose Dishonest and Incompetent Attorneys and Judges. [He] is a vocal critic of attorneys and judges. His web-site, amoralethics.com, serves as the vehicle for his dissemination of those views. One prominent area of his web-site advertises "Free Legal Advice." A visitor to the "Free Legal Advice" portion of the web-site would find the following preamble:
>
> > "We are all led to believe that whenever we are faced with some legal matter that we automatically are required to employ an attorney. There are many matters of a legal nature that we can and should resolve on our own without incurring unnecessary expenses of an attorney. Although I am not an attorney, I can assure you that it is not necessary to be a lawyer in order to provide some guidance and/or advice on how to deal with your legal problems. * * * "
>
> In a final section titled "Miscellaneous Legal Matters," Palmer states:
>
> > "If you have any questions or concerns regarding any legal matter, I would be more than happy to review it and provide you with guidance and/or advice within a reasonable amount of time. It is my

desire to assist you in trying to solve your own legal matters when possible without incurring unnecessary legal expenses. It is important to remember that employing an attorney should be the last resort and not your first option. Any guidance or advice that I provide to you is absolutely free. The only time I would seek reimbursement would be for the cost of any copies and postage to send them to you if necessary." * * *

The Ohio Board of Commissioners on the Unauthorized Practice of Law was unwilling to find this web-based advice to be unauthorized practice. It stated:

It is fair to say that Palmer's web-site offers a type of general advice on legal matters, but his comments are little different from what can be found in any number of publications found on newsstands every day. Books and magazine articles offered for sale in Ohio contain legal advice from authors not licensed to practice law in this state, yet the Supreme Court has never found those publications to constitute the unauthorized practice of law. One key element of the practice of law is missing in published advice offered to the general public: the tailoring of that advice to the needs of a specific person. The practice of law involves the rendering of legal advice to an individual. Legal publications offering general advice or opinions do not purport to customize the advice to the particularized needs of the reader.

The publication of general legal advice on Palmer's web-site, good or bad, is not of itself the unauthorized practice of law. More troubling is the offer to respond to "any questions about your rights" and "provide you with guidance and/or advice." If Palmer actually gave legal advice in specific response to a question from one of his readers, he would have engaged in the unauthorized practice of law.

The Board found, however, that there was insufficient evidence of advice in specific cases.

Contrast *Palmer* with *In re Reynoso*, 477 F.3d 1117 (9th Cir. 2007) which involved the use of "web-based software that prepares bankruptcy petitions." The owner/operator of the web sites selling the software was not a lawyer, yet the advertising for the software made claims like: "[T]he Ziinet engine is an *expert system*. It knows bankruptcy laws right down to those applicable to the state in which you live." The software was designed to "select bankruptcy exemptions for the debtor" and offered access to the web site's " 'Bankruptcy Vault,' " which would provide information on " 'loopholes' " as well as " 'stealth techniques.' " Because the software did not simply place unedited responses from debtors into the forms, but instead made selections as to appropriate forms, the court found that selling the software was the unauthorized practice of law.

6. ***Pro Se* Representation:** It is not the unauthorized practice of law for an individual to act on her own behalf, either in preparation or drafting of documents or in self-representation in court proceedings. *Bennion, Van Camp, Hagen & Ruhl v. Kassler Escrow, Inc.*, 635 P.2d 730, 734 (Wash. 1981).

While *pro se* appearances do not constitute the unauthorized practice of law, and while judges will often grant procedural leniency to such litigants, the *pro se* litigant can cause difficulties for the court, as in *Hollawell v. Leman*, No. CIV. A. 94–5730, 1994 WL 545451 (E.D.Pa. Sept. 30, 1994), where the court used its inherent power to dismiss, without prejudice, pleadings filed by a *pro se* federal prisoner. The envelope in which the pleading was filed contained "language denouncing, by name, a court administrator, assistant district attorney, two state judges and a member of this judicial body * * *." The envelope itself was 12″ x 15,″ and the language printed on it was about 3/4″ high. It referred taxpayers to the fact that they were paying "a 'Documented' 'sleazy pimp,' 'fraud' and 'thief', namely Federal Judge _____, (a/k/a, 'the Pimp')."

7. **Pro Se Activities by Corporations and Other Entities:** Juridical or artificial persons, such as partnerships and corporations, cannot appear *pro se*. As one court noted, "Corporations and partnerships, by their very nature, are unable to represent themselves and the consistent interpretation * * * is that the only proper representative of a corporation is a licensed attorney, not an unlicensed layman regardless of how close his association with the partnership or corporation." *United States v. W. Processing Co.*, 734 F.Supp. 930, 940 (W.D.Wash. 1990) (quoting *Turner v. American Bar Ass'n*, 407 F.Supp. 451, 476 (N.D.Tex. 1975), *aff'd sub nom. Taylor v. Montgomery*, 539 F.2d 715 (7th Cir. 1976)). Accordingly, it was proper for a court to enter a default when a partnership attempted to appear through a non-attorney. *See Eagle Assocs. v. Bank of Montreal*, 926 F.2d 1305 (2d Cir. 1991). Likewise, when a corporate president filed a bankruptcy petition on behalf of the corporation, the petition was dismissed as "null and void," even where the corporation obtained an attorney to represent it in the proceedings. *See In re Global Constr. & Supply Inc.*, 126 B.R. 573 (Bankr.E.D.Mo. 1991). Even a sole proprietorship operating as a limited liability company could not be represented as a plaintiff in federal court by its proprietor. *See Lattanzio v. COMTA*, 481 F.3d 137 (2d Cir. 2007).

Some states have allowed such representation in certain courts of limited jurisdiction. For example, the South Carolina Supreme Court adopted a rule proposed by the state bar that allowed businesses to appear via lay agents in civil magistrate court proceedings. *See In re Unauthorized Practice of Law Rules*, 422 S.E.2d 123 (S.C. 1992). This rule, incorporated into a statute that purported to authorize lay representation of businesses "in magistrate court," was held not to extend to such a representative acting as prosecutor in criminal misdemeanor charges for passing worthless checks to the business. *See In re Richland Cnty. Magis. Ct.*, 699 S.E.2d 161 (S.C. 2010).

8. **Aiding Unauthorized Practice:** Return to the problem at the beginning of this section. When Grant makes a deal with attorney Angela Hazendorf and Angela then refers "clients" to Grant for Divorce Kits, what potential pitfalls exist for Angela? Model Rule 5.5 renders unauthorized practice an issue not just for nonlawyers, but also for lawyers. Model Rule 5.5(a) prohibits a lawyer from assisting a nonlawyer in unauthorized practice. In *In re Juhnke*, 41 P.3d 855 (Kan. 2002), Juhnke employed Hyter as a part-time legal assistant. Hyter was a disbarred lawyer who had served two months in prison for tax evasion. When first hired, Hyter assisted Juhnke in

brief writing. "Thereafter, Mr. Hyter's responsibilities expanded to whatever was placed on his desk." *Id.* at 856. Hyter handled real estate cases, including writing contracts, meeting with clients personally, preparing pleadings, and providing legal advice. Juhnke was publicly censured for his assistance to Hyter in the unauthorized practice. While the case does not so mention, Hyter was also subject to sanction. It is unauthorized practice for a suspended or disbarred attorney to continue to practice law. The ABA Standards for Imposing Lawyer Sanctions (1992) call for disbarment for a lawyer who "intentionally or knowingly engages in further similar acts of misconduct" following a suspension. *Id.*, Standard 8.1(b).

D(2) MULTI–JURISDICTIONAL PRACTICE

PROBLEM

The law firm of Berks and Ross is a professional law corporation incorporated in New York, with its principal place of business in downtown Manhattan. Columbia Corporation, Inc. is a California corporation with its principal place of business in San Francisco. Columbia Corporation is a leading producer of sports memorabilia, primarily of professional football, baseball, and basketball players. Attorneys Neal Smithton and Anna Harwick are employed by Berks and Ross. Both are licensed to practice law in New York. Neither has ever been licensed to practice law in California. In fact, no attorney at Berks and Ross is licensed to practice law in California. Nonetheless, Columbia Corporation negotiated with Berks and Ross (specifically Smithton and Harwick) to have the firm perform legal services in connection with all claims and causes of action against Sheridan, Inc., a large sports memorabilia dealer, which is a Delaware corporation whose principal place of business is Sacramento, California.

While representing Columbia Corporation, Smithton and Harwick traveled to California on several occasions. During these meetings, the attorneys discussed various matters related to Columbia Corporation's dispute with Sheridan and strategy for resolving the dispute. They made recommendations and gave advice. During one trip to California, Smithton and Harwick also met with Sheridan representatives on four or five occasions during a two-day period. At the meetings, Smithton and Harwick spoke on Columbia Corporation's behalf—at one point demanding that Sheridan pay $1 million in damages to Columbia Corporation and indicating their belief that damages would exceed $2 million if the claim were litigated.

Eventually, Columbia Corporation settled its dispute with Sheridan. When Berks and Ross then made a claim for legal fees in connection with the matter, Columbia Corporation refused to pay. Berks and Ross then sued in California for the amount of those legal fees. Columbia Corporation defended on the basis that Berks and Ross, as well as Smithton and Harwick, were not admitted to the practice of law in California and should not be permitted to recover legal fees for their services.

QUESTIONS

Would you expect that situations like this are common, where lawyers admitted in one state are hired by an entity client whose interests, business and legal, are national? How will lawyers and law firms negotiate these issues if lawyers are admitted in one state, or only a handful of states?

RULE REFERENCES

Model Rule 5.5

RESTATEMENT § 4

SUPERADIO LIMITED PARTNERSHIP v. WINSTAR RADIO PRODUCTIONS, LLC.[1]

Supreme Judicial Court of Massachusetts, 2006.
844 N.E.2d 246.

GREANEY, J. * * *

Superadio and Baby Love entered a radio network agreement (agreement) wherein Superadio became the exclusive advertising sales agent for an existing radio program and a proposed new radio program produced by Baby Love. Under the agreement, the net revenues collected from the sale of advertising airing on the radio programs were to be divided equally between Superadio and Baby Love. The agreement provided that it "shall be interpreted" under Massachusetts law and that "[a]ny dispute arising under the [a]greement, including but not limited to any dispute concerning payments due, shall be arbitrated under the rules of the American Arbitration Association (AAA) before a panel of the [AAA] sitting in Boston, Massachusetts." After an extension, the agreement terminated on December 31, 1998.

A few months later, Superadio filed a demand for arbitration, alleging that Baby Love had withheld approximately $150,000 in advertising revenues that should have been shared with Superadio. The disputed revenue allegedly derived from advertisements that had been booked by Superadio during the term of the agreement * * *. Baby Love filed an answer and a counterclaim asserting that Superadio had violated the agreement by refusing to turn over advertising revenues that Superadio had collected on Baby Love's behalf for advertisements that had aired before the agreement terminated. Baby Love sought $841,239 in damages. Superadio agreed that Baby Love was entitled to approximately $75,000 of those revenues, but held the money to offset the amount which Superadio claimed it was owed.

The parties selected a panel of three arbitrators * * *. By agreement of the parties, the Commercial Arbitration Rules of the AAA * * * would

---

1. Winstar Radio Productions, LLC, is the successor in interest to the corporation involved in the underlying dispute, Walt "Baby" Love Productions, Inc. We collectively refer to these entities as Baby Love.

govern the proceeding. The panel entered a partial summary judgment award, finding that Superadio had no right to offset, and ordering Superadio to pay the withheld amount to Baby Love. * * *

At some point in the proceedings, Superadio objected to the appearance of Baby Love's attorney, an attorney licensed to practice law in New York, but not in Massachusetts, contending that the attorney was engaged in the unauthorized practice of law. The attorney had not sought admission pro hac vice in Massachusetts, and Baby Love had not retained local counsel.

The [arbitration panel held a hearing and ultimately] concluded that Baby Love had supported its claim that Superadio had underreported the amount of advertising revenues owed. The panel, however, could not enter an award for contract damages because of Baby Love's inability to prove its damages, an inability attributable to Superadio's failure in discovery to produce documents relevant to the damages issue. The panel concluded that * * * it had the authority to impose a sanction on Superadio for violating the panel's * * * discovery order, and imposed a sanction in the amount of $271,000. [T]he panel rejected Superadio's argument that the representation of Baby Love by a licensed out-of-State attorney constituted the unauthorized practice of law.

Superadio filed a complaint in the Superior Court seeking to vacate the arbitration award. Baby Love filed an answer and a counterclaim requesting confirmation of the award. [The trial court affirmed the panel's award, but the appellate court reversed it.] We granted Baby Love's application for further appellate review. * * *

We first take up Superadio's argument that the arbitration award was procured by undue means * * * because Baby Love's attorney, a New York attorney not licensed to practice law in Massachusetts, engaged in the unauthorized practice of law by representing Baby Love in the arbitration. As a general proposition, an attorney practicing law in Massachusetts must be licensed, or authorized, to practice law here. Whether representation of a party by an out-of-State licensed attorney at a Massachusetts arbitration proceeding constitutes the practice of law, is an issue of first impression.

Under the Massachusetts Rules of Professional Conduct, * * * a lawyer "shall not ... practice law in a jurisdiction where doing so violates the regulation of the legal profession in that jurisdiction." Mass. R. Prof. C. 5.5 * * *.

The parallel rule of the American Bar Association (ABA) Model Rules of Professional Conduct (2003) [Model Rule 5.5(c)][3] now expressly permits multijurisdictional practice in arbitration. * * *

3. While the matter is generally governed by rule, a few courts have decided the issue. See *Williamson v. John D. Quinn Constr. Corp.,* 537 F.Supp. 613, 616 (S.D.N.Y.1982) (rejecting claim that out-of-State attorney and firm were foreclosed from recovery obtained in connection with services rendered in arbitration proceeding because not authorized to practice law in that State); *Colmar, Ltd. v. Fremantlemedia N. Am., Inc.,* 344 Ill.App.3d 977, 989, 280 Ill.Dec. 72, 801 N.E.2d

Adoption of this rule is currently under consideration in Massachusetts[, and many states] have adopted a rule of professional conduct similar or identical to ABA Model Rule 5.5(c)(3). We note also that, while the Restatement (Third) of the Law Governing Lawyers § 3 (2000), does not expressly address arbitration, it generally permits an out-of-State attorney to "provide legal services" in another jurisdiction to a client so long as the matter is reasonably related to the attorney's home-State practice. * * * We conclude that, even assuming that the representation might constitute the unauthorized practice of law, the conduct would not provide a basis to vacate the [arbitration] award.

[The arbitration panel acted in conformance with AAA rules when imposing sanctions against Superadio.] The award here, based as it is on the monetary assessment imposed for Superadio's violation of discovery, gives Baby Love a measure of relief in damages that would otherwise have been impermissibly denied because of Superadio's intransigence, hardly an "injustice" * * *.

Judgment affirmed.

NOTES ON MULTI-JURISDICTIONAL PRACTICE

1. After the *Superadio* case, Massachusetts did adopt the ABA version of Model Rule 5.5(c). *See* Rule 3:07, MASS. RULES OF PROF. CONDUCT.

2. Prior to Model Rule 5.5(c), decisions were mixed on whether participation by an out-of-state lawyer in arbitration constituted the "practice of law," as noted in the *Superadio* court's footnote 3. Based on your review of the earlier section, generally dealing with "Unauthorized Practice," do you consider what lawyers do in representing a client in a contested arbitration proceeding the "practice of law"? If so, why do you think courts have held otherwise? Consider your answer in light of the question posed to you prior to *Superadio.*

The *Superadio* court's footnote 3 mentions the California case of *Birbrower, Montalbano, Condon & Frank, P.C. v. Superior Court*, 949 P.2d 1 (Cal. 1998). This case, which served as the basis for the problem, drew particular attention in the ABA's push to adopt Model Rule 5.5(c). In *Birbrower*, the court found that the New York lawyers were engaged in the unauthorized practice of law in California, then found that they therefore were not allowed to recover any legal fees for work done within the state, although they could

---

1017 (2003) (concluding that out-of-State attorney's representation of client during arbitration proceeding did not constitute unauthorized practice of law). But cf. *Matter of Creasy*, 198 Ariz. 539, 541–544, 12 P.3d 214 (2000) (concluding that disbarred attorney violated order of disbarment because [he] engaged in practice of law by representing party at private arbitration proceeding). Since the *Creasy* opinion, ABA Model Rule 5.5(c)(3) has been adopted in Arizona. See Ariz. R. Prof. C. 5.5(c)(3) (2005). Out-of-State attorneys engaging in arbitration proceedings in Arizona, however, must inform their clients that they are not admitted to practice in Arizona, and "must obtain the client's informed consent to such representation." Ariz. R. Prof. C. 5.5(e). We note that Superadio's reliance on *Birbrower, Montalbano, Condon & Frank, P.C. v. Superior Court,* 17 Cal.4th 119, 70 Cal.Rptr.2d 304, 949 P.2d 1, cert. denied sub nom. *Birbrower, Montalbano, Condon & Frank, P.C. v. ESQ Business Servs., Inc.,* 525 U.S. 920, 119 S.Ct. 291, 142 L.Ed.2d 226 (1998), is misplaced. In that case, it was determined that the out-of-State attorneys had engaged in the unauthorized practice of law, but "none of the time that the New York attorneys spent in California was spent in arbitration." *Id.* at 133.

recover for work performed in New York. 949 P.2d at 11. Although a substantial part of the work done in California involved preparation for arbitration that was preempted by settlement, the court declined to carve out an exception for such work. *Id.* at 9. Shortly after the *Birbrower* decision, the California legislature adopted a statute providing a procedure (analogous to *pro hac vice* admission to appear in court) whereby out-of-state lawyers could be permitted to represent parties in arbitration proceedings. *See* CAL.CIV.PROC. CODE § 1282.4(b) *et seq.* (1998, reenacted in 2010 and 2012). Finally, in 2004, the California Supreme Court adopted a Rule that parallels (but is not identical to) Model Rule 5.5(c) in providing a limited exemption from unauthorized practice rules for multijurisdictional practice. *See* Cal. Rules of Ct. Rule 9.48(h) (2007).

3. **Model Rule 5.5(c):** Consider two ethics opinions written by the Philadelphia Bar Association's Professional Guidance Committee. In the first, the ethics committee concluded that a lawyer from outside Pennsylvania was not engaged in the unauthorized practice when representing a client in an alternative dispute resolution proceeding in Pennsylvania. *Out-of-State Lawyer May Handle ADR Matter for Existing Client*, 72 U.S.L.W. 2389 (Jan. 13, 2004). In the second, the committee concluded that a lawyer licensed in India was engaged in the unauthorized practice when trying to advise a Pennsylvania citizen on Indian law in Pennsylvania. *Lawyer Who Is Admitted in Foreign Country Can't Be 'Legal Consultant' in Pennsylvania*, 72 U.S.L.W. 2375 (Jan. 6, 2004). Under Model Rule 5.5(c), are these correct results? Why or why not?

Then consider the lawyers in an Atlanta, Georgia law firm who were indicted for unauthorized practice in North Carolina. The lawyers assisted Gardner–Webb University, a North Carolina school, in an NCAA investigation concerning the university's basketball program. The North Carolina State Bar Authorized Practice Committee sent the lawyers a cautionary letter prior to the indictment. *Georgia Law Firm, Lawyers Are Indicted For Unauthorized Practice in North Carolina*, 20 Laws.Man. on Prof. Conduct (ABA/BNA) 203 (Apr. 21, 2004). Does anything in Model Rule 5.5(c) permit the lawyers' conduct?

Finally, consider *Rose–Velasquez v. Astrue*, No. 2:06–CV–297 TS, 2008 WL 1765659 (D. Utah Apr. 16, 2008), where the client's attorney was admitted in Utah, but hired an attorney who was not admitted in Utah to write briefs in the case. The client then opposed payment of legal fees to the non-admitted lawyer. To justify payment to the non-admitted lawyer, what would be required under Model Rule 5.5(c)?

Multi-jurisdictional practice issues cross not just state, but also national, borders. The ABA Ethics Committee has concluded that a U.S. lawyer "may outsource legal or nonlegal support services provided the lawyer remains ultimately responsible for rendering competent legal services to the client." ABA Standing Comm. on Ethics and Prof'l Resp., Formal Op. 08–451 (2008). Although many accept some outsourcing of legal work to those outside the United States, the practice remains somewhat controversial, due in part to the effect on the employment prospects of new attorneys. *See* Jose A. Arambulo, Comment, *O Where, O Where Has My Legal Job Gone?: Examining the Realities of "Offshoring" Legal Work and Why States Can Regulate the Practice Despite Congress' Broad Power Under the Foreign Commerce Clause,* 38 Sw.L.Rev. 195 (2008). There are still disputes about the extent of outsourcing, the supervisory duties of the U.S. lawyer, see Mark L. Tuft, *Supervising Offshore Outsourcing of Legal Services in a Global Environment: Re–Examining Current Ethical Standards,* 43 Akron L.Rev. 825 (2010), and other matters. For discussions of non-U.S. lawyers providing legal services, see Steven C. Bennett, *The Ethics of Legal Outsourcing,* 36 N.Ky.L.Rev. 479 (2009), and Jack P. Sahl, *Foreword: The New Era—Quo Vadis?,* 43 Akron L.Rev. 641 (2010).

4. **Multi–Jurisdictional Practice Following Major Disaster:** Following Hurricane Katrina's path of destruction through the Gulf region, the ABA adopted a "Model Court Rule on Provision of Legal Services Following Determination of Major Disaster" in 2007. Under that rule, the highest court of a state could determine the occurrence of a disaster affecting the justice system within the state or affecting out-of-state citizens who now needed legal services within the state. Further, the court could determine that a disaster in another state required assistance from in-state lawyers. In any such event, out-of-state lawyers would be permitted to provide legal services within the state and in-state lawyers could be permitted to perform services in other states, provided that all such services were provided on a pro bono basis. Comment [14] to Model Rule 5.5 references this model court rule.

5. ***Pro Hac Vice* Admission:** Admission *pro hac vice* takes place when a non-admitted lawyer is permitted by a court to practice before that court in connection with a particular matter. Such admission usually involves a lawyer from, for example, Arkansas, seeking admission to try a case in Texas. It could also involve a lawyer, for example, admitted in Virginia but not admitted in the federal court in Virginia, seeking admission to the federal court in Virginia to try a single case. In a case involving a lawyer who sought admission *pro hac vice* in West Virginia for the purpose of handling a series of asbestos-related tort cases, the Supreme Court of West Virginia discussed the concept:

> In *Leis v. Flynt,* 439 U.S. 438, 441–42, 99 S.Ct. 698, 700, 58 L.Ed.2d 717, 721–22 (1979), the United States Supreme Court discussed *pro hac vice* admissions in the American courts:
>
>> We do not question that the practice of courts in most states is to allow an out-of-state lawyer the privilege of appearing upon motion, especially when he is associated with a member of the local bar. In view of the high mobility of the bar, and also the trend toward specialization, perhaps this is a practice to be encouraged. But it is not a right granted either by statute or the Constitution.
>
> Although the opportunity to appear in a state court *pro hac vice* is a privilege and not a right, a court should grant a request to appear *pro hac vice* "unless some legitimate state interest is thwarted by admission of the out-of-state attorney." *Enquire Printing & Publishing Co., Inc. v. O'Reilly,* 193 Conn. 370, 375, 477 A.2d 648 (1984) * * *.
>
>> Where the Court is satisfied that the out-of-state attorney has sufficient training and expertise to represent his clients' interests

and is admitted and practicing law in good standing in another state
. . . the motion to admit *pro hac vice* will generally be granted. * * *

18 International Ltd. v. Interstate Express, Inc., 116 Misc. 2d 66, 455
N.Y.S.2d 224, 226 (1982).

These and other factors were considered by the Arkansas Supreme
Court in *McKenzie v. Burris*, 255 Ark. 330, 500 S.W.2d 357 (197[3]) * * *:

> The state has legitimate interests to be weighed in considering pro
> hac vice admissions in order to maintain a high level of professional
> ethics, to assure a high quality of representation in the courts and to
> protect the economic interests of the regularly licensed resident
> attorneys of the state. In order to properly protect these interests and
> to expedite the administration of justice, the courts are concerned
> with the qualifications and conduct of counsel, their availability for
> service of papers and amenability to disciplinary proceedings.

> [T]here are occasions when, because an out-of-state attorney has
> demonstrated considerable expertise in a specialized area of the law, a
> court will admit that attorney *pro hac vice* for the limited purpose of
> engaging in that type of litigation. * * *

> However, we emphasize that, like the practice of law, the *pro hac vice*
> admission of an out-of-state attorney not licensed to practice law in this
> State is a privilege, not a right. Trial court judges, in the conscientious
> exercise of their discretion, may refuse otherwise proper *pro hac vice*
> applications when there is evidence of misconduct or other procedural
> abuses by the attorney seeking admission.

State ex rel. H.K. Porter Co. v. White, 386 S.E.2d 25, 29–31 (W.Va. 1989).

6.   In a criminal case, where a defendant is normally entitled to the
effective assistance of counsel of her own choosing, the decision to deny
admission *pro hac vice* to counsel chosen by the defendant "necessarily
implicates constitutional concerns." *Panzardi–Alvarez v. United States*, 879
F.2d 975, 980 (1st Cir. 1989).

E.   DISCIPLINE

PROBLEM

Having been admitted to the bar in your state, you entered into practice
as an associate in the firm of McGann & Arnone, a medium size firm for your
area. A few weeks ago, Casey Forrester came to see you. Casey indicated that
she had been represented by Albert Hoching, a local lawyer that you have
met. Hoching represented Casey in a personal injury action and had told
Casey and her husband that the case was proceeding nicely. In fact, Hoching
had never filed the claim, and the statute of limitations has now run. Casey
found this out this morning, when she went to court for some sort of hearing
and Hoching did not appear. When Casey went to Hoching's office, she found
him packing the last of his office into the back of a truck. Hoching told Casey
that he was checking himself into a mental hospital in another state. Casey

went back to the court and was able to tell the judge what happened, in the presence of adversary counsel, whereupon the judge encouraged Casey to find a new lawyer.

Casey had heard your name from a friend and came to your office. Because you find Casey's story so bizarre, you tell her you want to bring in Susan Westin, your senior partner. When the two of you pop unannounced into Westin's office, you find she is with Ralph Waite, a local banker that you and Westin have represented on several occasions. When you tell Westin that Casey and you would like to talk to her about another local lawyer, Waite immediately chimes in: "Oh that reminds me, did you guys hear that Albert Hoching has just 'lost it'? He was in the bank this morning, closed all his accounts, took the money, and said he was moving to another state." Upon hearing this, you tell Waite and Westin what Casey has just told you. Casey listens and says nothing.

QUESTIONS

Waite and Casey leave soon thereafter, and Westin chastises you for repeating what a client told you to another client. Thereafter, Westin believes you, as well as adversary counsel in Casey's underlying case, have an obligation to reveal Hoching's misconduct to the bar's disciplinary authorities, but Westin wants you to check with Casey before you tell anyone. The next day, you call Casey and seek permission to involve the authorities. "What will happen?" she wants to know. You respond: "Well, by the time they do anything, he may be out of state. Most likely, other clients are involved and you may not be able to collect much if you sue Hoching for malpractice." Casey is then adamant: "Please don't tell anybody until you've had a chance to talk with him. Maybe you can work something out so I can get something for my trouble before everybody else finds out." Because of your conversation in the presence of Waite, Westin thinks the information about Hoching is no longer privileged and that you must reveal it to the disciplinary authorities. Can you properly follow the mandate from your client?

RULE REFERENCES

Model Rules 8.3 and 8.5

ABA Model Code of Judicial Conduct, Rule 2.15 (formerly Canon 3D)

RESTATEMENT § 5

ABA Standards for Imposing Lawyer Discipline (1986)

IN RE ETHICS ADVISORY PANEL OPINION NO. 92–1

Supreme Court of Rhode Island, 1993.
627 A.2d 317.

MURRAY, JUSTICE.

This matter came before us pursuant to a petition for review filed by the Rhode Island Chief Disciplinary Counsel (disciplinary counsel), requesting that this court review and rescind the Supreme Court Ethics

Advisory Panel Opinion No. 92–1, issued January 14, 1992. * * * According to the panel, it received a letter from an attorney requesting ethical advice. The letter stated that another attorney, "attorney X," had represented a corporation on various legal and business matters since 1987. Attorney X referred a litigation matter to the inquiring attorney regarding a lease agreement that attorney X had negotiated previously on behalf of the client. Pursuant to the lease agreement, attorney X held client funds in an escrow account. After several years of litigation the inquiring attorney negotiated a settlement of the dispute and the client agreed to the settlement. The inquiring attorney then called attorney X to arrange for the release of the funds from the escrow account. During that conversation, attorney X told the inquiring attorney that the funds were not available because attorney X had used the funds without the client's authorization.

The inquiring attorney then advised the client of the criminal nature of attorney X's conduct and stated that he or she had a duty to report the ethical violation to the disciplinary authorities. According to the brief submitted by the panel, "[t]he client would not authorize a disclosure and expressed a concern to have the client funds replaced. The client believed that to report the misconduct would interfere with the likelihood of the funds being replaced."

Subsequently, attorney X replaced the client's funds. The client was satisfied with the restoration of the funds and refused to authorize disclosure of the misconduct. According to the panel, the client continued to use attorney X's services on other legal matters.

The aforementioned facts implicate two of the most fundamental ethical obligations of attorneys engaged in the practice of law. The first is the lawyer's duty of confidentiality. This duty is set forth in Rule 1.6 of the Rules of Professional Conduct * * *. The second fundamental duty triggered by these facts is an attorney's duty to report to disciplinary authorities the professional misconduct of another attorney [pursuant to Rule 8.3].

The Ethics Advisory Panel reviewed these rules and issued the following opinion: * * *

"The Panel notes that pursuant to Rule 1.6, an attorney is given discretion to reveal information relating to the representation of a client in only two situations. If neither of these situations arise, the attorney is prohibited from making a disclosure. The Panel also notes the comment to Rule 1.6 which states in part, 'The confidentiality rule applies not merely to matters communicated in confidence by the client but also to all information relating to the representation, whatever its source.'

"Assuming the information the attorney received is confidential and within the attorney-client privilege, the Panel is of the opinion that absent the consent of the client, the attorney is prohibited * * * from revealing it, even in the context of reporting another attorney's misconduct. See also Rule 8.3(c) which states that a report regarding another attorney's misconduct is not required where it would involve violating Rule 1.6."

In this petition for review the disciplinary counsel argues that the Rules of Professional Conduct do not prohibit a lawyer from reporting the serious ethical misconduct of another attorney without client consent when the reporting attorney learned of the misconduct by way of an admission by the accused attorney and not by way of disclosure from the client. * * *

In this case none of the parties disputes the suggestion that attorney X's embezzlement of client funds is a violation of the Rules of Professional Conduct that raises a substantial question regarding attorney X's fitness to practice law. In addition, it is clear that on the basis of the admission by attorney X, the inquiring attorney had "knowledge" of the violation as required by Rule 8.3. Thus, absent a confidentiality issue, it is clear that the inquiring attorney would be under an ethical obligation to report the embezzlement and indeed would be subject to discipline if the inquiring attorney failed to report the embezzlement.

Rule 8.3(c), however, expressly exempts Rule 1.6 confidences from disclosure. Pursuant to Rule 1.6, an attorney "shall not reveal information relating to representation of a client unless the client consents after consultation, except for disclosures that are impliedly authorized." The official comment to Rule 1.6 helps define the phrase "shall not reveal information relating to the representation of a client." The comment states:

> "The principle of confidentiality is given effect in two related bodies of law, the attorney-client privilege (which includes the work product doctrine) in the law of evidence and the rule of confidentiality established in professional ethics. * * * *The confidentiality rule applies not merely to matters communicated in confidence by the client but also to all information relating to the representation, whatever its source.*" (Emphasis added.) * * *

Applying these rules, the Ethics Advisory Panel concluded that the inquiring attorney's knowledge of attorney X's embezzlement was confidential information because the inquiring attorney learned of the embezzlement during the course of his representation of a client. Moreover, the panel noted that neither of the two exceptions to Rule 1.6 applied, and accordingly Rule 1.6 required the inquiring attorney to keep his or her knowledge of the embezzlement confidential.

The disciplinary counsel * * * suggests that because the admission by attorney X was not a "privileged" communication pursuant to the rules regarding the attorney-client evidentiary privilege, the admission was not a protected communication pursuant to Rule 1.6. In support of this argument, the disciplinary counsel cites *In re Himmel*, 125 Ill.2d 531, 127 Ill.Dec. 708, 533 N.E.2d 790 (1988). In *Himmel* the Illinois Supreme Court interpreted [prior Disciplinary] Rule 1–103(a) [and] concluded that attorney Himmel did have knowledge of a communication that fell outside the attorney-client privilege. The fact that the communication was not "privileged," combined with the court's finding that Himmel stood to gain financially from the nondisclosure of the violation led the Illinois Supreme Court to discipline Himmel for failing to comply with the reporting requirements. * * *

The disciplinary counsel's reliance on *Himmel* in this case is misplaced. Unlike Illinois' rule, Rule 1.6 * * * protects from disclosure a broader range of information than would be protected under the attorney-client privilege. Even though the attorney-client evidentiary privilege may not protect this information, Rule 1.6 prevents the inquiring attorney from disclosing it because it relates to the representation of a client. * * *

This is not to say that we are not concerned with the ramifications of this decision. In this case a lawyer has engaged in criminal conduct as well as violated the Rules of Professional Conduct. The failure of the Rules of Professional Conduct to facilitate the investigation and prosecution of attorney X is correspondingly a failure of the legal profession to regulate itself effectively. This failure fuels the perception that under a cloak of confidentiality, the legal profession is engaged in a cover-up of attorney misconduct. [The study of the rule might be worthwhile to avoid this result in the future, but the Ethics Advisory Panel is affirmed.]

NOTES ON DISCIPLINE

1. **Extent of Knowledge Required:** Model Rule 8.3(a) requires a report only if the lawyer "knows" of the other lawyer's unfitness. What constitutes knowledge under Model Rule 1.0(f)? Consider two cases. First, in *In re Riehlmann*, 2004–0680 (La. 1/19/05), 891 So.2d 1239, Riehlmann, a criminal defense attorney, had worked as a prosecutor with Deegan, a law school classmate. In a 1994 conversation with Riehlmann, Deegan indicated that he was terminally ill and that he had deliberately suppressed blood evidence that could have exculpated a murder defendant Deegan prosecuted. He had obtained a conviction and sentence of death. After Deegan died, Riehlmann did not reveal this conversation until five years later, when the original defendant was about to be executed and new defense counsel found some hint of manipulation of the blood evidence. Did Riehlmann "know" of the misconduct of Deegan? Did Riehlmann fulfill his Model Rule 8.3 duty?

Second, in *Estate of Spencer v. Gavin*, 2008 WL 1899196 (N.J.Super.Ct.App.Div. Apr. 23, 2008), lawyer Gavin stole $400,000 while serving as personal representative of the estate of a client. Gavin then died of cancer. While serving as personal representative, Gavin hired Averna, an attorney in an unrelated firm, to do several small drafting assignments for the estate, for which Averna received total payment of less than $3,000. Averna was added as a defendant in subsequent civil suits against Gavin and his estate, with the plaintiffs claiming that Averna owed a duty to the estate, by virtue of Model Rule 8.3, to report Gavin. When Averna moved for summary judgment, the estate produced affidavits from another attorney who indicated that Averna was being groomed to take over Gavin's practice, that Averna used legal forms with Gavin's name, that Averna told the attorney that Gavin was " 'raping and pillaging' " the estate, and that Averna was aware that Gavin had purportedly stolen two rings from the estate, used them in Gavin's own marriage and, in fact, was buried in one. Averna maintained that he was not associated with Gavin in the practice of law and that he knew nothing of the theft. How should these facts be analyzed under Model Rule 8.3?

Is the Model Rule 8.3(c) exception applicable to either case? Why or why not? If not, why did each attorney who knew of the misconduct by the other attorney fail to report it? For discussions of the reluctance of attorneys to report misconduct by their fellow attorneys, see Fred C. Zacharias, *The Myth of Self–Regulation*, 93 Minn.L.Rev. 1147 (2009), and Thomas R. DeBray, Jr., Comment, *No One Likes a Tattletale: Why Alabama Should No Longer Force Attorneys to Report the Professional Misconduct of Other Attorneys*, 34 J. Legal Prof. 181 (2009).

2. **Disciplinary Sanctions:** Return to our problem. Assume that Hoching is turned in to the ethics authorities by Casey's adversary counsel. The case is heard and Hoching is found guilty of a disciplinary violation. What should be considered in imposing a sanction? The Standards for Imposing Lawyer Sanctions, adopted by the ABA in 1986 and reaffirmed in 2012, are often used by courts as an aid in determining the appropriate sanction. In general, courts are encouraged to review "the duty violated," "the lawyer's mental state," "the potential or actual injury caused by the lawyer's misconduct," and "the existence of aggravating or mitigating factors." *Id.*, Standard 3.0. Subject to these general factors, the Standards generally make recommendations depending on the severity of the injury and the mental state of the lawyer for *disbarment* (terminating the individual's status as a lawyer, either permanently or for a number of years after which the disbarred lawyer is required to reapply), *suspension* (removing the lawyer from practice indefinitely or for a specified period of time), *reprimand* (public censure), or *admonition* (private censure). *Id.*, Standards 2.2, 2.3, 2.5 & 2.6.

Other sanctions are also possible. Interim suspension is suggested when the lawyer should be removed from practice pending final disposition of some matter, such as final resolution of a criminal matter, or where the lawyer is physically or mentally unable to continue practice. *Id.*, Standard 2.4. The Standards also authorize probation, which can include supervision by another attorney, periodic audits of bank accounts, periodic mental or physical examinations, and re-passing of the bar examination or the Multistate Professional Responsibility Examination. *Id.*, Standards 2.7 & 2.8. Additional sanctions can include, among other things, restitution and assessment of the costs of the disciplinary process. *Id.*, Standard 2.8. In *Kentucky Bar Ass'n v. Greene*, 63 S.W.3d 182 (Ky. 2002), the attorney was required to satisfy a malpractice judgment against him as a condition of any application for reinstatement following a suspension.

3. **Process Required in Disciplinary Proceedings:** The United States Supreme Court has held that lawyer disciplinary proceedings, even though designed to protect the public, constitute a "punishment or penalty imposed on the lawyer." *In re Ruffalo*, 390 U.S. 544, 550 (1968). Accordingly, the proceedings are "quasi-criminal" and the lawyer charged is "entitled to

procedural due process, which includes fair notice of the charge." *Id.* at 550. Other than *Ruffalo*, where charges against the lawyer were amended after the lawyer testified at the disciplinary hearing but the lawyer was given no additional opportunity to defend those charges, the extent of the "due process" that is required in disciplinary matters has been somewhat unclear.

Rosenthal v. Justices of the Supreme Court of California, 910 F.2d 561 (9th Cir. 1990), provides an example of an attorney's due process rights. The attorney, who had been disbarred by the California Supreme Court, filed a federal action claiming that various provisions of the California disciplinary scheme were constitutionally deficient. In rejecting this challenge, the court pointed out several differences between disciplinary and criminal proceedings. In a lawyer disciplinary proceeding, according to the court:

(a) The criminal law's presumption of innocence does not apply.

(b) The criminal law's requirement of "proof beyond a reasonable doubt" does not apply.

(c) The confrontation requirements of the criminal law are not applicable. As a result, admission of documents from other proceedings is permitted in disciplinary hearings.

(d) The lawyer is entitled to limited procedural due process such as notice and an opportunity to be heard, as well as call witnesses and cross-examine them.

The limited due process to which the lawyer is entitled does not include the right to a court-appointed attorney if the lawyer is indigent. *See In re Harris*, 49 P.3d 778, 784 (Or. 2002) (holding that a disciplinary proceeding is not "criminal" for Sixth Amendment appointment of counsel purposes). The court also declined an invitation to compel attorneys to represent indigent subjects of disciplinary proceedings under the court's inherent power.

In *Spevack v. Klein*, 385 U.S. 511 (1967), the Court held that the privilege against self-incrimination applies to testimony in a lawyer disciplinary hearing and that a lawyer cannot be disciplined for non-cooperation solely because of his invocation of the privilege due to fear of criminal punishment. It is apprehension of *criminal* punishment that triggers the privilege, however, and there is no general right to remain silent in an attorney disciplinary proceeding. *See In re Zisook* 430 N.E.2d 1037 (Ill. 1981).

4. **Duty to Report Judges:** Model Rule 8.3(b) imposes a substantially similar duty on lawyers to report judicial misconduct as exists to report lawyer misconduct. In *In re Borders*, 665 A.2d 1381 (D.C. 1995), a lawyer sought readmission after being disbarred due to federal convictions for, among other things, conspiracy and obstruction of justice. The obstruction charge arose when Borders participated in a plot to obtain leniency from federal judge Alcee Hastings, who was later impeached. Borders refused to testify in response to a subpoena in both criminal and subsequent impeachment proceedings related to Judge Hastings. Borders was granted immunity for his testimony, but still refused to testify, and he was held in contempt. *See id.* at 1382–83. The District of Columbia Court of Appeals found this violation of Model Rule 8.3(b), among others, to justify denying Border's application for

readmission. *See* 665 A.2d at 1384. Judge Hastings went on to become a United States Congressman from Florida.

5. **"The Robing Room":** "The Robing Room" is a website whose subtitle is: "Where judges are judged." *See* www.therobingroom.com. One of the features of the site is its rankings of the "top 10" and "bottom 10" federal judges. One post states: "This judge is utterly contemptible. . . . Look, I'm a prosecutor. Have been my whole life[. The activities in this court are] totally disgusting and morally bankrupt. [The judge is] a disgrace to the bench [who] should be impeached." www.therobingroom.com/Judge.aspx?ID= 1517#comments. Does this prosecutor who penned this post have a duty to report the judge to judicial disciplinary authorities?

6. **Duty of Judges to Report Lawyer/Judge Misconduct:** Return to the problem at the beginning of this section. Does the judge who heard Casey's story have any obligation to report Hoching's misconduct? Does the judge have enough information? Under Rules 2.15(A) and (B) (formerly Canon 3D(1) and (2)) of the ABA Model Code of Judicial Conduct, if a judge has "knowledge" of the misconduct of either another judge or lawyer that raises "a substantial question" about the judge's or lawyer's "honesty, trustworthiness, or fitness," the judge must "inform the appropriate authority." "Knowledge" is defined the same for judges as it is for lawyers, i.e., "actual knowledge" which can be "inferred from circumstances." *Id.*, Terminology. If the judge does not have actual knowledge of misconduct, but has "information indicating a substantial likelihood" of misconduct of either another judge or lawyer, the judge must "take appropriate action" under Rules 2.15(C) and (D) (formerly Canon 3D(1) and (2)). "Appropriate action" can include discussion with the potentially offending individual, discussion with judge's supervisor, or reporting the possible violation. *Id.*, Rule 2.15, Comment [2].

7. **Reciprocal Discipline:** Return to the problem at the beginning of this section. Assume Hoching is disciplined in your state. Does he have any obligation to advise other states or federal courts where he is admitted? Will those states discipline Hoching? Lawyers licensed in multiple jurisdictions are usually required to report the fact that they have been disciplined by one jurisdiction to other jurisdictions where they are admitted, even if they are not actually practicing in the other jurisdictions. Failure to so report is itself a separate violation. *See In re Hawkins*, 2001 ND 55, 623 N.W.2d 431. This obligation applies when the attorney is disciplined in one state and admitted in another. *See In re Shea*, 760 N.Y.S.2d 492 (App.Div. 2003) (discipline in Connecticut; reciprocal discipline in New York). It also applies when the attorney is disciplined in the federal court and admitted in state court. *See In re Cohn*, 761 N.Y.S.2d 177 (App.Div. 2003) (discipline in federal court; reciprocal discipline in state court). Finally, the obligation applies when the attorney is disciplined in state court and admitted to federal court. *See In re Kramer*, 282 F.3d 721 (9th Cir. 2002) (discipline in state; reciprocal discipline in federal court). Comments to the ABA Standards for Imposing Lawyer Sanctions (1991) recognize that reciprocal discipline can be imposed without a hearing, but encourage the opportunity for the lawyer to be heard "to raise * * * due process challenge[s] or to show that a sanction different from the

sanction imposed in the other jurisdiction is warranted." *Id.* § 2.9, Commentary.

8. **Multi–Jurisdictional Discipline and Choice of Law:** Suppose, in the problem, that Hoching maintains his principal law office in an adjoining jurisdiction where he was going to check into a hospital. His office in your jurisdiction is only a part-time one. The adjoining state uses a former version of the Model Rules as its standard of attorney conduct. Whose disciplinary rules should be considered in disciplining Hoching? Under Model Rule 8.5(a), a lawyer admitted to practice in more than one jurisdiction is subject to discipline in any of the jurisdictions, regardless of where the misconduct occurs. Model Rule 8.5(b) is the ABA's effort to determine which state's law applies when a lawyer who is admitted in multiple jurisdictions faces discipline. Model Rule 8.5(b)(1) provides that the rules of professional conduct of the jurisdiction where a case is venued will apply to litigation-related conduct. For other matters, the rules of the jurisdiction in which the lawyer's conduct occurred apply, unless the lawyer's conduct had its "predominant effect" in a different jurisdiction, but a lawyer will not be disciplined if the lawyer's conduct conforms to the rules of the jurisdiction where the lawyer reasonably believed the conduct would have its predominant effect. *See* Model Rule 8.5(b)(2).

In the RESTATEMENT, the American Law Institute elected not to adopt a formal rule on the topic, although the comments acknowledge the ABA position. The ALI comments indicate "presumptive" jurisdiction in a state where a single lawyer engaging in non-litigation work is admitted, or if admitted in multiple states, in the state where the lawyer maintains his or her "principal place of law practice." In litigated matters, "presumptive" jurisdiction exists in the state where the litigation is pending. The Comment then notes: "Either presumptive preference can be displaced by a sufficient demonstration that the interests of another jurisdiction" are more compelling. RESTATEMENT, § 5, Comment *h.*

9. **Discipline of Attorneys Admitted *Pro Hac Vice*:** Once admitted to practice *pro hac vice*, the attorney is entitled to the same procedural rights regarding revocation for cause as are provided to a regularly admitted attorney subject to discipline. Thus, an attorney admitted *pro hac vice* cannot be disciplined under more stringent standards than those used for local counsel. While full-scale hearings to revoke *pro hac vice* status are unnecessary, the attorney must be given notice and an opportunity to be heard. *See United States v. Collins*, 920 F.2d 619, 626 (10th Cir. 1990).

F. REGULATION OF LAWYERS IN LAW FIRMS

PROBLEM

You have recently graduated from law school and have joined Smith, Stavros & Schwartz, a 10–person law firm in the capital city of your state, as a salaried associate. The firm has three partners (whose names make up the firm name) and six other associates. It maintains a general practice, with some emphasis on litigation, particularly plaintiffs' personal injury litigation. The firm has an excellent reputation and does fairly extensive radio and television advertising within the state.

Among the first tasks you are assigned is to research the feasibility of transforming the firm from its present partnership organization to a business structure that shields individual members of the firm from the business liabilities of the firm itself. Your state legislature has adopted statutes permitting the formation of three alternative types of companies for the provision of "licensed professional services": the professional corporation, the limited liability company, and the limited liability partnership. These statutes all provide that members of such organizations (that is, shareholders, partners, or other owners of equity interests) who practice a licensed profession remain personally liable (that is, to the extent of their personal assets) for their own acts in performance of their profession, but not for the acts of any other member or employee of the firm and not for any obligations incurred by the firm as such. The state supreme court, which has regulatory authority over the practice of law, has yet to rule on whether lawyers are permitted to utilize these alternative forms as provided by the statute. The Model Rules have been adopted by the supreme court without relevant modification.

At the same time, you are asked to research whether the firm, in its present form or in a limited liability form, could establish a business consulting service separate from the firm's law practice, providing advice on management and marketing strategies for business enterprises. One of the senior partners has a close friend with substantial experience in this field who is not a lawyer but who, the partner believes, would represent a very valuable investment for the firm.

On another matter, you are asked to work with Stavros, one of the partners, in the preparation of a plaintiff's personal injury case arising out of a one car accident caused by brake failure on the plaintiff's car. The defendant is the plaintiff's mechanic who, according to the plaintiff's deposition testimony, was asked to check and repair the brakes two days before the accident, but failed to do so. The mechanic claims that, although the worksheet for the job refers to the brakes, he told the plaintiff that he couldn't get to it that day, and plaintiff decided (against the mechanic's advice) to take the car back at the end of the day anyway. You have interviewed and obtained a signed statement from a friend and co-worker of plaintiff, who states that the plaintiff told *him*, the day after the car was in the shop, that he (the plaintiff) had done exactly as the defendant claims. You show Stavros this statement and recommend that the client be confronted with it. Stavros questions you very closely about the likelihood that the defendant or his counsel would have discovered this witness, whom you met quite by chance and who told you that he had not been contacted by anyone else and would not say anything unless he were asked. Stavros then tells you to file the statement away and forget it, saying "we're better off not knowing what the client would say about this."

Your experiences with Stavros have made you rethink your commitment to this firm. As a result, you have gone back and read some of the employment documents you signed when you joined the firm. First, your employment agreement provides, among other things, that if you leave the firm and continue to practice law, you will not advertise legal services on any media that can be viewed within ten miles of the firm's office. In addition, the agreement provides that after leaving the firm, you will not thereafter accept any client for whom you have worked while with the firm, for a period of two years from your departure, without written consent from the firm. The agreement also provides that if you leave after practicing with the firm for five years or more, you are entitled to two months' salary, as a bonus for your longevity, plus an additional "retirement" benefit of one additional month salary multiplied by the number of years you were associated with the firm, provided you do not practice law within the state for a period of two years from your departure. If you do practice law during the period, you are still entitled to the two month salary benefit, but not the additional "retirement" benefit. As you think about leaving the firm, you know you have some clients who would likely follow you, so you wonder if you can talk to them about your leaving before your actual departure.

RULE REFERENCES

Model Rules 1.0(c), 1.8(h), 5.4, 5.7, 5.2, 5.1, 5.3, 5.6, and 1.17

RESTATEMENT §§ 9 & 58

F(1) REGULATION OF LAW FIRMS

QUESTIONS

How do you reconcile the provisions of Model Rule 1.0(c) authorizing a firm to be organized as a professional corporation with your knowledge of the limited liability of the members of many such forms of professional corporations, especially considering the provision of Model Rule 1.8(h) making it impermissible for the lawyer to make "an agreement prospectively limiting the lawyer's liability to a client for malpractice"? What should be the response to the statement: "If the legislature authorizes business entities to limit liability, then lawyers and law firms can do the same"?

NOTES ON REGULATION OF LAW FIRMS

1. In *Henderson v. HSI Financial Services, Inc.*, 471 S.E.2d 885 (Ga. 1996), the Georgia Supreme Court reversed an earlier decision prohibiting use of a law firm professional corporation to shield liability for misconduct by individual members of the firm. *Henderson* approved the use of the professional corporation and validated a state statute that limited liability of members of the corporation. Use this case to first focus on the "inherent power" concepts you studied in section A of this chapter. In acknowledging that the legislature has spoken on the subject of corporate structure, is the court saying that it has no inherent power to regulate law firms that happen to be professional corporations? Or is the court recognizing the distinction Professor Wolfram drew between "affirmative" and "negative" inherent power? *See supra* section 2(A), note 3. Once the legislature acts, is the court saying that the court need not worry about acting, provided the conduct at issue can be adequately reconciled with the rules of the profession?

2. **Limiting Liability Under Statute:** If the court elects to follow a state statute, there is potential for lack of uniformity from state to state. In contrast to the general tenor of the Georgia court in *Henderson*, consider

Scarborough v. Napoli, Kaiser & Bern, LLP, *880 N.Y.S.2d 800 (App.Div. 2009). In* Scarborough, *associates of a limited liability partnership sought dismissal as individual defendants from a malpractice lawsuit. The court noted that applicable New York law allowed liability for individual employees of a limited liability partnership. As a result, the associates would be exempt from personal liability, even as members of a limited liability partnership, only if they could initially prove, "as a matter of law that [they] committed no negligent or wrongful act."* Id. at 802.

3. Under the American Law Institute's RESTATEMENT, a law firm is generally subject to liability for the wrongful actions of any employee. If a partnership is organized without a limitation of liability for partners, all partners are jointly and severally liable. If the firm is organized other than as a partnership, the liability of principals in the firm depends on the law of the jurisdiction. RESTATEMENT, § 58 (2000).

F(2) REGULATION OF LAW FIRMS' SUBSTANTIVE BUSINESS—LAW RELATED SERVICES AND MULTIDISCIPLINARY PRACTICE

QUESTIONS

In the problem, can the firm employ the business consultant and offer his services to the public under the firm's name? Can he be offered an equity interest in the firm and charged with the development of the consulting business? Can the firm acquire an equity interest in the friend's consulting business? As you read the next set of materials and Model Rule 5.7, consider what problems arise when an attorney for a client is part of a business in which the client is a participant/investor, or when a non-lawyer is part of a law firm.

FORMAL OPINION NUMBER 2003–1

The Supreme Court of Ohio Board of Commissioners on Grievances and Discipline, 2003. 2003 WL 1947992.

* * * OPINION:

This opinion addresses questions regarding a law firm's legal representation of buyers or sellers of business entities, a law firm's assistance in locating buyers and sellers of business entities either through the law firm or through an ancillary business, the use of business brokers, referrals to lenders, and fees for such services. * * *

INTRODUCTION

The purchase or sale of a business entity involves a wide range of legal services that vary in complexity. For example, the purchase or sale of a business entity may involve only the purchase or sale of assets; or it may also involve the negotiation of the purchase, sale, lease, exchange, or assignment of an interest in real estate. A purchase or sale of a business entity may also involve the purchase or sale of securities. * * *

This Board does not have authority to advise lawyers as to legal issues, including whether the proposed activities require licensure under the laws governing real estate or securities. * * * This opinion advises lawyers only as to ethical issues under the Ohio Code of Professional Responsibility.

QUESTION ONE

In representing a seller of a business entity, is it proper for a law firm to help locate a buyer and to charge the seller/client a fee based upon a percentage of the transaction price?

The law firm proposes to represent the seller, to locate a buyer, and to charge the seller/client a fee based upon a percentage of the transaction price. Three ethical concerns exist. Is it proper for a law firm to provide law related services, such as assisting a client in locating a buyer of a business? Is there a reasonable possibility that the law firm's professional judgment on behalf of the seller of a business entity may be adversely affected by the law firm's financial interest in receiving a percentage of the transaction price? Is the law firm's fee of a percentage of the transaction price illegal or clearly excessive?

Providing law related services

Providing legal representation to a client who wishes to buy or sell a business entity may naturally lend itself to assistance by the law firm in helping to locate a seller or buyer for the client. Through social, business, or professional connections, a lawyer may know of a potential buyer or seller to introduce to a law firm client. Assistance by a law firm in locating a buyer or seller of a business entity for a law firm client is a service related to the lawyer's legal representation of the client. * * *

ABA Model Rule 5.7(a) acknowledges that lawyers may provide law-related services either in circumstances that are not distinct from the lawyer's provision of legal services to clients or through a separate entity. The rule identifies law-related services as services that might reasonably be performed in conjunction with and in substance are related to the provision of legal services. The rule requires that lawyers who provide law-related services must comply with professional rules of conduct. [I]t is this Board's view that in the absence of a prohibitive rule, Ohio attorneys may, as they have by tradition and perhaps by unspoken rule, provide law-related services as part of the practice of law to legal clients of the law firm. The provision of law-related services through a law firm must comport with professional rules of conduct and to any applicable laws governing the law-related service.

As to the question presented, a law firm representing a seller of a business entity may assist the seller/client by helping to locate a buyer.

QUESTION TWO

In representing a buyer of a business entity, is it proper for a law firm to help locate a seller and to charge the buyer/client a fee based upon a percentage of the transaction price?

The law firm proposes to represent the buyer, to locate a seller, and to charge the buyer/client a fee based upon a percentage of the transaction price. Based upon the Board's response to Question One, the Board advises as follows. In representing a buyer of a business entity, a law firm may help locate a seller and charge the buyer/client a fee based upon a percentage of the transaction price; provided the fee is not illegal or excessive and there is full disclosure by the lawyer to the buyer/client and written informed consent by the buyer/client. The lawyer should clearly inform the seller, preferably both verbally and in writing, that the lawyer is representing the buyer, not the seller.

QUESTION THREE

If a law firm uses a business broker to help locate either a buyer or seller of a business entity for a law firm client, is it proper for the law firm to charge the client a fee based upon a percentage of the transaction price and share the fee with the business broker?

A lawyer may not share legal fees with a business broker [under Model Rule 5.4(a)]. * * *

Regardless of how the law firm bases its fee, hourly or as a percentage of a transaction price, a business broker's fee may not come from the law firm's legal fee. If the services of a business broker are used, the broker's fee must be independent of the legal fee.

QUESTION FOUR

If a law firm represents neither a buyer nor a seller of a business entity, is it proper for the law firm to introduce the buyer or seller to a lender and to receive from the lender a fee based upon the size of a loan transaction?

The context in which a law firm would introduce a buyer or a seller, not represented by the law firm, to a lender is unclear. For purposes of this opinion, the Board assumes that the buyer or seller sought assistance from the law firm because the buyer or seller knows, through personal, business, or professional contacts, that the law firm provides legal representation to business entities. The Board also assumes that the law firm did not improperly solicit the buyer or seller.

[Thus], the law firm questions the propriety of receiving a fee from a lender for referring a buyer or seller whom the law firm purports not to represent. * * * When a law firm provides a law-related service through the law firm, but does not provide other legal services to the person for whom the law-related service is performed, the rules governing professional conduct apply. *See e.g.*, ABA, Model Rule 5.7, Comment 2.

An agreement that a law firm will receive from the lender a fee based upon a loan transaction with a buyer or seller referred by the law firm may reasonably affect a lawyer's independent judgment regardless of whether the lawyer considers the buyer or seller to be represented by the law firm. Even if a law firm provides no other legal representation to a buyer or seller who has sought assistance from the law firm, the lawyer has exercised professional legal judgment in deciding to introduce a buyer or seller to a lender [under Model Rule 5.4(c)].

QUESTION FIVE

If an investment group asks a law firm to locate a seller of a business entity, is it proper for the law firm to receive a percentage of the transaction price from the buyer/investment group and is it proper for the law firm to represent the seller?

The context in which a law firm would assist an investment group to locate a seller of a business entity is unclear. For purposes of this opinion, the Board assumes that the investment group sought assistance from the law firm because the investment group knows through personal, business, or professional contacts, that the law firm provides legal representation to business entities. The Board also assumes that the law firm did not improperly solicit the investment group.

The law firm exercises professional independent judgment on behalf of the investment group when the firm provides assistance in locating a seller of a business entity. As stated in Question Four, when a law firm provides a law-related service through the law firm, but does not provide other legal services to the person or entity for which the law-related service is performed, the rules governing professional conduct apply. * * *

QUESTION SIX

Is it proper for a law firm to establish an ancillary business to locate buyers and sellers of business entities and for the law firm's ancillary business to charge its clients a percentage of the transaction price?

In Opinion 94–7, this Board addressed lawyers owning ancillary businesses. The Board advised:

> An attorney or several attorneys within a law firm may own an ancillary business that provides law-related services, for example, a Workers' Compensation Service Company that provides claims administration services for employers. Attorneys who operate such law-related businesses must do so in a manner consistent with the Ohio Code of Professional Responsibility. * * *

It is improper for attorneys who own an ancillary business to require that customers of the business agree to legal representation by the attorneys or their law firm as a condition of engagement of the services of the ancillary business. If customers of the ancillary business need legal services, they may be informed that the attorneys can provide the legal representation, but they must also be informed of the ownership interest and encouraged to seek legal counsel of their own choice.

An attorney's ownership interest in an ancillary business must be disclosed to customers of the business who may be in need of legal services. An attorney, before accepting employment by a client who is also a customer of the business, must fully disclose the ownership interest in the ancillary business and obtain client consent.

In keeping with Opinion 94–7, this Board advises as follows. It is proper for a law firm to establish an ancillary business to locate buyers and sellers of business entities and for the law firm's ancillary business to charge clients of the ancillary business a percentage of the transaction price, provided such fee is legally proper. An ancillary business must heed any applicable state laws, including the laws regulating the sale of real estate and securities. * * *

NOTES ON BUSINESS REGULATION OF LAW FIRMS

1. **Non–Law Services (Ancillary or Multidisciplinary Practice):** The ABA's position on the provision by lawyers or law firms of "ancillary services"—services that are not legal services in the strict sense of requiring a law license—has undergone considerable evolution. In Formal Opinion 328 (1972), the Standing Committee on Ethics and Professional Responsibility concluded that dual practice was not prohibited so long as advertising and solicitation restrictions were observed. It went on to say, however, that when the lawyer's other profession is *law-related*—one involving similar services such as accounting, real estate brokerage, marriage counseling, etc., so that it is difficult for the client to distinguish the legal from the non-legal services— the lawyer is to be regarded as practicing law in either setting, and therefore subject to the lawyer's obligations (confidentiality, conflict of interest, etc.) in both.

2. In the 1980s, a number of law firms began to acquire or establish businesses providing non-legal services, and the issue of their propriety became a live one. In most cases, the business operated separately with the law firm simply functioning as owner or shareholder, so that structural problems like the prohibition against partnership with a non-lawyer in the practice of law under Model Rule 5.4 were avoided. *See, e.g.,* James F. Fitzpatrick, *Legal Future Shock: The Role of Large Law Firms by the End of the Century*, 64 Ind.L.J. 461, 467–69 (1989). Other problems of lawyer-client relations, such as conflicts of interest, remained.

3. In response to this controversy, the ABA adopted a new provision, Model Rule 5.7, in 1991. At that time, it virtually prohibited dual practice by requiring that services be rendered only to law clients and only by employees of the firm, rather than through a separate entity. This rule was adopted by a narrow margin, and was so controversial that it was rescinded in 1992 by a similarly narrow margin. The present Model Rule 5.7 was adopted in 1994. It essentially codifies the principle of Formal Opinion 328 that lawyers providing law-related services are subject to lawyers' professional responsibility in so doing. As noted in the Ohio opinion, the rule also allows lawyers to form non-law firm businesses that provide services that do not amount to the practice of law. When this happens, Comment [11] to Model Rule 5.7 indicates that external law, rather than the Model Rules, governs the legal duties of the parties.

4.   Much of the discussion relating to the scope of law-related activities has focused on the lawyer who is also an accountant or the lawyer who is also involved in real estate. The field, however, is more extensive. In attempting to address the issue, the Florida Bar Ethics Hotline indicated that it had received questions "about combining a law practice with a used car lot, a coffee shop, a magnetic resonance imaging center, a doctor's office, accountants, financial planners, guardians, elder care helpers, stockbrokers, patent research companies, dentists, mental health counselors, mediators, arbitrators, lease audit firms, and sports agents." *In re Amendments to Rules Regulating the Fla. Bar*, 820 So.2d 210, 213 (Fla. 2002).

F(3) REGULATION OF LAW FIRM MEMBERS

QUESTION

In the problem, you are told that you have a statement from the client's friend indicating that the client did, indeed, take his car against the advice of the mechanic, who apparently told the client that the car needed brake work. You have shown this statement to the partner for whom you work, and the partner has told you to file the statement away and not ask the client about it. The client's deposition testimony was not consistent with this statement. Despite your strongly expressed conviction that the personal injury client's deposition testimony is false, Stavros insists on going ahead with the trial, featuring the client as the star witness. Stavros wants you to conduct the direct examination of the client according to the script Stavros has developed. What are your options and obligations?

JACOBSON v. KNEPPER & MOGA, P.C.

Supreme Court of Illinois, 1998.
706 N.E.2d 491.

JUSTICE NICKELS delivered the opinion of the court:

We are asked here to consider the issue of whether an attorney who has been discharged by his law firm employer should be allowed the remedy of an action for retaliatory discharge. We hold that an attorney may not maintain such an action.

BACKGROUND

Plaintiff, Alan P. Jacobson, filed a one-count complaint in the circuit court of Cook County against the law firm of Knepper & Moga, P.C. (hereinafter, the firm), alleging that he had been wrongfully discharged in retaliation for reporting the firm's illegal practices to a principal partner of the firm. In his complaint, plaintiff made the following factual allegations. In July 1994, plaintiff was hired as an associate attorney of the firm. Shortly thereafter, plaintiff discovered that the firm was filing consumer debt collection actions in violation of the venue provisions of the [Federal] Fair Debt Collection Practices Act * * * and the Illinois Collection Agency Act * * *. Plaintiff spoke with James Knepper, one of the firm's principal partners, regarding the filing practice and was advised that the matter would be remedied.

In April 1995, plaintiff was given the responsibility of reviewing and signing all complaints filed by the firm in consumer debt collection cases. In this role, plaintiff learned that the firm continued to file actions in violation of the venue provisions of the above-referenced acts. Plaintiff reiterated his complaint to Knepper, who again assured plaintiff that the practice would be corrected. Shortly thereafter, plaintiff was relieved of the responsibility to review and sign complaints in consumer debt collection cases. Less than three months later, plaintiff discovered that the firm had not ceased the practice of filing complaints in the improper venue. Plaintiff approached Knepper regarding the matter for a third time. Approximately two weeks later, plaintiff was terminated.

Plaintiff's complaint alleged that he had been discharged in retaliation for his insistence that the firm cease its practice of filing consumer debt collection actions in the wrong venue. The firm filed a motion to dismiss. [The issue is whether an attorney can maintain a cause of action] for the Tort of Retaliatory Discharge against his non-client law firm employer due to the pre-eminence of the Rules of Professional Conduct[.]

ANALYSIS

Generally, an employer may fire an employee-at-will for any reason or no reason at all. * * * Nevertheless, this court has recognized the limited and narrow tort of retaliatory discharge as an exception to the general rule of at-will employment. * * * To establish a cause of action for retaliatory discharge, a plaintiff must demonstrate that (1) he was discharged in retaliation for his activities; and (2) the discharge is in contravention of a clearly mandated public policy. * * *

While there is no precise definition of what constitutes clearly mandated public policy, a review of Illinois case law reveals that retaliatory discharge actions are allowed * * * when an employee is discharged in retaliation for the reporting of illegal or improper conduct, otherwise known as "whistle blowing." * * * Here, it is plaintiff's contention that the enactment of the provisions of the Fair Debt Collection Practice Act and the Illinois Collection Agency Act, violations of which are alleged in the complaint, articulate a clearly mandated public policy. Plaintiff argues that, because he alleged that he was terminated in retaliation for his reporting of the firm's violations of these acts, his complaint states a cause of action.

The tort of retaliatory discharge is a limited cause of action which "seeks to achieve ' "a proper balance * * * among the employer's interest in operating a business efficiently and profitably, the employee's interest in earning a livelihood, and society's interest in seeing its public policies carried out." ' " * * * In this case, the public policy to be protected, that of protecting the debtor defendants' property and ensuring them due process, is adequately safeguarded without extending the tort of retaliatory discharge to employee attorneys.

Plaintiff was a licensed attorney at all times throughout this controversy and, as such, he was subject to the Illinois Rules of Professional Conduct * * *. The firm's conduct of intentionally filing collection actions against debtors in a county which it knows venue is improper clearly violates Rule 3.3 of the Rules of Professional Conduct * * * (lawyer shall not make a statement of material fact or law to a tribunal which the lawyer knows or reasonably should know is false) * * *. Further, the Rules of Professional Conduct prohibit a lawyer from engaging in conduct involving dishonesty, fraud, deceit, or misrepresentation. [Rule] 8.4([c]). Because plaintiff possessed unprivileged knowledge that the firm engaged in conduct involving dishonesty, fraud, deceit, or misrepresentation, he was required to report such knowledge to a tribunal or other authority empowered to investigate or act upon such violation. [Rule] 8.3(a). * * *

Therefore, the attorney's ethical obligations serve to adequately protect the public policy established by the collection statutes. Because sufficient safeguards exist in this situation, it is unnecessary to expand the limited and narrow tort of retaliatory discharge to the employee attorney. * * *

Thus, we hold that plaintiff, as a licensed attorney employed as such by the defendant law firm, cannot maintain a cause of action for retaliatory discharge because the ethical obligations imposed by the Rules of Professional Conduct provide adequate safeguards to the public policy implicated in this case. * * * Accordingly, we reverse the judgments of the appellate and circuit courts and remand this cause with directions that defendant's motion to dismiss be granted. * * *

CHIEF JUSTICE FREEMAN, dissenting:

I respectfully dissent. [Under the court's ruling,] one class of employees in this state, attorneys, has been stripped of a remedy which Illinois clearly affords to all other employees in such "whistle-blowing" situations. Today's opinion serves as yet another reminder to the attorneys in this state that, in certain circumstances, it is economically more advantageous to keep quiet than to follow the dictates of the Rules of Professional Conduct.

NOTES ON REGULATION OF LAW FIRM MEMBERS

1.   Model Rules 5.1, 5.2, and 5.3 constitute the ABA's first attempt to address supervisory lawyers, subordinate lawyers, and non-lawyer law firm employees in formal rules.

2.   The harshness of the *Jacobson* result on the associate can only be understood by considering the decision in the context of Model Rule 5.2:

   a.   Under Model Rule 5.2, Jacobson cannot participate in filing the debt collection cases in the manner being done by the firm. As the court finds in *Jacobson*, the professional duty is not "arguable."

b. Thus, if during the period of time he was in charge of these cases, Jacobson was told to file them the way the firm had been doing, Jacobson's professional duty would not have been arguable, and he could not do so.

c. When fired because he did not endorse the firm's impermissible conduct, Jacobson, like most associates in law firms, was an "at-will" employee and could thus be fired with or without cause.

d. In Illinois, at least, even though the discharge was motivated by Jacobson's ethical conduct, he would not have a right to sue the firm for his discharge.

e. Moreover, according to the court, even if he remained in the firm, he had an obligation to turn the firm in to disciplinary authorities under Model Rule 8.3, because he possessed non-confidential information relating to conduct reflecting adversely on the fitness of other members of the firm.

f. In a business climate where most law firm associates have extensive student loans to repay, in addition to themselves and families to support, is it any wonder that the dissent predicts that associates in Jacobson's position will "keep quiet" rather than follow the dictates of the Model Rules?

For discussions of Model Rule 5.2 and its effect on subordinate attorneys, see Andrew M. Perlman, *The Silliest Rule of Professional Conduct: Model Rule 5.2(b)*, 19 ABA Prof'l Law. 14 (2009), and Douglas R. Richmond, *Academic Silliness About Model Rule 5.2(b)*, 19 ABA Prof'l Law. 15 (2009).

3. Not all cases are as harsh as *Jacobson*. In *Wieder v. Skala*, 609 N.E.2d 105, 108–10 (N.Y. 1992), plaintiff, an associate, asked the law firm to report a different associate following the second associate's admission of malpractice, fraud, and deceit. The plaintiff was then discharged. The New York court held:

> [I]n any hiring of an attorney as an associate to practice law with a firm there is implied an understanding so fundamental to the relationship and essential to its purpose as to require no expression: that both the associate and the firm in conducting the practice will do so in accordance with the ethical standards of the profession. * * *

> Intrinsic to [the law firm relationship] was the unstated but essential compact that in conducting the firm's legal practice both plaintiff and the firm would do so in compliance with the prevailing rules of conduct and ethical standards of the profession. Insisting that as an associate in their employ plaintiff must act unethically and in violation of one of the primary professional rules amounted to nothing less than a frustration of the only legitimate purpose of the employment relationship.

As a result, plaintiff was able to maintain a cause of action for retaliatory discharge.

4. **Duties of Supervising Lawyer:** To what extent must a supervising lawyer monitor the activities of both supervised lawyers and non-lawyer assistants, under Model Rules 5.1 and 5.3? The American Law Institute

indicates that the supervising lawyer must "take reasonable measures, given the level and extent of [the lawyer's] responsibility." RESTATEMENT § 11, Comment *c*. The RESTATEMENT adds: "Those measures, such as an informal program of instructing or monitoring another person, must often assume the likelihood that a particular lawyer or nonlawyer employee may not yet have received adequate preparation for carrying out that person's own responsibilities." *Id.*

5. **House Counsel:** Suppose the supervised lawyer is not an associate in a law firm, but is instead an employee of a corporation, employed as "house" or "inside" counsel. Illinois has also refused a claim for retaliatory discharge for lawyers who are "house counsel." *Balla v. Gambro, Inc.*, 584 N.E.2d 104 (Ill. 1991). Other courts have, however, disagreed. In *Crews v. Buckman Laboratories Int'l, Inc.*, 78 S.W.3d 852 (Tenn. 2002), the court held that "house counsel" was also an employee of the corporation who could bring a common law retaliatory discharge action after being fired for reporting to the board of bar examiners that her supervisor was not licensed to practice law in Tennessee. In addition, the discharged lawyer could reveal otherwise confidential client information to sustain the claim. *See also Lewis v. Nationwide Mut. Ins. Co.*, No. 3:02CV512 (RNC), 2003 WL 1746050 (D.Conn. Mar. 18, 2003) (recognizing such a cause of action for a discharged insurance company lawyer who claimed the company was compromising his independent judgment on behalf of his client, the company's insureds); *Heckman v. Zurich Holding Co. of Am.*, 242 F.R.D. 606 (D.Kan. 2007) (allowing retaliatory discharge action by in house counsel). Even where a retaliatory discharge action is available, however, the attorney must still withdraw from representing the corporate client. *See Gen. Dynamics Corp. v. Superior Court*, 876 P.2d 487 (Cal. 1994). As a result, even if the retaliatory discharge action is successful, reinstatement is not an available remedy.

F(4) REGULATION OF LAW FIRM EMPLOYMENT AGREEMENTS

QUESTIONS

Recall that in the problem, there are restrictions on the amount you can receive from your firm in the event you leave. Are these restrictions on your separate and post-departure practice imposed by the employment agreement valid and enforceable? If you decide to leave, can you contact firm clients to advise them of your impending departure and your interest in continuing to represent them? What does Model Rule 5.6 have to say on these issues? Consider the following case.

PIERCE v. MORRISON MAHONEY LLP

Supreme Judicial Court of Massachusetts, Suffolk, 2008.
897 N.E.2d 562.

CORDY, J.

In *Pettingell v. Morrison, Mahoney & Miller*, 426 Mass. 253, 256, 687 N.E.2d 1237 (1997) (*Pettingell*), we precluded the enforcement of a provision in the Morrison, Mahoney & Miller partnership agreement that "impose[d] adverse consequences on a withdrawing partner" who competed with the law firm. We precluded enforcement because the provision did not impose such adverse consequences on a withdrawing partner who did not compete with the firm. We concluded that the provision violated the public policy of protecting the rights of clients and potential clients to their choice of counsel, as embodied in * * * Mass. R. Prof. C. 5.6 * * *. In this case, we must decide whether that firm's amended partnership agreement, which imposes identical financial consequences on all partners who voluntarily withdraw from the firm, regardless of whether they compete with the firm after withdrawing, also violates rule 5.6. We conclude that it does not. * * *

The defendant Morrison Mahoney LLP (Morrison Mahoney or the firm) is a limited liability partnership engaged in the practice of law. The plaintiffs Joel F. Pierce, John J. Davis, Elizabeth M. Fahey, Mitchell S. King, and Alice Olsen Mann are lawyers admitted to the practice of law in Massachusetts who became partners of Morrison Mahoney (or its predecessor) in 1981, 1987, 1987, 1987, and 1985 respectively. On January 17, 1989, Morrison Mahoney adopted a new partnership agreement, which each plaintiff signed. The partnership agreement provided that any provision of the agreement could be amended by vote of the partners.

Under the 1989 partnership agreement Morrison Mahoney maintained its financial accounts and reported its income to the Internal Revenue Service on a cash basis. Morrison Mahoney also maintained its financial accounts on an accrual basis.

[T]he 1989 partnership agreement * * * allocated the increase or decrease in the net worth of the partnership resulting from each year's operation (i.e., net income or loss), determined on an accrual basis, among the partners. The increase or decrease in the firm's net worth was divided into portions and allocated to each partner as annual partnership interest credits (APICs). The amount of APICs allocated to each partner was noted on the accrual reports prepared by Morrison Mahoney's accountants and on yearly records kept for each partner. * * *

Partners departing from Morrison Mahoney could * * * receive APICs payments after their departure in certain circumstances. For example, departing partners who retired under the terms of the agreement after having been a Morrison Mahoney partner for twenty years or attaining the age of sixty could receive payment on account of their APICs after departing the firm. However, if such a partner subsequently resumed the practice of law "other than [at] the . . . firm," the agreement treated that partner as a voluntarily withdrawn partner. Departing partners who voluntarily withdrew from the firm would receive APICs payments only if they did not compete with the firm.

This forfeiture-for-competition provision for voluntarily withdrawing partners became the subject of litigation. * * * In * * * 1997, this court

* * * conclud[ed] that the forfeiture-for-competition provision violated the polices underlying [the predecessor rule to Rule 5.6].

While the [earlier] litigation was pending, the [firm] partners * * * voted to amend the * * * partnership agreement[. The new agreement] deleted the forfeiture-for-competition provision for voluntarily withdrawing partners and replaced it with a provision that provided that all partners voluntarily withdrawing from the firm would forfeit their APICs, regardless of whether the partners competed with Morrison Mahoney after withdrawal. [Three of the four plaintiffs here attended the meeting where these amendments were adopted. The fourth neither attended nor voted by proxy.]

The plaintiffs Pierce, Davis, and Fahey voluntarily withdrew from Morrison Mahoney * * * to form a new law firm. Mann voluntarily withdrew from Morrison Mahoney * * * to form her own law office. King voluntarily withdrew from Morrison Mahoney * * * to join another law firm. None of the plaintiffs had reached age sixty or served as a Morrison Mahoney partner for twenty years, and each planned to continue practicing law.[12] Relying on the [then existing partnership agreement], Morrison Mahoney made no payments on account of APICs to any of the plaintiffs.

[The five former members of the firm brought three separate suits which were then consolidated seeking] APICs payments from Morrison Mahoney. * * * The judge concluded that to the extent the 1995 amendments did not permit voluntarily withdrawn partners who continued to practice law to receive APICs payments, the amendments violated [R]ule 5.6, and ordered Morrison Mahoney to make APICs payments to the plaintiffs. * * * We granted Morrison Mahoney's application for direct appellate review. * * *

Rule 5.6 provides in pertinent part: "A lawyer shall not participate in offering or making ... a partnership or employment agreement that restricts the right of a lawyer to practice after termination of the relationship, except an agreement concerning benefits upon retirement...." Our cases make clear that [R]ule 5.6 exists primarily to protect the interests of clients, not lawyers.

[W]e previously reviewed the enforceability of the forfeiture-for-competition provision in Morrison Mahoney's 1989 partnership agreement, holding that it violated DR 2–108(A), the predecessor to [R]ule 5.6, and was therefore void as against public policy. *Pettingell, supra* at 255, 258, 687 N.E.2d 1237. We reasoned that such a provision would "discourage a lawyer who leaves a firm from competing with it," which "would tend to restrict a client or potential client's choice of counsel." * * *

We reached a similar conclusion in [*Eisenstein v. David G. Conlin, P.C.*, 827 N.E.2d 686 (Mass. 2005)]. At issue in that case was "whether a law firm may contractually bind former partners to share fees they earn

---

12. At the time of their respective withdrawals, the balances in the plaintiffs' APICs accounts were as follows: $1,076,855 for Pierce; $225,235 for Davis; $70,585 for Fahey; $94,876 for King; $177,999 for Mann.

from the firm's current and former clients after the partners leave the firm." * * * We held that such provisions are unenforceable because they "provide clear disincentives for former ... partners" to serve the firm's clients, even though "those clients [may] have determined that their own interests would best be served by such representation." * * * Thus, such fee-sharing provisions "impinge on the 'strong public interest in allowing clients to retain counsel of their choice.'" * * * "[R]ule 5.6 exists to protect the strong interests clients have in being able to choose freely the counsel they determine will best represent their interests. The rule furthers the client's right freely to select counsel by prohibiting attorneys from engaging in certain practices that effectively shrink the pool of qualified attorneys from which clients may choose." * * * Accordingly, "[t]he 'broad prophylactic object' of [R]ule 5.6 ... requires close judicial scrutiny of any partnership provision that imposes financial disincentives on attorneys who leave a firm *and then compete* with it" * * *.

Central to our [prior] holdings * * * were the different fates of a lawyer who withdrew and competed and one who withdrew but did not compete. In each case, the partnership agreement created a strong disincentive for withdrawing partners to represent clients who formerly had been represented by the prior firm, or whose representation might be viewed as competitive to the firm. The problem in *Pettingell* was not that a forfeiture occurred, but that after voluntarily withdrawing from Morrison Mahoney, a partner who wanted to compete had to choose between (1) representing Client A and forfeiting his APICs account or (2) declining to represent Client A and retaining his APICs. The problem in *Eisenstein* was similar in that after leaving the firm, the former partner had to choose between (1) representing the former firm's clients and remitting a portion of the fees from those clients to that firm or (2) declining to represent the former firm's clients in order to keep one hundred percent of the fees generated from other clients. The financial disincentives in those cases tended to limit a client's choice of counsel by discouraging former firm lawyers from representing certain clients. In this case, however, the fate of a lawyer who voluntarily withdraws and competes with Morrison Mahoney for its clients is precisely the same as the fate of a lawyer who voluntarily withdraws and does not: both forfeit their APICs on withdrawal. Thus, a Morrison Mahoney partner who voluntarily withdraws and competes is no longer faced with the choice that was problematic in *Pettingell*. Instead, that lawyer may accept the representation of any client without triggering a financial forfeiture. This does nothing to "shrink the pool of qualified attorneys from which clients may choose." * * *

Nevertheless, the plaintiffs argue that this constituted a "de facto forfeiture-for-competition provision" because no partner could voluntarily withdraw from Morrison Mahoney, compete with the firm, and receive APICs payments. However, the plaintiffs fail to acknowledge the difference between a loss of benefits that is triggered by the decision to compete and one that is triggered by the decision to leave, whether or not one later competes. Only the first limits client choice in violation of the public policy behind [R]ule 5.6. The purpose of [R]ule 5.6 is not to protect lawyer mobility. A provision that makes a lawyer reluctant to leave, but that does not restrict the lawyer's conduct after he or she departs, does nothing to prevent the lawyer from thereafter accepting clients in competition with the firm. In restructuring its partnership agreement in this fashion, Morrison Mahoney has created a financial disincentive for its partners to leave the firm before they reach age sixty or serve as partners for twenty years. There is nothing inherently violative of public policy in partners agreeing to such disincentives in the interests of the long-term financial and professional health of their enterprises.

The plaintiffs argue further that the partnership agreement's definition of "retirement" allows the firm to discriminate between partners who leave to compete and those who do not by classifying competing partners as "voluntarily withdrawn" (and thus not entitled to APICs) and classifying noncompeting partners as "retired." Notably, not all "retired" partners are entitled to APICs payments. As we have already explained, of the partners who meet the agreement's definition of retirement, only those who do so *after* reaching age sixty or serving as a partner for twenty years receive APICs payments upon their departure. * * * Regardless of whether Morrison Mahoney classifies a departing partner as "voluntarily withdrawn" or "retired," that partner is not eligible to receive APICs payments before reaching either the age or seniority benchmark.

The plaintiffs direct us to Morrison Mahoney's alleged "disparate treatment" of two partners who left the firm after reaching the age or seniority benchmarks for APICs payments. Although both of these partners met the definition of retirement on departing Morrison Mahoney, one later began to compete and had to forfeit APICs payments, while the other joined the Attorney General's office and continued to receive APICs payments. The plaintiffs point to this as evidence that Morrison Mahoney "had a singular goal of denying partners who competed with the Firm repayment of their APIC[s] accounts." Morrison Mahoney responds by characterizing APICs as "retirement benefits" that fit within the retirement benefits exception in [Rule 5.6(a)]. The plaintiffs dispute Morrison Mahoney's characterization of APICs as "retirement benefits" and argue that APICs in fact represent each partner's ownership interest in the firm, which was "fixed and vested at the time allocated and reflected a return of income that had been earned and deferred."

We need not decide, however, whether APICs are a "retirement benefit" or some other form of interest or expectancy. The answer to that question is only relevant to the class of partners whose receipt of APICs may be contingent on whether they compete, that is, partners who have reached age sixty or served as a Morrison Mahoney partner for twenty years. No plaintiff in this case had reached those benchmarks on departing from Morrison Mahoney. Whether Morrison Mahoney's amended partnership agreement shrinks the pool of attorneys who have reached the age or seniority benchmark in derogation of client choice is thus not before us. * * *

In sum, [w]e reverse the judgments for the plaintiffs on their claims that Morrison Mahoney's partnership agreement violates [R]ule 5.6 by depriving them of their APICs. * * * The case is remanded for entry of judgments in favor of Morrison Mahoney.

NOTES ON LAW FIRM COMPETITION

1. Model Rule 5.6 generally bars both direct and indirect restraints on competition. The problem is based on *Blackburn v. Sweeney*, 637 N.E.2d 1340, 1343–44 (Ind.Ct.App. 1994), in which the court noted that "prohibitions against soliciting customers have been viewed as an impermissible restraint of trade in other contexts." As a result, "[a] nonadvertisement agreement indirectly, but effectively, limits the pool of attorneys from which potential clients may choose." This decision, however, did not end the matter. The Blackburn side of the case also took the agreement to federal court, which found the agreement to be a "horizontal agreement to allocate markets among competitors" and therefore a *per se* violation of the federal antitrust laws. *See Blackburn v. Sweeney*, 659 N.E.2d 131, 132 (Ind. 1995) (citing *Blackburn v. Sweeney*, 53 F.3d 825 (7th Cir. 1995)).

2. In *Jacob v. Norris, McLaughlin & Marcus*, 607 A.2d 142 (N.J. 1992), the New Jersey court proclaimed its view that restrictive employment covenants for lawyers are almost universally banned because they violate public policy. The American Law Institute echoes this holding: "Only in California * * * are restrictive covenants in law-firm agreements enforced" in the face of the contrary position of Rule 5.6. RESTATEMENT, § 13, Reporter's Note (2000); *but see Fearnow v. Ridenour, Swenson, Cleere & Evans, P.C.*, 138 P.3d 723, 724 (Ariz. 2006) (following California's lead in finding that "a shareholder agreement requiring a departing lawyer to tender his stock to a professional corporation for no compensation if he thereafter competes with the corporation in the practice of law" did not violate Model Rule 5.6(a)). The California exception is epitomized by *Howard v. Babcock*, 863 P.2d 150 (Cal. 1993). About the professed need to protect both lawyer mobility and the client's right to choose, the court wrote:

> Upon reflection, we have determined that these courts' steadfast concern to assure the theoretical freedom of each lawyer to choose whom to represent and what kind of work to undertake, and the theoretical freedom of any client to select his or her attorney of choice is inconsistent with the reality that both freedoms are actually circumscribed. Putting aside lofty assertions about the uniqueness of the legal profession, the reality is that the attorney, like any other professional, has no right to enter into employment or partnership in any particular firm, and sometimes may be discharged or forced out by his or her partners even if the client wishes otherwise. Nor does the attorney have the duty to take any client who proffers employment, and there are many grounds justifying an attorney's decision to terminate the attorney-client relationship over the client's objection.

Id. at 158. In light of Model Rule 5.6, what is the difference between Morrison, Mahoney's initial partnership agreement, barred by the court, and the subsequent provision allowed by the court in *Pierce*? How does that difference affect the ability of a client to obtain counsel?

3. **Retirement Exception:** As noted by the court in *Pierce*, Model Rule 5.6 does allow law firm agreements that restrict a lawyer's right to receive retirement benefits. In *Schoonmaker v. Cummings & Lockwood of Connecticut, P.C.*, 747 A.2d 1017 (Conn. 2000), plaintiff was 60 years old and had been employed as an attorney for the firm for 35 years. He was thus eligible for a lump sum payment upon leaving the firm of 1x his average earnings for the preceding five years. Because he was at least 60 years old and had been employed in the firm for at least 20 years, plaintiff was also eligible for an additional 2x the same benefit if he "retired." Under the agreement, "retirement" referred not only to a full cessation of the practice of law, but to any circumstance in which the person was no longer a partner in the firm. Payment was forfeited, however, if the person leaving the firm practiced law for three years within a limited geographic area. Plaintiff left the firm and immediately began another practice within the prohibited geographic area. As a result, the firm paid the 1x benefit, but refused to pay the 2x benefit. *See id.* at 1020–21.

Plaintiff claimed that to be effective under Model Rule 5.6, "retirement" could only include a total cessation of practice. The court disagreed, finding that so long as the 2x payment was conditioned on "minimum age and longevity requirements," that portion of the agreement met the authorized exception of Model Rule 5.6. *See Schoonmaker*, 747 A.2d at 1029, 1035–36.

4. **Sale of Law Practice:** Model Rule 1.17 places substantial restrictions on the sale of all or part of a law practice. While the pre–2002 version of Model Rule 1.17 required the practice to be "sold as an entirety," the current Model Rule permits sale of "an area of practice."

5. **Dissolution of Law Firm or Termination of Partnership:** There are no specific rules on the obligations of partners or members of firms when the firm dissolves. The American Law Institute comments that issues surrounding the cessation of a firm, as well as the ability of lawyers departing a firm to solicit firm clients or other lawyers within the firm, are normally left to the law firm agreement. RESTATEMENT, § 9, Comments *i* & *j*. In the absence of any agreement to the contrary, a lawyer preparing to depart a law firm may solicit only those clients upon "whose matters the lawyer is actively and substantially working" and only after the lawyer advises the firm that the lawyer will be soliciting such clients. Once the lawyer has left the prior firm, the lawyer may solicit former clients and former firm clients without restriction. *See id.*, § 9(3). The courts will generally approve of law firm agreements dealing with termination and withdrawal of members, will assume that lawyers will comply with other rules of professional conduct in this activity, and will attempt to read the provisions consistent with the Rules of Professional Conduct if possible. *See Welch v. Davis*, 114 S.W.3d 285 (Mo.Ct.App. 2003).

CHAPTER 3

THE ATTORNEY–CLIENT RELATIONSHIP

■ ■ ■

INTRODUCTION

In the next three chapters we explore the relationship between attorney and client. This chapter explores some of the more formal elements of the relationship, as well as some of the basic responsibilities of the parties. The next two chapters deal with two of the sometimes more troublesome aspects of the relationship: confidentiality and conflict of interest.

The attorney-client relationship is most often understood to be a contractual one, presumptively founded upon mutual agreement. It is prototypically an agency contract, with the client as principal and the attorney as agent. In a modern world, however, the attorney-client relationship can also begin when the client relies on advice of an attorney, without the typical formalities of contract. In addition, attorney-client relationships can be formed through court order. This occurs when an attorney is asked by the court to represent a person or entity that cannot afford counsel.

Part A of this chapter explores the way in which lawyers obtain clients through advertising and solicitation. Part B discusses a question that looks deceptively easy—when does the relationship begin, both for individuals and for entities needing a lawyer? Once that relationship is formed, Part C discusses authority within the relationship. Thinking back to the *Sprung* case in Chapter One, when, if ever, would it be permissible for the plaintiff's lawyer to agree to extend the time when a defendant could answer, despite the client's express disapproval?

The balance of the chapter assumes the existence of a relationship and discusses duties of both parties within that relationship. Part D discusses the lawyer's obligation to hold money or other property received from third parties in trust. Part E discusses the client's obligation to pay fees. Part F discusses both civil liability for malpractice, including liability to non-clients, and constitutional concepts of ineffective assistance of counsel, for which a convicted criminal defendant might be afforded a new trial. Finally, Part G deals with the end of the relationship, either because

106

the lawyer is discharged or because the lawyer can or must withdraw from representing the client. This final section also discusses the lawyer's fee in such circumstances.

A. ATTRACTING CLIENTS

PROBLEM

Having graduated from your favorite law school, taken and passed the bar, and with a generous gift from your parents, you have decided to open up your own law office. The only foreseeable problem on your horizon is clients—you don't have any. As a result, you meet with a marketing specialist who gives you some ideas. Based on those ideas, you decide on a vigorous advertising and solicitation campaign.

Because you hope to do trial work, you contact the telephone company and are able to arrange "800" service for yourself within your state with the telephone number 529–7848. As a result, your telephone listing can read "1–800–LAWSUIT." Using this telephone number, you regularly advertise your practice on radio, television, and newspapers, and you set up a web page containing information about you, your practice, and the law generally. You change the name of your practice to "The Suit Shop" and agree to sponsor youth sports teams who will wear tee shirts with "The Suit Shop" and "call us at 1–800–LAWSUIT" emblazoned on them.

You also decide to check your newspaper daily to find out who has been injured in automobile and other types of accidents. That will allow you to write directly to those injured (or their families), to offer to discuss their legal rights with them. Because you think you can do some criminal work, you also check the newspaper section containing the names of those arrested and decide to write to these persons as well, offering your services.

QUESTIONS

(a) Is your advertising and solicitation strategy proper under your state's ethics rules?

(b) Assume that one of your first clients was employed at a local discount store. She tells you the store discriminated against her and a number of other employees. Assume you want to bring a class action on behalf of the employees who allege discrimination. Can you file suit, discover the names of other employees through discovery, and then solicit them?

RULE REFERENCES

Model Rules 7.1, 7.2, 7.3, 7.4, and 7.5

FLORIDA BAR v. PAPE

Supreme Court of Florida, 2005.
918 So.2d 240.

PARIENTE, C.J. * * *

We conclude that attorneys Pape and Chandler ("the attorneys") violated Rules Regulating the Florida Bar 4–7.2(b)(3) and 4–7.2(b)(4) by using the image of a pit bull and displaying the term "pit bull" as part of their firm's phone number in their commercial. Further, because the use of an image of a pit bull and the phrase "pit bull" in the firm's advertisement and logo does not assist the public in ensuring that an informed decision is made prior to the selection of the attorney, we conclude that the First Amendment does not prevent this Court from sanctioning the attorneys based on the rule violations. We determine that the appropriate sanctions for the attorneys' misconduct are public reprimands and required attendance at the Florida Bar Advertising Workshop.

BACKGROUND * * *

On January 12, 2004, The Florida Bar filed complaints against the attorneys, alleging that their law firm's television advertisement was an improper communication concerning the services provided, in violation of the Rules of Professional Conduct. The advertisement included a logo that featured an image of a pit bull wearing a spiked collar and prominently displayed the firm's phone number, 1–800–PIT–BULL. The Bar asserted that this advertisement violated the 2004 version of Rules Regulating the Florida Bar 4–7.2(b)(3) and 4–7.2(b)(4), which state:

(3) *Descriptive Statements.* A lawyer shall not make statements describing or characterizing the quality of the lawyer's services in advertisements and written communications; provided that this provision shall not apply to information furnished to a prospective client at that person's request or to information supplied to existing clients.

(4) *Prohibited Visual and Verbal Portrayals.* Visual or verbal descriptions, depictions, or portrayals of persons, things, or events must be objectively relevant to the selection of an attorney and shall not be deceptive, misleading, or manipulative. * * *

ANALYSIS * * *

A. Violation of Attorney Advertising Rules

As a preliminary matter, the pit bull logo and 1–800–PIT–BULL telephone number in the ad by the attorneys do not comport with the general criteria for permissible attorney advertisements set forth in the comments to section 4–7 of the Rules of Professional Conduct. The rules contained in section 4–7 are designed to permit lawyer advertisements that provide objective information about the cost of legal services, the experience and qualifications of the lawyer and law firm, and the types of cases the lawyer handles. * * *

B.   First Amendment Protection of Lawyer Advertising * * *

Lawyer advertising enjoys First Amendment protection only to the extent that it provides accurate factual information that can be objectively verified. This thread runs throughout the pertinent United State Supreme Court precedent.

The seminal lawyer advertising case is *Bates v. State Bar of Arizona,* 433 U.S. 350, 376, 97 S.Ct. 2691, 53 L.Ed.2d 810 (1977), which involved the advertising of fees for low cost legal services. In *Bates,* the Supreme Court held generally that attorney advertising "may not be subjected to blanket suppression," and more specifically that attorneys have the constitutional right to advertise their availability and fees for performing routine services. *Id.* at 383–84, 97 S.Ct. 2691. The cost of legal services, the Supreme Court concluded, would be "relevant information needed to reach an informed decision." *Id.* at 374, 97 S.Ct. 2691.

In reaching this conclusion the Supreme Court recognized that "[a]dvertising is the traditional mechanism in a free-market economy for a supplier to inform a potential purchaser of the availability and terms of exchange." *Id.* at 376, 97 S.Ct. 2691. "[C]ommercial speech serves to inform the public of the availability, nature, and prices of products and services, and thus performs an indispensable role in the allocation of resources in a free enterprise system. In short, such speech serves individual and societal interests in assuring informed and reliable decisionmaking." *Id.* at 364, 97 S.Ct. 2691 (citation omitted).

The Supreme Court emphasized that advertising by lawyers could be regulated and noted that "because the public lacks sophistication concerning legal services, misstatements that might be overlooked or deemed unimportant in other advertising may be found quite inappropriate in legal advertising." *Id.* at 383, 97 S.Ct. 2691. The Supreme Court specifically declined to address the "peculiar problems associated with advertising claims relating to the quality of legal services," but observed that "[s]uch claims *probably are not susceptible of precise measurement or verification and, under some circumstances, might well be deceptive or misleading to the public, or even false.*" *Id.* at 366, 97 S.Ct. 2691 (emphasis supplied).

After *Bates,* the Supreme Court considered a Missouri rule that restricted lawyer advertising to newspapers, periodicals, and the yellow pages, and limited the content of these advertisements to ten categories of information (name, address and telephone number, areas of practice, date and place of birth, schools attended, foreign language ability, office hours, fee for an initial consultation, availability of a schedule of fees, credit arrangements, and the fixed fee charged for specified "routine" services). *See In re R.M.J.,* 455 U.S. 191, 194, 102 S.Ct. 929, 71 L.Ed.2d 64 (1982). * * * In holding the Missouri restrictions per se invalid as applied to the lawyer, the Supreme Court concluded that the state had no substantial interest in prohibiting a lawyer from identifying the jurisdictions in which he or she was licensed to practice. *See id.* at 205, 102 S.Ct. 929. The Court noted that this "is *factual* and highly relevant information." *Id.* (emphasis supplied). Although the Court found the lawyer's listing in large capital letters that he was a member of the Bar of the Supreme Court of the United States to be "[s]omewhat more troubling" and in "bad taste," this alone could not be prohibited without a finding by the Missouri Supreme Court that "such a statement could be misleading to the general public unfamiliar with the requirements of admission to the Bar of this Court." *Id.* at 205, 102 S.Ct. 929. In short, the Supreme Court in *R.M.J.* was dealing with restrictions on clearly factual and relevant information that had not been found to be misleading or likely to deceive. As in *Bates,* the Supreme Court concluded that such restrictions violated the First Amendment.

In *Zauderer v. Office of Disciplinary Counsel of the Supreme Court of Ohio,* 471 U.S. 626, 629, 105 S.Ct. 2265, 85 L.Ed.2d 652 (1985), the Supreme Court addressed whether a state could discipline a lawyer who ran newspaper advertisements containing nondeceptive illustrations and legal advice. One advertisement published the lawyer's willingness to represent women injured from the use of the Dalkon Shield intrauterine device. *See id.* at 630, 105 S.Ct. 2265. The parties had stipulated that the advertisement was entirely accurate. *See id.* at 633–34, 105 S.Ct. 2265.

In holding that the lawyer could not be disciplined on the basis of the content of his advertisement, the Supreme Court observed that the advertisement did not promise results or suggest any special expertise but merely conveyed that the lawyer was representing women in Dalkon Shield litigation and was willing to represent other women with similar claims. *See id.* at 639–40, 105 S.Ct. 2265. * * * The Court then concluded that "[b]ecause the illustration for which appellant was disciplined is an accurate representation of the Dalkon Shield and has no features that are likely to deceive, mislead, or confuse the reader, the burden is on the State to present a substantial governmental interest justifying the restriction." *Id.* at 647, 105 S.Ct. 2265.

The most recent United States Supreme Court decision to address restrictions on the content of lawyer advertising involved an attorney who held himself out as certified by the National Board of Trial Advocacy (NBTA). *See Peel v. Attorney Registration & Disciplinary Comm'n of Illinois,* 496 U.S. 91, 110 S.Ct. 2281, 110 L.Ed.2d 83 (1990). The state supreme court had concluded that the claim of NBTA certification was "misleading because it tacitly attests to the qualifications of [petitioner] as a civil trial advocate." *Id.* at 98, 110 S.Ct. 2281 (plurality opinion) (quoting *In re Peel,* 126 Ill.2d 397, 128 Ill.Dec. 535, 534 N.E.2d 980, 984 (1989)) (alteration in original). [A] plurality of the Supreme Court concluded that the facts as to NBTA certification were "true and verifiable." *Id.* at 100, 128 Ill.Dec. 535, 534 N.E.2d 980 (plurality opinion). The plurality pointed out the important "distinction between *statements of opinion or quality and statements of objective facts that may support an inference of quality.*" *Id.* at 101, 128 Ill.Dec. 535, 534 N.E.2d 980 (plurality opinion) (emphasis supplied). A majority of the Court concluded that the letterhead was not actually or inherently misleading, and thus that the attorney could not be prohibited from holding himself out as a civil trial specialist certified by the NBTA. *See id.* at 106, 128 Ill.Dec. 535, 534 N.E.2d 980 (plurality opinion); *id.* at 111–12, 128 Ill.Dec. 535, 534 N.E.2d 980 (Marshall, J., concurring in the judgment).

The pit bull logo and "1–800–PIT–BULL" phone number are in marked contrast to the illustration of the Dalkon Shield intrauterine device at issue in *Zauderer,* which the United States Supreme Court found to be "an accurate representation [with] no features that are likely to deceive, mislead, or confuse the reader." 471 U.S. at 647, 105 S.Ct. 2265. The Dalkon Shield illustration *informed* the public that the lawyer represented clients in cases involving this device. The "pit bull" commercial produced by the attorneys in this case contains no indication that they specialize in either dog bite cases generally or in litigation arising from attacks by pit bulls specifically. Consequently, the logo and phone number do not convey objectively relevant information about the attorneys' practice. Instead, the image and words "pit bull" are intended to convey an image about the nature of the lawyers' litigation tactics. We conclude that an advertising device that connotes combativeness and viciousness without providing accurate and objectively verifiable factual information falls outside the protections of the First Amendment.

* * * CONCLUSION

* * * We find John Robert Pape and Marc Andrew Chandler guilty of violating rules 4–7.2(b)(3) and 4–7.2(b)(4) of the Rules Regulating the Florida Bar. We order that each attorney receive a public reprimand, which shall be administered by the Board of Governors of The Florida Bar upon proper notice to appear. We also direct Pape and Chandler to attend and complete the Florida Bar Advertising Workshop within six months of the date of this opinion.

It is so ordered.

NOTES ON ADVERTISING, SOLICITATION, AND FIRM NAMES

1. **Supreme Court Cases About Attorney Advertising:** The common thread in the Supreme Court cases striking state bar restrictions on advertising is truthfulness. The newspaper advertising in *Bates v. State Bar of Arizona,* 433 U.S. 350 (1977), and *Zauderer v. Office of Disciplinary Counsel of Supreme Court of Ohio,* 471 U.S. 626, 637 (1985), the letters in *Zauderer* and *Shapero v. Kentucky Bar Ass'n,* 486 U.S. 466, 472 (1988), the certification in *Peel v. Attorney Registration & Disciplinary Commission of Illinois,* 496 U.S. 91 (1990), and the field of practice advertising in *In re R.M.J.,* 455 U.S. 191 (1982), all contained truthful information about legal services conveyed in a non-deceptive fashion. Because each of these cases involved a writing, it was possible to later judge their truth and non-deceptiveness. Model Rules 7.1

(Communications Concerning a Lawyer's Services), 7.2 (Advertising), and 7.4 (Communication of Fields of Practice and Specialization) contain that same common thread. If the communication about legal service is both truthful and non-deceptive, it is likely to be permissible, due to the likely unconstitutionality of most state bar restrictions.

In light of the Supreme Court cases consistently rejecting state bar bans on truthful advertising, is the holding in *Pape* correct? Attorneys Pape and Chandler petitioned for certiorari to the U.S. Supreme Court, but the Court declined to grant it. *Pape v. Fla. Bar*, 547 U.S. 1041 (2006).

2. **Personal Solicitation:** Attorneys sometimes seek clients via personal solicitation, as in *Ohralik v. Ohio State Bar Ass'n*, 436 U.S. 447 (1978). Personal solicitation raises another problem, referred to by Wasserstrom in *supra* section 1(B)—the inherent inequality of the relationship between lawyer and client leading to the potential for the lawyer to manipulate the client. When the lawyer calls upon the client in person, given the inherent inequality of the relationship, it may later be impossible to determine if the lawyer's entreaties were either truthful or non-deceptive. As a result, Model Rule 7.3(a) bans the activity with *Ohralik*'s blessing.

3. **Cooling Off Periods:** The Supreme Court again addressed solicitation in *Florida Bar v. Went for It, Inc.*, 515 U.S. 618, 635 (1995), where the Court upheld the constitutionality of "the [Florida] Bar's 30–day [post-accident] restriction on targeted direct-mail solicitation of accident victims and their relatives." The Court noted that the Bar presented survey evidence that documented a "substantial interest both in protecting injured Floridians from invasive conduct by lawyers and in preventing the erosion of confidence in the profession that such repeated invasions have engendered." It also found that the "palliative devised by the Bar to address these harms is narrow both in scope and in duration." *Id.*

Justice Kennedy's dissent in *Went For It* emphasized the irony of preventing injured persons from hearing from lawyers offering their services in the often crucial period immediately following an accident, while permitting lawyers for potential adversaries "to contact the unrepresented [victims] to gather evidence or offer settlement." He also argued that the restriction was too broad, in that it unjustifiably assumes that all solicitations within 30 days would be unwelcome or unnecessary, that the problem of offense is "self-policing" in that "potential clients will not hire lawyers who offend them," and that the restriction falls most heavily on "those who most need legal representation," namely those who are too ill-informed to know that they need legal help. 515 U.S. at 635–45.

Following Justice Kennedy's concerns, suppose a state were to enact a 30–day direct mail ban similar to the one in *Went For It*, but applied that ban to attorneys who would write to those who had been arrested for criminal or traffic offenses. In *Ficker v. Curran*, 119 F.3d 1150 (4th Cir. 1997), the court found the interests balanced differently from those in *Went For It*. Noting that the Supreme Court "rested its conclusion largely on the principle that the privacy of accident victims * * * deserves protection," the court found "[t]he case before us lacks a similar justification for banning speech. While a criminal or traffic defendant may be shaken by his arrest, what he needs is representation, not time to grieve." 119 F.3d at 1155.

4. **Television, Radio, and the Internet:** None of the cases cited by the Court discusses television, radio, or internet advertising. The comments to Model Rule 7.2 make it clear that such advertising is included within the framework of "public media" in the rule. Model Rule 7.3, Comment [3]. If the internet is used to contact a specific client, the words "Advertising Material" are required by Model Rule 7.3(c). In addition, Model Rule 7.3(b) bans as impermissible solicitation direct contact with a prospective client over the internet in "real time" chatrooms. For further discussions of internet advertising, see William R. Denny, *How the Can–Spam Act of 2003 Affects Electronic Communication by Lawyers*, Practical Lawyer, Aug. 2005, at 17, and Nia Marie Monroe, Comment, *The Need for Uniformity: Fifty Separate Voices Lead to Disunion in Attorney Internet Advertising*, 18 Geo.J. Legal Ethics 1005 (2005). For discussions of ethical issues arising out of attorney websites, see ABA Standing Committee on Ethics & Professional Responsibility, Formal Opinion 10–457 (2010), and Margaret Hensler Nicholls, Comment, *A Quagmire of Internet Ethics Law and the ABA Guidelines for Legal Website Providers*, 18 Geo.J. Legal Ethics 1021 (2005). For a discussion of professional responsibility issues arising out of blogging by lawyers, see Judy M. Cornett, *The Ethics of Blawging: A Genre Analysis*, 41 Loy.U.Chi.L.J. 221 (2009).

5. **Firm Names:** In dealing with firm names, Model Rule 7.5 permits use of a "trade name" so long as the use is not false or misleading within the meaning of Model Rule 7.1 and so long as the trade name does not imply connection with a government or public agency or charity. While the Supreme Court has permitted restrictions on trade names incidental to otherwise commercial speech, *see Friedman v. Rogers*, 440 U.S. 1 (1979), one court has struck down a rule that would forbid firm names like "The Suit Shop." *See Michel v. Bare*, 230 F.Supp.2d 1147 (D.Nev. 2002) (invalidating a Nevada rule that limited firm names to those containing "the names of one or more living, retired or deceased members of the law firm"), *but see Rodgers v. Comm'n for Lawyer Discipline*, 151 S.W.3d 602 (Tex.App. 2004) (finding that a Yellow Pages advertisement promoting an "Accidental Injury Hotline" violated trade name restrictions, because it suggested that the telephone number would direct callers to an information service, while it actually referred them to an attorney); N.C. State Bar Ethics Comm., Op. 2004–9 (rejecting a proposed firm name that misleadingly suggest affiliation with a financial planning group).

Model Rule 7.5(d) also refers to the trade name that could be generated when two lawyers share office space, but are not partners. While it would be convenient to refer to the office sharing arrangement as "Jones and Smith, Attorneys at Law," the rule prohibits this usage unless the lawyers are, in fact, partners. This deception would also take place when the law firm name misleadingly suggests independence that does not exist. *See In re Foos*, 770 N.E.2d 335 (Ind. 2002), disciplining a lawyer for use of the name "Conover & Foos, Litigation Section of the Warrior Insurance Group, Inc." The "firm" was not a firm at all, but lawyer employees of the insurance company.

6. **Advertising, Solicitation, and Class Actions:** Rule 23(d) of the Federal Rules of Civil Procedure authorizes the court to provide notices and to impose conditions on the actions of counsel in class actions. The civil

procedure rules do not allow the court to issue a blanket ban preventing attorneys from contacting prospective class members through use of truthful advertising and permitted solicitation. *See Parris v. Superior Court*, 135 Cal.Rptr.2d 90 (Ct.App. 2003). The court can, however, restrict the content of mailings to prospective class members and can require such mailings to contain appropriate "Advertising" disclaimers, so they are not confused with notices from the court. *See In re McKesson HBOC, Inc. Sec. Litig.*, 126 F.Supp.2d 1239 (N.D.Cal. 2000). Finally, when counsel in one case uses information learned during discovery in that case to solicit potential clients for a subsequent class action, this is not impermissible barratry, champerty and maintenance. *See DaimlerChrysler Corp. v. Kirkhart*, 561 S.E.2d 276 (N.C.Ct.App. 2002).

7. **Multi–Jurisdictional Advertising:** Like Florida, most states have altered the Model Rules fairly substantially in the process of adopting, and later changing, their advertising rules. As a result, it is difficult for an attorney to advertise in a way that complies with the rules of all jurisdictions that the advertising might reach. Nonetheless, states often insist upon compliance with their rules, even by out-of-state attorneys, at least when their efforts are directly aimed at in-state potential clients. *See Lawyer Disciplinary Bd. v. Lakin*, 617 S.E.2d 484 (W.Va. 2005) (banning Illinois law firm from practice for twelve months and permanently prohibiting solicitation violating West Virginia rules). For discussions of the difficulties facing those who advertise in multiple jurisdictions, see Margaret Raymond, *Inside, Outside: Cross–Border Enforcement of Attorney Advertising Restrictions*, 43 Akron L.Rev. 801 (2010), and Emily Olson, Comment, *The Ethics of Attorney Advertising: The Effects of Different State Regulatory Regimes*, 18 Geo.J. Legal Ethics 1055 (2005).

8. **Lawyer Participation in Legal Services Plans:** Model Rule 7.2(b) permits legal services plans and lawyer referral services. Model Rule 7.3(d) allows in-person and telephone solicitation by legal services plans. According to Comment [6] to Model Rule 7.2:

> A legal service plan is a prepaid or group legal service plan or a similar delivery system that assists prospective clients to secure legal representation. [L]awyer referral service[s], on the other hand, * * * are understood by laypersons to be consumer-oriented organizations that provide unbiased referrals to lawyers with appropriate experience in the subject matter of the representation and afford other client protections, such as complaint procedures or malpractice insurance requirements.*

States are split on whether an attorney can pay an internet "matching" service to steer clients to the attorney. *Compare* Ariz. State Bar Comm. on Rules of Prof'l Conduct, Op. 2005–08 (opposing internet matching services); Tex. State Bar Prof'l Ethics Comm., Op. 561 (2005) (similar), *with* R.I. Sup. Ct. Ethics Advisory Panel, Op. 2005–01 (permitting payment of annual membership fee to internet matching service).

---

9. **Do the Advertising Rules Have Meaning?** One author has concluded that advertising rules are mostly meaningless. *See* Fred C. Zacharias, *What Lawyers Do When Nobody's Watching: Legal Advertising as a Case Study of the Impact of Underenforced Professional Rules*, 87 Iowa L.Rev. 971 (2002). Reviewing the yellow pages in San Diego, Professor Zacharias found that one in seven ads did not contain the name of a lawyer responsible for the content of the ad, as required by Model Rule 7.2(c). He also found that very few of these lawyers were disciplined for the content of their advertising. He determined that some could conclude, among other things, that regulators did not deem advertising offenses to be "important enough to prompt disciplinary action." Perhaps this is why the RESTATEMENT has no rules governing advertising, solicitation, or firm names.

B. NATURE, ESTABLISHMENT, AND SCOPE OF THE RELATIONSHIP

B(1) ESTABLISHING A CLIENT/ATTORNEY RELATIONSHIP

PROBLEM

Howard Smith is a disabled white man who lives on a modest income in an apartment building owned by a respected and politically active African American woman. He is an active member of the American Nazi party and has a disagreeable personality. When he had legal problems in the past, he tried to obtain assistance from the local legal aid society, but his meager income disqualified him from receiving assistance. He now comes to your office.

Smith, in a story laced with foul language and racial and sexual slurs, tells you about repairs that need to be made to his building and the substantial impairment of living conditions in the apartment without those repairs. He wants to force the landlord to make the repairs and wants your help. You indicate that the landlord may indeed have an obligation to fix the place up, but are not sure of the extent of that obligation. You also tell him you really don't have much time and are not sure that you and he could get along. You indicate that he should try to find another lawyer. About a week later, you get a phone message from your secretary telling you that Smith called and that he could not find another lawyer.

QUESTIONS

(a) Have you become Smith's attorney? What are your obligations, if any?

(b) Assume that, after Smith tells his story, you say: "I think you have a claim, but I am awfully busy. I'll write a letter to your landlord on my stationery telling her my opinion, but if that doesn't work, you'll have to get someone else to go to court for you." You write the letter, but the landlord remains adamant. Do you have any further obligations to Smith?

TOGSTAD v. VESELY, OTTO, MILLER & KEEFE

Supreme Court of Minnesota, 1980.
291 N.W.2d 686.

PER CURIAM.

[This is an appeal by the defendants in a legal malpractice action following a jury finding] that the defendant attorney Jerre Miller was negligent and that, as a direct result of such negligence, plaintiff John Togstad sustained damages in the amount of $610,500 and his wife, plaintiff Joan Togstad, in the amount of $39,000. Defendants (Miller and his law firm) appeal to this court from the denial of their motion for judgment notwithstanding the verdict or, alternatively, for a new trial. We affirm.

In August 1971, John Togstad began to experience severe headaches and on August 16, 1971, was admitted to Methodist Hospital where tests disclosed that the headaches were caused by a large aneurism[1] on the left internal carotid artery[2]. The attending physician, Dr. Paul Blake, a neurological surgeon, treated the problem by applying a Selverstone clamp to the left common carotid artery. The clamp was surgically implanted on August 27, 1971, in Togstad's neck to allow the gradual closure of the artery over a period of days.

The treatment was designed to eventually cut off the blood supply through the artery and thus relieve the pressure on the aneurism, allowing the aneurism to heal. It was anticipated that other arteries, as well as the brain's collateral or cross-arterial system would supply the required blood to the portion of the brain which would ordinarily have been provided by the left carotid artery. The greatest risk associated with this procedure is that the patient may become paralyzed if the brain does not receive an adequate flow of blood. In the event the supply of blood becomes so low as to endanger the health of the patient, the adjustable clamp can be opened to establish the proper blood circulation.

In the early morning hours of August 29, 1971, a nurse observed that Togstad was unable to speak or move. At the time, the clamp was one-half (50%) closed. Upon discovering Togstad's condition, the nurse called a resident physician, who did not adjust the clamp. Dr. Blake was also immediately informed of Togstad's condition and arrived about an hour

---

1. An aneurism is a weakness or softening in an artery wall which expands and bulges out over a period of years.

2. The left internal carotid artery is one of the major vessels which supplies blood to the brain.

later, at which time he opened the clamp. Togstad is now severely paralyzed in his right arm and leg, and is unable to speak.

Plaintiffs' expert [testified that the paralysis was caused by a lack of blood to the brain caused by the clamp and the negligence of the hospital and doctor in failing to open the clamp sooner. Dr. Blake and defendants' expert disputed that the clots were caused by the clamp procedure.]

About 14 months after her husband's hospitalization began, plaintiff Joan Togstad met with attorney Jerre Miller regarding her husband's condition. Neither she nor her husband was personally acquainted with Miller or his law firm prior to that time. John Togstad's former work supervisor, Ted Bucholz, made the appointment and accompanied Mrs. Togstad to Miller's office. Bucholz was present when Mrs. Togstad and Miller discussed the case.

Mrs. Togstad had become suspicious of the circumstances surrounding her husband's tragic condition due to the conduct and statements of the hospital nurses shortly after the paralysis occurred. One nurse told Mrs. Togstad that she had checked Mr. Togstad at 2 a.m. and he was fine; that when she returned at 3 a.m., by mistake, to give him someone else's medication, he was unable to move or speak; and that if she hadn't accidentally entered the room no one would have discovered his condition until morning. Mrs. Togstad also noticed that the other nurses were upset and crying, and that Mr. Togstad's condition was a topic of conversation.

Mrs. Togstad testified that she told Miller "everything that happened at the hospital," including the nurses' statements and conduct which had raised a question in her mind. She stated that she "believed" she had told Miller "about the procedure and what was undertaken, what was done, and what happened." She brought no records with her. Miller took notes and asked questions during the meeting, which lasted 45 minutes to an hour. At its conclusion, according to Mrs. Togstad, Miller said that "he did not think we had a legal case, however, he was going to discuss this with his partner." She understood that if Miller changed his mind after talking to his partner, he would call her. Mrs. Togstad "gave it" a few days and, since she did not hear from Miller, decided "that they had come to the conclusion that there wasn't a case." No fee arrangements were discussed, no medical authorizations were requested, nor was Mrs. Togstad billed for the interview.

Mrs. Togstad denied that Miller had told her his firm did not have expertise in the medical malpractice field, urged her to see another attorney, or related to her that the statute of limitations for medical malpractice actions was two years. She did not consult another attorney until one year after she talked to Miller. Mrs. Togstad indicated that she did not confer with another attorney earlier because of her reliance on Miller's "legal advice" that they "did not have a case."

On cross-examination, Mrs. Togstad was asked whether she went to Miller's office "to see if he would take the case of (her) husband * * *." She replied, "Well, I guess it was to go for legal advice, what to do, where shall we go from here? That is what we went for." Again in response to defense counsel's questions, Mrs. Togstad testified as follows:

Q And it was clear to you, was it not, that what was taking place was a preliminary discussion between a prospective client and lawyer as to whether or not they wanted to enter into an attorney-client relationship?

A I am not sure how to answer that. It was for legal advice as to what to do.

Q And Mr. Miller was discussing with you your problem and indicating whether he, as a lawyer, wished to take the case, isn't that true?

A Yes.

On re-direct examination, Mrs. Togstad acknowledged that when she left Miller's office she understood that she had been given a "qualified, quality legal opinion that (she and her husband) did not have a malpractice case."

Miller's testimony was different in some respects from that of Mrs. Togstad. Like Mrs. Togstad, Miller testified that Mr. Bucholz arranged and was present at the meeting, which lasted about 45 minutes. According to Miller, Mrs. Togstad described the hospital incident, including the conduct of the nurses. He asked her questions, to which she responded. Miller testified that "(t)he only thing I told her (Mrs. Togstad) after we had pretty much finished the conversation was that there was nothing related in her factual circumstances that told me that she had a case that our firm would be interested in undertaking." * * *

On cross-examination, Miller testified as follows:

Q Now, so there is no misunderstanding, and I am reading from your deposition, you understood that she was consulting with you as a lawyer, isn't that correct?

A That's correct.

Q That she was seeking legal advice from a professional attorney licensed to practice in this state and in this community?

A I think you and I did have another interpretation or use of the term "Advice." She was there to see whether or not she had a case and whether the firm would accept it.

Q We have two aspects; number one, your legal opinion concerning liability of a case for malpractice; number two, whether there was or wasn't liability, whether you would accept it, your firm, two separate elements, right?

A I would say so.

Q Were you asked on page 6 in the deposition, folio 14, "And you understood that she was seeking legal advice at the time that she was in your office, that is correct also, isn't it?" And did you give this answer, "I don't want to engage in semantics with you, but my impression was that she and Mr. Bucholz were asking my opinion after having related the incident that I referred to." The next question, "Your legal opinion?" Your answer, "Yes." Were those questions asked and were they given? * * *

A Yes, I gave those answers. Certainly, she was seeking my opinion as an attorney in the sense of whether or not there was a case that the firm would be interested in undertaking. * * *

This case was submitted to the jury by way of a special verdict form. The jury found that * * * there was an attorney-client contractual relationship between Mrs. Togstad and Miller * * *.

In a legal malpractice action of the type involved here, four elements must be shown[. The first required element is] that an attorney-client relationship existed * * *.

This court first dealt with the element of lawyer-client relationship in the decision of *Ryan v. Long*, 35 Minn. 394, 29 N.W. 51 (1886). The *Ryan* case involved a claim of legal malpractice and on appeal it was argued that no attorney-client relation existed. This court, without stating whether its conclusion was based on contract principles or a tort theory, disagreed:

> (I)t sufficiently appears that plaintiff, for himself, called upon defendant, as an attorney at law, for "legal advice," and that defendant assumed to give him a professional opinion in reference to the matter as to which plaintiff consulted him. Upon this state of facts the defendant must be taken to have acted as plaintiff's legal adviser, at plaintiff's request, and so as to establish between them the relation of attorney and client.

Id. (citation omitted). More recent opinions of this court, although not involving a detailed discussion, have analyzed the attorney-client consideration in contractual terms. *See, Ronnigen v. Hertogs*, 294 Minn. 7, 199 N.W.2d 420 (1972) * * *. For example, the *Ronnigen* court, in affirming a directed verdict for the defendant attorney, reasoned that "(u)nder the fundamental rules applicable to contracts of employment * * * the evidence would not sustain a finding that defendant either expressly or impliedly promised or agreed to represent plaintiff * * *." 294 Minn. 11, 199 N.W.2d 422. The trial court here * * * applied a contract analysis in ruling on the attorney-client relationship question. This has prompted a discussion by the Minnesota Law Review, wherein it is suggested that the more appropriate mode of analysis, at least in this case, would be to apply principles of negligence, i.e., whether defendant owed plaintiffs a duty to act with due care. 63 Minn.L.Rev. 751 (1979).

We believe it is unnecessary to decide whether a tort or contract theory is preferable for resolving the attorney-client relationship question raised by this appeal. The tort and contract analyses are very similar in a case such as the instant one,[4] and we conclude that under either theory

---

4. Under a negligence approach it must essentially be shown that defendant rendered legal advice (not necessarily at someone's request) under circumstances which made it reasonably

the evidence shows that a lawyer-client relationship is present here. The thrust of Mrs. Togstad's testimony is that she went to Miller for legal advice, was told there wasn't a case, and relied upon this advice in failing to pursue the claim for medical malpractice. In addition, according to Mrs. Togstad, Miller did not qualify his legal opinion by urging her to seek advice from another attorney, nor did Miller inform her that he lacked expertise in the medical malpractice area. Assuming this testimony is true, as this court must do, * * * we believe a jury could properly find that Mrs. Togstad sought and received legal advice from Miller under circumstances which made it reasonably foreseeable to Miller that Mrs. Togstad would be injured if the advice were negligently given. Thus, under either a tort or contract analysis, there is sufficient evidence in the record to support the existence of an attorney-client relationship.

[The malpractice aspects of this case are set forth at *infra* section 3(F)(1).]

NOTES ON THE ATTORNEY-CLIENT RELATIONSHIP

1. **Accidental Clients:** Some commentators refer to situations like *Togstad*, where an attorney enters into an attorney-client relationship without realizing it, as "accidental client" cases. For discussions of the dangers of unknowingly entering into such relationships, see Susan R. Martyn, *Accidental Clients*, 33 Hofstra L.Rev. 913 (2005), and Ingrid A. Minott, Note, *The Attorney–Client Relationship: Exploring the Unintended Consequences of Inadvertent Formation*, 86 U.Det. Mercy L.Rev. 269 (2009). For a discussion of the potential for accidental formation of attorney-client relationships via e-mail, see Douglas K. Schnell, Note, *Don't Just Hit Send: Unsolicited E–Mail and the Attorney–Client Relationship*, 17 Harv.J.L. & Tech. 533 (2004).

2. **Duties to Prospective Clients:** Model Rule 1.18 and section 15 of the RESTATEMENT both deal with duties to prospective clients like Mrs. Togstad. For a comprehensive overview of the relationship between attorneys and potential clients, see Fred C. Zacharias, *The Preemployment Ethical Role of Lawyers: Are Lawyers Really Fiduciaries?*, 49 Wm. & Mary L.Rev. 569 (2007). Both the Model Rules and the RESTATEMENT indicate that information coming from prospective clients is confidential and that the lawyer (and members of the lawyer's firm) cannot accept clients in the same or substantially related cases where use of the information from the prospective client could be harmful to the prospective client. The prospective client can consent to use of the information. The attorney in *Togstad* would not think of a violation of these rules because he simply assumed Mrs. Togstad was NOT a client.

---

foreseeable to the attorney that if such advice was rendered negligently, the individual receiving the advice might be injured thereby. * * * Or, stated another way, under a tort theory, "(a)n attorney-client relationship is created whenever an individual seeks and receives legal advice from an attorney in circumstances in which a reasonable person would rely on such advice." 63 Minn.L.Rev. 751, 759 (1979). A contract analysis requires the rendering of legal advice pursuant to another's request and the reliance factor, in this case, where the advice was not paid for, need be shown in the form of promissory estoppel. *See*, 7 C.J.S., Attorney and Client, § 65; Restatement (Second) of Contracts, § 90.

3. In his treatise, Professor Wolfram characterizes the attorney-client relationship this way:

> The law of contract defines the client-lawyer relationship for many, but hardly for all purposes. At the least, any duty that a lawyer has under the law of contract is owed to the client. But because the relationship is a fiduciary one, a lawyer may incur legal responsibilities that have no parallel in the law of contract. It is best, then, to speak of the lawyer's professional undertaking rather than the lawyer's contractual duties.

CHARLES W. WOLFRAM, MODERN LEGAL ETHICS § 4.1, at 146–47 (1986).

As noted in paragraph [17] of the Preamble and Scope section of the Model Rules, "Whether a client-lawyer relationship exists for any specific purpose can depend on the circumstances and may be a question of fact." The American Law Institute makes this point even more clearly, finding the existence of a relationship either when the lawyer manifests an intent to represent the client or fails to do so in circumstances in which the lawyer should reasonably know the client is relying on the lawyer to provide service. *See* RESTATEMENT, § 14.

4. **Who Decides if an Attorney–Client Relationship Exists?** If the existence of the attorney-client relationship is one of fact, then who decides the question? In *DeVaux v. American Home Assurance Co.*, 444 N.E.2d 355 (Mass. 1983), the Massachusetts Supreme Court answered:

> Where reasonable persons could differ as to the existence of an attorney-client relationship, this issue must be resolved by the trier of fact. [T]he question whether there was an attorney-client relationship depends on the reasonableness of the [client's belief]. The application of the reasonable person standard is uniquely within the competence of the jury.

See also Keatinge v. Biddle, 188 F.Supp.2d 3 (D.Me. 2002) (holding that the "existence of an attorney-client relationship is a factual question" for the jury, in an estate planning context); *Meyer v. Mulligan*, 889 P.2d 509, 513–14 (Wyo. 1995) (similar). What then would be the jury question to be resolved in your dealings with Smith in the problem?

5. **Model Rule 1.16:** What are the implications of cases like *Togstad*? What should a lawyer do when the lawyer does not want to take a case, but nonetheless has discussed the matter with the prospective client?

> A number of commentators, in assessing the importance of the case, have indicated that, in a situation where the lawyer chooses not to take the case after the initial consultation, the lawyer must send to the client a "non-engagement" letter. The fallacy in the use of this language is that, at this point in time, the lawyer is *already engaged* and if the lawyer wants to terminate the relationship, what is really needed is a *"breaking engagement"* letter.

James R. Devine, *Minnesota's* Togstad *Decision: Expanding the Ethical Responsibilities of All Lawyers*, 38 J.Mo. Bar 40, 41–42 (1982). For a discussion of the proper elements of a letter breaking the bond between an attorney and a potential client, see Lawrence J. Fox, *Non–Engaging, Engaging, and Disengaging Clients*, Litigation, Summer 2010, at 18.

6. ***Togstad* and the Internet:** Return to the problem, but assume that Smith did not come to your office, but instead saw your website, which encourages people to send email about legal problems to you. Assume Smith sent you an email filled with the same kind of foul language, racial and sexual slurs that are contained in the problem. Your office practice is to have an assistant go through the email that comes through your website and send a return message to all who send messages to you. Because of the tenor of this email, however, your assistant brings this email to you. You dictate a return email repeating your response as contained in the problem. Do you have any obligation to Smith?

If, as *Togstad*, the comments to the Model Rules, and the RESTATEMENT indicate, an attorney-client relationship can be formed by reliance, what are the implications for e-mail inquiries received by the lawyer? At least one ethics panel has determined that wholly unsolicited email inquiries sent to a lawyer who neither advertises on the internet or maintains a website will not create an attorney-client relationship. *See* Ariz. State Bar Comm. on Rules of Prof'l Conduct, Op. 2002–04, *digested in* Laws.Man. on Prof. Conduct (ABA/BNA) 1201:1404 (2003). In such a case, there is neither a manifestation of agreement to represent the client by the lawyer nor a failure to manifest lack of interest by the lawyer and reliance by the prospective client. Neither is the lawyer required to respect the confidentiality of such an unsolicited email under Model Rule 1.18. *See id.*

The situation could be different, however, if the lawyer maintains a website or advertises for clients on the internet. In this latter circumstance, the lawyer has manifested an interest in establishing an attorney-client relationship and some sort of disclaimer might be necessary. *See id.* Even with such a disclaimer, however, subsequent conduct could be inconsistent with the disclaimer and still form the relationship. *See* D.C. Bar Legal Ethics Comm., Op. 316 (2002), *digested in* Laws.Man. on Prof. Conduct (ABA/BNA) 1201:2303 (2003). In this opinion, the District of Columbia Bar Legal Ethics Committee found it permissible for lawyers to solicit clients through internet chat rooms, but cautioned against the inadvertent formation of an attorney-client relationship that would almost certainly be created when the lawyer provides legal advice to the inquiring prospective client. *See also* ABA Comm. on Ethics and Prof'l Resp., Formal Opinion 10–457 ("Lawyer Websites") (2010) (discussing in Part III the circumstances under which website visitor inquiries might give rise to prospective-client obligations under Model Rule 1.18).

7. **Must the Lawyer Accept All Clients?** Is the lawyer obligated to accept every prospective client that walks through the door? The American Bar Association, for many years, recommended an oath of admission that included the following pledge: "That I will never reject, from any consideration personal to myself, the cause of the defenseless or oppressed * * *." The current Model Rules contain nothing comparable. Comment [5] to Model Rule 1.2(b) does state that "representing a client does not constitute approval of the client's views or activities." In addition, Model Rule 1.16(a)(2) prohibits a lawyer from representing a client if "[t]he lawyer's physical or mental condition materially impairs the lawyer's ability to represent the client." Model Rule 1.16(b)(4) also permits an attorney to withdraw if "the client

insists upon taking action * * * with which the lawyer has a fundamental disagreement." The RESTATEMENT is a bit more direct, indicating that "a lawyer need not accept representation of a client." RESTATEMENT, Chapter 2, Introductory Note. Is the discretion envisioned by the RESTATEMENT completely unfettered? The next three notes should help answer this question.

8. **Discriminatory Practices:** Suppose the lawyer's personal beliefs, mainstream or not, preclude the lawyer's representation? What if the lawyer refuses to represent any African Americans, because the lawyer says, "I cannot get along with Blacks"? Suppose a lawyer of the Jewish faith refuses to represent any American Nazi, even though the lawyer recognizes that these potential clients have fundamental constitutional rights? Suppose a fundamentalist Christian turns down representation of lesbians seeking to enforce a state constitutional prohibition against discrimination? Today, amendments to the rules in California, among other jurisdictions, prohibit discrimination in accepting clients on the basis of "race, national origin, sex, sexual orientation, religion, age or disability." Cal.R.Prof.Cond. 2–400(B)(2).

The Americans with Disabilities Act prohibits discrimination against persons with disabilities in places of public accommodation and defines that term to include "offices." Civil rights statutes provide that all citizens have the same contract rights as white Americans. Some commentators argue that those statutes prevent discrimination against those protected groups. *See* Samuel Stonefield, *Lawyer Discrimination Against Clients: Outright Rejection—No; Limitations on Issues and Arguments—Yes*, 20 W. New Eng.L.Rev. 103, 113 (1998). In Massachusetts, a female attorney who limited her family law practice to the representation of women was found to have discriminated against a male who sought representation in a divorce case by the Massachusetts Commission Against Discrimination. *See Stropnicky v. Nathanson*, 19 M.D.L.R. (Landlaw, Inc.) 39 (Feb. 25, 1997). The case prompted a symposium on the duty to represent. *See* Martha Minow, *Foreword: Of Legal Ethics, Taxis, and Doing the Right Thing*, 20 W. New Eng.L.Rev. 5 (1998). What, if any, rules against discrimination exist in your state?

9. **Compelled Representation in Criminal Cases:** Return to the background facts in the problem, but assume that Smith gets into a heated discussion with his landlord and is arrested for assaulting her. While Smith has an interest in a small corporation, that interest cannot be liquidated, and he has no other money. The state public defender is not obligated to handle this municipal court matter, and the Municipal Judge has asked you to represent Smith on this misdemeanor charge that could lead to Smith being jailed. What are your obligations?

The American Law Institute notes that an attorney-client relationship exists when "a tribunal with power to do so appoints the lawyer to provide the service." RESTATEMENT, § 14(2). There is almost universal agreement that, in order to fulfill the obligation of the Sixth Amendment to the U.S. Constitution, courts have the power to appoint lawyers to represent indigent criminal defendants who face a real prospect of jail and to further order those lawyers to serve for little or no pay. Such appointment does not constitute an unlawful "taking" of the lawyer's time or services because acceptance of such appointments is considered to be part of the privilege of practicing law. Appointed counsel, however, cannot be required to absorb the cost of "necessary expenses" of this criminal litigation. Costs such as "investigatory services, deposition costs, witness fees, payment of expert witness, and similar outlays" must be borne by the state to avoid an impermissible taking from the lawyer. *Williamson v. Vardeman*, 674 F.2d 1211, 1215 (8th Cir. 1982). The RESTATEMENT makes clear that when the court appoints counsel, or when the court appoints a stand-by counsel to assist a criminal defendant pro se, consent to creation of the attorney-client relationship is implied, although the defendant can reject counsel. If counsel is rejected, the court can order the defendant to "choose between an unwelcome lawyer and self-representation," with the possible assistance of stand-by counsel. *Id.*, § 14, Comment *g*.

Before the 1960s, many courts relied heavily on their power to appoint attorneys in private practice to represent indigent criminal defendants. After the landmark decision in *Gideon v. Wainwright*, 372 U.S. 335 (1963), where the Supreme Court compelled states to provide counsel to indigent defendants, this practice waned, because public defender systems became commonplace. Courts still occasionally rely on their power to appoint private practice attorneys to represent criminal defendants, especially when public defender's offices have crushing caseloads. *See, e.g.*, Robin Troy, *Trial by [F]ire*, Mont. Law., Feb. 2005, at 12 (describing appointment of private practice attorneys to represent criminal defendants in Missoula County, Montana).

10. **Compelled Representation in Civil Cases:** Return to the background facts in the problem, but assume that Smith files a nearly incoherent *pro se* complaint in the local court. When he appears in court on this complaint, the judge asks if Smith has consulted a lawyer and your name comes up. The Judge then calls you and asks you, in the interests of justice, to represent Smith, even though it is likely to be without fee. What are your obligations?

If the court is not under constitutional compulsion to appoint counsel in a case, as in most civil cases, can the court still compel lawyers to serve without, or with substantially diminished, compensation? In *Mallard v. U.S. District Court*, 490 U.S. 296 (1989), the Supreme Court overturned the compulsory appointment of counsel in a federal case. The trial judge in the case, however, had relied on a federal statute authorizing, but not requiring, the appointment of counsel. The Court specifically did not answer "the question whether the federal courts possess inherent authority to require lawyers to serve." *Id.* at 310. Given the extent of the inherent power possessed by courts, which you studied in the last chapter, is there any question that the courts have the power to compel lawyers to represent indigent clients in civil cases? As stated by the Supreme Court of Florida, "uncompensated representation of indigents under court order is an obligation that lawyers accept as a condition of their license to practice law and a part of their public responsibility as officers of the court." The court then found that the attorney's obligation "is an absolute defense" to a claim that compulsory representation of indigents amounts to an unconstitutional "taking." *In re Amendments to Rules Regulating the Fla. Bar*, 573 So.2d 800, 805 (Fla. 1990). Not all courts agree. The South Carolina Supreme Court outlined the differing views in *South Carolina Dept. of Social Services v. Tharp*, 439 S.E.2d 854, 857 (S.C. 1994):

[C]ourts have split as to whether appointment of counsel, *pro bono,* to represent indigents amounts to a taking. A number of jurisdictions * * * find no taking in light of an attorney's obligation to represent the defenseless or oppressed. *See, e.g., In re Farrell,* 127 Misc.2d 350, 486 N.Y.S.2d 130 (1985); *Yarborough v. Superior Court,* 150 Cal.App.3d 388, 197 Cal.Rptr. 737 (1st Dist. 1983) *vacated on other grounds,* 39 Cal.3d 197, 216 Cal.Rptr. 425, 702 P.2d 583 (1985); *New Jersey Div. of Youth Services v. D.C.,* 118 N.J. 388, 571 A.2d 1295 (1990); *In re: Amendments to Rules Regulating the Florida Bar,* 573 So.2d 800 (1990); *see generally* Annot. 52 A.L.R.4th 1063 (1987).

Other jurisdictions equate the practice of law with a property right to hold that appointment without compensation constitutes a taking. *See* [*State ex rel Scott v. Roper,* 688 S.W.2d 757 (Mo. 1985); *Bedford v. Salt Lake County,* 447 P.2d 193 (Utah 1968); *Menin v. Menin,* 359 N.Y.S.2d 721 (Sup.Ct. 1974).]

Yet another approach has been to find that *pro bono* appointments do not constitute a *per se* taking but that, at some point, the burden on particular attorneys may become so excessive as to rise to the level of a taking. *See* [*Family Div. Trial Lawyers v. Moultrie,* 725 F.2d 695 (D.C.Cir. 1984).] *See also In Re: Amendments to Rules Regulating Florida Bar, supra* (attorneys may challenge appointments where they take a substantial portion of a lawyer's available services).

Some courts have limited appointment in non-criminal cases to situations that are "exceptional," leaving that determination to trial court discretion on a case-by-case basis. *See Gibson v. Tolbert,* 102 S.W.3d 710 (Tex. 2003). Other courts have adopted a more comprehensive test. *See Jackson v. Cnty. of McLean,* 953 F.2d 1070 (7th Cir. 1992). A summary of those tests creates a schematic that looks something like this:

First, the court should determine whether the indigent civil litigant has made a reasonable effort to independently obtain private counsel. Only after the court is satisfied that the indigent was unsuccessful in that effort or was "effectively precluded" from making an attempt to find private counsel could the court seek to appoint counsel.

Second, if the court has found the client unable to hire private counsel, then the court may request private counsel's assistance.

Third, a reviewing court can find the trial court's decision not to appoint private counsel an abuse of discretion only when the denial represents "fundamental unfairness infringing on due process rights." To determine if such fundamental unfairness exists, the reviewing court will look to the following factors, each of which must be specifically addressed in the trial court's determination of the request for appointment of counsel:

    a.   the merits of the underlying claim filed by the indigent;

    b.   the ability of the indigent to conduct a proper investigation into the claim;

    c.   whether the truth is more likely to be served if both sides are represented by counsel;

d. the ability of the indigent to effectively present the case at trial;

e. the complexity of the legal issues involved.

Courts sometimes appoint attorneys for purposes other than traditional civil case advocacy. In Arizona, the state supreme court has determined that courts have the power to require attorneys to serve as arbitrators. *Scheehle v. Justices of the Sup. Ct. of Ariz.*, 120 P.3d 1092 (Ariz. 2005).

11. **Non–Mandatory *Pro Bono*:** If the courts do not compel lawyers to represent indigent clients without fee, how will such persons obtain representation? First, what is the extent of the problem, given the existence of the federally subsidized Legal Services Corporation? Legal services programs funded by the Legal Services Corporation are eligible to serve clients with incomes up to 125% above the poverty level, or about one in five Americans. Legal Services Corporation funded offices are not permitted to represent clients in "class actions, challenges to welfare reform, collection of attorneys' fees, rulemaking, lobbying, litigation on behalf of prisoners, representation in drug-related public housing evictions, and representation of certain categories of aliens." Kellie Isbell & Sarah Sawle, *Pro Bono Publico: Voluntary Service and Mandatory Reporting*, 15 Geo.J. Legal Ethics 845, 846 (2002). Because of the number of citizens eligible for legal services and the limitations on such programs, a 1994 ABA study showed that almost 80% of poor people facing legal difficulty did not have access to legal services. *Id.* at 847.

In part as a result of the perceived unmet legal needs of the poor, during the 1980s debate over the Model Rules, considerable attention was devoted to a proposal to substitute a mandatory obligation to perform *pro bono* service in place of Model Rules 6.1 and 6.2. In 1980, the ABA's Kutak Commission [the drafters of the Model Rules] proposed the following:

> A lawyer shall render unpaid public interest legal service. A lawyer may discharge this responsibility by service in activities for improving the law, the legal system, or the legal profession, or by providing professional services to persons of limited means or to public service groups or organizations. A lawyer shall make an annual report concerning such service to appropriate regulatory authority.*

ABA Comm'n on Evaluation of Prof'l Standards, Model Rules of Prof'l Conduct (Discussion Draft, Jan. 30, 1980), Model Rule 8.1. The negative reaction in the bar, particularly to the problems of definition and enforcement of a mandatory obligation, was strong enough to cause the Commission in its final recommendations to revert to a standard suggesting an aspiration to provide at least 50 hours of *pro bono* service, primarily to those who need legal services and cannot afford it. *See* Model Rule 6.1.

The debate resurfaced in the Ethics 2000 Commission, which originally proposed revisions to Model Rule 6.1 requiring 50 hours of service or a $100 per hour substitute. Opposition to this revision came largely from the "legal services community," which feared that bar resentment of mandatory service would overshadow the real "crisis in unmet legal needs." It was also argued that compulsory service by "reluctant attorneys" could diminish the quality of legal services to the poor. *See* Judith L. Maute, *Changing Conceptions of Lawyers' Pro Bono Responsibilities: From Chance Noblesse Oblige to Stated*

Expectations, 77 Tul.L.Rev. 91, 140–41 (2002). After further debate, the Ethics 2000 Commission was almost equally divided on the issue of mandatory service, ultimately voting not to require it. *See id.* at 140–46. Instead, the commission added the first sentence of current Model Rule 6.1, making it clear that all lawyers have an obligation to provide *pro bono* services, and also added Comment [11], encouraging law firms to provide a work environment satisfactory to accomplishing the obligation to provide *pro bono* services. *See* Maute, *supra*, at 146–47.

As of a 2002 survey in the Georgetown Journal of Legal Ethics, only New Jersey required mandatory *pro bono* and only Florida mandated the reporting of voluntary *pro bono* hours worked. *See* Isbell & Sawle, *supra*, at 856, 859. In 2006, Illinois added a similar reporting requirement. *See* Ill.S.Ct.R. 756(f). The issue remains active with numerous ABA leaders calling for increased awareness of the lawyer's obligation to provide *pro bono* services. *See* Maute, *supra*, at 142. Initiatives such as the Pro Bono Challenge, sponsored by the Pro Bono Institute, have caused many large firms to commit a "certain percentage of work to pro bono matters." In addition, one lawyer magazine "ranks the amount of pro bono work by the 100 largest firms." Terry Carter, *Building a Pro Bono Base*, 89 A.B.A.J., June 2003, at 30, 32. These efforts are designed to show lawyers and firms that " '[p]ro bono is good for business.' It is good for recruiting and training; it is good for making a name and making an impact; it is good for client relationships; and it is good as a glue within the firm." *Id.* at 30.

12. **Limited Representation:** Model Rule 1.2(c) permits the lawyer to limit the scope of the representation upon the consent of the client. In *Lerner v. Laufer*, 819 A.2d 471 (N.J.Super.Ct.App.Div. 2003), plaintiff had been married for 24 years to her husband, who then decided to divorce her. Because plaintiff and her husband had accumulated considerable wealth, they agreed to allow a lawyer business associate of the husband to mediate a property settlement agreement. After several mediation sessions, a property settlement agreement was drafted and plaintiff was given a list of attorneys to consult before signing the agreement. She consulted with defendant who, at the outset, produced a letter that the plaintiff was asked to read and sign. The letter indicated that the defendant had done no investigation or discovery of the assets of the husband and was not giving an opinion on the fairness of the underlying property settlement. Rather, the letter stated, the defendant was retained only to assure the plaintiff understood the terms and conditions of the property settlement agreement. After the property settlement agreement became part of the divorce decree, plaintiff discovered that husband had been less than truthful about a company owned by the parties and that the company was actually worth considerably more than represented in the parties' negotiations. Plaintiff then sued defendant claiming that defendant failed to conduct discovery to properly locate assets subject to equitable distribution. The court granted the defendant lawyer's motion for summary judgment, holding that the plaintiff's consent letter created a representation limited under Model Rule 1.2(c) to the terms of the negotiated agreement only: "[I]t is not a breach of the standard of care for an attorney under a signed[,] precisely drafted consent agreement to limit the scope of representa-

tion to not perform such services * * * that he or she might otherwise perform absent such a consent." *Id.* at 483. Whether representation for a limited purpose has indeed been created is a question of fact. *See Marcano v. Litman & Litman, P.C.*, 741 N.Y.S.2d 522 (App.Div. 2002) (concerning a claim by a plaintiff who was injured in a job-related accident that the workers compensation law firm to which he was referred was negligent in not advising him of the possibility of suing third parties).

13. **Law Student *Pro Bono*:** Should law students be required to help solve the problem by providing *pro bono* legal assistance to the poor as a graduation requirement? Would this be a good way for students to acquire "field experience"? As of 2002, approximately nine law schools, including Harvard, Columbia, and the University of Pennsylvania, required some form of *pro bono* work by students. *See* Christina M. Rosas, *Mandatory Pro Bono Publico for Law Students: The Right Place to Start*, 30 Hofstra L.Rev. 1069 (2002) (arguing in favor of mandatory *pro bono* for students).

B(2) IDENTIFYING THE CLIENT

PROBLEM

The "Big Five" Athletic Conference is a combination of major colleges all located within 50 miles of your city. The "Big Five" schedules games, negotiates media contracts, hires officials, and does other activities to promote the marketing of competitive sports of the conference. It is organized as a not-for-profit corporation. All revenues generated by the conference are returned to the individual schools. The "Big Five" has retained the law firm of Page and LaRussa to represent it on all matters. East Central Suburban University and City North University are both members of the "Big Five." Because of their geographic proximity and their knowledge of higher education issues, the law firm of Young and Winslow represents both East Central Suburban and City North on most higher education matters. Last week, the "Big Five" conference determined that Albert Delong, a highly recruited high school football player, was academically ineligible to play for perennial "Big Five" football power Southside University because of a question about one of his high school grades. Delong and his parents consulted with Young and Winslow, and that law firm has filed suit on behalf of Delong against the Big Five Conference and Southside University.

QUESTIONS

At a hearing to determine if preliminary injunctive relief should be granted, the judge, upon request from conference lawyers Page and LaRussa, asked Young and Winslow if they have a "conflict of interest" in appearing against the conference in a matter in which they also represent two of the five member institutions. What issues are involved? Do you need further information?

RULE REFERENCES

Model Rules 1.13 and 1.8(f)

RESTATEMENT § 96

J.G. RIES & SONS, INC. v. SPECTRASERV, INC.

Superior Court of New Jersey, Appellate Division, 2006.
894 A.2d 681.

WEFING, P.J.A.D.

Plaintiff J.G. Ries & Sons, Inc. ("Ries") appeals, pursuant to leave granted, from a trial court order disqualifying the firm of Pearce Fleisig, LLC ("Pearce") from representing it in this matter. After reviewing the record in light of the contentions advanced on appeal, we reverse.

Ries owns property located at 65 Jacobus Avenue in Kearny. Defendant Spectraserv has its principal place of business on property owned by defendant Modern Transportation Company and located at 75 Jacobus Avenue. Spectraserv is in the business of receiving sewage sludge, processing it and then disposing of the resulting sludge cake. In June 2004, represented by Pearce, Ries filed suit against Spectraserv, Modern and certain of their related companies [("Spectraserv")], seeking damages for the noxious odors and fumes Ries alleged were generated by Spectraserv in the course of its business operations and which Ries contended affected the use of its own property. * * *

The area in question is in the portion of Kearny referred to generally as South Kearny. Trucking companies are one of the principal businesses in the area * * *. Approximately fifty of the businesses located in South Kearny banded together several years prior to the incidents giving rise to this appeal to form Lincoln North Development Corporation to advance and promote the business interests of its members and the area. Both Ries and Spectraserv are members of Lincoln North. * * *

In November 2004, Kearny amended its zoning ordinance and divided what had been the SKM [(South Kearny Manufacturing)] zone into SKM–N and SKM–S zones. This amended ordinance included certain restrictions on the maintenance and operation of trucking terminals and the storage of trailers that had not been in the prior ordinance, and in December 2004, Lincoln North filed a prerogative writ action, challenging this zoning ordinance on behalf of its members. The Pearce firm, counsel to Ries in its suit against Spectraserv, represented Lincoln North in its challenge to the Kearny zoning ordinance.

In April 2005, Spectraserv filed a motion to bar Pearce from continuing as the attorney for Ries in its suit against Spectraserv. This appeal follows upon the trial court granting Spectraserv's motion.

On appeal, Ries contends that no conflict of interest exists between the Pearce firm representing it in its suit against Spectraserv, as well as representing Lincoln North in the challenge to the Kearny zoning ordinance. * * * Spectraserv, on the other hand, responds that a conflict of interest exists that requires the disqualification of the Pearce firm under *RPC* 1.7 * * *. We are satisfied that Ries is correct in this regard. * * *

I

We turn first to the effect, if any, of Pearce representing Lincoln North, of which both Ries and Spectraserv are members, upon its ability to represent Ries in its suit against Spectraserv. * * * The trial court concluded in its oral opinion that the Pearce firm was disqualified under *RPC* 1.7[, which governs conflicts of interest,] and that *RPC* 1.13 did not apply. * * * Whether the Pearce firm is, indeed, disqualified under *RPC* 1.7(a) depends, in part, upon whether Spectraserv should be deemed a Pearce client in light of its membership in Lincoln North. * * *

A

Both parties find support for their respective positions in *Glueck v. Jonathan Logan, Inc.*, 653 F.2d 746 (2d Cir.1981). The plaintiff in that case, a former executive with the defendant, sued for breach of employment contract. *Id.* at 748. He was represented in that suit by the firm of Phillips, Nizer, Benjamin, Krim & Ballon. *Ibid.* Logan moved to disqualify the firm because it also represented a trade association, Apparel Manufacturers Association, Inc., of which R & K Originals, one of Logan's divisions, was a member. *Ibid.* The sole purpose of the Association was to negotiate collective bargaining agreements for its members with the International Ladies Garment Workers' Union. *Ibid.* The president of R & K was a vice-president of the Association and had occasion to meet with Phillips, Nizer to discuss labor matters. *Ibid.* The District Court concluded that Phillips, Nizer's representation of the Association precluded it from representing Glueck in his suit against Logan, and the Court of Appeals affirmed. *Ibid.* The Court of Appeals formulated the following principle:

> Disqualification will ordinarily be required whenever the subject matter of a suit is sufficiently related to the scope of the matters on which a firm represents an association as to create a realistic risk either that the plaintiff will not be represented with vigor or that unfair advantage will be taken of the defendant. Moreover, once that risk appears, it is appropriate to assess the risk that prosecution of a plaintiff's lawsuit by an association's law firm will inhibit the free flow of information from the defendant to the firm that is necessary for the firm's proper representation of the association.

[*Id.* at 750.]

The court stressed that in the course of representing the Association in labor negotiations, the firm could have learned whether Logan had cause to terminate Glueck. *Ibid.* It also noted that the firm could have become privy to Logan's termination policies or practices that might bear upon the merits of Glueck's suit. *Ibid.* Thus, the court found the presence of a "substantial relationship" between the firm representing the Association and representing Glueck against an Association member and granted Logan's motion to disqualify the firm. *Id.* at 749–50.

[W]e are unable to perceive a "substantial relationship" between Ries's lawsuit against Spectraserv and Lincoln North's prerogative writ action against the municipality of Kearny. The only real connection between the two is that they involve property located in South Kearny. The two suits have completely separate subject matter and litigation goals. The Lincoln North action is a challenge to Kearny's revision of its zoning ordinance; its object is to permit trucking companies to continue operating their businesses in the same manner they had been permitted to under the prior ordinance. The Ries suit is entirely unrelated to the maintenance of a trucking business; it is premised upon Ries's allegation that Spectraserv's business generates noxious fumes and odors that carry onto the Ries property. We are satisfied that the principles enunciated in *Glueck* do not warrant disqualifying the Pearce firm for the Spectraserv litigation.

B

The trial court also cited, as additional support, *Formal Opinion of the Committee on Ethics and Professional Responsibility of the American Bar Association,* Formal Op. 92–365 (1992). The question posed to the Committee was whether "a law firm representing a trade association may also represent a client litigating against an individual member of that association." *Ibid.* The Committee reached no direct conclusion to the question but rather set forth an analytical framework to consider the matter in the context of the then-governing Model Rules of Professional Responsibility. The Committee noted that the proper method of analysis would, in large measure, depend upon whether the individual member of the trade association could be considered a client of the attorney. *Ibid.* * * *

The Committee distinguished between what it referred to as a member of the trade association being considered a "direct" client of the attorney representing the association and the member being considered a "derivative" or "vicarious" client. The Committee noted that the formation of an attorney-client relationship is not dependent upon the parties having specifically agreed to the creation of such a relationship and pointed to *Westinghouse Elec. Corp. v. Kerr–McGee Corp.,* 580 F.2d 1311 (7th Cir.1978).

In that case, the firm of Kirkland and Ellis was retained by the American Petroleum Institute to oppose certain legislation which Congress was considering which would require the divestiture of certain businesses by Institute members. *Westinghouse, supra,* 580 F.2d at 1312–13. As part of that representation, the firm solicited information from various Institute members, including Kerr–McGee, as to the potential impact of the proposed legislation. The firm noted in its solicitation that the information was not publicly available and would be held in confidence. *Id.* at 1313–14. Kerr–McGee replied and provided the material requested, and the firm prepared and released a report on the extent of competition in the industry, attempting to demonstrate that divestiture was not required or appropriate. *Id.* at 1314.

The Kirkland firm, however, also represented Westinghouse Electric Corporation. *Id.* at 1313. On the same day that the firm released the report on behalf of the Institute, it filed suit on behalf of Westinghouse against Kerr–McGee and others, alleging they were acting to establish an illegal conspiracy in restraint of trade. *Id.* at 1312. Shortly after the filing of the complaint, Kerr–McGee moved to disqualify the firm. *Id.* at 1313. The District Court denied the motion, but the Court of Appeals reversed. *Ibid.* The court, after noting that "[a] fiduciary relationship may result because of the nature of the work performed and the circumstances under which confidential information is divulged", *id.* at 1320, concluded that a fiduciary relationship existed between the Kirkland firm and Kerr McGee in view of the sharing of confidential information that had occurred. *Id.* at 1321. * * *

Spectraserv contends that it is a "direct" client of the Pearce firm in light of information it has supplied to the firm in conjunction with its representation of Lincoln North. It also contends that in the alternative, it should be considered a vicarious client under *Glueck, supra.* We are satisfied that in the context of this case, Spectraserv is neither a direct nor a vicarious client of the Pearce firm, and thus no conflict of interest exists.

Spectraserv stresses that it provided certain information to Lincoln North and analogizes that to the situation in *Westinghouse, supra.* We are unable to consider the two situations comparable. First, the information in question was not requested by the Pearce firm but by an individual named Karl Petry on behalf of the Association to assist it with an earlier challenge to another Kearny zoning ordinance. * * * Further, there was no representation that the information would be treated as confidential nor did Spectraserv request such treatment. Much of the information, moreover, such as real estate taxes and square footage, is publicly available. In addition, Spectraserv maintains a website from which it is possible to learn many of the details about its business operations. The only information that Spectraserv provided to Lincoln North that would not be readily available to a diligent researcher was the amount of federal and state income taxes that Spectraserv had paid. Spectraserv's tax liability, however, is totally unrelated to either of these two lawsuits. [T]here could have been no reasonable expectation that the information Spectraserv supplied to Lincoln North would not be disclosed. Indeed, it was intended for disclosure, to advance the purposes of the Lincoln North litigation. * * * We are satisfied that Spectraserv was not a direct client of the Pearce firm.

[T]here is not a substantial relationship between the two matters, and thus, Spectraserv was not a vicarious client of the Pearce firm. The closest analogy our research has uncovered in reported New Jersey authority is *Greate Bay Hotel & Casino, Inc. v. Atlantic City,* 264 N.J.Super. 213, 624 A.2d 102 (Law Div.1993). Plaintiff in that case filed suit to compel Atlantic

City to acquire a certain small parcel of land and keep it vacant for public access. *Id.* at 214, 624 A.2d 102. After suit was filed, an entity known as Square Brighton, which had a leasehold interest in the property, was permitted to intervene. *Ibid.* Square Brighton was represented by the firm of Clapp & Eisenberg, which also served as counsel to certain business trusts created by various Atlantic City casinos to operate a computerized link of their respective progressive slot machines. *Ibid.* Plaintiff Greate Bay was a member of several of these business trusts and sought to disqualify Clapp & Eisenberg from representing Square Brighton. *Id.* at 216, 624 A.2d 102. The trial court denied the application, concluding that the business trusts were separate entities and that the firm's representation of the entity did not create an attorney-client relationship between the members of the entity and the firm representing the entity. *Id.* at 221, 624 A.2d 102.

We find that analogy persuasive here. Lincoln North is an entity separate and apart from Spectraserv. Just as the firm of Clapp & Eisenberg was permitted to represent both the business trusts and the intervenor, the Pearce firm should be permitted to represent both Lincoln North and Ries in these wholly unrelated actions.

* * * For the reasons stated, the order under review is reversed, and the matter is remanded to the trial court for further proceedings in accordance with this opinion. * * *

NOTES ON DETERMINING CLIENT IDENTITY

1. In *Kilpatrick v. Wiley, Rein & Fielding*, 2001 UT 107, 37 P.3d 1130, plaintiffs were partners of a limited partnership formed to purchase a television station. Defendants were unquestionably the lawyers for the limited partnership. Plaintiffs, however, claimed the defendant firm also represented the partners. In reversing a directed verdict for the plaintiffs on the issue, the court found that the individual limited partners could only be clients of the attorneys if they "reasonably believed" they were so represented. This issue was a question of fact.

In *Sickler v. Kirby*, 805 N.W.2d 675 (Neb.Ct.App. 2011), on the other hand, it was held that the two shareholders in a closely held corporation formed to franchise their successful coffee house business, who were also its only officers, had personal malpractice claims against attorneys purporting to represent the entity, where the essence of the alleged malpractice was failure to properly advise the entity concerning the fact that its franchising operations had been conducted in violation of state and federal laws. On the relationship between a closely held corporation and its shareholders, the court said:

> In the instance of closely held corporations, it seems clear that the financial well-being of the directors, officers, and owners of the corporation is usually inseparable from the interests and fate of the corporation. And, we suggest that the more closely held the corporation, the less separable the directors, officers, and owners are from the corporation.

Here, there is substantial evidence that the interests and fates of [the owners] are indistinguishable from those of [the corporation].

[T]here is no evidence showing a clear understanding on the part of [the owners] that [the lawyer's] representation was solely of [the corporation] to the exclusion of [the owners'] personal interests as the directors, officers, and owners of [the corporation]. In fact, the evidence is to the contrary.

805 N.W.2d at 689–90.

2. **What if No Entity Exists?** Multiple individuals want to form a corporation and hire a lawyer to represent ONLY the corporation to be. Is this possible? Relying on a Wisconsin case, *Jesse* ex rel. *Reinecke v. Danforth*, 485 N.W.2d 63 (Wis. 1992), the Arizona State Bar Committee on the Rules of Professional Conduct in Opinion 02–06 (2002) concluded that it was possible for a lawyer to represent only the future corporation. Even though there was no client until the corporation's articles of incorporation are filed, a lawyer, in an agreement with the incorporators, can provide that the lawyer only represents the entity. The lawyer should counsel the incorporators that they are not being individually represented, and the corporation should ratify the acts of counsel once the corporation comes into existence.

3. **What About Insurance Defense?** When an insured buys a liability insurance policy, the section dealing with claims normally provides language something like: "We [the insurer] have the right and duty to defend any suit against you [the insured] seeking damages under this policy." By controlling the litigation from the outset, the insurer exercises optimal control of potential loss in the litigation. When the insurer hires the lawyer, however, who is the client—the insurer, the insured, or both? Clearly the lawsuit is against the "insured," who is the named party. But equally clearly, particularly where the suit seeks damages within the limits of the insurance policy, the insurer is the entity that will pay any judgment and any attorney fees arising out of the suit.

Is the client, then: (1) the insured, who bought the policy, had the accident, and in whose name the proceeding is filed; (2) the insurer, who will probably suffer a higher financial loss than the insured; or (3) both the insurer and the insured?

4. **Conflict of Interest:** The answer to the question "who is the client?" often implicates conflict of interest concerns. Model Rule 1.13(a) provides that a lawyer retained by an organization ordinarily works for that organization, not for its managers, employees, or other constituents. If the lawyer knows or should know that a constituent's interests conflict with those of the organization the lawyer is representing, the lawyer must explain to the constituent that the organization, not the constituent, is the lawyer's client. *See* Model Rule 1.13(f). If there is no conflict between the lawyer's organizational client and its constituent, and if the conflict of interest provisions of Model Rule 1.7 do not prohibit joint representation, the lawyer can represent both the organization and the client. *See* Model Rule 1.13(g).

The answers to the insurance questions provide another point of reference regarding the conflict of interest issues in identifying the client. They are discussed in *infra* section 5(A)(1)(c).

C. AUTHORITY WITHIN THE RELATIONSHIP

PROBLEM

In a civil suit filed against him, Carl Baker is alleged to have assaulted plaintiff Maude Aikens. The suit seeks damages against Baker in the amount of $25,000. Carl Baker comes to your office and you agree to defend the case, thereafter filing an answer generally denying the allegations of the complaint. You follow your answer with interrogatories to the plaintiff. Baker, who knows little about the law, but who has seen a lot of lawyer shows on television, demands that you depose the plaintiff. Though you explain that interrogatories will accomplish the same result, Carl insists. He also insists that you seek a change of venue and that, for trial, you subpoena all of Maude's tax records for the past ten years, although the issue of Maude's wealth has no bearing on the case. After you thoroughly discuss these matters with Baker, he grudgingly acquiesces to your handling of discovery, venue, and subpoena matters, although he encourages you to "do it my way." After further discussion, Baker also sees the benefit of settlement negotiations with the attorney for Maude Aikens, and he specifically authorizes you to pursue such discussions.

In discussions with Maude's lawyer, you learn that Maude will accept a settlement of the matter whereby Carl Baker pays Maude $100 and apologizes to her in court. In telephone discussions with Carl Baker about this proposed settlement, you infer his agreement to such a settlement and so advise the attorney for Maude Aikens, whereupon you both sign an agreement embodying it on behalf of your respective clients. The next day, you ask Baker to stop by your office where you advise him that the settlement has been finalized. Baker becomes irate. He expresses shock that you would accept such a deal. He insists that he will never pay Maude a dime, let alone apologize to her. You also advise him that even if the matter must go to trial, you will not subpoena all of Maude's tax records. He becomes even more irate, then stomps out of your office mumbling something like "well, we'll just see about that!" After you calm down, you call the attorney for Maude and advise her that Baker does not, in fact, consent and that there can be no settlement under the terms suggested.

QUESTIONS

(a) Assume that Maude Aikens' attorney immediately files a motion to specifically enforce the settlement. On what legal theory could Maude's attorney argue that Baker should be bound by your actions?

(b) Assume that, after the meeting in your office, Carl Baker consulted a lawyer who is member of your State's ethics committee about your conduct. Specifically, Baker complained that your failure to subpoena Maude's tax records, which went directly against his wishes, as well as your conduct in not deposing Maude and not seeking a change of venue, must have violated some obligation you owed him. How should this lawyer respond to Baker's complaints?

RULE REFERENCES

Model Rules 1.2 and 1.14

RESTATEMENT §§ 21–23

ACKERMAN v. SOBOL FAMILY PARTNERSHIP, LLP

Supreme Court of Connecticut, 2010.
4 A.3d 288.

ZARELLA, J. * * *

In the underlying cases, the plaintiffs alleged, inter alia, breach of contract, breach of fiduciary duty, unjust enrichment, civil conspiracy and violation of the Connecticut Unfair Trade Practices Act, General Statutes § 42–110a et. seq. The cases were scheduled for a combined jury and court trial to commence on July 8, 2008, after the completion of jury selection. On July 3, 2008, however, the Sobol defendants and the defendant Bank of America each filed a motion to enforce a settlement agreement purportedly reached with the plaintiffs on July 1, 2008. On July 8, 2008, the trial court, *Eveleigh*, J., conducted a hearing * * * to determine whether the settlement agreement was enforceable, at which the plaintiffs argued that there was no agreement and the defendants argued that there was. On July 9, 2008, the court issued an oral decision from the bench containing the following findings of fact and conclusions of law.

[The trial court found that, after a mediation that did not resolve the dispute, plaintiff's attorney Glenn Coe] "made an offer to settle the litigation in a series of conversations with [Robert Wyld, who represented the Sobol defendants,] and [Attorney David] Schneider[, who represented the Bank of America,] on Thursday, June 26, and Friday, June 27, 2008. * * *

"[Wyld], who was negotiating the settlement on behalf of ... the Sobol defendants ... notified [Coe] on Monday, June 30, 2008, that the offer of settlement made by [Coe] on behalf of all [of the] plaintiffs was accepted by the Sobol defendants. The Sobol defendants understood that the settlement between the plaintiffs and the Sobol defendants was part of a global settlement proposal made by [the] plaintiffs' counsel, and, therefore, both [Wyld] and [Coe] awaited word from [Schneider], who represented the Bank of America in the separate actions in which Tamar Ackerman ... and [Tzvi Rakoszynski] were named plaintiffs. * * *

["]The Bank of America, through [Schneider], accepted the $1.1 million settlement proposal in the early afternoon of July 1, 2008, prior to the 5 p.m. deadline. The global settlement offer thus [had] been accepted by all [of the] defendants.

"The plaintiffs Rena Ackerman, [Rakoszynski], and [Mical Mann], were all present on the day that the Bank of America accepted the offer, July 1, 2008. * * * At no time prior to the acceptance of the settlement proposal on July 1, 2008, were [the] defendants or their attorneys notified that the offer had been withdrawn, unauthorized, or otherwise ineffective. During that same period [Rena] Ackerman never manifested to [the] defendants or their attorneys that the settlement authority of her attorney was limited or had been terminated. * * * "

I

The plaintiffs first claim that the trial court improperly granted the defendants' motions to enforce the purported settlement agreement. * * * The defendants respond that the trial court's finding of apparent authority was not clearly erroneous because it was properly supported by the evidence. We agree with the defendants. * * *

With respect to the governing legal principles, "it is a general rule of agency law that the principal in an agency relationship is bound by, and liable for, the acts in which his agent engages with authority from the principal, and within the scope of the agent's employment.... An agent's authority may be actual or apparent.... Actual authority exists when [an agent's] action [is] expressly authorized ... or ... although not authorized, [is] subsequently ratified by the [principal]." (Citations omitted; internal quotation marks omitted.) *Maharishi School of Vedic Sciences, Inc. (Connecticut) v. Connecticut Constitution Associates Ltd. Partnership*, 260 Conn. 598, 606–607, 799 A.2d 1027 (2002). In contrast, "[a]pparent authority is that semblance of authority which a principal, through his own acts or inadvertences, causes or allows third persons to believe his agent possesses.... Consequently, apparent authority is to be determined, not by the agent's own acts, but by the acts of the agent's principal.... The issue of apparent authority is one of fact to be determined based on two criteria.... First, it must appear from the principal's conduct that the principal held the agent out as possessing sufficient authority to embrace the act in question, or knowingly permitted [the agent] to act as having such authority.... Second, the party dealing with the agent must have, acting in good faith, reasonably believed, under all the circumstances, that the agent had the necessary authority to bind the principal to the agent's action....

"Apparent authority terminates when the third person has notice that: (1) the agent's authority has terminated; (2) the principal no longer consents that the agent shall deal with the third person; or (3) the agent is acting under a basic error as to the facts. 1 Restatement (Second), Agency § 125, comment (a) (1958). Unless otherwise agreed, there is a notification by the principal to the third person of revocation of an agent's [apparent] authority or other fact indicating its termination: (a) when the principal states such fact to the third person; or (b) when a reasonable time has elapsed after a writing stating such fact has been delivered by the principal (i) to the other personally.... 1 Restatement (Second), [*supra*, at

§ 136(1)]. In addition, the principal can properly give notification of the termination of the agent's authority by ... (b) giving publicity by some ... method reasonably adapted to give the information to such third person. [*Id.*, § at 136(3)]." * * * *Tomlinson v. Board of Education*, 226 Conn. [704,] 734–35, 629 A.2d 333[, 349 (1993) (quoting Restatement (Second) of Agency, at § 136(3))].

The same principles apply to the relationship between attorneys and their clients. * * * In the context of settlement agreements, the authority to determine whether and on what terms to settle a claim is reserved to the client *except* when the client has validly authorized the attorney to make such decisions. See 1 Restatement (Third), The Law Governing Lawyers § 22(1), p. 180 (2000). Thus, an attorney with apparent authority may enter into a settlement agreement that is binding on the client. * * *

Both the Restatement of Agency and the Restatement of the Law Governing Lawyers provide that the mere act of retaining an attorney, without more, is insufficient to create apparent authority to bind the client to a settlement. * * * Rather, manifestations of apparent authority must take the form of "conduct by a person, observable by others, that expresses meaning." 1 Restatement (Third), Agency, *supra*, at § 1.03, comment (b), p. 56. Such conduct, however, "is not limited to spoken or written words.... Silence may constitute a manifestation when, in light of all the circumstances, a reasonable person would express dissent to the inference that other persons will draw from silence. Failure then to express dissent will be taken as a manifestation of affirmance." Id., at p. 57. Apparent authority also may be conveyed to the third person "from authorized statements of the agent, from documents or other indicia of authority given by the principal to the agent, or from third persons who have heard of the agent's authority through authorized or permitted channels of communication. Likewise ... apparent authority can be created by appointing a person to a position ... which carries with it generally recognized duties ... to do the things ordinarily entrusted to one occupying such a position...." 1 Restatement (Second), Agency, *supra*, at § 27, comment (a), p. 104. The Restatement (Third) of Agency similarly explains that * * * "If a principal has given an agent general authority to engage in a class of transactions, subject to limits known only to the agent and the principal, third parties may reasonably believe the agent to be authorized to conduct such transactions and need not inquire into the existence of undisclosed limits on the agent's authority." (Citations omitted.) 1 Restatement (Third), Agency, *supra*, at § 3.03, comment (b), pp. 174–75.

We are also guided by the Rules of Professional Conduct, which provide the framework for the ethical practice of law in this state. See generally Rules of Professional Conduct, preamble. Among these rules are that an attorney shall be truthful when dealing with others on a client's behalf; Rules of Professional Conduct 4.1(1); an attorney shall abide by the client's decision whether to settle a matter; Rules of Professional Conduct 1.2(a); and an attorney shall promptly consult with the client and secure the client's consent prior to taking action on any matter with respect to which the client's informed consent is required. Rules of Professional Conduct 1.4(a)(1). Mindful of these principles, we thus examine the record to determine whether the evidence supports the trial court's factual findings under *Tomlinson*.

A

We begin by considering whether the plaintiffs held Coe out as possessing sufficient authority to settle the litigation as required under the first prong of *Tomlinson v. Board of Education*, supra, 226 Conn. at 734, 629 A.2d 333. * * * The defendants [contend] that the trial court's finding that Coe had apparent authority was based on a course of dealing that began, at the latest, during the court-ordered mediation on May 29, 2008, continued under court supervision through the month of June and concluded on July 1, during which time the plaintiffs consistently held Coe out as their sole spokesman on settlement matters with the power to receive, reject and make settlement offers. We agree with the defendants that the plaintiffs clothed Coe with apparent authority to settle the litigation.

[T]he trial court's finding that the plaintiffs clothed Coe with apparent authority to settle the litigation is supported by evidence of a course of dealing involving the plaintiffs, Coe, the defendants and the parties' attorneys that was well established before the Sobol defendants and the Bank of America accepted the global settlement offer. * * * Coe represented all of the plaintiffs at the court-ordered mediation on May 29, 2008, [and later rejected the defendants' settlement offer and] made the anticipated counteroffer on behalf of all of the plaintiffs in his June 16 letter to the Sobol defendants. It is clear that Coe was authorized to make this offer, which would have settled the litigation if accepted, because the letter contained language indicating that it pertained to all of the pending litigation and was "for settlement purposes only." * * *

Furthermore, after the Sobol defendants rejected the counteroffer, [defense attorney] Wyld observed Rena Ackerman conferring with Coe at a hearing on June 25, 2008, to determine which issues would be tried to a jury. Thereafter, Coe made the global settlement offer to the defendants in a series of conversations with Schneider and Wyld, repeatedly assuring them that he had authority to settle the litigation for the terms under discussion. On July 1, one day after the Sobol defendants accepted the offer, the plaintiffs Rena Ackerman, Rakoszynski and Mann were present with Coe at the Hartford offices of Shipman and Goodwin[. Defense attorneys] Wyld and Schneider both observed Rena Ackerman and her husband at the offices, where they met with Coe from time to time and were seen conferring with Coe before Schneider called to inform them that the Bank of America had accepted the offer, thus settling the litigation. There was no apparent discord or distance in the relationship between Coe and Rena Ackerman and no one objected to Coe's extension of the deadline for the Bank of America to respond from noon until 5 p.m. In other words, Ackerman manifested by her conduct during the times she was observed with Coe prior to the offer's acceptance that she was aware of, and fully supported, the global settlement offer.

In addition, none of the plaintiffs, including Rena Ackerman, who was described by the trial court as "a very bright person who is vigilant in pursuing and protecting her interests," indicated by their conduct prior to the Bank of America's acceptance of the offer that Coe did not have continued authority to settle the litigation. Specifically, there is no evidence that the plaintiffs notified any third person that they had revoked Coe's authority following the defendants' rejection of their counteroffer, or that Coe no longer was representing Rakoszynski and Mann during the negotiations in June. * * *

The plaintiffs * * * rely on *New England Educational Training Service, Inc. v. Silver Street Partnership*, 148 Vt. 99, 100, 528 A.2d 1117 (1987), in which the Vermont Supreme Court rejected the claim that the defendant's attorney had apparent authority to settle the litigation. In that case, the defendant had given its attorney express authority to conduct negotiations with the plaintiff and to settle the case for $10,000, but, after the plaintiff rejected that offer, the attorney settled the case for $60,000. *Id.*, at 101, 528 A.2d 1117. The trial court granted the plaintiff's motion for summary judgment on the ground that the settlement agreement was enforceable. *Id.* On appeal, the Vermont Supreme Court concluded that, because there was no evidence that the defendant had authorized its attorney to settle the case for $60,000, the trial court's decision could be sustained only if the evidence demonstrated that the defendant's counsel had implied or apparent authority to settle the case for the higher amount. *Id.*, at 103, 528 A.2d 1117. After determining that the attorney had no such implied authority, the court concluded that he also had no apparent authority because there was "absolutely no evidence in the record of conduct on the part of the principal ... which could reasonably have been relied on by [the] plaintiff as a manifestation of the authority of its agent to conclude a binding settlement agreement." *Id.*, at 105, 528 A.2d 1117. Mere retention of the attorney to conduct settlement negotiations and an " 'atmosphere of offers' " was no substitute for conduct on the part of the principal to support a finding of apparent authority. *Id.*, at 106, 528 A.2d 1117. The Vermont Supreme Court therefore reversed the judgment. *Id.*

We conclude that *New England Educational Training Service, Inc.* * * * is inapposite because Coe engaged in a course of dealing with the defendants for more than one month during which the plaintiffs indicated by their conduct that Coe had authority to receive, reject and make settlement offers, beginning with the court-ordered mediation on May 29, continuing with his rejection of the defendants' written offer and his June 16 counterproposal, and culminating in the final days of June, when he made the global settlement offer, assured Schneider and Wyld that he had the authority to make the offer and was observed several times conferring with Rena Ackerman. Accordingly, we conclude that the first prong of the test set forth in *Tomlinson v. Board of Education, supra,* 226 Conn. at 734, 629 A.2d 333, is satisfied because the trial court's factual finding that the plaintiffs held Coe out as having sufficient authority to settle the litigation is supported by the evidence.

B

We next consider whether the trial court properly found that the defendants reasonably could have believed that Coe had apparent authority to settle the litigation as required under the second prong of *Tomlinson v. Board of Education,* supra, 226 Conn. at 734–35, 629 A.2d 333. [T]he second prong of the test set forth in *Tomlinson* requires evidence that "the party dealing with the agent must have, acting in good faith, reasonably believed, under all the circumstances, that the agent had the necessary authority to bind the principal to the agent's action." (Internal quotation marks omitted.) *Tomlinson v. Board of Education,* supra, 226 Conn. at 734–35, 629 A.2d 333 * * *. In the present case, it is undisputed that Coe represented all of the plaintiffs when he rejected the defendants' written settlement offer and when he made the counteroffer to the defendants in his letter of June 16. Thereafter, the plaintiffs gave no notice to the defendants or their counsel that Coe no longer had authority to continue settlement negotiations or to make settlement offers on their behalf. Rather, Rena Ackerman was seen conferring with Coe at a court proceeding in late June and at the depositions on July 1, when settlement negotiations intensified. Thus, simply on the basis of this course of dealing among the parties, the defendants reasonably could have believed that Coe continued to have authority to discuss settlement terms and to make settlement offers during the middle and latter part of June. * * *

[The defense attorneys were] further justified in believing that Coe's statements were authorized because * * * Connecticut attorneys are required to conduct their professional affairs in accordance with the Rules of Professional Conduct. Accordingly, [the defense attorneys] reasonably relied on Coe's repeated assurances that he had secured the plaintiffs' consent to the terms of the global settlement offer because, to borrow the plaintiffs' own language, an attorney with Coe's "abundance of experience and exemplary reputation" never would have misrepresented his authority in such a matter in violation of the rules. [G]iven the circumstances in the present case, namely, that Coe and the plaintiffs were in an attorney-client relationship subject to the expectations that normally apply to attorneys involved in complex negotiations with other attorneys, we conclude that the evidence was sufficient to support the trial court's conclusion as to Coe's apparent authority under the second prong of *Tomlinson v. Board of Education,* supra, 226 Conn. at 734–35, 629 A.2d 333. * * *

Insofar as the plaintiffs claim that it was unreasonable for the defendants to believe that, because the oral agreement was not in writing, it was not fully authorized, we disagree. The trial court correctly noted that "the fact that an oral agreement was later to be memorialized in writing does not make it any less enforceable." * * * We thus conclude that the trial court's finding that Coe had apparent authority to settle the litigation is supported by the evidence and is legally correct, and, accordingly, that the plaintiffs' claim that the settlement agreement is unenforceable under *Tomlinson v. Board of Education*, supra, 226 Conn. at 734–35, 629 A.2d 333, has no merit.

* * * The judgment is affirmed.

NOTES ON AUTHORITY

1. **Actual Authority:** Consider the case and the problem first from an agency law perspective. The court recognizes "actual authority," as does section 2.01 of the American Law Institute's RESTATEMENT (THIRD) OF AGENCY (2006). In our problem, actual authority is "express" in that you agree to defend the case filed by Maude Aikens. By agreeing to defend Carl Baker, you have the "implied" authority to negotiate with Maude's attorney toward a resolution favorable to your client, Baker. Both "express" and "implied" authority are "actual" authority because they arise from the agreement between agent and principal.

2. **Apparent Authority:** The *Ackerman* court also mentions "apparent" authority, which might exist when there is no actual authority. "Apparent" authority is outlined in section 8 of the RESTATEMENT (SECOND) OF AGENCY. While "actual" authority arises from the agreement between principal and agent, "apparent" authority, as the court makes clear, arises outside and in spite of the contractual relationship and is dependent on the principal's (Carl's) manifestations to a third party (Maude or Maude's attorney). Suppose attorney and client specifically agree that attorney has no power to settle a case for the client, but the attorney tells the judge that the case has been settled. At the time the attorney so indicates, the client is standing next to the attorney and says "yes" when the judge, in response to the attorney's statement, asks the client, "Did you hear and agree with what the attorney just said?" Can the client repudiate this settlement on the theory that the attorney had no authority to represent to the court that there was a settlement? In this situation, one court held that the attorney had "apparent authority" to settle, based on the representations and failure to object by the client, even if the attorney's representations go well beyond the specific provisions of the actual contract between client and attorney. *See Navajo Tribe of Indians v. Hanosh Chevrolet–Buick, Inc.*, 749 P.2d 90 (N.M. 1988). The trial and appellate courts in *Ackerman* reached similar conclusions.

3. **Authority and Model Rule 1.2:** The *Ackerman* court relied in part upon the Connecticut version of Model Rule 1.2(a). *See also Attorney Grievance Comm'n of Md. v. Stern*, 19 A.3d 904, 926 (Md. 2011) (disbarring attorney for, inter alia, settling a client's claim without the client's "knowledge or consent"). As to the objectives of the representation, it is the client, the principal in the principal/agent relationship, who controls. As to the means by which those objectives are accomplished, the attorney must keep the client informed, as required by Model Rule 1.4. Thereafter, however, decisions about the means to accomplish the client's objectives are left largely to the

lawyer's training. If, in communicating the means of accomplishing the client's objectives, the lawyer and client disagree over the means, Comment [2] to Model Rule 1.2(a) indicates the lawyer may need to withdraw. Based on this decision, which of your actions, taken on Carl's behalf, would be considered part of the "means" of accomplishing *Carl's* "objectives"?

4. **Evidentiary Issues:** Note that the *Ackerman* court reaches a result different from that in a case it discusses, *New England Educational Training Service*. Will the courts' willingness or skepticism about enforcing settlements reached by attorneys affect future settlement negotiations? When Maude Aikens' attorney files the motion to enforce the settlement, the *New England Educational Training Service* court seems to imply that Maude's attorney will have to prove that you have authority from Carl to settle the case. Model Rule 4.2 makes it absolutely clear that Maude's attorney cannot contact Carl directly to ask if you, as Carl's attorney, have full settlement authority while negotiations are pending. How, then, will Maude's attorney prove that you had settlement authority in a jurisdiction that follows *New England Educational Training Service*? As the *Ackerman* opinion's discussion of authority based upon the hiring of a professional with generally recognized duties suggests, some courts hold that the hiring of an attorney creates a presumption that the attorney has the authority to settle. This presumption might be overcome by testimony from the client to the effect that the attorney had no authority. *See, e.g., Barton v. Snellson*, 735 S.W.2d 160 (Mo.Ct.App. 1987).

5. **Test Your Understanding of Authority:** To test your understanding of this material, consider the following: In *Barton v. Snellson*, the court found that the client's failure to tell the adversary that the client's lawyer had no authority to settle was sufficient to create "apparent" authority in that lawyer to settle. The apparent authority then created the evidentiary presumption used by the court. After the client was then held to be bound by the lawyer's settlement, the client sued the lawyer, claiming the lawyer breached the employment agreement under which the lawyer had no authority to settle. The lawyer defended this second suit on the basis of "issue preclusion," arguing that the issue of the lawyer's authority had already been resolved affirmatively in the lawyer's favor. The court held the authority issue in the second suit was different from that in the first suit and, as a result, issue preclusion did not apply. Can you see why? *See Barton v. Tidlund*, 809 S.W.2d 74 (Mo.Ct.App. 1991).

6. **Duties to Clients with Diminished Capacity:** Model Rule 1.14 concerns clients with diminished capacity because of age, illness, or some other reason. It first requires an attorney to attempt as normal a client-attorney relationship as possible. It then allows the lawyer to take reasonable steps that are needed to protect the client, including consulting with appropriate persons and seeking the appointment of a guardian, conservator, or guardian *ad litem. See In re Clark*, 688 S.E.2d 484, 498 (N.C.Ct.App. 2010) (affirming trial court's finding that an attorney fulfilled his "duty to exercise his best judgment on behalf of his client" in refusing to follow his incapacitated client's expressed desire to have her competency legally restored, because doing so would have facilitated potential loss of her personal injury settlement); *In re Kuhn*, 2010 ND 127, ¶ 20, 785 N.W.2d 195, 202 (suspending

attorney who failed to communicate with an incapacitated clients' guardian, because his "understandable desire to give his client attention and respect does not overcome [the client's] incapacity to make legal decisions on his own behalf"). Finally, it reminds attorneys that information related to the representation of a client with diminished capacity is nonetheless protected by Model Rule 1.6, except when the attorney must reveal it to protect the client's interests. An attorney who represents a client with diminished capacity should peruse the extensive comments to this Model Rule. For commentary on Model Rules 1.14(a) & (b), see James R. Devine, *The Ethics of Representing the Disabled Client: Does Model Rule 1.14 Adequately Resolve the Best Interests/Advocacy Dilemma?*, 49 Mo.L.Rev. 493 (1984); *see also* Va. State Bar Standing Comm. on Legal Ethics, Op. 1816 (2005) (concluding that a criminal defense attorney can mount a defense in a death penalty case, despite his suicidal client's desire to be executed).

D.   THE TRUST ACCOUNT

PROBLEM

Gerald and Sandra MacMillan come into your office with two matters. First, Gerald has a personal injury claim against his neighbor, on whose icy sidewalk he slipped and fell. You determine on the basis of MacMillan's medical and other bills that the claim is worth at least $100,000. You know that reports from the hospital and doctors will cost at least $1,000, and that you will need them before you can proceed too far on the case. You enter into a fee agreement with him that calls for a fee of $1,000 plus 33% of any net amounts recovered (after expenses) in excess of $10,000. You ask for an advance against expenses of $1,500. MacMillan gives you a check for that amount and authorizes you to obtain medical records on his behalf.

The second matter is a little more complicated. Sandra MacMillan's uncle Ray, who had been living in a nursing home, has just died. He had named Sandra as executor of his estate. Sandra assumed her uncle had little property but when she went to the nursing home to pick up her uncle's property, she had been presented with several large boxes of baseball cards and old coins. Sandra has two sisters and a cousin, all of whom will inherit equally under the uncle's estate. Sandra thinks the baseball cards and coins are pretty valuable and wants you both to represent her in handling the estate and to keep these items. You agree to both requests and establish your fee of $150 per hour, plus expenses. You request an advance of $500 on your fee and expenses. Sandra agrees to pay this amount by the end of the week.

QUESTIONS

(a) What should you do with the $1,500 check MacMillan gives you? Why?

(b) Assume that the next day, you contact MacMillan's doctor on the personal injury claim, obtain reports from her at a cost of $550, and also obtain photocopies of hospital records at a cost of $250. How do you pay for the report and the records? What documents will you create to assure MacMillan of the amounts you spent?

(c) Assume you filed suit against Gerald MacMillan's neighbor. After brief negotiations, the matter is settled for $150,000, and you receive a check for that amount from the neighbor's insurer. The check is made payable to you and MacMillan. How should you deal with this check? What options are available to you?

(d) Assume MacMillan came to your office, and you deposited the check into your trust account and made payment to both him and yourself of the full amount due each of you. Two days later, the insurance company fails, and their check is dishonored. You then hear from an angry MacMillan who tells you that your Trust Account check has "bounced." The same day, you also receive a telephone call from the statewide disciplinary authority expressing concern over the fact that the check to MacMillan was returned for insufficient funds. The attorney calling you suggests that an audit of your trust account may be in order. What problems exist and what rights do you have?

(e) What do you do with the baseball cards and coins?

(f) Assume that in connection with Sandra MacMillan's uncle's estate, you file his will in the local probate court at a cost of $75 and you incur other legitimate expenses in the amount of $125. You also spend two hours working on this matter before Sandra comes in and gives you a check in the requested amount of $500. What do you do with that check?

RULE REFERENCES

Model Rule 1.15

RESTATEMENT § 44

D(1) THE NATURE OF TRUST OBLIGATIONS AND SANCTIONS FOR VIOLATIONS

IN RE WILSON

Supreme Court of New Jersey, 1979.
409 A.2d 1153.

WILENTZ, C. J.

In this case, respondent knowingly used his clients' money as if it were his own. We hold that disbarment is the only appropriate discipline. * * *

Misappropriation[1] of clients' funds is both a crime * * * and a direct violation of [the Rules]. * * *

Like many rules governing the behavior of lawyers, this one has its roots in the confidence and trust which clients place in their attorneys. Having sought his advice and relying on his expertise, the client entrusts

---

1. Unless the context indicates otherwise, "misappropriation" as used in this opinion means any unauthorized use by the lawyer of clients' funds entrusted to him, including not only stealing, but also unauthorized temporary use for the lawyer's own purpose, whether or not he derives any personal gain or benefit therefrom.

the lawyer with the transaction including the handling of the client's funds. Whether it be a real estate closing, the establishment of a trust, the purchase of a business, the investment of funds, the receipt of proceeds of litigation, or any one of a multitude of other situations, it is commonplace that the work of lawyers involves possession of their clients' funds. That possession is sometimes expedient, occasionally simply customary, but usually essential. Whatever the need may be for the lawyer's handling of clients' money, the client permits it because he trusts the lawyer.

It is a trust built on centuries of honesty and faithfulness. Sometimes it is reinforced by personal knowledge of a particular lawyer's integrity or a firm's reputation. The underlying faith, however, is in the legal profession, the bar as an institution. No other explanation can account for clients' customary willingness to entrust their funds to relative strangers simply because they are lawyers. * * *

We have no doubt that the bar is as anxious as we are to preserve that trust. Its preservation is essential to public acceptance of reforms that may be proposed by the bench and bar together. Mistrust may provoke destructive change. Public confidence is the only foundation that will support constructive reform in the public interest while preserving the finest traditions of the profession. * * *

That confidence is so important that mitigating factors will rarely override the requirement of disbarment. If public confidence is destroyed, the bench and bar will be crippled institutions. * * *

NOTES ON THE TRUST ACCOUNT AND SANCTIONS

1. **Sanctions and the ABA:** While most courts agree with the sentiment expressed in *Wilson*, a sanction of "automatic" disbarment has not generally gained much support. In fact, it is endorsed by the American Bar Association only in certain circumstances. Section 4.1 of the 1986 Standards for Imposing Lawyer Sanctions, which were reaffirmed by the ABA in 2012 (with rescission of the previous Commentary), deals specifically with misuse of property:

4.1   Failure to Preserve the Client's Property

Absent aggravating or mitigating circumstances, * * * the following sanctions are generally appropriate in cases involving the failure to preserve client property:

4.11   Disbarment is generally appropriate when a lawyer knowingly converts client property and causes injury or potential injury to a client.

4.12   Suspension is generally appropriate when a lawyer knows or should know that he is dealing improperly with client property and causes injury or potential injury to a client.

4.13   Reprimand is generally appropriate when a lawyer is negligent in dealing with client property and causes injury or potential injury to a client.

4.14 Admonition is generally appropriate when a lawyer is negligent in dealing with client property and causes little or no actual or potential injury to a client.*

2. **The Temptation of the Trust Account:** Despite the widespread recognition that using client funds for personal or office purposes is one of the surest and quickest ways to lose a law license, some attorneys continue to succumb to the temptation to use trust account funds improperly. Sometimes attorneys mistakenly convince themselves that communication and other problems with clients justify such misuse of client property. *See In re Midlen*, 885 A.2d 1280 (D.C. 2005) (providing an 18 month suspension of an attorney who converted disputed funds to his own use, even though the attorney took no more in fees than he was due under the fee agreement with his client). Sometimes attorneys simply succumb to financial pressure. *See In re Blumstein*, 801 N.Y.S.2d 299 (App.Div. 2005) (disbarring an attorney at one of the nation's most prestigious law firms for converting more than half a million dollars belonging to his client, his own elderly aunt, to his own use).

D(2) THE MECHANICS OF TRUST ACCOUNTING & LOCATION OF DEPOSITS

DAVID E. JOHNSON, TRUST AND BUSINESS ACCOUNTING FOR ATTORNEYS

© 2006 David E. Johnson, Jr.

KEY CONCEPT #1

Separate Clients are Separate Accounts

Individualism is the single most important concept in trust accounting. Client A has nothing whatsoever to do with Client B. Consequently, each client's funds must be looked on as totally separate from those of all other clients, and they must, therefore, be separately maintained. **Never** can you allow one client's funds to be used, even momentarily, to satisfy another client's obligations or, of course, your own. * * *

Classically, the way to maintain individual identity is to establish totally separate accounts for each client. In the modern business world this is not usually practical, given the volume of funds that pass transitorily through an attorney's trust account as a consequence of handling many different matters for many different clients. To accommodate the needs of modern commerce, [Model Rule 1.15(a)] authorizes attorneys to establish a general (or common) trust account through which many clients' monies (usually held for short periods of time) will pass. Separation is obtained by maintaining a separate record (called a client ledger) for each individual client. The client ledger, together with other parts of our mandatory recordkeeping system, is virtually as good as opening a separate account. The lawyer is able to instantly account for all money received on behalf of each client, as well as all money disbursed for that client's legal matter.

A general (common) trust account can be viewed as a great funnel into which many clients' monies flow via deposits and disbursements. If client ledgers and other required records are properly maintained, the attorney is always able to tell exactly whose monies are in the general trust account at any given time. If client ledgers and associated records are not maintained, it is very difficult for the attorney to segregate the various clients' funds. This failure results in a commingling of one client's funds with those of other clients. Then, when monies are needed and the trust account spigot is turned on, the individuality of the funds used is blurred. Money comes out, but it is very difficult for the attorney to know whose money is being used. * * *

KEY CONCEPT #2

You Can't Spend What You Don't Have

Accountants['] analogies notwithstanding, attorneys are not banks. Therefore, they do not have inexhaustible supplies of "available" funds at their disposal. Of course, many attorneys do have on deposit in their attorney trust account, from time to time, large amounts of clients' funds which have cleared the banking process. These funds, however, are not "available" for use by anyone other than the individual client who owns them. This we know from our first Key Concept. * * *

KEY CONCEPT #3

Timing is Everything

Implicit in Key Concept #2 is the additional issue of timing. Every attorney who signs trust account checks should contact the firm's financial institution and be personally aware of that institution's clearing time for (a) intrastate checks (b) interstate checks and (c) other unusual instruments. * * *

If Client A brings in $5,000 in cash and it is deposited and credited to the attorney's trust account today, it can surely be disbursed tomorrow at that client's direction. However, if Client A brings in to an attorney a personal check drawn on a * * * financial institution, the attorney who deposits that check in the trust account today probably cannot draw against that check tomorrow at the client's request. This is due to the fact that the client's personal check has to clear the banking process. * * * Attorneys must recognize that this hiatus will almost always exist and that there is almost always a delay * * * between the time the lawyer actually makes a deposit at a financial institution and the time that institution actually collects those monies and gives you credit for their receipt. It is not until the latter event that the lawyer can disburse against those funds. * * *

KEY CONCEPT #4

Always Maintain An Audit Trail

The purpose of all recordkeeping requirements and procedures is to help clients know, and attorneys explain, what happened to clients' funds that were entrusted to the attorney's care. Accountability requires that all aspects of the transaction be traceable through an accurate audit trail, from the time of receipt of the fund up to and including, not only disbursement of the funds (usually by check), but proper negotiation of that check by the payee and clearance through the banking process. * * *

In a normal transaction, where a client gives money to an attorney who then puts that money in the firm's trust account and pays the money out at the direction of the client, the following minimum documents (sometimes referred to as source documents) will provide the audit trail:

(a) the initial deposit slip (or a duplicate copy or bank receipt), which should show the date the slip was made up, the amount of the deposit, the name or file number of the client on whose account the money has been received, the source of the funds and the date stamp showing the day the deposit was actually received by the bank;

(b) the bank statement, which will show when the deposit was actually credited;

(c) the checkbook stub, which will show when disbursements were made and to whom, as well as the amount;

(d) the disbursement check which will show the date it was drawn, the amount, the name of the payee, the purpose of the check (or notation of the matter it pertains to), the order of negotiation (from the endorsement) and the date deposited for collection; and

(e) the bank statement, which will show the date the trust account was actually charged for the check. * * *

KEY CONCEPT #6

There Is No Such Thing As A Negative Balance

In trust accounting, there is no such thing as a negative balance. All balances must either be positive (while monies are being held for clients) or zero (when the matter is closed and no monies remain in the trust account). * * *

NOTES ON TRUST ACCOUNT RECORDKEEPING

1. **Model Rules for Client Trust Accounts:** Although some modern financial transactions occur in electronic form, rather than via checks and paper deposit slips, the basic concepts outlined above remain applicable. Model Rule 1.15 has not been changed since the Ethics 2000 changes adopted by the ABA in 2002. However, in 2010 the ABA adopted the Model Rules for Client Trust Account Records. These new rules, which replaced the 1993 Model Rule on Financial Recordkeeping, require attorneys to keep trust account records for five years (or some other period, if adopted by a state) of both traditional and electronic transactions. Model Rules for Client Trust Account Records, Rule 1. The rules also require withdrawals to be made only via check or electronic transfer. *Id.*, Rule 2. The new ABA trust account rules allow the records to be maintained in electronic or other media, as long as print copies can be produced. *Id.*, Rule 3.

2. **Attorney Responsibility for Recordkeeping:** Attorneys are responsible for keeping all required trust account records. System failures caused by unexpected problems like computer viruses do not excuse an attorney from recordkeeping requirements. *See In re Ward*, 2005 ND 144, ¶¶ 13–14, 701 N.W.2d 873, 877–78.

D(3) INTEREST ON LAWYER TRUST ACCOUNTS (IOLTA)

BROWN v. LEGAL FOUNDATION OF WASHINGTON

Supreme Court of the United States, 2003.
538 U.S. 216.

JUSTICE STEVENS delivered the opinion of the Court.

The State of Washington, like every other State in the Union, uses interest on lawyers' trust accounts (IOLTA) to pay for legal services provided to the needy. Some IOLTA programs were created by statute, but in Washington, as in most other States, the IOLTA program was established by the State Supreme Court pursuant to its authority to regulate the practice of law. In *Phillips v. Washington Legal Foundation*, 524 U.S. 156, 118 S.Ct. 1925, 141 L.Ed.2d 174 (1998), a case involving the Texas IOLTA program, we held "that the interest income generated by funds held in IOLTA accounts is the 'private property' of the owner of the principal." * * * We did not, however, express any opinion on the question whether the income had been "taken" by the State or "as to the amount of 'just compensation,' if any, due respondents." * * * We now confront those questions.

I

As we explained in *Phillips, id.,* at 160–161, 118 S.Ct. 1925, in the course of their legal practice, attorneys are frequently required to hold clients' funds for various lengths of time. It has long been recognized that they have a professional and fiduciary obligation to avoid commingling their clients' money with their own, but it is not unethical to pool several clients' funds in a single trust account. Before 1980 client funds were typically held in non-interest-bearing federally insured checking accounts. * * *

In 1980, Congress authorized federally insured banks to pay interest on a limited category of demand deposits referred to as "NOW accounts." [Thereafter, every state authorized lawyers to place client funds in NOW accounts.] The result is that, whereas before 1980 the banks retained the value of the use of the money deposited in non-interest-bearing client trust accounts, today, because of the adoption of IOLTA programs, that value is transferred to charitable entities providing legal services for the poor. The aggregate value of those contributions in 2001 apparently exceeded $200 million. In 1984, the Washington Supreme Court established its IOLTA program by amending its Rules of Professional Conduct.

[The program was later amended to apply not only to lawyers, but also to Limited Practice Officers (LPOs).]

In its opinion explaining the order, the court noted that earlier Rules had required attorneys to hold client trust funds "in accounts separate from their own funds," * * * and had prohibited the use of such funds for the lawyer's own pecuniary advantage, but did not address the question whether or how such funds should be invested. Commenting on then-prevalent practice the court observed:

> "In conformity with trust law, however, lawyers usually invest client trust funds in separate interest-bearing accounts and pay the interest to the clients whenever the trust funds are large enough in amount or to be held for a long enough period of time to make such investments economically feasible, that is, when the amount of interest earned exceeds the bank charges and costs of setting up the account. However, when trust funds are so nominal in amount or to be held for so short a period that the amount of interest that could be earned would not justify the cost of creating separate accounts, most attorneys simply deposit the funds in a single noninterest-bearing trust checking account containing all such trust funds from all their clients. The funds in such accounts earn no interest for either the client or the attorney. The banks, in contrast, have received the interest-free use of client money." * * *

The court then described the four essential features of its IOLTA program: (a) the requirement that *all* client funds be deposited in interest-bearing trust accounts, (b) the requirement that funds that cannot earn net interest for the client be deposited in an IOLTA account, (c) the requirement that the lawyers direct the banks to pay the net interest on the IOLTA accounts to the Legal Foundation of Washington (Foundation), and (d) the requirement that the Foundation must use all funds received from IOLTA accounts for tax-exempt law-related charitable and educational purposes. * * *

In its opinion the court responded to three objections that are relevant to our inquiry in this case. First, it rejected the contention that the new program "constitutes an unconstitutional taking of property without due process or just compensation." *Id.*, at 1104. Like other State Supreme Courts that had considered the question, it distinguished our decision in *Webb's Fabulous Pharmacies, Inc. v. Beckwith*, 449 U.S. 155, 101 S.Ct. 446, 66 L.Ed.2d 358 (1980), on the ground that the new " 'program creates income where there had been none before, and the income thus created would never benefit the client under any set of circumstances.' " * * *

Second, it rejected the argument that it was unethical for lawyers to rely on any factor other than the client's best interests when deciding whether to deposit funds in an IOLTA account rather than an account that would generate interest for the client. The court [rejected this argument because in any case, if the money could "produce a net benefit for the client," it must be invested on the client's behalf.] "Only if the money cannot earn net interest for the client is the money to go into an IOLTA account." * * *

The court also rejected the argument that it had failed to consider the significance of advances in computer technology [in holding] that the Rule expressly requires attorneys to give consideration to the capability of financial institutions to calculate and pay interest on individual accounts * * *. Given the court's explanation of its Rule, it seems apparent that a lawyer who mistakenly uses an IOLTA account as a depositary for money that could earn interest for the client would violate the Rule. Hence, the lawyer will be liable to the client for any lost interest, however minuscule the amount might be.

II

This action was commenced by a public interest law firm and four citizens to enjoin state officials from continuing to require LPOs to deposit trust funds into IOLTA accounts. [Pretrial discovery in the case revealed at least two cases where lawyers' clients' monies were deposited into IOLTA accounts under the law and which earned in one case minimal interest and, in another case, $4.96 interest.] After discovery, the District Court granted the defendants' motion for summary judgment [concluding] "that in no event can the client-depositors make any net returns on the interest accrued in these accounts. Indeed, if the funds were able to make any net return, they would not be subject to the IOLTA program." * * * As a legal matter, the court concluded that the constitutional issue focused on what an owner has lost, not what the " 'taker' " has gained, and that petitioners Hayes and Brown had "lost nothing." * * *

While the case was on appeal, we decided *Phillips v. Washington Legal Foundation*, [*supra*]. Relying on our opinion in that case, a three-judge panel of the Ninth Circuit decided that the IOLTA program caused a taking of petitioners' property and that further proceedings were necessary to determine whether they are entitled to just compensation. * * * The Court of Appeals then reconsidered the case en banc. * * * The en banc majority affirmed the judgment of the District Court, reasoning that * * * there was no taking because petitioners had suffered neither an actual loss nor an interference with any investment-backed expectations, and that the regulation of the use of their property was permissible. Moreover, in the majority's view, even if there were a taking, the just compensation due was zero.

III

While it confirms the State's authority to confiscate private property, the text of the Fifth Amendment imposes two conditions on the exercise of such authority: the taking must be for a "public use" and "just compensation" must be paid to the owner. In this case, the first condition is unquestionably satisfied. * * * The fact that public funds might pay the legal fees of a lawyer representing a tenant in a dispute with a landlord who was compelled to contribute to the program would not undermine the public character of the "use" of the funds. * * * Even if there may be occasional misuses of IOLTA funds, the overall, dramatic success of these programs in serving the compelling interest in providing legal services to literally millions of needy Americans certainly qualifies the Foundation's distribution of these funds as a "public use" within the meaning of the Fifth Amendment.

Before moving on to the second condition, the "just compensation" requirement, we must address the type of taking, if any, that this case involves. * * *

In their complaint, [plaintiffs] separately challenge (1) the requirement that their funds must be placed in an IOLTA account (Count III) and (2) the later transfers to the Foundation of whatever interest is thereafter earned (Count II). [This case resembles *Loretto v. Teleprompter Manhattan CATV Corp.*, 458 U.S. 419, 102 S.Ct. 3164, 73 L.Ed.2d 868 (1982), which used a *per se* analysis when the government occupied a small portion of a rooftop for cable TV purposes.] We therefore assume that [plaintiffs] retained the beneficial ownership of at least a portion of their escrow deposits until the funds were disbursed at the closings, that those funds generated some interest in the IOLTA accounts, and that their interest was taken for a public use when it was ultimately turned over to the Foundation. [As a result,] we must determine whether any "just compensation" is due.

IV * * *

All of the Circuit Judges and District Judges who have confronted the compensation question, both in this case and in *Phillips*, have agreed that the "just compensation" required by the Fifth Amendment is measured by the property owner's loss rather than the government's gain. This conclusion is supported by consistent and unambiguous holdings in our cases. * * *

Applying the teaching of these cases to the question before us, it is clear that neither [plaintiff] is entitled to any compensation for the nonpecuniary consequences of the taking of the interest on his deposited funds, and that any pecuniary compensation must be measured by his net losses rather than the value of the public's gain. For that reason, both the majority and the dissenters on the Court of Appeals agreed that if petitioners' net loss was zero, the compensation that is due is also zero.

[The dissenters in the Court of Appeals posed several hypotheticals to argue that in some cases lawyers might deposit funds into an IOLTA account mistakenly—that is, in cases where the interest that could be earned would, in fact, benefit the client.] It does not follow, however, that there is a need for further hearings to determine whether [plaintiffs are] entitled to any compensation from the respondents.

The Rules adopted and administered by the Washington Supreme Court unambiguously require lawyers and LPOs to deposit client funds in non-IOLTA accounts whenever those funds could generate net earnings for the client. * * * Thus, if the LPOs who deposited petitioners' money in IOLTA accounts could have generated net income, the LPOs violated the court's Rules. Any conceivable net loss to petitioners was the consequence of the LPOs' incorrect private decisions rather than any state action. Such mistakes may well give petitioners a valid claim against the LPOs, but they would provide no support for a claim for compensation from the State, or from any of the respondents. * * *

VI

To recapitulate: It is neither unethical nor illegal for lawyers to deposit their clients' funds in a single bank account. A state law that requires client funds that could not otherwise generate net earnings for the client to be deposited in an IOLTA account is not a "regulatory taking." A law that requires that the interest on those funds be transferred to a different owner for a legitimate public use, however, could be a *per se* taking requiring the payment of "just compensation" to the client. Because that compensation is measured by the owner's pecuniary loss— which is zero whenever the Washington law is obeyed—there has been no violation of the Just Compensation Clause of the Fifth Amendment in this case. It is therefore unnecessary to discuss the remedial question presented in the certiorari petition. Accordingly, the judgment of the Court of Appeals is affirmed.

JUSTICE SCALIA, with whom THE CHIEF JUSTICE, JUSTICE KENNEDY, and JUSTICE THOMAS join, dissenting.

The Court today concludes that the State of Washington may seize private property, without paying compensation, on the ground that the former owners suffered no "net loss" because their confiscated property was created by the beneficence of a state regulatory program. In so holding the Court creates a novel exception to our oft-repeated rule that the just compensation owed to former owners of confiscated property is the fair market value of the property taken. * * * Our precedents compel the conclusion that petitioners are entitled to the fair market value of the interest generated by their funds held in interest on lawyers' trust accounts (IOLTA). I dissent from the Court's judgment to the contrary. * * *

JUSTICE KENNEDY, dissenting.

[Justice Kennedy first agrees with Justice Scalia's dissent.] It does seem appropriate to add this further observation. By mandating that the interest from these accounts serve causes the justices of the Washington Supreme Court prefer, the State not only takes property in violation of the Fifth and Fourteenth Amendments to the Constitution of the United States but also grants to itself a monopoly which might then be used for the forced support of certain viewpoints. Had the State, with the help of Congress, not acted in violation of its constitutional responsibilities by taking for itself property which all concede to be that of the client, * * * the free market might have created various and diverse funds for pooling small interest amounts. These funds would have allowed the true owners of the property the option to express views and policies of their own choosing. Instead, as these programs stand today, the true owner cannot even opt out of the State's monopoly.

The First Amendment consequences of the State's action have not been addressed in this case, but the potential for a serious violation is there. * * *

NOTES ON *IOLTA*

1. **Use of IOLTA Funds:** As the Court points out, typically, IOLTA funds are used to help fund such projects as legal services and other programs designed to improve the administration of justice. According to one source, in 2003, the year of the Supreme Court's opinion, IOLTA programs generated some $200 million nationally for such programs. *See Alabama Law Foundation's IOLTA Program Gets Good News from U.S. Supreme Court*, 64 Ala. Law. 261 (2003).

2. **ABA Rules Requiring Banks to Accept IOLTA Funds:** To enforce the obligation to place client funds into an account separate from the lawyer's own, ABA Model Rule for Lawyer Disciplinary Enforcement 29 (1999), which is only applicable to lawyers if adopted by an individual state, places obligations on banks. In order to be permitted to accept lawyer trust account funds, a bank must agree to notify a state disciplinary authority if there is an overdraft on a lawyer's trust account. In addition, if probable cause exists to believe a lawyer is not properly maintaining a trust account, the chief lawyer disciplinary officer is authorized to audit that account. A rule similar to the ABA version was upheld against a challenge that it violated the rights of privacy of both attorney and client, was an impermissible intrusion into the attorney-client relationship, was constitutionally vague, and constituted a constitutionally impermissible search, in *In re Kennedy*, 442 A.2d 79 (Del. 1982).

D(4) SAFEGUARDING TANGIBLE PERSONAL PROPERTY

IN RE JENKINS

Supreme Court of Kansas, 1995.
907 P.2d 825.

PER CURIAM: * * *

The facts, as determined by the Board, are not disputed by respondent. * * * The following pertinent findings were made by the panel in this matter: * * *

> "2. In 1989 the respondent undertook to represent the complainant, Gary A. Brooks, in a divorce action. Following a trial a decree was entered wherein complainant was to receive certain items of personal property.

"3. Complainant's ex-wife delivered to the respondent certain items of said personal property. However, the respondent did not inspect, inventory or receipt for such items received and they were apparently placed in a garage at the home of respondent's wife. Respondent claimed to be also involved in a divorce action and claimed to have no access to the garage at that point in time.

"4. At some later time complainant did receive certain items of the subject property but claims that certain other items have not been returned. Throughout the relevant time period complainant experienced great difficulty in communicating with respondent and obtaining responses to his inquiries regarding his property.

"5. The complainant acknowledged that his ex-wife originally claimed to have returned property which was not, in fact, returned and the panel is unable to make specific findings with regard to any items of personal property which respondent may have received and failed, for whatever reasons, to deliver to complainant." * * *

We adopt the recommendation of the panel that respondent receive indefinite suspension from the practice of law, such suspension to run concurrent with and upon the same terms and conditions as the indefinite suspension ordered in *In re Jenkins*, 255 Kan. 797, 877 P.2d 423. We shall consider additional requirements if respondent seeks reinstatement * * *.

MRPC 1.15 (1994 Kan.Ct.R.Annot. 332) (safekeeping property) sets out guidelines for lawyers when holding clients' property of any form. We emphasize that Rule 1.15 also applies to tangible personal property. * * *

The comment to Rule 1.15, in pertinent part, offers further guidance in handling personal property of a client.

"A lawyer should hold property of others with the care required of a professional fiduciary. Securities should be kept in a safe deposit box, except when some other form of safekeeping is warranted by special circumstances. All property which is the property of clients or third persons should be kept separate from the lawyer's business and personal property and, if monies, in one or more trust accounts....

"Third parties, such as a client's creditors, may have just claims against funds *or other property* in a lawyer's custody. A lawyer may have a duty under applicable law to protect such third-party claims against wrongful interference by the client and accordingly, may refuse to surrender the property to the client. However, a lawyer should not unilaterally assume to arbitrate a dispute between the client and the third party.

"The obligations of a lawyer under this Rule are independent of those arising from activity other than rendering legal services. For example, a lawyer who serves as an escrow agent is governed by the applicable law relating to fiduciaries even though the lawyer does not render legal services in the transaction...

"Rule 1.15 of the Model Rules of Professional Conduct requires that lawyers in the practice of law who are entrusted *with the property* of law clients and third persons must hold that property with the care required of a professional fiduciary. The basis for Rule 1.15 is the lawyer's fiduciary obligation to safeguard trust property and to segregate it from the lawyer's own property, and not to benefit personally from the possession of the property." (Emphasis added.)

We adopt the panel's recommendation that respondent be directed to reasonably negotiate with the complainant in an attempt to resolve any remaining controversy regarding return of personal property.

IT IS THEREFORE ORDERED that Howard L. Jenkins, II, be suspended from the practice of law indefinitely in accordance with Supreme Court Rule 203(a)(2) (1994 Kan.Ct.R.Annot. 189) for his violations herein.

NOTE ON PERSONAL PROPERTY

1. **Substantial Sanctions:** As in *Jenkins*, courts tend to adopt severe sanctions for failure to protect a client's interest in personal property. This sometimes occurs even when disciplinary authorities recommend lighter penalties. *See Toledo Bar Ass'n v. Scott*, 2011–Ohio–4185, 953 N.E.2d 831 (adopting two-year suspension for attorney who used his client's Cleveland Browns tickets, among other violations, despite the parties' stipulation to a one-year suspension).

E. CLIENT LIABILITY: FEES

E(1) THE FEE AGREEMENT AND THE AMOUNT

PROBLEM

When Fred Loesch, a well-to-do businessman, died, he was survived by his second wife Delores, two daughters by his first marriage, and two wills. The earlier-dated will left his estate to his daughters; the latter-dated will left everything to Delores. When Delores offered her will for probate, her stepdaughters filed an action to contest the will, alleging that it had been procured by fraud and undue influence. Delores then hired Max Walters to be her "counsel in all matters relative to the estate of Fred Loesch." Delores' agreement with Walters called for a legal fee of 2.5 percent "of the total fair market value of the probate estate" in return for "customary legal services to me as personal representative of the estate." The contract further provided "that in addition to the above services, additional compensation may be necessary for extraordinary services, including: defense of any lawsuit; any travel related to the estate or any property of the estate; and photocopying, computer research, or telefaxing." The agreement also provided that these additional services would be billed at a rate of $300 per hour over and above the 2.5 percent of the estate's value. Finally, the contract contained a "personal guarantee" obligating Delores personally to pay Walters any amounts due to him, in the event she was not appointed by the court or did not continue as personal representative.

Walters represented Delores for several years in conjunction with the estate, including the sale of businesses Fred Loesch had owned, the defense of the will contest brought by the daughters, and the defense of a constructive-trust suit brought by the daughters, who charged Delores with embezzling assets of the estate. Delores lost both of these suits, being found in the will contest to have exercised undue influence on the testator. After four years, Delores discharged Walters because she thought he was moving too slowly in selling one of Fred's assets.

The estate was valued at almost a million dollars, which under the contract with Delores made Walters' fee for the "customary legal services" that he rendered to her in her capacity as executrix $24,000. To this Walters added hourly billings of $102,000 for the extra services rendered (in the will contest and the constructive trust suit) and demanded a total of $126,000 under the contract.

QUESTIONS

(a) Is Walters' $126,000 fee "reasonable"? Are parts of it reasonable?

(b) Suppose in computing hourly fees, Walters did the following:

(1) Rounded to the nearest 15 minutes—that is, every time he worked on the file, his time sheets reflected at least 15 minutes worth of work. Walters did this because every time he worked on the file, he had to spend some time getting "up to speed" on the matter.

(2) Charged at least $75 for every phone call, regardless of duration. Walters did this because phone calls interrupted other work and, he believed, caused him to miss at least 10 minutes worth of billing on whatever he was previously doing. If a phone call went beyond 15 minutes, Walters used a 1/2 hour billing rate.

(3) Added a surcharge to each litigation file in the amount of $500; $300 of which was to cover costs of doing computer research and $200 was to cover the cost of photocopying.

Are these billing practices acceptable?

(c) Suppose while traveling by airplane to a closing of one of Loesch's business properties, Walters dictated letters and wrote a brief memorandum on another file unrelated to anything being done for Loesch. Could Walters charge his regular hourly fee both for traveling on behalf of Loesch and for working on the other file?

RULE REFERENCES

Model Rule 1.5

RESTATEMENT §§ 34 & 38

E(1)(a) Defining "Reasonable" Fees

FOURCHON DOCKS, INC. v. MILCHEM INC.

United States Court of Appeals, Fifth Circuit, 1988.
849 F.2d 1561.

EDITH H. JONES, CIRCUIT JUDGE:

This diversity case involves the breach of an anti-sublease provision in a Louisiana property lease. The district court awarded the accelerated rent as damages for breach, but fixed attorneys' fees considerably less than would have been provided by the lease. Both sides appeal.

BACKGROUND

[After a 1981 lease on unimproved property between Caillouet, Inc. ("Caillouet"), as lessor, and Joseph Blanchard, as lessee, was assigned to Fourchon, Inc. ("Fourchon"), a portion was subleased by Fourchon to "Milchem," with Caillouet's consent.] The Fourchon/Milchem sublease contained a provision [prohibiting further subleases without the written permission of Fourchon and Caillouet. When] Milchem subleased the property to Chromalloy Land Corporation ("Chromalloy") without notice to, or the consent of, Fourchon or Caillouet * * *, Fourchon brought this action * * *. [The action was removed to federal court, which ruled in Fourchon's favor, voided the sublease and awarded damages. The district court also] awarded attorneys' fees to Fourchon as stipulated in the Fourchon/Milchem sublease. [T]he fee award[, however,] was reduced to $51,750.00, the "reasonable value" of legal services rendered to Fourchon in connection with this litigation.

[Only the cross-appeal of Fourchon dealing with the district court's award of legal fees follows. Eds.]

II. CROSS-APPEAL OF FOURCHON

Fourchon raises several points of error on cross-appeal with respect to the district court's reduction of its attorneys' fee award from $216,000 to $57,750. The initial award was based on the applicable Fourchon/Milchem sublease provision,[12] while the final award represented the court's finding of a reasonable sum owed for the hours worked by Fourchon's attorneys.

Fourchon first argues that the district court lacked jurisdiction to review its contractual fee agreement * * *.

[B]ecause of a prohibition in Louisiana's Code of Professional Responsibility against a lawyer's collecting a "clearly excessive fee," courts may inquire into the reasonableness of a fee. [W]e find that the district court was justified in its review and reduction of the fee award. * * *

---

12. That provision states: . . . Should it become necessary for sublessor to retain an attorney at law for the purpose of collection of monies due under the provisions of this sublease, sublessee agrees and binds itself to pay additionally twenty percent (20%) of the amount due and owing.

Fourchon also challenges the district court's method of calculating a reasonable fee. Fourchon urges that the court erred in fixing a "reasonable amount" rather than a "maximum reasonable amount," and that it failed to consider all the factors listed in Rule 1.5(a) for determining attorneys' fees. The case law is bereft of authority requiring the fixing of a "maximum reasonable" fee, but instead equates nonexcessiveness with reasonableness. * * * Similarly, Rule 1.5 of the Rules of Professional Conduct requires that a lawyer's fee be "reasonable" and then lists factors to be considered in determining "reasonableness." The trial court's apparent formula for calculating the final fee award, multiplying the attorney hours worked by an hourly rate it deemed reasonable, did not abuse the broad discretion accorded him in setting fees. * * * We also find no error in his failure expressly to consider all eight [Rule 1.5(a)] factors because the language of that provision as well as the interpretive state court decisions have held that the guidelines are permissive and that consideration of them all is not mandatory.

For these reasons, the decision of the district court is AFFIRMED.

FORMAL OPINION 93–379*

American Bar Association Standing Committee on
Ethics and Professional Responsibility, 1993.a

Billing for Professional Fees, Disbursements and Other Expenses * * *

The Model Rules of Professional Conduct provide important principles applicable to the billing of clients * * *. The Committee has decided to address several practices that are the subject of frequent inquiry, with the goal of helping the profession adhere to its ethical obligations to its clients despite economic pressures.

The first set of practices involves billing more than one client for the same hours spent. In one illustrative situation, a lawyer finds it possible to schedule court appearances for three clients on the same day. He spends a total of four hours at the courthouse, the amount of time he would have spent on behalf of each client had it not been for the fortuitous circumstance that all three cases were scheduled on the same day. May he bill each of the three clients, who otherwise understand that they will be billed on the basis of time spent, for the four hours he spent on them collectively? In another scenario, a lawyer is flying cross-country to attend a deposition on behalf of one client, expending travel time she would ordinarily bill to that client. If she decides not to watch the movie or read her novel, but to work instead on drafting a motion for another client, may she charge both clients, each of whom agreed to hourly billing, for the time during which she was traveling on behalf of one and drafting a document on behalf of the other? A third situation involves research on a particular topic for one client that later turns out to be relevant to an inquiry from a second client. May the firm bill the second client, who

a. This opinion is published at ABA/BNA Lawyers' Manual on Professional Conduct 1001:209 (1994). Eds.

agreed to be charged on the basis of time spent on his case, the same amount for the recycled work product that it charged the first client?

The second set of practices involves billing for expenses and disbursements, and is exemplified by the situation in which a firm contracts for the expert witness services of an economist at an hourly rate of $200. May the firm bill the client for the expert's time at the rate of $250 per hour? Similarly, may the firm add a surcharge to the cost of computer-assisted research if the per-minute total charged by the computer company does not include the cost of purchasing the computers or staffing their operation? * * *

Professional Obligations Regarding the Reasonableness of Fees

Implicit in the Model Rules and their antecedents is the notion that the attorney-client relationship is not necessarily one of equals, that it is built on trust, and that the client is encouraged to be dependent on the lawyer, who is dealing with matters of great moment to the client. The client should only be charged a reasonable fee for the legal services performed. Rule 1.5 explicitly addresses the reasonableness of legal fees. The rule deals not only with the determination of a reasonable hourly rate, but also with total cost to the client. The Comment to the rule states, for example, that "[a] lawyer should not exploit a fee arrangement based primarily on hourly charges by using wasteful procedures." The goal should be solely to compensate the lawyer fully for time reasonably expended, an approach that if followed will not take advantage of the client. * * *

The lawyer's conduct should be such as to promote the client's trust of the lawyer and of the legal profession. * * * An unreasonable limitation on the hours a lawyer may spend on a client should be avoided as a threat to the lawyer's ability to fulfill her obligation under Model Rule 1.1 to "provide competent representation to a client." * * * Certainly either a willingness on the part of the lawyer, or a demand by the client, to circumscribe the lawyer's efforts, to compromise the lawyer's ability to be as thorough and as prepared as necessary, is not in the best interests of the client and may lead to a violation of Model Rule 1.1 if it means the lawyer is unable to provide competent representation. * * *

On the other hand, the lawyer who has agreed to bill on the basis of hours expended does not fulfill her ethical duty if she bills the client for more time than she actually spent on the client's behalf. In addressing the hypotheticals regarding (a) simultaneous appearance on behalf of three clients, (b) the airplane flight on behalf of one client while working on another client's matters and (c) recycled work product, it is helpful to consider these questions, not from the perspective of what a client could be forced to pay, but rather from the perspective of what the lawyer actually earned. A lawyer who spends four hours of time on behalf of three clients has not earned twelve billable hours. A lawyer who flies for six hours for one client, while working for five hours on behalf of another, has not earned eleven billable hours. A lawyer who is able to reuse old work product has not re-earned the hours previously billed and compensated when the work product was first generated. Rather than looking to profit from the fortuity of coincidental scheduling, the desire to get work done rather than watch a movie, or the luck of being asked the identical question twice, the lawyer who has agreed to bill solely on the basis of time spent is obliged to pass the benefits of these economies on to the client. The practice of billing several clients for the same time or work product, since it results in the earning of an unreasonable fee, therefore is contrary to the mandate of * * * Model Rule 1.5.

Moreover, continuous toil on or overstaffing a project for the purpose of churning out hours is also not properly considered "earning" one's fees. One job of a lawyer is to expedite the legal process. Model Rule 3.2. * * *

It goes without saying that a lawyer who has undertaken to bill on an hourly basis is never justified in charging a client for hours not actually expended. If a lawyer has agreed to charge the client on this basis and it turns out that the lawyer is particularly efficient in accomplishing a given result, it nonetheless will not be permissible to charge the client for more hours than were actually expended on the matter. When that basis for billing the client has been agreed to, the economies associated with the result must inure to the benefit of the client, not give rise to an opportunity to bill a client phantom hours. * * * The point here is that fee enhancement cannot be accomplished simply by presenting the client with a statement reflecting more billable hours than were actually expended. On the other hand, if a matter turns out to be more difficult to accomplish than first anticipated and more hours are required than were originally estimated, the lawyer is fully entitled (though not required) to bill those hours unless the client agreement turned the original estimate into a cap on the fees to be charged.

Charges Other Than Professional Fees

In addition to charging clients fees for professional services, lawyers typically charge their clients for certain additional items which are often referred to variously as disbursements, out-of-pocket expenses or additional charges. * * * The Rules provide no specific guidance on the issue of how much a lawyer may charge a client for costs incurred over and above her own fee. However, we believe that the reasonableness standard explicitly applicable to fees under Rule 1.5(a) should be applicable to these charges as well.

The Committee * * * has identified three different questions which must be addressed. First, which items are properly subject to additional charges? Second, to what extent, if at all, may clients be charged for more than actual out-of-pocket disbursements? Third, on what basis may clients be charged for the provision of in-house services? We shall address these one at a time.

A. General Overhead

* * * In the absence of disclosure to the client in advance of the engagement to the contrary, the client should reasonably expect that the

lawyer's cost in maintaining a library, securing malpractice insurance, renting of office space, purchasing utilities and the like would be subsumed within the charges the lawyer is making for professional services.

B. Disbursements

At the beginning of the engagement lawyers typically tell their clients that they will be charged for disbursements. * * * Thus, if the lawyer hires a court stenographer to transcribe a deposition, the client can reasonably expect to be billed as a disbursement the amount the lawyer pays to the court reporting service. Similarly, if the lawyer flies to Los Angeles for the client, the client can reasonably expect to be billed as a disbursement the amount of the airfare, taxicabs, meals and hotel room.

It is the view of the Committee that, in the absence of disclosure to the contrary, it would be improper if the lawyer assessed a surcharge on these disbursements over and above the amount actually incurred unless the lawyer herself incurred additional expenses beyond the actual cost of the disbursement item. In the same regard, if a lawyer receives a discounted rate from a third-party provider, it would be improper if she did not pass along the benefit of the discount to her client rather than charge the client the full rate and reserve the profit to herself. * * *

C. In–House Provision of Services

Perhaps the most difficult issue is the handling of charges to clients for the provision of in-house services. In this connection the Committee has in view charges for photocopying, computer research, on-site meals, deliveries and other similar items. Like professional fees, it seems clear that lawyers may pass on reasonable charges for these services. Thus, in the view of the Committee, the lawyer and the client may agree in advance that, for example, photocopying will be charged at $.15 per page, or messenger services will be provided at $5.00 per mile. However, the question arises what may be charged to the client, in the absence of a specific agreement to the contrary, when the client has simply been told that costs for these items will be charged to the client. We conclude that under those circumstances the lawyer is obliged to charge the client no more than the direct cost associated with the service (i.e., the actual cost of making a copy on the photocopy machine) plus a reasonable allocation of overhead expenses directly associated with the provision of the service (e.g., the salary of a photocopy machine operator). * * *

NOTES ON REASONABLE FEES

1. **Reasonableness of Fees:** The overarching standard regarding the fees attorneys charge their clients is reasonableness. *See* Model Rule 1.5(2) (prohibiting an agreement for, as well as the charging or collecting of, an unreasonable fee or unreasonable expenses). Many factors go into determining the reasonableness of the fee. *See Nischwitz v. Miskovic (In re Airspect Air, Inc.),* 385 F.3d 915, 922 (6th Cir. 2004) (stating that a fee agreement "should

be judged by the totality of the circumstances''). As one would expect with so widespread an inquiry, there is some disagreement regarding whether certain charges are reasonable. For example, despite the ABA ethics opinion above, the Pennsylvania Bar Association opined that a law firm can charge a client a pro rata share of monthly computer legal research fees, as long as the client gave informed consent. Pa. Bar Ass'n Comm. on Legal Ethics and Prof'l Resp., Op. 2006–30.

2. **Subsequent Events:** Subsequent events may alter the amount of a reasonable fee. In *Cotton v. Kronenberg*, 44 P.3d 878 (Wash.Ct.App. 2002), the client hired a lawyer to defend the client against rape charges. The lawyer estimated the fee between $10,000 and $30,000 and took, as a "nonrefundable fee," real estate belonging to the client and a mobile home. The lawyer recorded the deed to the property and sold it and the mobile home for $42,000. Before the case came to trial, the trial court disqualified the lawyer for improper contact with a witness. When the client sought a refund of unearned legal fees, the lawyer refused, noting the nonrefundable nature of the fee agreement. The court, in ordering a disgorgement of legal fees, noted that the fact the fee agreement is reasonable at the time it is entered is not a defense when events require reevaluation of the agreement's reasonableness. "For example, if a client offers an attorney an interest in a fledgling company in exchange for legal representation, and the value of that share * * * unexpectedly increases greatly, the value of the fee may become unreasonably large in proportion to the work performed." *Id.* at 885; *see also Holmes v. Loveless*, 94 P.3d 338 (Wash.Ct.App. 2004) (refusing to enforce fee agreement that had become unreasonable over passage of three decades). Attorneys should also be wary of underestimating fees and not alerting clients when they should have known the fees would substantially exceed their original estimates, because their clients could sue them for misrepresentation. *See Updike, Kelly and Spellacy, P.C. v. Beckett*, 850 A.2d 145, 167 (Conn. 2004).

3. **Retainers and Advance Fee Payments:** Often, lawyers receive money in advance, as was the case in *Kronenberg*. When the money is received only because the lawyer is agreeing to be available to provide legal services to the client over a given period of time, this is a true *retainer*. It is earned when paid because the lawyer need not provide any service during the given period. Instead, the lawyer only needs to be available to the client if the client wants service during the period. A true *retainer*, therefore, does not need to be deposited into a trust account, because the money has been earned. In many cases, legal work done while on retainer will be separately billed rather than be billed against the retainer. A *retainer* can still be unreasonable, particularly where its amount does not "[bear] a reasonable relationship to the income the lawyer sacrifices or expense the lawyer incurs by accepting it, including such costs as turning away other clients." RESTATEMENT, § 34, Comment *e*. When, however, the money is received in advance to secure payment of the legal fees in the future, as was the case in *Kronenberg*, the lawyer has received an *advance fee payment*. In this circumstance, the funds will be deposited into a trust account, then depleted as the lawyer does the work. For a discussion of both types of payments, see *Iowa Supreme Court Board of Professional Ethics and Conduct v. Apland*, 577 N.W.2d 50, 54–55 (Iowa 1998). For a comprehen-

sive discussion of retainers, see Douglas R. Richmond, *Understanding Retainers and Flat Fees*, 34 J. Legal Prof. 113 (2009).

4. **Nonrefundable Retainers:** Model Rule 1.5 prohibits "an unreasonable fee." Model Rule 1.16 requires the lawyer, upon termination of the representation to "[refund] any advance payment of fee * * * that has not been earned." Applying these two rules, can any legal fee ever be truly "nonrefundable"? Is that what the court held in *Kronenberg* when it ordered the attorney to return the fees? For cases in addition to *Kronenberg* and *Apland* that hold that "nonrefundable" retainers are impermissible in cases involving "advance fee payments," see *In re Datesman*, No. 98–30369DWS, 1999 WL 608856 (Bankr.E.D.Pa. Aug. 9, 1999) (and cases cited therein). For a case adopting a three-part test for determining whether a retainer is reasonable, see *Stalls v. Pounders*, No. W2003–02933–COA–R3–CV, 2005 WL 181687, at *5 (Tenn.Ct.App. Jan. 27, 2005) (identifying the three factors as client understanding of the retainer's meaning and effect, attorney-client agreement, and the reasonableness of the terms of the retainer).

5. **Is a Written Retainer Agreement Required?** *Fourchon Docks* considers legal fees in the context of a definitive, apparently written, fee agreement. Indeed, Model Rule 1.5(b) strongly encourages an agreement concerning fees at the outset of the relationship, particularly where the lawyer has not "regularly represented the client." New York has gone even further, requiring under 22 NYCRR § 1215.2 (2002) that unless the legal fee is expected to be under $3,000 or the attorney has previously represented the client, New York lawyers must have written fee agreements with their clients. The writing must state the scope of legal services, an explanation of the fees and billing practices, and, where applicable, notice of the client's right to fee arbitration. A similar provision was previously required of all New York attorneys in matrimonial actions.

6. **What if No Fee Is Discussed?** Suppose, however, that there is no such discussion and the lawyer goes about doing the work for the client? Is the attorney entitled to any fee? Section 39 of the RESTATEMENT provides that in such cases the client is obligated to pay the lawyer "the fair value of the legal services." This rule would apply if lawyer and client had not arrived at any fee agreement, *see Heninger & Heninger, P.C. v. Davenport Bank & Trust Co.*, 341 N.W.2d 43 (Iowa 1983) (parties never had a meeting of the minds as to how legal fees were to be paid), or where the fee agreement entered into by the parties fails for some reason. *See, e.g., Mulholland v. Kerns*, 822 F.Supp. 1161 (E.D.Pa. 1993) (providing that, where a client discharges a lawyer hired on a contingent fee basis, so that the contingent fee contract is no longer applicable, the attorney can recover a legal fee based on the reasonable value of the services). The RESTATEMENT has more difficulty in defining "fair value," indicating that "some measures of price from a competitive market might be inappropriate," and that a "conservative evaluation is usually appropriate" in such cases. *Id.*, § 39, Comment *b(ii)*.

7. **Judicial Review of Fee Contracts:** *Fourchon Docks* discusses the ability of the court to review fee contracts when asked to do so by one of the parties. Upon what is that ability based? Under equitable principles, the courts would intercede to prevent unfairness by the lawyer in the fiduciary

relationship existing between lawyer and client. *See* 3 John N. Pomeroy, A Treatise on Equity Jurisprudence, § 960, at 829–30 (5th ed. 1941).

8. **Conflict of Interest Issues:** After a lawyer begins representation of a client, the lawyer's obligation is to the client. As a result, under Model Rules 1.7(a) and 1.8(b), any conduct that benefits the lawyer at the expense of the client is likely to be a conflict of interest, to which the client must consent. Suppose, then, that a fee is not discussed at the outset of the representation, and the representation commences. Later, the attorney wants to discuss a fee with the client and wants to receive a fee other than the "fair value," as described in section 39 of the RESTATEMENT. Now Model Rule 1.4(a)(1) and the definition of "informed consent" in Model Rule 1.0(e) come into play. It cannot be assumed that the lawyer and the client are in an arms' length transaction. Instead, the lawyer must provide "adequate information" concerning the proposed fee agreement, as well as the risks associated thereof and any "available alternatives."

9. **Suits over Legal Fees:** A similar self-dealing conflict of interest arises when a lawyer decides to sue a client over a past due fee that the client has failed or refused to pay. While section 41 of the RESTATEMENT prohibits fee collection methods that harass a client, neither the rules nor the courts prohibit an attorney from suing a client to recover an unpaid legal fee on public policy grounds. *See Swanson & Lange v. Miner*, 623 A.2d 976 (Vt. 1992). Does such a suit, however, make good, practical sense?

10. **Fee Arbitration:** Numerous states and many bar associations have adopted provisions calling for arbitration of fee disputes between attorney and client. *See* James R. Devine, *Mandatory Arbitration of Attorney–Client Fee Disputes: A Concept Whose Time Has Come*, 14 U.Tol.L.Rev. 1205, 1226–35 (1983). As stated in Comment [9] to Model Rule 1.5, "If a procedure has been established for resolution of fee disputes, such as an arbitration or mediation procedure established by the bar, the lawyer must comply with the procedure when it is mandatory, and, even when it is voluntary, the lawyer should conscientiously consider submitting to it." In upholding the constitutionality of its mandatory arbitration provision, the New Jersey Supreme Court recognized the benefits flowing from the position of attorney and, consequently, had "no difficulty in imposing a concomitant responsibility * * * to submit to arbitration of fee disputes when such arbitration is necessary to maintain public confidence in the Bar as a whole." *See In re LiVolsi*, 428 A.2d 1268, 1280 (N.J. 1981). In ABA Standing Comm. on Ethics and Prof'l Resp., Formal Op. 02–425 (2002), the American Bar Association agreed that lawyers could insert a clause in a retainer agreement compelling arbitration of all fee disputes and malpractice claims by the client against the lawyer. Again, however, an issue in such clauses is conflict of interest. Such a clause cannot be used in the absence of communication to the client of both the benefits and the risks associated with such a clause.

QUESTIONS AND NOTES ON COURT-ORDERED LEGAL FEES

1. Return to the problem involving Delores Loesch and attorney Max Walters. Assume that Loesch is African American, and that she is having difficulty with the City of Redwood, where her late husband owned a number

of rental properties. Since her husband's death and Delores' assumption of control over the estate, it seems as though the entire city bureaucracy has descended on these rental properties. Delores believes, and Walters reasonably believes, after investigation, that the difficulties Delores is having with these rental properties are the result of racial discrimination by city agencies. Walters successfully files suit in federal court against the city alleging a violation of Delores' civil rights. Federal law provides that Walters is entitled to recover attorney fees from the city once the suit is successful. How should the federal judge determine the amount of those fees?

2. **The "American Rule" and Exceptions:** "It is well established that, under the 'American Rule,' 'the prevailing litigant is ordinarily not entitled to collect a reasonable attorneys' fee from the loser.' " * * * *Pennsylvania v. Del. Valley Citizens' Council for Clean Air*, 478 U.S. 546, 561 (1986), *opinion supplemented by* 483 U.S. 711 (1987). "There are exceptions to this principle, the major one being Congressional authorization for the courts to require one party to award attorney's fees to the other. There are over 100 separate statutes providing for the award of attorney's fees * * *." 478 U.S. at 561–62. States also have statutes authorizing fee awards to attorneys. California, for example, reportedly had "at least 210 fee-shifting statutes" in 1986. *See* Robert L. Rossi, *Attorneys Fees*, Chapter 6: Recovery of Attorneys' Fees from Non–Client Parties; General Principles (3d ed. 2011).

The U.S. Supreme Court held that a party suing under the Fair Housing Discrimination and Americans with Disabilities Acts must secure a judgment on the merits or court-ordered consent decree to be considered a prevailing party entitled to attorneys' fees. *See Buckhannon Bd. and Care Home, Inc. v. W. Va. Dept. of Health & Human Res.*, 532 U.S. 598 (2001). While applying a state private attorney general statute, the California Supreme Court disagreed, by allowing that states courts to award attorneys' fees to parties who serve as "catalysts" whose suits lead to changes in defendants' conduct without judgments or decrees. *See Graham v. DaimlerChrysler Corp.*, 101 P.3d 140 (Cal. 2004). Then the U.S. Supreme Court allowed attorneys' fees to Employee Retirement Income Security Act (ERISA) plaintiffs who show some degree of success on the merits, under a specific ERISA attorneys' fees statute that does not require the plaintiff to be a "prevailing party" to receive fees. *See Hardt v. Reliance Standard Life Ins. Co.*, 130 S.Ct. 2149 (2010).

3. **The Lodestar:** Courts often use the term "lodestar" to refer to the base amount an attorney should receive from the other side, and often calculated it by multiplying a reasonable number of hours times a reasonable hourly rate in the forum, *see Interfaith Cmty. Org. v. Honeywell Int'l, Inc.*, 426 F.3d 694, 703–11 (3d Cir. 2005). Regardless of the futuristic name, the essential component for awarding such fees remains the same: "[T]he benchmark for the awards under nearly all of these statutes is that the attorney's fee must be 'reasonable.' " The "lodestar" amount can account for the fact that different lawyers working on a case bill at different hourly rates. *See Del. Valley Citizens' Council*, 478 U.S. at 562.

4. **Adjustments to the Lodestar:** The central issue in *Delaware Valley* was not the "lodestar" amount, but whether that amount could be increased

because of the contingency of the work or because of the exceptional quality of the lawyer's services. In the second opinion in the case, the Court considered whether to increase the "lodestar" amount:

> The bar and legal commentators have been much interested in the issue. Some writers unqualifiedly have endorsed the concept of increasing the fee award to insure that lawyers will be adequately compensated for taking the risk of not prevailing. * * *
>
> Others have been considerably more reserved in their endorsement of a contingency bonus, focusing on four major problems with the use of this factor. First, evaluation of the risk of loss creates a potential conflict of interest between an attorney and his client, for in order to increase a fee award, a plaintiff's lawyer must expose all of the weaknesses and inconsistencies in his client's case, and a defendant's attorney must either concede the strength of the plaintiff's case in order to keep down the fee award, or "allo[w] the fee to be boosted by the contingency bonus [by] insisting that the plaintiff's victory was freakish." * * * Second, in order to determine the proper size of the contingency bonus, a court must retroactively estimate the prevailing party's chances for success from the perspective of the attorney when he first considered filing the suit. * * *
>
> The third problem * * * is the same one identified by the courts which have questioned this practice: it penalizes the defendant with the strongest defense * * *. Finally, because the contingency bonus cannot be determined with either certainty or accuracy, it "cannot be justified on the ground that it provides an appropriate incentive for litigation." * * *
>
> There are other considerations. Fee-shifting removes the interest a paying client would have in ensuring that the lawyer is serving the client economically; the task of monitoring the attorney is shifted to the judge in separate litigation over fees if the plaintiff wins. Fee litigation occurs on a case-to-case basis and is often protracted, complicated and exhausting. There is little doubt that it should be simplified to the maximum extent possible.

Del. Valley Citizens' Council, 483 U.S. 711, 721–23 (1987).

The Court then considered the underlying legislation and found Congressional intent inconclusive on the concept of increasing the "lodestar" amount. The Court then concluded that truly "exceptional" cases could justify increasing the "lodestar" amount, but that this was not such a case. *See id.; see also Perdue v. Kenny A. ex rel. Winn,* 130 S.Ct. 1662, 1673 (2010) (reversing an upward adjustment to the lodestar amount while noting that "there is a 'strong presumption' that the lodestar figure is reasonable, but that presumption may be overcome in those rare circumstances in which the lodestar does not adequately take into account a factor that may properly be considered in determining a reasonable fee.").

It is not unusual for a court to adjust fees downward from the lodestar amount claimed by an attorney. *See, e.g., Dibler v. Metwest, Inc.,* No. CA3:95–CV–1046–BC, 1997 WL 222910, at *6 (N.D.Tex. Apr. 29, 1997) ("exclud[ing] from an attorneys' fee award all time that is excessive, duplicative, inadequately documented, or otherwise unnecessary," including all 40.1 hours billed for a specified date due to "the blatant impossibility of a 40.1 hour day"); *Heavener v. Meyers*, 158 F.Supp.2d 1278, 1280 (E.D.Ok. 2001) (reducing requested fees substantially due to "the excessive billing and fee padding practices" in a "simple, straightforward" civil rights case). Indeed, at least one court has denied fees that would have otherwise been due to a prevailing party as sanctions altogether, due to the prevailing attorney's "exorbitant" requests for fees and costs. *Budget Rent–A–Car Sys., Inc. v. Consol. Equity LLC*, 428 F.3d 717 (7th Cir. 2005) (citing several similar holdings).

E(1)(b) Types of Legal Fees

REPORT OF ABA COMMISSION ON BILLABLE HOURS
American Bar Association, 2001–2002.*

Preface

In this report, the Commission on Billable Hours * * * challenges the profession to look at value over cost when determining fair payment for services rendered. The billable hour is fundamentally about quantity over quality, repetition over creativity. With no gauge for intangibles such as productivity, creativity, knowledge or technological advancements, the billable hours model is a counter-intuitive measure of value. Alternatives that encourage efficiency and improve processes not only increase profits and provide early resolution of legal matters, but are less likely to garner ethical concerns. * * *

The Corrosive Impact of Emphasis on Billable Hours

[Among other problems, hourly billing:]

Results in a Decline of the Collegiality of Firm Culture and an Increase in Associate Departures * * *

Unfortunately, the increased need for billable hours has caused the pace of law practice to become frenetic and has had a negative effect on mentoring, associate training and collegiality. Lawyers no longer are being recognized primarily for the quality of their work and their talent. As a result, the quality of law firm cultures are in decline and the pressure for hours makes it impossible for many lawyers to achieve balance in their lives. * * *

Discourages Pro Bono Work

Another unfortunate and unintended result of the higher hourly billing requirements is a loss of available time for pro bono work. The well-meaning associate who desires to participate in pro bono work is often challenged by the attitude of law firms that value only billable work. * * *

Provides No Predictability of Cost for Client

Most clients want some level of predictability in their legal costs. Hourly billing does not offer any predictability for the client. * * *

Does Not Reward the Lawyer for Productive Use of Technology

Lawyers' overhead has increased dramatically due to the need for improved technology. The new technology has allowed the lawyers to be more efficient and to produce their work in fewer hours. As a result, the profession is facing increased costs and fewer hours to bill. * * * As a result, instead of seeing monetary rewards for their improved efficiency and investment in technology, lawyers are seeing their profit margin decrease which ironically creates additional pressure to bill more hours.

Puts Client's Interests in Conflict with Lawyer's Interests

Normally, the client's interest is to resolve a matter or complete a project efficiently and quickly. If hourly billing is utilized, the efficient and quick lawyer will earn a lower fee than an inefficient and slow lawyer. Because of this, hourly billing fails to align the interests of the lawyer and client, and under many circumstances puts their interests in conflict. * * *

Why Billable Hours are so Entrenched

[Among other reasons, the billable hour remains because:]

The Method is Simple

Law firms find it very simple to multiply hours worked by a billing rate; law departments find it simple to understand and review such bills. Alternative methods of billing inevitably introduce more complexity without obvious benefit and, therefore, do not challenge the incumbent system.

Comfortable Standard Completely Familiar to All Sides

An obvious reason supporting billable hours is longevity—the fact that by now everyone is wholly familiar with the system. A generation of partners knows no other way to bill * * *.

Serves When No One Can Calculate Value of a Service

Support for billing on an hourly basis rests strongly on the difficulty of determining ahead of time the value of a particular legal service. * * * For law firms, the value of the same amount and quality of legal work to one client could be completely different than the value of the same work to a second client. Yet, it simplifies life to stay with the lowest common denominator—hours worked. * * *

Lets Law Firms Make More Money

Hourly billing allows, indeed may encourage, profligate work habits. * * *

Works Regardless of Volume or Type of Services

Whatever the legal service, [l]aw firms, being conservative entities, welcome the risk adverse arrangement of hourly billing. They willingly engage in fixed fee work if the volume is large enough, but for episodic work, they are concerned that the risk of loss is higher than the opportunity for gain. * * *

Alternative Billing Methods

Fixed or Flat Fees

[T]he most frequently used alternative fee arrangement in firms of all sizes was fixed or flat fees. Fifty-five percent of respondents said their firms had used the method in the last year. Between 54 percent and 63 percent of firms with between 2 to 50 lawyers have used this alternative [in the consumer bankruptcy area. One] firm now offers clients a "fixed menu of services," which are flat fee options for defined services or total cases. However, another attorney countered that "Flat fees in litigation have proven to be counterproductive to settlement and unfairly burden the court system."

[F]irms use fixed or flat fees far more often for transactional work than for litigation * * *. Firms may find it difficult to segment their litigation into discreet pieces for which flat fees can be recovered (for instance, a flat fee for drafting a complaint or a motion). [One attorney] suggested a special category of fixed fees, dubbed *fixed fees in stages*, may be the answer for litigation matters. The attorney attested that her/his firm has successfully used flat fees for transactional work and has been experimenting with incremental flat fee hybrids for litigation stages. The lawyer said the key to creating meaningful fixed/flat fees in litigation is to set them based on stage instead of per project. For example, charging $x for interrogatories, $y for pretrial motions, and $z for summary judgment motions would provide clients with "some degree of certainty as to the total litigation expense, an incentive to settle or at least consider settlement, and an incentive for law firms to become more efficient (and reward those firms who in fact are efficient)." * * *

Discounting

Perhaps the easiest variation on straight billable hours is a discount on hourly rates. This method was the most frequently cited method by law department respondents, cited by more than a third of them. Although hourly billing is very common, discounts on those rates are relatively uncommon. Slightly more than half the departments said that 20 percent or less of their hourly bills have been shaved by a discount. This finding may indicate that departments that do not often use outside counsel lack the leverage to insist on discounts. It may also bear witness to the sentiment that discounts on hourly rates prove to be ineffective for cost control. Though a law firm may discount the hourly rates charged, the number of hours worked may rise proportionately. [Discounted billing is often applied to all attorneys and does not therefore improve efficiency.] The work of some lawyers perhaps should be discounted heavily, whereas the work of other lawyers perhaps should receive premiums. * * *

Blended Billing Rate

The *blended billing rate,* which allows firms to bill a set hourly rate regardless of who is doing the work, found favor with a fair amount of law departments and law firms. Almost one out of every two in-house respondents and between a fifth and a third of their private practice counterparts said they used the blended rate method in the past twelve months. Fourteen percent of in-house respondents said that between 11–20 percent of their bills are calculated on this basis. The data also showed that blended rates are used [more in litigation matters.]

Contingent Fee

Thirty-six percent of in-house respondents used contingent fees in 2001. Some variations of contingent fees include outcome-based billing and a base fee plus a success fee * * *. A once-claims manager for a major insurance carrier suggested the use of *outcome-based billing,* a rewards-based system grounded on budgetary compliance and case results. His current company is establishing preferred defense counsel networks for its clients. Building on that, an attorney practicing in Japan suggested a *base fee topped with a success fee* structure. * * *

Hybrid

Twenty-four percent of in-house counsel have used some mixture of alternative arrangements (*hybrid*), while less than 20 percent of the law firm respondents answered questions about hybrid fees, which included the *flat fee plus hourly* and the *hourly rate plus contingency.* Of the hybrid possibilities, the most popular in the firms was the *flat fee plus hourly rate* approach (ranging from 22 percent to 67 * * * percent of the 35 respondents) * * *.

Other Methods

A law firm billing by *retrospective fees based on value, unit fees and relative fees based on value,* or taking *equity,* would be in a minority. The rare use of these methods are also reflected in law department feedback, as only 8–9 percent have experience with them, and they comprise less than 20 percent of those departments' legal fees. One * * * respondent is upfront about charging a reasonable value. He tells clients:

> That I do not charge by the hour but seek to charge for what I believe to be the reasonable value of the services. I also remind clients that if they are not satisfied with my charges based on the nature of the work performed, they obviously do not have to return with a repeat assignment. Most are quite happy to have their fees based on the reasonable value of the results achieved. * * *

NOTES ON BILLING

1. For the story of one attorney whose clients think of him as "Superman," see Karen Dillon, *6022 Hours,* Am.Law., July/Aug. 1994, at 57. As the title suggests, the lawyer billed more than 6,000 hours per year for four

consecutive years. In the year studied by the author, the lawyer billed 6,022 hours, an average of just under 16.5 hours per day for a 365–day year. " 'I really dedicated my life to help my clients and get a good result.' " the lawyer was quoted as saying. The author calls this lawyer "a case study of the need for firms to move away from hourly billing."

2. **Discipline for Unreasonable Fees:** Model Rule 1.5(a)'s requirement of reasonable attorneys' fees and expenses is frequently cited and applied in litigated or arbitrated fee disputes between attorneys and clients. Nonetheless, some attorneys go so far afield of reasonable fees and expenses that they find themselves sanctioned in the disciplinary process. *See, e.g., In re Silverton*, 113 P.3d 556 (Cal. 2005) (disbarring recently reinstated attorney for excessive fees); *In re Tun*, 26 A.3d 313 (D.C. 2011) (suspending attorney for double billing); *In re Shalant*, No. 01–0–04627, 2005 WL 1926522 (Cal.Bar. Ct. May 18, 2005) (disbarring attorney for pattern of excessive fees); *Disciplinary Counsel v. Holland*, 2005–Ohio–5322, 835 N.E.2d 361 (suspending attorney for one year for double billing); *Disciplinary Counsel v. Johnson*, 2005–Ohio–5323, 835 N.E.2d 354 (same). One court even suspended a law firm associate for inflating the number of hours on his firm's internal time sheets, even though the client was not billed for the inflated time because the firm had agreed to a contingent fee for the case. *In re Lawrence*, 2004–0019 (La. 10/19/04); 884 So.2d 561.

E(2) SPECIAL PROBLEMS WITH CONTINGENT FEES

PROBLEMS AND QUESTIONS

(a) Attorney regularly handles personal injury actions and normally does so on a contingent fee basis. In her experience, most of her clients cannot afford to hire an attorney on an hourly basis while recovering from the trauma of either a personal injury or the death of a family member. Last week, Attorney was hired by Husband, whose wife was killed in an automobile accident in which she was struck by a drunken driver. Husband agreed to pay Attorney a fee consisting solely of 40% of any amounts recovered by Husband pursuant to judgment or settlement in the matter.

(1) Who decides if a case should be funded on a contingent fee basis? What considerations are involved in the decision?

(2) What additional terms or elements, if any, would be required in order for this agreement to be permissible under the Model Rules?

(3) Assume that a proper contingent fee agreement is made between Husband and Attorney and that, after a petition is filed, the insurance company for the drunken driver offers the full amount of its $500,000 insurance policy. Further minimal investigation convinces Attorney that drunken driver has no other assets. When Husband comes to Attorney's office to settle up the matter, Attorney wants $200,000 for her fee. How should this bill be presented by Attorney to Husband? Is $200,000 a "reasonable fee"?

(4) Assume, instead, that after a proper contingent fee agreement is made, the case proceeds and it turns out that the drunk driver has fairly

substantial assets, in addition to insurance. After trial, but before a jury verdict, the drunk driver defendant offers to settle the litigation by paying Husband $100,000 now and $25,000 per year for the next 25 years, with payments to cease if Husband dies or remarries during the 25–year period. Husband wants to accept this offer. How should Attorney calculate the amount of the fee? How should it be collected?

(b) Wife hires Lawyer to obtain a divorce from Husband, which Husband is expected to contest. Are any of the following fee arrangements proper?

(1) $2,000 plus $200 per hour in court time if successful; $100 per hour if unsuccessful?

(2) 30% of all property awarded to Wife in excess of the marital home and child support?

(3) $2,000 plus 20% of all property awarded to Wife in excess of the marital home and child support?

Would any of your answers be different if Husband contested only the amount of property distribution?

(c) Suppose in Problem (b) that the court awarded Wife support for herself and the children of the marriage in the amount of $2,000 per month. Several years went by and Husband has paid nothing for any month. Wife returns to Lawyer, but is now practically penniless. Can Lawyer attempt collection of the past due amounts on the basis of a contingent fee?

(d) Widow is primary beneficiary on Deceased's Life Insurance policy in the amount of $250,000. Widow has no other assets. Widow is accused of murdering Deceased and, if convicted, Widow will be precluded by law from collecting on the insurance policy. Widow asks Lawyer to represent her in the murder case and in the insurance claim. Can Lawyer accept the criminal case without fee so long as he collects 25% of the insurance proceeds?

RULE REFERENCES

Model Rules 1.5(c)–(d) and 1.8(e) & (i)

RESTATEMENT §§ 34 & 38

ROHAN v. ROSENBLATT

Superior Court of Connecticut, 1999.
25 Conn.L.Rptr. 287 (unpublished), 1999 WL 643501.

VERTEFEUILLE, JUDGE

The plaintiff Jeffrey Rohan brings this action against the defendant Leon Rosenblatt, his former attorney, to recover an allegedly unreasonable and excessive legal fee paid by Rohan to Rosenblatt. The defendant charged Rohan a one-third contingency fee to collect the proceeds of a $100,000 life insurance policy insuring his wife. * * *

On January 24, 1991, the plaintiff's wife, Patricia Moore–Rohan, applied for a $100,000 life insurance policy to be issued by First Colony

Life Insurance Company. The beneficiary was to be her husband, the plaintiff. On February 14, 1991, less than one month later, Moore–Rohan was diagnosed as having terminal lung cancer. Shortly after that, Rohan spoke with the defendant about the likelihood of First Colony paying the proceeds of the new life insurance policy. * * *

First Colony issued its policy in March 1991. On April 29, 1991, Moore–Rohan died. After her death, Rosenblatt represented the plaintiff with respect to [collection of the policy].

Rosenblatt told Rohan repeatedly in June that he believed suit would be necessary to collect the proceeds of the First Colony policy. He also told Rohan that the litigation would be "horrendous." Rosenblatt's beliefs about the litigation were based on the chronological facts, i.e., that Moore–Rohan was diagnosed with cancer so soon after she applied for the insurance and that she died so soon after the policy was issued. He had no factual basis for his conclusions. * * *

On June 14, 1991, Rohan and Rosenblatt met and discussed a fee arrangement. The defendant asked Rohan what type of fee arrangement he wanted. Rohan initially said an hourly fee, but also said that he had no money to pay a fee on that basis. They therefore agreed to a one-third contingency fee. They did not discuss whether the contingency fee would apply if the matter was resolved without the need to file suit. Because Rosenblatt repeatedly stated that litigation was inevitable, Rohan believed filing suit would be necessary and the contingency fee was therefore appropriate. * * *

On August 20, 1991, First Colony paid the face amount of the policy plus interest from the date of death [directly to Rohan]. Rohan promptly called Rosenblatt to inform him that the policy had been paid. Rohan also asked Rosenblatt how much of a fee he owed. Rosenblatt told him it was "a lot of money, $33,333.33." * * *

Some months later Rohan [a police officer] had second thoughts about the amount of Rosenblatt's bill. He * * * wrote to First Colony to find out how much work Rosenblatt had done. In July 1992, he consulted a new attorney and retained him to seek the return of most of the $33,333.33 that he paid Rosenblatt. * * *

An attorney-client relationship imposes a fiduciary duty on the attorney. * * * This fiduciary relationship is characterized by a unique degree of trust and confidence between the parties; the attorney has superior knowledge and expertise and has the duty to represent the interests of his or her client.

The attorney as fiduciary bears * * * the burden of proving fair dealing with the client. Our courts have always given close scrutiny to attorney-client relationships. * * * The superior position of the fiduciary provides opportunity for abuse of the confidence placed in him or her. * * * Because a distressed plaintiff may yield too uneasily to unfair demands from his or her attorney, courts will look closely at a contract for contingent fees and will declare it void if the compensation is unfair or excessive. * * *

A contingent fee is appropriate only where there is a genuine risk whether the attorney will be able to bring an asset into the client's possession. * * * Before an attorney enters into a contingency fee agreement with a client, the client needs to be fully informed as to the degree of risk involved. * * * If there is no significant risk with regard to the representation, a contingency fee agreement is not appropriate. * * * "The clearest case where there would be an absence of real risk would be a case in which an attorney attempts to collect from a client a supposedly contingent fee for obtaining insurance proceeds for a client when there is no indication that the insurer will resist the claim. * * * " Attorneys should be careful about charging contingent fees for the collection of insurance proceeds because contingent fees can be unreasonably large when it takes little effort on the attorney's part to collect the policy proceeds. * * * Just such a situation occurred here.

The circumstances as they actually existed in June 1991 did not warrant a contingency fee agreement and a contingent fee agreement was not reasonable at that time. Rosenblatt's belief that "horrendous" litigation would be necessary was based only on the chronology of events relating to the issuance of the policy, not on any objective facts. First Colony never indicated to Rosenblatt or Rohan that it would resist payment of the policy. * * * Therefore, in June 1991, when the parties agreed to a one-third contingency fee agreement, there was not a significant risk that the policy would not be paid and a contingency fee agreement was not appropriate. * * *

[We must consider not only the circumstances at the time the contingent fee contract was entered, but also subsequent events through the conclusion of the representation, in determining the reasonableness of the fee.] Under the circumstances here, all of the events relating to the reasonableness of a contingent fee, including the events subsequent to the making of the agreement, should be considered in determining the reasonableness of that fee. Indeed, given that the "result obtained" and the "time and labor required" to perform the legal service are factors to be considered by the court under [Model Rule 1.5], and those factors can only be determined at the conclusion of the representation, the court believes it necessarily must consider facts subsequent to the making of the contingency fee agreement. * * *

Rosenblatt's actions * * * were unethical and oppressive. He charged a fee that was not reasonable, in violation of [Rule 1.5] and he took advantage of Rohan, his client, for his own personal financial gain. Finally, Rosenblatt's actions caused substantial injury to Rohan, a person of modest means who has been deprived at all times of the significant amount of money, $33,333.33, which he paid Rosenblatt in 1991 and which Rosenblatt has failed to refund. [The court entered judgment for that amount.]

NOTES ON CONTINGENT FEES

1. Unlike other fee agreements covered by Model Rule 1.5, a contingent fee agreement requires a writing. In fact, a reasonable reading of Model Rule 1.5(c) requires separate writings at the outset and at the conclusion of the matter. Suppose the lawyer delays thirty-three months in placing the initial writing before the client? In *Starkey, Kelly, Blaney & White v. Estate of Nicolaysen*, 796 A.2d 238, 241 (N.J. 2002), the New Jersey Supreme Court held the delay meant the attorney had not fulfilled the writing requirement within a " 'reasonable time' " and was therefore not entitled to recover the contingent fee.

2. If a contingent fee is an exception to the general rule prohibiting a lawyer from having an interest in the outcome of a client's case, as they appear to be under Model Rule 1.8(i)(2), are contingent fees to be used only as an exception—that is, when other types of fee agreements are not possible? Does the attorney have any obligation to first offer a non-contingent fee arrangement? The ABA Standing Committee on Ethics and Professional Responsibility, in Informal Opinion 86–1521 ("Offering Alternatives to Contingent Fees") (1986), declared that generally a lawyer does have such an ethical obligation. However, it relied in part on former Comment [5] to Model Rule 1.5, which provided: "When there is doubt whether a contingent fee is consistent with the client's best interest, the lawyer should offer the client alternative bases for the fee and explain their implications." This language was removed from the comments to Model Rule 1.5 in 2002. The committee found that "contingent fees are not necessarily improper even when the client has the money to pay a fixed fee." Under the same then-existing comments to Model Rule 1.5, however, "when a client is in a position to pay a fixed fee, the lawyer should not seek unilaterally to determine whether a contingent fee is consistent with the client's best interest, but should provide the client with the opportunity to make that determination after consultation." Informal Opinion 86–1521. The Committee confirmed this position in Formal Opinion 94–389 (1994).

The current comments to Model Rule 1.5 now state, more generally, "In determining whether a particular contingent fee is reasonable, or whether it is reasonable to charge any form of contingent fee, a lawyer must consider the factors that are relevant under the circumstances." Model Rule 1.5, Comment [3].

3. **Contingent Fees and Structured Settlements:** Suppose the client's case results in a "structured settlement," one in which the client does not receive all of the money at one time, but will receive it in payments over time, a method that may (or may not) include an initial payment at the time of settlement. If lawyer and client had negotiated a contingent fee, how is the money to be paid to the lawyer? Illustration 4 following Comment *e* to section 35 of the RESTATEMENT provides an example: Lawyer and client have a contingent fee agreement in a personal injury case in which the lawyer will receive 30% of the recovery. Eventually, the case is resolved in a structured settlement in which the client will receive $100,000 up-front (apparently from

an annuity that will cost the defendant $200,000) and then $1,500 per month for life. How do you calculate the attorney's fee?

Under the RESTATEMENT, if there has been no advance agreement about how to pay attorney's fees in the event of a structured settlement, the attorney is entitled to receive the attorney's share from each payment actually received by the client. The RESTATEMENT comment also provides that when, by advance agreement, the attorney is to receive the entire fee at the time the structured settlement is entered, and the advance agreement does not state how that amount is to be calculated, the entire fee is to be calculated on the then present value of the entire settlement.

Thus, in the example, the attorney would receive $30,000 from the up-front payment (30% of $100,000) and then $450 per month (30% of $1,500) from each month that payment is actually made to the client. In *In re Chow*, 656 P.2d 105 (Haw.Ct.App. 1982), the court first ordered that all out-of-pocket expenses be paid from the up-front payment before calculating the attorney's fee. Presumably, this issue would now be resolved based on the initial writing required for any contingent fee under Model Rule 1.5(c).

In *Johnson v. Sears, Roebuck & Co.*, 436 A.2d 675 (Pa.Super.Ct. 1981), a child was struck by a truck. After negotiating for a structured settlement, the attorney claimed all the fee from the up-front amount. The child died shortly after settlement was reached, so very few time payments were made. The parents argued that the attorney should receive payments only as received, but the court ordered that payment be made based on the amount of the up-front payment, plus the cost of the long term annuity.

4. **Income Tax Treatment of Contingent Fees:** Resolving a split between two circuits, the Supreme Court has held that the fees paid to an attorney working under a contingent fee agreement usually are part of the taxable income from the plaintiff's recovery in the suit. *Comm'r of Internal Rev. v. Banks*, 543 U.S. 426 (2005).

5. **Contingent Fees and the Lawyer's Trust Account:** In *supra* section 3(D), you learned that money in which the client has an interest MUST be deposited into a trust account. Most resolutions of litigation are paid by check or insurance company draft. Assume the lawyer settles a client's case for $1,000,000, with a 30% contingent fee. The defendant's insurance company delivers a draft to the lawyer made payable to the client and the lawyer, because the insurance company knows of the lawyer's interest in the outcome. The lawyer promptly notifies the client of the check's arrival, pursuant to Model Rules 1.4 and 1.15(d), and asks the client to come to the lawyer's office to sign the check. When the client signs the check, can the lawyer immediately make payment to the client of the client's share of the proceeds? Assuming the answer is "no," because the check or draft is just an order to pay, rather than actual payment, how will the client react to being told to come back in about a week to receive the client's share? How would you draft a provision of the retainer agreement to resolve this problem in a way that frustrates the client less?

6. **The Counterclaim Issue:** Assume a lawyer is hired on a 30% contingent fee basis in an automobile accident case and files a personal injury action on the client's behalf. The other driver defends the action and files a

counterclaim against the client. At trial, client is awarded $100,000 from defendant, but defendant is awarded $50,000 from client on the counterclaim. Does attorney receive $30,000 (30% of $100,000) or $15,000 (30% of the $100,000 claim minus the $50,000 lost on the counterclaim)? In *Levine v. Bayne, Snell & Krause, Ltd.*, 40 S.W.3d 92 (Tex. 2001), the court held that section 35(2) of the RESTATEMENT controlled. Under that section, "Unless the [attorney-client fee agreement] indicates otherwise * * *, the lawyer is entitled to receive the specified fee only when and to the extent the client receives payment." Because there was no contrary provision in the fee contract, the court held the attorney to the net recovery, after deduction for the amount recovered by the adversary on a counterclaim.

As a result of *Levine*, one author suggests the following provision for a retainer agreement:

> "Attorney's fees shall be calculated as ____% of any amounts received from the client's following causes of action: [insert each cause of action]. Attorney's fees shall be based exclusively on the above mentioned causes of action and shall not be reduced by any counterclaim, offset, or any other claim for relief asserted by any other party."

Hudson Jobe, *Contingent Fee Agreements: Drafting for Potential Counterclaims After* Levine v. Bayne, Snell & Krause, Ltd., 55 Baylor L.Rev. 297, 310 (2003).

7. **Suggested Fee Agreement Provisions in Contingent Fee Cases:** Based on the foregoing notes, what should be contained in any "client retention agreement"? In William C. Becker, *The Client Retention Agreement—The Engagement Letter*, 23 Akron L.Rev. 323, 329–41 (1990), the author studied written fee agreements used by Ohio lawyers, finding these agreements to contain some of the following provisions. After reading them, what additional provisions would you want to add? Which provisions are mandatory?

COSTS

[A]lmost all agreements [provided] that costs and expenses, sometimes generally referred to as "out-of-pocket" expenses are the responsibility of the client * * *. However, retention agreements vary considerably as to the specificity concerning what items of cost are to be charged * * *.

OBLIGATION TO ADVANCE?

Lawyers may advance costs. Must they do so? Does the obligation of competence and diligence demand it? * * *

It is no secret that some cases (especially large, complex, original product liability or anti-trust claims) require enormous investments of money and it is probably no secret that lawyers, on occasion, run out of funds and ability to advance them. Moreover, there could be a legitimate disagreement between the lawyer and the client arising from the different perceptions of risk and benefit. This different perception could very well lead to a difference in attitude toward investment or advance. I saw no agreement that provided for handling this problem.

FEES—IN GENERAL

[Rule 1.5 sets] forth, in general, the considerations which should be taken into account in the establishment of fees. Within the overall limitation that fees not be excessive, the factors which test that determination include time spent, results achieved, novelty or difficulty of the problem and fees customarily charged. * * *

CLOSING CALCULATION—WHAT COMES FIRST?

One of the key items of accounting for final distribution to the client has to do with the order in which various items are deducted from the gross recovery. The following example illustrates the differences that may occur in the final amount which a client may receive. Assume a $100,000.00 recovery, a 33 1/3 percent contingent fee, and costs of $10,000.00. If costs come out first, and the 33 1/3% contingency is applied to the remainder the lawyer receives $30,000 and the client $60,000 as a final, bottom-line number. If on the other hand, the 33 1/3% comes off the top, the result is different. That scenario results in $57,667 for the client. In short, if the contingent fee comes first, the lawyer receives $3,333 more than if costs come out first, and, conversely, client receives $3,333 less. Using recovery of $250,000, same contingency and $50,000 costs, the difference to the client is approximately $17,000 depending on calculation method. * * *

FEE CALCULATION: STRUCTURE? * * *

It would appear sensible to make provision for this increasingly common event. If provision is made for applying the appropriate percentage to the current value or current cost of the structure, it might be well also to reference the method by which this valuation will be reached (an agreed upon actuary or computation system), and further provide (as in one agreement) that the cost of obtaining this valuation is a cost which will be included in costs chargeable to the client.

POST TRIAL COMPENSATION

An important consideration in retention agreements is providing for what will happen should there be post-trial action or activity. In short, what happens in case of an appeal? * * *

Some agreements which provide for varying fee percentages depending upon the time that the final settlement is made provide for the highest percentage to be applied should an appeal be necessary before final payment. (Some agreements do not provide for appeal and simply set out one percentage to be applied to the final payment.) Interestingly, however, several agreements provide separately for the appeal process. These agreements provide for a "new and separate" agreement for any post-trial activity, presumably for more fees. While these agreements simply state that there *will* be a new agreement on appeal, the terms of that agreement are not spelled out and it is not clear if the client is, in some way, obligated to reach such an agreement and, if so, on what terms. It is also not clear whether such an agreement will be for a fixed fee or for an additional percentage fee. One such agreement specifically provided that the agreement for post-trial activity would provide for "additional" payment to the lawyer. * * *

While there may be no specific ethical or professional responsibility considerations here, it would seem appropriate to spell out the matter of an appeal somewhat more clearly. The use of different percentages for various stages of effort might be an appropriate solution.

Frankly, the provision for an additional (undefined) contract for the appeal process is one which seems fraught with peril as it is impossible to understand exactly what the client's obligations are or, indeed, the lawyers'. * * *

CLOSING

Some agreements provide for closing statements and, of course, closing statements are now mandated [under the Rules in contingent fee cases]. Some retention agreements include proposed or sample closing forms which would appear to be helpful and which serve to highlight the question of whether costs come out of the gross amount or out of the net amount after contingency. * * *

8. **Prohibited Contingent Fees—Criminal Cases:** To be within the rule prohibiting contingent fees in a criminal case, the contingent event must be the result of the criminal case. Thus, an agreement whereby the attorney would receive $5,000 if the client is convicted, but $10,000 if the client is acquitted, is clearly within the prohibition. Where a criminal defendant assigned a portion of any possible judgment in a separate and unrelated civil action to criminal defense counsel to partially pay the criminal lawyer's set fee, however, there was no impropriety. *See Colson v. Mitchell*, 798 F.Supp. 966 (E.D.N.Y. 1992).

Suppose, instead, the facts of our problem. The defendant was charged with murdering her husband. The defendant was named as beneficiary of her husband's life insurance policy, but if convicted of murder, would be ineligible to collect on the life insurance. If the criminal defense counsel's fee includes a contingent interest in the proceeds of the life insurance, does this arrangement effectively preclude counsel from seeking potential plea agreements for anything short of acquittal and, in that sense, is the fee contingent on the outcome of the criminal case? *See Commonwealth v. Simon*, 285 A.2d 861 (Pa. 1971).

The mere existence of a contingent fee in a criminal case will not render counsel ineffective in a Sixth Amendment sense. To be successful in a constitutional claim, the defendant would have to show that the contingent fee resulted in a conflict of interest that actually affected counsel's performance in the criminal trial. *See People v. Winkler*, 578 N.Y.S.2d 582 (App.Div. 1992). Ineffective assistance is discussed more thoroughly in *infra* section 3(F)(1), Questions and Notes on Attorney Negligence in Criminal Cases.

9. **Prohibited Contingent Fees—Domestic Relations Cases:** The rule prohibiting a contingent fee in a domestic relations matter generally applies not only to a divorce action itself, but to a contingent fee based upon

the value of property awarded to the client or the amount of support for either the spouse or child(ren). This is true regardless of whether the parties were married or were unmarried but cohabitating with one another. Or. State Bar, Formal Op. 2005–13. Once the original action is over, however, and the amount owed is determined by the original judgment in the domestic relations matter, it is permissible to charge a contingent fee for attempts to recover the unpaid arrears. N.J. Supreme Court Advisory Comm. on Prof'l Ethics, Op. 618 (1988); *see also* Mont. Bar Ass'n Ethics Comm., Op. 040804 (2004) (allowing contingent fee agreement for attorney's attempt to locate marital assets concealed by opposing party in original divorce action). What is the difference? Assume that, in the divorce action, a husband and wife agree that the husband will dispose of his interest in one business and use the proceeds to start another, but will provide the wife with a 40% interest in the second business. After the granting of the divorce, the wife learns that her ex-husband is selling his entire interest in the new, second business and she is concerned with her security. She hires an attorney on a contingent fee basis, and the attorney files a new action titled "Post–Decree Petition to Modify and Enforce Dissolution Judgment." Is this new case more like the factual situation in the Oregon or New Jersey ethics opinion? *See Licciardi v. Collins*, 536 N.E.2d 840 (Ill.App.Ct. 1989).

10. **Prohibited Contingent Fees—Public Policy Cases:** Occasionally, it is argued that public policy should prohibit contingent fee contracts in some circumstances. In *Lawyer Disciplinary Board v. Morton*, 569 S.E.2d 412 (W.Va. 2002), the West Virginia court refused to discipline an attorney who took a contingent fee in the collection of medical payments on behalf of a client injured in a vehicle accident. The court found the case was not one in which the lawyer faced little or no risk in collecting for the client, an argument similar to the one in *Rohan v. Rosenblatt*, the principal case. The court also found that a contingency fee agreement in the case was not prohibited by statute and that such agreements should not be *per se* impermissible in medical payments cases. The court thus enforced the contingent fee agreement. In *Gisbrecht v. Barnhart*, 535 U.S. 789 (2002), the Supreme Court held contingent fee agreements appropriate in cases in which the client recovers social security benefits. The Court also enforced the provision of a federal statute that limited contingent fees to 25% in such cases.

E(3) DIVISION OF FEES

PROBLEM

Stuart Smith's only daughter, who was about to graduate from law school, died on the operating table at the local hospital. Smith comes to your office wanting to sue the hospital and the doctors involved. Although you have known Smith for years and have done most of his legal work, neither you nor your partners do litigation or know very much about medical malpractice. Therefore, you refer Smith to Ralph Wilson, a good friend of yours from law school who does a substantial amount of medical malpractice litigation.

QUESTIONS

(a) Assume you continue to handle other legal business for Smith, but always refer him to Wilson when the malpractice case is mentioned. The day after you read in the paper that the malpractice case resulted in a jury verdict for $1.8 million for Smith, you receive a note and check from Wilson. The note reads:

> Total fee—$600,000; your share—$200,000; enclosed is our check for that amount. Thank you for referring this matter to us.
>
> /s/ R. Wilson

What should you do with this check?

(b) Assume instead that when you referred Smith to Wilson, you and Wilson entered into the following written agreement:

> It is agreed between [you] and Wilson (1) that we will equally split all attorney fees received to which Wilson may be entitled as a result of the Smith malpractice matter; (2) that Wilson will primarily handle the litigation of the malpractice case; (3) that [you] will assume responsibility for the Smith malpractice matter as if [you] were a partner of Wilson; (4) that Wilson will make disclosure of this fee arrangement to Smith and secure Smith's written consent to it; (5) no fee collected will exceed a reasonable fee.

You may assume that Wilson did get Smith's written consent to this agreement. However, after a jury verdict of $1.8 million and a reasonable legal fee of $600,000, Wilson refuses to pay you a legal fee of $300,000, claiming that such a fee would not be in proportion to the work done by each of you. Will this argument be successful?

RULE REFERENCES

Model Rules 1.5(e) & 5.4(a)

RESTATEMENT §§ 10 & 47

JUDGE v. PARKER McCAY

United States District Court for the Eastern District of Pennsylvania, 2007.
500 F.Supp.2d 521.

DALZELL, DISTRICT JUDGE

A lawyer has brought a breach of contract claim against a law firm to which he referred a case, alleging that the firm failed to pay him the referral fee it owed him under an oral agreement. Because the clients were in the dark about this alleged agreement, the controlling jurisprudence obliges us to deny the lawyer's claim.

I. *Factual Background*

Glenn Judge worked as an insurance adjuster for Amica Insurance Company in southern New Jersey. * * * Amica was a client of the law firm of Parker McCay, P.A., and Judge worked regularly on insurance defense cases with lawyers at that firm, including then-associate J. Brooks DiDonato. * * * Judge is also a lawyer [admitted in Massachusetts, New Jersey, and Pennsylvania], though in early 2001 he was not an active member of any state's Bar.

On January 11, 2001, Judge's neighbor, Timothy Carroll, was injured in an accident at a construction site in New York City. * * * Judge learned of Carroll's injuries and called DiDonato to ask if Parker McCay would be "interested in handling" the legal representation of Timothy Carroll and his wife, Cindy. * * * DiDonato spoke with Gary Piserchia, a certified civil trial attorney at Parker McCay who handles personal injury cases. * * * DiDonato then told Judge that the firm was interested in representing the Carrolls and faxed Judge a retainer agreement for the Carrolls to execute. * * *

"[A]s a neighbor," Judge visited Timothy Carroll in a New Jersey hospital and delivered the retainer agreement between the Carrolls and Parker McCay. * * * During Judge's visit, Timothy Carroll signed the Parker McCay retainer agreement. * * * Judge delivered that document to Parker McCay. * * * Cindy Carroll later signed the retainer agreement, so the parties to it were Timothy and Cindy Carroll and Parker McCay. * * * That contingent fee agreement said nothing about fee sharing with anyone.

On September 28, 2002, Parker McCay filed a lawsuit on behalf of the Carrolls in the Superior Court * * *. The jury "verdict and settlement" came to $1,894,744. * * * After the jury verdict, Judge called the Carrolls and, for the first and only time, discussed with them the matter of him receiving a fee. * * * Cindy Carroll asked him if he was "trying to get money out of this case." * * *

Parker McCay received $511,829.39 for its legal fees in the Carroll's civil action. * * * According to Judge, Parker McCay also received $25,140.00 for its work on Timothy Carroll's workers' compensation claim. * * *

Judge demanded a referral fee of $175,637.80 from Parker McCay, claiming they had an agreement that the law firm would pay him a referral fee of one-third of what it received on the third party case and one-fifth on the workers' compensation matter. Parker McCay denied that it had entered such an agreement. On February 28, 2007, Judge filed a complaint against Parker McCay[.] Before us now are the parties' cross-motions for summary judgment, their responses thereto, and a joint stipulation of facts.

II. Legal Analysis

The complaint states one claim for breach of contract of a referral fee agreement. It is undisputed that the parties never entered into a written agreement for Parker McCay to share its fee with Judge, but they disagree as to whether they entered into such an oral agreement. Notably, it is undisputed that no one discussed a referral fee with the Carrolls until after the verdict, nor did the Carrolls ever give written or oral consent to such an agreement. Because of this, we need not address whether an oral fee-splitting or referral fee agreement actually existed, but shall assume that it did. For the reasons discussed below, such a contract is unenforceable under New Jersey law.

A. *Choice of Law* * * *

The parties agree that New Jersey law applies, and they are correct. Judge and Parker McCay entered into the alleged oral agreement in New Jersey, which is also where the Carrolls executed the retainer agreement. Judge delivered the retainer agreement to Parker McCay at the firm's office in New Jersey, and Parker McCay filed the Carroll's lawsuit in that state. These contacts weigh overwhelmingly in favor of applying New Jersey contract law, so we apply that law as the New Jersey courts and legislature have declared it. * * *

B. *The Breach of Contract Claim*

Parker McCay contends that, even if there were an oral agreement for a referral fee, it would be unenforceable because the Carrolls were not notified of, nor did they consent to, the payment of any referral fee, as the New Jersey Court Rules and Rules of Professional Conduct require. Judge contends that Parker McCay cannot use his failure to get the Carroll's consent as a "shield" to avoid paying him a referral fee.

New Jersey Rule of Professional Conduct 1.5(e) ("R.P.C.1.5(e)")[3] addresses lawyers' fees and provides [in language similar, but not identical to Model Rule 1.5(e)] that:

> Except as otherwise provided by the Court Rules, a division of fee between lawyers who are not in the same firm may be made only if:
>
> > (1) the division is in proportion to the services performed by each lawyer, or, by written agreement with the client, each lawyer assumes joint responsibility for the representation; and
> >
> > (2) the client is notified of the fee division; and the client consents to the
> >
> > (3) participation of all the lawyers involved; and
> >
> > (4) the total fee is reasonable.

New Jersey Court Rule 1:39–6(d) ("Rule 1:39–6(d)") provides an exception to certain provisions of R.P.C. 1.5(e). It allows certified attorneys, such as Piserchia, to divide a fee with a referring lawyer without regard to whether the division is proportional to the services each lawyer

---

3. Even if Judge was unaware of New Jersey's R.P.C. 1.5(e) because he was not licensed in New Jersey when the alleged agreement was formed, Massachusetts has a similar client consent requirement:

> A division of a fee between lawyers who are not in the same firm may be made only if, after informing the client that a division of fees will be made, the client consents to the joint participation and the total fee is reasonable....

Mass. R. Prof. Conduct 1.5(e).

performed[, but] lawyers who agree to share fees pursuant to Rule 1:39–6(d) must have the client's informed consent to the arrangement. Here, it is undisputed that Judge did not timely inform the clients or ever obtain their consent to the alleged fee referral agreement.

Judge nevertheless contends that the agreement *is* enforceable. The New Jersey courts, however, take a dim view of fee-sharing agreements that plainly violate the Rules of Professional Conduct.

In the recent decision in *Goldberger, Seligsohn & Shinrod, P.A. v. Baumgarten,* 378 N.J.Super. 244, 875 A.2d 958 (N.J.Super.App.Div. 2005), a lawyer who represented the child of a deceased sued another lawyer who represented the deceased's estate in a wrongful death action, alleging, *inter alia,* that the defendant breached a fee-sharing contract whereby the plaintiff was to receive twenty-five percent of the fee earned in the action the defendant brought on behalf of the estate. The trial court granted defendant's motion for summary judgment, and the plaintiff appealed. The appellate court upheld the judgment in favor of the defendant for the breach of contract claim, agreeing with the trial court that the plaintiff was not entitled to relief on the breach of contract claim because the alleged agreement failed to conform to R.P.C. 1.5(e). *Id.* at 963. Among the alleged agreement's deficiencies, the appellate court noted that:

> [T]here is no evidence that the clients were notified of the alleged fee division, nor is there any evidence that the clients consented to the participation of all of the lawyers involved. In the circumstances, the judge correctly found that the alleged agreement did not satisfy the requirements of *R.P.C.* 1.5(e). Relief could not be awarded for a breach of the alleged agreement because it was contrary to law....

Id.

Thus, under *Goldberger,* where a lawyer seeking payment from an alleged fee-sharing agreement gives no evidence that the clients consented to it, the lawyer cannot prevail on a breach of contract claim. * * * Judge has not cited any New Jersey jurisprudence that undermines *Goldberger*'s authority as a predictor of New Jersey law. He points to several cases in *other* jurisdictions,[5] but even if some states will in certain circumstances

---

5. For instance, Judge cites *Saggese v. Kelley,* 445 Mass. 434, 837 N.E.2d 699 (2005), where the Massachusetts Supreme Judicial Court, addressing a state rule of professional conduct similar to New Jersey's R.P.C. 1.5(e), found that a fee-sharing agreement between lawyers that did not comply with disciplinary rules was "not necessarily unenforceable." *Id.* at 441, 837 N.E.2d 699. Notably, though, that court found it "significant" that the client *was* informed of, and consented to, the fee-sharing agreement toward the end of the attorney-client relationship, thereby ratifying conduct that otherwise would constitute a breach of fiduciary duty. *Id.* at 442, 837 N.E.2d 699. Here, the Carrolls never ratified the alleged fee-sharing agreement.

Judge also cites several other cases, none decided under New Jersey law and all differing from our case. In *Freeman v. Mayer,* 95 F.3d 569 (7th Cir.1996), the referring attorney fully disclosed the fee-sharing arrangement with the clients, who then consented to the joint representation and the fee arrangement, *id.* at 570–71, 575. The court enforced the agreement between the lawyers even though they did not enter into a written agreement with the clients concerning the joint representation, as Indiana Rule of Professional Conduct 1.5(e) required. *Id.* at 574–75. Unlike the referring attorney in *Freeman,* Judge never bothered to disclose the alleged fee-sharing agreement to the Carrolls or obtain their consent. In *Daynard v. Ness, Motley, Loadholt, Richardson & Poole, P.A.,* 188 F.Supp.2d 115 (D.Mass.2002), the court, applying Massachusetts jurisprudence,

enforce fee-sharing agreements that violate their rules of professional conduct, as a court sitting in diversity we are not free to apply their jurisprudence where, as here, New Jersey law governs and there is no evidence that the New Jersey Supreme Court would follow other states' reasoning contrary to *Goldberger* and the New Jersey Advisory Committee.

When Judge brought the Parker McCay retainer agreement to the hospital, the Carrolls then and there were entitled to know why Judge was recommending that law firm, particularly if one of the reasons was Judge's personal financial interest. Such information was unquestionably relevant to the Carrolls' informed decision-making about legal representation. Indeed, the New Jersey Rules of Professional Conduct ensure that the Carrolls should have received that information. But Judge chose not to reveal it, a decision the New Jersey courts do not reward.

New Jersey has elected not to enforce contracts that violate the state's Rules of Professional Conduct and Court Rules, as the alleged oral agreement here does. If New Jersey will not enforce fee-sharing agreements entered into without client consent, we cannot.

III. Conclusion

For the reasons discussed herein, we find that the alleged oral agreement for a referral fee is unenforceable. We shall therefore grant the motion for summary judgment of Parker McCay and deny that of Glenn Judge.

NOTES ON FEE SPLITTING

1. **Split of Authority on Fee Splitting:** As the *Judge* court's footnote 5 documents, some courts do not reject all claims by attorneys for shared fees, even when the client has not signed an agreement to fee-splitting among attorneys in different firms. In *Daynard v. Ness, Motley, Loadholt, Richardson & Poole, P.A.*, 188 F.Supp.2d 115 (D.Mass. 2002), plaintiff was a law professor who assisted the defendant law firm in representing plaintiffs in tobacco litigation. Plaintiff alleged that he had an oral agreement, apparently not agreed to by the client, whereby plaintiff was to receive 5% of any fees received by the defendant. After the defendant received approximately $2,000,000,000 in legal fees, plaintiff received nothing and filed suit. The court concluded that Massachusetts' courts are reluctant "to let a violation of public policy spoil entirely an otherwise valid agreement." *Id.* at 124–25. Similarly, in *Davies v. Grauer*, 684 N.E.2d 924, 930 (Ill.App.Ct. 1997), the court found that an attorney who refused to comply with a fee splitting

---

refused to void a fee-splitting agreement because the lawyers had not informed the clients of the agreement, *id.* at 131. The court noted that the case did *not* implicate referral fees because the referring lawyer had worked on the tobacco cases at issue for over a decade. *Id.* Finally, the court in *Potter v. Peirce*, 688 A.2d 894 (Del.1997), held that a lawyer could not assert his non-compliance with his state's rules of conduct as a defense to an agreement with an out-of-state referring lawyer who was not charged with compliance with that rule or a similar rule in his own jurisdiction, *id.* at 897. In contrast, New Jersey and Massachusetts both required Judge to obtain the Carrolls' consent to the alleged agreement.

agreement that did not comply with the rule was both breaching a contract and violating a fiduciary relationship. In allowing an action to enforce the agreement to proceed, the court would not allow the breaching attorney to be rewarded for such misconduct. In *Mink v. Maccabee*, 17 Cal.Rptr.3d 486, 488 (Ct.App. 2004), the court held that client permission prior to the division of fees was sufficient under the California rule requiring client permission. Are these holdings consistent with the Model Rule 1.5(e) requirement of client permission?

2. **Punitive Damages in Fee Splitting Cases:** Where a fee splitting agreement was admitted by the breaching attorney, the court found the breaching attorney had committed the tort of conversion and allowed the trial court to award punitive damages. *See Francis Bernhardt III, P.C. v. Needleman*, 705 A.2d 875 (Pa.Super.Ct. 1997).

3. **Disciplinary Sanctions for Non–Compliant Fee Splitting:** As *Judge* and the decisions it cites document, courts often apply Model Rule 1.5(e)'s provisions, including its client consent requirement, in civil suits by an attorney attempting to collect a portion of the fee from another attorney. Nonetheless, Model Rule 1.5(e) is a rule that, if violated, can lead to discipline. *See Ky. Bar Ass'n v. Mills*, 318 S.W.3d 89, 92 (Ky. 2010) (disbarring attorney for, inter alia, dividing fees with non-firm attorneys not in proportion to services performed, in the absence of client consent); *Disciplinary Counsel v. McCord*, 2009–Ohio–1517, ¶ 36, 905 N.E.2d 1182, 1189 (suspending attorney for, inter alia, improperly sharing fees with an attorney who was not a member of his firm without a fee-sharing agreement).

4. **Fee Splitting Agreements and Conflicts of Interest:** The conflict of interest rules can trump even a permitted agreement to divide a legal fee. Thus, where multiple passengers in an automobile were represented by the firm that represented the driver of the automobile involved in a fatal accident, the firm representing the driver could not ethically accept even a permitted referral fee from the firm to which were referred the cases of the passengers in the driver's car. *See Evans & Luptak, PLC v. Lizza*, 650 N.W.2d 364 (Mich.Ct.App. 2002).

5. **Fee Splitting After Firm Break–Up:** The fee splitting rule does not apply when lawyers in the same firm begin a case, the firm breaks up, and one of the lawyers continues to handle the matter in a new firm. *See Norton Frickey, P.C. v. James B. Turner, P.C.*, 94 P.3d 1266 (Colo.App. 2004); *Piaskoski & Assocs. v. Ricciardi*, 686 N.W.2d 675, 682 (Wis.Ct.App. 2004).

6. **Fee Splitting with Nonlawyers:** The fee splitting prohibitions of Model Rule 1.5 affect the relationship of lawyers with each other and with clients. Model Rule 5.4(a) is concerned with the professional independence of lawyers. To prevent improper outside influence on a lawyer's thinking, it prohibits any split of a legal fee with a nonlawyer except in well-defined situations involving the payment of a fee to the family of a deceased lawyer, the purchase of the practice of another lawyer, or the inclusion of nonlawyer members of an office in a pension, profit-sharing or retirement plan. Thus, where an attorney entered an agreement with "We The People" Paralegal Services whereby the attorneys would pay "We The People" a referral fee for personal injury cases, which came to light after the attorneys refused to pay

the referral fee and were sued by "We The People," the attorneys were suspended for one year and one day for violation of Model Rule 5.4, among other violations. *See In re Watley*, 2001–1775 (La. 12/7/01); 802 So.2d 593.

Ethics opinions routinely prohibit any legal fee split that involves a non-lawyer. Thus, it was considered impermissible for an attorney-member of a law firm made up exclusively of lawyer-mediators "to participate in an arrangement with non-lawyers whereby the 'mediation firm' obtains referrals [from non-lawyers] in return for the payment of fees * * * to the non-lawyers." *See* Ill. Judicial Ethics Comm., Op. No. 01–05 (2002). Similarly, a law firm was allowed to hire an outside management firm comprised of non-lawyers, provided the law firm did not assign a share of legal fees to the management firm, because such an assignment would violate Model Rule 5.4(a). *See* N.C. State Bar, Formal Ethics Op. 2 (2001).

Will the same rules apply to a lawyer who accepts *pro bono* referrals from a charitable organization's "Lawyer Referral Service," whose rules require that the lawyer share any court ordered fees with the charitable organization? The American Bar Association has suggested that they do not. *See* ABA Standing Comm. on Ethics and Prof'l Resp., Formal Op. 93–374 (1993). Model Rule 5.4(a)(4) codifies this opinion. In addition, one ethics committee has approved an attorney's agreement to split any statutory attorneys' fees awarded with a client. *See* L.A. Cnty. Bar Ass'n Ethics Comm., Formal Op. 515 (2005).

F. ATTORNEY MALPRACTICE: DAMAGES AND OTHER REMEDIES

F(1) THE BASIC OBLIGATION OF CARE

PROBLEM

On May 22, five years ago, John Teague was injured in an automobile accident. Teague was a passenger in a vehicle being driven by his friend, Ron Reynolds. The Reynolds vehicle was struck in the middle of an intersection controlled by a four-way stop sign. Reynolds had stopped at the stop sign and then proceeded into the intersection, as had the other vehicle.

John Teague was referred by a family friend to Albert Webster, a local attorney. Teague saw Webster shortly after being discharged from the hospital, where he had been confined following the accident. Webster agreed to represent Teague in the personal injury action.

During the intervening five years, Teague received several phone calls from the adjuster from Reynolds' insurance company. He always referred those calls to Webster. Teague also kept in touch with Webster and sought information about the progress of the case. Webster's responses always sought to deflect the question.

Teague has come to you because he learned yesterday that Webster forgot to file the lawsuit against Reynolds, and the statute of limitations has expired. When Teague today called the adjuster for Reynolds' insurer, with whom he has spoken in the past, the adjuster indicated she was sorry, but the insurer would offer no money to settle the case.

Teague wants you to advise him about his remedies against Webster.

QUESTIONS

(a) On what legal theory or theories might Webster be liable to Teague?

(b) What must Teague prove in order to succeed?

(c) Assuming that Webster is held liable, is he entitled to a credit against any judgment for the legal fees he would have received if a suit against Reynolds had been successful?

RULE REFERENCES

Model Rules 1.1 and 1.3 and Scope ¶ [20]

RESTATEMENT §§ 16 & 48–54

TOGSTAD v. VESELY, OTTO, MILLER & KEEFE

Supreme Court of Minnesota, 1980.
291 N.W.2d 686.

[The facts of this case are found at *supra* section 3(B). In the action, plaintiff sought damages for legal malpractice. Only that portion of the opinion dealing with the sufficiency of the evidence of malpractice is reproduced here.]

PER CURIAM

* * * The jury found that the defendant attorney Jerre Miller was negligent and that, as a direct result of such negligence, plaintiff John Togstad sustained damages in the amount of $610,500 and his wife, plaintiff Joan Togstad, in the amount of $39,000.

[At the meeting at Miller's office between Mrs. Togstad, her husband's former work supervisor Ted Bucholz and Miller,] Miller * * * claimed he related to Mrs. Togstad "that because of the grievous nature of the injuries sustained by her husband, that this was only my opinion and she was encouraged to ask another attorney if she wished for another opinion" and "she ought to do so promptly." He testified that he informed Mrs. Togstad that his firm "was not engaged as experts" in the area of medical malpractice, and that they associated with the Charles Hvass firm in cases of that nature. Miller stated that at the end of the conference he told Mrs. Togstad that he would consult with Charles Hvass and if Hvass's opinion differed from his, Miller would so inform her. Miller recollected that he called Hvass a "couple days" later and discussed the case with him. It was Miller's impression that Hvass thought there was no liability for malpractice in the case. Consequently, Miller did not communicate with Mrs. Togstad further. * * *

Kenneth Green, a Minneapolis attorney, was called as an expert by plaintiffs. He stated that in rendering legal advice regarding a claim of medical malpractice, the "minimum" an attorney should do would be to request medical authorizations from the client, review the hospital records, and consult with an expert in the field. John McNulty, a Minneapolis attorney, and Charles Hvass testified as experts on behalf of the defendants. McNulty stated that when an attorney is consulted as to whether he will take a case, the lawyer's only responsibility in refusing it is to so inform the party. He testified, however, that when a lawyer is asked his legal opinion on the merits of a medical malpractice claim, community standards require that the attorney check hospital records and consult with an expert before rendering his opinion.

Hvass stated that he had no recollection of Miller's calling him in October 1972 relative to the Togstad matter. He testified that [in medical malpractice cases,] "I have to make a decision as to whether or not there probably is or probably is not * * * medical malpractice. And if, in my judgment, based upon what the client has told me, there is not medical malpractice, I will so inform the client." Hvass stated, however, that he would never render a "categorical" opinion. In addition, Hvass acknowledged that if he were consulted for a "legal opinion" regarding medical malpractice and 14 months had expired since the incident in question, "ordinary care and diligence" would require him to inform the party of the two-year statute of limitations applicable to that type of action.

This case was submitted to the jury by way of a special verdict form. The jury found that Dr. Blake and the hospital were negligent and that Dr. Blake's negligence (but not the hospital's) was a direct cause of the injuries sustained by John Togstad; * * * that Miller was negligent in rendering advice regarding the possible claims of Mr. and Mrs. Togstad; that, but for Miller's negligence, plaintiffs would have been successful in the prosecution of a legal action against Dr. Blake; and that neither Mr. nor Mrs. Togstad was negligent in pursuing their claims against Dr. Blake. The jury awarded damages to Mr. Togstad of $610,500 and to Mrs. Togstad of $39,000. * * *

In a legal malpractice action of the type involved here, four elements must be shown: (1) that an attorney-client relationship existed; (2) that defendant acted negligently or in breach of contract; (3) that such acts were the proximate cause of the plaintiffs' damages; (4) that but for defendant's conduct the plaintiffs would have been successful in the prosecution of their medical malpractice claim. * * *

[We find that an attorney-client relationship existed.]

Defendants argue that even if an attorney-client relationship was established the evidence fails to show that Miller acted negligently in assessing the merits of the Togstads' case. They appear to contend that, at most, Miller was guilty of an error in judgment which does not give rise to legal malpractice. * * * However, this case does not involve a mere error of judgment. The gist of plaintiffs' claim is that Miller failed to perform the minimal research that an ordinarily prudent attorney would do before rendering legal advice in a case of this nature. The record, through the testimony of Kenneth Green and John McNulty, contains sufficient evidence to support plaintiffs' position.

In a related contention, defendants assert that a new trial should be awarded on the ground that the trial court erred by refusing to instruct the jury that Miller's failure to inform Mrs. Togstad of the two-year statute of limitations for medical malpractice could not constitute negligence. The argument continues that since it is unclear from the record on what theory or theories of negligence the jury based its decision, a new trial must be granted. * * *

The defect in defendants' reasoning is that there is adequate evidence supporting the claim that Miller was also negligent in failing to advise Mrs. Togstad of the two-year medical malpractice limitations period and thus the trial court acted properly in refusing to instruct the jury in the manner urged by defendants. One of defendants' expert witnesses, Charles Hvass, testified:

> **Q** Now, Mr. Hvass, where you are consulted for a legal opinion and advice concerning malpractice and 14 months have elapsed (since the incident in question), and you hold yourself out as competent to give a legal opinion and advice to these people concerning their rights, wouldn't ordinary care and diligence require that you inform them that there is a two-year statute of limitations within which they have to act or lose their rights?

> **A** Yes. I believe I would have advised someone of the two-year period of limitation, yes.

Consequently, based on the testimony of Mrs. Togstad, i.e., that she requested and received legal advice from Miller concerning the malpractice claim, and the above testimony of Hvass, we must reject the defendants' contention, as it was reasonable for a jury to determine that Miller acted negligently in failing to inform Mrs. Togstad of the applicable limitations period. * * *

There is also sufficient evidence in the record establishing that, but for Miller's negligence, plaintiffs would have been successful in prosecuting their medical malpractice claim. Dr. Woods, in no uncertain terms, concluded that Mr. Togstad's injuries were caused by the medical malpractice of Dr. Blake. Defendants' expert testimony to the contrary was obviously not believed by the jury. Thus, the jury reasonably found that had plaintiff's medical malpractice action been properly brought, plaintiffs would have recovered.

Based on the foregoing, we hold that the jury's findings are adequately supported by the record. Accordingly we uphold the trial court's denial of defendants' motion for judgment notwithstanding the jury verdict. * * *

Defendants also contend that the trial court erred by refusing to instruct the jury that plaintiffs' damages should be reduced by the amount of attorney fees plaintiffs would have paid defendants had Miller prosecuted the medical malpractice action. [An earlier Minnesota court presented with this question refused to answer it but noted:]

> (T)he record would indicate that, in the trial of this case, the parties probably proceeded upon the assumption that the element of attorneys' fees, which plaintiff might have had to pay defendant had he successfully prosecuted the suit, was canceled out by the attorneys' fees plaintiff incurred in retaining counsel to establish that defendant failed to prosecute a recoverable action. * * *

Decisions from other states have divided in their resolution of the instant question. The cases allowing the deduction of the hypothetical fees do so without any detailed discussion or reasoning in support thereof. * * * The courts disapproving of an allowance for attorney fees reason * * * that a reduction for lawyer fees is unwarranted because of the expense incurred by the plaintiff in bringing an action against the attorney. * * *

We are persuaded by the reasoning of the cases which do not allow a reduction for a hypothetical contingency fee, and accordingly reject defendants' contention. * * *

NOTES ON LEGAL MALPRACTICE

1. **Contract and Tort Actions:** The court in *Togstad* recognizes two distinct causes of action for legal malpractice. What are the elements of both the tort and contract actions? The RESTATEMENT sees both contract and tort actions as "Professional Negligence." *See* RESTATEMENT, § 48, Comment *c* (2000).

2. **Damages:** Damages in malpractice actions have included the amount of personal injuries the client would have recovered in the underlying action, as well as other damages "proximately caused" by the lawyer's malpractice, such as additional legal fees. Damages have also included the loss of the benefit of the underlying bargain. *See* Charles W. Wolfram, Modern Legal Ethics, § 5.6.3 (1986). However, one court has held that a legal malpractice plaintiff is not entitled to recover punitive damages that allegedly would have been recovered in the underlying lawsuit, because allowing such recovery would not advance the public policy of punishing the wrongdoer and deterring others from engaging in similar misconduct. *Tri–G, Inc. v. Burke, Bosselman & Weaver*, 856 N.E.2d 389, 417 (Ill. 2006).

3. **Causation:** Traditionally, causation in legal malpractice actions is proved by showing that " 'but for' the negligence [of the attorney], the harm would not have occurred." In addition, the attorney can also be liable if "the negligence was a concurrent independent cause of the harm." This test is used in both litigation and transactional malpractice. *See Viner v. Sweet*, 70 P.3d 1046, 1051 (Cal. 2003).

4. **Contribution and Indemnity:** In our problem, once Webster is found liable to Teague, can Webster seek contribution from Reynolds, the original tortfeasor? In an action subsequent to the principal case, *Vesely, Otto, Miller & Keefe v. Blake*, 311 N.W.2d 3 (Minn. 1981), the law firm sought contribution from the doctor whose negligence first brought Mrs. Togstad to Miller's office. The court found that the lawyers and the doctor committed distinct torts at different times. As a result, there was no common injury to the plaintiff to which the two tortfeasors each contributed a proportionate share. This is likely to be true in most legal malpractice cases: "An attorney retained to pursue a client's cause of action or to protect the client from the wrongful conduct of another does not by his own negligence act in concert with or participate in the wrongful conduct of the client's adversary." *Id.* at 5. California found no public policy violation, however, when a lawyer sued a co-counsel for indemnification in a malpractice case. *Musser v. Provencher*, 48 P.3d 408 (Cal. 2002).

5. **Malpractice Insurance:** There is no requirement under the Model Rules that lawyers maintain malpractice insurance. However, in 2004 the ABA adopted the Model Court Rule on Insurance Disclosure. *ABA Delegates, in Close Vote, Approve Rule Requiring Lawyers to Report Insurance Status*, 20 Laws.Man. on Prof. Conduct (ABA/BNA) 411 (2004). In states where this rule has been adopted, attorneys must advise the state supreme court about whether they have malpractice coverage. Some have proposed going even further, by adding provisions to Model Rule 1.4 that would require attorneys to keep their clients informed about their malpractice insurance status. *See* ABA Standing Comm. on Client Protection, Proposed Amendments for Malpractice Coverage Disclosure. About half of the states now require actively practicing attorneys to disclose their malpractice insurance status in some form.

6. **Suit Within a Suit:** A damage action against an attorney for malpractice in asserting a claim is often described as "a suit within a suit," because the client must prove not only the negligence of the attorney, but also the likely success of the underlying action. As stated by one court: " 'Where the plaintiff bringing suit for legal malpractice has lost another suit * * *, plaintiff must prove that: (1) The original claim was valid [and] (2) It would have resulted in a judgment in [plaintiff's] favor * * *.' " *See Little v. Matthewson*, 442 S.E.2d 567, 569 (N.C.Ct.App. 1994), *quoting Rorrer v. Cooke*, 329 S.E.2d 355, 369 (N.C. 1985). In "a case within a case within a case," a state supreme court dismissed a malpractice action against a plaintiff's third attorney because the plaintiff failed to present evidence that his second attorney (the target of the current, second malpractice action) should have prevailed in a first malpractice action against the plaintiff's first attorney for failing to adequately represent him in an underlying employment law suit. *Dennis v. Northcutt*, 923 So.2d 275, 280 (Ala. 2005).

7. **Breach of Fiduciary Duty:** In the attorney-client relationship, the attorney, as agent of the client principal, is always in a "fiduciary" relationship with the client. Does that then mean that any attorney error that supports a cause of action for legal malpractice under either a tort or contract theory will also support a cause of action for breach of fiduciary duty? A Utah court separated breach of fiduciary duty claims from those involving negli-

gence: "Legal malpractice based on negligence concerns violations of a standard of care; whereas, legal malpractice based on breach of fiduciary duty concerns violations of a standard of conduct." The court then found that breach of fiduciary duty claims "are grounded on the fundamental principle that attorneys must be completely loyal to their clients and must never use their position of trust to take advantage of client confidences for themselves or for other parties." *Kilpatrick v. Wiley, Rein & Fielding*, 909 P.2d 1283, 1290 (Utah Ct.App. 1996). A Texas court further clarified by finding that the breach of fiduciary claim often "involves the attorney's failure to disclose conflicts of interest, failure to deliver funds belonging to the client, placing personal interests over the client's interests, improper use of client confidences, taking advantage of the client's trust, engaging in self-dealing, and making misrepresentations." *Goffney v. Rabson*, 56 S.W.3d 186, 193 (Tex.App. 2001). The RESTATEMENT agrees, indicating that breach of fiduciary duty is available as a cause of action when the lawyer violates client confidences, misuses client property, impermissibly engages in conflict of interest, deals dishonestly with the client, or uses "advantages arising from the client-lawyer relationship in a manner adverse to the client." RESTATEMENT, §§ 49 & 16(3).

8. **Underlying Judgment Uncollectible:** If the defendants in the underlying lawsuit would have been unable to satisfy any judgment against them, how should this fact be raised in the malpractice action? *Little v. Matthewson*, for example, indicated that the malpractice plaintiff must prove that any underlying judgment " 'would have been collected.' " 442 S.E.2d at 569. At least one court has declared this position to be the "majority approach." *Lavigne v. Chase, Haskell, Hayes & Kalamon, P.S.*, 50 P.3d 306 (Wash.Ct.App. 2002). Other courts, however, hold that uncollectability is an affirmative defense, to be pleaded and proved by the defending attorney. *See, e.g., Teodorescu v. Bushnell, Gage, Reizen & Byington*, 506 N.W.2d 275 (Mich.Ct.App. 1993); *Carbone v. Tierney*, 864 A.2d 308, 319 (N.H. 2004) (describing this holding as the minority position among the states); *Lindenman v. Kreitzer*, 775 N.Y.S.2d 4, 8 (App.Div. 2004).

9. **Malpractice on Appeal:** When the alleged malpractice involves the mishandling of an appeal, "causation in fact" is proved by showing first, that the attorney's conduct caused an unfavorable appellate result and second, that the unfavorable appellate result caused an unfavorable result in the underlying action. *See Charles Reinhart Co. v. Winiemko*, 513 N.W.2d 773, 776 (Mich. 1994).

10. **Need for Expert Testimony:** In *Wong v. Ekberg*, 807 A.2d 1266, 1270–71 (N.H. 2002), the court considered whether, and when, expert testimony is needed in a legal malpractice action:

Other jurisdictions that have addressed this issue have held that, except in clear or palpable cases, "[i]n an action for legal malpractice, expert testimony is generally needed to establish both the level of care owed by the attorney under the particular circumstances and the alleged failure to conform to that benchmark." * * * The reason for this requirement is that "[w]ithout expert testimony, lay juries cannot understand most litigation issues, local practices, or the range of issues that influence how an attorney should act or advise." * * * Thus, "to avoid liability being imposed solely upon a disgruntled client's version of what happened or what he or she believes should have happened," * * * expert testimony is necessary to inform the jury regarding the skill and care ordinarily exercised by lawyers, a measure not ordinarily within the common knowledge of lay persons.

[E]xpert testimony may not be required when "the evidence of negligence is so patent and conclusive that reasonable persons can reach only one conclusion * * *."

In the case, all of the errors alleged were tactical or strategic decisions, such as failing to object to allegedly improper statements or failing to locate or subpoena certain witnesses, and the court concluded that expert testimony was necessary. Comments to the RESTATEMENT agree with the court by indicating that in any malpractice case, including a breach of fiduciary case, the plaintiff client must introduce expert testimony concerning both the applicable attorney standard of care and the failure of the defendant attorney to abide by that standard. Examples of conduct "so patent and conclusive" that expert testimony is not needed would include missing the statute of limitations or withdrawing from the case without telling the client. RESTATEMENT, § 52, Comment *g.*

11. **Violation of Ethics Rules as Malpractice:** Should violation of one of the Model Rules give rise to a malpractice action? The pre–2002 version of the Model Rules indicated that "[v]iolation of a Rule should not give rise to a cause of action." American Bar Association, Model Rules of Prof'l Conduct Scope ¶ [6] (2001). The current rule prevents the earlier statement from being read literally by providing that violation "should not itself give rise to a cause of action." Model Rules, Scope ¶ [18]. The RESTATEMENT provides that the factfinder may use any lawyer conduct rules as an "aid" to understanding the standard of care owed by the lawyer and that the Model Rules can be used and referred to by experts and others in the trial as setting forth the standards for the lawyer's conduct. *See* RESTATEMENT, § 52(2) & Comment *f.*

The courts have taken differing views of the relevance of a violation of an applicable rule of professional conduct in a malpractice action against an attorney. The Alabama Supreme Court held that "[t]he trial judge properly held that the evidence of a violation of the Rules of Professional Conduct could not be used in a legal malpractice action." *Ex parte Toler*, 710 So.2d 415, 416 (Ala. 1998). The Indiana Supreme Court held that the rules "have limited application outside of the attorney discipline process" and disavowed previous decisions providing for civil liability based upon rules violations. *Liggett v. Young*, 877 N.E.2d 178, 182–83 (Ind. 2007). A New York court granted summary judgment dismissing a legal malpractice action even though the defendant attorney "clearly violated" a rule that prohibited him from engaging in a sexual relationships with his client. *Guiles v. Simser*, 804 N.Y.S.2d 904, 907 (App.Div. 2005). The Nevada Supreme Court adopted what it described as the position of a "majority of jurisdictions * * * that the violation of professional rules of responsibility does not create a private right of action, but is relevant to the standard of care." *Mainor v. Nault*, 101 P.3d 308, 320 (Nev. 2004).

12. **Judicial Malpractice:** Are judges liable for making incorrect decisions or for negligence in decision making? If they were, how would that affect a judge's ability to be independent? A good summary of the law is set out by the Seventh Circuit in *Johnson v. McCuskey*, 72 Fed.Appx. 475, 476 (7th Cir. 2003):

> Judges are immune from lawsuits seeking monetary damages, * * * and that immunity extends even to acts made in bad faith or with malice * * *. There are two circumstances, however, when a plaintiff can overcome judicial immunity. First, "a judge is not immune from liability for nonjudicial actions, *i.e.,* actions not taken in the judge's judicial capacity." * * * Second, "a judge is not immune for actions, though judicial in nature, taken in the complete absence of all [subject matter] jurisdiction."

See also supra section 2(B), note 6 (discussing judicial immunity from civil rights damages suits, but not from civil rights suits seeking declaratory or injunctive relief).

QUESTIONS AND NOTES ON ATTORNEY INADEQUACY IN CRIMINAL CASES

1. Assume that the driver of the other vehicle in the problem was Bill Stevens. Stevens, although not driving negligently when interacting with Reynolds and Teague, was actually in a rush. He had become the focus of a criminal investigation after three women complained to the police that a man wearing a green ski mask and carrying a knife had sexually assaulted them. The police investigation of the incidents began to focus on Bill Stevens. Stevens was already on probation for indecent exposure and, after questioning by his parole officer, Stevens agreed to a "lie detector" test. During questioning, Stevens denied any involvement. The polygraph examiner indicated that Stevens was being deceptive in his answers. When Stevens' wife consented to a search of their two cars, police found a knife and a green stocking cap. Stevens was arrested, and attorney Darnell Jordan was appointed to represent him. Jordan obtained court permission to hire an investigator and to have a psychiatric examination of Stevens performed, but ultimately did not do either. Jordan did not interview any of the three victims.

Two days before trial, Jordan told Stevens that the state had a strong case and advised Stevens to consider a plea. Jordan indicated his belief, based on no research, that the polygraph evidence would be admitted against Stevens. Jordan also told Stevens that the state would be allowed to use the prior indecent exposure incident, even though Jordan had been assured by the prosecutor that would not be done. Acting on his attorney's advice, Stevens pleaded no contest to the criminal charges, was sentenced to ten years in prison, and began serving his sentence immediately. There was no appeal, so Jordan's representation of Stevens ended upon the conclusion of trial. Assume that, in fact, Stevens did not commit the crimes. Assuming that time still permits an appeal or post-conviction review in the criminal case on the ground that Jordan was ineffective as defense counsel, what standards govern such a claim? Suppose that, unbeknownst to Stevens, Jordan represented one of the victims, who would be able to obtain a fairly substantial sum from a state "crime victims fund" if Stevens was convicted. Would the result change?

2. **Malpractice in Criminal Cases—Ineffective Assistance of Counsel:** "Malpractice" in criminal cases takes two forms. First, following conviction, the criminal defendant can assert a claim under the Sixth Amendment to the United States Constitution alleging a denial of the defendant's right to effective assistance of counsel. If successful, the criminal conviction can be overturned. The United States Supreme Court, in *Strickland v. Washington*, 466 U.S. 668, 686–96 (1984), set out the standards necessary to overturn a criminal conviction on ineffective assistance grounds:

> [T]he Court has recognized that "the right to counsel is the right to the effective assistance of counsel." * * * The benchmark for judging any claim of ineffectiveness must be whether counsel's conduct so undermined the proper functioning of the adversarial process that the trial cannot be relied on as having produced a just result. * * *

> A convicted defendant's claim that counsel's assistance was so defective as to require reversal of a conviction or death sentence has two components. First, the defendant must show that counsel's performance was deficient. This requires showing that counsel made errors so serious that counsel was not functioning as the "counsel" guaranteed the defendant by the Sixth Amendment. Second, the defendant must show that the deficient performance prejudiced the defense. This requires showing that counsel's errors were so serious as to deprive the defendant of a fair trial, a trial whose result is reliable. Unless a defendant makes both showings, it cannot be said that the conviction or death sentence resulted from a breakdown in the adversary process that renders the result unreliable. * * *

> Prevailing norms of practice as reflected in American Bar Association standards and the like, e.g., ABA Standards for Criminal Justice 4–1.1 to 4–8.6 (2d ed. 1980) ("The Defense Function"), are guides to determining what is reasonable, but they are only guides. No particular set of detailed rules for counsel's conduct can satisfactorily take account of the variety of circumstances faced by defense counsel or the range of legitimate decisions regarding how best to represent a criminal defendant. Any such set of rules would interfere with the constitutionally protected independence of counsel and restrict the wide latitude counsel must have in making tactical decisions. * * *

> Judicial scrutiny of counsel's performance must be highly deferential. * * * Because of the difficulties inherent in making the evaluation, a court must indulge a strong presumption that counsel's conduct falls within the wide range of reasonable professional assistance[. A] court deciding an actual ineffectiveness claim must judge the reasonableness of counsel's challenged conduct on the facts of the particular case, viewed as of the time of counsel's conduct. * * *

> An error by counsel, even if professionally unreasonable, does not warrant setting aside the judgment of a criminal proceeding if the error had no effect on the judgment. * * * Accordingly, any deficiencies in counsel's performance must be prejudicial to the defense in order to constitute ineffective assistance under the Constitution.

In certain Sixth Amendment contexts, prejudice is presumed. Actual or constructive denial of the assistance of counsel altogether is legally presumed to result in prejudice. * * * Prejudice in these circumstances is so likely that case by case inquiry into prejudice is not worth the cost. * * *

One type of actual ineffectiveness claim warrants a similar, though more limited, presumption of prejudice. [P]rejudice is presumed when counsel is burdened by an actual conflict of interest. In those circumstances, counsel breaches the duty of loyalty, perhaps the most basic of counsel's duties. Moreover, it is difficult to measure the precise effect on the defense of representation corrupted by conflicting interests. Given the obligation of counsel to avoid conflicts of interest and the ability of trial courts to make early inquiry in certain situations likely to give rise to conflicts, * * * it is reasonable for the criminal justice system to maintain a fairly rigid rule of presumed prejudice for conflicts of interest. Even so, the rule is not quite the per se rule of prejudice that exists for the Sixth Amendment claims mentioned above. Prejudice is presumed only if the defendant demonstrates that counsel "actively represented conflicting interests" and that "an actual conflict of interest adversely affected his lawyer's performance."

[In all other cases, the defendant must show] that particular errors of counsel were unreasonable [and] that they actually had an adverse effect on the defense. * * * The defendant must show that there is a reasonable probability that, but for counsel's unprofessional errors, the result of the proceeding would have been different. A reasonable probability is a probability sufficient to undermine confidence in the outcome. * * *

In making this determination, a court hearing an ineffectiveness claim must consider the totality of the evidence before the judge or jury. Some of the factual findings will have been unaffected by the errors, and factual findings that were affected will have been affected in different ways. Some errors will have had a pervasive effect on the inferences to be drawn from the evidence, altering the entire evidentiary picture, and some will have had an isolated, trivial effect. Moreover, a verdict or conclusion only weakly supported by the record is more likely to have been affected by errors than one with overwhelming record support. Taking the unaffected findings as a given, and taking due account of the effect of the errors on the remaining findings, a court making the prejudice inquiry must ask if the defendant has met the burden of showing that the decision reached would reasonably likely have been different absent the errors. * * *

When the Court first announced it would consider standards for ineffective assistance of counsel, there was some belief that the decision would provide new hope for many criminal defendants. In practice, however, the *Strickland* standard has resulted in a situation in which "the vast majority of ineffective assistance of counsel claims are denied even when the claims concern deplorable legal assistance." Meredith J. Duncan, *The (So–Called) Liability of Criminal Defense Attorneys: A System in Need of Reform*, 2002 B.Y.U.L.Rev. 1, 18–20. The perceived ineffectiveness of *Strickland's* ineffectiveness standard ultimately caused Justice Blackmun to issue this scathing critique of the criminal defense system while dissenting from a denial of certiorari in *McFarland v. Scott*, 512 U.S. 849 (1994):

> The impotence of the *Strickland* standard is perhaps best evidenced in the cases in which ineffective-assistance claims have been denied. John Young, for example, was represented in his capital trial by an attorney who was addicted to drugs and who a few weeks later was incarcerated on federal drug charges. The Court of Appeals for the Eleventh Circuit rejected Young's ineffective-assistance-of-counsel claim on federal habeas, *Young v. Zant*, 727 F.2d 1489 (1984), and this Court denied review, 470 U.S. 1009, 105 S.Ct. 1371, 84 L.Ed.2d 390 (1985). Young was executed in 1985. John Smith and his codefendant Rebecca Machetti were sentenced to death by juries selected under the same Georgia statute. Machetti's attorneys successfully challenged the statute under a recent Supreme Court decision, *Taylor v. Louisiana*, 419 U.S. 522, 95 S.Ct. 692, 42 L.Ed.2d 690 (1975), winning Machetti a new trial and ultimately a life sentence. *Machetti v. Linahan*, 679 F.2d 236 (CA11 1982). Smith's counsel was unaware of the Supreme Court decision, however, and failed similarly to object at trial. *Smith v. Kemp*, 715 F.2d 1459 (CA11 1983). Smith was executed in 1983.

> Jesus Romero's attorney failed to present any evidence at the penalty phase and delivered a closing argument totaling 29 words. Although the attorney later was suspended on unrelated grounds, Romero's ineffective-assistance claim was rejected by the Court of Appeals for the Fifth Circuit, *Romero v. Lynaugh*, 884 F.2d 871, 875 (1989), and this Court denied certiorari, 494 U.S. 1012, 110 S.Ct. 1311, 108 L.Ed.2d 487 (1990). Romero was executed in 1992. Larry Heath was represented on direct appeal by counsel who filed a 6–page brief before the Alabama Court of Criminal Appeals. The attorney failed to appear for oral argument before the Alabama Supreme Court and filed a brief in that court containing a 1–page argument and citing a single case. The Eleventh Circuit found no prejudice, *Heath v. Jones*, 941 F.2d 1126, 1131 (1991), and this Court denied review, 502 U.S. 1077, 112 S.Ct. 981, 117 L.Ed.2d 144 (1992). Heath was executed in Alabama in 1992.

> James Messer, a mentally impaired capital defendant, was represented by an attorney who at the trial's guilt phase presented *no* defense, made no objections, and emphasized the horror of the capital crime in his closing statement. At the penalty phase, the attorney presented no evidence of mental impairment, failed to introduce other substantial mitigating evidence, and again repeatedly suggested in closing that death was the appropriate punishment. The Eleventh Circuit refused to grant relief, *Messer v. Kemp*, 760 F.2d 1080 (1985) (Johnson, J., dissenting), and this Court denied certiorari, 474 U.S. 1088, 106 S.Ct. 864, 88 L.Ed.2d 902 (1986). Messer was executed in 1988. Even the attorney who could name only *Miranda* and *Dred Scott* twice has survived ineffective-assistance challenges. See *Birt v. Montgomery*, 725 F.2d 587, 596–601 (CA11) (en banc), cert. denied, 469 U.S. 874, 105 S.Ct. 232, 83 L.Ed.2d 161 (1984); *Williams v. State*, 258 Ga. 281, 368 S.E.2d 742 (1988), cert. denied, 492 U.S. 925, 109 S.Ct. 3261, 106 L.Ed.2d 606 (1989). None of these cases

inspires confidence that the adversarial system functioned properly or "that the trial ca[n] be relied on as having produced a just result." *Strickland*, 466 U.S., at 686, 104 S.Ct., at 2064. Yet, in none of these cases was counsel's assistance found to be ineffective.

McFarland v. Scott, 512 U.S. 1256, 1259–61 (1994).

In *Rompilla v. Beard*, 545 U.S. 374 (2005), though, the Supreme Court held that a defendant who was given the death penalty was entitled to relief under *Strickland*, due to his trial attorneys' failure to investigate the file regarding his prior conviction that the prosecutor used at the trial's penalty phase. Regarding the deficiency prong of *Strickland*, the Court found, "If the defense lawyers had looked in the file on Rompilla's prior conviction, it is uncontested they would have found a range of mitigation leads." *Id.* at 390. Regarding the prejudice prong, the Court found that the potential mitigation "evidence adds up to a mitigation case that bears no relation to the few naked pleas for mercy actually put before the jury, and although we suppose it is possible that a jury could have heard it all and still have decided on the death penalty, that is not the test," then held the available mitigation evidence about the defendant's severely disadvantaged upbringing and mental capacity undermined confidence in the sentencing outcome. *Id.* at 393. The *Rompilla* decision was the third in half a decade where the Supreme Court applied the *Strickland* test and found that defendants whose trial counsel did not adequately investigate and present potential mitigating evidence at the penalty phases of death penalty trials had been denied their right to effective assistance of counsel. *See Wiggins v. Smith*, 539 U.S. 510 (2003); *Williams v. Taylor*, 529 U.S. 362 (2000).

Although many ineffective assistance claims are unsuccessful, lower courts also sometimes grant relief to criminal defendants due to their trial attorneys' ineffective representation. *See, e.g., United States v. Williams*, 372 F.3d 96 (2d Cir. 2004) (reversing sentence because defense counsel allegedly engaged in criminal transactions with defendant and, therefore, had an actual conflict of interest); *Canaan v. McBride*, 395 F.3d 376 (7th Cir. 2005) (holding that counsel's failure to advise defendant that he could testify at the penalty phase was ineffective assistance); *Summerlin v. Schriro*, 427 F.3d 623 (9th Cir. 2005) (holding that counsel failed to adequately investigate potential mitigation evidence in death penalty case); *People v. Turner*, 5 N.Y.3d 476, 806 N.Y.S.2d 154, 840 N.E.2d 123 (2005) (holding that trial counsel's failure to adequately resist lesser-included offense instruction on timeliness grounds violated state constitutional right to counsel).

3. **Renewed Supreme Court Interest in Representation of Criminal Defendants:** In 2009 and 2010, the Supreme Court granted *certiorari* and applied *Strickland* to a flurry of cases, though convicted defendants lost most of these cases. In *Wood v. Allen*, 130 S.Ct. 841 (2010), the Court held that a state court had reasonably determined that trial counsel's failure to investigate and present evidence of mental deficiencies at the penalty phase of a capital case was an acceptable tactical decision, so the defendant was not entitled to federal habeas relief. Similarly, in *Bobby v. Van Hook*, 130 S.Ct. 13 (2009), the Court held that trial counsel did not represent a criminal defendant deficiently in their investigation of the defendant's penalty phase mitiga-

tion evidence, so the convicted defendant was not entitled to habeas relief. Reaching the same result under the other prong of *Strickland*, in *Wong v. Belmontes*, 558 U.S. 15 (2009), the Court held that a convicted defendant had not been denied the effective assistance of counsel, because his trial attorney's deficiencies did not prejudice him to the extent required by *Strickland*. Also, in *Smith v. Spisak*, 558 U.S. 139 (2010), the Court assumed that defendant's attorney gave an inadequate closing argument, but nonetheless reinstated the conviction because there was "no 'reasonable probability' that a better closing argument without these defects would have made a significant difference."

However, in *Padilla v. Kentucky*, 130 S.Ct. 1473 (2010), the Court held that counsel engaged in deficient representation by failing to advise the defendant that his guilty plea would result in automatic deportation, then remanded the case to the Kentucky courts for a determination of whether the defendant established sufficient prejudice to require post-conviction relief. *See infra* section 6(A)(4)(b) (discussing *Padilla*). Also, in a case where *Strickland* did not directly apply, because it involved habeas procedural issues for a defendant who sought post-conviction relief and therefore did not have a constitutional right to counsel at that stage, the Court reversed the lower courts' denial of a petition for habeas relief as untimely, where errors by counsel led to the petition's tardiness. *See Holland v. Florida*, 130 S.Ct. 2549 (2010).

Has the Supreme Court breathed new life into *Strickland* and given those convicted of crimes new hope for their appeals based on alleged ineffective assistance of counsel? In the alternative, does the Court's tendency, even after granting *certiorari* somewhat more frequently than in the past, to uphold convictions under *Strickland* suggest that criminal defendants will continue to succeed only very rarely when pursuing ineffective assistance claims?

4. **Law Student Representation of Criminal Defendants:** When a law student represents a criminal defendant under a student practice rule and is properly supervised under that rule, the student's conduct is judged, for ineffective assistance of counsel purposes, under the same standard as other attorneys. *See, e.g., State v. Glenn*, 935 P.2d 679, 682–83 (Wash.Ct.App. 1997). When written permission to an appearance by a law student is necessary, failure to obtain the writing will be considered only a procedural misstep, rather than ineffective assistance, provided the defendant is actually notified of the student representation. *See, e.g., Jones v. State*, 902 P.2d 686, 695–96 (Wyo. 1995).

5. **Malpractice in Criminal Cases—Civil Malpractice Suits:** Return to our problem. Assuming the state statute of limitations on legal malpractice claims is two years, and assuming that a judge reverses Stevens' conviction two years and nine months after the end of the plea hearing, would a malpractice claim be barred by the statute of limitations?

The RESTATEMENT notes that a criminal defense attorney can be liable for malpractice to the criminal defendant if the defendant proves both that the lawyer performed negligently or in breach of contract, or if the lawyer breached a fiduciary duty, and that, but for those errors, the result in the criminal proceeding would have been different. RESTATEMENT, § 53, Comment *d*. The second requirement is the traditional "but for" proximate causation of most legal malpractice cases. In the criminal context, however, does this mean that a malpractice action will not lie until the criminal conviction is over-turned? While the RESTATEMENT indicates the defendant should not need to prove innocence, the comment-writers acknowledge that the overwhelming majority of jurisdictions require the criminal conviction to be overturned. *See id.*, Reporter's Notes; *see also* Meredith J. Duncan, *Criminal Malpractice: A Lawyer's Holiday*, 37 Ga.L.Rev. 1251, 1266–68 (2003); Kevin Bennardo, Note, *A Defense Bar: The "Proof of Innocence" Requirement in Criminal Malprac-tice Claims*, 5 Ohio St.J.Crim.L. 341 (2007). Because of the interrelationship between the ineffective assistance claim and the legal malpractice claim, once the criminal defendant alleges ineffective assistance of counsel, and loses that claim, many courts hold that the defendant is then issue-precluded from raising the malpractice of the lawyer for the same conduct. *See, e.g., McNeeley v. Spencer*, No. 1999–CA–003017–MR, 2002 WL 31126910 (Ky.Ct.App. Sept. 27, 2002) (unpublished decision); Duncan, *supra*, at 1270–72. Some courts disagree, though, and do not require reversal of the conviction, proof of innocence, or post-conviction relief prior to a legal malpractice suit. *See, e.g., Rantz v. Kaufman*, 109 P.3d 132 (Colo. 2005); *Godby v. Whitehead*, 837 N.E.2d 146 (Ind.Ct.App. 2005); *Mrozek v. Intra Fin. Corp.*, 2005 WI 73, 699 N.W.2d 54 (allowing malpractice case to proceed despite plaintiff's guilty plea in underlying criminal case).

Problems also arise in dealing with the statute of limitations. If a cause of action accrues when the criminal defendant's conviction is final, the statute of limitations begins to run when the last appeal is over—presumably while the defendant is serving time in prison. In many states, then, the statute will expire before the criminal defendant is exonerated, thereby barring the claim before the defendant had a real chance to prosecute it. *See* Duncan, *supra*, at 1274–76; *Holmes v. Boal*, No. Civ.A. 04–2591–CM, 2005 WL 2122315 (D.Kan. Aug. 22, 2005); *Morrison v. Goff*, 91 P.3d 1050 (Colo. 2004). The several schools of thought on this issue are discussed in *Gebhardt v. O'Rourke*, 510 N.W.2d 900 (Mich. 1994). Acknowledging a split of authority, *id.* at 905 n.11,[11] the court refused to "accept the 'no relief-no harm' rule because it is a legal fiction with serious analytical flaws.[13]" *Id.* at 906. The court instead adopted a two-track approach whereby the civil case and any criminal appeals

---

11. Jurisdictions considering the issue are split regarding whether appellate relief should be a required element [of the legal malpractice action in criminal cases]. Those answering yes include: Alaska, *Shaw [v. State Dep't of Admin., Pub. Defender Agency*, 816 P.2d 1358 (Alaska 1991)]; New York, *Carmel v. Lunney*, 70 N.Y.2d 169, 518 N.Y.S.2d 605, 511 N.E.2d 1126 (1987); Massachu-setts, *Glenn v. Aiken*, 409 Mass. 699, 569 N.E.2d 783 (1991); and Oregon, *Stevens v. Bispham*, 316 Or. 221, 851 P.2d 556 (1993). Those answering no include: Missouri, *Jepson v. Stubbs*, 555 S.W.2d 307 (Mo. 1977); District of Columbia, *McCord v. Bailey*, 204 U.S.App.D.C. 334, 636 F.2d 606 (1980); Alabama, *Mylar v. Wilkinson*, 435 So.2d 1237 (Ala. 1983); Kansas, *Bowman v. Doherty*, 235 Kan. 870, 686 P.2d 112 (1984); Ohio, *Krahn v. Kinney*, 43 Ohio St.3d 103, 538 N.E.2d 1058 (1989); and Pennsylvania, *Quick v. Swem*, 390 Pa.Super. 118, 568 A.2d 223 (1989).

13. Rather than being a legal definition of harm, the rule is a legal fiction that divorces the law from reality. "[P]ersons convicted of a crime will be astonished to learn that, even if their lawyers' negligence resulted in their being wrongly convicted and imprisoned, they were not harmed when they were wrongly convicted and imprisoned but, rather, that they are harmed only if and when they are exonerated."

This legal fiction of "harm" subverts the policy of a statute of limitations by extending indefinitely the time in which this type of legal malpractice claim could potentially accrue. Rather than the two years after last day of service or six months after discovery limitation periods the

could both proceed at the same time. Filing of the civil case would put the attorney on notice of a claim. Thereafter, the civil plaintiff could seek a stay of the civil case pending resolution of the criminal matter. If the civil case was stayed, and relief was granted in the criminal case, the court indicated that issue preclusion would work in the civil plaintiff's favor to prevent a relitigation of the "ineffective assistance" issues already resolved in the criminal case. *Id.* at 907.

6. **Public Defender Immunity from Malpractice:** Both federal and state public defenders are often, though not always, immune from malpractice liability to their criminal clients, under variations of the sovereign immunity doctrine. *See, e.g., Sullivan v. United States,* 21 F.3d 198 (7th Cir.1994); *Briggs v. Lawrence,* 281 Cal.Rptr. 578 (Ct.App. 1991); *Schreiber v. Rowe,* 814 So.2d 396 (Fla. 2002); *Dziubak v. Mott,* 503 N.W.2d 771 (Minn. 1993).

F(2) DUTIES TO THIRD PARTIES

PROBLEM

Ruth Ann and Elmer Lebett, brother and sister, have come to you seeking information about a possible legal malpractice claim against attorney Rona Delb. Delb had been attorney for Ruth Ann and Elmer's mother and, upon Mrs. Lebett's request, Rona had prepared a will for Mrs. Lebett. Mrs. Lebett told Ruth Ann and Elmer that she wished to exclude their sister Nita from her will and divide her estate equally between Ruth Ann and Elmer. Rona Delb apparently drafted this will, and Mrs. Lebett executed it one day after undergoing major surgery. She died approximately four weeks later.

Mrs. Lebett's husband had predeceased her. During his lifetime, he had created a marital trust, giving his wife a testamentary power of appointment over the trust's assets. At the time of Mrs. Lebett's death, the trust had a value of over $600,000. Unfortunately, Mrs. Lebett's power of appointment was not exercised in the will drawn by Delb, nor was any reference made to it. Consequently, under the terms of the trust, the assets were distributed to Ruth Ann, Elmer, and Nita, in equal shares.

Other than this error, Mrs. Lebett's will survived a challenge by Nita, who claimed that her mother was mentally incompetent and that Ruth Ann and Elmer had exercised undue influence on her.

Ruth Ann and Elmer believe they should have divided the $200,000 share of their father's marital trust that Nita received, and they claim they should now get it from attorney Delb, although Delb has never represented either of them. They have come to you for help.

QUESTIONS

(a) *Togstad* indicated that one of the elements of a malpractice action is the existence of an attorney-client relationship. Without such a relationship, how might Ruth Ann and Elmer seek to hold Delb liable for malpractice under a tort, contract, or any other theory?

Legislature has set forth, there would be no definite limitation period. *Stevens,* n.11 *supra*[,] 316 Or. at 239, 851 P.2d 556 (Unis, J., concurring).

(b) What proof would be necessary to sustain any cause of action you think exists?

RULE REFERENCE

Restatement § 51

IN RE GUARDIANSHIP OF KARAN

Court of Appeals of Washington, 2002.
38 P.3d 396.

SWEENEY, J.

Trask v. Butler[, 872 P.2d 1080 (Wash. 1994),] establishes a six-point analysis to determine whether a lawyer owes a duty to a nonclient. In this guardianship case, a mother hired a lawyer to help her set up a guardianship for her child's estate following the death of the child's father. The father had designated the child as the beneficiary of his life insurance policy. The lawyer petitioned the court for a guardianship. But the resulting guardianship order neither required a bond for the guardian, nor blocked the account from access in lieu of the bond. The mother depleted the funds. The dispositive issue is whether the lawyer owed the child a duty, and thereby created standing for the child to bring this action for malpractice. We conclude that the lawyer did owe a duty and reverse and remand for trial. * * *

GUARDIANSHIP STATUTE REQUIREMENTS

Washington's guardianship statutes are designed to protect a person of diminished capacity. The guardianship order *must* provide a meaningful remedy in the event the estate assets are depleted. It does so by requiring the guardian to post a bond. RCW 11.88.100. As an alternative protection for the ward, where posting a bond would work a hardship, the statute allows the funds to be deposited in a bank or other secure account, subject to withdrawal only by court order—a blocked account. RCW 11.88.105.

Compliance with these provisions is a condition precedent to the appointment of a guardian whenever the estate is worth over $3,000. RCW 11.88.100; *In re Guardianship of Whitish,* 47 Wash.2d 652, 658, 289 P.2d 340 (1955). Failure to post bond deprives the nominal guardian of the legal authority to assume the duties of the office. *Id.* at 657, 289 P.2d 340. Here, the guardianship order did not require either a bond or blocked account. * * *

STANDING

The general rule is that only an attorney's client may file a claim for legal malpractice. *Trask v. Butler,* 123 Wash.2d 835, 840, 872 P.2d 1080 (1994). But an attorney may owe a nonclient a duty even in the absence of this privity. *Stangland v. Brock,* 109 Wash.2d 675, 680, 747 P.2d 464 (1987). When the facts underlying the alleged attorney-client relationship are disputed, the fact-finder makes the determination after weighing the evidence and the credibility of the witnesses. *Stiley v. Block,* 130 Wash.2d 486, 502, 925 P.2d 194 (1996). Here, the facts are not in dispute. The only question is one of standing. And that is a question of law to be decided by us. *Trask,* 123 Wash.2d at 842–43, 872 P.2d 1080 * * *.

To determine whether a lawyer owes a duty to a nonclient which then creates standing to sue for malpractice, Washington applies a six-element test. *Trask,* 123 Wash.2d at 842, 872 P.2d 1080. There is an older, third party beneficiary test. There, the court asks whether the plaintiff is an intended beneficiary of the contract for services. *Id.* The first element of the multi-factor test incorporates the third party beneficiary test. We do not, therefore, address it separately here, even though Ms. Janssen raises it as a separate issue.

TRASK TEST

In the absence of an express lawyer-client relationship, Washington courts use a multi-factor balancing test set forth in *Trask.* To establish whether the lawyer owes the plaintiff a duty of care in a particular transaction, the court must determine:

1. The extent to which the transaction was intended to benefit the plaintiff;

2. The foreseeability of harm to the plaintiff;

3. The degree of certainty that the plaintiff suffered injury;

4. The closeness of the connection between the defendant's conduct and the injury;

5. The policy of preventing future harm; and

6. The extent to which the profession would be unduly burdened by a finding of liability.

Trask, 123 Wash.2d at 843, 872 P.2d 1080. The threshold question is whether the nonclient plaintiff is an intended beneficiary of the transaction. If not, there is no further inquiry. *Id.*

TRASK

In *Trask,* the personal representative of the parents' estate was one of two heirs. The heirs were brother and sister, who from the outset were legal adversaries. When the father died, the personal representative immediately hired a lawyer. Brother and sister litigated title to a real estate parcel which had been quitclaimed to the brother by the father without the surviving mother's signature. They also litigated whether the brother had encroached on estate lands from his neighboring property. To meet the mother's medical expenses, the personal representative sold the home at a bargain price, in part because of the litigation. *Trask,* 123 Wash.2d at 837–38, 872 P.2d 1080.

After the mother died, the personal representative acceded to all the brother's demands in exchange for his agreement not to sue her for breach of her duty as personal representative. The brother instead sued the personal representative's lawyer for malpractice. *Id.* at 838–39, 872 P.2d 1080. He alleged the lawyer negligently advised the personal representative to file the quiet title action against the quitclaimed property. And this had the effect of reducing the property's value. He claimed that the lawyer owed him a duty of care as a beneficiary of the estate. *Id.* at 839, 872 P.2d 1080.

The *Trask* court weighed the six factors and concluded that the lawyer for the personal representative of a probated estate owes no duty to beneficiaries for advice given to the personal representative which results in loss of the value to the estate. The court held that, in a probate situation, the relationship between the lawyer and personal representative is not intended to benefit the estate beneficiaries. The court found that the brother was at best an incidental beneficiary of the lawyer's services. *Id.* at 845, 872 P.2d 1080. The court determined that its holding would not create future harm to estate beneficiaries, who have recourse to other legal remedies for breach of duty by a personal representative. The profession would be greatly burdened by a finding of a duty on these facts because lawyers cannot fulfill conflicting duties to parties whose interests are adversarial. * * *

Mr. Topliff argues that *Trask's* holding must be applied as a bright-line rule. In fact, both parties ask for a bright-line rule that a guardian's lawyer either does or does not owe a duty of care to the ward. But there is no bright-line rule; nor should there be. The lesson of *Trask* is that each case must be evaluated on its own facts. * * *

Trask is factually distinguishable. The *Trask* case resolved a dispute between an adult, competent beneficiary of a will who was in an adversarial relationship with another adult beneficiary. The second beneficiary was also both the personal representative of the deceased father's estate and attorney-in-fact for the surviving mother. *Trask,* 123 Wash.2d at 838, 872 P.2d 1080. And the lawsuit against the lawyer was over day-to-day judgment calls in managing the estate.

By contrast, here we have: (1) a legally incompetent infant ward, (2) a non-adversarial relationship, and (3) legal services solely consisting of setting up the guardianship.

The *Trask* court recognized that not every estate beneficiary is "incidental" to every transaction between every estate administrator and his or her lawyer. For instance, in the matter of a botched will, third-party intended beneficiaries may have a cause of action in negligence against the drafting attorney under the multi-factor balancing test. *Trask,* 123 Wash.2d at 843, 872 P.2d 1080 (citing *Stangland,* 109 Wash.2d at 681, 747 P.2d 464). * * *

APPLICATION OF THE *TRASK* FACTORS

Here, the *Trask* factors establish a duty owed by Mr. Topliff to Amanda.

1. *Intended Beneficiary:* The primary reason to establish a guardianship is to preserve the ward's property for his or her own use. It is not for the benefit of others. *In re Guardianship of Michelson,* 8 Wash.2d 327, 335, 111 P.2d 1011 (1941) (guardianship held unnecessary). Therefore, the attorney-client relationship between Mr. Topliff and Ms. Schafer was established to benefit Amanda.

The remaining *Trask* factors also support a finding of duty.

2. *Foreseeability of Harm:* It is foreseeable that failure to put in place the statutory safeguards for the protection of the estate will leave the ward vulnerable to the kind of losses Amanda incurred. This is why the Legislature required the safeguards.

3. *Certainty Plaintiff Suffered Injury:* It is not disputed that Amanda suffered harm. She lost three-quarters of her estate. And she had no meaningful recourse against the judgment-proof guardian.

4. *Connection between Lawyer's Conduct and Injury:* If established, the connection between the alleged conduct and the injury is direct. The lawyer bypassed the statutory safeguards that protect a ward from a guardian's squandering the funds.

5. *Future Harm:* In matters involving the welfare of minors and other legally incompetent individuals, the courts assume a particular duty to protect the interests of the ward. *Durham v. Moe,* 80 Wash.App. 88, 91, 906 P.2d 986 (1995). Policy considerations favor finding a duty in the interests of preventing future harm. *In re Guardianship of Ivarsson,* 60 Wash.2d 733, 738, 375 P.2d 509 (1962).

The *Trask* court found that a cause of action against the personal representative's lawyer was not necessary because the probated estate's beneficiary had an independent cause of action against the personal representative for breach of fiduciary duty. *Trask,* 123 Wash.2d at 843–44, 872 P.2d 1080. Here, however, the conditions precedent for establishing a guardianship—bond or blocked account—were not established.

Moreover, direct action for breach against the guardian is likely to be an empty remedy absent a bond. In contrast to *Trask,* the injury to the ward in this case is precisely that she was left without any meaningful remedy. The remedy would have been secured by the statutorily required bond, or rendered unnecessary by a properly blocked account.

The *Trask* court based its decision in part on the premise that a beneficiary can take an active role in estate matters by retaining an attorney or communicating with the personal representative. *Id.* at 844, 872 P.2d 1080. But a three-year-old cannot do this.

6. *Burden on the Profession:* Finally, *Trask* notes that imposing liability in that case would create an impossible ethical conflict for lawyers, because the interests of beneficiaries and the personal representative of a deceased's estate are frequently at odds. The parties are legal adversaries. *Id.* But, again, that is not the case here. A potential conflict of interest arises when the lawyer simultaneously represents clients with opposing interests. *Kidney Ass'n of Or., Inc. v. Ferguson,* 315 Or. 135, 145, 843 P.2d 442 (1992). In contrast to *Trask,* the legitimate interests of the guardian here are inseparable from those of the ward.

The profession will not be unduly burdened by finding a duty in this case, because the applicable law mandates either a bond or a blocked account. The obligation to protect the interests of wards in circumstances such as this does not put lawyers in an ethical bind. To require them to inform a would-be guardian that Washington statutes mandate either a bond or a blocked account is not a burden on the profession. * * *

We have applied the *Trask* factors. In doing so, we conclude that Mr. Topliff owed a duty of care to the ward, Amanda Karan.

PROFESSIONAL NEGLIGENCE

Once a relationship giving rise to a duty is established, the elements of a malpractice claim are the same as for any other negligence action. *Stangland,* 109 Wash.2d at 679, 747 P.2d 464. Those elements are: breach * * *; proximate cause * * *; and damages * * *.

Questions of breach, proximate cause, or damages will be questions of fact on remand. We reverse and remand for trial on the remaining elements of negligence.

NOTES ON LAWYER LIABILITY TO THIRD PARTIES

1. **The Multi–Factor Test:** The *Trask* court identified two prominent tests from other states for determining whether an attorney could be sued by a third party to the attorney-client relationship. According to *Trask,* the Illinois "third party beneficiary test is summarized in Neal v. Baker, [551 N.E.2d 704 (Ill.App.Ct. 1990), which] extended the traditional concept of attorney liability to include third parties who were 'intended beneficiaries of the relationship between the client and the attorney.'" *Trask,* 872 P.2d at 1084. To create liability under this test, the "nonclient must prove that the primary purpose and intent of the attorney-client relationship is to benefit or influence the third party." *Id.* (quoting *Neal*).

The *Trask* court noted that the California "multi-factor balancing test" analyzes the six factors listed in the *Trask* and *Karan* opinions. *Id.* at 1083. To some extent, the *Trask* court combined the Illinois and California tests, by adopting the six-factor test with an emphasis on the first factor, i.e., whether the malpractice plaintiff was an intended beneficiary of the attorney-client relationship. *See id.* at 1084 (noting that "the threshold question is whether the plaintiff is an intended beneficiary of the transaction to which the advice pertained" and that, "[w]hile the answer to the threshold question does not totally resolve the issue, no further inquiry need be made unless such an intent exists").

The *Trask* court held that there was no duty owed by the attorney hired by the personal representative of the estate to the estate's beneficiaries, because "(1) the estate and its beneficiaries are *incidental,* not intended, beneficiaries of the attorney-personal representative relationship; (2) the

estate heirs may bring a direct cause of action against the personal representative for breach of fiduciary duty; and (3) the unresolvable conflict of interest
an estate [that an attorney would encounter] in deciding whether to represent
the personal representative, the estate, or the estate heirs unduly burdens the
legal profession." *Id.* at 1085. In *Guardianship of Karan*, the court found that
there was a duty to a person other than the attorney's direct client. Are these
holdings correct? Are the facts in the two cases distinguishable? Does the
decision in *Osornio v. Weingarten*, 21 Cal.Rptr.3d 246 (Ct.App. 2004), where
the court applied the six-factor test and found that an attorney owed a duty to
the intended beneficiary of a will drafted for the client, reduce your confidence
in the *Trask* holding or simply reinforce the reality that multi-factor tests are
fact-bound inquiries that can lead to different outcomes in cases with some
factual similarities?

Consider *Perez v. Stern*, 777 N.W.2d 545 (Neb. 2010). A mother of two
minor children hired a lawyer to pursue a wrongful death action as representative of her deceased husband's estate against persons alleged to be responsible for his death in an auto accident. The lawyer filed the suit, but failed to
perfect service, resulting in the case being dismissed. By the time the mother
hired another lawyer to a malpractice action against the original lawyer on
behalf of herself, their children, and the husband/father's estate for negligent
loss of the wrongful death claim, the statute of limitations had run against the
malpractice claim as to the mother and the estate, but the statute was tolled
as to the children because of their minority. When the mother sought to
continue the claim for the children, the defense was that there was no
attorney-client relationship with the children and no duty owed to them. The
court rejected the defense, applying the six factor test for the first time in
Nebraska. It held that, because the children were statutory beneficiaries of
the decedent under the wrongful death law and therefore direct beneficiaries
of the mother's services as estate representative, the attorney had a duty to
exercise reasonable care in representing their interests. The court reviewed all
of the potential conflicts justifying the contrary results in cases like *Trask*,
but found them absent in the case at hand. It also noted that a number of
other jurisdictions had reached the same conclusion in this context.

2. **Intent to Benefit:** The *Trask* court intimates that the extent of the
intent to "benefit" the third party is the most important of the six factors to
be considered. In *Johnson v. Wiegers*, 46 P.3d 563, 566 (Kan.Ct.App. 2002),
the court set out the multi-factor test in a slightly different form: First, if the
third party is an adversary of the attorney's client, there can be no duty to
that third party. "It is eminently sensible that a lawyer's duty * * * leaves no
room for an additional—and almost certainly conflicting—duty to the client's
adversary." Second, there must be some intent of the client to benefit the
third party. Third, if there is such an intent, then the court can use the multi-
factor analysis.

3. **Litigation Cases:** Some courts have expanded upon the first prong
of the test used in Kansas. In *Trask*, the court found that the attorney for the
estate was required to act in the best interests of the estate, not in the
interests of any individual beneficiary. In essence, the court found no third-
party liability because of the conflict of interest that would befall the estate
attorney in having to act to benefit one of the beneficiaries or face a

malpractice suit. Other courts have taken this finding to hold that while the *Trask* multi-factor analysis "may be effective when used to address the duties of attorneys in transactional matters or estate planning and probate practice, [it] is not appropriate to define an attorney's duties while representing clients in adversarial proceedings[, because] an adverse party has no basis for reliance on the actions of an adversary's counsel." *Rhode v. Adams*, 1998 MT 73, ¶ 19, 957 P.2d 1124, 1127 (and cases cited therein).

4. **Third–Party Beneficiary:** The difficulty of the "intended beneficiary" theory can be seen in cases like *Minnich v. Yost*, 817 A.2d 538 (Pa.Super.Ct. 2003). When Minnich's mother died, Minnich's father took his own and his deceased wife's will to Yost for estate planning advice. Yost did not advise Minnich's father of the need to have the wife's will probated and, apparently as a result, Minnich did not receive the benefit from his mother's estate that he might have otherwise received. The court denied liability from Yost to Minnich because Minnich was only the incidental beneficiary of the consultation between Minnich's father and Yost over the father's estate plan.

5. **Corporate Representation:** One area in which third-party liability of attorneys may be increasing is in representation of corporations and other entities following the Enron and similar corporate scandals. Areas of concern appear to be liability of business promoters' lawyers to investors, liability of lawyers to pension plan beneficiaries for faulty pension plan investments, and liability of lawyers for corporations to investors for securities fraud violations of the corporation. *See Attorneys Who Represent Companies Face Higher Possibility of Liability to Nonclients*, 19 Laws.Man. on Prof. Conduct (ABA/BNA) 176 (2003).

6. **Opinion Writing:** Where a lawyer drafts an opinion letter or other documents that are sent to third parties, the lawyer can be held liable for malpractice, but only where the court finds some duty to disclose to the third party. *See Vanguard Prod., Inc. v. Martin*, 894 F.2d 375 (10th Cir. 1990) (attorney for mortgage lender owed common law duty of ordinary care to mortgagee who relied on the lawyer's opinion); *Prudential Ins. Co. v. Dewey, Ballantine, Bushby, Palmer & Wood*, 605 N.E.2d 318 (N.Y. 1992) (relationship between the lender and the attorney for borrower was close enough to privity to allow the lender to sue the lawyer for malpractice, when the lender relied on the borrower's attorney's opinion letter). *See also infra* section 6(B)(2).

7. **RESTATEMENT Attempts Restatement:** Section 51 of the RESTATEMENT attempts to summarize the many cases on third-party liability holding a lawyer liable to a nonclient. Under the RESTATEMENT, a lawyer may be liable to a nonclient:

First, when the lawyer or the lawyer's client, with the lawyer's assent, "invites the nonclient to rely on the lawyer's opinion or * * * other legal services," provided the nonclient is not more remote from the lawyer than permitted by applicable tort law;

Second, when the lawyer "knows" that one of the primary objectives of the client is to benefit the nonclient, provided that creation of a duty to the nonclient would not "significantly impair" the lawyer's professional obligations to the client and provided that, without recognizing a duty to the nonclient, the responsibility to the client probably would not be enforced;

Third, where the lawyer's client is a personal representative, such as a trustee, guardian or executor, and the lawyer knows that the lawyer needs to act "to prevent or rectify the breach of a fiduciary duty owed by the client to the nonclient," provided that the nonclient is not otherwise "reasonably able to protect its rights," and provided that creation of a duty to the nonclient would not "significantly impair" the lawyer's professional obligations to the client.

G. TERMINATION OF THE RELATIONSHIP

G(1) WITHDRAWAL

PROBLEM

You were hired by Client to pursue a personal injury claim against Defendant. At the outset of the representation, you and Client agreed to a contingent fee arrangement of 40%. You begin to investigate the case and, with the consent of your client and the attorney for Defendant, enter into settlement negotiations with Defendant's attorney and insurance adjuster.

QUESTIONS

(a) After extensive negotiations with Defendant's insurance company, you are offered $75,000 in full settlement of your client's claim, an amount you consider reasonable. You discuss this amount with Client, who immediately rejects it. You honestly do not believe that Client will recover anywhere near that much if the case goes to trial. What are your options?

(b) Client gave you the names of two "eyewitnesses" to the incident that caused Client's injuries. Client insists that these witnesses be allowed to testify. You have interviewed both witnesses and reviewed the facts and are convinced, beyond any possible doubt, that the witnesses were not present at the scene. After you confer with Client, who again insists that these witnesses be allowed to testify, you immediately withdraw from the case. Have you acted properly?

(c) Assume that instead of a contingent fee, you and Client had agreed that Client would pay your hourly rate of $175 and that you would bill monthly. After two months of billings totaling $6,900, Client has not paid you any money. When you confer, Client admits to being financially strapped, but swears to make payment "soon." Can you withdraw? What considerations are involved?

RULE REFERENCES

Model Rule 1.16

RESTATEMENT §§ 31–32

SOBOL v. DISTRICT COURT OF ARAPAHOE COUNTY

Supreme Court of Colorado, En Banc, 1980.
619 P.2d 765.

ROVIRA, JUSTICE.

Ellis J. Sobol and the law firm of Zuckerman & Sobol, P.C., petitioners, filed this original proceeding * * * seeking relief in the nature of prohibition * * *. The petitioners ask that we order the respondent trial court to reverse a ruling denying their motion for leave to withdraw as counsel for Helen M. Sterling, individually, and * * * as administratrix * * * of the Estate of Ernst H. Sterling * * *.

Several years ago, the petitioners were retained by Sterling to represent her in her capacity as the administratrix * * * of the estate of her deceased husband. Subsequently she requested petitioners to initiate a civil action against the law firm of Simon, Eason, Hoyt & Malone. The petitioners agreed to undertake such representation and, from what appears in the record before us, a contingent fee agreement was entered into between the parties. * * *

During the course of the representation by petitioners of Sterling * * *, certain disputes and disagreements arose. Petitioners argue that Sterling was uncooperative, critical of their handling of the litigation, deliberately withheld material information, repeatedly contacted the attorney for the defendants, and has made effective representation impossible.

Sterling has denied responsibility for these disputes and disagreements and has rejected petitioners' characterization of their dealings with one another. She claims that she is entitled to be represented by petitioners because a contingent fee agreement had been agreed to and because she has not been able to secure the services of other counsel.

[T]en months before [the case] was scheduled to go to trial, petitioners filed motion for leave to withdraw as counsel. After a hearing * * *, the respondent trial court granted the motion and gave Sterling thirty days to obtain new counsel. She filed *pro se* a Motion for Rehearing [whereupon] the trial court affirmed its prior ruling, but further ordered the petitioners to use their best efforts in assisting Sterling to find other counsel and report back to the court within ninety days.

[A]nother hearing was held, and the respondent trial court was advised by both petitioners and Sterling that new counsel had not been obtained. Although recognizing an obvious antagonistic relationship between the petitioners and Sterling and the handicap this presented in preparation of the case at issue, the court held that Sterling would be even more prejudiced if she were required to appear *pro se*. The court, therefore, reversed its prior decision and denied petitioners' motion for leave to withdraw.

I.

The question of whether an attorney should be permitted to withdraw his general appearance on behalf of a litigant in a civil case is, under ordinary circumstances, within the discretion of the trial court; and its decision will not be reversed unless this discretion has been demonstrably abused. * * * As a general rule, an attorney who undertakes to conduct an action impliedly agrees that he will pursue it to some conclusion; and he is not free to abandon it without reasonable cause. * * * Even where cause may exist, the attorney's withdrawal must be undertaken in a proper manner, duly protective of his client's rights and liabilities. * * *

The court's inherent power to require an attorney to appear derives from its responsibility to conduct its business efficiently, effectively, and fairly. * * * However, in some cases a court abuses its discretion in failing to permit an attorney's withdrawal from his client's case. * * * We find that such an abuse occurred here when * * * the court ordered petitioners to represent Sterling * * *.

Implicit in the court's [original] order * * * was the finding that the mutual antagonism which existed between lawyers and client was so intense that it rendered it unreasonably difficult for petitioners to carry out their employment effectively. * * * There were no special or unusual circumstances of which the court was made aware at the February 7 hearing that would have justified a refusal to grant petitioners' motion. * * * The client had ample time to procure new counsel to handle [the] case. When the court granted petitioners' motion, this responsibility became the client's. * * *

Petitioners were scrupulous in their efforts to find alternative counsel, and conscientiously assisted Sterling and the trial court in this process after the motion to withdraw was granted. * * * Sterling had sufficient time and opportunity before her trial date to secure representation * * *. The trial court was rightfully concerned that Sterling's lack of legal representation might prejudice her ability to litigate * * *. But Sterling had and continues to have primary responsibility for solving this problem. By the time the trial court reversed its ruling to permit withdrawal * * *, nothing in the dealings between Sterling and the petitioner had improved and, if anything, their mutual lack of confidence and mistrust had deepened. The court, therefore, abused its discretion in ordering petitioners to reenter a relationship which had already been properly severed. * * *

NOTES ON WITHDRAWAL

1. **Discretion of the Court:** The court in *Sobol* indicates that normally, the attorney "impliedly agrees" to pursue representation until "some conclusion." The motion to withdraw, then, is addressed to the discretion of the trial court. The court will often be required to balance the interests of the attorney, the client, and the court. Factors considered by the courts include whether the case is a criminal or civil matter, the proximity of trial, the complexity of the case, the ability of the client to obtain new counsel, the prejudice to the remaining parties, and the reason given for withdrawal. In *Commonwealth v. Sweeney*, 533 A.2d 473 (Pa.Super.Ct. 1987), the appellate court found that the trial court abused its discretion where the attorney was

hired for the limited purpose of representing the client in pretrial and trial stages of the case and the trial court refused to allow the attorney to withdraw during an appeal.

2. **Good Cause for Withdrawal:** The "permissive withdrawal" provisions of Model Rule 1.16(b) outline circumstances in which the attorney may withdraw, but is not required to withdraw. After detailing the specific circumstances that allow an attorney to seek to withdraw in Model Rule 1.16(b)(1)–(6), Model Rule 1.16(b)(7) permits the attorney to withdraw for "good cause." What does that mean?

In *Ryan v. State*, 51 P.3d 175 (Wash.Ct.App. 2002), attorney Hugo was hired to represent the plaintiff in a personal injury case on a contingent fee basis. Hugo hired attorney Stein to assist. As the case progressed, Hugo left the practice of law in Washington and moved to Florida. Stein then took on primary, rather than secondary, responsibility for the case. As Stein's caseload in his own firm increased, Stein wrote Hugo, withdrawing from the case. After Hugo successfully negotiated a $150,000 settlement for the plaintiff, Stein wanted to be paid a portion of the legal fee, either as part of a contingency fee agreement with Hugo or on the basis of a reasonable fee for the work he had done on the case. The court held that neither Stein's increased workload nor his transfer from secondary to primary responsibility justified withdrawal and that, because Stein therefore withdrew without cause, he was entitled to no fee for the work done on the case. The court set out the standard for withdrawal for good cause:

> Courts have found 'good cause' where the attorney knows that the client's claim is fraudulent, the attorney has professional objections to the client's retention of additional counsel, the client is uncooperative, the attorney and client suffer a 'breakdown' in communication, the client degrades the attorney (usually by claiming the attorney was dishonest), the client refuses to pay justified attorney fees and costs or ethical rules require the attorney to withdraw.... It has been held unjustifiable for an attorney to withdraw from a case because the client has retained other counsel, the attorney does not believe the negotiated contract with the client is sufficiently compensatory, the attorney feels that the case has no potential or the client refuses to accept a settlement offer.

51 P.3d at 178–79, *quoting Ausler v. Ramsey*, 868 P.2d 877, 880 n.4 (Wash.Ct. App. 1994). Note the distinction the court makes between the lawyer having a "professional objection" to the hiring of additional counsel and the mere hiring of that counsel. For this court, the former is likely covered by Model Rule 1.16(b)(4), while the latter is not.

3. **Fee Disputes:** One of the bases for permissive withdrawal under Model Rule 1.16(b)(5) is the failure of the client to fulfill an obligation to the lawyer. This almost always involves the failure by the client to pay all or a portion of the lawyer's fee. In *Fidelity National Title Insurance Co. v. Intercounty National Title Insurance Co.*, 310 F.3d 537 (7th Cir. 2002), the attorney had amassed unpaid legal fees and expenses over $400,000, but the trial court refused to allow counsel to withdraw. The court of appeals first ruled that the denial of a motion to withdraw is an appealable interlocutory

order because it is not related to the merits of the dispute, because any error cannot be rectified at the end of the case, and because of the burden it places on counsel. The court found that unpaid legal fees of $470,000, together with a prospect of an additional $500,000 worth of uncompensated legal fees prior to trial, justified withdrawal and overturned the court's exercise of discretion.

Not all attorney financial difficulties, however, will lead to successful motions to withdraw. Indeed, the *Fidelity National Title Court* itself said, "A lawyer engaged in strategic conduct may forfeit any right to withdraw. One form of strategic behavior is waiting until the client is over a barrel and then springing a demand for payment." *Id.* at 540. Judges do occasionally deny requests by attorneys to withdraw due to non-payment of their legal bills or litigation expenses, where prejudice to the client, other parties, and/or the court is found to outweigh the burden on the attorney. *See In re Tutu Wells Contamination Litig.*, 164 F.R.D. 41 (D.V.I. 1995); *Haines v. Liggett Grp., Inc.*, 814 F.Supp. 414 (D.N.J. 1993). In *In re Ryan*, No. 07–63072–aer7, 2008 WL 762203 (Bankr.D.Or. Mar. 20, 2008), a bankruptcy debtor discharged her lawyer just before scheduled hearings on the U.S. Trustee's motion to dismiss her bankruptcy petition, solely because she could not afford to continue paying legal fees. The court treated this ground for her lawyer's motion to withdraw as indistinguishable from that of simple failure to pay fees. It conditioned the granting of the lawyer's motion on her firm's refunding fees already received.

4. **Withdrawal for Other Ethical Reasons:** Issues relating to withdrawal, whether mandatory or permissive, often arise in the context of other ethical problems. Withdrawal when the client seeks to commit perjury is discussed in *infra* section 4(C). The professional responsibility concerns when a client seeks to file a frivolous lawsuit, which can include a withdrawal duty, are discussed in *infra* section 6(A)(1)(a).

5. **Obligations upon Withdrawal:** An attorney who withdraws, regardless of the reason, must do so in a way that protects the client's interests "to the extent reasonably practicable." *See* Model Rule 1.16(d). Therefore, an attorney must take steps like allowing time for the client to hire another attorney, surrendering papers and property to the client, and refunding unearned advance fee payments. *Id.* This obligation applies to attorneys who have been discharged. *Malonis v. Harrington*, 816 N.E.2d 115, 123 (Mass. 2004) (noting that "a discharged attorney must take all reasonable steps to protect the client's interests, including surrendering papers and property to which the client is entitled and discussing with the client the consequences of the discharge"). Courts have disciplined attorneys who failed to protect their client's interests while withdrawing. *See, e.g., In re Swanson*, 200 P.3d 1205, 1217 (Kan. 2009) (suspending attorney for, inter alia, failing to protect a client's interests after being discharged); *In re Henry*, 684 S.E.2d 624 (Ga. 2009) (disbarring attorney who failed to provide files to clients after discharge and engaged in other misconduct); *In re Cruse*, 2007–1716 (La. 8/22/07); 963 So.2d 377 (suspending attorney for, inter alia, not returning files and unearned fees to clients).

G(2) DISCHARGE, TERMINATION, AND LEGAL FEES

PROBLEM

As attorney for the Diamond Corporation, you have been working on the defense of a significant personal injury action for several years. At a recent pretrial conference, the judge suggested that she thought a settlement of the matter for around $200,000 might be possible. Because you agree that a $200,000 settlement would be a good deal for Diamond, given its potential multi-million dollar exposure, you recommend this figure to the Board of Directors.

At the Board of Directors meeting at which potential settlement is discussed, one of the directors says: "You're selling us out. I read about a case just like this in the newspaper and the jury only awarded $50,000 to the plaintiff with no punitives." Although you try to explain the significant differences between the cases, the other directors are swayed and, at the end of the discussion, the chair says: "Sorry, we just don't feel right about our relationship any more. You're fired." In fact, you have not "sold the client out" and $200,000 is a very fair settlement. At the time of your discharge, you have spent about 150 hours on the case. Your regular hourly charge is $300, a rate standard in your legal community and one which has been accepted by the courts as fair in this type of litigation.

QUESTIONS

(a) How much are you entitled to as a fee?

(b) When should it be paid?

RULE REFERENCES

Model Rules 1.5(c) and 1.16

RESTATEMENT §§ 30–33, 37 & 40

SOMUAH v. FLACHS

Court of Appeals of Maryland, 1998.
721 A.2d 680.

CHASANOW, JUDGE.

This appeal arises out of a suit filed by Jeremy Flachs (Respondent) * * * against Millicent Somuah (Petitioner) to recover compensation for the legal services Respondent provided to Petitioner. * * *

I.

The underlying dispute arises out of an automobile accident involving a taxicab in which Petitioner and her daughter were severely injured. * * * Petitioner retained Respondent to represent her regarding a possible personal injury claim as a result of this accident. * * * The retainer agreement entered into by the parties provided, *inter alia,* for a one-third contingency fee to be deducted before the payment of expenses * * *.

After [an] initial interview with Petitioner, Respondent began investigating Petitioner's claim, expending considerable effort, as well as a substantial amount of money as he took steps to collect and preserve evidence. Petitioner moved to Maryland [and shortly] thereafter, Respondent began to explore the possibility of a lawsuit in Maryland state courts. * * * Respondent asked a Maryland attorney * * * to assist him in a Maryland lawsuit, and [when introducing this Maryland attorney to Petitioner, Respondent first notified Petitioner that Respondent was licensed to practice law in Virginia and the United States District Court for the District of Virginia, as well as the District of Columbia, but that Respondent was not licensed to practice in Maryland. Apparently because Respondent was not licensed in Maryland, and before Respondent could arrange for local counsel], Petitioner discharged Respondent as her attorney * * *. After his termination, Respondent sent Petitioner a letter requesting payment for the time spent and expenses incurred in investigating Petitioner's claim. Petitioner refused this request. * * *

Respondent filed suit against Petitioner seeking to recover the reasonable value of services rendered and expenses paid during the course of his representation of Petitioner. Specifically, Respondent requested $11,324.66 for expenses paid and $8,685.00 for time spent investigating Petitioner's claim. The automobile accident case for which the Petitioner retained Respondent was still pending. Both parties filed motions for summary judgment and moved for judgment at trial; all were denied. The jury subsequently returned a verdict in favor of Respondent and awarded compensation in the amount of $19,946.01. * * * On appeal, the Court of Special Appeals * * * affirmed the judgment against Petitioner * * *. Petitioner timely filed a petition for writ of certiorari which was granted by this Court. * * *

III. * * *

Petitioner alleges that she had cause to terminate Respondent as a matter of law because he failed to disclose at their initial meeting the fact that he was not licensed to practice law in Maryland, and thus Respondent is precluded from recovering any compensation. The Court of Special Appeals in this case limited what constitutes cause for terminating an attorney's representation [concluding] that "a lawyer's failure to tell a prospective client that he is not licensed to practice in the jurisdiction where suit likely will be brought does not constitute the kind of fraud or other undue influence necessary to invalidate a lawyer-client contract." * * * As we shall explain, a client's right to terminate an attorney-client relationship is not as limited as the Court of Special Appeals concluded.

It is a well-settled rule in this State that a client has great latitude in discharging his or her attorney. An attorney's authority to act for a client is freely revocable by the client. *See Skeens v. Miller,* 331 Md. 331, 335,

628 A.2d 185, 187 (1993) * * *. The client's right to terminate the attorney-client relationship is necessary given the confidential nature of such a relationship and "the evil that would be engendered by friction or distrust." * * * Because the power of the client to discharge his or her attorney is an "implied term of the retainer contract," the client does not breach the contract when he or she terminates the attorney-client relationship based on a reasonable subjective dissatisfaction with the attorney's services, even if the client does not have "good cause." * * * Furthermore, the fact that an attorney has been retained under a contingent fee agreement does not affect the client's absolute right to discharge an attorney. * * *

Although this Court has not previously explained what constitutes a proper basis for terminating an attorney-client relationship, this Court has addressed to some extent the circumstances in which an attorney's compensation may be forfeited. [We have] indicated that a fee agreement in violation of the Maryland Lawyers' Rules of Professional Conduct may result in the forfeiture of an attorney's compensation.

[M]any jurisdictions found * * * cause for termination but still permitted *quantum meruit* recovery by the attorney. These courts have indicated that almost any good faith reason asserted by the client may constitute cause to discharge an attorney, ranging from whatever causes the client to lose faith in the attorney, *Fracasse v. Brent*, 6 Cal.3d 784, 100 Cal.Rptr. 385, 494 P.2d 9, 13 (Cal. 1972) * * * to an attorney's breach of contract. * * *

A client discharges an attorney without just cause when the client has no basis for being dissatisfied with the attorney's services or the discharge is in bad faith. Under these circumstances, the attorney has an immediate cause of action for breach of the fee contract. On the other hand, a client has cause to discharge his or her attorney when the client has any good faith basis for being dissatisfied with the attorney, even though the attorney has performed competently. [C]ause for discharging an attorney can be divided into two groups: First, where the attorney commits serious misconduct, *i.e.*, fraud or illegal conduct, etc.; and second, where the attorney acts competently and there is no serious misconduct, but the client has a good faith basis to be dissatisfied with the attorney. In the former situation, the attorney is not entitled to any fee. In the latter situation, the attorney is entitled to be compensated for the work done prior to discharge, but in a contingent fee contract, the attorney must await the occurrence of the contingency. [T]his is based on the agreement that no fee will be payable unless and until the contingency occurs.

Respondent points out, and Petitioner concedes, that Respondent performed competently prior to his discharge, and we note that there was no misrepresentation, fraud, or deceit on the part of Respondent. [As a result, there was no "cause" to discharge Respondent. The court, however, did] conclude for the following reasons that Petitioner had a good faith basis for being dissatisfied with Respondent's representation. * * *

Respondent did not explain to Petitioner at their initial meeting, or in the retainer contract, that he [was not licensed in Maryland and] would be unable to try the case and would need local counsel if the case were filed in Maryland state court. In fact, Respondent did not inform Petitioner of such a limitation on his ability to represent Petitioner until * * * three months after he was retained. * * * Petitioner had a basis for losing confidence in and being dissatisfied with the Respondent's continued representation.

IV. * * *

We hold that where a client has a good faith basis to terminate the attorney-client relationship but there is no serious misconduct warranting forfeiture of any fee, the attorney is entitled to compensation based on the reasonable value of services rendered prior to discharge, considering as factors the reasonable value of the benefits the client obtained as a result of the services rendered prior to discharge and the nature and gravity of the cause that led to the attorney's discharge. * * *

The primary rationale for permitting *quantum meruit* recovery is to prevent unjust enrichment to the client of the benefits of the attorney's services prior to discharge. * * * In awarding a discharged attorney the reasonable value of the services he or she rendered prior to discharge, the court "preserve[s] the client's right to discharge his attorney without undue restriction, and yet acknowledge[s] the attorney's right to fair compensation for work performed." [We thus] strike a balance between the client's absolute right to discharge his or her attorney and the attorney's right to fair compensation for services competently rendered prior to discharge. In determining the reasonable value of the services of a discharged attorney to the client, we note that factors which may be considered by the court are listed in Maryland Lawyers' Rule of Professional Conduct 1.5 * * *.

V.

The result in this case requires us to address another issue: Where the attorney was retained on a contingency basis and discharged by a dissatisfied client prior to the fulfillment of the contingency, when may the attorney recover compensation in *quantum meruit?*

[C]ourts in other jurisdictions are split as to when a discharged attorney may sue his or her former client for *quantum meruit* recovery. [*Skeens*,] 331 Md. at 337–40, 628 A.2d at 188–90 (discussing rationales behind the "California rule" requiring an attorney to wait until the contingency is met and the "New York rule" permitting an attorney to sue immediately upon discharge). Following the "New York rule," this Court held that, where an attorney has been discharged without cause, the attorney's cause of action in *quantum meruit* accrues immediately upon the termination of the contingent agreement, and the attorney is not required to wait until the contingency is fulfilled. 331 Md. at 343–44, 628 A.2d at 191 (reasoning that "a client who without cause terminates a contingent fee agreement may not thereafter resurrect the contingency term as a defense when the discharged attorney files a fee claim").

The *Skeens* decision does not require a similar result in the instant case as Respondent was discharged because the client had a good faith basis for being dissatisfied with the attorney-client relationship. Where any fee is contingent on recovery by the client and where, as in this case, there has been some basis for the client being dissatisfied with the attorney, the contingency generating the fee must occur prior to the attorney's recovery. We conclude that the attorney's claim accrues upon the fulfillment of the contingency, *i.e.,* where the plaintiff/former client obtains a final judgment. Respondent therefore must wait until Petitioner recovers in her action against Chrysler in order to maintain his action for compensation. * * *

JUDGEMENT OF THE COURT OF SPECIAL APPEALS REVERSED. CASE REMANDED * * * FOR FURTHER PROCEEDINGS CONSISTENT WITH THIS OPINION.

RODOWSKY, JUDGE, dissenting. * * *

Prior to today's decision Maryland law concerning the rights of the parties to an attorney-client retainer contract was relatively well-settled in five aspects. First, "the authority of an attorney to act for a client is revocable at the will of the client. The client's power to discharge the attorney is an implied term of the retainer contract." * * * Second, "[b]ecause the client's power to end the relationship is an implied term of the retainer contract, the modern rule is that if the client terminates the representation, with or without cause, the client does not breach the retainer contract, and thus, the attorney is not entitled to recover on the [express] contract." * * * Third, "[i]f the client discharges the attorney for cause, the prevailing rule is that the attorney may not recover any compensation." * * * Fourth, "if the representation is terminated either by the client without cause or by the attorney with justification, the attorney is entitled to be compensated for the reasonable value of the legal services rendered prior to termination." * * * Fifth, the attorney's claim for the reasonable value of services rendered prior to termination may be asserted when the client terminates the representation without cause, even where the parties had agreed on a contingent fee. This fifth rule was the holding in *Skeens.* [331 Md.] at 344, 628 A.2d at 191. * * *

Here, the majority opinion in effect asserts that "cause" for termination comes in two varieties. The first, which I shall call "High Grade" cause, carries that degree of substantiality which excuses the promisor from paying promised compensation. The second variety, which I shall call "Low Grade" cause, is a creature of the majority opinion and is not "cause" at all as conventionally used in the employment context.

What I call "High Grade" cause, the majority terms " 'cause' for the forfeiture of an attorney's compensation." * * * This is an objective determination. The majority and I agree that if the client has "High Grade" cause for terminating the retainer contract, the attorney is not entitled to any compensation for services. What I call "Low Grade" cause, the majority calls "a 'basis' for an attorney's discharge." * * * The majority's "basis" seems to be no more than a bona fide dissatisfaction on the client's part with the attorney's performance. It is a subjective standard. [T]he Court holds that, if the client terminates because of a bona fide dissatisfaction, this "basis" does not bar *quantum meruit* recovery by the attorney for services rendered prior to the termination, but the *quantum meruit* claim becomes contingent and accrues only if, as, and when there is a recovery in the litigation underlying the terminated retainer contract. On this aspect of the case the majority and I part company. * * *

The majority in the instant matter postpones accrual of the claim for restitution in a contingent fee retainer contract that has been terminated by a client for Low Grade cause until "the fulfillment of the contingency, *i.e.,* where the plaintiff/former client obtains a final judgment." * * * This is contrary to what we held in *Skeens* and, in my opinion, *Skeens* was correctly decided. The contingency is a provision of the express contract, but here the client terminated that contract without cause, that is, without any material breach by the attorney. The attorney's claim then becomes one for restitution, and the damages are the value of the services rendered prior to the date of termination. Because the plaintiff/former client, who has been benefitted by the services of the first attorney, makes those benefits available, at the time of termination, to the replacement attorney, the claim in *quantum meruit* unconditionally accrues at the time of termination. * * * Therefore, in my view, the judgment of the Court of Special Appeals should be affirmed. * * *

NOTES ON LEGAL FEES AND DISCHARGE

1. **Discharge Without Cause:** In *AFLAC, Inc. v. Williams*, 444 S.E.2d 314 (Ga. 1994), the court indicated that the client has the "absolute right to discharge" the lawyer with or without cause at any time and further that, because of that right, the client who discharges their lawyer is not in breach of any retainer agreement with the lawyer. The comments to Model Rule 1.16(a)(3) agree, stating the client has the "right to discharge a lawyer at any time, with or without cause * * *." Model Rule 1.16, Comment [4]. As noted in the RESTATEMENT: "A client is not forced to entrust matters to an unwanted lawyer. * * * A discharged lawyer loses actual authority to act." RESTATEMENT, § 32, Comment *b* (2000). An attorney who fails to withdraw in a timely fashion after a client discharges the attorney faces possible discipline. *See, e.g., In re Newman*, 958 N.E.2d 792, 797 (Ind. 2011) (suspending attorney for, inter alia, waiting six weeks until after being discharged to withdraw); *In re Swanson*, 200 P.3d 1205, 1217 (Kan. 2009) (suspending attorney for, inter alia, failing to properly withdraw after being discharged); *Attorney Grievance Comm'n v. Steinberg*, 910 A.2d 429, 445 (Md.Ct.App. 2006) (disbarring attorney for, inter alia, waiting six months after being discharged to withdraw).

2. **Getting Paid After Getting Fired:** How does the lawyer who has been discharged without cause get paid? This is particularly tricky if the attorney was working under a contingent fee agreement, and the contingency, the client's recovery, has not been met when the client fires the attorney.

The comments to Model Rule 1.16 state that the client's right to discharge the lawyer without cause is "subject to liability for payment for the lawyer's services." Model Rule 1.16, Comment [4]. Under early decisions, in such a situation, the lawyer could elect either of two remedies. First, the lawyer could treat the contract as breached, thereby allowing the attorney to await the outcome of the contingent event and then sue for the entire value of the contract. Second, the lawyer could treat the client's discharge of the lawyer without cause as a repudiation of the contract, thereby allowing the lawyer to sue for the fair value of the lawyer's services up to the point of discharge. *See* RESTATEMENT, § 40, Comment *b*. Recent decisions often reject the breach of contract theory, because the right to discharge the attorney is seen as an implicit term of the contract between the client and the attorney. *See Campbell v. Bozeman Investors of Duluth*, 1998 MT 204, ¶ 21, 964 P.2d 41, 44. Thus, most courts now allow the attorney to recover solely upon the *quantum meruit* theory. *See Rangel v. Save Mart, Inc.*, 142 P.3d 983, 991 (N.M.Ct.App. 2006) (noting that "it appears to be the general rule in other jurisdictions that discharged attorneys are reimbursed on a quantum meruit basis, even when there is a contingency fee contract"). Because the *quantum meruit* approach is based upon the concept that the client should not be unjustly enriched by the discharged lawyer's services, the amount the attorney can recover will be based upon the "the value conferred on the client, not the effort expended by the lawyer, although the two may be the same in many instances." *Farmer v. Lawson (In re Estate of Johnson)*, 855 N.E.2d 686, 702 (Ind.Ct.App. 2006); *see also Malonis v. Harrington*, 816 N.E.2d 115, 123 (Mass. 2004) (noting that a "client should never be made to pay twice").

If the client in a contingent fee case discharges the attorney before the client recovers, when is the attorney allowed to receive payment for services rendered to the client? *Somuah* mentions the California and New York rules, which attempt to reconcile the lawyer's right to be compensated for services already rendered in a way that does not penalize the client for exercising the client's absolute right to discharge the lawyer. *Skeens v. Miller*, discussed by the *Somuah* court, discusses the relative merits of the alternative rules:

> Courts following the California rule hold "that the cause of action to recover compensation for services rendered prior to the revocation of a contingent fee contract does not accrue until the occurrence of the stated contingency." * * * Under that rule, it follows that the discharged attorney will be denied compensation in the event recovery is not obtained in the case which was being handled under a contingent fee agreement. * * *

The Supreme Court of California adopted its rule for two reasons.

"First, one of the significant factors in determining the reasonableness of an attorney's fee is 'the amount involved and the result obtained.' It is apparent that any determination of the 'amount involved' is, at best, highly speculative until the matter has finally been resolved. Second, and perhaps more significantly, we believe it would be improper to burden the client with an absolute obligation to pay his former attorney regardless of the outcome of the litigation. * * *"

Courts following the California rule have amplified the reasons for deferring the accrual of the cause of action until the occurrence of the contingency. Courts have stated that such a rule furthers the public policy of allowing clients to freely discharge their attorneys, * * * deferring the cause of action does not harm the attorney because the attorney would not have benefited earlier until the occurrence of the contingency, * * * the rule promotes the broad objective of promoting greater confidence in the profession and the attorney-client relationship, * * * and any possible injustice to the attorney is avoided because a judgment could be worthless if the client's underlying suit is not successful * * *.

Courts following the New York rule hold that the discharged attorney's cause of action accrues immediately upon the termination of the attorney's services without cause, rather than being deferred until the happening of the contingency. [The New York courts] provided two reasons for adoption of the rule * * *. First, the client cannot make the attorney's recovery dependent upon a contract term when the client has terminated the contract. * * * Second, ["the] value of one attorney's services is not measured by the result attained by another[." T]he Supreme Court of Illinois expanded on the rationale for the New York rule by providing three additional reasons for its adoption. First, the court stated that *quantum meruit* is based on the implied promise to pay for those services which are of value to a recipient, and the recipient would be unjustly enriched if he were able to retain the services without paying for them. * * * Second, the court believed that the outcome of the litigation is not an indispensable element that must be considered in calculating the value of an attorney's services. * * * Finally, the court opined that because the former client is liable only for the reasonable value of the services received prior to discharge, if the attorney's services were of little or no value to the former client, any injustice to the client would be avoided by no award or a minimal award of attorney's fees.

Skeens v. Miller, 628 A.2d 185, 188–89 (Md. 1993).

Similar issues can arise in non-contingent fee cases. In *Franklin & Marbin, P.A. v. Mascola*, 711 So.2d 46 (Fla.Dist.Ct.App. 1998), the attorney withdrew, without any fault, from representing a client under an hourly fee explicitly set out in a written fee agreement. The Florida court found the California rule applicable to both fixed fee and contingent fee contracts, but was unwilling to award the attorney only the reasonable value of the attorney's services from an hourly fee agreement, instead recognizing the contracted for amount as the appropriate remedy. In *McQueen, Rains & Tresch, LLP v. Citgo Petroleum Corp.*, 2008 OK 66, ¶ 12, 195 P.3d 35, 40, the Oklahoma

Supreme Court found that a liquidated damages clause of a fix-fee, fixed-term contract between a client and a law firm might be enforceable after the client discharged the law firm.

3. **"High Grade" Discharge:** Return to the background facts of the problem, but assume that upon being advised of the settlement, and your recommendation that it be accepted, a member of the Board of Directors says: "It's no wonder you want to accept that settlement; your brother is the partner of the plaintiff's attorney. How can we accept a settlement when the plaintiff has admitted fault in the accident and our witnesses indicate we have none?" Assume that all of what this member of the Board says is true and that, in negotiating with your brother's partner, it is clear that you were attempting to do him a favor. With client's consent, you withdraw. Your regular hourly billing rate is $300, and you have spent 150 hours on the case. How much are you entitled to as a fee?

The *Somuah* court recognizes that in some circumstances, the client does have cause to discharge the attorney and the attorney is, because of the cause, entitled to no fee. The court specifically mentions some conflict of interest situations, cases involving fraud or undue influence by the attorney, situations where the attorney abandons the client without reason, and fee agreements that violate the Model Rules. As noted by the dissent, these "high grade discharge" cases involve an objective determination about the attorney's conduct. The reasons used by the court generally mirror those contained in the RESTATEMENT, which authorizes partial or total forfeiture of the lawyer's fee for "clear and serious" violations of the attorney's professional duty to the client. RESTATEMENT, § 37. The view of the dissent in *Somuah* was that either the client had no cause for discharging the lawyer, whereupon the Maryland lawyer was entitled to the reasonable value of the lawyer's services immediately, or the client had cause for "high grade" discharge and the lawyer was entitled to no compensation.

4. **"Low Grade" Discharge:** Disagreeing with the dissent, the majority in *Somuah* recognized that a number of courts have found "cause" for the client to discharge the lawyer, but have not required the lawyer to thereby forfeit the entire legal fee. Consider the following cases:

In *Mulholland v. Kerns*, 822 F.Supp. 1161 (E.D.Pa. 1993), an attorney hired to represent clients in a damage action arising out of an automobile accident proved to be unfamiliar with local practice and unable to substantially move the case forward. By the time of discharge, the "case was, at this point, floundering, and plaintiffs had lost confidence in him." The court distinguished cases in which the attorney had committed either "illegal or immoral acts" from those in which the attorney is discharged merely "for cause." When dismissed for cause, the attorney was entitled to receive a fee based on *quantum meruit*. The court noted that the phrase *quantum meruit* means " 'as much as deserved,' " thereby allowing the court to consider the "cause" for the discharge.

In *International Materials Corp. v. Sun Corp.*, 824 S.W.2d 890 (Mo. 1992), the court found: "It was or should have been apparent * * * that the case was too difficult for [the attorneys] because they did not have the resources of time and staff available to successfully prosecute this claim." The court found that total fee forfeiture is justified only when there is a "serious violation of duty to a client" that causes a destruction of the attorney-client relationship. Where the lawyer has done nothing "willfully blameworthy," a *quantum meruit* measure of recovery should be used. *Id.* at 893.

In *Searcy, Denney, Scarola, Barnhart & Shipley, P.A. v. Scheller*, 629 So.2d 947 (Fla.Dist.Ct.App. 1993), ten years of litigation and two trials had netted the client a $26 million judgment. During the course of those proceedings, however, the attorneys and client had executed several new and changing contingent fee agreements. Ultimately, the attorneys wrote the client "an ultimatum giving him three alternatives." The client could either sign a fee agreement sought by the attorneys, acknowledge a certain stated portion of the case as being within the fee agreement, or hire a new lawyer. The client chose the last of the three and fired the attorney. The trial court found that the attorneys' ultimatum "amounted to a material breach of the entire contract of representation," and ordered a fee forfeiture. The court followed the RESTATEMENT view. Section 37 of the RESTATEMENT provides:

> A lawyer engaging in clear and serious violation of duty to a client may be required to forfeit some or all of the lawyer's compensation for the matter. Considerations relevant to the question of forfeiture include the gravity and timing of the violation, its willfulness, its effect on the value of the lawyer's work for the client, any other threatened or actual harm to the client, and the adequacy of other remedies.

The court then held that a court should order total forfeiture "only after exhausting the aptness of all other remedies to cure the specific act of misconduct in issue." 629 So.2d at 953. Thus, both the court in *Searcy* and the RESTATEMENT envision the type of subjective determination opposed by the dissent in *Somuah*.

5. **Acts Constituting Discharge:** An attorney is usually discharged by the express words of the client. It is possible, however, for a discharge to be effected in more subtle ways. Thus, where the client, during the pendency of the representation, files an ethics charge against the lawyer, the actions of the client evidence such distrust as to amount to a discharge. *Brown v. Johnstone*, 450 N.E.2d 693, 695 (Ohio Ct.App. 1982). Similarly, where the client hires a new attorney, that often amounts to a repudiation of the prior attorney-client relationship and therefore to a discharge. Even in that situation, though, it is not always clear whether the client has completely discharged the first attorney. *See Brown v. Silvern*, 45 P.3d 749, 752 (Colo.App. 2001) (reversing summary judgment dismissing malpractice claim against the client's first attorney because there was a factual issue about whether the attorney was still representing the client even though "it is undisputed that [the client] obtained his case file from [the first attorney] and that two months later he retained a second attorney").

When counsel believes that acts of the client amount to a discharge of the lawyer, however, the lawyer may still be required formally to withdraw. As long as counsel remains the attorney of record in the case, she will bear ultimate responsibility for the handling or mishandling of the action. *See, e.g., Blakely v. State*, 649 S.W.2d 187, 188 (Ark. 1983).

The RESTATEMENT recognizes other events as discharging the lawyer: The client dies or a corporation loses its capacity to function; the lawyer dies or is physically or mentally incapable of representing clients; or the lawyer is disbarred or suspended or is disqualified from representing the client by a tribunal. RESTATEMENT, § 31. In each of these cases, either the principal-client is no longer capable of having an agent, or the agent-lawyer is no longer capable of acting as such.

6. **Discharge and the Court:** The client's right to discharge the lawyer is not completely unfettered. Under Model Rule 1.16(c), even a discharged lawyer can only withdraw with the court's permission. Courts deny motions to withdraw more often than one might think, for a variety of reasons. One common reason is a concern that granting an attorney's motion to withdraw would substantially disrupt the court proceedings. *See, e.g., Miller v. Dunn & Phillips, P.C.,* 839 F.Supp.2d 383 (D.Mass. 2011); *Alzheimer's Inst. of Am., Inc. v. Avid Radiopharmaceuticals,* No. 10–6908, 2011 WL 6088625 (E.D.Pa. Dec. 7, 2011); *SEC v. Poirier,* No. 96–02243–PHX–EHC, 2007 WL 2462173 (D.Ariz. Aug. 24, 2007).

As noted in the Reporter's Notes to the RESTATEMENT, a lawyer who does not obtain the required permission of the court to withdraw continues to represent the client, so that lawyer can be held liable for malpractice. If the court denies the lawyer's request to withdraw, the lawyer is required to reasonably attempt to further the client's "lawful objectives." RESTATEMENT, §§ 31, Reporter's Notes & 32, Comment *d*.

7. **Criminal Case Discharge and Standby Counsel:** Issues often arise when counsel attempts to withdraw in a criminal case, where the court is obligated to preserve the client's constitutional right to effective assistance of counsel. Courts are often reluctant to grant motions to withdraw when they suspect that a defendant in a criminal case is attempting to disrupt the justice system by discharging counsel or engaging in other actions that force counsel to move to withdraw. *See United States v. Allen,* No. 06–40056–01–SAC, 2008 WL 2622872 (D.Kan. July 1, 2008) (denying motion to withdraw by the defendant's third attorney, after granting motions to withdraw from his first two attorneys); *State v. Stovall,* 227 P.3d 1010 (Table), No. 100, 704, 2010 WL 1379512 (Kan.Ct.App. Feb. 4, 2010); *State v. Foye,* 2008 WL 5056206 (N.J.Super.Ct.App.Div. Dec. 2, 2008); *see also Tutt v. State,* 339 S.W.3d 166, 169 (Tex.App. 2011) (affirming trial court that informed defendant, who wished to discharge his court-appointed attorney and be granted a continuance to find and hire an attorney, that "he could either proceed with his current court-appointed counsel or represent himself").

Sometimes a criminal defendant expresses a desire to fire his or her attorney and proceed *pro se*. When faced with such a request by an indigent defendant, the court must determine whether the defendant is competent to "voluntarily and intelligently" waive the *Gideon v. Wainwright,* 372 U.S. 335 (1963), right to be represented by counsel at the government's expense, with the many attendant benefits of representation by an attorney. *Faretta v. California,* 422 U.S. 806, 807 (1975); *United States v. Moreland,* 622 F.3d 1147, 1155–57 (9th Cir. 2010); *State v. Hartsoe,* 2011 MT 188, ¶ 39, 258 P.3d 428, 437.

If the court grants the defense attorney's motion to withdraw and allows the defendant to proceed *pro se*, it often simultaneously orders the attorney to serve as "standby counsel" for the defendant. *See, e.g., United States v. Isaac*, 655 F.3d 148, 152–53 (3d Cir. 2011); *State v. Dethman*, 2010 MT 268, ¶ 7, 245 P.3d 30, 32–33. In *United States v. Bertoli*, 994 F.2d 1002 (3d Cir.1993), the court explained its reasons for ordering a discharged law firm to remain in the case as "standby" counsel:

> The Supreme Court noted the benefits of standby counsel in *Faretta v. California*, 422 U.S. 806, 95 S.Ct. 2525, 45 L.Ed.2d 562 (1975), stating that an appointment may be made "to aid the accused if and when the accused requests help, and to be available to represent the accused in the event that termination of the defendant's self-representation is necessary." * * * Such an appointment facilitates the accused's Sixth Amendment right to proceed *pro se* and conduct one's own defense. * * * The appointment of standby counsel may be made even over the objection of the defendant. [If so ordered by the court,] an attorney who has entered an appearance for a criminal defendant has a duty to continue in a standby role not only to his former client but also to the court itself. * * *

> Essentially, standby counsel has two purposes—to act as a safety net to insure that the litigant receives a fair hearing of his claims and to allow the trial to proceed without the undue delays likely to arise when a layman presents his own case. Alternately, we can identify at least four functions that standby counsel can serve:

> (1) Standby counsel must be available if and when the accused requests help. * * *

> (2) Standby counsel must be ready to step in if the accused wishes to terminate his own representation. * * *

> (3) The court may appoint standby counsel in order to explain and enforce the basic rules of courtroom protocol to the accused. * * *

> (4) The court may appoint standby counsel in order to overcome routine obstacles that may hinder effective *pro se* representation.

994 F.2d at 1017–19. The court of appeals refused to overturn the trial court's appointment of the law firm as standby counsel. *See also United States v. Young*, 428 Fed.Appx. 9 (D.C.Cir. 2011) (approving trial court's explanation to the defendant and the jury that defendant "was representing himself, even though standby counsel was present to help with procedure and protocol").

Although courts often appoint standby counsel when indigent defendants waive their constitutional right to be represented by counsel at the government's expense, they are not required to do so. *See United States ex rel. Jordan v. Walls*, No. 02 C 2906, 2002 WL 31455971 (N.D.Ill. Nov. 1, 2002). Because there is no constitutional right to standby counsel, a defendant who is convicted cannot seek to overturn the conviction due to ineffective assistance of standby counsel. *See United States v. Oliver*, 630 F.3d 397, 413–14 (5th Cir. 2011).

8. **Attorneys' Liens:** Like others who perform services for clients, attorneys attempt to protect their interest in collecting for their services

through legal processes. Historically, courts have recognized two types of attorneys' liens.

The first type of attorneys' lien is a "charging lien." It attaches to funds recovered by an attorney to secure payment of her fees and expenses in obtaining the funds. The basis of the lien is discussed in *Cherpelis v. Cherpelis*, 959 P.2d 973, 975–76 (N.M.Ct.App. 1998):

> [T]he attorney's charging lien "has its origin in the common law, and is governed by equitable principles." * * * It is an attorney's right to "recover his fees and money expended on behalf of his client from a fund recovered by his efforts, and also the right to have the court interfere to prevent payment by the judgment debtor to the creditor in fraud of his right to the same." * * * The attorney's charging lien is intended "to protect attorneys against dishonest clients, who, utilizing the services of the attorney to establish and enable them to enforce their claims against their debtors, sought to evade payment for the services which enabled them to recover their demand." [T]he traditional attorney's charging lien is solely an equitable remedy administered by the court in its discretion.

Although the charging lien has its origin in common law, many states now have statutes outlining circumstances when an attorney can attach a lien to the potential recovery by a client. *See, e.g.*, Wyo.Stat.Ann. § 29–9–102; *Hughes v. Cole*, 465 S.E.2d 820, 833 (Va. 1996) (noting that a state statute allowed a discharged attorney to attach a lien to potential recovery to protect the attorney's *quantum meruit* recovery). In at least one state, a defendant who settles with a plaintiff without procuring the written consent of an attorney with a qualifying charging lien is liable to that attorney for the amount of the charging lien. *See* Mo.Rev.Stat. 484.140. To protect their clients' interests, defense attorneys usually advise their clients to make their settlement checks payable to the plaintiff and all of the plaintiff's attorneys. However, one court has held that this is not a required practice. *Block v. Bernard, Cassisa, Elliott & Davis*, 2004–1893 (La.App. 1 Cir. 11/4/05); 927 So.2d 339, 350 (finding there was no duty to include the plaintiff's attorney's name on settlement check under existing law, but also noting that the legislature or state supreme court could create such a duty).

The second type of attorneys' lien is called a "retaining lien." It does not attach to the money or property obtained by the lawyer in a particular matter, as does the charging lien, but instead attaches to any "papers, documents, securities, and monies of the client coming into the hands of the attorney in the course of the professional employment." *Britton & Gray, P.C. v. Shelton*, 2003 OK CIV APP 40, ¶ 9, 69 P.3d 1210, 1212. The *Britton & Gray* court noted that the purpose of the retaining lien is to obtain satisfaction of the lawyer's fee, then considered whether the prejudice to the client is inconsistent with Model Rule 1.16(d)'s requirement that the lawyer, upon termination of the representation, take reasonable steps to preserve the client's rights, including surrendering client papers and property to the client:

> Generally, the only advantage an attorney derives from the "ancient retention power" "recognized since earliest time" is some leverage to induce the client to settle the fee dispute. Most often, a client settles because of embarrassment or inconvenience:

[T]he effectiveness of the lien is proportionate to the inconvenience of the client in being denied access to his property. The focal point is not upon the objective worth of the property, but upon its subjective worth to the client and those who represent him. If the property loses this latter value, the attorney's possession becomes meaningless, and his passive lien, to all effects, worthless. Therefore, *it is the inconvenience suffered by the client which determines the value of the lien,* and if the client or his representative considers the elimination of this inconvenience to be as valuable as the amount of the attorney's charges, then the client will satisfy the charges, the lien will dissolve, and the client's property will be returned. * * *

At some point * * * an attorney's claimed retaining lien may cross the line from mere inconvenience or embarrassment to potential harm or prejudice.

Other jurisdictions have occasionally addressed this issue. For public policy reasons, some courts have refused to enforce the retaining lien when a client's important liberty interests are at stake, such as when the papers in the attorney's possession are essential to defense of a criminal charge. * * * California has held that where the subject matter of an attorney's lien is of no economic value to the attorney, but is used only to extract disputed fees from his client, the lien is void as against public policy and unenforceable. [Under Model Rule 1.16(d), even] if the lawyer has been unfairly discharged by the client, a lawyer must take all reasonable steps to mitigate the consequences to the client. * * * The rule imposes a *mandatory* obligation on an attorney to mitigate the consequences of the severed attorney-client relationship, and *requires* the attorney to "surrender" the client's papers. * * *

The rule also *permits* an attorney to retain the client's papers to secure payment of *earned* and *unpaid* fees, but *only* as allowed by law. The contrast between the *mandatory* obligation to surrender the client's papers, and the *permissive* retention right, suggests to us that, all other things being equal, the right of the client to possession of *his or her* books and papers prevails over the attorney's retaining lien rights in the case of conflict between the two. This must be so because the assertion of a retaining lien that causes prejudice to a client is inconsistent with the lawyer's continuing duty to his client, particularly since other legal methods are available to collect the fee. * * *

Consequently, where[,] as here, a client furnishes to an attorney original documents needed for anticipated litigation, and the client alleges that he or she cannot pursue the claim further without those documents, the trial court must determine (1) whether the client will suffer serious consequences without them, and (2) whether any prejudice to the client can be mitigated by means other than a return of the documents. If not, the attorney's right to possession of the client's documents—inconsistent with the continuing duty to the client—must yield. While each case will turn on its own particular facts and circumstances, only in this way may the rights of the attorney and client be balanced.

2003 OK CIV APP at ¶¶ 15–21, 69 P.3d at 1213–15.

The RESTATEMENT generally prohibits the "retaining lien" by refusing a lien on client papers for the purpose of securing payment of the lawyer's fee. RESTATEMENT, § 43. Other professional responsibility authorities agree with this prohibition on withholding papers and other client property, at least when retaining these items would prejudice the client's interests. *See, e.g.,* Alaska Bar Ass'n Ethics Comm., Op. 2004–1 (concluding that a lawyer may not withhold a report from an expert or investigator, despite client non-payment, if withholding would harm the client); Ariz. State Bar Comm. on Rules of Prof'l Conduct, Op. 04–01 (2004) (determining that the attorney could retain materials only when doing so would not prejudice the client); Mont. State Bar Ethics Comm., Op. 000210 (2000) (asserting that a retaining lien was improper, absent written consent from the client); *see also Bonner v. Goonewardene*, 800 N.Y.S.2d 821 (Civ.Ct. 2005) (holding that a retaining lien could not attach to a client's passport). Of course, if the withholding of client papers and property will not harm the client, the retaining lien usually has little or no power to influence the client to pay outstanding bills, so this prohibition renders the retaining lien ineffective in most instances.

The RESTATEMENT, however, allows the attorney and the client to provide by contract for a reasonable "charging lien." The RESTATEMENT also exempts "work product" generated by the lawyer from the general prohibition on retaining liens. *See* RESTATEMENT, § 43. Perhaps the latter provision recognizes that these documents are not the property of the client, but are, instead, the property of the lawyer, with the client having, at most, a right of access. *See Corrigan v. Armstrong, Teasdale, Schlafly, Davis & Dicus*, 824 S.W.2d 92 (Mo.Ct.App. 1992).

CHAPTER 4

CONFIDENTIALITY

■ ■ ■

INTRODUCTION

The attorney's obligation of confidentiality has its roots in two distinct but related bodies of law: the rules of evidence and the rules of agency. In the law of evidence, which governs the functioning of the courts and other public agencies, the rule of confidentiality is embodied in the attorney-client privilege and its newer procedural cousin, the "work product" doctrine. These protections are subject to numerous qualifications reflecting accommodation of the private interest in confidentiality with the public interest in informed decisions. Privilege and work product may be claimed against an authoritative demand for information by, or under the sanction of, the government (subpoena, discovery request, or testimony under oath), or a formal offer of evidence by another party in a legal proceeding. In the law of agency, in principle a relationship based on private agreement, the rule of confidentiality is an expression of the agent's duty to protect the principal's interests, and it is understood to apply without regard to the source of the information or to the public or private status of the person to whom unauthorized disclosure might be made. The duty of confidentiality restricts voluntary disclosure of information by the lawyer/agent to persons other than the client. The agent's duty of confidentiality generally covers a much greater range of information than does the attorney-client privilege.

In Section A, we explore the principal limitations of the privilege in relation to the general "ethical" duty of confidentiality expressed in the professional rules. In succeeding sections, we examine several of the most important—and often contested—exceptions to the duty of confidentiality. These exceptions purport to respond to overriding obligations of the attorney to the courts, to non-client third persons, or to the attorney herself. If the attorney is an "agent of the highest order," these sections ask: are there special limits to her devotion to her principal, which might not be applicable to other kinds of agents? Might the attorney be permitted or required to disclose information to others, the use of which in official proceedings would remain limited by the privilege? The debate on these questions continues to occupy our profession.

A. PRIVILEGE AND CONFIDENTIALITY

A(1) THE ROLE OF THE PRIVILEGE IN GENERAL

A(1)(a) The Threshold Concept of "Legal Services"

PROBLEM

Harris Cleveland comes to attorney Jesse Astor and asks Astor to make a large payment of money in Astor's own name to the Baron Corporation, without disclosing from where it came. When asked why he wants to remain anonymous, Cleveland explains that he had embezzled the money from the corporation as its employee and wants to make restitution, but also wants to avoid prosecution. Cleveland explains further that he has already retained other counsel concerning the issues of civil and criminal liability, and is following that attorney's advice in coming to Astor with this request. Astor agrees to make the payment and accepts a substantial fee for the service.

QUESTION

If Baron reports the payment to the police and they demand disclosure from Astor of the identity of the source of the money as well as an explanation of why the payment was made, can Astor be required to disclose?

RULE REFERENCES

Model Rules Preamble ¶ [2] and Model Rule 1.18(a)–(b)
RESTATEMENT § 14

HUGHES v. MEADE

Court of Appeals of Kentucky, 1970.a
453 S.W.2d 538.

CLAY, COMMISSIONER.

This is an original proceeding for a writ of prohibition against the Honorable N. Mitchell Meade, Judge of the Fayette Circuit Court. Petitioner, an attorney, seeks to restrain the respondent from enforcing a contempt ruling entered against him because of his refusal to answer a question as a witness in a criminal trial. Petitioner was not a party to, nor did he represent anyone as an attorney in such proceeding.

The proceeding in which he was called as a witness was the trial of one Williams on a criminal charge involving the theft of an IBM typewriter. Petitioner had participated in the return of an IBM typewriter to the Lexington Police Department. His testimony with respect thereto, and so much thereof as is pertinent to the question presented, is as follows:

Q. "Would you tell the jury the circumstances and how you happened to deliver that typewriter?

---

a. [Before 1976, the Court of Appeals was Kentucky's highest state court. Eds.]

A.   "Well, a certain party called me and employed me because of, first of all, my relationship with the Lexington Police Department, which is very good, and I do entirely criminal law and know all of the policemen and members of the Police Department, and asked me if I could get some property returned without getting me involved in it.

Q.   "Without getting who involved—you or him?

A.   "Without getting me involved. * * *

"So I called Morris Carter, who was then either assistant chief or a major. I know Morris well, and I asked him, I said, 'Morris, are you all interested in getting some stolen property back?' And he said 'Yes we are,' and he said, 'What is it?' I said 'I don't know, I have no idea,' and I said, 'Morris, I don't want to get involved in this thing, I don't want to be called as a witness, all I want to do is get this taken care of.' He said, 'All right, how is it going to be delivered?' And I said, 'Well, I'm watching the cartoons.' It was Saturday morning, and I said, 'Somebody is going to leave it on my front porch,' and the shades were down and I heard a car come up and left, and I called Morris back and I said 'Morris, it's out here,' and he said, 'Okay I'll send somebody out to get it,' * * *.

(Officer Sparks arrived and a taped box was opened disclosing a typewriter.)

Q.   "Can you identify it as to brand or model?

A.   "It was an IBM typewriter, I don't know what model it was.

Q.   "And then did Officer Sparks take possession of the box and the typewriter at that time?

A.   "He took it and took it down town, I guess. * * *

Q.   "And do I understand you correctly that during the period of time from when it arrived and up until Officer Sparks got there you had not seen this typewriter?

A.   "Never seen it. * * *

Q.   "Was this delivered on your property?

A.   "Yes, it was.

Q.   "You didn't want to see who it was?

A.   "No, that's right.

Q.   "You say that the certain party called you and employed you to do what you have just described and said you did, is that correct?

A.   "Yes, sir.

Q.   "Was this the extent of your employment?

A.   "Yes, sir.

Q.   "Have you been paid for that service?

A.   "Yes, sir.

Q. "And I'll ask you now if you will tell us the name of the individual who employed you?

A. "I refuse to answer."

Petitioner was found in contempt of court for failure to identify the person who had called him. It is his contention that this information was a privileged communication * * * and the trial court improperly sought to compel him to disclose it. That subsection of the statute provides (insofar as pertinent):

"No attorney shall testify concerning a *communication* made to him, *in his professional character*, by his client, or his advice thereon without the client's consent * * *." (Emphasis added)

This statutory provision generally conforms to the common law policy and principle of attorney-client privilege (developed since 1800) and it is generally recognized in the United States. See 8 Wigmore, Evidence § 2291 (McNaughton rev. 1961). * * *

Wigmore states the object * * * "is to protect the perfect working of a special relation, wherever confidence is a necessary feature of that perfect working."

Some question has been raised as to whether an attorney-client relationship generally existed between the unknown person and the petitioner, but we believe the question presented is narrower in compass. * * *

[In] NLRB v. Harvey (C.A.4 1965), 349 F.2d 900, 16 A.L.R.3d 1035[,] a detective had been employed by an attorney to take under surveillance a union organizer. In a matter before the National Labor Relations Board[b] the attorney declined to name the client who had employed him to hire the detective. On an appeal from an order [in favor of] the lawyer, the court remanded the case for the district judge to determine the nature and character of the lawyer's employment with respect to the transaction involved.

The affidavit of the lawyer established clearly that the undisclosed person had been his regular and continuing client, for whom various legal services had been furnished and performed. In a well-considered opinion the court * * * concluded that under special circumstances the privilege involving the client's identity may be invoked, but since the "character" of the lawyer's retainer with respect to this transaction was not unequivocally established, the question could be decided only after further proof. [T]he court set forth the criteria to determine this issue in the following language:

"If the District Judge finds from the nature and character of Harvey's employment that Harvey was retained by his client to

---

b. [The Board was investigating charges by the organizer that the surveillance had been ordered by his employer for the purpose of interfering with his federally protected organizing activities. The lawyer denied that his client was the employer but would not otherwise identify him, and the Board sought a court order requiring him to disclose the client's identity. Eds.]

render a legal opinion, perform a legal service or afford representation in legal proceedings and as an incident to this employment he hired the detective, the privilege should be recognized. On the contrary, if Harvey was engaged to obtain information for his client without being retained to furnish a legal opinion, services or representation, in connection with the request for information, the privilege does not exist and he must disclose the name of his client and comply with the subpoena." * * *

[I]t is the opinion of the majority of the court that whether or not a bona fide attorney-client relationship existed between the petitioner and the undisclosed person, the principal transaction involved, i.e., the delivery of stolen property to the police department, was not an act in the professional capacity of petitioner nor was it the rendition of a legal service. He was acting as an agent or conduit for the delivery of property which was completely unrelated to legal representation. While repose of confidence in an attorney is something much to be desired, to use him as a shield to conceal transactions involving stolen property is beyond the scope of his professional duty and beyond the scope of the privilege. * * *

The petition for a writ of prohibition is denied.

DEAN v. DEAN

District Court of Appeal of Florida, Fourth District, 1992.
607 So.2d 494.

FARMER, JUDGE.

The issue raised here is whether the attorney-client privilege can be used to prevent the disclosure of the identity of a person who had previously consulted an attorney regarding the return of stolen property belonging to one of the parties in a civil case. As we explain along the way, under the circumstances of this case the privilege bars such disclosure.

The facts are unusual, to say the least. During the pendency of the Deans' dissolution of marriage case, the husband's place of business was allegedly burgled, resulting in the loss of two duffel bags containing various personal items belonging to husband's daughter, and from $35,000 to $40,000 in cash. Sometime after the theft, an unidentified person telephoned Krischer at his office. He related the conversation as follows:

I received a telephone call from an individual who knew that I was an attorney; knew I was an attorney that was involved in the Baltes[1] matter and the individual asked me for advice with regard to returning property. I advised this person on the telephone that the experience that I have had in the State Attorney's office was that the best avenue was to turn the property over to an attorney and let the

1. This refers to a widely publicized case in which a hit-and-run driver consulted Krischer for advice and, afterwards, Krischer asserted the attorney-client privilege when asked to disclose the name of the driver. The fact that the person consulting Krischer in this case referred to the widely publicized case when Krischer kept the identity of his contact confidential might reasonably be taken as evidencing the contact's strong interest in confidentiality.

attorney bring it to the State Attorney's office or to the law enforcement.

At another point, Krischer added:

> Obviously I have been through this before and I knew all the questions to ask this person and I got all the responses back which indicate[d] to me this person knew I was a lawyer, was asking for legal advice and did not want their identity revealed.

Krischer met twice and had one telephone conversation with this person. Nearly six weeks after the second meeting, the two duffel bags containing only the daughter's personal property were delivered to Krischer's office by someone who told his receptionist that he "would know what they are." No cash was included with the returned items. Krischer then delivered the bags to the police, telling them that they "may have some connection with" husband.

In a twist of irony, these events came to light through Krischer's former secretary, who had also by then become a client of husband's lawyer. Soon after, husband's lawyer served Krischer with a subpoena for a deposition, seeking the identity of Krischer's contact. Krischer asserted the privilege at the deposition. Husband then moved to compel the testimony. After a hearing, the trial court granted the motion * * *.

It is * * * necessary in this case that we focus not on what Krischer did but on what the client intended. Krischer testified that his contact sought legal advice from him—which is, he contends, paradigmatically a legal service—and hence became his client for the purpose of invoking the privilege. We agree.

Krischer's testimony makes plain the intent of his client.

Q. Is it true that the employment by you, by person "x" was predicated on the fact that you would keep person "x's" identity confidential?

A. Yes, that was the condition of the employment.

Q. Was your employment also a condition that you were person "x's" lawyer for all purposes?

A. Correct. The individual called—I can expedite this if I can state a couple of things, judge. I had obviously been through this previously in another case. I was well aware of what was needed to be established in order to protect this client. I inquired of this client if that individual knew I was an attorney. That individual indicated that they did. I inquired if they were seeking legal advice. They indicated that they did. They discussed a legal problem with me. I gave them legal advice.

A condition precedent to this person discussing the legal problem with me was that I not divulge their identity. This person came to me with knowledge of my previous actions in a previous case and felt that I could be trusted, and on that condition precedent I listened to the problem, gave advise [sic] and rendered legal services. * * *

[W]e conclude that the trial court has misinterpreted the privilege and the policies underlying it. It is indisputable that his contact, like the client in *Anderson* [*v. State*, 297 So.2d 871 (Fla.Dist.Ct.App. 1974)], consulted Krischer as an attorney. It is indisputable that the client sought legal advice about a specific matter. It is indisputable that the specific matter concerned a crime that had already been committed, not a planned or future act which might be a crime. And it is indisputable that the client insisted on confidence.

The focus, as we have seen from the common law development of the privilege and our own [statutory] definition of "client", is on the perspective of the person seeking out the lawyer, not on what the lawyer does after the consultation. As we have also seen, it has long been understood that the representation of a client in a court or legal proceeding is not indispensable for the invocation of the privilege. That Krischer's client sought him out for purely legal advice was enough. Legal advice, after all, is by itself a legal service. It is not necessary to the existence of the privilege that the lawyer render some additional service connected with the legal advice. Nor, as we know, is it even necessary that the lawyer appear in court or contemplate some pending or future legal proceeding.

And even if it were, the engagement of an attorney to effect the return of stolen property should certainly qualify. Surely there is a public purpose served by getting stolen property in the hands of the police authorities, even if the identity of the thief is not thereby revealed. Here the consultation resulted in exactly that. Krischer advised his client to turn over the property to the state attorney or the police. A lawyer's advice can be expected to result in the return of the property if the confidentiality of the consultation is insured.

[T]he mere fact that the consulted attorney acts as a "conduit" for the return of stolen property does not support the conclusion that the attorney has engaged in unprotected consultation with the person seeking the advice.[7] A legal service has been rendered just as surely as when the lawyer represents the accused thief in a criminal trial.

NOTES ON LEGAL SERVICES, CONFIDENTIALITY, AND THE ATTORNEY-CLIENT RELATIONSHIP

1. **Does the Relationship or the Service Determine the Availability of the Privilege?** In *Hughes*, was an attorney-client relationship created

---

7. In contrast, the attorney in [*Hughes v. Meade*, 453 S.W.2d 538 (Ky. 1970),] testified that he had been contacted only to deliver stolen property to the police. His contact reached out for him, not because he was a lawyer, but instead because he was a good friend of many members of the police force. Unlike Krischer here, he gave no legal advice. His services amounted to a phone call informing the police that, if they were interested in the return of stolen property, they could pick it up on the attorney's front porch. Not surprisingly, the court determined that this attorney rendered no legal service, and therefore could not invoke the attorney-client privilege. 453 S.W.2d at 542.

by the "client's" request for assistance in returning the stolen typewriter? Clearly the Kentucky court considered the requested service not to be a "legal service." Therefore, if that were the only relationship between the two it was not a "client-lawyer relationship." The court is at some pains to point out, however, that even if such a relationship existed for other purposes, it would not support a claim of privilege with respect to the particular service at issue if that were not a "legal service." See also Section 68 of the RESTATEMENT, which makes clear that the privilege applies only to communications made "for the purpose of obtaining or providing legal assistance for the client."

Does the *Dean* court persuasively distinguish between its case and that in *Hughes* in this respect? Is it consistent, for example, with the principle of the *NLRB* case on which the *Hughes* court relies? Is there an important difference, in terms of the policies underlying the special status of the relationship, between a client who tells a lawyer, "I want you to return certain stolen property to the police without telling them where you got it, and without yourself getting involved with ownership or possession of the property," and one who tells a lawyer, "I want to get certain stolen property returned without being implicated. Can I do that, and, if so, how"? The next problem and associated materials and notes, exploring the parameters of the privilege, may help to answer that question.

2. **How Should the Lawyer Respond to Such Requests?** Is our problem more like *Hughes* or *Dean*? Can you construct a dialogue for Jesse Astor to initiate, having heard Cleveland's request, that would lead to his being able to assure Cleveland that the client's identity will be protected?

3. **The Duty of Confidentiality:** Did the lawyer in *Hughes*, once he agreed to perform the requested service, have a professional duty of confidentiality with respect to his client's identity, so that, for example, he could be disciplined for telling a friend about it over a cocktail? It is not clear whether the RESTATEMENT's limiting definition of the relationship is incorporated into Model Rule 1.6, the general rule on the duty of confidentiality owed to a "client." Careless breach of a promise made in a non-professional capacity could, however, be "professional misconduct" within the meaning of Model Rule 8.4(c), as "involving dishonesty, fraud, deceit or misrepresentation."

The Model Rule 1.6 duty of confidentiality covers substantially more information than the communications protected by the attorney-client privilege, because the attorney's Model Rule 1.6 duty of confidentiality applies to all "information relating the representation of a client." As a result of this wide reaching duty, attorneys must be careful to not disclose any information about their clients. This broad duty of confidentiality also applies to modern electronic communications. *See, e.g.*, L.A. Cnty. Bar Ass'n Prof'l Resp. & Ethics Comm., Formal Op. 514 (2005) (noting that attorney's listserv postings should not include details about clients' cases); Or. State Bar Legal Ethics Comm., Op. 2011–184 (similar); N.Y. State Bar Ass'n Comm. on Prof'l Ethics, Op. 782 (2004) (concluding that attorneys must be careful to protect from disclosure of confidential information in metadata).

4. **Confidentiality Duty to Prospective Clients:** Would there be such a duty if the lawyer had ultimately refused to accept the assignment? Model Rule 1.18(a), briefly discussed in *supra* section 3(B)(1), note 2, consid-

ers any person who discusses the "possibility of forming a client-lawyer relationship" with a lawyer to be a "prospective client." Model Rule 1.18(b) imposes a general duty of confidentiality; but this rule, too, lacks a definition of the relationship. Section 15 of the RESTATEMENT sets forth the same "prospective client" rule, but section 14's definition of the relationship would presumably preclude application of section 15 to the *Hughes* situation.

A(1)(b) Attorney–Client Privilege

PROBLEM

Benjamin Harris, a sole practitioner, has been retained as general outside attorney for Smarr Machine Corporation. The company manufactures small electric machines for industrial use. Shortly after being retained, Harris takes a regular tour of the company's main plant designed to acquaint new employees and other interested persons with the operation. During the tour, while the foreman of one assembly line is explaining the process to Harris' group, a malfunction occurs on the line, signaled by a buzzer and a red warning light. The foreman explains the nature of the malfunction to the group and points out that, as a matter of routine, the machine being assembled at that point will be caught at the end of the line and rejected.

A few months later, an employee of another company sues Smarr for personal injuries suffered as a result of a breakdown allegedly caused by a defect in a machine sold by Smarr to the plaintiff's employer. Harris investigates and discovers that the machine complained of was assembled on the date of his tour, and the alleged defect is one that would have been produced by the malfunction that the group observed. Harris talks to the foreman, and she tells him that she has no record of having rejected any product on that day.

Harris also talks to John Jones, the owner of a manufacturing company which uses a substantial number of Smarr machines, who was in the group taking the plant tour on the day in question. At the close of this interview, Harris prepares and Jones signs a statement setting forth what Jones observed that day, including what the foreman said to the group.

Harris meets an old friend at a cocktail party and regales him with the story of the tour and the subsequent lawsuit. The friend, who turns out to be married to a partner in the plaintiff's law firm, passes the story on to her.

QUESTIONS

(a) Plaintiff's counsel now serves notice of Harris' deposition. May Harris refuse to answer questions (i) about what he observed, (ii) about what the foreman told him on the day of the tour, or (iii) about what the foreman told him later in the course of his investigation?

(b) As a result of the cocktail party conversation, plaintiff's counsel is able to locate other witnesses and establish the facts surrounding the line malfunction. Is Harris subject to disciplinary action for his disclosure?

RULE REFERENCES

Model Rule 1.6 and commentary

RESTATEMENT §§ 68–73

NOTES ON THE SCOPE OF THE PRIVILEGE

1. **Wigmore View:** Perhaps the most widely quoted definition of the attorney-client privilege is that of Professor Wigmore:

> (1) Where legal advice of any kind is sought (2) from a professional legal adviser in his capacity as such, (3) the communications relating to that purpose, (4) made in confidence (5) by the client, (6) are at his instance permanently protected (7) from disclosure by himself or by the legal adviser, (8) except the protection be waived.

8 Wigmore, Evidence § 2292, at 554 (McNaughton rev. ed., 1961).

While other authorities such as McCormick on Evidence, ch. 10 (Broun et al. eds., 6th ed. 2006), the Model Code of Evidence Rule 209 (A.L.I. 1942), the Uniform Rules of Evidence, Rule 502 (2005), section 68 of the RESTATEMENT, and the ABA Task Force on Attorney–Client Privilege, *see Report of the American Bar Association's Task Force on the Attorney–Client Privilege*, 10 Bus.Law. 1029 (2005), take a broader view of the privilege on particular issues, there is agreement on several points. The privilege belongs to the client, and can be invoked by the attorney only on behalf of the client, although the attorney's authority to do so is presumed. *See* Unif.R.Evid., Rule 502(c). Only the client can waive the privilege, and only the client (if a party to the proceedings) can appeal from an erroneous denial of privilege. *See* McCormick on Evidence § 92. It is a protection against unauthorized disclosure by the attorney or anyone else, as well as a right to refuse to disclose. *See* Unif.R.Evid., Rule 502(b). Its purpose is to protect the attorney-client relationship, and especially its role in the adversary system, by promoting full disclosure and free communication. *See* McCormick on Evidence § 87.

The following notes, without pretense to completeness, illustrate some of the more important substantive issues reflected in Wigmore's definition.

2. **"Legal Adviser":** As indicated by *Hughes* and *Dean*, a privileged communication must be made to or received from someone believed by the client to be an attorney acting as such. *See also* McCormick on Evidence § 88; 8 Wigmore, Evidence § 2302. In *Fisher v. United States*, 425 U.S. 391 (1976), taxpayers under IRS investigation for possible civil or criminal liability obtained certain documents from their accountants relating to the accountants' preparation of their tax returns, and shortly thereafter turned the documents over to their lawyers. The IRS then subpoenaed the documents from the lawyers, all of whom refused to comply on the ground of the client's privilege. The Court held that: (i) the client's Fifth Amendment privilege against self-incrimination is not violated by compelling production from the client's attorney; (ii) the attorney-client privilege does not protect pre-existing

documents transferred to the attorney, unless they would be protected in the hands of the client; (iii) accountants' working papers do not involve testimonial communication by the taxpayer, and therefore are subject to compelled production in the hands of the taxpayer. The subpoenas were thus enforceable.

3. **"Communications":** Facts that are observed by the attorney as a result of privileged communications are themselves also privileged, *see Rubin v. State*, 602 A.2d 677 (Md. 1992), although information acquired or facts observed not in any way attributable to client communications are not, *see* McCormick on Evidence § 89. In particular, it is clear that the privilege does not extend to physical evidence received by the attorney from third persons not acting as agents for the client. In *Morrell v. State*, 575 P.2d 1200 (Alaska 1978), the client filed a motion to suppress a legal pad containing an apparent kidnapping plan. The legal pad was given to the client's lawyer by the client's tenant and then turned over to the prosecution. The pad was not suppressed. It has also been held proper to admit attorney testimony concerning the circumstances of receipt of evidence from such third person. *Dyas v. State*, 539 S.W.2d 251 (Ark. 1976). Moreover, the privilege does not extend to physical evidence received from the client. A subpoena *duces tecum* directed to an attorney, which sought production of money delivered to the attorney by clients suspected of bank robbery, was sustained in *In re January 1976 Grand Jury*, 534 F.2d 719 (7th Cir. 1976). In both *Hughes* and *Dean*, then, there was no dispute about the physical evidence being privileged. It was not.

4. **"Made in Confidence":** The privilege applies only to communications that the client intends to be confidential, McCormick on Evidence § 91; 8 Wigmore, Evidence § 2311. It does not apply to communications clearly intended to be disclosed, such as a suicide note, *People v. Doe*, 375 N.E.2d 975 (Ill.App.Ct. 1978). Nor does it apply to statements knowingly made in the presence of third persons, *see Lynch v. Hamrick*, 968 So.2d 11 (Ala. 2007) (holding that privilege did not apply to conversation between attorney and client, because the client's daughter was present); *People v. Urbano*, 26 Cal.Rptr.3d 871, 875–76 (Ct.App. 2005) (holding that attorney-client privilege did not apply when a client "spoke to his attorney loudly enough" in a courtroom that spectators sitting in the last row of seats could hear), if they are not agents of the attorney or the client reasonably needed to protect the interests of the litigants, *United States v. Landof*, 591 F.2d 36 (9th Cir. 1978), or if their intended function is that of public witness, such as witness to a will, *Cubbage v. Gray*, 411 S.W.2d 28 (Ky. 1967). On the other hand, a court has held that the mere fact that the information conveyed is public knowledge does not destroy the privilege if the client intended it to be confidential, *State v. Valdez*, 618 P.2d 1234 (N.M. 1980).

Some modern forms of communication have made it harder to assert that communications were made in confidence, especially when the persons communicating knew about possible interception of the communications by third parties. For example, even though a state statute provided that access to electronic communications by those facilitating or storing electronic communication did not defeat the attorney-client privilege, a California court held that an employee of a company that warned in its employee handbook that employees had no right to privacy in e-mails sent via company computers did not communicate in confidence when she sent an e-mail on the company computer. *Holmes v. Petrovich Dev. Co.*, 119 Cal.Rptr.3d 878, 893–99 (Ct.App. 2011); *see also Alamar Ranch, LLC v. Cnty. of Boise*, No. CV–09–004–S–BLW, 2009 WL 3669741, at *4 (D. Idaho Nov. 2, 2009) (similar); *but see Convertino v. U.S. Dept. of Justice*, 674 F.Supp.2d 97, 108–10 (D.D.C. 2009) (holding that a DOJ employee's e-mails from his work account to his personal attorney were protected by attorney-client privilege); *Stengart v. Loving Care Agency, Inc.*, 990 A.2d 650 (N.J. 2010) (finding an expectation of privacy despite use of employer's computer, where employee used her personal, password-protected e-mail account). For a discussion of the application of privilege to electronic communications, see John M. Barkett, *The Challenge of Electronic Communications: Privilege, Privacy, and Other Myths*, Litig., Fall 2011, at 17.

5. **"By the Client":** While Wigmore's statement was once understood to restrict the privilege to communications by the client, protecting attorney communications only insofar as they would disclose information obtained from the client, *United States v. King*, 536 F.Supp. 253, 261 (C.D.Cal. 1982), the prevailing view today is that it extends to communications between lawyer and client without regard to direction. Unif.R.Evid., Rule 502(b); McCormick on Evidence § 89. Section 68 of the RESTATEMENT takes the broader view, protecting communications "between privileged persons," who are defined in section 70 to include the client, the lawyer, and their agents for the representation.

6. **Corporate/Entity Clients:** Where the client is a corporation or other juridical entity, the question arises: To which corporate agents does the privilege extend? The next case helps to answer this question.

UPJOHN CO. v. UNITED STATES

Supreme Court of the United States, 1981.
449 U.S. 383.

[Upjohn's general counsel Thomas was informed by independent accountants auditing one of Upjohn's foreign subsidiaries that it had made payments to foreign governments. After consulting with outside counsel and his Board chairman, Thomas decided to conduct a confidential internal investigation of such payments among all foreign subsidiaries, which included a questionnaire directed to "All Foreign General and Area Managers" * * * to be returned directly to Thomas. The company eventually submitted a report to the SEC and IRS concerning certain payments, and disclosed to IRS investigators a list of respondents to the questionnaire. An IRS demand for the questionnaires themselves was resisted on the ground of privilege and work product. On certiorari from rulings adverse to the company, the Supreme Court reversed. The portion of JUSTICE REHNQUIST's opinion dealing with the claim of privilege follows:]

II

Federal Rule of Evidence 501 provides that "the privilege of a witness ... shall be governed by the principles of the common law as they may be interpreted by the courts of the United States in light of reason and experience." The attorney-client privilege is the oldest of the privileges for confidential communications known to the common law. 8 J. Wigmore, Evidence § 2290 (McNaughton rev. 1961). Its purpose is to encourage full and frank communication between attorneys and their clients and thereby promote broader public interests in the observance of law and administration of justice. The privilege recognizes that sound legal advice or advocacy serves public ends and that such advice or advocacy depends upon the lawyer's being fully informed by the client. As we stated last Term in *Trammel v. United States*, 445 U.S. 40, 51, 100 S.Ct. 906, 913, 63 L.Ed.2d 186 (1980): "The lawyer-client privilege rests on the need for the advocate and counselor to know all that relates to the client's reasons for seeking representation if the professional mission is to be carried out." And in *Fisher v. United States*, 425 U.S. 391, 403, 96 S.Ct. 1569, 1577, 48 L.Ed.2d 39 (1976), we recognized the purpose of the privilege to be "to encourage clients to make full disclosure to their attorneys." * * *

The Court of Appeals, however, considered the application of the privilege in the corporate context to present a "different problem," since the client was an inanimate entity and "only the senior management, guiding and integrating the several operations, ... can be said to possess an identity analogous to the corporation as a whole." * * * The first case to articulate the so-called "control group test" adopted by the court below, *Philadelphia v. Westinghouse Electric Corp.*, 210 F.Supp. 483, 485 (ED Pa.), petition for mandamus and prohibition denied *sub nom. General Electric Co. v. Kirkpatrick*, 312 F.2d 742 (CA3 1962), cert. denied, 372 U.S. 943, 83 S.Ct. 937, 9 L.Ed.2d 969 (1963), reflected a similar conceptual approach:

> "Keeping in mind that the question is, Is it the corporation which is seeking the lawyer's advice when the asserted privileged communication is made?, the most satisfactory solution, I think, is that if the employee making the communication, of whatever rank he may be, is in a position to control or even to take a substantial part in a decision about any action which the corporation may take upon the advice of the attorney, ... then, in effect, *he is (or personifies) the corporation* when he makes his disclosure to the lawyer and the privilege would apply." (Emphasis supplied.)

Such a view, we think, overlooks the fact that the privilege exists to protect not only the giving of professional advice to those who can act on it but also the giving of information to the lawyer to enable him to give sound and informed advice. * * *

In the case of the individual client the provider of information and the person who acts on the lawyer's advice are one and the same. In the corporate context, however, it will frequently be employees beyond the control group as defined by the court below—"officers and agents ... responsible for directing [the company's] actions in response to legal advice"—who will possess the information needed by the corporation's lawyers. Middle-level—and indeed lower-level—employees can, by actions within the scope of their employment, embroil the corporation in serious legal difficulties, and it is only natural that these employees would have the relevant information needed by corporate counsel if he is adequately to advise the client with respect to such actual or potential difficulties. * * *

The control group test adopted by the court below thus frustrates the very purpose of the privilege by discouraging the communication of relevant information by employees of the client to attorneys seeking to render legal advice to the client corporation. The attorney's advice will also frequently be more significant to noncontrol group members than to those who officially sanction the advice, and the control group test makes it more difficult to convey full and frank legal advice to the employees who will put into effect the client corporation's policy. * * *

The narrow scope given the attorney-client privilege by the court below not only makes it difficult for corporate attorneys to formulate sound advice when their client is faced with a specific legal problem but also threatens to limit the valuable efforts of corporate counsel to ensure their client's compliance with the law. In light of the vast and complicated array of regulatory legislation confronting the modern corporation, corporations, unlike most individuals, "constantly go to lawyers to find out how to obey the law" * * *. The test adopted by the court below is difficult to apply in practice, though no abstractly formulated and unvarying "test" will necessarily enable courts to decide questions such as this with mathematical precision. But if the purpose of the attorney-client privilege is to be served, the attorney and client must be able to predict with some degree of certainty whether particular discussions will be protected. An uncertain privilege, or one which purports to be certain but results in widely varying applications by the courts, is little better than no privilege at all. The very terms of the test adopted by the court below suggest the unpredictability of its application. The test restricts the availability of the privilege to those officers who play a "substantial role" in deciding and directing a corporation's legal response. * * *

The communications at issue were made by Upjohn employees to counsel for Upjohn acting as such, at the direction of corporate superiors in order to secure legal advice from counsel. As the Magistrate found, "Mr. Thomas consulted with the Chairman of the Board and outside counsel and thereafter conducted a factual investigation to determine the nature and extent of the questionable payments *and to be in a position to give legal advice to the company with respect to the payments.*" (Emphasis supplied.) * * * Information, not available from upper-echelon management, was needed to supply a basis for legal advice concerning compliance with securities and tax laws, foreign laws, currency regulations, duties to shareholders, and potential litigation in each of these areas. The communications concerned matters within the scope of the employees' corporate duties, and the employees themselves were sufficiently aware that they were being questioned in order that the corporation could obtain legal advice. The questionnaire identified Thomas as "the company's General

Counsel" and referred in its opening sentence to the possible illegality of payments such as the ones on which information was sought. * * *

A statement of policy accompanying the questionnaire clearly indicated the legal implications of the investigation. The policy statement was issued "in order that there be no uncertainty in the future as to the policy with respect to the practices which are the subject of this investigation." It began "Upjohn will comply with all laws and regulations," and stated that commissions or payments "will not be used as a subterfuge for bribes or illegal payments" and that all payments must be "proper and legal." Any future agreements with foreign distributors or agents were to be approved "by a company attorney" and any questions concerning the policy were to be referred "to the company's General Counsel." * * * This statement was issued to Upjohn employees worldwide, so that even those interviewees not receiving a questionnaire were aware of the legal implications of the interviews. Pursuant to explicit instructions from the Chairman of the Board, the communications were considered "highly confidential" when made, * * * and have been kept confidential by the company. Consistent with the underlying purposes of the attorney-client privilege, these communications must be protected against compelled disclosure.

The Court of Appeals declined to extend the attorney-client privilege beyond the limits of the control group test for fear that doing so would entail severe burdens on discovery and create a broad "zone of silence" over corporate affairs. Application of the attorney-client privilege to communications such as those involved here, however, puts the adversary in no worse position than if the communications had never taken place. The privilege only protects disclosure of communications; it does not protect disclosure of the underlying facts by those who communicated with the attorney:

> "[T]he protection of the privilege extends only to *communications* and not to facts. A fact is one thing and a communication concerning that fact is an entirely different thing. The client cannot be compelled to answer the question, 'What did you say or write to the attorney?' but may not refuse to disclose any relevant fact within his knowledge merely because he incorporated a statement of such fact into his communication to his attorney." *Philadelphia v. Westinghouse Electric Corp.*, 205 F.Supp. 830, 831 (ED Pa.1962). * * *

Here the Government was free to question the employees who communicated with Thomas and outside counsel. Upjohn has provided the IRS with a list of such employees, and the IRS has already interviewed some 25 of them. While it would probably be more convenient for the Government to secure the results of petitioner's internal investigation by simply subpoenaing the questionnaires and notes taken by petitioner's attorneys, such considerations of convenience do not overcome the policies served by the attorney-client privilege. As Justice Jackson noted in his concurring opinion in *Hickman v. Taylor*, 329 U.S., at 516, 67 S.Ct., at 396: "Discovery was hardly intended to enable a learned profession to perform its functions . . . on wits borrowed from the adversary."

[W]e conclude that the narrow "control group test" sanctioned by the Court of Appeals, in this case cannot, consistent with "the principles of the common law as . . . interpreted . . . in the light of reason and experience," Fed. Rule Evid. 501, govern the development of the law in this area.

NOTES ON PRIVILEGE AND ITS EXCEPTIONS

1. **Corporate Privilege:** As *Upjohn* noted, many courts used the "control group" test before this decision. After *Upjohn*, the Uniform Rules of Evidence were amended to incorporate its holding by defining "representative of the client" as including a "person who, for the purpose of effectuating legal representation for the client, makes or receives a confidential communication while acting in the scope of employment for the client." Rule 502(a)(2) (1986). For a helpful discussion of the principal alternatives to the "control group" test rejected in *Upjohn*, with extensive references to the literature, see Note, *The Attorney–Client Privilege and the Corporate Client: Where Do We Go After* Upjohn?, 81 Mich.L.Rev. 665 (1983).

As is typical with U.S. Supreme Court cases, even in areas dominated by state law, *Upjohn* has been highly influential, with several states adopting its subject-matter approach. Edward J. Imwinkelried & Andrew Amoroso, *The Application of The Attorney–Client Privilege to Interactions Among Clients, Attorneys, and Experts in the Age of Consultants: The Need for a More Precise, Fundamental Analysis*, 48 Hous.L.Rev. 265, 296–97 (2011). However, some states still retain the control group test. *See* Thomas R. Mulroy & Eric J. Muñoz, *The Internal Corporate Investigation*, 1 DePaul Bus. & Com.L.J. 49, 54 (2002) (listing fourteen states with *Upjohn* test and eight with control group test).

2. **Exceptions to Privilege—Aid to Future Crime or Fraud**: A client calls his attorney by operator-assisted long distance telephone and tells him that he has killed another person. The attorney asks the client if he has gotten rid of the weapon, and the client says "no." The attorney instructs the client to get rid of the weapon and to sit tight, making sure not to talk to anyone until the attorney arrives. The telephone company operator overhears the conversation, contrary to company rules. The Texas Court of Criminal Appeals held that the trial judge did not err in receiving the operator's testimony. The conversation was not privileged, because its purpose was to counsel commission of the further crime of, essentially, obstruction of justice. *Clark v. State*, 261 S.W.2d 339 (Tex.Crim.App. 1953).

Is there a risk here of punishing a client intending no further crime, for his attorney's lawlessness? Rule 502(d)(1) of the Uniform Rules of Evidence presupposes that the advice is obtained to "commit what the client knew or reasonably should have known was a crime or fraud." On the other hand, if the client seeks advice from an attorney with the intent to further a crime, the crime-fraud exception to the attorney-client privilege applies even if the attorney who is consulted does not know the client has that intent. *See United States v. Doe*, 429 F.3d 450 (3d Cir. 2005).

Note that in *Clark* the attorney-client conversation that showed the improper purpose of the consultation just happened to be overheard by a third party. Absent such a stroke of luck for the prosecution, how can the improper purpose be proven? It is clear that the prosecution bears the burden of proof on this exception, *see In re Grand Jury Proceedings*, 401 F.3d 247, 251 (4th Cir. 2005) (noting that "[t]he party asserting the crime-fraud exception, [usually the prosecution,] must make a prima facie showing that the privileged communications fall within the exception"); *Purcell v. Dist. Att'y*, 676 N.E.2d 436 (Mass. 1997), and that the evidence for it would almost always lie in otherwise protected communications. In *Purcell*, the client in the initial interview made statements to the attorney threatening to set fire to the building from which he was about to be evicted, while seeking legal advice on how to prevent the eviction. The attorney thought the threats were serious, and reported them to the police to prevent them from being carried out. The prosecution relied on the attorney's report to claim, in support of its subpoena to the attorney to testify against the client in the ensuing prosecution for possession of incendiary devices found in the process of eviction, that the purpose of the consultation was to get advice on how to commit the arson or avoid prosecution for it. The court held that there was nothing in the attorney's report or his representation of the client on the eviction matter to warrant a finding of such improper purpose, but that the additional circumstance of client's having been found the next day with incendiary devices could justify an *in camera* hearing of the attorney's testimony concerning the circumstances in which the threatening statements were made to determine whether the improper purpose was shown.

3. **Exceptions to Privilege—Identity of Client**: It is generally said that the identity of the client and the fact of employment are not privileged. *See* McCormick on Evidence § 90. Nonetheless, as in *Dean*, some courts have been willing to protect the client's identity, where under the circumstances of the case disclosure of the client's identity would (i) result in disclosure of a confidential communication (e.g., the client's motive in making the payment or the client's reason for consulting the lawyer), or (ii) would constitute the "last link" in a chain of evidence necessary to convict the client, not simply aid in bringing criminal charges or civil suit against the client. *Id.*

4. **Scope of Privilege Following Client's Death**: Assume that an attorney has otherwise privileged information from a client, who has since died, that the client was responsible for a murder for which an innocent man is currently on trial. Can the attorney's testimony to that effect be introduced in the innocent man's proceeding? Three cases support a case-by-case "balancing approach" to overriding the privilege taking into account extraordinary circumstances.

In *Cohen v. Jenkintown Cab Co.*, 357 A.2d 689 (Pa.Super.Ct. 1976), a tort action brought by a woman severely injured when struck by one of the defendant's cabs, an attorney consulted by one of its drivers who had claimed that he had observed the plaintiff being struck by a hit-and-run car was allowed after the driver's death to testify that the latter had admitted to having driven the car that caused the injury. The court found that the client's rights or interests, in the particular context, could not be adversely affected by admission of the testimony, because he died without any assets or estate and the attorney's information had already been provisionally disclosed by agreement of the parties in a deposition. The court also found that the evidence was not available from any other source.

In *Morales v. Portuondo*, 154 F.Supp.2d 706 (S.D.N.Y. 2001), an attorney was consulted by a person who—with the encouragement of his priest—had confessed to the mother of one friend and the lawyer for a second friend that he had participated in the murder whereas the other two had not. Both of them had been convicted of murder. The factually guilty person was scheduled to testify in support of a motion to set aside the verdict. His attorney advised him to remain silent, in part because the attorney did not believe that his testimony would cause the judge to set aside the verdict. After the client's death eight years later, the priest and others testified at a post-conviction relief hearing in state court, but the request for a new trial was denied because their testimony was inadmissible hearsay and would not have changed the verdict anyway. Finally, a federal habeas corpus proceeding was initiated, and this time the lawyer's testimony was also proffered. The federal judge admitted it despite the privilege, because exclusion of the other witnesses was improper under a hearsay exception and the cumulative effect of the attorney's testimony made it clear that this exclusion constituted harmful error requiring retrial. The fact that the client had wanted to come forward, but refrained from doing so on advice of counsel, was undoubtedly a factor favoring the ruling.

In *People v. Vespucci*, 745 N.Y.S.2d 391 (Nassau Cnty.Ct. 2002), a lawyer in this situation, acting pursuant to advice from a professional responsibility professor, told defense counsel that he had exculpatory information but could not reveal it unless a court ordered him to do so. While the trial judge acknowledged some support in New York law for a *Cohen*-style exception and found most of its criteria to be met, he denied a motion to compel such testimony on the ground that the information was available from another source—the client's former domestic partner.

The RESTATEMENT characterizes a "good cause" exception to the posthumous privilege as "desirable * * * on a litigated issue of pivotal significance," although "[t]he law recognizes no [such] exception." RESTATEMENT, § 77, Comment *d*. The Reporter's Note to this comment cites scholars favoring the exception, but does not acknowledge *Cohen*. *See id.* vol. 1 p. 593. Also, the New York cases were decided after the RESTATEMENT's publication. In *Swidler & Berlin v. United States*, 524 U.S. 399 (1998), the U.S. Supreme Court rejected a balancing test for the criminal context that would have allowed the attorney of a deceased client to be subpoenaed to testify as to the client's disclosures to him regarding possible crimes by government officials, including the deceased, being investigated by an independent counsel and a federal grand jury.

5. **Privilege and Its Relationship to Confidentiality**: Attorney-client privilege is not the only doctrine governing confidentiality. Model Rule 1.6 outlines the attorney's duty of confidentiality regarding client information,

including, but by no means limited to, attorney-client communications. As we will see in the next sections, the Model Rules recognize exceptions to the lawyer's Model Rule 1.6 duty of confidentiality, at least permitting and sometimes even requiring disclosure of otherwise confidential information (i.e., that defined in Model Rule 1.6(a) as "information relating to the representation"). The issues of admissibility of evidence in judicial and quasi-judicial proceedings and the right of an adversary to require disclosure of evidence, however, continue to be governed by the law of privilege and work product. Thus, an attorney whose client leaves voice mail messages threatening a judge who has just ruled against him with violence may be permitted, under Model Rule 1.6(b), to disclose the threatening communication to the judge and to law enforcement authorities in so far as necessary to prevent the client from carrying out the threats, without thereby making the lawyer's testimony concerning the communication admissible in evidence in a criminal proceeding against the client. *In re Grand Jury Investigation*, 902 N.E.2d 929 (Mass. 2009). On the question of whether the privilege should apply at all to such communications, the Massachusetts court declared:

> We * * * hold that [the client's] communications were made in furtherance of the rendition of legal services and thus protected by the attorney-client privilege. * * * Scholars, commentators, and courts have formulated a number of tests for determining the germaneness of a client's communication. However, none of these formulations appears to give clients breathing room to express frustration and dissatisfaction with the legal system and its participants. The expression of such sentiments is a not uncommon incident of the attorney-client relationship, particularly in an adversarial context, and may serve as a springboard for further discussion regarding a client's legal options. If a lawyer suspects that the client intends to act on an expressed intent to commit a crime, the lawyer may attempt to dissuade the client from such action, and failing that, may make a limited disclosure to protect the likely targets. * * *

> Requiring the privilege to yield for purposes of a criminal prosecution not only would hamper attorney-client discourse, but also would discourage lawyers from exercising their discretion to make such disclosures, as occurred here, and thereby frustrate the beneficial public purpose underpinning the discretionary disclosure provision of rule 1.6. * * * Furthermore, any test to ascertain the germaneness of an ostensibly threatening communication on a case-by-case basis would make the privilege's applicability uncertain, rendering the privilege "little better than no privilege." * * *

> Warning clients that communications deemed irrelevant to the matter for which they have retained counsel will not be protected not only may discourage clients from disclosing germane information, but also may disincline clients to share their intentions to engage in criminal behavior. In the latter circumstance, a lawyer's ability to aid in the administration of justice by dissuading a client from engaging in such behavior is impaired. * * * The lawyer also may never receive the very information necessary for him or her to determine whether to make a limited disclosure to prevent the harm contemplated by the client.

Id. at 933–34.

A(1)(c) The Work Product Doctrine

Questions

Return to the problem concerning the plant tour. Assume that plaintiff's counsel serves a subpoena on Harris, demanding a copy of Jones' statement. Must Harris produce the statement? Under what conditions?

UPJOHN CO. v. UNITED STATES

Supreme Court of the United States, 1981.
449 U.S. 383.

[The portion of Justice Rehnquist's opinion concerning the claim of attorney-client privilege is excerpted in *supra* section 4(A)(1)(b). The portion of his opinion dealing with the company's work product claim, which also helpfully explains the distinction between the privilege and the work product doctrine, follows:]

III

Our decision that the communications by Upjohn employees to counsel are covered by the attorney-client privilege disposes of the case so far as the responses to the questionnaires and any notes reflecting responses to interview questions are concerned. The summons reaches further, however, and Thomas has testified that his notes and memoranda of interviews go beyond recording responses to his questions. * * * To the extent that the material subject to the summons is not protected by the attorney-client privilege as disclosing communications between an employee and counsel, we must reach the ruling by the Court of Appeals [rejecting Upjohn's work product claim].

[The work product] doctrine was announced by the Court over 30 years ago in *Hickman v. Taylor*, 329 U.S. 495, 67 S.Ct. 385, 91 L.Ed. 451 (1947). In that case the Court rejected "an attempt, without purported necessity or justification, to secure written statements, private memoranda and personal recollections prepared or formed by an adverse party's counsel in the course of his legal duties." * * * The Court noted that "it is essential that a lawyer work with a certain degree of privacy" and reasoned that if discovery of the material sought were permitted

> "much of what is now put down in writing would remain unwritten. An attorney's thoughts, heretofore inviolate, would not be his own. Inefficiency, unfairness and sharp practices would inevitably develop in the giving of legal advice and in the preparation of cases for trial. The effect on the legal profession would be demoralizing. And the interests of the clients and the cause of justice would be poorly served." * * *

The "strong public policy" underlying the work-product doctrine * * * has been substantially incorporated in Federal Rule of Civil Procedure 26(b)(3).[7] * * *

While conceding the applicability of the work-product doctrine, the Government asserts that it has made a sufficient showing of necessity to overcome its protections. The Magistrate apparently so found * * *. The Government relies on the following language in *Hickman*:

> "We do not mean to say that all written materials obtained or prepared by an adversary's counsel with an eye toward litigation are necessarily free from discovery in all cases. Where relevant and nonprivileged facts remain hidden in an attorney's file and where production of those facts is essential to the preparation of one's case, discovery may properly be had.... And production might be justified where the witnesses are no longer available or can be reached only with difficulty." * * *

The Government stresses that interviewees are scattered across the globe and that Upjohn has forbidden its employees to answer questions it considers irrelevant. The above-quoted language from *Hickman*, however, did not apply to "oral statements made by witnesses ... whether presently in the form of [the attorney's] mental impressions or memoranda." * * * As to such material the Court did "not believe that any showing of necessity can be made under the circumstances of this case so as to justify production.... If there should be a rare situation justifying production of these matters petitioner's case is not of that type." * * * Forcing an attorney to disclose notes and memoranda of witnesses' oral statements is particularly disfavored because it tends to reveal the attorney's mental processes * * *.[8]

Rule 26 * * * permits disclosure of documents and tangible things constituting attorney work product upon a showing of substantial need and inability to obtain the equivalent without undue hardship. This was the standard applied by the Magistrate * * *. Rule 26 goes on, however, to state that "[i]n ordering discovery of such materials when the required showing has been made, the court shall protect against disclosure of the

---

7. This provides, in pertinent part:

"[A] party may obtain discovery of documents and tangible things otherwise discoverable under subdivision (b)(1) of this rule and prepared in anticipation of litigation or for trial by or for another party or by or for that other party's representative (including his attorney, consultant, surety, indemnitor, insurer, or agent) only upon a showing that the party seeking discovery has substantial need of the materials in the preparation of [the party's] case and that [the party] is unable without undue hardship to obtain the substantial equivalent of the materials by other means. In ordering discovery of such materials when the required showing has been made, the court shall protect against disclosure of the mental impressions, conclusions, opinions, or legal theories of an attorney or other representative of a party concerning the litigation."

[Ed.: Rule 26 has been amended since this case. For the latest version of the work product provisions, as of the publication of this text, see *infra* note 2.]

8. Thomas described his notes of the interviews as containing "what I considered to be the important questions, the substance of the responses to them, my beliefs as to the importance of these, my beliefs as to how they related to the inquiry, my thoughts as to how they related to other questions. In some instances they might even suggest other questions that I would have to ask or things that I needed to find elsewhere." * * *

mental impressions, conclusions, opinions or legal theories of an attorney or other representative of a party concerning the litigation." Although this language does not specifically refer to memoranda based on oral statements of witnesses, the *Hickman* court stressed the danger that compelled disclosure of such memoranda would reveal the attorney's mental processes. It is clear that this is the sort of material the draftsmen of the Rule had in mind as deserving special protection. * * *

Based on the foregoing, some courts have concluded that *no* showing of necessity can overcome protection of work product which is based on oral statements from witnesses. * * * Those courts declining to adopt an absolute rule have nonetheless recognized that such material is entitled to special protection. * * *

We do not decide the issue at this time. It is clear that the Magistrate applied the wrong standard when he concluded that the Government had made a sufficient showing of necessity to overcome the protections of the work-product doctrine. * * * The notes and memoranda sought by the Government here, however, are work product based on oral statements. If they reveal communications, they are, in this case, protected by the attorney-client privilege. To the extent they do not reveal communications, they reveal the attorneys' mental processes in evaluating the communications. As Rule 26 and *Hickman* make clear, such work product cannot be disclosed simply on a showing of substantial need and inability to obtain the equivalent without undue hardship.

While we are not prepared at this juncture to say that such material is always protected by the work-product rule, we think a far stronger showing of necessity and unavailability by other means than was made by the Government or applied by the Magistrate in this case would be necessary to compel disclosure. Since the Court of Appeals thought that the work-product protection was never applicable in an enforcement proceeding such as this, and since the Magistrate whose recommendations the District Court adopted applied too lenient a standard of protection, we think the best procedure with respect to this aspect of the case would be to reverse the judgment of the Court of Appeals for the Sixth Circuit and remand the case to it for such further proceedings in connection with the work-product claim as are consistent with this opinion.

NOTES ON WORK PRODUCT

1. The uncertainty expressed in the *Upjohn* opinion about when denial of immunity for lawyer impressions, opinions, etc., would be justified remains unresolved. Section 87(2) of the RESTATEMENT, relying primarily on federal rules and cases, distinguishes between "opinion work product," which consists of "the opinions or mental impressions of a lawyer," and all other work product. Section 89 provides that opinion work product is immune from discovery unless it is waived or "extraordinary circumstances justify disclosure." Comment *d* states that the latter concept "has never been intelligibly defined" and indicates that the courts which invoke it appear simply to be

expressing unwillingness fully to equate work product immunity with the attorney-client privilege.

To test the significance of this uncertainty, consider the facts of *Hickman v. Taylor*: Following a boat accident, the boat manufacturer hired an attorney to investigate and represent the company. In the course of the investigation, the attorney talked to numerous employees, all of whom talked to the attorney in the normal course of their duties so the attorney could make recommendations to the company. The attorney also talked to witnesses, including both passengers and others who observed the events surrounding the accident. From some of these witnesses, the attorney took statements, written in the witness' own hand and signed by them. From other witnesses, the attorney wrote interview notes. Included within those notes were the attorney's impressions of the witnesses, such as "this is a good witness who really seems to know what she saw," or "we need to check the eyesight of this witness[, because it] looks like she wears glasses but did not have them on when I talked to her."

As to each of the actions of the attorney, decide if the activities are protected by attorney-client privilege, are discoverable without limitation as factual information, are discoverable only upon a showing of exceptional circumstance, or are non-discoverable mental impressions.

2. As amended after the *Upjohn* case, the work product provisions of Rule 26 of the Federal Rules of Civil Procedure state:

(b) Discovery Scope and Limits. * * *

(3) *Trial Preparation: Materials.*

(A) *Documents and Tangible Things.* Ordinarily, a party may not discover documents and tangible things that are prepared in anticipation of litigation or for trial by or for another party or its representative (including the other party's attorney, consultant, surety, indemnitor, insurer, or agent). But, subject to Rule 26(b)(4), those materials may be discovered if:

> **(i)** they are otherwise discoverable under Rule 26(b)(1); and

> **(ii)** the party shows that it has substantial need for the materials to prepare its case and cannot, without undue hardship, obtain their substantial equivalent by other means.

(B) *Protection Against Disclosure.* If the court orders discovery of those materials, it must protect against disclosure of the mental impressions, conclusions, opinions, or legal theories of a party's attorney or other representative concerning the litigation.

(C) *Previous Statement.* Any party or other person may, on request and without the required showing, obtain the person's own previous statement about the action or its subject matter. If the request is refused, the person may move for a court order, and Rule 37(a)(5) applies to the award of expenses. A previous statement is either:

> **(i)** a written statement that the person has signed or otherwise adopted or approved; or

(ii) a contemporaneous stenographic, mechanical, electrical, or other recording—or a transcription of it—that recites substantially verbatim the person's oral statement.

A similar protection for work product is provided in the procedural rules of most states, but there is considerable variation in detail. Generally, however, there is enhanced protection for materials that directly reflect a lawyer's mental processes, as in federal Rule 26(b)(3)(B).

A(2) DIRECT EVIDENCE IN THE LAWYER'S POSSESSION

PROBLEM

James Pollin owns a small business that has been failing, and his marriage threatens to break up due to his financial struggles. He has been represented for some years by Mary Barton, a local attorney. Early one morning, Pollin comes to Barton's office in a highly agitated state, carrying a canvas bag which proves to contain a skier's face mask, a pair of gloves, a sawed-off shotgun, and $20,000 in currency of various denominations. He tells Barton a disjointed story about robbing a supermarket the night before, taking the night watchman hostage, and going out into the country with the hostage. He remembers the location where he held the hostage, and thinks he may have killed him, but cannot sort out enough details to be sure. Barton advises Pollin to go to the police, but he refuses. She then persuades him to go to his doctor (whose office is in the same building), leaving the bag and its contents with her. The doctor immediately hospitalizes him, on the basis of a mental breakdown.

By mid-morning of that day, the robbery has been discovered, and a search is on for the watchman. Barton, being careful not to be detected, drives to the remote spot Pollin had mentioned to her, finds the watchman's horribly mutilated body in a hollow tree, takes numerous photographs of the scene, and returns to her office with a set of keys which she found 50 yards or so away from the tree. The keys turn out, as she suspects, to belong to Pollin.

QUESTIONS

(a) After several days of searching, the police are unable to locate the watchman. His family issues a tearful broadcast for help in locating him. Pollin is still in the hospital, and there is no indication of suspicion of him in the matter. What can Barton do, if anything, to respond to the distress of the family?

(b) Eventually, suspicion begins to center on Pollin, who is still in the hospital unable to talk. The police, acting on a hunch, come to Barton with questions. What can she tell them?

RULE REFERENCES

Model Rules 1.6, 3.4(a), and 8.4(c)–(d)

RESTATEMENT § 119

THE CASE OF ROBERT GARROW'S LAWYERS

After a man with a rifle was reported to have kidnapped four young campers in a remote area of New York's Adirondack Mountains, a massive twelve day manhunt resulted in the wounding and capture of Robert Garrow. By that time, one of the bodies of the four had been discovered, and Garrow was charged with his murder. Two Syracuse lawyers, Frank Armani and Francis Belge, were appointed to defend him.

During consultation with his lawyers, Garrow admitted having killed three other persons: one of the remaining bodies had already been found, and Garrow told Armani and Belge how to find the other two, both young women. The lawyers found the bodies by following Garrow's directions, and photographed them—perhaps reassembling one of the bodies in order to photograph it. Within the next several months, each body was found accidentally by passersby.

Both of the deceased were the subjects of intensive search and advertising by their families prior to the discovery of their bodies. The parents of one of the girls came to the lawyers and asked for help in locating her. They would only say that they could not tell them anything. A year after the incident, Garrow was tried for the first murder, and testified, in support of his plea of insanity, not only about that murder but also about the others. The disclosure that the lawyers had known about the bodies months before their discovery, but had remained silent, unleashed a wave of public indignation and debate about lawyers' ethics. The propriety of the lawyers' silence was addressed in two different judicial proceedings. First, in connection with their representation of Garrow by appointment, Armani and Belge submitted claims for compensation beyond the statutorily prescribed amount, alleging not only unusual expenditure of time, but also damage to their practices resulting from the public outcry over their conduct. Second, as a result of the public pressure, Belge was indicted under the New York public health laws for failure to give a dead person a decent burial and for failure to report the death of a person without medical attendance. The two county courts each vindicated the lawyers, granting the additional compensation, on the one hand, and dismissing the indictments on the other. Relevant portions of the opinions follow.

IN RE ARMANI

Hamilton County Court, 1975.
371 N.Y.S.2d 563.

Marthen, Judge. * * *

Who can imagine the anguish of these attorneys, fathers themselves, at having to carry inviolate this confidence knowing full well the agonies endured by the parents of the missing girls? Who can appreciate the torment, after the disclosure was made public, suffered by them as a result of the poisoned pens and poisoned tongues of the self-righteous? Who, indeed, in the legal profession can truly and objectively look back from the comfortable chair of the Monday morning quarterback and say, "I would have done thus and so in spite of the ethic of confidentiality which I am sworn to uphold."? Indeed, who can understand the anguish of having to defend oneself months later against a charge of criminal wrongdoing where one has acted in the highest tradition of the legal profession? * * *

[The court relieved both Armani and Belge from the operation of a state law that would have limited each to a maximum fee of $500 for the case, and awarded them a combined fee of approximately $12,000.]

PEOPLE v. BELGE

Onondaga County Court, 1975.
372 N.Y.S.2d 798, *affirmed*, 376 N.Y.S.2d 771 (1975).

ORMAND N. GALE, JUDGE. * * *

The National Association of Criminal Defense Lawyers, as Amicus Curiae, citing *Times Publishing Co. v. Williams*, 222 So.2d 470, 475 (Fla.App. 1969) succinctly state[s] the issue in the following language:

If this indictment stands,

"The attorney-client privilege will be effectively destroyed. No defendant will be able to freely discuss the facts of his case with his attorney. No attorney will be able to listen to those facts without being faced with the Hobson's choice of violating the law or violating his professional code of Ethics." * * *

The effectiveness of counsel is only as great as the confidentiality of its client-attorney relationship. If the lawyer cannot get all the facts about the case, he can only give his client half of a defense. This, of necessity, involves the client telling his attorney everything remotely connected with the crime.

Apparently, in the instant case, after analyzing all the evidence, and after hearing of the bizarre episodes in the life of their client, [the lawyers] decided that the only possibility of salvation was in a defense of insanity. For the client to disclose not only everything about this particular crime but also everything about other crimes which might have a bearing upon his defense, requires the strictest confidence in, and on the part of, the attorney.

When the facts of the other homicides became public, as a result of the defendant's testimony to substantiate his claim of insanity, "Members of the public were shocked at the apparent callousness of these lawyers, whose conduct was seen as typifying the unhealthy lack of concern of most lawyers with the public interest and with simple decency." A hue and cry went up from the press and other news media suggesting that the attorneys should be found guilty of such crimes as obstruction of justice or becoming an accomplice after the fact. From a layman's standpoint, this certainly was a logical conclusion. However, the constitution of the United States of America attempts to preserve the dignity of the individual and to do that guarantees him the services of an attorney who will bring to the bar and to the bench every conceivable protection from the inroads of the state against such rights as are vested in the constitution for one accused of crime. Among those substantial constitutional rights is that a defendant does not have to incriminate himself. His attorneys were bound to uphold that concept and maintain what has been called a sacred trust of confidentiality.

The following language from the brief of the Amicus Curiae further points up the statements just made:

> "The client's Fifth Amendment rights cannot be violated by his attorney. There is no viable distinction between the personal papers and criminal evidence in the hands or mind of the client. Because the discovery of the body of Alicia Hauck would have presented 'a significant link in a chain of evidence tending to establish his guilt' * * *, Garrow was constitutionally exempt from any statutory requirement to disclose the location of the body. And Attorney Belge, as Garrow's attorney, was not only equally exempt, but under a positive stricture precluding such disclosure. Garrow, although constitutionally privileged against a requirement of compulsory disclosure, was free to make such a revelation if he chose to do so. Attorney Belge was affirmatively required to withhold disclosure. The criminal defendant's self-incrimination rights become completely nugatory if compulsory disclosure can be exacted through his attorney."

In the recent and landmark case of *United States v. Nixon*, 418 U.S. 683, at page 713, 94 S.Ct. 3090, at page 3110, 41 L.Ed.[2d] 1039, at page 1061 the Court stated:

> "The constitutional need for production of relevant evidence in a criminal proceeding is specific and neutral to the fair adjudication of a particular criminal case in the administration of justice. Without access to specific facts a criminal prosecution may be totally frustrated."

In the case at bar we must weigh the importance of the general privilege of confidentiality in the performance of the defendant's duties as an attorney, against the inroads of such a privilege, on the fair administration of criminal justice as well as the heart tearing that went on in the victim's family by reason of their uncertainty as to the whereabouts of Alicia Hauck. In this type [of] situation the Court must balance the rights of the individual against the rights of society as a whole. There is no question but Attorney Belge's failure to bring to the attention of the authorities the whereabouts of Alicia Hauck when he first verified it, prevented bringing Garrow to the immediate bar of justice for this particular murder. This was in a sense, obstruction of justice. This duty, I am sure, loomed large in the mind of Attorney Belge. However, against this was the Fifth Amendment right of his client, Garrow, not to incriminate himself. If the Grand Jury had returned an indictment charging Mr.

Belge with obstruction of justice under a proper statute, the work of this Court would have been much more difficult than it is.

There must always be a conflict between the obstruction of the administration of criminal justice and the preservation of the right against self-incrimination which permeates the mind of the attorney as the alter ego of his client. But that is not the situation before this Court. We have the Fifth Amendment right, derived from the constitution, on the one hand, as against the trivia of a pseudo-criminal statute on the other, which has seldom been brought into play. Clearly the latter is completely out of focus when placed alongside the client-attorney privilege. An examination of the Grand Jury testimony sheds little light on their reasoning. The testimony of Mr. Armani added nothing new to the facts as already presented to the Grand Jury. He and Mr. Belge were co-counsel. Both were answerable to the [Model Rules]. The Grand Jury chose to indict one and not the other. It appears as if that body were grasping at straws.

It is the decision of this Court that Francis R. Belge conducted himself as an officer of the Court with all the zeal at his command to protect the constitutional rights of his client. Both on the grounds of a privileged communication and in the interests of justice the Indictment is dismissed.

NOTES ON ARMANI AND BELGE

1. **Ethics Proceedings Against Armani and Belge:** See New York State Bar Association Committee on Professional Ethics, Formal Opinion 479, 50 N.Y.St.B.J. 259 (1978), finding no impropriety in the lawyers' conduct (other than possible tampering with physical evidence).

From the extensive contemporary discussion of this case, see Monroe H. Freedman, Lawyers' Ethics in an Adversary System (1975); Elgin Edwards, *Hard Answers for Hard Questions: Dissenting in Part from Dean Freedman's Views on the Attorney–Client Privilege*, 11 Crim.L.Bull. 478 (1975), *with a reply by* Monroe Freedman, *Legal Ethics: Confidentiality and the Case of Robert Garrow's Lawyers*, 25 Buff.L.Rev. 211 (1975); J. Michael Callan & Harris David, *Professional Responsibility and the Duty of Confidentiality: Disclosure of Client Misconduct in an Adversary System*, 29 Rutgers L.Rev. 332 (1976).

2. **Obstruction of Justice:** The court in *People v. Belge* indicates that it would have more difficulty with a charge of "obstruction of justice." Why? The New York crime that might have been charged in the case is defined in New York Penal Law §§ 205.50–.65. Section 205.50 provides as follows:

§ 205.50. Hindering prosecution; definition of term

As used in sections 205.55, 205.60 and 205.65 [defining variants of the generic crime], a person "renders criminal assistance" when, with intent to prevent, hinder or delay the discovery or apprehension of, or the lodging of a criminal charge against, a person who he knows or believes has committed a crime or is being sought by law enforcement officials for the commission of a crime, or with intent to assist a person in profiting or benefiting from the commission of a crime, he:

1. Harbors or conceals such a person; or

2. Warns such a person of impending discovery or apprehension; or

3. Provides such person with money, transportation, weapon, disguise or other means of avoiding discovery or apprehension; or

4. Prevents or obstructs, by means of force, intimidation or deception, anyone from performing an act which might aid in the discovery or apprehension of such person or in the lodging of a criminal charge against him; or

5. Suppresses, by any act of concealment, alteration or destruction, any physical evidence which might aid in the discovery or apprehension of such person or in the lodging of a criminal charge against him; or

6. Aids such person to protect or expeditiously profit from an advantage derived from such crime.

See also Model Penal Code § 242.3. Would it be unethical for a lawyer to engage in conduct that violates this criminal law? *See* Model Rule 8.4(b), (c) & (d). The next case addresses the implications of applying such a criminal statute to lawyers representing criminal defendants, while recognizing their duty to turn physical evidence over to the prosecution.

QUESTIONS ON PHYSICAL AND OTHER EVIDENCE

Return to the night watchman problem. Are the canvas bag and its contents, the keys, or the photographs subject to compelled production on demand of the police? What should Barton do with them?

COMMONWEALTH v. STENHACH

Superior Court of Pennsylvania, 1986.
514 A.2d 114.

HESTER, JUDGE:

Two criminal defense attorneys have appealed from convictions for hindering prosecution and tampering with evidence arising from their conduct while representing a defendant in a murder trial. Appellants George and Walter Stenhach were young public defenders appointed to represent Richard Buchanan, a man charged with first degree murder. Following Buchanan's directions, appellants recovered a rifle stock used in the homicide. Allegedly believing that disclosure of the rifle stock would be legally and ethically prohibited, appellants did not deliver it to the prosecutor until ordered to do so by the court during the prosecution's case. After Buchanan's conviction of third degree murder, appellants were charged with hindering prosecution, * * * tampering with physical evidence, * * * criminal conspiracy, * * * and criminal solicitation * * *. A jury found both appellants guilty of hindering prosecution, a third degree felony, and tampering, a second degree misdemeanor. In addition, George was convicted of solicitation, and Walter of conspiracy. Each was sentenced to twelve months probation and a fine of $750. * * *

We reject appellants' argument that their retention of physical evidence was proper under existing law. We hold, however, that the statutes under which they were convicted are unconstitutionally overbroad as applied to criminal defense attorneys. Accordingly, we do not address appellants' claims of trial error, but order appellants discharged.

BACKGROUND

In March, 1982, Theodore Young was killed in Potter County. The following day Richard Buchanan and an accomplice were arrested and charged with first degree murder. Appellant George Stenhach, part-time Public Defender of Potter County, undertook Buchanan's defense immediately. He petitioned for appointment of an investigator to assist in Buchanan's defense, and former police officer Daniel Weidner was appointed as Buchanan's investigator. During a confidential conference among Stenhach, Weidner and Buchanan, Buchanan described the death of Theodore Young. He said that Young had attacked him with two knives and that during the attack, Young had died after he was shot, hit by Buchanan's car, then struck by Buchanan's rifle, causing the stock of the rifle to break off. Buchanan and his accomplice had then disposed of the weapons and other items relating to Young's death. During the conference, Weidner and Buchanan prepared a map identifying the location of some of these items. * * *

On the same day, Weidner found the broken rifle stock and brought it back to appellants' office. He did not find the barrel, which was eventually discovered by the prosecutor and introduced into evidence at Buchanan's trial. Weidner was unable to locate the knives allegedly used by the victim, and no knives were ever found. When Weidner delivered the rifle stock to appellants, they stored it inside a paper bag in a desk drawer in their office. * * *

On the fourth day of Buchanan's murder trial, during an in-camera hearing, the prosecutor questioned Weidner about the rifle stock. Appellants objected on the ground that an answer would violate the attorney-client privilege. The trial judge overruled the objection, holding the privilege inapplicable to physical evidence, and ordered Weidner to answer. After Weidner testified how he had located and retrieved the rifle stock, the judge ordered its production, and appellants brought it from their office. The stock was not entered into evidence during Buchanan's trial by the prosecution or by the defense.

After Buchanan's conviction, the prosecutor, District Attorney Leber, charged appellants with hindering prosecution and tampering with evidence for withholding the rifle stock. * * *

POLICIES

[The court outlined the principal policy considerations on both sides: the privilege against self-incrimination, the right to effective assistance of counsel, zealous representation, and fair administration of justice on the appellants' side; obedience to law and the truth-seeking function of the criminal trial on the appellee's side.]

It is important to identify the rights and policies underlying this appeal, but they are so general they do not lend themselves readily to resolution of the narrow issues we must decide. Furthermore, it is obvious that there are significant policies supporting each side of this appeal, policies seemingly at war with each other. We do not believe it is helpful to explain our decision in terms of balancing policies, as if Buchanan's fifth amendment rights were more weighty than the truth-seeking function of the judicial system. Such explications are a form of begging the question. Finally, these broad considerations focus far too much attention on the Buchanan case. We are not reviewing Buchanan's conviction, nor his right to effective assistance of counsel; we are reviewing appellants' convictions.

What is relevant to this case is the protection of constitutional rights inuring directly to appellants. We believe the primary question is whether appellants have been denied due process of law by application of a penal statute which is vague or overbroad. In this country we do not tolerate criminal statutes like those of the emperor Caligula, who wrote his laws in very fine print and displayed them high on tall pillars, "the more effectually to ensnare the people." 1 W. Blackstone, Commentaries 46. We insist that "a statute which either forbids or requires the doing of an act in terms so vague that men of common intelligence must necessarily guess at its meaning and differ as to its application, violates the first essential of due process...." *Connally v. General Construction Co.*, 269 U.S. 385, 391, 46 S.Ct. 126, 127, 70 L.Ed. 322, 328 (1926). Within this context, we proceed to address appellants' arguments.

DUTY TO DELIVER

Appellants' first argument is that they had no duty to turn over the rifle stock to the prosecutor until ordered to do so by the court. We reject this argument. Although we have no Pennsylvania cases on point, the decisions in other jurisdictions appear to be virtually unanimous in requiring a criminal defense attorney to deliver physical evidence in his possession to the prosecution without court order. It is true that most of the cases arose in the context of appeals from criminal convictions challenging the effectiveness of counsel who had turned over physical evidence, or in the context of litigation of discovery orders or in the context of contempt proceedings against attorneys who failed to produce evidence. The sole case in which an attorney was charged with a criminal offense resulted in the only holding that the concealed evidence was protected by the attorney-client privilege. We join the overwhelming majority of states which hold that physical evidence of crime in the possession of a criminal defense attorney is not subject to a privilege but must be delivered to the prosecution.

In re Gartley, 341 Pa.Super. 350, 491 A.2d 851 (1985), while not directly on point, provides guidance and support for our decision. Although the case was decided after the commission of the offenses charged against appellants herein, this court affirmed the proper execution of a carefully-tailored search warrant to seize a client's business records from an attorney's office. We stated that the use of an attorney's office

> as a haven for evidence material to an ongoing criminal investigation does not place it beyond the reach of a proper search pursuant to a warrant issued on probable cause; we will not restrain the Commonwealth's efforts to obtain otherwise seizable evidence *merely* because it has been placed in the hands of an attorney. To hold otherwise would mean that a criminal suspect could shield evidence from discovery by the simple expedient of delivery to an attorney, a result we deem patently unreasonable. * * *

Though the case did not involve the question of whether the attorney had a duty to deliver physical evidence sua sponte, we believe the quoted language provides strong support for our holding in this case.

Turning to the law in other jurisdictions, we note the much-quoted case of *State v. Olwell*, 64 Wash.2d 828, 394 P.2d 681 (1964). A criminal defense attorney had been held in contempt of court following his refusal to answer questions or produce weapons at a coroner's inquest, in defiance of a subpoena duces tecum. The appellate court reversed the finding of contempt, holding that the subpoena was defective on its face for invading the confidential relationship between attorney and client so that refusal to testify against the client was not contemptuous. * * * The court went on to state that the attorney was required to produce the weapon on his own motion, and that the jury was not to learn the source of the evidence.

> We do not, however, by so holding, mean to imply that evidence can be permanently withheld by the attorney under the claim of the attorney-client privilege. Here, we must consider the balancing process between the attorney-client privilege and the public interest in criminal investigation. We are in agreement that the attorney-client privilege is applicable to the knife held by appellant, but do not agree that the privilege warrants the attorney, as an officer of the court, from withholding it after being properly requested to produce the same. The attorney should not be a depository for criminal evidence (such as a knife, other weapons, stolen property, etc.), which in itself has little, if any, material value for the purposes of aiding counsel in the preparation of the defense of his client's case. Such evidence given the attorney during legal consultation for information purposes and used by the attorney in preparing the defense of his client's case whether or not the case ever goes to trial, could clearly be withheld for a reasonable period of time. It follows that the attorney, after a reasonable period, should, as an officer of the court, on his own motion turn the same over to the prosecution.
>
> We think the attorney-client privilege should and can be preserved even though the attorney surrenders the evidence he has in his possession. The prosecution, upon receipt of such evidence from an

attorney, where charge against the attorney's client is contemplated (presently or in the future), should be well aware of the existence of the attorney-client privilege. Therefore, the state when attempting to introduce such evidence at the trial, should take extreme precautions to make certain that the source of the evidence is not disclosed in the presence of the jury and prejudicial error is not committed. By thus allowing the prosecution to recover such evidence, the public interest is served, and by refusing the prosecution an opportunity to disclose the source of the evidence, the client's privilege is preserved and a balance is reached between these conflicting interests. * * *

We have quoted at length from *Olwell* because most of the cases which follow[, cite,] or quote it * * * raise the same issues addressed in the above passage.

People v. Meredith, 29 Cal.3d 682, 175 Cal.Rptr. 612, 631 P.2d 46 (1981), reached similar conclusions. A murder defendant told his attorney where he had abandoned physical evidence of the crime. The attorney's investigator retrieved the evidence, the attorney examined it and then turned it over to the police, and the evidence was admitted at trial along with testimony of the investigator describing the location of the evidence. On appeal from his conviction, the defendant conceded the admissibility of the physical evidence, but challenged the admissibility of the testimony regarding its location. The court held that the testimony did not violate the attorney-client privilege. "When defense counsel alters or removes physical evidence, he necessarily deprives the prosecution of the opportunity to observe that evidence in its original condition or location.... To extend the attorney-client privilege to a case in which the defense removed evidence might encourage defense counsel to race the police to seize critical evidence." * * *

In *People v. Lee*, 83 Cal.Rptr. 715, 3 Cal.App.3d 514 (1970), the court also concluded that physical evidence in the possession of an attorney was not privileged. The defendant's wife had given incriminating evidence to his attorney, and the attorney in turn gave it to a third party to hold pending judicial resolution of the proper disposition of the evidence, giving the prosecutor notice of his action. The prosecutor obtained a search warrant from the trial court, seized the evidence and introduced it at trial, together with testimony identifying the defendant's wife as the source. * * * The court also approved the testimony regarding the source, for the attorney-client privilege does not protect information coming to the attorney from a third person unless such person is the client's agent. * * *

These California decisions were followed by the Court of Appeals for the Ninth Circuit * * * in *Clutchette v. Rushen*, 770 F.2d 1469 (9th Cir. 1985). The defendant told his attorney where certain evidence was located and the attorney told his investigator to retrieve it; the investigator did so, but gave it directly to the police. The evidence was introduced at trial along with the investigator's description of its location. The court held that neither the sixth amendment right to effective assistance of counsel nor the attorney-client privilege had been violated. The trial court had "scrupulously" prevented the prosecution from disclosing the source of information leading to discovery of the evidence; the source was privileged but the evidence itself lost its privileged character when the attorney ordered it removed from its original location. The court stated that "California law requires that a defense attorney must, after a reasonable time, turn evidence taken from its original resting place over to the prosecution[."]

Morrell v. State, 575 P.2d 1200 (Alaska Supreme Ct.1978), is another direct appeal from a criminal conviction raising the issue of ineffectiveness of trial counsel following his delivery of incriminating physical evidence to the police. A third party had discovered the evidence and brought it to the attorney. Unsure of his duties, he sought guidance from the ethics committee of the state bar association. The committee advised him to return the evidence to the finder, explaining the laws pertaining to concealment of evidence. Counsel did so, and assisted the third party in delivering the evidence to the police. The court held that counsel was not ineffective * * *. After reviewing cases involving duties of attorneys in possession of incriminating physical evidence, the court summarized their holdings.

> From the foregoing cases emerges the rule that a criminal defense attorney must turn over to the prosecution real evidence that the attorney obtains from his client. Further, if the evidence is obtained from a non-client third party who is not acting for the client, then the privilege to refuse to testify concerning the manner in which the evidence was obtained is inapplicable. * * *

With the exception of [*People v.*] *Belge*, [*supra*,] the foregoing cases provide a consistent body of law, which we adopt. To summarize, a criminal defense attorney in possession of physical evidence incriminating his client may, after a reasonable time for examination, return it to its source if he can do so without hindering the apprehension, prosecution, conviction or punishment of another and without altering, destroying or concealing it or impairing its verity or availability in any pending or imminent investigation or proceeding. Otherwise, he must deliver it to the prosecution on his own motion. In the latter event, the prosecution is entitled to use the physical evidence as well as information pertaining to its condition, location and discovery but may not disclose to a fact-finder the source of the evidence. We thus reject appellants' contention that their conduct was proper and that they had no duty to deliver the rifle stock to the prosecution until they were ordered to do so.

DUE PROCESS: OVERBREADTH * * *

We hold that the statutes at issue in this case are overbroad when applied to attorneys representing criminal defendants. The literal language of each section is relatively clear. [One section] states that a person is guilty of hindering prosecution "if, with intent to hinder the ... conviction ... of another for crime, he ... conceals ... evidence of the crime ... regardless of its admissibility in evidence...." [Another section] provides that a person is guilty of tampering with physical evidence "if, believing that an official proceeding ... is pending ..., he ... conceals or removes any record, document or thing with intent to impair its verity or availability in such proceeding...." The clarity of the language is delusive, for it prohibits conduct which cannot constitutionally be prohibited along with conduct which clearly can. In certain circumstances, an attorney might conceal evidence with the intent of impairing its availability in his client's criminal trial and with the intent of hindering his client's conviction.

An example of such circumstances might involve an attorney whose client gives him a handwritten account of involvement in the crime he is charged with committing. If the attorney were to destroy the statement or retain it in his file, he would be guilty of violating the literal terms of the statutes against hindering prosecution and tampering with evidence. Yet no one would suggest the attorney should give the document to the prosecutor; indeed, to do so would be an egregious violation of the attorney's duties to his client.

The functions of the attorney counseling a criminal defendant have a constitutional dimension. In opposing unreasonable searches and seizures, in preventing self-incrimination and in rendering effective assistance of counsel, the defense attorney is charged with the protection of fourth, fifth and sixth amendment rights. In performing these functions, the defense attorney might run afoul of the statutes against hindering prosecution and tampering with evidence; thus he may not have adequate notice of what conduct might be a crime, and he is subject to the threat of arbitrary and discriminatory prosecution.

Beyond the obvious example stated above, there is little or no guidance for an attorney to know when he has crossed the invisible line into an area of criminal behavior. There are no prior cases in this jurisdiction in which a criminal defense attorney has been convicted of violating these statutes. We have discussed many of the similar cases from other jurisdictions, none of which addresses the precise issues facing us in this case. Although we focused on the uniformity we found in those cases as to disposition of physical evidence, they express a great deal of doubt and reflect great diversity as to the grayer areas of ethical usage of evidence of all sorts. Attorneys face a distressing paucity of dispositive precedent to guide them in balancing their duty of zealous representation against their duty as officers of the court. Volumes are filled with other potential sources of guidance, such as ethical codes and comments thereto, both proposed and adopted, advisory opinions by ethics committees and myriad articles in legal periodicals. The plethora of writings exemplifies the profession's concern with the problem, and although they may help to clarify some of the issues, they fail to answer many of the difficult questions in this area of legal practice. * * *

Even if it were possible, it is not the function of this court to provide an advisory opinion as to various examples of attorney conduct not involved in this case which might or might not violate the statutes we are reviewing. We note that other jurisdictions have enacted criminal statutes which address the unique role of defense attorneys in the administration of criminal justice and do not subject them to rules identical with those applicable to the public. *See Clark v. State*, 159 Tex.Cr.R. 187, 261 S.W.2d 339, *cert. denied*, 346 U.S. 855, 74 S.Ct. 69, 98 L.Ed. 369 (1953) (statute specifically excluded from liability one who aids an offender in preparing his defense). * * *

For these reasons, we hold that the statutes which prohibit hindering prosecution and tampering with physical evidence are unconstitutionally overbroad when applied to attorneys representing criminal defendants.

Accordingly, the judgments of sentence are vacated and appellants discharged.

NOTES ON PHYSICAL AND OTHER EVIDENCE

1. **Authentication and Chain of Custody:** In *Stenhach*, the court allowed evidence turned over by a lawyer to be used by the prosecution, but cautioned against revealing how it came into the prosecution's possession. Suppose, however, that the only way the prosecution can provide a chain of custody for the evidence is through testimony by the lawyer. In *Commonwealth v. Ferri*, 599 A.2d 208 (Pa.Super.Ct. 1991), clothing worn by a murder defendant at the scene of a crime was given to the defendant's former attorney and then turned over by that attorney to a public defender. The prosecution learned about the clothing via statements made by the defendant and another individual implicated in the crime. Over a claim of privilege, the court admitted the former attorney's testimony concerning receipt of the clothing so as to provide a chain of custody necessary to admission of the evidence in court. *See also People v. Sanchez*, 30 Cal.Rptr.2d 111, 116 (Ct.App. 1994) (quoting *Meredith* decision's citation of *Lee* and *Morrell* as support for the proposition that " 'an attorney must not only turn over evidence given him by *third parties*, but also testify as to the source of that evidence,' " and noting that " '[b]oth decisions emphasized that the attorney-client privilege was inapplicable because the third party was not acting as an agent of the attorney or the client' ") (emphasis in original). The court noted that the defendant can avoid such testimony by stipulating to the original source of the physical evidence (citing *Meredith*). *See also* 1 Geoffrey C. Hazard, Jr. & W. William Hodes, The Law of Lawyering, § 9.29 (3d ed. 2004). Do you think the court's decision would have been different if the lawyer still represented the defendant?

2. **Due Process:** In its "Due Process: Overbreadth" analysis, the *Stenhach* court sees a fatal conflict between the hindering and tampering statutes and the constitutional duties of the defense lawyer. The court referred to a hypothetical situation involving the client's handwritten account of his involvement in the crime being turned over to the lawyer. Is this document privileged as a communication from client to lawyer? If so, can the statute

sensibly be read as requiring the lawyer to make it available to the prosecution? If it cannot be so interpreted, where is the "overbreadth"? For criticism of the Pennsylvania court's "overbreadth" rationale for letting the appellants off the hook, see Susan P. Koniak, *The Law Between the Bar and the State*, 70 N.C.L.Rev. 1389 (1992).

3. **Options: Return to Original Location or Source—or Do Not Take Possession?** The *Stenhach* court indicates that once a lawyer has removed evidence and had it tested, there is an option other than turning the evidence over to prosecutors: The lawyer can "return [the evidence] to its source if he can do so without hindering the apprehension, prosecution, conviction or punishment of another and without altering, destroying or concealing it or impairing its verity or availability in any pending or imminent investigation or proceeding." This option was embraced and elaborated by the ABA Standards for Criminal Justice Defense Function, Standard 4–4.6 (1993). This standard advises that a defense attorney who receives such evidence should disclose the location of or deliver it to law enforcement authorities *only* if (1) that is required by law or court order, or (2) if the item is contraband. The standard argues that the appropriate general rule for counsel absent such obligations is to return it to the source "unless there is reason to believe that the evidence might be altered or destroyed or used to harm another or return is otherwise impossible." *Id.* at 4–4.6(c). A general rule requiring prompt delivery to authorities, it argues, would "hamper defense counsel's obligation to undertake as full a factual investigation as possible," whereas "counsel must be encouraged to acquire physical evidence if he or she believes the client's defense might genuinely be enhanced thereby," *id.*, Commentary. For a comprehensive analysis and critique of the Standard from defense counsel's perspective, with references and examples, see Rodney J. Uphoff, *The Physical Evidence Dilemma: Does ABA Standard 4–4.6 Offer Appropriate Guidance?*, 62 Hastings L.J. 1177 (2011); *cf.* RESTATEMENT, § 119, Comment *c* (dismissing the return-to-the-source option as either mostly impractical or as likely to enable others who know about the evidence to prevent it from being discovered by proper authorities).

Perhaps the best option for the attorney is to refuse to take possession of the evidence in the first instance. Taking possession and moving the evidence to a location where it is less likely to be found can result in discipline against the attorney. *In re Ryder*, 381 F.2d 713 (4th Cir. 1967) (affirming eighteen month suspension of defense attorney for moving sawed-off shotgun and stolen money from client's safe deposit box to attorney's safe deposit box).

4. **Photographs:** Recall that the lawyer in the problem, after talking to the client, went to the scene and took photographs. How are these photographs to be treated? Are they physical evidence, or work product? Consider the following case.

FLETCHER v. UNION PACIFIC RAILROAD CO.

United States District Court, S.D. California, 2000.
194 F.R.D. 666.

BROOKS, UNITED STATES MAGISTRATE JUDGE.

[Fletcher, a Union Pacific Railroad (UPRR) employee, fell while working on a moving train when a grab iron he was holding broke. He claimed substantial and permanent injuries, and sued UPRR under the Federal Employers' Liability Act for damages in excess of $5 million. The defendant obtained a medical examination of Fletcher by a physician of its choice, who submitted a report finding "no objective signs of serious or permanent injury." Fletcher then sought production of any surveillance films that UPRR took after his injury, claiming that they would show evidence of the extent of his injury.]

III.   DISCUSSION * * *

B. *Surveillance Films Constitute Work Product And Are Entitled To Qualified Immunity From Discovery.*

Numerous courts have held that surveillance films constitute work product and are subject to qualified immunity. * * * A party may only discover an opponent's surveillance films or other trial preparation materials upon a showing that he or she has substantial need for the items and cannot obtain their substantial equivalent without undue hardship. * * *

Whether films will be used at trial is a significant factor in determining whether the party seeking to discover them has a "substantial need" for the material. * * *

C. *Judicial Application Of The Rule 26(b)(3) "Substantial Need" Test To Surveillance Films.*

Courts have not taken a uniform approach in applying the "substantial need" test. * * * Courts following [a] two-prong approach require a party seeking discovery of an opponent's trial preparation material to demonstrate "substantial need" and "undue hardship." "The burden is squarely on [the requesting party] to meet both prongs of this test." * * *

The substantial need prong examines: 1) whether the information is an essential element in the requesting party's case and 2) whether the party requesting discovery can obtain the facts from an alternate source. * * *

The extent to which a party needs information contained in an opponent's work product depends, in large part, on whether the work product is unique. * * *

The undue hardship prong examines the burden obtaining the information from an alternate source would impose on the party requesting discovery. * * * Examples of undue hardship include instances when witnesses cannot recall statements contained in interviews. * * * Unusual expense involved in obtaining equivalent information is another factor that may establish undue hardship. * * *

Courts following [a] three-factor approach consider: 1) whether there is "substantial need" for the work product—something more than relevancy under rule 26(b)(1); 2) whether substantially equivalent information can be obtained from another source; and 3) whether doing so would create an undue hardship (not merely expense or inconvenience) for the party seeking discovery. * * *

E. *Should Defendant's Work Product Be Produced?*

In determining whether Fletcher has demonstrated a substantial need for Defendant's work product, the Court will ask three questions: 1) Are the facts depicted in the films essential to proving Fletcher's prima facie case; 2) can Fletcher obtain substantially equivalent information from an alternate source; and 3) would doing so create an undue burden? * * *

1. *The Surveillance Films Are Not Essential To Fletcher's Prima Facie Case.* * * *

Defendant's surveillance tapes contain information on Fletcher's physical condition. Union Pacific will not introduce the tapes at trial. * * * Defendant has conceded that the films depict Fletcher performing day-to-day activities such as walking and getting into a car. * * * The films may show that Plaintiff engaged in these activities with some degree of difficulty, corroborating his claim that he was injured. The surveillance occurred on various dates two months after the accident and again approximately one year later.

The films are not the only available evidence that Plaintiff is injured. Fletcher's medical records, his testimony, testimony of coworkers and his spouse, and the testimony and reports of his treating physician and retained experts will be offered to show that he was injured in the * * * accident. Under these circumstances, the surveillance films would be offered to corroborate Plaintiff's claims. * * * However, corroborative evidence is rarely "necessary." * * * "It is often thought cumulative...." * * * Plaintiff has not carried his burden of establishing a substantial need for his opponent's attorney work product.

2. *Fletcher Has Not Demonstrated That He Cannot Obtain The Information Contained In The Surveillance Films From An Alternate Source.* * * *

Plaintiff maintains that the films are unique because they lack the taint of bias associated with alternate sources of information. The same argument can be made for most of an opposing counsel's work product. However, more is required before work product is turned over to the other side.

Fletcher's emphasis on the weight of his evidence and the surveillance material misconstrues rule 26(b)(3). Substantial equivalence focuses on the *quality* of the information a party can obtain from alternate sources. * * * A requesting party has been required to depose witnesses to show that they could not recall information, thus providing substantially equivalent information, before attorney work product would be produced. * * *

Case law recognizes that some items are so unique that they lack a substantial equivalent. For example, a videotape of the incident giving rise to a suit or a witness statement taken shortly after the incident often lack any substantial equivalent. * * *

The surveillance films in this case do not provide unique information. The films do not contain footage of the accident itself. They depict

Fletcher engaging in day-to-day activities two to fifteen months after the accident. * * * The films depict Fletcher's physical condition on seven days; Plaintiff is familiar with his physical condition from the day he was injured to the present. * * *

Fletcher does not claim he is unable to testify about his physical condition since the accident. Further, Plaintiff does not contend that his wife and other individuals with whom he interacts on a regular basis are unable to provide testimony about his injuries. Finally, Plaintiff has not alleged that his treating physician and expert witnesses, armed with his medical records, are unable to testify to the nature and extent of his injuries. On the contrary, Fletcher seeks Defendant's films to bolster the testimony he and his treating physician will offer. * * *

3. *Fletcher Has Not Shown That Obtaining Substantially Equivalent Information From Other Sources Would Create An Undue Burden.*

Assuming that Fletcher has a substantial need for Defendant's trial preparation materials, he may only discover the films by showing that obtaining equivalent information from another source would create an undue burden. * * *

At the hearing on Fletcher's second motion to compel production of the surveillance films, the Court held that Plaintiff failed to demonstrate undue burden because he had made no attempt to obtain equivalent information from alternate sources. * * * Rather than cure this deficiency, Fletcher simply maintains that "scour[ing]" his neighborhood for potential witnesses would be futile.

[Fletcher's motion to compel was therefore denied.]

QUESTION

In *Stenhach*, the court finds the attorney has a duty to volunteer evidence of a crime. In *Fletcher*, the court refuses to compel an attorney to volunteer evidence that could help "make or break" the adversary's case. Can you articulate why the two cases come out differently?

B. PROTECTING THIRD PERSONS FROM HARM BY THE CLIENT

PROBLEM

Joan Smith makes an appointment with attorney Harriet Madison, for herself and her husband Walter, to discuss a farm boundary dispute between them and their neighbor Norman Adams. The dispute relates to a twenty acre tract of woods that Adams now plans to clear and plant. Smith's deed from his predecessor includes the tract, but Adams has a previously unrecorded deed from the predecessor, dated prior to Smith's, purporting to convey the woods to Adams. Under applicable law, the tardily recorded deed is effective against Smith only if he knew about it when he took his own title. When she makes the appointment with Madison, Mrs. Smith indicates concern that her husband has been violently angry about the matter.

At the interview, Smith begins with an agitated narrative of the arguments he has had with Adams, and concludes by saying that he knows that the unrecorded deed isn't any good against him, but that he has got a little insurance anyway. He explains that his insurance is in the form of a letter from the predecessor, dated on the same day as Smith's deed, to the effect that Adams wanted to buy the woods but he had decided not to sell. Further conversation discloses that the letter is a fake, and that Smith actually knew about the deed to Adams. Madison explains that fraudulent use of the letter to dissuade Adams from his claim would expose Smith to civil and possibly even criminal liability, and that under the law Adams' deed is good against him. Madison expresses the opinion that Smith would have, at most, a minor civil claim arising out of their arguments.

At this point, Smith flies into a rage, shouting that he is going to show Adams the letter no matter what, and if Adams doesn't back off he'll burn his house down. Smith storms out of the office. Before she follows him, Mrs. Smith tells Madison that she's afraid her husband, who has had ten years' experience as a fire inspector, will follow through with his threats.

QUESTIONS

(a) May Madison now get on the phone to Adams or the police to warn them? About what?

(b) If Madison says nothing, Adams refuses to back off, and Smith in fact burns the Adams house down, is Madison subject to discipline? To civil liability to Adams? Would the situation be different if one of the Adams children is in the house at the time of the fire and is severely and permanently injured by burns?

(c) If Madison says nothing, Adams backs off as a result of Smith's showing him the letter and pays Smith $2,000 in settlement of other claims, then Smith sells the twenty acres for a housing development, is Madison subject to discipline? To civil liability to Adams?

RULE REFERENCES

Model Rules 1.2(d), 1.6, and 4.1(b)

RESTATEMENT §§ 66 & 67(1)

HAWKINS v. KING COUNTY

Court of Appeals of Washington, Division 1, 1979.
602 P.2d 361.

SWANSON, ACTING CHIEF JUDGE.

Michael Hawkins, acting through his guardian ad litem, and his mother Frances M. Hawkins, appeal from a summary judgment dismissing attorney Richard Sanders from an action sounding in tort. Appellants contend Sanders, court-appointed defense attorney for Michael Hawkins, was negligent and committed malpractice by failing to divulge information regarding his client's mental state at a bail hearing. We find no error and affirm. * * *

Michael Hawkins was [arrested and] booked for possession of marijuana. Following his court appointment as Hawkins' defense counsel * * *, Richard Sanders conferred with Hawkins for about 45 minutes, at which time Hawkins expressed the desire to be released from jail.

[On the same day,] Sanders talked with Palmer Smith, an attorney employed by Hawkins' mother Frances Hawkins, to assist in having Hawkins either hospitalized or civilly committed. Smith told Sanders then, and reiterated by letter, that Hawkins was mentally ill and dangerous. [Several days later], Dr. Elwood Jones, a psychiatrist, telephoned and wrote Sanders and averred Hawkins was mentally ill and of danger to himself and others and should not be released from custody. Sanders represented that he intended to comply with his client's request for freedom.

[The following day], a district judge released Hawkins on a personal surety bond. At the bail hearing, Sanders did not volunteer any information regarding Hawkins' alleged illness or dangerousness, nor were any questions in that vein directed to him either by the judge or the prosecutor. Smith, Jones, and Mrs. Hawkins were informed of Hawkins' release, and all parties later met on two occasions in a counseling environment.

[A]bout 8 days after his release, Michael Hawkins assaulted his mother and attempted suicide by jumping off a bridge, causing injuries resulting in the amputation of both legs. The Hawkinses commenced an action for damages against King County, the State of Washington, Community Psychiatric Clinic, Inc., and one of its employees [and later] amended the suit * * * to name Sanders a party defendant. Sanders filed a motion to dismiss for failure to state a claim. [The trial court granted the motion, treating it as one for summary judgment, thereby permitting] Hawkins an interlocutory appeal.

On appeal, the Hawkinses essentially present two arguments: First, that by his failure at the bail hearing to disclose the information he possessed regarding Michael Hawkins' mental state, defense counsel Sanders subjected himself to liability for malpractice, as court rules and the [Model Rules] mandate such disclosure on ethical and legal grounds. Second, that by the same omission Sanders negligently violated a common law duty to warn foreseeable victims of an individual he knew to be potentially dangerous to himself and others. See *Tarasoff v. Regents of University of California*, 17 Cal.3d 425, 131 Cal.Rptr. 14, 551 P.2d 334 (1976).

Sanders asserts the Hawkinses have failed to demonstrate that he breached any duty owed to them * * *.

We believe that the duty of counsel to be loyal to his client and to represent zealously his client's interest overrides the nebulous and unsupported theory that our rules and ethical code mandate disclosure of information which counsel considers detrimental to his client's stated interest. Because disclosure is not "required by law," appellants' theory of liability on the basis of ethical or court rule violations fails for lack of substance.

Turning then to the Hawkinses' theory of a common law duty to warn or disclose, we note common law support for the precept that attorneys must, upon learning that a client plans an assault or other violent crime, warn foreseeable victims. See *Tarasoff v. Regents*, supra * * *. The difficulty lies in framing a rule that will balance properly "the public interest in safety from violent attack" against the public interest in securing proper resolution of legal disputes without compromising a defendant's right to a loyal and zealous defense. We are persuaded by the position advanced by amicus "that the obligation to warn, when confidentiality would be compromised to the client's detriment, must be permissive at most, unless it appears beyond a reasonable doubt that the client has formed a firm intention to inflict serious personal injuries on an unknowing third person." * * *

In *Tarasoff*, the defendant psychologists had first-hand knowledge of Poddar's homicidal intention and knew it to be directed towards Tatiana Tarasoff, who was wholly unaware of her danger. The knowledge of the defendants in *Tarasoff* was gained from statements made to them in the course of treatment and not from statements transmitted by others. * * *

In the instant case Michael Hawkins' potential victims, his mother and sister, knew he might be dangerous and that he had been released from confinement, contrary to Tatiana Tarasoff's ignorance of any risk of harm. Thus, no duty befell Sanders to warn Frances Hawkins of a risk of which she was already fully cognizant. Further, it must not be overlooked that Sanders received no information that Hawkins planned to assault anyone, only that he was mentally ill and likely to be dangerous to himself and others. That Sanders received no information directly from Michael Hawkins is the final distinction between the two cases.

The common law duty to volunteer information about a client to a court considering pretrial release must be limited to situations where information gained convinces counsel that his client intends to commit a crime or inflict injury upon unknowing third persons. Such a duty cannot be extended to the facts before us. * * *

The decision of the superior court granting summary judgment dismissing the respondents as party defendants is affirmed.

IN RE GOEBEL

Supreme Court of Indiana, 1998.
703 N.E.2d 1045.

PER CURIAM.

[Attorney Goebel was charged in a disciplinary proceeding with violating Indiana Rule of Professional Conduct 1.6 by revealing to his client confidential information about another client of the firm where he worked. The hearing officer found no violation, and the Disciplinary Commission (charging authority) petitioned for review.]

The facts are essentially undisputed. The respondent was a partner in a Crawfordsville law firm. During relevant periods, another partner (the "partner") represented a client of the firm (the "guardianship client") in a guardianship matter. The partner sent correspondence about the guardianship proceeding to the client at 3813 East 300 South [Street] in a specified Indiana city. The mail was returned marked "No Such Street–NSS."

While the partner was representing the guardianship client, the respondent represented a client (the "criminal client") against criminal charges. The guardianship client's husband was a witness for the prosecution in the criminal proceeding pending against the criminal client. The criminal client informed the respondent of his intent to locate and kill the guardianship client and her husband, being aware that the respondent's firm represented her. The respondent attempted to dissuade the criminal client from doing so.

On December 16, 1993, the criminal client appeared in the respondent's law office and demanded the respondent reveal the location or address of the guardianship client. The respondent showed the envelope which had been mailed by the partner to the guardianship client at 3813 East 300 South and which had been returned with the notation "No Such Street–NSS." The criminal client copied the address. The respondent did not report the criminal client's actions to police or the guardianship client. Two days later, the criminal client murdered the guardianship client's husband at her home at the actual address of 3813 South 300 East. The criminal client was convicted of the murder and sentenced to life in prison without the possibility of parole.

The hearing officer found the respondent showed the returned envelope to the criminal client to substantiate that the respondent did not know the guardianship client's real address and, therefore, to thwart any efforts of the criminal client to locate (and murder) the guardianship client or her husband. * * *

The evidence reveals that the criminal client had been searching for the guardianship client's home for months and had even traveled to Bowling Green, Kentucky, in search of it. The criminal client had told the respondent he wanted to kill the guardianship client, her husband, and the two police investigators handling the criminal client's case. During a police interview after the murder, the respondent expressed his fear of the criminal client and revealed that the criminal client had threatened both the respondent and his family.

Professional Conduct Rule 1.6(b) provides that a lawyer may reveal information relating to the representation of a client to the extent the lawyer believes is reasonably necessary to prevent the client from committing any criminal act. The respondent's counsel claimed during final arguments before the hearing officer, and the hearing officer found, that the respondent revealed the address on the envelope to "dissuade" his client from committing murder. However, the colloquy between the respondent and police during the respondent's interview after the murder does not support that conclusion:

> Police: At some point did [the criminal client] relay to you that there was going to be a hearing [. . .]?
>
> Respondent: Yes, he was aware of that and uh he was aware that my partner represented the [guardianship client].
>
> Police: And during that uh or close to that date uh did [the criminal client] come to your office and was shown A. [sic] an address where uh [the guardianship client] was reportedly living at [. . .]?
>
> Respondent: I believe, I think so. I'm almost positive. I think what the conversation was. Was he pressing me to find out the address and uh I ask [the partner] about it and she said every piece of mail that she had sent to the address given to her by [the guardianship client] had been returned and I believe I showed him an envelope to substantiate that I didn't know her address by showing him an envelope with whatever address it was.
>
> Police: Did he write that address down?
>
> Respondent: I think he did. Yes.
>
> Police: And
>
> Respondent: Pretty sure he did.
>
> Police: All the information that he was trying to gather from you and other sources was for what purpose?
>
> Respondent: To track down [the guardianship client's husband], it appeared.
>
> Police: To do what?
>
> Respondent: To get rid of him. I assume.
>
> Police: To kill him?
>
> Respondent: Yes. I think so.

Commission's Exhibit 1, at pp. 8–9.

After giving the information to the criminal client, the respondent did not notify local police, the sheriff, or the guardianship client.[1] Both the content of the respondent's interview with police and his lack of action after showing the envelope to the criminal client to prevent him from locating the guardianship client demonstrate that the respondent did not display the envelope to prevent commission of a criminal act, but rather that he did so based on the criminal client's forceful demand.[2] Accordingly, we find that the respondent's divulging of the information relating to his firm's representation of the guardianship client was not excepted from Rule 1.6's confidentiality requirements. We conclude that the respondent violated the rule. * * *

A client must be able to trust her attorney to keep confidential information gained in the course of representation. Otherwise, full dialogue critical to the attorney-client relationship and, thus, to the best possible resolution of legal matters, will be compromised. The observance of the ethical obligation of a lawyer to hold inviolate confidential information of the client not only facilitates the full development of facts essential to proper representation of the client but also encourages individuals to seek early legal assistance. We are aware, of course, that the respondent faced very difficult circumstances when his threatening client confronted him as to the whereabouts of the guardianship client. While the respondent's fear for his own safety is understandable under the circumstances, such fear did not justify his revelation of confidential information. The respondent, like all attorneys admitted to practice in this state, stated in his oath of office that he would, *inter alia*, "maintain the confidence and preserve the secrets of my client *at every peril to myself* . . ." Admis.Disc.R. 22. (Emphasis supplied). That the respondent revealed the information in this instance under conditions of severe duress is a strong and compelling mitigating factor, but does not change the fact that he violated the rule.

[T]he respondent was motivated by self interest in revealing the information, albeit understandably so for his own interest of self-preservation. Moreover, the information which the respondent conveyed to the criminal client could not be obtained from other sources outside that law office. [We] conclude that a public reprimand adequately addresses the misconduct.

NOTES ON PREVENTIVE DISCLOSURE

1. **Tort Duty to Disclose:** Application of the *Tarasoff* rule (from *Tarasoff v. Regents of the University of California*, 551 P.2d 334 (Cal. 1976),

---

1. We note, however, that the respondent was not required under the *Rules of Professional Conduct* to inform the guardianship client or law enforcement officials of the criminal client's threats. Professional Conduct Rule 1.6(b) provides that a lawyer "may reveal" confidential information to prevent the client from committing any criminal act. This provision does not *require* that an Indiana attorney report a client's threats to commit a criminal act.

2. We point out that there is no evidence in the record that the information consisting of the erroneous address was a causal factor in the murder of the guardianship client's husband.

cited in *Hawkins*) to health professionals, and especially to psychotherapists, is increasingly accepted, although the cases are not numerous. *See* 3 David W. Louisell & Harold Williams, Medical Malpractice, § 17A.15 (2009). The *Tarasoff* decision itself, as applied to psychotherapists, was superseded in California by a statute that forecloses tort liability unless "the patient has communicated to the psychotherapist a serious threat of physical violence against a reasonably identifiable victim or victims," and if the psychotherapist in those circumstances has discharged the duty to warn and protect "by making reasonable efforts to communicate the threat to the victim or victims and to a law enforcement agency." Cal.Civ. Code, § 43.92 (1985, amended 2006). That provision has been interpreted as (1) requiring that the information received actually lead the psychotherapist to believe that the patient poses such a serious threat, and (2) extending to a threat communicated by a family member for the purpose of advancing the patient's therapy, *Ewing v. Goldstein*, 15 Cal.Rptr.3d 864 (Ct.App. 2004); *see also Munstermann ex rel. Rowe v. Alegent Health–Immanuel Med. Ctr.*, 716 N.W.2d 73 (Neb. 2006) (holding that while a Nebraska statute identical to the California one does not directly apply to physician-psychiatrists, its principle and limitations should apply to them as a matter of common law). In general, tort liability does not extend to threats of suicide or threats to property, or to threats to persons already aware of the danger. *See* 3 Louisell & Williams, *supra*, § 17A.15.

Is it appropriate to extend such liability to lawyers? To all "professionals," including accountants, investment brokers, etc.? To everyone regardless of special training in the analysis of human behavior? In *Munstermann*, the Nebraska court based its common-law extension of tort liability to physician-psychiatrists in part on the ALI's RESTATEMENT (SECOND) OF TORTS, § 315 (1993), which denies a "duty so to control the conduct of a third person as to prevent him from causing physical harm to another unless" the preventer has a special relation to the actor imposing such a duty or to the victim imposing a duty of protection. None of the examples of such duties in the succeeding sections 316–20 (parent-child, master-servant, licensor/licensee those in charge of persons having dangerous propensities, persons having custody of others) involves a relationship comparable to lawyer-client as such. So far, it appears that *Hawkins* is the only case in which such liability has been contemplated for lawyers.

For extended discussion of the implications of *Tarasoff*, not only for psychotherapists but also for lawyers and other professionals, see Vanessa Merton, *Confidentiality and the "Dangerous" Patient: Implications of Tarasoff for Psychiatrists and Lawyers*, 31 Emory L.J. 263 (1982).

2. **Ethics Rules Permitting Unconsented Disclosure:** What kinds of threatened harm justify unconsented disclosure of confidential information? The discussion generally centers around hierarchies of value in comparison with the confidentiality of the attorney-client relationship, and the progression of the ABA's positions illustrates the typical range discussed: personal injury or death, physical injury to property, and financial injury (usually resulting from fraud). The pre-Model Rules ABA position, outlined in Model Code Disciplinary Rule 4–101(C)(3), permitted even greater disclosure of any intended crime, without reference to the nature of the threatened harm. A majority of states revising their rules after the adoption of the Model Rules

retained the position that, as a matter of disciplinary law, a lawyer may disclose her client's intention to commit a crime threatening substantial property or financial interests. Section 67 of the RESTATEMENT also took this view. The ABA clung to the narrow view in the comprehensive revisions of the Model Rules adopted in 2002, but in 2003 it finally yielded and revised its own Model Rule 1.6 to permit disclosure of crimes or frauds that have resulted, or are "reasonably certain to result," in substantial financial injury. Model Rule 1.6(b)(2) & (3). For a review of the evolution of Model Rule 1.6, see Michael Ariens, *"Playing Chicken": An Instant History of the Battle Over Exceptions to Client Confidences*, 33 J. Legal Prof. 239 (2009).

3. **Saving a Life:** Go back to our where-the-bodies-are-buried problem at *supra* section 4(A)(2), and suppose that our lawyer goes to the scene in the woods and finds the watchman still barely alive, but obviously in danger of bleeding to death. Can she get life-saving help without breaching confidentiality? If not, do the rules authorize such disclosure? Would a professional rule that prohibited such disclosure be morally acceptable?

Model Rule 1.6(b) was amended in 2002 to remove its former limitation to the prevention of a client's intended future *act*, drawing on section 66 of the RESTATEMENT. That section for the first time permitted unconsented disclosure—always as a last resort after efforts to get the client to respond have failed—regardless of whether or not the act itself (e.g., an assault or the planting of a bomb or incendiary device) had already occurred, whether or not the act was or would be criminal, and whether or not it was or would be attributable to the client. At least one court, however, subsequently interpreted the old language as permitting disclosure of client's information as to the whereabouts of his victims to the authorities. The court's decision turned upon the lawyer's reasonable belief that the victims *might* still be alive, "where an attorney's or a client's *omission* to act *could* result in 'imminent death or substantial bodily harm' constituting a separate and more severe crime from the one already committed." *McClure v. Thompson*, 323 F.3d 1233, 1245 (9th Cir. 2003) (emphasis added).

4. **Wrongful Conviction or Detention as Preventable Harm:** Assume that a lawyer's client tells his lawyer that he is solely responsible for a murder for which a third person is being tried with a possible death sentence or life imprisonment, but refuses to allow the lawyer to tell anyone. Could unconsented disclosure to the third person's defense counsel be justified as "reasonably necessary ... to prevent reasonably certain death or substantial bodily harm" within the meaning of Model Rule 1.6(b)(1)? How would the lawyer evaluate the tradeoff between confidentiality and innocence?

One jurisdiction, at least, has adopted a version of Model Rule 1.6(b) that specifically allows disclosure of confidential information "to prevent the wrongful execution or incarceration of another," explained in a comment as permission to disclose "in the specific situation where such information discloses that an innocent person has been convicted of a crime and has been sentenced to imprisonment or execution," Massachusetts Rules of Professional Conduct 1.6(b)(1), Comment 9A (1998). A committee of the ABA Criminal Justice Section proposed an amendment to Model Rule 1.6 to add an exception for such disclosure after the client's death. *See* Peter A. Joy & Kevin C.

McMunigle, *Confidentiality and Wrongful Conviction*, Criminal Justice, Summ. 2008, at 46 (also noting the ambiguity of the Massachusetts rule as to whether or not it includes pre-conviction disclosure). For extended analyses of the issues of interpretation of current rules as well as of policy, see Inbal Hasbani, Comment, *When the Law Preserves Injustice: Issues Raised by a Wrongful Incarceration Exception to Attorney–Client Confidentiality*, 100 J.Crim.L. & Criminology 277 (Winter 2010) (indicating skepticism of liberal interpretations of current Model Rules), and Ken Strutin, *Preserving Attorney–Client Confidentiality at the Cost of Another's Innocence: A Systemic Approach*, 17 Tex. Wesleyan L.Rev. 499 (2011) (calling for a comprehensive solution to the wrongful conviction problem that does not rest solely on relaxed ethics rules).

5. **Mandatory Child Abuse Reporting Statutes:** Most, if not all, states now have statutes requiring persons who have reason to believe that a child is being abused to report the abuse to government officials. Sometimes these statutes require specified groups of professionals (such as teachers, physicians, nurses, and others) to report, but sometimes they require all individuals to report. In a state with a statute that lists attorneys as individuals who must report or requires all individuals, presumably including attorneys, to report, is an attorney required to report evidence of child abuse obtained while working on a client's behalf? Asked another way, does the Model Rule 1.6 duty of confidentiality trump the statutory reporting duty, or vice versa? Does it matter if the attorney believes that there is a possibility of future abuse? If so, does it matter if the attorney is aware of a specific target of potential future abuse? Is this an instance where court-adopted rules governing attorney behavior trump statutory provisions, as discussed in *supra* section 2(A)? For discussion of these and related issues, see Nev. Standing Comm. on Ethics and Prof'l Resp., Op. 30 (2005), Adrienne Jennings Lockie, *Salt in the Wounds: Why Attorneys Should Not Be Mandated Reporters of Child Abuse*, 36 N.M.L.Rev. 125 (2006), Donald R. Lundberg, *Mandatory Child Abuse Reporting by Lawyers*, Res Gestae, Dec. 2011, at 31, Katharyn I. Christian, Comment, *Putting Legal Doctrines to the Test: The Inclusion of Attorneys as Mandatory Reporters of Child Abuse*, 32 J. Legal Prof. 215 (2008), and Stephanie Conti, Note, *Lawyers and Mental Health Professionals Working Together: Reconciling the Duties of Confidentiality and Mandatory Child Abuse Reporting*, 49 Fam.Ct.R. 388 (2011).

6. **Disclosure Permitted or Required?** Should preventive disclosure, if permitted at all, be mandatory as a matter of disciplinary rule, or entirely discretionary for the lawyer? Following its predecessors, ABA Model Rule 1.6(b) does not require attorney disclosure, but only permits it in some circumstances; and most state versions, like the Indiana rule in *Goebel*, follow suit. At least 13 states, however—Arizona, Connecticut, Florida, Hawai'i, Illinois, Nevada, New Jersey, North Dakota, Texas, Vermont, Virginia, Washington, and Wisconsin—have adopted variations on the Model Rule that require disclosure of confidential information in some situations. See the links to state rules at ABA/BNA Lawyers Manual on Professional Conduct at http://lawyersmanual.bna.com/mopw2. A majority of these variants require disclosure of information necessary to prevent the client from committing an act (usually a criminal act) that would cause physical harm; two (New Jersey and

Vermont) also require it in case of a fraudulent act threatening injury to financial interests or property. Florida and Virginia extend the requirement to prevention of any client crime. Illinois, North Dakota, and Washington require disclosure of any information necessary to prevent any substantial physical harm (regardless of who would cause it and whether it would be criminal). Hawaii limits the requirement to rectifying the consequences of substantial injury to financial interests or property caused by completed criminal or fraudulent acts of the client in furtherance of which the lawyer's services had been used. For the history of such a mandate to correct client fraud in the ABA's prior rules, see the notes following the next problem.

Essentially all jurisdictions reject the idea, argued for by some, that such disclosure should be prohibited under all circumstances. Would such a universal prohibition—as applied, for example, to a planned murder—be either morally acceptable or practically enforceable? *See* 1 Geoffrey C. Hazard, Jr. & W. William Hodes, The Law of Lawyering § 9.20 (3d ed. 2012).

An attorney's confidentiality duties under Model Rule 1.6 are not coextensive with the attorney-client privilege. Therefore, even when disclosure is allowed or required under a state's version of Model Rule 1.6, the client might be allowed to assert attorney-client privilege to prevent the attorney's testimony from being introduced against the client. In *Newman v. State*, 863 A.2d 321, 324 (Md.Ct.App. 2004), a client told her divorce attorney that she planned to kill one of the couple's two sons, so that her husband would be blamed for that son's death, which would cause the court to award her custody of the other son. Acting pursuant to Maryland's version of Model Rule 1.6, the attorney told a judge about the client's plans. The appellate court reversed the client's conviction for conspiracy to commit murder and other crimes, due to the trial court's admission of the attorney's testimony about the conversation with his client, despite the client's privilege objection. 863 A.2d at 325–27. In the appellate court's view, "To permit a Rule 1.6 disclosure to destroy the attorney-client privilege and empower the attorney to essentially waive his client's privilege without the client's consent is repugnant to the entire purpose of the attorney-client privilege in promoting candor between the attorney and client." 863 A.2d at 333. The court also held that the crime-fraud exception to the privilege did not apply when the client merely informed the attorney of her plans, because she did not seek the attorney's assistance in carrying out those plans. *Id.* at 335–37. Do you agree with the court's reasoning and holdings?

7. **Disclosure and Client with Diminished Capacity:** To what extent is the duty of confidentiality changed by a client's disability or limited capacity affecting communication and decision-making? The original version of Model Rule 1.14 addressed the issue indirectly, without making clear the consequences for confidentiality. Under the original version, the lawyer was permitted to seek a guardian or take other action when the lawyer reasonably believed the client could not act in the client's own interest. The ABA Committee on Ethics and Professional Responsibility concluded in Informal Opinion 89–1530 (1989) that the permission to seek a guardianship in Model Rule 1.14(b) necessarily implies permission to make such disclosures of confidential information as are necessary to initiate and pursue such a procedure. The Michigan State Bar Committee on Professional and Judicial

Ethics reached the same conclusion in Opinion RI–51 (1990), after having taken the opposite view under the prior Model Code of Professional Responsibility in Opinion CI–882 (1983). California's State Bar Committee on Professional Responsibility and Conduct also rejected the option of seeking a conservatorship under Rules of Professional Conduct that did not adopt Model Rule 1.14, Opinion 89–112 (1989), as have most opinions applying the former Model Code. *See* ABA Annotated Model Rules of Professional Conduct 240–41 (2d ed. 1992). For a critical assessment of the old Model Rule 1.14, see James R. Devine, *The Ethics of Representing the Disabled Client: Does Model Rule 1.14 Adequately Resolve the Best Interests/Advocacy Dilemma?*, 49 Mo.L.Rev. 493 (1984).

In 2002, the ABA added a provision to Model Rule 1.14 that finds implied authorization in Model Rule 1.6 for disclosures "reasonably necessary to protect the client's interests." Model Rule 1.14(c). Some elaboration of the relevant considerations is found in Comment [8], entitled, "Disclosure of the Client's Condition."

8. **Disclosure of Fraud:** Much of the literature deals with the attorney's duty or prerogative to disclose confidential information to *prevent* client wrongs. In the wake of numerous large-scale corporate frauds in the late 1990s and early 2000s, attention has refocused on the attorney's disclosure to *correct* a client fraud (or other wrong) that has already been committed. The next set of materials addresses some of the issues created by these cases.

PROBLEM

Arlen Smith and Dale Shaster, Attorneys and Counselors at Law, represent Ajax Leasing Company, which leases luxury automobiles to corporate executives. Smith & Shaster drafts leases for the Company and represents the Company in negotiating the purchase of new automobiles from their manufacturer, secured by assignment of prospective lease payments. After dozens of such leases are negotiated, Smith & Shaster learns that Ajax is setting rentals due under the leases at an artificially low level, and is accepting under-the-table lump sum payments from its executive customers. The effect is to reduce substantially the security the manufacturers are entitled to have for the Company's payments to them under the purchase agreements. Dale Shaster confronts the Company's officers, who agree to stop the practice but reject Shaster's demand that they take appropriate steps to rectify the consequences of their fraudulent activities. Smith & Shaster thereupon withdraw from the representation, having provided no further services to the Company.

QUESTION

Having failed to persuade the Company to rectify their fraud, and assuming that Smith & Shaster were not negligent in failing to discover the fraud sooner, what are the lawyers' responsibilities to the manufacturers?

RULE REFERENCES

Model Rules 1.2, 1.6, 1.13, and 4.1

RESTATEMENT § 67(2) & (4)

NOTES ON CORRECTIVE DISCLOSURE

1. **History of Disclosure Rules:** In 1969, the ABA adopted a *mandatory* disclosure rule for information "clearly establish[ing]" that the client had committed a fraud on a person in the course of the representation, where the client was unwilling to self-disclose. American Bar Association, Model Code of Professional Responsibility, Disciplinary Rule 7–102(B)(1). This rule was amended in 1974 to provide an exception from the duty where the information clearly establishing the fraud was privileged, and the ABA Ethics Committee interpreted that exception as extending to all *confidential* information whether or not privileged, *see* Formal Op. 341 (1975). However, by the time it was replaced by the Model Rules as the official position of the ABA in 1983, only a minority of states had adopted the amendment to the disciplinary rule. *See* Geoffrey C. Hazard, Jr., *Rectification of Client Fraud: Death and Revival of a Professional Norm*, 33 Emory L.J. 271, 294 n.38 (1984). The Model Code of Professional Responsibility, as adopted in most jurisdictions, thus imposed a corrective disclosure requirement only with respect to client frauds committed during the representation, as distinguished from other crimes or wrongs. Do legal services have some special relationship with potential fraud that justifies a special responsibility to protect third parties from the consequences of such client misconduct merely because it occurred on the lawyer's watch?

The Kutak Commission, the drafters of the Model Rules, focused on the lawyer's duty not to *assist* the client in criminal or fraudulent activity, and proposed *permissive* disclosure, under Model Rule 1.6(b), "to rectify the consequences of a client's criminal or fraudulent act *in the commission of which the lawyer's services had been used.*" Proposed Final Draft of Model Rules of Professional Conduct Rule 1.6(b)(3) (1981) (emphasis added); *see* Hazard, *supra,* at 296–97. This proposal was rejected by the ABA and no disclosure provision, permissive or mandatory, appeared in its Model Rule 1.6. This left an absolute prohibition against a lawyer's disclosing the intent by the client to commit a crime of fraud in the future. However, a substantial minority of jurisdictions adopted variants on the Commission's proposal. The lawyer was, however, prohibited from counseling the client to engage in fraud or assisting the client in so engaging under Model Rule 1.2(d). If the matter was in litigation, the lawyer was also obligated to prevent fraud upon the tribunal under Model Rule 3.3, as discussed in *infra* section 4(C). The current version of Model Rule 1.6(b)(3), as amended in 2003, finally adopts permissive corrective disclosure, as does the current version of Model Rule 1.13(c), which was also amended in 2003.

A factually more complicated case than our problem gained national attention in the early 1980s. That case nicely illustrates practical difficulties presented by the Model Rules' apparent dual command directed to lawyers whose clients contemplate or commit fraud: (a) do not do anything to assist the client's fraud, and (b) at the same time, preserve the client's confidences. In the case of O.P.M. Leasing Services, Inc., and its New York law firm, when the lawyers first confronted the client they received a solemn commitment that future transactions would be certified as genuine, and withdrew only after discovering the clients were not honoring this commitment. After withdrawal, they refused to disclose their knowledge even to the successor law firm (which asked why they withdrew), until the fraud came out into the open, the clients were charged with crime, and both they and the new lawyers were sued for damages. Questions were raised about whether the lawyers should have discovered the fraud much sooner in the first place, whether they too readily accepted the officers' assurance of mended ways, and whether they should have informed at least their successor lawyers about the reasons for withdrawal. *See, e.g., Advice or Consent: O.P.M. Fraud Raises Questions About Role of a Criminal's Lawyer*, Wall Street J., Dec. 31, 1982, at 1; Larry Lempert, *O.P.M. Lawyers: Could, Should They Have Known?*, Legal Times, Jan. 3, 1983, at 1; Robert N. Treiman, Comment, *Inter–Lawyer Communication and the Prevention of Client Fraud: A Look Back at O.P.M.*, 34 UCLA L.Rev. 925 (1987). We draw more directly on the O.P.M. facts for our lawyer self-defense problem in *infra* section 4(D).

An attorney who has no pre-existing duty to disclose harmful information might create such a duty by disclosing related information. In *Vega v. Jones, Day, Reavis & Pogue*, 17 Cal.Rptr.3d 26 (Ct.App. 2004), the Jones, Day firm represented the acquiring company in a merger. The plaintiffs, shareholders of the acquired company, agreed to exchange their shares in the acquired company for shares of the acquiring company. The plaintiffs alleged that Jones, Day provided them with a " 'sanitized version' " of a disclosure schedule, which omitted harmful information about the acquiring company. The appellate court held that this fraud case could proceed, because someone—even a lawyer—who voluntarily provides information cannot withhold harmful information that renders the provided information misleading. *See id.* at 31–35.

Events of the late 1990s and early 2000s caused Congress and the Securities and Exchange Commission to enter the picture, for those who represent publicly held corporations. The position of the SEC with respect to corrective disclosure by attorneys in the securities context has now been clarified by 15 U.S.C. § 7245 (2006), part of the Sarbanes–Oxley Act, which was adopted by Congress in response to a spate of accounting scandals involving publicly held corporations such as the energy trading company Enron. It calls for the SEC to promulgate rules of conduct for lawyers who represent issuers when practicing before the Commission. The rules the SEC was obligated to enact include rules

(1) requiring an attorney to report evidence of a material violation of securities law or breach of fiduciary duty or similar violation by the company or any agent thereof, to the chief legal counsel or the chief executive officer of the company (or the equivalent thereof); and

(2) if the counsel or officer does not appropriately respond to the evidence (adopting, as necessary, appropriate remedial measures or sanctions with

respect to the violation), requiring the attorney to report the evidence to the audit committee of the board of directors of the issuer or to another committee of the board of directors comprised solely of directors not employed directly or indirectly by the issuer, or to the board of directors. 15 U.S.C. § 7245 (2006). The Commission adopted rules that became effective in 2003. 17 C.F.R. § 205 (2003).

It is interesting to note, however, that under the Commission's rules the lawyer's disclosure *to the Commission itself* is only permissive, and limited to (i) preventing a material violation by the issuer or perjury before the Commission about their conduct, or (ii) rectifying the consequences of a material violation that has or may cause substantial harm to financial interests of the issuer or of investors. 17 C.F.R. § 205.3(d)(2) (2003).

2. **"Noisy Withdrawal":** Suppose, in a situation similar to O.P.M. Leasing, that the law firm had issued an opinion letter in support of the application for bank loans, to the effect that the leases were legally enforceable assets of the client. Suppose further that upon withdrawal after the client refuses to make good on the outstanding fraudulent loans, the law firm is unable to acquire assurance from the client that it will not continue to utilize the opinion letter to support further loan applications from present creditors, even though the letter was clearly based on factual assumptions now known by the lawyers to be false. Without that assurance, the firm has good reason to believe that the client in fact intends such use. Under the ABA's pre–2002 Model Rules, which did not permit either preventive or corrective disclosure for client fraud generally, could the law firm nonetheless notify creditors that it no longer stands by its opinion letter, in order to prevent such future use?

The pre-Ethics 2000 commentary to Model Rule 1.6 ("Withdrawal," then Comment [16]) said so, stating that a lawyer who withdraws because his services will otherwise be used by the client to further a course of criminal or fraudulent conduct may not only give notice of such withdrawal but also "withdraw or disaffirm any opinion, document, affirmation, or the like." This comment was confirmed as a reasonable interpretation of the Model Rule by the ABA's Committee on Ethics and Professional Responsibility, Formal Opinion 92–366, *in* Laws.Man. on Prof. Conduct (ABA/BNA) 1001:134 (1992), third conclusion. Formal Opinion 92–366 is criticized on other grounds, but supported on the "noisy withdrawal" point, in Geoffrey C. Hazard, Jr., *Lawyers and Client Fraud: They Still Don't Get It*, 6 Geo.J. Legal Ethics 701 (1993). *See also* Charles W. Wolfram, *Parts and Wholes: The Integrity of the* Model Rules, 6 Geo.J. Legal Ethics 861, 864–71 (1993) (noting the intended tension between the black letter and the commentary in Model Rule 1.6).

The commentary was retained as Comment [14] in the 2002 version of Model Rule 1.6. This comment was removed in the summer of 2003, however, presumably because the new permission to engage in *corrective* disclosure where the lawyer's services have been used in the commission of a crime or fraud (new Model Rule 1.6(b)(3)) would clearly allow a "noisy withdrawal" of this sort. *See supra* note 1.

At the same time, the ABA amended Model Rule 1.13 to require an attorney who believes that she has been discharged or forced to withdraw as a result of her efforts to prevent injury to an organizational client, including efforts to make authorities in the organization aware of potential problems under Model Rule 1.13(b) or revealing of information under Model Rule 1.13(c), to "proceed as the lawyer reasonably believes necessary to assure that the organization's highest authority is informed of the lawyer's discharge or withdrawal." Model Rule 1.13(e). For a discussion of noisy withdrawal in this context, see Patrick H. Pugh, *The SEC Standards of Professional Responsibility for Attorneys: A Balanced Solution to Noisy Withdrawal*, 14 Kan.J.L. & Pub. Pol'y 659 (2005).

C. PROTECTING THE COURTS: CLIENT PERJURY

PROBLEM

You represent, by appointment, Arnold Howard, who has been accused of armed robbery and felony murder at a local bar. Howard maintains that he was at home alone the night of the crime, but has no witness to prove it. The state eventually discloses a witness who will identify Howard as present at the scene of the crime, although the only direct assertion that Howard was actually involved in the robbery comes from a co-defendant.

QUESTIONS

(a) You advise Howard to remain silent in the face of this evidence, but he insists on taking the stand to tell his alibi story, which you are now convinced is false. How should you proceed?

(1) Under what circumstances would you be permitted to withdraw? If you seek to withdraw, to whom should you address your motion for leave to withdraw? How much should you disclose in your motion of the reasons for it?

(2) If you do not seek to withdraw, or if your motion is denied, how should you handle the client on direct examination?

(b) The client admits to you, after you confront him with the likely testimony from the state, that he was at the bar that night, but he insists he had nothing to do with the robbery, and says it was committed by a friend of his who is now falsely implicating him. After firming up this story with further questioning, you advise the client to take the stand to tell it. But in response to your first substantive question on direct examination, the client blurts out the alibi story instead. You did not make an opening statement directly contradicting this story. How should you proceed?

(c) Assume that you have moved for leave to withdraw, and the judge has granted the motion. The judge further decides, in order to avoid possible prejudice, to declare a mistrial and have the defendant retried before a new judge and defended by a new lawyer. When the new trial occurs, you happen to be in the courtroom awaiting the next case, and you observe the defendant testifying to the alibi. Assuming that the state's evidence was exactly as it was known to you before you withdrew, what are your obligations?

(d) Assume instead that you concluded on the information available to you that the eyewitness statement was unreliable, and that the client's alibi was sincere and tenable. You present the client's testimony in the usual way, and the client is acquitted of the criminal charges.

(1) Some weeks after the acquittal, client comes into your office to clear up some fee issues, and says to you: "Boy, I sure had 'em fooled on that phony alibi, didn't I? I could have sworn you believed it too!" What are your obligations?

(2) A parallel civil case was brought against the client by the family of the murder victim for damages. After the criminal acquittal, but before the conversation described in (1) above, the plaintiffs proceed to trial of the civil case anyway. The client repeats the alibi testimony, and the jury hands down a verdict for the client. The above-described conversation occurs the day after the verdict and judgment in the civil case. What are your obligations?

RULE REFERENCES

Model Rules 3.3 and 1.16

RESTATEMENT § 120

NIX v. WHITESIDE

Supreme Court of the United States, 1986.
475 U.S. 157.

CHIEF JUSTICE BURGER delivered the opinion of the Court.

We granted certiorari to decide whether the Sixth Amendment right of a criminal defendant to assistance of counsel is violated when an attorney refuses to cooperate with the defendant in presenting perjured testimony at his trial.

I

A

Whiteside was convicted of second-degree murder by a jury verdict which was affirmed by the Iowa courts. The killing took place * * * in Cedar Rapids, Iowa. Whiteside and two others went to one Calvin Love's apartment late [in the evening], seeking marihuana. Love was in bed when Whiteside and his companions arrived; an argument between Whiteside and Love over the marihuana ensued. At one point, Love directed his girlfriend to get his "piece," and at another point got up, then returned to his bed. According to Whiteside's testimony, Love then started to reach under his pillow and moved toward Whiteside. Whiteside stabbed Love in the chest, inflicting a fatal wound.

Whiteside was charged with murder, and when counsel was appointed he objected to the lawyer initially appointed, claiming that he felt uncomfortable with a lawyer who had formerly been a prosecutor. Gary L.

Robinson was then appointed and immediately began an investigation. Whiteside gave him a statement that he had stabbed Love as the latter "was pulling a pistol from underneath the pillow on the bed." Upon questioning by Robinson, however, Whiteside indicated that he had not actually seen a gun, but that he was convinced that Love had a gun. No pistol was found on the premises; shortly after the police search following the stabbing, which had revealed no weapon, the victim's family had removed all of the victim's possessions from the apartment. Robinson interviewed Whiteside's companions who were present during the stabbing, and none had seen a gun during the incident. Robinson advised Whiteside that the existence of a gun was not necessary to establish the claim of self-defense, and that only a reasonable belief that the victim had a gun nearby was necessary even though no gun was actually present.

Until shortly before trial, Whiteside consistently stated to Robinson that he had not actually seen a gun, but that he was convinced that Love had a gun in his hand. About a week before trial, during preparation for direct examination, Whiteside for the first time told Robinson * * * that he had seen something "metallic" in Love's hand. When asked about this, Whiteside responded:

> "[I]n Howard Cook's case there was a gun. If I don't say I saw a gun, I'm dead."

Robinson told Whiteside that such testimony would be perjury and repeated that it was not necessary to prove that a gun was available but only that Whiteside reasonably believed that he was in danger. On Whiteside's insisting that he would testify that he saw "something metallic" Robinson told him, according to Robinson's testimony:

> "[W]e could not allow him to [testify falsely] because that would be perjury, and as officers of the court we would be suborning perjury if we allowed him to do it; ... I advised him that if he did do that it would be my duty to advise the Court of what he was doing and that I felt he was committing perjury; also, that I probably would be allowed to attempt to impeach that particular testimony." * * *

Robinson also indicated he would seek to withdraw from the representation if Whiteside insisted on committing perjury.

Whiteside testified in his own defense at trial and stated that he "knew" that Love had a gun and that he believed Love was reaching for a gun and he had acted swiftly in self-defense. On cross-examination, he admitted that he had not actually seen a gun in Love's hand. Robinson presented evidence that Love had been seen with a sawed-off shotgun on other occasions, that the police search of the apartment may have been careless, and that the victim's family had removed everything from the apartment shortly after the crime. Robinson presented this evidence to show a basis for Whiteside's asserted fear that Love had a gun.

The jury returned a verdict of second-degree murder, and Whiteside moved for a new trial, claiming that he had been deprived of a fair trial by

Robinson's admonitions not to state that he saw a gun or "something metallic." The trial court held a hearing, heard testimony by Whiteside and Robinson, and denied the motion. The trial court made specific findings that the facts were as related by Robinson.

The Supreme Court of Iowa affirmed respondent's conviction. * * * That court held that the right to have counsel present all appropriate defenses does not extend to using perjury, and that an attorney's duty to a client does not extend to assisting a client in committing perjury. Relying on [Iowa's Ethics Rules, which expressly prohibit] an attorney from using perjured testimony, and [provisions of the Iowa Code, which criminalize] subornation of perjury, the Iowa court concluded that not only were Robinson's actions permissible, but were required. The court commended " * * * Mr. Robinson * * * for the high ethical manner in which this matter was handled."

B

Whiteside then petitioned for a writ of habeas corpus in the United States District Court for the Southern District of Iowa. In that petition Whiteside alleged that he had been denied effective assistance of counsel and of his right to present a defense by Robinson's refusal to allow him to testify as he had proposed. The District Court denied the writ. Accepting the state trial court's factual finding that Whiteside's intended testimony would have been perjurious, it concluded that there could be no grounds for habeas relief since there is no constitutional right to present a perjured defense.

The United States Court of Appeals for the Eighth Circuit reversed and directed that the writ of habeas corpus be granted. * * * We granted certiorari, * * * and we reverse.

II * * *

B

In *Strickland* v. *Washington*, [466 U.S. 668 (1984),] we held that to obtain relief by way of federal habeas corpus on a claim of a deprivation of effective assistance of counsel under the Sixth Amendment, the movant must establish both serious attorney error and prejudice. To show such error, it must be established that the assistance rendered by counsel was constitutionally deficient in that "counsel made errors so serious that counsel was not functioning as 'counsel' guaranteed the defendant by the Sixth Amendment." * * * To show prejudice, it must be established that the claimed lapses in counsel's performance rendered the trial unfair so as to "undermine confidence in the outcome" of the trial. * * *

In *Strickland*, we acknowledged that the Sixth Amendment does not require any particular response by counsel to a problem that may arise. Rather, the Sixth Amendment inquiry is into whether the attorney's conduct was "reasonably effective." To counteract the natural tendency to fault an unsuccessful defense, a court reviewing a claim of ineffective assistance must "indulge a strong presumption that counsel's conduct falls within the wide range of reasonable professional assistance." * * * In giving shape to the perimeters of this range of reasonable professional assistance, *Strickland* mandates that

> "[p]revailing norms of practice as reflected in American Bar Association Standards and the like, ... are guides to determining what is reasonable, but they are only guides." * * *

Under the *Strickland* standard, breach of an ethical standard does not necessarily make out a denial of the Sixth Amendment guarantee of assistance of counsel. * * * Here we need not face that question, since virtually all of the sources speak with one voice.

C * * *

In *Strickland*, we recognized counsel's duty of loyalty and his "overarching duty to advocate the defendant's cause." * * * Plainly, that duty is limited to legitimate, lawful conduct compatible with the very nature of a trial as a search for truth. * * *

Disciplinary Rule 7–102 of the Model Code of Professional Responsibility (1980), entitled "Representing a Client Within the Bounds of the Law," provides:

> "(A) In his representation of a client, a lawyer shall not: * * *

> "(4) Knowingly use perjured testimony or false evidence. * * *

> "(7) Counsel or assist his client in conduct that the lawyer knows to be illegal or fraudulent."

This provision has been adopted by Iowa, and is binding on all lawyers who appear in its courts. See Iowa Code of Professional Responsibility for Lawyers (1985). * * *

Both the Model Code of Professional Responsibility and the Model Rules of Professional Conduct also adopt the specific exception from the attorney-client privilege for disclosure of perjury that his client intends to commit or has committed. DR 4–101(C)(3) (intention of client to commit a crime); Rule 3.3 (lawyer has duty to disclose falsity of evidence even if disclosure compromises client confidences). Indeed, both the Model Code and the Model Rules do not merely *authorize* disclosure by counsel of client perjury; they *require* such disclosure. See Rule 3.3(a)([3]); DR 7–102(B)(1); *Committee on Professional Ethics and Conduct of Iowa State Bar Assn.* v. *Crary*, 245 N.W.2d 298 (Iowa 1976). * * *

It is universally agreed that at a minimum the attorney's first duty when confronted with a proposal for perjurious testimony is to attempt to dissuade the client from the unlawful course of conduct. Model Rules of Professional Conduct, Rule 3.3, Comment; [Charles W.] Wolfram, Client Perjury, 50 S. Cal. L. Rev. 809, 846 (1977). A statement directly [on] point is found in the commentary to the Model Rules of Professional Conduct under the heading "False Evidence":

"When false evidence is offered by the client, however, a conflict may arise between the lawyer's duty to keep the client's revelations confidential and the duty of candor to the court. Upon ascertaining that material evidence is false, the lawyer *should seek to persuade the client that the evidence should not be offered* or, if it has been offered, that its false character should immediately be disclosed." Model Rules of Professional Conduct, Rule 3.3, Comment (1983) (emphasis added).

The commentary thus also suggests that an attorney's revelation of his client's perjury to the court is a professionally responsible and acceptable response to the conduct of a client who has actually given perjured testimony. Similarly, the Model Rules and the commentary * * * expressly permit withdrawal from representation as an appropriate response of an attorney when the client threatens to commit perjury. Model Rules of Professional Conduct, Rule 1.16(a)(1), Rule 1.6, Comment (1983) * * *. Withdrawal of counsel when this situation arises at trial gives rise to many difficult questions including possible mistrial and claims of double jeopardy. * * *

D

Considering Robinson's representation of respondent in light of these accepted norms of professional conduct, we discern no failure to adhere to reasonable professional standards that would in any sense make out a deprivation of the Sixth Amendment right to counsel. Whether Robinson's conduct is seen as a successful attempt to dissuade his client from committing the crime of perjury, or whether seen as a "threat" to withdraw from representation and disclose the illegal scheme, Robinson's representation of Whiteside falls well within accepted standards of professional conduct and the range of reasonable professional conduct acceptable under *Strickland.* * * *

The Court of Appeals' holding that Robinson's "action deprived [Whiteside] of due process and effective assistance of counsel" is not supported by the record since Robinson's action, at most, deprived Whiteside of his contemplated perjury. Nothing counsel did in any way undermined Whiteside's claim that he believed the victim was reaching for a gun. Similarly, the record gives no support for holding that Robinson's action "also impermissibly compromised [Whiteside's] right to testify in his own defense by conditioning continued representation ... and confidentiality upon [Whiteside's] *restricted* testimony." The record in fact shows the contrary: (a) that Whiteside did testify, and (b) he was "restricted" or restrained only from testifying falsely and was aided by Robinson in developing the basis for the fear that Love was reaching for a gun. Robinson divulged no client communications until he was compelled to do so in response to Whiteside's post-trial challenge to the quality of his performance. We see this as a case in which the attorney successfully dissuaded the client from committing the crime of perjury. * * *

Whatever the scope of a constitutional right to testify, it is elementary that such a right does not extend to testifying *falsely*. In *Harris* v. *New*

York, we assumed the right of an accused to testify "in his own defense, or to refuse to do so" and went on to hold:

> "[T]hat privilege cannot be construed to include the right to commit perjury. See *United States* v. *Knox*, 396 U.S. 77 [(1969)]; cf. *Dennis* v. *United States*, 384 U.S. 855 [(1966)]. Having voluntarily taken the stand, petitioner was under an obligation to speak truthfully...." 401 U.S., at 225, 91 S.Ct., at 645. * * *

The paucity of authority on the subject of any such "right" may be explained by the fact that such a notion has never been responsibly advanced; the right to counsel includes no right to have a lawyer who will cooperate with planned perjury. A lawyer who would so cooperate would be at risk of prosecution for suborning perjury, and disciplinary proceedings, including suspension or disbarment. * * *

E

We hold that, as a matter of law, counsel's conduct complained of here cannot establish the prejudice required for relief under the second strand of the *Strickland* inquiry. Although a defendant need not establish that the attorney's deficient performance more likely than not altered the outcome in order to establish prejudice under *Strickland*, a defendant must show that "there is a reasonable probability that, but for counsel's unprofessional errors, the result of the proceeding would have been different." * * *

Whether he was persuaded or compelled to desist from perjury, Whiteside has no valid claim that confidence in the result of his trial has been diminished by his desisting from the contemplated perjury. Even if we were to assume that the jury might have believed his perjury, it does not follow that Whiteside was prejudiced. * * *

Whiteside's attorney treated Whiteside's proposed perjury in accord with professional standards, and since Whiteside's truthful testimony could not have prejudiced the result of his trial, the Court of Appeals was in error to direct the issuance of a writ of habeas corpus and must be reversed.

Reversed.

[BLACKMUN, BRENNAN, STEVENS and MARSHALL, JJ., concurred solely on the ground of the absence of prejudice as a requirement of constitutional violation, and dismissed the majority's discussion of ethical standards as *obiter dictum.*]

NOTES ON NIX

1. *Nix v. Whiteside* responds to the attorney's duty when the client threatens to commit perjury, holding that the client is not denied effective counsel when the lawyer refuses to put such evidence into the case. This is the teaching of Model Rule 3.3(a)(3). The tension in *Nix* is between the client's usual right to testify and the attorney's duty not to present false testimony.

2. Short of revealing the client's intent to lie, is there anything that a lawyer should, or could, do that would be more fair to the client's interest? The next case helps answer this question.

COMMONWEALTH v. MITCHELL

Supreme Judicial Court of Massachusetts, 2003.
781 N.E.2d 1237.

GREANEY, J.

A jury convicted the defendant of two indictments charging murder in the first degree by reason of deliberate premeditation and extreme atrocity or cruelty. The defendant's motion for a new trial was denied by the trial judge, on the basis of affidavits, without an evidentiary hearing. The defendant is represented on appeal by the counsel who represented him in connection with his motion for a new trial. The defendant argues that he was denied constitutionally effective assistance of counsel (and incurred violations of other constitutional rights) when his trial counsel, relying on Mass. R. Prof. C. 3.3(e), 426 Mass. 1383 (1998), set forth below,[1] advised the judge at trial that the defendant would testify and present false testimony to the jury, that counsel had attempted to persuade the defendant from testifying falsely, that counsel had decided that he would not seek to withdraw from representing the defendant in the ongoing trial, and that counsel needed instruction from the judge on how to proceed before the jury. After receiving instruction, counsel presented the defendant's testimony in narrative form and made a closing argument that reflected his understanding of his ethical obligations.

[A couple to whom Mitchell had been selling drugs were brutally murdered in their apartment in the late evening of June 13, 1996. This occurred a few hours after Mitchell's supplier and neighbor, Adams, had been arrested in a drug raid on the latter's apartment. At trial, Adams testified that after he posted bond and returned home, he told the defendant that he believed the couple had tipped off the police. He said that Mitchell then asked him whether he wanted to do anything about this and that he said no. He said that later that evening Mitchell told him that he had "done" the couple. Mitchell's former girlfriend (Freitas) testified that she had been in his apartment before he came home after

---

1. Paragraph (e) of Rule 3.3 of the Massachusetts Rules of Professional Conduct, 426 Mass. 1383 (1998), entitled, "Candor Toward the Tribunal," provides, in pertinent part:

"In a criminal case, defense counsel who knows that the defendant, the client, intends to testify falsely may not aid the client in constructing false testimony, and has a duty strongly to discourage the client from testifying falsely, advising that such a course is unlawful, will have substantial adverse consequences, and should not be followed.... If a criminal trial has commenced and the lawyer discovers that the client intends to testify falsely at trial, the lawyer need not file a motion to withdraw from the case if the lawyer reasonably believes that seeking to withdraw will prejudice the client. If, during the client's testimony or after the client has testified, the lawyer knows that the client has testified falsely, the lawyer shall call upon the client to rectify the false testimony and, if the client refuses or is unable to do so, the lawyer shall not reveal the false testimony to the tribunal. In no event may the lawyer examine the client in such a manner as to elicit any testimony from the client the lawyer knows to be false, and the lawyer shall not argue the probative value of the false testimony in closing argument or in any other proceedings, including appeals." * * *

midnight, that he confessed to her in bed that he'd killed two people, that he told her the next morning that she couldn't stay because people would be asking questions, and that when he saw her again he asked her to tell police that he had been with her all that night. Two female friends whom he saw in the next two days (Gaspar and Rose) testified that he had told them he had murdered two people that night. Another witness testified that she sold Mitchell a gun that night, that he said he needed it for the people who snitched on Adams, that he had returned it to her a week later because it hadn't worked, and that a gun found at the scene was the same type. Patterson, an across-the-corridor neighbor of the victims who found the bodies the next day, testified that he had seen the defendant enter the victims' apartment that night after knocking and identifying himself, and later heard a sound like a "large branch" snapping. A policeman testified that Mitchell had called him and asked him not to question Freitas.]

On June 27, 1996, the defendant made contact with the Fall River police. After being given Miranda warnings and signing a written Miranda form, the defendant told the police that the victims used to buy drugs through him, and that he bought his drugs from Adams and dealt for Adams. The defendant stated that he went to Martha's Vineyard out of fear of being raided by the police. He indicated his view that more than one person had to have committed the killings because Shurtliff was "a big girl, and . . . it would have taken more than one [person] to hang her." The interrogating officer asked the defendant how he knew Shurtliff had been "hanged," and the defendant said he had just heard that. The defendant said he would help the police in trying to locate the murderers.

The defendant contended at trial that someone else, probably Adams, had killed the victims. The defendant called an analyst employed by Cellmark Diagnostics, who testified that DNA testing excluded the defendant as a source of DNA obtained from hairs found in Shurtliff's hand. The defendant also called Willie Smith. Smith testified that, during the early morning of June 14, 1996, he saw the defendant while talking to Adams on the porch to Adams's apartment. Smith stated that the porch lights were on, that he had not noticed any blood on the defendant's clothing, and that the defendant was not wearing any gloves. He denied paying attention to the conversation between Adams and the defendant.

The defendant testified. After his trial counsel had him state his name, counsel asked, "Mr. Mitchell, what do you wish to tell these jurors?" The defendant then proceeded to testify at length in a narrative fashion. The defendant recounted his dealings with Adams and recounted events that tended to implicate Adams as the killer. The defendant denied that he had killed the victims, denied that he had prayed while with Freitas, denied the statements Freitas, Gaspar, and Rose attributed to him, denied that he had told police not to question Freitas, and denied buying a gun from Hamilton.

The defendant's trial counsel did not argue the defendant's testimony in his closing argument. He emphasized the Commonwealth's high burden of proof and stressed that Adams had a motive to harm the victims. The defendant's trial counsel stated that the defendant was a small time dealer with no motive to kill the victims. He pointed out inconsistencies in Freitas's story to police and suggested that she had implicated the defendant out of fear of Adams. The defendant's trial counsel emphasized the failure of the police seriously to investigate suspects other than the defendant. He also argued that one of the victims' daughters had identified several people who had been in the victims' apartment, but not the defendant, as the possible killer or killers. He attacked Patterson's credibility based on his criminal record and inconsistent statements to police, and he attacked Adams's credibility, noting that Smith, who had been with Adams when they allegedly met the defendant after the killings, had not observed any blood on the defendant's hands. The defendant's trial counsel further called to the jury's attention the lack of physical evidence tying the defendant to the crimes, and what he considered failures in the police investigation. * * *

The defendant's allegations of ineffective assistance of his trial counsel, and related claims of constitutional violations, by reason of his trial counsel's invocation of rule 3.3(e), arose out of the following events. After both the Commonwealth and defense had rested, the defendant's trial counsel and the prosecutor approached the bench, where the defendant's trial counsel informed the judge that the defendant now wished to testify. In the absence of an objection by the prosecutor, the judge reopened the evidence to permit the defendant (and Smith, Adams's brother-in-law) to testify. The defendant's trial counsel stated that he had concerns about participating in a fraud on the court and could not reveal more without violating the attorney-client privilege, but that he wanted to put the defendant on the stand, ask him his name, and let him tell his story to the jury. The judge then took a recess to read rule 3.3(e). When the sidebar conference resumed, the defendant's trial counsel indicated that he would remain as counsel in order not to prejudice the defendant. He also assured the judge that he had tried to dissuade the defendant from testifying falsely. The judge instructed the defendant's trial counsel to remain standing during the defendant's narrative testimony on direct and to make objections to the prosecutor's cross-examination one question at a time, as appropriate, keeping in mind that he could not assist the defendant in presenting false testimony.

The trial proceeded in accordance with the judge's instructions. When the defendant finished testifying, his counsel was granted a recess to confer with him. The defendant's trial counsel reported back to the judge that he had "carried out [his] responsibilities under the disciplinary rule." The prosecutor then cross-examined the defendant. The defendant's trial counsel did not argue the defendant's testimony during his closing argument, but argued as summarized above. The defendant's request to make an unsworn statement to the jury was denied by the judge.

In his motion for a new trial, the defendant argued that his trial counsel did not have an adequate basis to invoke rule 3.3(e), that the judge unconstitutionally applied the rule by failing to conduct a colloquy with him, and that his constitutional rights were violated because he was not present at the sidebar when his trial counsel invoked rule 3.3(e). The defendant also claimed that he should have been afforded the opportunity to be represented by independent counsel, and that he should have been allowed to give an unsworn statement to the jury or to argue his own testimony in closing. In support of his contentions, the defendant offered his affidavit and the affidavit of his trial counsel. In the defendant's affidavit, he stated that "[t]he testimony that I gave at trial was true. I never told [my trial counsel] that I was going to testify falsely and commit perjury." The defendant's trial counsel, in his affidavit, made the following statements:

> "When I first interviewed [the defendant], he told me he did not kill the victims in this case.

> "Later on in the course of my representation, he told me that he did. My subjective belief was that this inculpatory story was true. I had no additional inculpatory information other than that provided by the Commonwealth in discovery and by the witnesses at trial. . . .

> "Prior to the defendant's testimony, I advised him that he was not permitted to give perjured testimony, and that I could not present perjured testimony or argue it.

> "I believed it was perjurious because it contradicted his earlier version of events and was contrary to the evidence provided to me in discovery and presented in the Commonwealth's case.

> "The defendant asked me if he could argue his case in addition to my argument. I told him that the judge would not allow it and I thought it would hurt rather than help him. . . ."

* * *

a. We first address the defendant's contention that the judge applied the wrong standard to inform the word "knows" in rule 3.3(e). The question what a criminal defense attorney should do when confronted with client perjury at trial has been a subject of considerable debate. The problem raises both ethical and constitutional concerns. Defense counsel must furnish zealous advocacy and preserve client confidences, but, at the same time, defense counsel has a duty under rule 3.3(e) to the court. In addition, the problem has constitutional implications by reason of its potential to deprive a defendant of his right to effective assistance of counsel, and his rights to due process and a fair trial, which include his right to testify in his own defense.

Not unexpectedly, courts have adopted differing standards to determine what an attorney must "know" before concluding that his client's testimony will be perjurious. The standards include the following: "good cause to believe the defendant's proposed testimony would be deliberately untruthful," *State v. Hischke,* 639 N.W.2d 6, 10 (Iowa 2002); "compelling support," *Sanborn v. State,* 474 So.2d 309, 313 n. 2 (Fla.Dist.Ct.App.1985);

"knowledge beyond a reasonable doubt," *Shockley v. State*, 565 A.2d 1373, 1379 (Del.1989); a "firm factual basis," *United States ex rel. Wilcox v. Johnson*, 555 F.2d 115, 122 (3d Cir.1977); a "good-faith determination," *People v. Bartee*, 208 Ill.App.3d 105, 108, 153 Ill.Dec. 5, 566 N.E.2d 855, cert. denied, 502 U.S. 1014, 112 S.Ct. 661, 116 L.Ed.2d 752 (1991); and "actual knowledge," *United States v. Del Carpio–Cotrina*, 733 F.Supp. 95, 99 (S.D.Fla.1990) (applying "actual knowledge" standard to require firm factual basis). The judge properly rejected standards that were too lenient (good cause to believe) or too rigid, particularly the standard sought by the defendant, knowledge beyond a reasonable doubt. The knowledge beyond a reasonable doubt standard essentially would eviscerate rule 3.3(e). That standard, as described by one court, is "virtually impossible to satisfy unless the lawyer had a direct confession from his client or personally witnessed the event in question." *State v. Hischke*, [639 N.W.2d] at 10. The standard would also tend to compel defense attorneys to remain silent in the face of likely perjury that a sharp private warning could nip in the bud. *See Nix v. Whiteside*, 475 U.S. 157, 169, 106 S.Ct. 988, 89 L.Ed.2d 123 (1986).

The judge correctly settled on the firm basis in fact standard. This standard satisfies constitutional concerns because it requires more than mere suspicion or conjecture on the part of counsel, more than a belief and more information than inconsistencies in statements by the defendant or in the evidence. Instead, the standard mandates that a lawyer act in good faith based on objective circumstances firmly rooted in fact. The lawyer may act on the information he or she possesses, and we decline to impose an independent duty on the part of counsel to investigate because such a duty would be "incompatible with the fiduciary nature of the attorney-client relationship," *United States v. Del Carpio–Cotrina*, [733 F.Supp.] at 99, n.9, and is unnecessary when an attorney relies, in significant part, on incriminating admissions made by the client.

b.   Under the standard articulated, we are satisfied that the defendant's trial counsel, a lawyer with thirty-five years' experience, acted properly under rule 3.3(e). Contrary to the defendant's contentions, his trial counsel was not faced with mere inconsistent statements. Rather, the defendant initially told his trial counsel that he did not kill the victims, but later stated that he had murdered them. The defendant's admission was different in kind from inconsistencies in details, or in statements by a defendant who, under all accounts, consistently denies culpability. The defendant's trial counsel was not faced with mere discrepancies in details told to him by the defendant at various times; he was faced with a direct admission from the defendant's own lips combined with substantial evidence produced by the Commonwealth that corroborated the defendant's admission, including the defendant's incriminating conduct and his inculpatory statements to others. The record amply supports the judge's finding that counsel had a firm basis in objective fact for his good faith determination that the defendant intended to commit perjury.

c. As the judge acknowledged in his posttrial ruling, the defendant should have been present at the sidebar conference during which his trial counsel invoked rule 3.3(e). The conference was a critical stage of the proceedings. * * * The defendant argues that had he been at the sidebar, he would have been able to convince the judge that his testimony would be truthful; that he would have asked that his trial counsel be discharged and new counsel appointed; and that he would have asked to make his own closing argument and renewed his request to make an unsworn statement to the jury.

The judge disposed of these contentions by pointing out that he would not have accepted the defendant's assertion that his testimony would be truthful; would not have allowed the defendant to make his own closing argument; and would not have reconsidered his previous ruling denying the defendant an opportunity to make an unsworn statement. As to the possibility of changing counsel, the judge ruled:

> "[I] would not have permitted [the defendant's trial counsel] to withdraw in the middle of a complicated trial and would not have appointed successor counsel. * * * Appointment of new counsel would simply have shifted the ethical dilemma from one attorney to another. In addition, it would be entirely impracticable, likely prejudicial, and unworkable to bring in a new lawyer in the middle of a lengthy trial in a murder charge. * * * Moreover, the defendant was not entitled to new counsel who might fail to recognize the problem of fabricated testimony or who might be unethical enough to present it. * * *

We agree with these rulings, and conclude, as did the judge, that the defendant's absence from the conference was harmless beyond a reasonable doubt. * * *

f. The narrative form of testimony was properly directed. This approach was adopted by the ABA in 1971. See ABA Standards for Criminal Justice 4–7.7 (Approved Draft 1971). Although the ABA later rejected this approach and currently suggests that the lawyer may examine as to truthful testimony, and although the approach has been criticized, * * * "the narrative [approach] continues to be a commonly accepted method of dealing with client perjury," *Shockley v. State,* 565 A.2d 1373, 1380 (Del.1989). See * * * *People v. Bartee,* 208 Ill.App.3d 105, 108, 153 Ill.Dec. 5, 566 N.E.2d 855 (1991). [The court rejected as impracticable the defendant's suggestion that counsel should have examined him as to the truthful portions of his testimony and argued them to the jury. The court also rejected as inconsistent with the Rule his arguments that he should have been allowed to submit a closing statement to the jury and that the judge should have held an evidentiary hearing before allowing counsel to proceed with the narrative approach.]

We affirm the judgments of conviction and the orders denying the motion for a new trial * * *.

NOTES ON ANTICIPATION OF CLIENT PERJURY AND PREVENTIVE MEASURES

1. **When Does the Attorney "Know" Enough to Act?** The first question for counsel in the "client perjury" cases—whether dealing with the prospect of the client's false testimony or with the fact of its having been given on the stand—is a factual one: Was that testimony, or will it be, knowingly false? The *Mitchell* court follows the prevailing "firm factual basis" standard in instructive detail, aided by the unique Massachusetts Rule 3.3(e). *See* Model Rule 1.0(f) (" 'Knowingly,' 'known,' or 'knows' denotes actual knowledge of the fact in question."); *see also* Joseph P. Williams, Current Developments, *Client Perjury and the Duty of Candor*, 6 Geo.J. Legal Ethics 1005, 1007–09 (1993).

Which standard was in fact applied in *Nix*? The Iowa Supreme Court had approved of counsel's decision to dissuade Nix from testifying that he had seen a gun, concluding that he "was convinced with good cause to believe defendant's proposed testimony would be deliberately untruthful," *State v. Whiteside*, 272 N.W.2d 468, 471 (Iowa 1978). This formulation was reaffirmed in *State v. Hischke*, 639 N.W.2d 6, 10 (Iowa 2002), cited in *Mitchell*. For a critique of this standard as the equivalent of "a 'good faith belief' test," and arguing that Whiteside's counsel did not have "actual knowledge" of his intention to perjure himself because there were alternative explanations of what Whitesides said, see Norman Lefstein, *Client Perjury in Criminal Cases: Still in Search of An Answer*, 1 Geo.J. Legal Ethics 521, 532–33 (1988).

Was the fact that Mitchell had admitted his guilt to his counsel an essential element of his "firm factual basis"? Consider the following statement from the Wisconsin Supreme Court:

> "[A]n attorney may not substitute narrative questioning for the traditional question and answer format unless counsel knows that the client intends to testify falsely. Absent the most extraordinary circumstances, such knowledge must be based on the client's expressed admission of intent to testify untruthfully. While we recognize that the defendant's admission need not be phrased in 'magic words,' it must be unambiguous and directly made to the attorney."

State v. McDowell, 681 N.W.2d 500, 513 (Wis. 2004). This view is evaluated as "perhaps the strictest standard yet for defining knowledge," in Erin K. Jaskot and Christopher J. Mulligan, *Witness Testimony and the Knowledge Requirement: An Atypical Approach to Defining Knowledge and Its Effect on the Lawyer as an Officer of the Court*, 17 Geo.J. Legal Ethics 845, 851 (2004).

2. **First Response—Dissuasion:** There is agreement, on all sides, that when the lawyer reaches the properly supported conclusion that her client intends to testify falsely, her first duty is to attempt to dissuade the client from doing so. How should the lawyer go about this? One essential element, illustrated most forcefully by *Nix*, is informing the client of the consequences of carrying out the plan, including most prominently what the lawyer herself will do if the client insists on lying. One cannot approach the task of dissuasion, therefore, without knowing what one's options are when dissuasion fails. Would dissuasion from perjury by means of a *misrepresentation* of

what one would do itself violate the client's constitutional rights, after *Nix*? Would it be a violation of professional duty?

3. **The Lawyer's Procedural Options—Withdrawal:** If dissuasion fails, should the lawyer seek to withdraw from the representation—a move that, because proceedings will already have begun in which the lawyer is counsel of record for the client, will almost always be subject to the discretion of the court? Until the 2002 amendments to the Model Rules, the ABA's positions generally favored this move as the next step. *See, e.g.,* pre–2002 Model Rule 3.3, Comment [7]. How likely is it, in a criminal case in which the defendant has a constitutional right to counsel, that withdrawal of counsel, even if allowed, will prevent the perjury? For arguments that withdrawal is unlikely to do more than salve the particular lawyer's conscience, see Monroe H. Freedman, Lawyers' Ethics in an Adversary System 33–34 (1975), and Lefstein, *supra* note 1, at 525–27. They suggest that successful withdrawal will probably be followed by appointment of new counsel who will not be informed about the client's intentions, and who will therefore be a more effective instrument of the perjury. Comment [15] to current Model Rule 3.3 now indicates a presumption that withdrawal will not always be required in order to comply with the lawyer's obligations. However, as a practical matter, withdrawal will often be necessary, because the client's desire to testify falsely and the attorney's Model Rule 3.3 duty to refuse to participate in the presentation of false evidence will often result in an irreconcilable conflict between the client and the attorney.

Seeking leave to withdraw (as distinguished from simply notifying the client of one's unwillingness to continue) also directly raises the question of how much confidential information to disclose to the judge in support of the motion. Former Model Rule 3.3 did not address this issue; rather, former Comment [7] simply assumed that the lawyer "ordinarily can withdraw" unless trial is either imminent or already begun. Since prevention of "fraud on a tribunal" or perjury was (and still is) not an expressly recognized exception to the obligation of confidentiality in Model Rule 1.6, the lawyer was left to ponder whether in the motion for leave to withdraw under such circumstances she must avoid disclosing confidential information. The lawyer also had to wonder whether Model Rule 1.6 would be violated even by identifying of the general nature of the lawyer's reason for seeking withdrawal. Comment [15] to current Model Rule 3.3 addresses the issue by limiting disclosure of otherwise protected confidential information to that which is "reasonably necessary" to comply with the Model Rule.

In fact it appears, as suggested in *Mitchell*, that courts have most often denied such motions—at least at the relatively late stage at which the issue comes to a head—on the ground of prejudice to the defendant's right to effective counsel, or because insufficient explanation is given in the motion. *See* Williams, *supra* note 1, at 1020. The motion to withdraw in such a case may at least have the effect of alerting the judge to the possibility of perjury in the defendant's testimony, without making it clear precisely in what respects the testimony is false.

4. **The Lawyer's Procedural Options—"The Free Narrative":** *Mitchell* is also a near textbook example of the use of the "free narrative"

approach to anticipated perjury in the case of criminal defendants. Its premise is that if the attorney does not put questions to the defendant that would elicit the anticipated lies she doesn't *offer* them, and will not be obligated to disclose their falsehood afterwards to the court, but only to avoid arguing their truth before the trier of fact, and to seek to persuade the client to rectify his perjury after the fact.

Note that Massachusetts' apparently unique Rule 3.3(e) *forbids* disclosure to the tribunal after the testimony is complete but counsel's efforts to persuade the client to rectify fail. A comment to the Rule reinforces the court's conclusion that the free narrative is consistent with this rule: "If the lawyer learns of the client's intention to commit perjury during the trial, and is unable to dissuade the client from testifying falsely, the lawyer may not stand in the way of the client's absolute right to take the stand and testify." Mass. Rules of Prof'l Conduct 3.3, Comment 9 (1998).

At least one jurisdiction has adopted a rule explicitly authorizing the attorney to put the client on the stand to testify narratively if he is unable to dissuade the client or to withdraw without seriously harming him, D.C. Bar Rules of Prof'l Conduct, Rule 3.3(b) (2007). Other states authorizing it have done so without clear support in the formal rules.

While the ABA's Defense Standards of 1971 embraced the free narrative, as the *Mitchell* opinion points out, the ABA's Committee on Professional Ethics found that Model Rule 3.3 as originally adopted in 1983—after *Nix* had established that a criminal defendant did not have a constitutional right to testify falsely—foreclosed use of the device because it would not relieve the lawyer of responsibility for the perjury, *see* ABA Formal Opinion 87–353 (1987). Current Model Rule 3.3(b) and its Comment [7] express continued disapproval of the approach, and make clear that the lawyer using it will not be absolved from the duty to take remedial action, unless the rules of the local jurisdiction *require* that it be used. Comments *h* and *i* to section 120 of the RESTATEMENT take the same position.

After *Nix*, on what rationale would such a method be *required*? Might a trial judge direct that defense counsel proceed with that method, in order to avoid granting a motion to withdraw while preserving the defendant's right to testify? Might this be appropriate in the face of some degree of uncertainty—notwithstanding the "firm factual basis" test—as to whether the testimony will actually be perjured? It remains likely, despite the narrative technique's advantages in accommodating competing interests, that it will send the message to the trier of fact that counsel does not believe those portions of the client's testimony that she does not mention. This prompted one scholar to reject it as "even less satisfactory than informing the judge of the defendant's guilt." Monroe H. Freedman, *Professional Responsibility of the Criminal Defense Lawyer: The Three Hardest Questions*, 64 Mich.L.Rev. 1469, 1477 (1966).

Despite the objections of the drafters of the Defense Standards, the Model Rules, and the Restatement, as well as others, the free narrative approach seems to be an at least somewhat common response to the defense attorney's notification to the trial court judge that the attorney expects the defendant to present perjured testimony, via the classic mid-trial motion to withdraw due to ethical concerns. Many courts deny these motions and allow the defendant to testify using a free narrative form. *See, e.g., Wilkins v. Scribner*, 263 Fed.Appx. 638, 640 (9th Cir. 2008) (affirming denial of writ of habeas corpus because the state court's "[u]se of the free narrative was not prejudicial"); *United States v. Baker*, 65 M.J. 691, 694 (Army Ct.Crim.App. 2007); *Scott v. State*, 2005–CT–00915–SCT, ¶ 10, 8 So.3d 855, 859 (Miss. 2009); *see also People v. Andrades*, 828 N.E.2d 599 (N.Y. 2005) (affirming conviction after trial court denied counsel's motion to withdraw during a pre-trial suppression hearing, then allowed the defendant to testify about circumstances of his alleged confession via free narrative).

5. **Narrative Combined with Attorney's Withdrawal:** Note that the judge in *Mitchell*, in granting the lawyer's request to put the client on the stand to testify narratively, directed the lawyer—at his request but without engaging the defendant in a colloquy on the issue—to remain at the counsel table and make appropriate objections to the prosecution's cross-examination. Might he have been allowed instead to withdraw from further representation? In *Brown v. Commonwealth*, 226 S.W.3d 74 (Ky. 2007), after defense counsel informed the judge in the absence of the jury that defendant intended to testify to facts that she did not feel she could support, the judge told defendant in colloquy that he could choose to make a limited narrative testimony and make his own closing argument and either have counsel remain at the table or withdraw from the courtroom altogether, but that counsel indicated that defendant might be better off if she were not there being silent. Upon hearing this, the defendant chose to proceed without counsel's presence, though she remained on call for the sentencing phase. On appeal from the defendant's conviction, the Kentucky Supreme Court held that this violated the defendant's right to counsel. Using *Mitchell* as its primary model for a permissible free narrative, and after praising the judge for the thoroughness of her colloquy, the court said:

> However, the court did err in advising Appellant and counsel that counsel could leave the courtroom during the narrative testimony. * * * By completely leaving the courtroom, in the presence of the jury, counsel telegraphed a problem to the jury. This was improper absent a knowing and voluntary waiver of counsel by Appellant as to representation beyond the perjured testimony. Counsel should have remained to assist when he could, since only counsel knew what he believed to be a proper question or an improper one. It remains unknown whether counsel had a good faith, firm factual basis to believe the testimony would be perjury. [G]iven that no one other than counsel and Appellant knew the contested area of testimony, requiring Appellant to testify wholly on his own and without benefit of counsel's objections on cross examination (which would have been directed at evidentiary rules rather than content), Appellant was unconstitutionally deprived of his right to assistance of counsel. This was compounded by requiring him to make his own closing argument and allowing counsel to return to conduct the sentencing phase.

226 S.W.3d at 85.

6. **Civil Cases:** Do any of the above considerations apply when a client proposes to testify falsely in a civil case? Specifically, does a party to a civil case have a constitutional right to testify on his own behalf? If not, does Model Rule 3.3, in conjunction with Model Rule 1.2 on the scope of the

attorney's authority, control the issue entirely by permitting the lawyer to override the client's wish to testify? For an affirmative answer with further references, see Williams, *supra* note 1, at 1011 & nn. 44–47.

7. **Nonclient Witnesses:** If the client insists on presenting third persons as witnesses, but the lawyer believes they intend to commit perjury, the lawyer has authority under Model Rules 1.2 and 3.3 to simply refuse to offer the witnesses. For a decision to that effect under the Model Code, see *People v. Schultheis*, 638 P.2d 8 (Colo. 1981) (en banc). The *obligation* not to offer such a witness is triggered under Model Rule 3.3(a)(3) by *knowledge* of the falsity of the prospective testimony. However, a criminal defendant's right to effective assistance of counsel requires such a decision to have an adequate foundation. Thus, where a defense attorney relied on the reports of detectives' non-belief in potential defense witnesses, without actually interviewing those witnesses, the lawyer's conduct did fall below that of effective assistance. *See Lord v. Wood*, 184 F.3d 1083 (9th Cir. 1999).

8. **Accomplished Perjury and the Disclosure Requirement:** Suppose the client has indicated a willingness to testify truthfully. The lawyer then puts the client on the stand, and the client begins to lie. If the lawyer reveals to the court that the client is testifying falsely, as seems to be required by Model Rule 3.3(a)(3) if all else fails, can the trial continue? Comment [10] says that it is up to the judge to determine how to proceed after being so informed, but does not offer guidance as to which alternative to choose. Is such a continued trial likely to be "fair" in a constitutional sense? If the trial cannot continue, what is to prevent future criminal defendants from promising to tell the truth, then lying in order to have the case mistried?

9. **Unanticipated Perjury and Civil Cases:** If a client has testified falsely in a civil case, do confidentiality considerations inhibit the remedial measures outlined in Model Rule 3.3, Comment [10]? As a matter of professional responsibility law, a few jurisdictions have modified Model Rule 3.3 in favor of confidentiality even in civil cases. *See, e.g.*, Washington Rule 3.3(c) & (d):

> (c) If the lawyer has offered material evidence and comes to know of its falsity, the lawyer shall promptly disclose this fact to the tribunal unless such disclosure is prohibited by Rule 1.6.

> (d) If the lawyer has offered material evidence and comes to know of its falsity, and disclosure of this fact is prohibited by Rule 1.6, the lawyer shall promptly make reasonable efforts to convince the client to consent to disclosure. If the client refuses to consent to disclosure, the lawyer may seek to withdraw from the representation in accordance with Rule 1.16.

Should the fact that perjury is a crime even in civil proceedings inhibit disclosure by the lawyer?

10. **Timing of Discovery of Perjury:** Suppose the lawyer does not discover until after trial and acquittal—or after final judgment and expiration of all appeals in a civil case—that his client had lied on the stand? Does the obligation to take appropriate remedial action still apply? Model Rule 3.3(c) explicitly ends the obligation at "the conclusion of the proceeding," and Comment [13] defines this to include final judgment and all appeals until the

time for further review has expired. What priority of values is reflected in the current rule and comment—a preference for corrective action over punishment? Is that an appropriate priority, for the liar's lawyer? Because there is generally no opportunity for appeal after an acquittal in a criminal case, is there really an option for post-acquittal corrective disclosure?

11. **Duty of Prosecutor:** In addition to obligations under Model Rule 3.3, prosecutors have an obligation under Model Rule 3.8(d) to disclose any evidence "that tends to negate the guilt of [an] accused." ABA Standing Comm. on Ethics and Prof'l Resp., Formal Opinion 09–454 (2009) (emphasizing that the Model Rule goes beyond what is required by constitutional decisions such as *Brady v. Maryland*, 373 U.S. 83 (1963)). Where a prosecution witness lied on the witness stand, and the prosecutor knew of the lie, the prosecutor had a duty to immediately correct any misperception caused by the perjury, a duty many prosecutors fulfill by immediately asking for a bench conference to work out the dynamics of how the jury will be advised of the witness' lying. A prosecutor may not wait until the prosecution's final closing argument, after the defense has had no chance to challenge the witness, to disclose the false testimony to the jury. *See United States v. LaPage*, 231 F.3d 488, 492 (9th Cir. 2000) (noting that "[a]ll perjury pollutes a trial, making it hard for jurors to see the truth"). Model Rule 3.8(g), added in 2008, imposes analogous post-conviction disclosure and remedial obligations with respect to "new, credible and material evidence creating a reasonable likelihood that a convicted defendant did not commit an offense of which the defendant was convicted." *See also* Model Rule 3.8(h) (creating an obligation for a prosecutor who "knows of clear and convincing evidence establishing that a defendant . . . was convicted of an offense that the defendant did not commit [to] seek to remedy the conviction").

D. PROTECTING THE ATTORNEY: SELF–DEFENSE

PROBLEM

Orville Larson operates a retail electronics store. One day he comes to the office of his attorney, John Cicero, for advice on how to set up a leasing arrangement whereby he could purchase certain pieces of large equipment and rent them to customers who don't wish to make a heavy initial capital investment. He has talked to a local bank, which has indicated a willingness to lend him the money to purchase the equipment, secured by assignment of a percentage of the rental payments. Cicero drafts a form of lease agreement suitable for the purpose, advises Larson on the bank's proposed contract, and represents Larson in the closing of several of the loan agreements with the bank. Over the next year, Larson makes about 50 such loan-purchase-lease transactions.

About a year after the initial transaction, Larson comes to Cicero's office and admits that most of the leases were either totally nonexistent or substantially inflated, that he had spent the money first on a wildly speculative and ultimately worthless investment, and that he has been using the proceeds of later loans to pay amounts due on earlier ones. He now finds himself unable to get the money to make the next set of payments, and wants to know what to do. Cicero advises him to come clean, but Larson is unwilling to give up the hope of finding the money. Cicero then tells Larson that there is nothing further he can do, and urges him to get another lawyer.

Shortly thereafter, the bank discovers that one of the leases is fraudulent, and approaches Cicero with a threat to sue him as well as Larson if restitution is not made, and to report both to the prosecutor. Cicero contacts Larson, who insists that Cicero remain silent.

QUESTIONS

Can Cicero disclose to the bank the extent of his knowledge concerning the transactions in which he participated, to defend against the charge of complicity in the fraud? If the bank goes to the prosecutor, can Cicero talk to the latter in similar terms?

RULE REFERENCES

Model Rule 1.6(b)(4)–(5)

RESTATEMENT §§ 64 & 65

IN RE BOELTER

Supreme Court of Washington, 1999.
985 P.2d 328.

ALEXANDER, J.

Attorney Arthur H. Boelter appeals the Washington State Bar Association (WSBA) Disciplinary Board's recommendation * * * that he receive a six-month suspension from the practice of law due to three counts of misconduct. The alleged misconduct arose out of a fee dispute between Boelter and a client, Robert Withey. The Board found that Boelter threatened to reveal Withey's confidences in a suit to collect fees and falsely claimed that a disclosable tape recording of a conference with Withey existed. It also found that the amount Withey was billed for the legal services was unreasonable. Boelter contends that a clear preponderance of the evidence does not support the findings of misconduct, and that the aggravating and mitigating factors were not properly weighed in determining his sanction.

FACTS

Boelter was admitted to practice in Washington in 1979. At the time of the alleged misconduct he was a principal in the Seattle law firm of Boelter, Silver and Gale, a firm that was known for a portion of the time material to this appeal as Boelter and Gale. Boelter was hired by Withey in 1990 to represent him before the Internal Revenue Service (IRS) in a tax dispute. During their initial conference, which occurred in August

1990, Withey revealed confidential information to Boelter regarding his past dealings with the IRS, including information that led Boelter "to conclude that Withey had concealed assets from the IRS and a bank." * * *

Most of the legal work for Withey was performed by two associate attorneys at Boelter's law firm, Deborah Lyons and John White. The law firm did no substantive legal work for Withey after November 1990. At that time a balance of fees was owing. In January and September of 1991, Boelter directed White to write letters to Withey in an effort to collect the unpaid fees. On October 8, 1991, Boelter wrote a letter to Withey that is at issue here. The letter alleged that Withey owed $1,824.33 for legal services performed and it warned that

> if we are not paid in full by October 15, 1991, we will file suit for the fees. You should understand that if we are forced to file suit, you forgo the attorney-client privilege and I would be forced to reveal that you lied on your statements to the IRS and to the bank as to your financial condition. This would entail disclosure of the tapes of our conversations about your hidden assets. There is a federal statute 18 U.S.C. § 1001 which provides for up to one year in jail for such perjury. The choice is yours. * * *

Following receipt of this letter, Withey formed an opinion that Boelter had a tape recording of their August 1990 conversation, and believed that Boelter would reveal confidential information about Withey's financial condition and assets if Withey did not pay his bill. Boelter followed this letter with a handwritten "speed-memo" * * * confirming a telephone conversation with Withey. At the bottom it read that "[a] copy of this letter is also being sent by certified mail. Our preparations to file suit have begun. I would suggest that you liquidate one of the undisclosed art works you have & pay us by November 25, 1991[.] Your choice[.]" * * *

In January 1992 Boelter and Withey reached a verbal understanding concerning settlement of Withey's account, and Boelter confirmed the agreement in a January 3, 1992, letter to Withey. Withey thereafter made a $400 payment to Boelter's firm, but failed to make the other payments outlined in the letter.

On March 3, 1992, at Boelter's behest, Boelter's associate, White, filed suit * * * against Withey and Withey's wife. Withey's attorney, Harry Platis, then contacted White and told him ["]that he had received $1,803.97 from Withey and had placed it in his trust account, and that he was authorized to pay those funds to Respondent [Boelter] upon return of the tape recordings of Respondent's conference with Withey and on condition that Respondent give Withey all of his files and retain no copies.["] White told Platis that he did not know of any tape recordings, and had not seen either the October 8, 1991, letter or the lower portion of the November 15, 1991, "speed-memo" in the file Boelter had given to him.

[White became concerned over what appeared to be threats by Boelter involving the tapes, confronted him, and got assurance that they had been erased and no longer existed. Platis requested an affidavit from Boelter to that effect, which White drafted and Boelter signed.] Relying upon this document, White wrote a letter to Platis on March 25, 1992, to confirm that the lawsuit was ready for settlement. Prior to consummating this agreement, Withey filed the grievance with the WSBA that is at issue here. The collection lawsuit against Withey did, however, proceed and was eventually settled in October 1993, upon Withey's payment to Boelter of $1,300. * * *

[The Court's analysis of the threat to disclose contained in the letter of Boelter to Withey of October 9, 1991, follows:]

The WSBA alleges that this letter misrepresents the applicability of an exception to the protection of attorney-client confidentiality that is guaranteed by [Model Rule] 1.6. [Model Rule] 1.6(a) provides that "[a] lawyer *shall not* reveal [information] relating to [the] representation of a client [unless the client gives informed consent, the disclosure is impliedly authorized in order to carry out the representation or the disclosure is permitted by paragraph (b)]." (Emphasis added.) Under the relevant exception, "[a] lawyer *may* reveal [information relating to the representation of a client] to the extent the lawyer reasonably believes necessary . . . [t]o establish a claim or defense on behalf of the lawyer in a controversy between the lawyer and the client." [Model Rule] 1.6(b)([5]) (emphasis added). Accordingly, Boelter would have been *able* to reveal Withey's confidences or secrets in litigation to recover fees if he reasonably believed that disclosure to be necessary. However, he would certainly not, as he claimed in his October 1991 letter to Withey, have been "*forced* to reveal that you lied on your statements to the IRS and to the bank as to your financial condition." * * * It is a leap in logic even to claim that such a disclosure could reasonably be made *voluntarily,* for even that claim necessarily assumes that Withey would raise inability to pay as a defense to this hypothetical lawsuit. Boelter admits that he made this assumption. We see a couple of problems with this. First, inability to pay is not a valid defense to an entry of a judgment, and thus it seems unlikely that Withey would have offered it. Second, and more important, Boelter failed to consider Withey's other defenses in their fee dispute, including a defense that he could have readily anticipated: principally, the argument that Withey was grievously overcharged by almost 1,000 percent. Implicit in the [Model Rule] 1.6(b)([5]) exception to [the confidentiality duty] is that it should not be carelessly invoked. Yet Boelter's letter creates the following impression: (1) *full* payment, *on terms dictated by Boelter,* must be received in *one week* or (2) Boelter will be *forced* to reveal Withey's *confessed crimes.*

Boelter admitted in his May 1992 response to Withey's WSBA grievance that his October 1991 letter was "poorly drafted," and "that the phrasing of my statement could have been better." * * * He claims that his warning was based upon the supposition that "Withey would say that he did not have any assets to pay the bill[,]" and he was merely "giving fair warning to Mr. Withey of my intent to use information as authorized by [Model Rule] 1.6." * * * He wrote that "[i]n hindsight, I can see that I should have worded my entire letter of October 8, 1991 differently so that Mr. Withey would have better understood what I was saying about the permissible use of attorney/client confidences in a fee dispute." * * * In his testimony he addressed questions concerning this issue as follows:

> Q. You agree, do you not, that the letter ... is an incomplete statement of what circumstances would permit you to make disclosures about client confidences or secrets?
>
> A. Yes. It should have been fleshed out more.
>
> Q. And do you also agree that the statement regarding any liability—or rather the implication that there is liability under that federal statute for perjury is somewhat incomplete?
>
> A. Yes. The letter, again, should have been fleshed out.

* * * Boelter would admit that his implication that Withey had violated 18 U.S.C. § 1001 was not researched. He characterized the letter, however, as being the product of *concern* for Withey, and not any desire to scare him into making payment.

The most innocuous interpretation of this language would be that it is unsolicited legal advice to Withey given in his best interest, warning him of the risk of his confidences being revealed in a legal dispute. This risk, avoidable through payment, is undeniable under [Model Rule] 1.6(b)([5]). The letter, however, does not read that innocently. Moreover, the letter cannot be read uncoupled from the November 1991 "speed-memo." The hearing examiner found that this "was in continuation" of the misconduct inherent in the October letter. * * * That second document, again, reads as follows: "Our preparations to file suit have begun. I would suggest that you liquidate one of the undisclosed art works you have & pay us by Nov. 25, 1991[.] Your choice [.]" * * * Going so far as to dictate the sale of an asset whose existence Boelter was aware of only through a client confidence reinforces the impression that he intended to convey a threat—a threat that closely resembles extortion.

Boelter asserts that under [Model Rule] 1.6 a lawyer should be able to " 'threaten' a former client" with disclosure of client confidences in order to resolve a fee dispute. * * * We disagree. Even if we assumed that Boelter's outrageous position is correct, and the protections of [Model Rule] 1.6 are so readily subjugated by its permissive [Model Rule] 1.6(b)([5]) exception, that would not excuse *misrepresenting* the applicability of that exception.[2]

---

2. Withey was asked about his first meeting with Boelter:

"Q. Did Mr. Boelter tell you during that first meeting anything about what would happen with the information that you were telling him?

"A. No. I would assume that it would be between he and I." * * *

[The court then proceeded to sustain the findings of impropriety by misrepresenting the existence of tapes and by grossly overstating the fees owing from Withey, and to sustain the imposition of the more severe six-month suspension.]

NOTES ON DISCLOSURE IN SELF-DEFENSE
OR TO ESTABLISH A CLAIM AGAINST A CLIENT

1. **Permitted Disclosure in Self–Defense:** In *Meyerhofer v. Empire Fire & Marine Insurance Co.*, 497 F.2d 1190 (2d Cir. 1974), a lawyer in a corporate law firm worked on a public offering of stock by a client company. He became persuaded that the law required certain information concerning the law firm's fees to be disclosed in a registration statement, and sought to persuade the senior members of the firm, as well as the client, that to omit such information from the statement would be a significant violation of securities laws. When the firm and the client refused to correct the statement before filing it, and the firm also refused to include this information in another registration statement on which the lawyer worked, the lawyer resigned from the firm. On the same day, he went to the Securities and Exchange Commission and filed an affidavit describing his own involvement in the relevant registration statements.

As a result of this disclosure, the first statement was corrected by the firm and client, and purchasers of the stock on the basis of the original statement sued the firm, the company, and the individual lawyer for damages for losses allegedly suffered because of the misinformation. The lawyer then proceeded to show the SEC affidavit to the plaintiffs' lawyers, and he was dropped from the suit as defendant. The defendant then moved to disqualify the plaintiffs' lawyers because of the (allegedly improper) disclosure, and to enjoin them, as well as the disclosing lawyer, from disclosing any of this information to others. The trial court granted the motion, but the Court of Appeals reversed, holding that the disclosing lawyer was entitled under the Model Code of Professional Responsibility Disciplinary Rule 4–101(C) (essentially identical to Model Rule 1.6(b)(5)) to make the disclosures in order to defend himself against the plaintiffs' claims.

Today, Comment [10] to Model Rule 1.6 allows the lawyer to disclose in self defense when "an assertion" of complicity by the lawyer has been made. Consider this comment in light of *In re National Mortgage Equity Corp. Mortgage Pool Certificates Securities Litigation*, 120 F.R.D. 687, 692–93 (C.D.Cal. 1988). In that complex litigation, counsel for a securities issuer was named as defendant, and the lawyers gave notice of their intention at an appropriate time to disclose client confidential information necessary to establish their own defense. After considerable discovery proceedings, the firm

For future guidance to attorneys, we would note that any expression of confidences by a client that can, potentially, be used against the client should be based upon an informed decision. That informed decision necessarily requires knowing about the exceptions to RPC 1.6. *See* RPC 1.4(b) ("A lawyer shall explain a matter to the extent reasonably necessary to permit the client to make informed decisions regarding the representation."). So that clients do not make the reasonable, if incorrect, assumption that their perhaps self-incriminating confidences are sacrosanct under all circumstances, it follows that an attorney should explain the exceptions to RPC 1.6 to his or her clients at the outset of representation.

notified the client of its intention to disclose, and the client sought a protective order prohibiting such disclosure. After a hearing, the court issued an order authorizing the disclosure, citing *Meyerhofer* for the proposition that the self-defense exception applied. The order (i) limited the disclosure to counsel of record in those cases in which the firm remained a contesting defendant, (ii) required disclosure of all attorney-client communications "concerning the same discrete subject matter," (iii) required that all persons to whom disclosure was made be prohibited from disclosing the information to any third person, and (iv) required that all such persons be informed of the order and the fact that they were bound by it.

For the proposition that a self-defense exception of similar scope applies to the attorney-client privilege as well as to the duty of confidentiality, see *First Federal Savings & Loan Ass'n of Pittsburgh v. Oppenheim, Appel, Dixon & Co.*, 110 F.R.D. 557 (S.D.N.Y. 1986). As an Ohio court noted, "Attorney-client privilege is generally held to be waived in cases where the asserting party has placed the information at issue by bringing [a malpractice] suit or by some other affirmative act." *Hahn v. Jennings*, 2004–Ohio–4789, ¶ 31, 2004 WL 2008474, at *8 (Ct.App.).

2. **Anticipatory Disclosure:** Given the extension of self-defense disclosure to third-party accusations, may the attorney anticipate the accusation, as by providing information to a grand jury which is investigating but has not yet indicted the attorney? *See* Model Rule 1.6, Comment [10]. In *In re Friend*, 411 F.Supp. 776 (S.D.N.Y. 1975), the court granted an attorney's application for permission to disclose certain exculpatory documents to a sitting grand jury, some of which were subject to his client's claim of privilege, on the ground that it would be senseless to require him to wait for the "stigma" of a criminal indictment.

3. **Necessity:** How "necessary" must the self-defense disclosure be in order to satisfy the rule, and who should decide? In *First Federal Savings & Loan, supra* note 1, the court in ruling on a motion for discovery following an *in camera* inspection of documents that the lawyer proposed to reveal, as well as all those originally listed as privileged, derived a "reasonable necessity" standard from the Model Rules comment, and defined that in turn as follows:

> In effect, disclosure is authorized for those items that, as a practical matter, seem likely to provide significant assistance to [the lawyer's] defense. [Further,] fairness would require disclosure of all documents pertaining to the communications at issue, whether [the lawyer] volunteered them or not.

110 F.R.D. at 567.

In *Levin v. Ripple Twist Mills, Inc.*, 416 F.Supp. 876, 886–87 (E.D.Pa. 1976), it was held improper for defense counsel, in response to plaintiff's motion to disqualify him for conflict of interest based on having previously represented the plaintiff, to disclose confidential information received from the plaintiff in an unrelated matter, simply to show the former client's impeachable character.

See also *In re Huffman*, 983 P.2d 534 (Or. 1999), where Huffman's client declared bankruptcy and obtained a discharge of his outstanding fee obligation. Huffman later sued the client for fraudulent transfer of certain assets prior to the bankruptcy, obtaining judgments declaring the transfers void and subjecting the proceeds to payment of the fees outstanding. The client hired another lawyer, who wrote to Huffman threatening to have the judgments vacated and to sue Huffman for abuse of process. Huffman responded with a long letter to the other lawyer claiming that he had not received notice of the bankruptcy. The letter also accused the former client of a long list of crimes and frauds against a variety of third persons. Several of these alleged wrongs related to matters on which he had previously advised the client. The letter stated that the client's character would be an issue in any suit between them. In a disciplinary proceeding instituted on the client's complaint, Huffman claimed, among other things, that his disclosures to the new lawyer were in self-defense. In sustaining the disciplinary charge, the Oregon Supreme Court said:

> We reject the accused's contention that his conduct falls under the exception in [Model Rule 1.6(b)(5)]. That exception is limited, by its terms, to disclosures that are *necessary* to establish a claim or defense on behalf of the lawyer in a controversy between the lawyer and the client. The accused already had established his claims against [the client], and there was no pending action against the accused by [the client] that required the accused to assert a defense. The disclosures were not required for the assertion of the accused's legal claims that his judgments against [the client] were valid. The accused's letter was little more than a veiled attempt to intimidate [the client] and [his new lawyer] in order to deter them from challenging the accused's judgments. The accused was not entitled to reveal [the client's] secrets under [the Model Rule].

Id. at 543.

CHAPTER 5

CONFLICTS OF INTEREST

■ ■ ■

INTRODUCTION

Conflict of interest is among the most pervasive problems of professional responsibility, and yet often among the least understood by law students and lawyers alike. The peculiar difficulty with conflict of interest rules is that they are premised not so much on concrete harm to the client as on the *potential* for such harm. *Actual* failure to provide competent service, neglect of a client's cause, breach of confidentiality, overreaching in the professional relationship—all are dealt with directly by prohibitions or duties, breach of which can result in malpractice liability or disciplinary action, as already discussed in previous chapters. In this chapter, we deal primarily with a client's *confidence and trust* in the subjective sense, with situations that provide the attorney with a specific *opportunity and motivation* to short-change the client and that therefore tend to undermine that confidence. Because the problems are subtle and frequently depend on turns of events not entirely predictable, the key to successful avoidance is anticipation and imagination.

Like the duty of confidentiality, the duty of loyalty has multiple sources and is not necessarily captured entirely in the Model Rules, which are primarily designed for application in disciplinary proceedings. Specifically, one of the most important remedies—one that has given rise to perhaps the majority of reported cases—is that of disqualifying the conflicted lawyer or firm from a particular representation. While this remedy is most often invoked in the context of a pending proceeding, by means of a motion addressed to the court's discretion, it can also be invoked in the context of non-litigation representation by means of an action for an injunction. The following case illustrates the nature and private law origins of the duty, as well as the variety of remedial approaches to its breach.

MARITRANS GP INC. v.
PEPPER, HAMILTON & SCHEETZ

Supreme Court of Pennsylvania, 1992.
602 A.2d 1277.

PAPADAKOS, JUSTICE. * * *

Maritrans is a Philadelphia-based public company in the business of transporting petroleum products along the East and Gulf coasts of the United States by tug and barge. Maritrans competes in the marine transportation business with other tug and/or barge companies, including a number of companies based in New York. Pepper is an old and established Philadelphia law firm. Pepper and [one of its partners, J. Anthony Messina,] represented Maritrans or its predecessor companies in the broadest range of labor relations matters for well over a decade. In addition, Pepper represented Maritrans in a complex public offering of securities, a private offering of $115 million in debt, a conveyance of all assets, and a negotiation and implementation of a working capital line of credit. Over the course of the representation, Pepper was paid approximately $1 million for its labor representation of Maritrans and, in the last year of the representation, approximately $1 million for its corporate and securities representation of Maritrans.

During the course of their labor representation of Maritrans, Pepper and Messina became "intimately familiar with Maritrans' operations" and "gained detailed financial and business information, including Maritrans' financial goals and projections, labor cost/savings, crew costs and operating costs." * * * This information was discussed with Pepper's labor attorneys, and particularly with Messina, for the purpose of developing Maritrans' labor goals and strategies. In addition, during the course of preparing Maritrans' public offering, Pepper was furnished with substantial confidential commercial information in Maritrans' possession—financial and otherwise—including projected labor costs, projected debt coverage[,] projected revenues * * *, and projected rates * * *. Pepper and Messina, during the course of their decade-long representation of Maritrans, came to know the complete inner-workings of the company along with Maritrans' long-term objectives, and competitive strategies in a number of areas including the area of labor costs, a particularly sensitive area in terms of effective competition. In furtherance of its ultimate goal of obtaining more business than does its competition, including the New York-based companies, Maritrans analyzed each of its competitors with Pepper and Messina. These analyses included an evaluation of each competitor's strengths and weaknesses, and of how Maritrans deals with its competitors.

[Pepper and Messina then undertook to represent several of Maritrans' New York competitors in labor negotiations designed to reduce costs and improve competitiveness. Maritrans got wind of this and objected, but the lawyers insisted it was a "business conflict" and not a "legal conflict." Nonetheless they agreed with Maritrans that they would not take on any more of the competitors than they already had, that Messina would no longer be the Pepper partner representing Maritrans, and that he would be screened from participation in that representation. With Messina's help two other competitors hired a lawyer at another firm, with whom Messina and Pepper were in fact negotiating to move to the Pepper firm. Within a month after an extensive conference with Maritrans executives on strategy in the event of a threatened strike against the New York competitors, Pepper terminated its representation of Maritrans, accepted the New York competitors as general clients, and took on the other lawyer as a partner, who in turn brought with him the remaining competitors as clients. Maritrans then sued to enjoin the firm from representation of these competitors, and the trial court granted the injunction, based on evidence showing that (i) the competitors themselves considered the type of information which Pepper and Messina had about Maritrans to be confidential and would not want it revealed to their competitors, (ii) that they would like to have such information about Maritrans, (iii) that labor costs were crucial to competitiveness, and (iv) that the information was not readily available in public records.

The trial court relied on the then applicable Model Code of Professional Responsibility. The Superior Court reversed on the ground that those rules do not support injunctive relief. The Supreme Court reversed in turn, agreeing that the professional rules do not normally support injunctive relief, but sustaining the injunction on independent common law grounds.]

I.

*Actionability and Independent Fiduciary Duty at Common Law of Avoiding Conflicts of Interest—Injunctive Relief * * ***

Activity is actionable if it constitutes breach of a duty imposed by statute or by common law. Our common law imposes on attorneys the status of fiduciaries *vis a vis* their clients; that is, attorneys are bound, at law, to perform their fiduciary duties properly. Failure to so perform gives rise to a cause of action. It is "actionable." Threatened failure to so perform gives rise to a request for injunctive relief to prevent the breach of duty. * * *

> There are few of the business relations of life involving a higher trust and confidence than those of attorney and client or, generally speaking, one more honorably and faithfully discharged; few more anxiously guarded by the law, or governed by sterner principles of morality and justice; and it is the duty of the court to administer them in a corresponding spirit, and to be watchful and industrious, to see that confidence thus reposed shall not be used to the detriment or prejudice of the rights of the party bestowing it. * * *

Adherence to those fiduciary duties ensures that clients will feel secure that everything they discuss with counsel will be kept in confidence. * * * Pepper and Messina, as attorneys, had a duty to administer properly their responsibilities to respect the confidences of Maritrans. * * *

Our courts clearly have the power to enjoin an attorney from breaching his duty to a client * * *.

Accordingly, the trial court's preliminary injunction was a proper mechanism to abate an unlawful and actionable breach of fiduciary duties to Maritrans where the facts support such a conclusion.

II.

An Attorney's Common Law Duty [I]s Independent of the Ethics Rules * * *

Long before the Code of Professional Responsibility was adopted, and before the Rules of Professional Conduct were adopted, the common law recognized that a lawyer could not undertake a representation adverse to a former client in a matter "substantially related" to that in which the lawyer previously had served the client. * * *

The legal obligation of a lawyer to refrain from misuse of a client's confidences goes even further back, predating the ABA Canons of Professional Ethics promulgated in 1908. *See, e.g., Bowman v. Bowman*, 153 Ind. 498, 55 N.E. 422 (1899), which was also a disqualification case. The threatened violation of this duty thus has been recognized as the basis for an injunction for at least virtually a century, as stated in the leading treatise on attorneys of about the same vintage. See, 1 Thornton on Attorneys at Law, § 180 (1914) * * *.

III.

Scope of Duties at Common Law * * *

Attorneys have always been held civilly liable for engaging in conduct violative of their fiduciary duties to clients, despite the existence of professional rules under which the attorneys could also have been disciplined.

Courts throughout the country have ordered the disgorgement of fees paid or the forfeiture of fees owed to attorneys who have breached their fiduciary duties to their clients by engaging in impermissible conflicts of interests. * * *

Notwithstanding that the attorneys in those cases could have been disciplined under applicable rules of professional conduct, disgorgement or forfeiture of fees for services rendered were ordered. Likewise, the United States Supreme Court has said:

A fiduciary . . . may not perfect his claim to compensation by insisting that although he had conflicting interests, he served his several masters equally well or that his primary loyalty was not weakened by the pull of his secondary one. Only strict adherence to these equitable principles can keep the standard of conduct for fiduciaries "at a level higher than that trodden by the crowd."

Woods v. City Nat'l. Bank & Trust Co., [312 U.S. 262, 269, 61 S.Ct. 493, 497, 85 L.Ed. 820 (1941)] (quoting Justice Cardozo).

Courts have also allowed civil actions for damages for an attorney's breach of his fiduciary duties by engaging in conflicts of interest. * * *

Courts throughout the United States have not hesitated to impose civil sanctions upon attorneys who breach their fiduciary duties to their clients, which sanctions have been imposed separately and apart from professional discipline. What must be decided in this case is whether, under the instant facts, an injunction lies to prohibit a potential conflict of interest from resulting in harm to Appellant Maritrans. Resort to simple equitable principles, as applied to the facts of this case, renders an affirmative answer to this question.

IV.

Equity

Injunctive relief will lie where there is no adequate remedy at law. * * * The purpose of a preliminary injunction is to preserve the status quo as it exists *or previously existed before the acts complained of*, thereby preventing irreparable injury or gross injustice. * * * A preliminary injunction should issue only where there is urgent necessity to avoid injury which cannot be compensated for by damages. * * *

Pepper and Messina argue that a preliminary injunction was an abuse of discretion where it restrains them from representing a former client's competitors, in order to supply the former client with a "sense of security" that they will not reveal confidences to those competitors where there has been no revelation or threat of revelations up to that point. We disagree. Whether a fiduciary can later represent competitors or whether a law firm can later represent competitors of its former client is a matter that must be decided from case to case and depends on a number of factors. One factor is the extent to which the fiduciary was involved in its former client's affairs. The greater the involvement, the greater the danger that confidences (where such exist) will be revealed. Here, Pepper and Messina's involvement was extensive as was their knowledge of sensitive information provided to them by Maritrans. We do *not* wish to establish a blanket rule that a law firm may not later represent the economic competitor of a former client in matters in which the former client is not also a party to a law suit. But situations may well exist where the danger of revelation of the confidences of a former client is so great that injunctive relief is warranted. This is one of those situations. There is a substantial relationship here between Pepper and Messina's former representation of Maritrans and their current representation of Maritrans' competitors such that the injunctive relief granted here was justified. It might be theoretically possible to argue that Pepper and Messina should merely be enjoined from revealing the confidential material they have acquired from Maritrans but such an injunction would be difficult, if not impossible, to administer. * * * As fiduciaries, Pepper and Messina can be fully enjoined from representing Maritrans' competitors as that would create too great a danger that Maritrans' confidential relationship with Pepper and Messina would be breached.

Here, the trial court did not commit an abuse of discretion. On these facts, it was perfectly reasonable to conclude that Maritrans' competitive position could be irreparably injured if Pepper and Messina continued to represent their competitors and that Maritrans' remedy at law, that is their right to later seek damages, would be difficult if not impossible to sustain because of difficult problems of proof, particularly problems related to piercing what would later become a confidential relationship between their competitors and those competitors' attorneys (Pepper and Messina).

NOTES ON COMMON LAW DUTIES

1. In *Maritrans*, dissenting opinions argued that the client Maritrans had consented to an "ethical wall" arrangement between the firm and Messina that provided it with sufficient assurance of confidentiality to make it inappropriate to issue an injunction under the circumstances. For more on the "ethical wall" exception to the prohibition against conflicting representations (sometimes called the "Chinese wall" in reference to the Great Wall of China), see *infra* sections 5(D)–(E). On the nature of the conflict between the clients, and whether it should qualify as a disqualifying one, see Geraldine Rowe, Maritrans G.P. Inc. v. Pepper, Hamilton & Scheetz: *Is Economic Competition Enough to Create a Conflict of Interest?*, 8 Geo.J. Legal Ethics 1171 (1995).

2. **Common Law Duties:** For confirmation of the common law origins of lawyer conflict of interest principles, consider a lawyer-client dispute arising more than twenty-five years before the adoption of the 1908 ABA Canons of Ethics. In *Chatfield v. Simonson*, 92 N.Y. 209 (1883), a New York lawyer represented an estate. The lawyer privately entered into a contract with another party whereby assets of the estate were released from the estate in exchange for payment to the lawyer of $1,500. After the conclusion of the case, and non-payment of the legal fee by the lawyer's client, the lawyer sued to recover the fee. The New York court wrote of the common law duty of loyalty to the client's interest:

> The contract, which the law implies from an attorney's employment is, that he shall render faithful and honest service to his client in the conduct of the business in which he is employed, and that he shall not use the knowledge gained therein * * * to the prejudice of his client * * *.

> The conduct of the plaintiff * * * was a violation of his professional duty and the obligations which he owed to his client, and tended directly to defeat the object of the employment * * *. We are, therefore, of the opinion that the facts were established showing a breach of his agreement, and a good defense to the plaintiff's claim thereon * * *.

Id. at 215 (1883). *See also* Edward P. Weeks, Attorneys at Law § 260 (2d ed. 1892) (duty to disclose adverse interests). The common law duties mentioned in *Maritrans* are also part of two Restatements. Section 78 of the AMERICAN LAW INSTITUTE's RESTATEMENT (THIRD) OF TRUSTS (2007) obligates the lawyer as a fiduciary to administer trust assets solely in the interest of the beneficiary. Sections 8.02 to 8.06 of the RESTATEMENT (THIRD) OF AGENCY (2006) define duties of loyalty to the client/principal, including a prohibition against the lawyer/agent's dealing adversely with the client/principal (§ 8.03).

A. CONFLICTS OF INTEREST OF MULTIPLE CLIENTS

A(1) MULTIPLE CLIENTS IN THE SAME MATTER

PROBLEM

James Jones and Harold Harmon are life-long friends and neighbors. Jones owns a vacation home at a lake near their home town, which Harmon has frequently used for vacations with his family. Jones' children are older and have moved out of the home, showing no interest in continuing to use the vacation home. Jones and his wife have tired of keeping the place up and want to sell, though they would like to use the house occasionally. Jones and Harmon tentatively agree that Jones will sell the vacation home to Harmon for $150,000, but that Jones will have the right to use it for two weeks out of every year at a mutually agreeable time. Jones owns a boat that Harmon doesn't want to buy, so they agree that Jones can continue to keep his boat at the dock on the property.

After a weekend at the vacation home, during which the sale agreement is reached, Jones and Harmon are driving back to town when their car collides with another car at an intersection. Jones is driving and is slightly injured, while Harmon, the only passenger, suffers severe and permanent injury to his legs. Both tell the police officer and Jones' insurance company that the other driver failed to stop at the intersection and that Jones had the right of way, but the other driver insists that it was Jones who failed to stop.

QUESTION

Jones and Harmon now come to you and ask you (i) to draw up a contract and deed for them reflecting the vacation home sale agreement, and (ii) to represent them in a suit against the other driver for personal injuries and property damage. Can you properly accept either representation? If so, under what conditions?

RULE REFERENCES

Model Rules 1.0(e), 1.7, 1.8(f) & (g), and 5.4(c)

RESTATEMENT §§ 121, 128 & Comment *f*

A(1)(a) Non–Litigation Matters

IOWA SUPREME COURT BOARD OF PROFESSIONAL ETHICS AND CONDUCT v. WAGNER

Supreme Court of Iowa, 1999.
599 N.W.2d 721.

LAVORATO, JUSTICE.

This disciplinary proceeding is a textbook example of the pitfalls that await an attorney who decides to represent both the buyer and the seller in a large commercial transaction. * * *

I. FACTS * * *

Before April 1995, Carl Oehl and his family operated a restaurant known as Colony Market Place in South Amana. Titles to the business and the real estate upon which the restaurant was located were in the name of Colony Market Place, Inc., a corporation whose shareholders included Oehl and his family. The restaurant had been in existence for twenty-eight years and included a gift shop and a specialty food line.

In December 1993, Oehl closed all but the gift shop and specialty food line and decided to sell the business. [For over a year he listed the property for sale, most recently at a price of $600,000 after having it appraised at $750,000, without success.]

In February 1995, Oehl and [attorney John C.] Wagner agreed that, if Wagner found a buyer and would represent Oehl in the sale, Oehl would pay him a commission of ten percent of the gross sale price as compensation for all of Wagner's services. If the property were sold on contract, Wagner was to receive ten percent of the down payment and ten percent of each payment on principal until the purchase price was paid in full.

Shortly thereafter, Wagner and his intern, Jeff Ritchie, visited the restaurant, viewed the appraisal, and reviewed the books and records of the business. Ritchie then prepared a sales brochure listing the asking price at $600,000. At one place in the brochure under the heading, Financial Information, appear the words "assurance of a profitable operation" and "a low risk factor for new ownership." Apparently, Oehl prepared this part of the brochure. Between March 16 and April 18, Ritchie contacted a number of people about buying the business but was unsuccessful in receiving any offers.

On April 18 David Childers met with Wagner at Wagner's Amana office to gather information about Oehl's restaurant. Childers knew that the restaurant had been closed for about fifteen months, but he did not know whether the restaurant was for sale. (At the time, Childers was a kitchen manager at another local restaurant.) Childers went to Wagner because Wagner had represented him in the past and Wagner was the only attorney he knew.

In that first meeting, Childers discussed buying the restaurant and starting his own business. He offered that he had never owned a business and had limited financial resources. Wagner told Childers that he represented Oehl in regard to the sale of Oehl's restaurant, but he could not be involved in negotiating a purchase price. Wagner also told Childers that it may be in his best interest to have independent counsel, but he did not explain why. And Wagner never mentioned he would receive a ten percent commission if he found a buyer for the restaurant. Additionally, Wagner mentioned that Childers could have his own appraisal but this would cost $1000 to $2000. Wagner, however, did not advise Childers that he ought to pay the money and obtain the appraisal. Wagner charged Childers for this meeting and for all subsequent work he did for Childers.

The following day Childers signed a confidentiality agreement regarding any financial information he learned about Oehl's restaurant and received a copy of the sales brochure. Wagner and Ritchie then accompanied Childers to Oehl's restaurant to meet Oehl and view the restaurant.

On the same day, Wagner began making inquiries to a local bank about financing for Childers. Those efforts continued for several more days and resulted in the bank agreeing to finance a portion of the purchase price. Wagner prepared several documents the bank required as a condition for the loan. One of the documents was a subordination agreement for which he charged Childers one-half of the preparation time because the services benefited both Childers and Oehl. Apparently, the bank required the titleholder to subordinate its vendor's interest to the bank's loan to Childers.

Childers and Oehl agreed to a purchase price of $400,000 with a down payment of $150,000. Wagner prepared the offer to buy, which included these amounts. After Childers signed the offer on April 24, Wagner presented it to Oehl that evening. Oehl wanted some additional terms that Wagner included in a counteroffer. Childers accepted the counteroffer the next day. On the same day, Wagner and Oehl amended their fee agreement, reducing the total amount of compensation from $40,000 to $37,500 and providing that Wagner receive $30,000 immediately instead of $15,000 and the balance a year later.

Two days after the counteroffer was signed, Wagner sent a congratulatory letter to Oehl and Childers in which he stated:

> I know I have repeatedly explained my legal ethics to all of you as this matter progressed, but I want to reiterate that I have represented all of you in the past. In regard to this transaction, it is my opinion that I can continue to provide representation to the Oehl family and to the Childers family as long as you are fully informed of such representation, and as long as there are no controversies. This will also confirm that I took no part with either of you in the development of the purchase price amount or any negotiations relating thereto.

Wagner invited responses only if either party disagreed with these representations.

Wagner prepared the documents for closing, which included required real estate filings, a title opinion to Childers, the real estate contract between the parties, and closing statements for both parties. The closing took place on May 26. Oehl's closing statement disclosed Wagner's commission, but Childers' statement did not. Childers never received a copy of Oehl's closing statement.

In his title opinion to Childers, Wagner wrote:

Prospective purchasers are also advised that the title examiner also represents the seller on this transaction. Buyers are advised that such representation is a conflict of interest as the interest of the parties are different and likely adverse. Buyers are advised that it would be prudent for them to consult with other counsel concerning this opinion.

To complete the purchase, Childers borrowed the $150,000 down payment from the bank; $50,000 of this amount was secured by a mortgage on his home and $100,000 was secured by the business. Additionally, Childers borrowed $54,000 as working capital from his brother.

Childers took possession of the restaurant on May 26. The first contract payment of $9375 was due December 31. Childers only paid $6000 of that payment. Childers asked Wagner for help regarding his financial problems. In response, Wagner tried to convince the bank to renegotiate the loan but was unsuccessful.

On December 27 Wagner told Childers to retain other counsel. Wagner wrote Oehl a letter telling him the same thing. Childers and Oehl thereafter retained other counsel.

Eventually, Oehl forfeited Childers' contract. Childers, however, still owed the bank nearly $150,000. He also owed his brother the $54,000 he had borrowed from him. Additionally, Childers owed some outstanding restaurant bills.

Wagner found another buyer, a former client, Todd Markillie. Markillie bought the restaurant on contract, agreeing to pay $348,000 with $25,000 down on August 1, 1996. Wagner loaned Markillie $50,000 toward the purchase price. Markillie suffered the same fate as Childers had: Oehl forfeited the contract in January 1997. Wagner was only able to recover $9000 of the $50,000 Wagner had loaned Markillie.

Thereafter, Wagner and his wife purchased the restaurant on contract for $322,000 and a down payment of $2500 on February 21, 1997. Oehl gave Wagner a $6500 credit on the purchase price because of the partially unpaid commission owing on the sale to Childers. The Wagners are presently leasing the property to a couple who apparently are running the business successfully.

Meanwhile, Childers' new attorney learned of Wagner's fee arrangement with Oehl in May 1996. Childers sued Wagner, and the parties later settled. There is no record evidence of the grounds for the suit or the terms of the settlement.

II. ETHICAL VIOLATIONS

[The court applied Iowa's Code of Professional Responsibility, DR 5–105, which defined conflict of interest among clients in terms of whether "the exercise of * * * independent professional judgment in behalf of a client will be or is likely to be adversely affected by" accepting employment by or continuing to represent another client. DR 5–105(D) allowed multiple representation to continue "if it is obvious that the lawyer can adequately represent the interest of each and if each consents to the representation after full disclosure of the possible effect of such representation on the exercise of the lawyer's independent professional judgment on behalf of each." This is now covered by Rule 32:17 of the Iowa Rules of Professional Conduct.]

[W]e find that from Childers' initial meeting with Wagner, Wagner was representing both Oehl as a seller and Childers as a buyer. Wagner concedes this fact. Although we stop short of finding that Wagner had any role in negotiating the purchase price, we agree with the commission that this fact did not eliminate the conflict. In fact, Wagner recognized this conflict in his title opinion to Childers. As one commentator notes, the differing interests between buyer and seller are obvious, and price is only one of many areas in which those interests differ:

> The process by which a buyer and seller of property transact their business is fraught with conflicts of interests. Indeed, a lawyer's simultaneous representation of a buyer and a seller in the same transaction is a paradigm of a conflict of interest. Beginning with such basic elements as determining the price and describing the property to be sold, what one party gets the other must concede. Terms of payment, security for unpaid balances, warranties of quality and of title, date of closing and risk of loss in the interim, tax consequences, and a host of other details should be addressed by each party or the party's adviser in a well-thought-out transaction. When the transaction is a large one—such as the purchase and sale of a residence, commercial property, or a business—the transaction typically becomes further complicated because the additional interests of banks, brokers, tenants, and title insurance companies may intrude.

Charles Wolfram, *Modern Legal Ethics* § 8.5, at 434 (West 1986) (footnotes omitted) [hereinafter Wolfram].

We also find * * * that Wagner's own financial stake in the transaction—the ten percent commission—brought his interests into conflict with Childers' interest, a fact that Wagner concedes. Given the uncertainty of the value of the restaurant and the lack of offers from other interested parties, the purchase of the restaurant was a risky proposition. In these circumstances, Childers had a right to expect competent, disinterested advice that would allow him to make an informed decision on whether to proceed with the purchase at all. Wagner's own interest, on the other hand, was to make sure that the sale went through so he could earn his commission.

Wagner's interests conflicted with Childers' interests in two other respects. Childers' interest naturally called for achieving a rock bottom purchase price. In contrast, Wagner's interest called for achieving the highest price possible to maximize his commission. In addition, it was in Wagner's and Oehl's interest that Childers make a sizable down payment. Wagner's up-front commission payment depended upon the size of the down payment. Oehl's interest was what any contract seller would want: the higher the down payment the greater the security. Obviously, Childers' interest was to obtain as small a down payment as possible.

[The court noted that both of these conflicts gave rise to a duty of full disclosure to the clients, including the advisability of obtaining independent counsel, in order to obtain their informed consent to the continued representation. With respect to Wagner's own interest, it was admitted that he made no disclosure whatever. With respect to the dual representation, the court said:]

In a dual representation situation, it is not enough for a lawyer simply to inform the client that the lawyer is representing both sides. Full disclosure * * * requires the "attorney not only to inform the prospective client of the attorney's relationship with the seller, but also to explain in detail the pitfalls that may arise in the course of the transaction which would make it desirable that the buyer obtain independent counsel." * * *

Such a disclosure is crucial in a large commercial transaction as the one here because as one court put it:

> A client cannot foresee and cannot be expected to foresee the great variety of potential areas of disagreement that may arise in a real estate transaction of this sort. The attorney is or should be familiar with at least the more common of these and they should be stated and laid before the client at some length and with considerable specificity.

In re Lanza, 65 N.J. 347, 352, 322 A.2d 445, 448 (1974). * * *

It is true that Wagner informed Childers and Oehl that he was representing both of them in the transaction and that if any controversies arose he would withdraw. In addition, Wagner told Childers about a possibility of a conflict. Wagner, however, did not advise Childers what possible conflicts might arise and why independent counsel was advisable. These disclosures to Childers were not adequate. * * * Wagner did not shed his duty to point out the advantages of obtaining independent counsel even though he shied away from negotiating the purchase price. * * *

We conclude Wagner violated [the conflict of interest Rules]. On this point, we note that Wagner now "recognizes that he should not have attempted to undertake even a circumscribed and limited representation of both parties in the real estate transaction." [The court ordered a three month suspension from the practice of law.]

NOTES ON MULTIPLE REPRESENTATION IN REAL ESTATE TRANSACTIONS

1. **Model Rule 1.7 on Dual Representation:** The Iowa court rightly describes Wagner's situation as a "textbook example of the pitfalls that await an attorney" undertaking dual representation in a large transaction. The case was decided, as noted, under an earlier version of the ABA's ethics standards, the Model Code of Professional Responsibility. Iowa has since adopted the Model Rules of Professional Conduct, including a rule that is identical in all relevant respects to the current Model Rule 1.7. Compare the essential terms of Model Rule 1.7(a)(2) concerning dual representation ("significant risk that the representation * * * will be materially limited by the lawyer's responsibilities to another client"), along with Model Rule 1.0(e) defining "informed consent," with those of the Iowa Code as applied in *Wagner*. Is there any reason to believe that the Iowa court would decide Wagner's case differently now?

2. **Common Problems:** In *State v. Callahan*, 652 P.2d 708 (Kan. 1982), an attorney who had been and continued to be the regular attorney for the buyer agreed, at the buyer's suggestion, to represent both parties, but improperly failed to disclose to the seller his close relationship to the buyer, failed adequately to explain the extent of seller's security for installment payments in the contract of sale, and failed adequately to protect seller's interests after buyer's default. *See also Baldasarre v. Butler*, 625 A.2d 458 (N.J. 1993), where a lawyer asked to represent the sellers negotiated a contract of sale with a buyer who was a long-time client of the lawyer, and represented the buyer in pursuing zoning variances to allow development of the property. The lawyer disclosed the multiple representation to both parties and obtained their written consent, but failed to disclose to the sellers during the zoning process the fact that the buyer had obtained an assignee—a fact that the buyer was not obligated to disclose to the seller, but which a truly independent lawyer would be obligated to disclose to his client. The representation was held improper, and the court took the occasion to announce a "bright line rule" that a lawyer may not represent both buyer and seller in a complex real estate transaction even with the informed consent of both.

One of the most common dual representations in real estate transactions is that of lender and borrower/purchaser. It has been held that where one attorney acted for both buyer and lender in searching and rendering a title opinion, there is no inherent conflict (though there is potential for it), due to similar interests in securing an accurate title opinion letter. *Westport Bank and Trust Co. v. Corcoran, Mallin and Aresco*, 605 A.2d 862 (Conn. 1992). If the dual representation is more general, such as representation of both buyer and lender at the closing, the potential for conflict may be greater. The positions of the Vermont Bar Association on the question are instructive. After declaring in 1990 that such a representation was categorically unconsentable under the Code's standard that it must be "obvious" that both parties can be adequately represented, it concluded in 2001 that it was potentially consentable under the original Model Rule 1.7's "lawyer reasonably believes" standard and reaffirmed this view under the 2002 revision of Model Rule 1.7. Vt. Bar Ass'n, Formal Opinion 2011–2 (2011). The opinion characterizes Model Rule 1.7 as substituting "a method for assessing when representing multiple parties is appropriate" for an absolute prohibition, and discusses factors to be considered, such as rules and regulations applicable to real estate closings, the circumstances and relative sophistication of each of the prospective clients, and the complexity of the transaction. The opinion notes one circumstance in which representation would be inappropriate: where the buyer wants to negotiate concessions from the seller that exceed the closing costs and the lender has a policy against such concessions.

3. **Lawyer as Scrivener:** Should a lawyer asked by a buyer and seller to draft certain instruments for them urge them to consider full separate representation, and warn them of risks involved in limiting the lawyer's responsibility to that of a draftsman? In *Boles v. Simonton*, 791 P.2d 755 (Mont. 1990), *overruled on other grounds by Uhler v. Doak*, 885 P.2d 1297 (Mont. 1994), a seller and buyer agreed to have a contract for deed drafted for them by an attorney. The contract contained a ninety day default clause permitting the seller to terminate the contract on buyer's default. After buyer's default and seller's termination, the buyer sued the attorney for failure to include a grace period in the contract, and for failure to check the accuracy of the legal description provided to him by the seller and prepare a preliminary title report. The court held, over a dissent arguing that a lawyer should be "more than a scrivener," that the lawyer was asked only to draft the contract and not to attend to other matters like the condition of the title. When a lawyer acts only as a "scrivener," should the lawyer treat the representation as one for a limited purpose under Model Rule 1.2(c)?

4. **Representing One Party to a Transaction When the Other Is Unrepresented:** The Iowa court clearly agrees that Wagner should not have undertaken the dual representation. Presumably, that would have meant representing only his first client, the seller. What pitfalls lie in such a situation, if the buyer is not represented by counsel? In *Florida Bar v. Belleville*, 591 So.2d 170 (Fla. 1991), a lawyer represented the buyer in a real estate transaction in which the seller, who had agreed with the buyer to pay the latter's attorney's fee, was unrepresented. The buyer presented terms to the attorney that were clearly one-sided: the seller's residence was to be transferred as well as the apartment building that had been the sole object of negotiation between buyer and seller, and the buyer was to give an unsecured promissory note that would terminate on the elderly seller's death. The court held that the contract was so one-sided as to put the drafting attorney on notice of possible unconscionability, and therefore imposed a duty on him to make sure that the seller understood both the nature and consequences of the specific terms, and that the attorney was acting on behalf of the buyer only. The attorney was suspended for thirty days for failure to do so.

The Florida court's opinion referred only to Rule 1.7. Consider Model Rule 4.3, which addresses "dealing on behalf of a client with a person who is not represented." Does its third sentence (added in 2002) discourage such communication as the Florida court required, as "legal advice ... other than to secure counsel"? *See* Comment [2].

In such a situation as the Florida case, did the lawyer also have a duty to consult with his own client about the apparently unconscionable features of the contract?

A(1)(b) Litigation Matters—Generally

SHILLEN'S CASE

Supreme Court of New Hampshire, 2003.
818 A.2d 1241.

BROCK, C.J. * * *

The referee's findings of fact and the record below support the following facts. The respondent is licensed to practice law in Vermont, where he has a law office. * * * Vincent and Pamela Hammond contacted the respondent regarding a New Hampshire automobile accident in which they had been involved. From the Hammonds' description of the accident and from the police report, the respondent understood that the other driver, Craig Scheller, caused the accident by failing to yield while making a left turn. Pamela Hammond was seriously injured in the accident. Vincent Hammond suffered relatively minor injuries.

Vincent Hammond was driving at the time of the accident. The car was owned and insured by his mother, Nina Hammond, through the Traveler's Insurance Company (Traveler's). Scheller was insured by Merchants Mutual Insurance Company (Merchants).

On December 7, 1993, Pamela and Vincent Hammond each retained the respondent to represent them in their claims for damages arising from the accident. Each signed a separate contingency fee agreement. The next day, the respondent made a first party claim against Traveler's on behalf of Pamela and Vincent Hammond for medical payments, property damage and uninsured motorist coverage. He also advised Merchants that he represented the Hammonds in connection with their personal injury claims. Sometime early in his representation of the Hammonds, the respondent received a copy of the police report indicating that Vincent Hammond had stated that he had been traveling at 40 mph in a 30 mph zone.

[Following respondent's demand against Merchants and negotiations,] Pamela Hammond's case against Merchants was ultimately settled for $215,000. Vincent Hammond's case against Merchants was settled for $8,000. The respondent prepared a release in connection with the settlement with Merchants * * * which the Hammonds signed * * *.

Sometime during the negotiations with Merchants, Merchants advised the respondent that it had a statement from Deborah Bickford, an eyewitness to the accident, stating that Vincent Hammond had been speeding. Among other things, the Bickford statement placed the speed of the Hammond vehicle at the time of the accident at upwards of 65 mph. At some point thereafter, the respondent met with the Hammonds[,] who read and discussed the Bickford statement. Vincent Hammond acknowledged that he had been speeding at the time of the accident, and informed the respondent that, after a discussion with his mother, he and his wife wished to pursue a claim against Vincent Hammond and Traveler's on behalf of Pamela Hammond. The respondent explained the possibility of a conflict of interest and the potential consequences, including the possibility of [a verdict in excess of the Hammond's insurance coverage], and believed that he had their consent to pursue an action against Traveler's.

[Just] prior to the Hammonds signing the release in the Merchants settlement, the respondent put Traveler's on notice of Pamela Hammond's claim against Vincent Hammond. In the letter, the respondent referred to "my clients: Pamela and Vincent Hammond." The respondent later provided Traveler's with a copy of the accident report, the Bickford statement, and photographs of the damage to Nina Hammond's vehicle.

Sometime thereafter, Vincent Hammond insisted that his acknowledgement of responsibility be put in writing for use in negotiations with Traveler's. [As a result], the respondent prepared an affidavit which declares: (1) that Mr. Hammond had read the Bickford statement and that he agreed that Bickford's observation of his speed was correct; (2) Mr. Hammond felt that had he not been traveling at such an excessive rate of speed, the accident would not have occurred; and (3) Mr. Hammond believed that his excessive speed and failure to operate his vehicle in a safe and prudent fashion caused the accident and injuries to his wife. The respondent forwarded the affidavit to Pamela Hammond for her husband's review and signature. Vincent Hammond signed the affidavit * * *. When the affidavit was returned to the respondent, included was a note stating, "Just so you know, we have dropped our insurance policy with Traveler's since they feel no responsibility for the accident. We are ready for court or whatever it takes. Thank you, Pam and Vinny Hammond."

Traveler's took the position that Pamela Hammond had essentially received full value for her injuries from Merchants and offered to settle her claim for $10,000. At no point during the course of the respondent's representation of the Hammonds in this matter did he disclose the affidavit to Traveler's.

[Later, respondent] retained local counsel, Claude T. Buttrey, to file suit against Vincent Hammond on behalf of Pamela Hammond. Buttrey moved to have the respondent admitted *pro hac vice*. Once suit was filed, the respondent ceased all communication with Vincent Hammond, and Vincent Hammond was represented by Attorney Robert Whaland. * * *

Whaland wrote to the respondent and advised him that under Kelley's Case, 137 N.H. 314, 627 A.2d 597 (1993), the respondent was not allowed to bring a claim against a client and therefore could not continue to represent Pamela Hammond. Upon review of *Kelley's Case*, the respondent concluded that he did have a conflict that could not be waived by Vincent Hammond's consent to his representation of Pamela Hammond. He withdrew from the case, and [thereafter] performed no work on Pamela Hammond's behalf. After finding successor counsel for her, the respondent had no further involvement in, and did not accept any fees from, the case.

At trial in the case of *Hammond v. Hammond*, Mr. Hammond testified on direct examination that he was traveling at 35 to 40 mph at the time of the accident. He then admitted that he had executed the affidavit, that he understood "pretty much all of it" when he had signed it, but that he had not been traveling "at a high rate of speed," as he had previously averred. He acknowledged that he had seen the Bickford statement, and that it was the statement referenced in the affidavit, but that he disagreed with Bickford's observations concerning his rate of speed.

Concerned that Mr. Hammond might have committed perjury, that Mr. Hammond's attorney hired by the insurance company might have a conflict as a potential witness against Mr. Hammond in a criminal case, and that Mr. Hammond's personal attorney had not reviewed the Bickford statement prior to advising his client to take the stand, the trial judge indicated that he would refer Mr. Hammond's testimony to the attorney general's office as possible perjury. He then declared a mistrial.

Mrs. Hammond's attorney immediately made demand upon Traveler's to settle her case within the policy limits of $300,000. The case was subsequently settled for $275,000, and Mr. Hammond received a full release.

The attorney general's office apparently chose not to pursue any case against Mr. Hammond for perjury and/or insurance fraud. [An assistant attorney general, however,] filed a formal complaint against [Respondent] Shillen with the professional conduct committee. The Committee determined that there was clear and convincing evidence that Shillen violated certain Rules, and filed a petition for public censure with this court. * * *

"In professional conduct matters, although we defer to the referee's factual findings if supported by the record, we retain the ultimate authority to determine whether, on the facts found, a violation of the rules governing attorney conduct has occurred and, if so, the appropriate sanction." * * * We review the findings made by the referee to determine "whether a reasonable person could reach the same conclusion as the referee based upon the evidence presented." * * *

We address first the judicial referee's finding that the respondent did not violate Rule 1.7, which [generally prohibits concurrent representation by the same lawyer of clients directly adverse to each other unless each client consents after consultation and the lawyer reasonably believes that the relationship will not adversely affect either client.] While a client may consent to representation notwithstanding a conflict, [the rule] makes clear that "when a disinterested lawyer would conclude that the client should not agree to the representation under the circumstances, the lawyer involved cannot properly ask for such agreement or provide representation on the basis of the client's consent." * * *

We conclude from our review of the record that no reasonable person could conclude that the Committee failed to prove by clear and convincing evidence that the respondent violated Rule 1.7 * * *. When the respondent first agreed to represent Pamela and Vincent Hammond * * *, he did not consider the possibility of a conflict of interest. At that time, the Hammonds had a mutual interest in recovering for their respective injuries from Scheller. The record supports the conclusion that at that time, the respondent did not know that Vincent Hammond's actions might have contributed to the accident. However, at some point during the negotiations with Scheller's insurer, the respondent learned of the Bickford statement and was therefore on notice that there was evidence that Mr. Hammond's speed had contributed to the accident, and, as a consequence, to his wife's injuries.

Rather than withdraw from representation of one or both of his clients, the respondent met with them to discuss the contents of the Bickford statement. After apparently obtaining their consent to proceed in an action against Traveler's, the respondent wrote a demand letter to Traveler's. At that point, it should have been clear to the respondent that he was representing two clients whose interests were directly adverse, in violation of [the Rules].

[Despite respondent's claim that he did not represent Mr. Hammond when the demand letter was written, the court found the record proved otherwise. In fact, the demand letter referred to both Hammonds as "his clients."] Finally, it is clear that the respondent continued to treat Mr. Hammond as a client, and that both Hammonds considered the respondent their attorney. The respondent testified that in response to his [demand letter], Traveler's

> wrote back to me and they claimed that there was no liability on behalf of Mr. Hammond, and that basically I should go pound sand. In effect, they were denying liability on the claim, period. I had told *Mr. and Mrs.* Hammond about this development, and at this point in time, *Mr. Hammond* became enraged and said, "You have to do something to convince them, Traveler's, that I am accountable. I have read Mrs. Bickford's statement and I agree with it."

(Emphasis added.) Thereafter, the respondent prepared an affidavit for Mr. Hammond's signature confessing liability, and forwarded the affidavit to Mrs. Hammond. When the Hammonds returned the signed affidavit to the respondent * * *, they included a handwritten note indicating that they were *both* prepared to proceed against Traveler's. Following the preparation of the affidavit, Mr. Hammond contacted the respondent on a regular basis to find out the status of the negotiations. He also informed the respondent of the status of Mrs. Hammond's medical care.

Whether the respondent explained the possibility of a conflict of interest and the potential consequences and obtained Vincent and Pamela Hammond's consent to pursue an action against Traveler's is irrelevant to the consideration of whether he violated Rule 1.7 * * *. A disinterested lawyer would conclude under these circumstances that a client should not agree to be represented by the same attorney who has been hired by his wife to sue him. When the driver of a motor vehicle is involved in an accident that results in serious injury to a passenger and it is clear that the driver may have contributed to the cause of the accident, an attorney cannot undertake to represent both parties. *Cf. Tornquist v. Perkowski,* 208 N.J.Super. 88, 504 A.2d 1226, 1228, n.1 (1984) (noting New Jersey Ethics committee statement that one attorney may represent driver and passenger who are husband and wife in a suit against a third party only when it is obvious that the third party is exclusively liable), *overruled on other grounds by Tichenor v. Santillo,* 218 N.J.Super. 165, 527 A.2d 78, 81 (1987). * * *

[The court then found that the respondent was negligent rather than willful in his misconduct, but that it clearly injured his client Vincent, among other things, by exposing him to the risk of a perjury charge; and ordered public censure as the appropriate disciplinary sanction.]

NOTES ON SIMULTANEOUS MULTIPLE REPRESENTATION IN LITIGATION

1. **Actual Conflict in Same Case:** Simultaneous representation of actually conflicting interests in litigation is understood to be a classic impropriety. *See, e.g., Fund of Funds, Ltd. v. Arthur Andersen & Co.,* 567 F.2d 225 (2d Cir. 1977). While prior versions of the Model Rules did not explicitly forbid it, a requirement that a reasonable lawyer would find that both sides could be adequately represented made room for a virtually per se rule. *See* Texas Rule 1.06(a) (1990) ("A lawyer shall not represent opposing parties to the same litigation."). *See also* RESTATEMENT, § 122(2)(b) (2000) (declaring representation of opposing parties in litigation to be improper regardless of consent).

The principle was applied in *Jedwabny v. Philadelphia Transportation Co.,* 135 A.2d 252 (Pa. 1957). There, the same lawyer represented the driver and two passengers in one vehicle in a suit against the owner of the other vehicle involved in a collision, a city streetcar whose motorman was alleged to be negligent. Thereafter, the defendant filed a counterclaim against the driver-plaintiff alleging contributory negligence. The lawyer for the plaintiffs then attempted to defend a claim for negligence against his client-driver by the defendant, but did not assert a claim for negligence against the same driver by the two passenger clients. The trial resulted in verdict and judgment against both drivers/owners in favor of both passenger plaintiffs, and against the car driver's claim for damages. The lone plaintiffs' lawyer filed no after-verdict motions. The court granted the original defendant's motion for new trial, however, on the sole ground that the driver-plaintiff was prejudiced by conflicted representation to which he had not had an opportunity to give informed consent. The granting of the new trial was affirmed on appeal, with the court noting that the same conflicted lawyer sought to have that ruling overturned and the verdict against his driver client reinstated! Apparently because cases like *Shillen* did not make the virtually per se rule clear to some lawyers, the current version of Model Rule 1.7(b)(3) and Comment [17] makes clear that even informed consent will not permit this type of representation.

2. **After–Acquired Conflicts:** When a conflict does subsequently arise in a multiple representation that was proper in the first place, what is the

attorney to do? In *In re H. Children*, 608 N.Y.S.2d 784 (Fam.Ct. 1994), a law guardian (called "guardian *ad litem*" in other jurisdictions) was appointed to represent a son and a daughter in a child abuse proceeding against their father. The guardian then interviewed the two children and determined that they had differing views on whether or not the abuse—alleged to have occurred only with respect to the daughter—in fact occurred, and that the son was likely to be called as a witness by the father. The guardian sought to withdraw as to the son but to remain as counsel for the daughter. The court, however, held that since the guardian had likely obtained confidential information from both children, she was required to withdraw from both representations in the absence of effective consent of both clients.

In *First American Carriers, Inc. v. Kroger Co.*, 787 S.W.2d 669 (Ark. 1990), two different insurance carriers insuring the owners of different vehicles involved in a mass accident retained different members of the same law firm on the same day to represent their insureds. A few days later a lawsuit was filed against both clients (among others) and shortly thereafter the two partners discovered their conflict. One of the lawyers had done very substantial work investigating the matter while the other had done only routine legal research. The latter notified the insurer that retained him that he was obligated to withdraw from the representation. This client then hired another lawyer and moved to disqualify the firm from the first representation as well. Again, the court held the lawyer was properly disqualified.

Disqualification in both these cases does not come from Model Rule 1.7. Instead, when the lawyers withdrew under Model Rule 1.16 from representing the son in *H. Children* and one of the drivers in *First American Carriers*, the client from whom the lawyer withdrew became a "former client" within the meaning of Model Rule 1.9. This is pointed out in Model Rule 1.7, Comment [33]. Under Model Rule 1.9(a), the only way either lawyer could continue to represent the current client is with the written consent of the now-former client.

3. **Consent to Future Conflicts:** In either *H. Children* or *First American Carriers*, could the lawyer have carefully drafted a retainer agreement that allowed the lawyer to continue to represent one of the clients if a future conflict developed, even over the disagreement of the remaining client? The answer, according to Model Rule 1.7, Comment [22] as introduced in 2002 along with the more specific statement of the conditions of informed consent in 1.7(b), is that "it depends." Consent to future conflict is governed by the reasonable understanding of the client at the time the waiver is obtained. "The more comprehensive the explanation of the types of future representations * * * and the actual and reasonably foreseeable adverse consequences," the more likely the waiver will be effective. "If the consent is general and open-ended," it is not likely to be effective. The implications of this revision are explained in ABA Formal Opinion 05–436 (2005), withdrawing a more restrictive opinion issued under the prior version of the Model Rule.

If a single attorney or law firm represents multiple clients in litigation, there is the potential that the clients will later disagree among themselves regarding a proposed course of action. One common disagreement among clients concerns the wisdom of accepting the opposing party's offer to settle.

Under Model Rule 1.8(g), a lawyer cannot participate in an aggregate settlement unless each client gives informed consent in a writing signed by the client. The New Jersey Supreme Court has held that the attorney is not allowed to attempt to resolve a conflict among clients regarding settlement in advance, simply by adopting a retainer agreement where each client agrees to settle if a majority of clients so agrees. *See Tax Auth., Inc. v. Jackson Hewitt, Inc.*, 898 A.2d 512 (N.J. 2006).

4. **One Client with Multiple Interests:** Suppose a single client has distinct and conflicting "interests" in the same matter. Can a single attorney properly represent her in both capacities? A negative answer was given in *McTaggart v. Lindsey*, 509 N.W.2d 881 (Mich.Ct.App. 1993), where the mother of a child who was killed in a hotel fire was both personal representative of the child's estate and a wrongful death claimant in her own right. It was held improper for one attorney to represent the mother in both capacities, where the estate would be distributed in part to persons other than the mother and where the defendant sought to settle both the wrongful death claim and the estate's claim for the child's pain and suffering in the same agreement. Would the result be the same if all of the proceeds were to be distributed to the mother as the only heir?

In *Boyd v. Trent*, 731 N.Y.S.2d 209 (App.Div. 2001), a father was injured in a car accident while his wife was driving his car. The father sued the driver of the other vehicles in two capacities. First, he sued to recover for his own injuries. He also sued as guardian of his infant children for their injuries. The father was represented in both capacities by the same lawyers. The trial judge granted a motion to remove the father as guardian of his children, and to disqualify the lawyers from both representations, on the ground that the father as owner of the car was vicariously liable for any negligence of his wife as driver. On appeal, it was held that removal of the father as guardian and disqualifying the lawyers from continuing to represent the children was enough, and that there was no reason that the lawyers could not continue to represent the father in his individual capacity. The court also held that a guardian *ad litem* should be appointed to represent the child.

A(1)(c) Litigation Matters—Insurance

QUESTIONS

In the problem at the beginning of this section, assume that the other driver has filed suit against Jones for damages suffered in the accident, and you are asked by Casualty Company, Jones' liability insurer, to represent Jones in defense of that suit. May you properly accept this representation? What problems may arise from such an arrangement?

ROGERS v. ROBSON, MASTERS, RYAN, BRUMUND AND BELOM

Appellate Court of Illinois, Third District, 1979.
392 N.E.2d 1365.

STOUDER, JUSTICE:

[A medical malpractice action filed against Dr. Rogers, who was represented by a law firm appointed by his liability insurance carrier, was settled by the firm, at the insistence of the carrier, against Dr. Rogers' explicit instructions. He sued the firm for damages for wrongful settlement without his consent. The trial court entered summary judgment for the firm, on the ground that the insurance contract expressly permitted settlement without the insured's consent where, as in this case, the doctor was no longer a current insured. The appellate court agreed that the policy permitted settlement without the insured's consent, but held that not to be dispositive as against the lawyers.]

Plaintiff argues * * * that defendant's conduct breached a duty to plaintiff independent of any duty associated with the insurance policy. Whether such a duty is owed to plaintiff by defendant and if so, whether that duty has been breached, depends on the relationship between plaintiff, defendant, and the insurance company. Since defendant is a group of attorneys, inquiry into this tripartite relationship focuses initially on the question, "Whom does the defendant represent?"

[W]hen an insurance company retains an attorney to defend an action against one of its insureds, the insured is the client and the company the attorney's employer. * * * The attorney-client relationship between the insured and the attorney imposes upon the attorney the same professional obligations that would exist had the attorney been personally retained by the insured. * * * The fact that the attorney also represents the insurer in no way alters his obligations or responsibilities to the insured. * * *

Ordinarily, since the interests of insurer and insured are harmonious, there is no conflict and the attorney is able to exercise independent judgment for both clients. Therefore, in the usual instance, there is nothing improper or unethical about representing the interests of both. * * * However, situations can arise where those interests may become conflicting. * * *

When a conflict does arise, serious ethical considerations prohibit an attorney from continuing to represent both the interests of the insured and the insurer. * * * However, the attorney does not necessarily have to withdraw from the case. In many situations, if, after full and frank disclosure, the clients are willing to consent to the attorney's continued representation on their behalf, ethical considerations are satisfied and the attorney may continue to represent the conflicting interests. * * *

What facts must be revealed depends on the circumstances. When an attorney represents two clients with divergent or conflicting interests in the same subject matter, the attorney must disclose all facts and circumstances which in the judgment of a lawyer of ordinary skill and capacity, are necessary to enable his client to make a free and intelligent decision regarding the representation. * * *

While the foregoing discussion has focused on the risks of conflict inherent in dual representation, the principle to be gleaned is that the attorney does represent the insured and assumes all of the duties imposed by the attorney-client relationship. Not only does the attorney owe his client fidelity and loyalty, but also is required to exercise reasonable skill in the performance of his duties. * * *

Well in advance of the settlement, defendant was informed by its client, the plaintiff, that no settlement should be made. According to plaintiff, defendant responded that the action would be defended. Despite the plaintiff's demands that the case not be settled, settlement negotiations took place culminating in settlement * * *. Plaintiff was not informed prior to settlement of the intention of the defendant attorneys to settle the action [or of the actual settlement]. * * *

By failing to inform plaintiff of the proposed settlement, defendant foreclosed plaintiff from alternatives that were available to him. Plaintiff could have consented to continued representation by the defendant at the expense of the insurance company with the accompanying likelihood that the case would be settled without his consent, for, as we have held, the insurance company by virtue of the contract could settle without plaintiff's consent. If plaintiff believed such a course of action was not in his best interests, he could release the insurance company from its obligation under the policy, select different counsel, defend the action at his own expense and bear the risk of an adverse decision.

Having failed to provide plaintiff with the proper disclosure of the facts and then obtaining plaintiff's consent to continued representation, defendant breached a duty which, if damages and proximate cause are established, will make defendant liable to plaintiff for the loss caused by the lack of disclosure. We believe the trial court erred in holding for defendant on its motion for summary judgment.

NOTES ON REPRESENTING INSURED AND INSURER

1. In *Rogers*, the court holds the lawyer liable independent of the contract of insurance by which the insured/plaintiff is provided a defense. For a case in which the insurance contract did not give the insurer the right to settle without the insured's consent, but the court held the insurer-appointed attorney liable for unauthorized settlement based on the attorney-client relationship rather than on the insurance contract, see *Lieberman v. Employers Insurance of Wausau*, 419 A.2d 417 (N.J. 1980).

2. **The Tripartite Relationship:** The characterization of the relationship between attorney, insurer, and insured as one of dual representation, where the attorney is retained by the insurer to defend the insured, has

prevailed in most jurisdictions since ABA Committee on Professional Ethics and Grievances, Formal Opinion 282 (1950). That opinion stated, however, that if a conflict arises between insurer and insured after the attorney has been retained, the latter's duty of loyalty is owed *to the insured*. This view has also prevailed in most jurisdictions, unchanged by any of the historical versions of the Model Rules. *See* Randall Riopelle, *When May an Insurer Fire Counsel Hired to Represent the Insured?*, 7 Geo.J. Legal Ethics 247, 249 (1993). Confusion resulting from the notion of a dual representation in which one client must be favored over the other is discussed in Robert E. O'Malley, *Ethics Principles for the Insurer, the Insured, and Defense Counsel: The Eternal Triangle Reformed*, 66 Tul.L.Rev. 511 (1991).

Some jurisdictions still hold that only the insured is the client. *See State Farm Fire & Cas. Co. v. Weiss*, 194 P.3d 1063 (Colo.App. 2008) (holding, after a canvass of the views of other jurisdictions, that an insurer does not have a malpractice claim against a lawyer for the insured, that malpractice claims are not assignable, and that therefore the insurer also cannot be equitably subrogated to the insured's malpractice claim); *Pine Island Farmers Coop v. Erstad & Riemer, P.A.*, 649 N.W.2d 444 (Minn. 2002) (holding that the insurer—otherwise simply a third-party payer of the lawyer's fee under Model Rule 1.8(f)—can only become a client (and therefore entitled to sue the lawyer for malpractice) with the informed consent of the insured). Indeed, the Hawaii Supreme Court has characterized the single-representation theory as "the modern view." *Finley v. Home Ins. Co.*, 975 P.2d 1145, 1153 (Haw. 1998), *citing* Douglas R. Richmond, *Walking a Tightrope: The Tripartite Relationship Between Insurer, Insured, and Insurance Defense Counsel*, 73 Neb.L.Rev. 265, 294 (1994).

One consequence of viewing the relationship between insurer and independent counsel, hired by the insurer to defend the insured, as one in which the insured is the client and the insurer only the one paying for the service is that the insurer will not be vicariously liable to the insured for the lawyer's negligence in handling the defense. *See State Farm Mut. Auto. Ins. Co. v. Traver*, 980 S.W.2d 625 (Tex. 1998).

3. **Conflicts in the Insurer/Insured/Counsel Relationship:** In the liability insurer-insured relationship, other sources of conflict include not only issues of strategy and tactics in defense but also the possible existence of facts that would exclude coverage of the particular claim or insured altogether. For a comprehensive survey of conflict issues in five stages of insurance defense (discovery and investigation, coverage and exclusion, communication and disclosure, negotiation and settlement, and litigation), see Eric Mills Holmes, *A Conflicts-of-Interest Roadmap for Insurance Defense Counsel: Walking an Ethical Tightrope Without a Net*, 26 Willamette L.Rev. 1 (1989). *See also* Conn. Bar Ass'n Comm. on Prof'l Ethics, Informal Op. 92–7 (1992), *digested in* Laws.Man. on Prof. Conduct (ABA/BNA) 1001:2030 (1992).

One example of such a conflict is a claim against the insured for punitive damages based on alleged willful or malicious conduct, which the insurer claims is not covered by the policy. Typically the insurer's contractual duty to defend is distinct from the duty to indemnify, so that the insurer may be obligated in such a conflict situation to allow the insured to retain independent counsel at the insurer's expense. *See Ill.Mun. League Risk Mgmt. Ass'n v. Siebert*, 585 N.E.2d 1130 (Ill.App.Ct. 1992); *Nandorf, Inc. v. CNA Ins. Cos.*, 479 N.E.2d 988 (Ill.App.Ct. 1985) (also holding that insured is not entitled to insurer financed independent counsel when punitive damages are sought).

Most courts insist, however, that the right of the insured to retain his own counsel at the insurer's expense is not automatically triggered by the insurer's "reservation of rights" warning of a potential coverage defense, without a specific showing that the dispute over coverage will generate a conflict of interest concerning defense of the lawsuit. Two cases illustrate the problem.

In *Emery v. Progressive Casualty Insurance Co.*, 2010–0327 (La.App. 1 Cir. 9/10/10); 49 So.3d 17, plaintiffs were injured when their car was rear-ended by another car; they sued the driver-owner of the other car along with the driver's employer and its insurer, alleging that the driver was acting in the scope of his employment and the employer was vicariously liable. The insurer had issued a no-coverage letter to the employer when notified of the claim, asserting that the policy did not cover the particular vehicle because it was not among those listed in a schedule, but when the suit was filed the insurer appointed a single attorney to represent both itself and the insured employer without ever having explained the conflict to the employer or sought informed consent to the dual representation. That lawyer proceeded to file an answer on behalf of both clients, including the insurer's defense of non-coverage, and (over a year later) participated in a deposition of the driver-employee that included specific questions relevant to insurance coverage. Only at that point did the insurer appoint a second lawyer to represent the employer on the issue of vicarious liability. On appeal from a judgment for the plaintiffs against the insurer along with the employer, it was held that the insurer had a duty immediately to address with the insured the inherent conflict created by its reservation of rights, and that it waived its coverage defense by failing to do so.

On the other hand, in *National Casualty Co. v. Forge Industry Staffing Inc.*, 567 F.3d 871 (7th Cir. 2009), an employer's liability insurer was asked to defend the employer against charges filed with the EEOC for discriminatory and/or retaliatory firing in violation of federal law. It agreed to do so, but under a reservation of rights under the policy excluding coverage for punitive damage awards and for "willful failure ... to comply with any law ... or regulations relating to employment practices," with "willful" defined as "acting with intentional or reckless disregard" of such laws. Upon receiving this reservation of rights, the employer requested appointment of independent counsel, and when the insurer refused the employer hired its own lawyer to defend the EEOC charges. The insurer then sought a declaratory judgment clarifying the coverage issue, and the employer counterclaimed for a declaration that the insurer was obliged to cover its defense costs. The court held that there was no conflict, and therefore no duty to pay for independent counsel, where: (1) no punitive damages award was available before the EEOC; (2) the mere fact that the claims asserted in a federal administrative proceeding "could result in lawsuits in which plaintiffs might request punitive damages" was not sufficient; and (3) the fact that there were no allegations in the complaints before the EEOC relating to "willfulness" (as distinguished from merely intentional violation of the law) precluded a finding of a conflict between insurer and insured in defense of the administrative charges. "Simply put, if no fact issues appear on the face of the underlying complaint that can be conclusively resolved in such a way that insurance coverage is necessarily precluded under the policy, then appointment of independent counsel is not warranted." *Id.* at 878.

Is either of these decisions inconsistent with Model Rule 1.7's Comment [13]? It takes the position that there is no inherent conflict in a lawyer being paid by someone other than the client, so long as the client understands the source of payment and so long as the lawyer's independent judgment is not compromised. It is only upon compromise of the lawyer's independent judgment or where payment from the third party "presents a significant risk that the lawyer's representation of the client will be materially limited" that a problem arises.

A(1)(d) Other Third Party Payment Cases

NOTES ON OTHER THIRD PARTY PAYMENT SITUATIONS

1. **Drafting a Will for a Client's Family Member:** Assume that you have regularly represented Mary Anderson and her husband, Brian, for some period of time. Mary now comes to you and wants you to help her Uncle Ralph write his will and plan his estate. Mary says that she and her husband will pay your legal fee.

This is a situation analogous to that of insurer/insured/lawyer. One party is paying a fee to the lawyer to represent another party. In this situation, Model Rule 1.8(f) addresses the risk that your independent judgment on behalf of the uncle may be influenced by the fee payer. Even if the client does not offer to pay the uncle's fees, but has expectations about being a beneficiary that she expects you to protect, you are presented with a classic conflict among current clients governed by Model Rule 1.7. ABA Formal Opinion 02–428 (2002) addresses these issues and points to the number of ethics problems involved in what appears to be a relatively simple case. First, under Model Rule 5.4(c), the lawyer must make sure that the lawyer's independent professional judgment on behalf of the testator is not compromised by the fact the lawyer is being paid by the beneficiary. Second, to be paid by the beneficiary, the requirements of Model Rule 1.8(f) must be met. Thus, the client/testator must give "informed consent" under Model Rule 1.0(e)— therefore the lawyer must fully inform the testator about material risks and advantages of consulting another lawyer. In addition, under Model Rule 1.8(f), the lawyer is again warned about compromise to the lawyer's independent professional thinking. Finally, under Model Rule 1.8(f), the lawyer must exercise care to protect client confidences under Model Rule 1.6. If, as is often the case, the person paying the lawyer is also a client of the lawyer, the lawyer must assure that the confidences of each client will be adequately protected. In addition, because the lawyer now has two clients in dealing with the same factual situation, the lawyer must comply with all of the requirements of Model Rule 1.7.

Less than a year after Formal Opinion 02–428 was published, a disciplinary case was decided that neatly illustrates the potential pitfalls. In *In re Blair*, 2002–2164 (La. 2/25/03); 840 So.2d 1191, a lawyer was consulted by the niece of his mother-in-law's elderly next door neighbor on how to protect the interests of her aunt, in light of her failing health and of her fear that other relatives were trying to take advantage of her and get her property. He recommended that the aunt execute a power of attorney in favor of the niece, with his mother-in-law as co-attorney for when the niece (who lived in New York) was unavailable. At the same time he had both the aunt and the niece sign separate retainer agreements calling for fees to be paid to him for his services. He also prepared guardianship papers in case the aunt should be incapacitated. Finally, he prepared a will for the aunt after extensive consultations with her, which (at her insistence) provided bequests not only to the niece but also to certain charities, other relatives and friends, including the lawyer's mother-in-law (her closest friend). The will named the mother-in-law as executrix. For all this work he received fees only from the aunt, and (at the aunt's request) did not disclose the contents of the will to the niece. Two years later the aunt died, and the niece—having expected that she and her daughter would be the sole beneficiaries—challenged the will. The lawyer appeared on behalf of his mother-in-law as executrix. After he was disqualified and other counsel hired to represent the estate, the niece's challenge was settled, but she filed a complaint against the lawyer with the bar disciplinary authority for misconduct. The authority found that the niece was his client on the basis of the retainer agreement (although she had not actually paid any fees for the lawyer's work) and that the lawyer was guilty of a conflict of interest among current clients in violation of Model Rule 1.7, as well as a conflict with his own interests in violation of Model Rule 1.8(c). He was suspended for three months. On the problem presented by his and his mother-in-law's individual interests, see *infra* section 5(B).

2. **Criminal Cases:** Assume that a state criminal defendant is charged with domestic violence. A lawyer is paid $200 to represent the defendant by the defendant's girlfriend, the person whom the defendant is alleged to have battered. In addition, the defendant was already on probation from another battering incident regarding the same girlfriend. Because the lawyer provided no explanation of potential conflict problems to either the defendant or the girlfriend, the lawyer was suspended. *See People v. Rivers*, 933 P.2d 6 (Colo. 1997). What explanation would have been necessary under Model Rule 1.8(f)? To whom?

3. **Statutory Duty Cases:** Assume that a police officer is charged with assault while in performing the officer's duties. The alleged victim of the assault also filed a civil proceeding for damages arising from the same conduct. Under state statute, a police officer charged or sued for assault as a result of acts in performance of the officer's duties is entitled to a lawyer paid for by the government entity in which the officer serves. As a result of this statute, the county appoints a lawyer to defend the officer in both the criminal and civil proceeding. The agreement between counsel and the county provided that the county's position was that the officer was acting outside the

scope of his employment and that the county intended to seek contribution from the officer for any damages the county was obligated to pay in the civil proceeding. It was thus in the county's interest to have the officer convicted of the criminal charge so as to assist its contention that the officer was acting outside the course of his duties. On appeal of the criminal conviction, the officer alleged that he was denied effective assistance of counsel because of the conflict of interest. Although the intermediate appellate court agreed with the officer, the Hawaii Supreme Court disagreed, holding counsel not ineffective. The court found that the officer voluntarily asked for assignment of an attorney at county expense, with knowledge that the county was seeking to hold the officer responsible. The court also found that there was no evidence that the lawyer allowed the contract with the county or the contentions of the county to affect his independent representation of the officer. *See Fragiao v. State*, 18 P.3d 871 (Haw. 2001).

A(1)(e) Positional Conflicts

PROBLEM

You are retained by John Smith Gun Company in defense of a product liability action. Smith Guns makes handguns that can be customized so that the trigger mechanism will respond more quickly, giving the guns what is known as a "hair trigger." The plaintiff in the action used the customizing feature to create a "hair trigger" mechanism on one of Smith's guns and then promptly shot himself with it. In defense of Smith Gun Company, you will argue that the plaintiff is substantially at fault and that your client cannot be held liable for idiots like the plaintiff.

Because you have become something of an expert in handgun cases, you are also retained by Angela Hartwig, who purchased a handgun, made by a different manufacturer, customized the trigger mechanism to a "hair trigger" level, and then promptly shot herself. In this case, you will argue that the customizing feature is a design defect and, additionally, gun manufacturers should be held strictly liable for injuries to consumers as a result of such defects. Under the applicable jurisdiction's law, holding the gun manufacturer strictly liable will prevent the manufacturer from arguing either contributory or comparative negligence of the plaintiff.

QUESTIONS

Are you prevented from accepting either the representation of Smith Gun Company or Angela Hartwig? What problems arise?

RULE REFERENCES

Model Rule 1.7

RESTATEMENT § 128, Comment *f*

WILLIAMS v. STATE

Supreme Court of Delaware, 2002.
805 A.2d 880.

HOLLAND, JUSTICE:

The appellant Joseph Williams filed these consolidated appeals from his conviction and death sentence for first-degree murder. Williams' lawyer, Bernard J. O'Donnell, has filed a motion to withdraw. The motion also requests that substitute counsel be appointed by this Court to represent Williams on appeal.

O'Donnell asserts that, on appeal, Williams could raise an arguable issue that the Superior Court erred when it concluded it was required to give "great weight" to the jury's 10–2 recommendation in favor of the death penalty for Williams. O'Donnell contends, however, that he may have a conflict in presenting this argument because he has advocated a contrary position on behalf of a different client in another capital murder appeal pending before this Court. In *Garden v. State* * * *, O'Donnell argued in his opening brief that the Superior Court erred when it *failed* to give great weight to the jury's 2–10 vote rejecting the imposition of the death penalty for Garden.

O'Donnell is concerned that his representation of both clients on this issue will create the risk that an unfavorable precedent will be created for one client or the other. O'Donnell also is concerned that it may invite questions about his credibility with this Court and his clients' perception of his loyalty to each of them. The State agrees that O'Donnell has a conflict of interest that disqualifies him from representing Williams in this appeal.

POSITIONAL CONFLICT

The potential conflict identified by O'Donnell is termed a "positional" conflict of interest. It arises when two or more clients have opposing interests in unrelated matters. [Under Model Rule 1.7(a)(2), it is impermissible for a lawyer to represent a client if "there is a significant risk that the representation of" the client "will be materially limited by the lawyer's responsibilities to another client * * *." Comment [24] allows the lawyer to take "inconsistent legal positions in different tribunals at different times on behalf of different clients," unless the position taken on behalf of one of the clients will "materially limit the lawyer's effectiveness in representing another client in a different case."]

In determining whether a positional conflict requires a lawyer's disqualification, the question is whether the lawyer can effectively argue both sides of the same legal question without compromising the interests of one client or the other. The lawyer must attempt to strike a balance between the duty to advocate any viable interpretation of the law for one client's benefit versus the other client's right to insist on counsel's fidelity to their legal position.[5]

---

5. Douglas R. Richmond, *Choosing Sides: Issue or Positional Conflicts of Interest*, 51 FLA. L.REV. 383, 386 (1999). *See generally* Peter Margulies, *Multiple Communities or Monolithic*

Under the circumstances presented in Williams' case, we find that O'Donnell has identified and demonstrated the existence of a disqualifying positional conflict. It would be a violation of the Delaware Rules of Professional Conduct for O'Donnell to advocate conflicting legal positions in two capital murder appeals that are pending simultaneously in this Court. Both the United States Constitution and the Delaware Constitution guarantee each of O'Donnell's clients a right to the effective assistance of counsel in a direct appeal following a capital murder conviction. Given his clients' disparate legal arguments, O'Donnell's independent obligations to his clients may compromise the effectiveness of his assistance as appellate counsel for one or both clients, unless his motion to withdraw is granted.

Conclusion

Accordingly, O'Donnell's motion to withdraw must be granted and substitute counsel will be appointed. O'Donnell and the State are both commended for their recognition of and adherence to the highest standards of professional conduct.

Note on Positional Conflicts

1. Under prior versions of the Model Rules, positional conflicts were generally permitted in trial courts, but not in appellate courts. *See* Comment [9] to pre–2002 version of Model Rule 1.7. The ABA committee rejected this approach in 1993 in an opinion requiring lawyers to exercise care in any positional conflict. *See* ABA Comm. on Ethics and Prof'l Responsibility, Formal Op. 93–377 (1993). This standard has been adopted into current Model Rule 1.7, Comment [24]. For critical analysis of this position, arguing that positional conflicts are not true conflicts of interest and that a rule discouraging lawyers from espousing different legal positions in unrelated matters encourages them to favor more powerful clients and therefore make themselves less available to poor or middle income clients without any corresponding benefit to the rights of the latter, see Helen A. Anderson, *Legal Doubletalk and the Concern with Positional Conflicts: A "Foolish Consistency"?*, 111 Penn St.L.Rev. 1 (2006).

A(2) UNRELATED REPRESENTATION OF A CURRENT CLIENT'S ADVERSARY

Problem

You represent the defendant in an auto accident case. In preparation for trial, the plaintiffs announce the deposition of a bystander witness, who

---

Clients: Positional Conflicts of Interest and the Mission of the Legal Services Lawyer, 67 FORDHAM L.REV. 2339 (1999); Norman W. Spaulding, *The Prophet and the Bureaucrat: Positional Conflicts in Service Pro Bono Publico,* 50 STAN.L.REV. 1395 (1998); John S. Dzienkowski, *Positional Conflicts of Interest,* 71 TEX.L.REV. 457 (1993); Nancy Ribaudo, *Issue Conflicts,* 2 GEO.J. LEGAL ETHICS 115 (1988); *see also* RESTATEMENT (THIRD) OF THE LAW GOVERNING LAWYERS, § 128 cmt. f (1998).

claimed to have observed the accident and says your client had been speeding. It turns out that this witness is also your client in an otherwise unrelated matter, namely her claim for social security disability benefits due to failing eyesight. What problems arise, and how should you deal with them?

RULE REFERENCES

Model Rules 1.7 and 1.8(b)

WORLDSPAN, L.P. v. SABRE GROUP HOLDINGS, INC.

United States District Court, Northern District of Georgia, Atlanta Division, 1998.
5 F.Supp.2d 1356.

MOYE, DISTRICT JUDGE.

This case is before the Court on the plaintiffs' motion to disqualify the defendants' local law firm in this active tort litigation. For the reasons set forth below, the motion is GRANTED.

The law firm has served for several years, and currently is still serving, as counsel for plaintiffs in state tax matters in Georgia and Tennessee. This litigation as well as the tax matters all involve in different ways and to different degrees plaintiffs' computer airline reservations operation. The main computer located physically in Atlanta, Georgia, is the heart of plaintiff's entire business.

[The court pointed out that its local rule requires lawyers to follow the Code of Professional Responsibility adopted by the State Bar of Georgia and its own interpretations of the Code's rules and principles, set forth the relevant text of Disciplinary Rule 5–105(A) and (C), and noted that the Georgia provision is virtually identical to that of the ABA's Model Code of Professional Responsibility.]

The ABA/BNA Lawyer's Manual on Professional Conduct addresses the issues covered by those sections and here involved (ABA/BNA Lawyers' Manual on Professional Conduct, Practice Guide, § 51:101):

"A lawyer may not represent one client whose interests are adverse to those of another current client of the lawyer's, even if the two representations are unrelated, unless the clients consent and the lawyer believes he or she is able to represent each client without adversely affecting the other. Courts and ethics panels generally take a broad view of this restriction, and a specific adverse effect probably will not have to be shown. All that need be present is that one lawyer or firm is representing two clients, even in unrelated matters with potentially conflicting interests. The rules with respect to concurrent representation of conflicting interests are rooted in a lawyer's duty of loyalty to the client. This is generally considered a somewhat greater obligation than the one the lawyer owes to a former client, which is to protect client confidences and secrets.["]

In this case, it is clear that defendants have given their informed consent, and while plaintiffs question the adequacy of their representation in the highly partisan context of this case, the court believes there is little reason to question the law firm's competent and adequate representation of plaintiff's interests in the pending state tax matters. * * *

It is clear that when informed specifically that the law firm had undertaken to represent the defendants in this instant lawsuit brought by plaintiffs, the plaintiffs strenuously objected. The law firm, however, relies on its "standard" engagement letter sent to plaintiffs when their first representation was undertaken, September 16, 1992, to show that plaintiffs then prospectively gave the required consent to the present simultaneous, dual representation in this lawsuit commenced over five years subsequent to the claimed consent. * * *

In this connection, it is necessary to refer to the language of that letter (Exhibit A to plaintiffs' motion to disqualify). Its relevant language follows:

> "As we have discussed, because of the relatively large size of our firm and our representation of many other clients, it is possible that there may arise in the future a dispute between another client and WORLDSPAN, or a transaction in which WORLDSPAN's interests do not coincide with those of another client. In order to distinguish those instances in which WORLDSPAN consents to our representing such other clients from those instances in which such consent is not given, you have agreed, as a condition to our undertaking this engagement, that during the period of this engagement we will not be precluded from representing clients who may have interests adverse to WORLD-SPAN so long as (1) such adverse matter is not substantially related to our work for WORLDSPAN, and (2) our representation of the other client does not involve the use, to the disadvantage of WORLDSPAN, of confidential information of WORLDSPAN we have obtained as a result of representing WORLDSPAN.

> "We have advised you that we have served as special counsel to Delta Air Lines for certain types of matters, including state and local tax matters. We do not view our work for Delta to be in conflict with our representation of WORLDSPAN, and Delta ... has consented to our representation of WORLDSPAN. We have also advised you that we have represented American Airlines. We do not believe our representation of American Airlines is in conflict with our representation of WORLDSPAN. We have also represented various other airlines from time-to-time on limited matters ... we do not view our representation of any of these carriers to be in conflict with our proposed representation of WORLDSPAN." * * *

The substance * * * of the law firm's evidence with respect to the letter is that there was no response thereto by plaintiffs and the representation was thereupon commenced * * *.

The substance of plaintiffs' testimony with respect to the letter is that plaintiffs, by house counsel, took immediate objection, in 1992, to the possibility of future direct litigation against [them] by the law firm, and insisted upon immediate written notice of any such intended adverse litigation. Plaintiffs' witness asserts this position was conveyed by fax to the law firm, and followed by a telephone conversation with the lawyer in charge of plaintiffs' matters at the law firm, the result of which was that the lawyer stated there would be no change in the standard letter, and the representation simply continued. * * *

Looking only at the original letter itself, the Court finds that its very language is ambiguous. The phrase "will not be precluded from representing clients who may have interests adverse to WORLDSPAN so long as (1) such adverse matter" does not necessarily or even impliedly foreshadow future directly adverse litigation. It is the opinion of this Court that future directly adverse litigation against one's present client is a matter of such an entirely different quality and exponentially greater magnitude, and so unusual given the position of trust existing between lawyer and client, that any document intended to grant standing consent for the lawyer to litigate against his own client must identify that possibility, if not in plain language, at least by irresistible inference including reference to specific parties, the circumstances under which such adverse representation would be undertaken, and all relevant like information. * * *

The Court believes the above point to carry added weight when, as here, the future conflict is caused by undertaking the representation of a client with whom the law firm has no present relationship. The law firm points out that at the time the letter was sent, the law firm advised the plaintiffs that it either currently, or in the past ("we have represented American Airlines"—a valid construction of that phrase would be that no current representation existed) had represented American Airlines, stating however: "We do not believe our representation of American Airlines is in conflict with our representation of WORLDSPAN." The record shows that American Airlines is a subsidiary of AMR Corporation (AMR). The Sabre Group are 80% owned by AMR. There was no suggestion that the Law Firm had ever represented AMR, or the Sabre Group, and no suggestion that it considered it had a standing obligation to represent any entity owned by or connected to either AMR or American Airlines, or, indeed, that it had the expectation of being so requested. The defendants here are simply new clients requesting representation by the law firm five years after the "standard" letter of representation was sent. Without in any way suggesting such to be the case here, to weaken the requirement of informed consent so that general letters of standing consent, that is, waivers of professional obligations as set forth in the applicable codes of professional responsibility, suffice would, in this Court's opinion, drastically denigrate the lawyer's unique position of trust with his client and go far towards permitting the relationship to depend merely upon the non-appearance of a more substantial client. For this reason, * * * the Court * * * holds that, absent informed consent, a conflict situation cannot be resolved after the conflicted representation has occurred by the law firm's withdrawal from the least desired representation. * * *

The Court has found most useful in this regard the [RESTATEMENT § 128(2) and Comment [e], in proposed final draft form]. The Restatement is particularly helpful by reason of its recognition of the evolving nature of the legal profession.

The Court now finds that the law firm's representation of defendants herein is in prohibited conflict with its ethical duties to[,] and position of trust with[,] plaintiffs, and orders it disqualified from further representation of defendants. As the result of this disqualification, it shall be necessary for the defendants to secure new local counsel * * *.

NOTES ON SIMULTANEOUS *"UNRELATED"* REPRESENTATION

1. **The *Worldspan* Court's Sources:** Although the court in *Worldspan* operated under a local rule adopting the Model Code of Professional Responsibility of the state in which it sat, it felt obliged to interpret that Code in the light of "the mainstream of current legal thought and law," and placed primary reliance not only on the ABA/BNA Lawyers' Manual of Professional Responsibility, which was based on Model Rule 1.7, but also on the RESTATEMENT, which is not based on any single set of formal rules. Although the representation of adverse interests in the same proceeding is unconsentable under Model Rule 1.7(b)(3), representation of differing interests in separate, unrelated proceedings is potentially permissible. Comments [3] and [8] to the pre–2002 version of Model Rule 1.7 and Comment [6] to the post–2002 version of Model Rule 1.7 make clear that simultaneous unrelated representation is a situation of "directly adverse" representation, but one that can be remedied by informed consent. *See also* RESTATEMENT § 128, Comment *e* (citing mostly cases decided before adoption of the Model Rules, when the Model Code was predominant).

For another example of simultaneous unrelated representation see *Thaler v. Jacoby & Meyers Law Offices*, 742 N.Y.S.2d 241 (App.Div. 2002). In *Thaler*, the law firm of Jacoby & Meyers and several of its members were sued for malpractice by a former client. Among the individual lawyers named as defendants was Thaler. An unnamed law firm represented all of the defendants, including Thaler. While this lawsuit was pending Thaler left Jacoby & Meyers, and then claimed that Jacoby & Meyers had not paid him substantial sums of money that he earned with the firm. Pursuant to the partnership agreement, this claim was referred to arbitration. In the arbitration, the unnamed law firm appeared on behalf of Jacoby & Meyers, asserting that Thaler did not perform competently for Jacoby & Meyers and was therefore not entitled to the additional compensation he was seeking. Thaler sought to have the unnamed law firm disqualified from representing Jacoby & Meyers in the arbitration, on the ground that such representation conflicts with the unnamed firm's duties to Thaler as a client in the malpractice action. The court found that in the arbitration proceeding, the unnamed firm would be questioning Thaler's competence as an attorney. As a result, Thaler would effectively be prevented from discussing with the firm any issue that might relate to his competence in the malpractice action "for fear that his confidences might be used against him in the arbitration." The court disqualified the unnamed law firm.

Compare *Thaler* with *Culbreth v. Covington Board of Education*, No. 07–73–DLB, 2007 WL 3124711 (E.D.Ky. Oct. 24, 2007), which involved a suit against the Board and its Superintendent by one of its employees for violation of her due process rights in being demoted from administrator to teacher with a reduction in pay, without proper notice. At the same time the lawyer representing the plaintiff was representing an individual member of the Board in defense of a suit brought by the state attorney general challenging the member's qualifications to sit on the Board. On motion of the civil rights defendants to disqualify the lawyer from representing the employee, alleging a conflict of interest because of the dual representation, the court denied the motion, holding (1) that the representations were not directly adverse because the individual member was not a party to the civil rights suit (only the Board as an entity was a party) and (2) that there were no common issues or other facts creating a risk of material limitation of either representation.

2. **Client in Unrelated Matter as Material Witness in a Proceeding Opposing Another Client:** Consider the problem preceding the *Worldspan* case. Is the "directly adverse" criterion of Model Rule 1.7(a) met, where one of the clients is not an opposing party to the other, but only a witness offered by the opposing party? If not, is there a significant risk that your representation of one of the clients will be materially limited by your responsibilities to the other, under Model Rule 1.7(a)(2)? If either, is informed consent of both clients possible under Model Rule 1.7(b)? What, exactly, would the risk be for either client if you continue? Are the matters truly "unrelated"?

The cases indicate that the answers depend on the nature of the testimony. In *Committee on Legal Ethics v. Frame*, 433 S.E.2d 579 (W.Va. 1993), a law firm represented a plaintiff suing a closely held corporation for personal injuries suffered on the premises of the corporation's mobile home sales facility. A member of the firm not involved with that representation then agreed to represent the vice president and manager of the company, who was also the majority shareholder, in her divorce proceedings. When the manager discovered the dual representation she caused the corporation's counsel to move to disqualify the firm from representing the personal injury plaintiff, and when this was unsuccessful she discharged the firm from her divorce representation. Her complaint to the disciplinary authorities resulted in a public reprimand by the state supreme court. The court held that the representations were "directly adverse" within the meaning of Model Rule 1.7(a), where the manager appeared as a witness in the personal injury matter and was cross-examined by a member of the firm. The facts that no confidential information appeared to have been exchanged, and that neither the manager nor the corporation could show any actual prejudice to their positions, were not dispositive, since the potential for such harm existed. The firm should have sought informed consent to the dual representation.

On the other hand, in *Jaggers v. Shake*, 37 S.W.3d 737 (Ky. 2001), the court denied the motion to disqualify where a firm's client in lawsuit A was likely to be a secondary witness for the firm's opponent in lawsuit B, but the credibility of that witness was probably not going to be a crucial issue in that suit.

3. **Reasonable Belief that the One Representation Will Not Be Adversely Affected by the Other:** In *In re Boyle's Case*, 611 A.2d 618 (N.H. 1992), it was held in a disciplinary proceeding that it was a violation of Model Rule 1.7 for a lawyer to defend a father in a criminal matter and simultaneously to act as guardian *ad litem* for his children in a marital dispute in which custody of the children was at issue. The lawyer argued that under the applicable state law his role as guardian *ad litem* (GAL) was not that of representing a "client" but of acting as a party to the proceeding, and that he had obtained the informed consent of the father to the dual role. In fact it was not the father, but the mother, who initiated the complaint. The court held, however, that "[t]he responsibilities of the two roles accepted by the respondent are in fundamental conflict," so that the lawyer could not reasonably believe that the representation of the father would not be adversely affected. According to the court, "There was a reasonable possibility that, by virtue of the respondent's duties as GAL, he might discover facts that would inure to the detriment of his client. [The father], however, was entitled to have unconflicted representation." 611 A.2d at 620.

In the marital proceeding the lawyer's recommendation as GAL was that the father should be given custody. In the disciplinary proceeding, he argued that he had already "taken sides" in the marital dispute by the time he agreed to defend the father in the criminal case. The court simply noted that his continuing obligation as GAL was to act in the best interest of the children, an interest that could conflict with the father's interest. If the court's real concern had been for the adequacy of the lawyer's advocacy *for the children*, would Model Rule 1.7 have been a proper basis for discipline?

4. **Risk of Tactical Employment of Potential Opposing Counsel:** Does the strict rule against simultaneous unrelated adverse representation present an opportunity for companies involved in frequent litigation to neutralize major law firms from future adverse representation by spreading minor business among them? In denying a motion to disqualify on discretionary grounds despite a minor conflict of this character, one court said:

> Were this court to rule that disqualification was mandated by [the law firm's] breach of Rule 1.7 in this case, the implications would be overwhelming. Clients of enormous size and wealth, and with a large demand for legal services, should not be encouraged to parcel their business among dozens of the best law firms as a means of purposefully creating the potential for conflicts. With simply a minor "investment" of some token business, such clients would in effect be buying an insurance policy against that law firm's adverse representation. Although lawyers should not be encouraged to sue their own clients (hence the sanctions discussed above), the law should not give large companies the incentive to manufacture the potential for conflicts by awarding disqualification automatically.

SWS Fin. Fund A v. Salomon Bros., Inc., 790 F.Supp. 1392, 1402–03 (N.D.Ill. 1992).

The Professional Ethics Committee for the State Bar of Texas, in its Opinion No. 585 (2008), addressing the question of whether a lawyer could properly counsel his client in a lawsuit to hire all the lawyers in the small town where they reside so as to prevent the opposing party from hiring a local lawyer, said that the Texas rules did not directly address the question, except in their Rule 4.04 (identical to Model Rule 4.4), which forbids a lawyer representing a client from using "means that have no substantial purpose other than to embarrass, delay or burden a third person...."

Opinion 1724 of the Standing Committee on Legal Ethics of the Virginia State Bar (2004), cited by the Texas committee, addressed a slightly different hypothetical, that of a husband who intends to hire lawyer A to represent him in his upcoming divorce proceeding and who decides on his own to undertake preliminary interviews with all the other lawyers in town, not intending to hire them but only to give them some confidential information that would preclude them from representing his wife. The Virginia committee reached two conclusions: (1) that the lawyers so interviewed would not be conflicted because the husband's purpose precluded any expectation of confidentiality within the meaning of Model Rule 1.6; and (2) that if lawyer A had counseled the husband to undertake that project, A would have violated the Virginia equivalent of Model Rule 4.4 (the language prohibited a lawyer from taking an action "when the lawyer knows or when it is obvious that such action would merely serve to harass or maliciously injure another"). *See also* Model Rule 1.18(d) (providing some protection for the law firm, though not the individual attorney, who is consulted by one pretending to be a potential client).

5. **Concurrent or Successive Representation?** A number of courts have held, under different ABA formulations, that when a conflict arises between current clients in separate matters of the sort involved in *Worldspan*, the lawyer(s) cannot thereafter simply withdraw from one of the representations and thereby transform the situation into a former client one governed by the less demanding test of "substantial relationship" under Model Rule 1.9 or its equivalent. In *Flying J. Inc. v. TA Operating Corp.*, No. 1:06–CV–30 TC, 2008 WL 648545 (D. Utah Mar. 10, 2008), the court dubbed this tactic "the hot potato doctrine." The court discussed, but found inapplicable to the particular facts, the "thrust-upon" exception that, where the conflict resulted from an unforeseeable action on the part of the client or otherwise through no fault of the lawyer, withdrawal might be effective.

However, see *Airis SFO, LLC v. San Francisco*, No. A112473, 2006 WL 2949329 (Cal.Ct.App. Oct. 17, 2006), a case later withdrawn from publication, where a law firm had represented the city in various matters in the past, and had entered into an agreement making it eligible to do legal work for the city when asked, then had filed an action against the city on behalf of a third person. The city asked the firm to withdraw from that representation on the sole ground that it was a current client of the firm at that time, invoking a California rule making it *per se* impermissible to oppose a current client even in an unrelated matter. The firm dismissed the original federal action before a motion to disqualify could be filed, but shortly thereafter filed an essentially identical suit in state court. After the city moved to disqualify the firm on the same ground, the appellate court held that trial court properly denied the motion. The crucial finding—based on contract language and actual practice of the city under it, but contested by the city—was that the particular relationship between the firm and the city had become one of matter-by-matter offers of employment rather than a continuous relationship. The court found that, at the time of first filing the suit, the firm had completed all of its active work for the city and had refused further assignments, so the city was not a current client within the meaning of California's rule.

Whether a client is a current or a former client can be a tricky factual issue, even when it is not treated as a "hot potato." In *Shearing v. Allergan, Inc.*, No. CV–S–93–866–DWH (LRL), 1994 WL 382450 (D.Nev. Apr. 5, 1994), the plaintiff's law firm had been outside counsel for the defendant company for thirteen years, doing a variety of work with total billings in excess of two million dollars. Its last matter for the company had been solicited by the firm, accompanied by a reminder that the firm considered the relationship to be an indefinite one, and had been completed more than a year before the plaintiff's case came into the office. The court held that the defendant was a current client, thereby disqualifying the firm from representing the plaintiff despite the absence of any relationship between this matter and any work done for the defendant.

B. PERSONAL INTERESTS OF THE ATTORNEY

PROBLEM

Hamilton Holmes is a retired high school math teacher whose pension and social security payments barely meet his normal living expenses. Holmes is unmarried but has two nephews to whom he is quite close. An inveterate tinkerer in his basement workshop, Holmes has invented a new puzzle that he believes will be a substantial money-maker. He goes to the office of James Jorgensen, an attorney in general practice who has acquired some expertise in patent law through a graduate program, for advice on how to exploit the invention.

QUESTIONS

(a) Holmes offers Jorgensen a one-third interest in the enterprise in exchange for Jorgensen's doing the legal work in obtaining a patent, establishing the appropriate corporate structure for a marketing company, etc. May Jorgensen accept such an arrangement? What issues of professional responsibility may arise?

(b) Assume that the business is established with Jorgensen's legal help, and is successful enough to make Holmes a moderately wealthy man. Jorgensen sells his interest in the enterprise to Holmes, but remains general counsel to the company and acts as personal attorney for Holmes in numerous transactions. Jorgensen becomes Holmes' closest friend. Holmes then develops a degenerative neurological disease that, his doctors say, will kill him within a few years. He comes to Jorgensen with a plan for leaving the bulk of his estate to his nephews, after a sizeable gift to his college. He also owns a summer cottage in the Adirondacks in which Jorgensen and his family have spent several vacations, which he wishes to leave to Jorgensen. The cottage is worth $150,000. He wants Jorgensen to draft the will and to be his executor, saying "of course I wouldn't trust anyone else to do it." How should Jorgensen respond to this request?

(c) At the height of Holmes' new-found success, another school teacher named Sarah Church appears, claiming that the puzzle was her idea. She says she had shared the idea, including the general marketing scheme, with Holmes over coffee at a teachers' convention, asking his advice. He allegedly said, "Give it up, it won't work." She had done so. Church files suit against Holmes for an amount that would practically make him a pauper again. Jorgensen concludes that she has a chance of winning, but that compromise is impossible. He is reluctant to put his friend in the position of having, after losing the lawsuit, to exhaust the rest of his estate for attorney's fees. He and Holmes had already talked about writing a book about the invention, to indulge their shared literary ambitions. May he offer to defend Holmes in the lawsuit for no fee other than an equal share of royalties from Holmes' biography?

RULE REFERENCES

Model Rules 1.7(a) & (b) and 1.8(a)–(d) & (j)

RESTATEMENT §§ 125–27

B(1) TRANSACTIONS WITH CLIENTS

MONCO v. JANUS

Appellate Court of Illinois, First District, First Division, 1991.
583 N.E.2d 575.

JUSTICE BUCKLEY delivered the opinion of the court:

In February 1987, plaintiff Dean Monco (Monco) petitioned to dissolve on the grounds of deadlock JI–SCO–NI Enterprises, Inc. (Jisconi), an Illinois corporation, owned 50% each by Monco and defendant Ronald Janus (Janus). Jisconi's sole asset is its ownership of patent rights to an invention which Monco and Janus had assigned to Jisconi. Janus counterclaimed against Monco seeking to vacate the assignment and to compel Monco to turn over the Jisconi shares he owned on the grounds that the invention was Janus' idea, that Monco was Janus' personal attorney, and that the assignment and Monco's stock ownership in Jisconi were the result of Monco's undue influence and breach of fiduciary duty to Janus. Monco responded in part to the counterclaim with a motion for sanctions pursuant to [the Illinois version of Fed.R.Civ.P. 11] against Janus and his attorneys.

[The trial court dismissed Janus' counterclaim, finding that he had ratified the arrangement. Janus appealed from that ruling. The appellate court's discussion of the trial court's denial of Monco's motion for procedural sanctions against Janus and his attorney is omitted.]

The facts of this case defy succinct summary. The record shows that Janus is a college graduate, a certified teacher, and the sole proprietor of his own landscaping business for over 17 years. Monco is an attorney admitted to practice in Illinois and before the United States Patent and Trademark Office. Monco is also a shareholder in a Chicago law firm.

Prior to the transaction in question, Janus and Monco had been social acquaintances since 1970. In 1981 and 1984, Janus contacted Monco to discuss possible patentable ideas. These ideas were not pursued. In the spring of 1985, Monco engaged Janus to perform landscaping services for his home. On Memorial Day weekend, while performing such services, Janus sat down with Monco at Monco's kitchen table and drew a sketch of an idea for a beverage container to be worn around the neck of the user. The contents of the conversation which next transpired [are] disputed by the parties and nothing in writing exists to verify either party's version of the agreement.

Janus testified that after Monco told him that his idea was fantastic, Janus asked Monco if he was interested in pursuing the idea together. Janus told Monco that Monco could help him with the idea and share in any profits. Janus testified that he and Monco agreed to share expenses equally and that Monco would provide business contacts and free legal services to the venture. Janus denied that Monco told him to obtain independent legal advice and denied that he and Monco were "50/50" partners.

Monco testified that Janus specifically asked him to go into business and offered Monco a 50% interest in the venture. Monco accepted Janus' offer and the two shook hands. Monco testified [that] they discussed various matters, including licensing the patent to a manufacturing concern, from which they would receive royalties, versus assigning the patent to a separate corporation owned by them equally, which would avoid personal liability but would require business capital and marketing. Monco testified that he specifically advised Janus to obtain outside counsel to make sure that Janus' interests were represented. Janus agreed. Monco's wife, who was present for much of the conversation, corroborated Monco's testimony.

Significantly, at the kitchen table meeting, or any time thereafter, Monco admitted that he never advised Janus that if Janus were to assign the patent to a jointly-owned corporation, Janus would lose exclusive control over the patent in the event of corporate dissolution. In such situation, Janus and Monco as co-owners of the patent would have equal rights to market the patent without accounting to the other for profits. Monco also testified that he did not inform Janus of the option of licensing the patent to Jisconi as opposed to a full assignment. Monco explained that Janus was not his client and that anything less than a full assignment to a jointly-owned company would be inconsistent with their agreement to be "50/50" partners.

In the summer months following the "kitchen table" meeting, Janus and Monco communicated by telephone and letter and exchanged ideas on numerous matters involving the beverage container, including what entity would be best for liability and tax purposes. Ultimately, the parties agreed to incorporate and name the entity using the first names of their children. Monco also suggested and conducted a "prior art" search to determine if Janus' idea was patentable. Based on the results of this search, Monco concluded and Janus agreed that a patent application was appropriate.

On September 19, 1985, Janus and Monco met with Mark Fine, an attorney and friend of Monco, about incorporating Jisconi. Fine prepared draft articles of incorporation and testified that Monco and Janus told him that they were equal partners in the new business. Fine heard nothing during this conversation to indicate to him that Monco and Janus were anything other than business partners. Fine also testified that he advised Janus to obtain independent counsel to prepare a buy/sell and shareholders' agreement in order to protect Janus' interests. Janus' recollection about this meeting conflicted with Fine's. Janus denied ever discussing anything regarding specific ownership interests, and he could not remember Fine's advice to obtain independent counsel.

After the meeting with Fine, Janus asked Monco to prepare the incorporation papers. Monco was reluctant to prepare these papers because he did not practice corporate law. However, using Fine's draft, Monco prepared the papers and forwarded them to Janus for his review and signature. Janus admitted that Monco told him to have his own counsel review the papers but Janus never did. Janus testified that he considered Monco his attorney and thought that Monco would assure that Janus' interests were protected. Jisconi was incorporated on October 2, 1985.

Following the incorporation of Jisconi, Monco prepared the initial patent application for the beverage container. The application, related documents, and the assignment of the patent to Jisconi were forwarded to Janus for his review. Monco testified that he again told Janus to have his own counsel review the documents, but Janus denied ever receiving this advice. On October 28, 1985, without the aid of independent counsel, Janus executed the parent patent application and an initial assignment. Monco filed the parent patent application and related documents on November 12, 1985.

[In early 1986 Janus consulted an independent patent lawyer, who reviewed a second patent application submitted to Janus by Monco for improvements, on which Monco was co-applicant because, as he said, he had participated in its development. In July 1986 Monco wrote a letter to Janus on various matters, in which for the first time in writing he advised Janus to obtain independent legal advice on matters connected with the corporation and their agreements. Janus hired a second independent lawyer, who accompanied Janus in reviewing and signing various corporate documents including pre-incorporation agreements and ratifying shareholder instruments making Monco and Janus equal shareholders and assigning all patents to the corporation. By the end of the summer controversy over control had surfaced, and by the end of the year they were in total deadlock. Monco filed his petition to dissolve the corporation in early 1987. In his counterclaim Janus specifically asserted that he had never been told that, as a matter of patent law, each partner would have 100% nonexclusive rights under the patents on dissolution of the corporation. He demanded damages, as well as forfeiture of Monco's 50% interest as an excessive legal fee.]

The first issue we address is whether a client's subsequent conduct can cure an attorney-client transaction which is the product of the attorney's undue influence. This is an issue of first impression in Illinois.

Transactions between attorneys and clients are closely scrutinized. When an attorney engages in a transaction with a client and is benefited thereby, a presumption arises that the transaction proceeded from undue influence. [*See Klaskin v. Klepak*, 534 N.E.2d 971 (Ill. 1989).] Once a presumption is raised, the burden shifts to the attorney to come forward with evidence that the transaction was fair, equitable and just and that the benefit did not proceed from undue influence. * * * Because a strong presumption of undue influence arises when an attorney engages in a transaction with a client and is benefitted thereby, courts require clear and convincing evidence to rebut this presumption. * * * Some of the factors the courts deem persuasive in determining whether the presumption of undue influence has been overcome include a showing by the attorney (1) that he or she made a full and frank disclosure of all relevant information; (2) that adequate consideration was given; and (3) that the client had independent advice before completing the transaction. (*McFail v. Braden* (1960), 19 Ill.2d 108, 118, 166 N.E.2d 46, 52.) Once the presumption has been rebutted, the burden of production and persuasion is again on the client to show undue influence. * * *

Initially, we agree with the circuit court that an attorney-client relationship existed between Monco and Janus. The evidence supports that Monco was acting as the attorney for Jisconi as well as for both himself and Janus. While the evidence also shows that Monco and Janus were business partners, Monco's role as Janus' partner does not foreclose the conclusion that Monco was also Janus' personal attorney.

We also agree with the circuit court that Monco entered into a beneficial business transaction with Janus. Accordingly, under relevant supreme court precedent, Monco was required to prove by clear and convincing evidence the three *McFail* factors. We agree that Monco failed to meet his burden.

Under the first factor, it cannot be readily disputed that Monco failed to give Janus a "full and frank disclosure of all relevant information" prior to Janus making the first assignment of all his rights in the patent to Jisconi. Monco admitted at trial that he did not learn of the effect of Jisconi's dissolution under the patent laws until shortly before he filed his petition for dissolution in February 1987. Thus, there is no way Monco could have timely given Janus the required information.

Under the second factor, Monco did not present clear and convincing evidence to show that he gave adequate consideration to support the 50% ownership interest in Jisconi he received. Admittedly, Monco was the "brains" behind taking the appropriate measures to assure that Janus' idea became patented and that the idea was marketed profitably. In this regard, Monco spent, as he testified, hundreds of hours of his own time working on Jisconi matters. While Monco worked on Jisconi at a time when he was fully compensated by his firm, Monco testified that his work on Jisconi prevented him from billing firm clients which in turn contributed to a lower yearly salary. Aside from the legal and non-legal time Monco contributed towards Jisconi, the record shows that Monco contributed over $13,000 in capital contributions. These expenses were never reimbursed by Jisconi. Moreover, Monco fronted Janus' one-half of the expenses from time to time when Janus became unable to pay his share.

Notwithstanding the above consideration contributed by Monco, we agree that it was not clear and convincing evidence of adequate consideration. Monco's 50% interest gave him an equal voice in Jisconi affairs. If Janus and Monco disagreed, Monco's interest gave him the ability to deadlock Jisconi's affairs and potentially hold Janus hostage. It must be remembered that this extreme leverage was given to Monco at a time when an attorney-client relationship existed. More importantly, the beverage container idea originated with Janus. Even in Monco's opinion, the idea had great money-making potential. We agree that Monco's labor and capital contributions were not adequate consideration to support the benefits which Monco could ultimately reap.

As for the third factor, the record shows that Janus did not have independent counsel before executing the first assignment. According to Janus, at this stage of their relationship, Monco was his personal attorney and was looking out for his interests. Although Monco advised Janus to have independent counsel to look over his work, this advice was insufficient. Janus' trust in Monco was great. The two had been personal acquaintances since 1970, and Janus had consulted Monco on two prior occasions regarding other patentable ideas. In light of Janus' extreme trust in Monco, Monco's suggestion that Janus have someone look over his work was insufficient to satisfy Monco's obligation to assure that Janus had independent counsel before executing the assignment. * * *

As previously discussed, Monco did not present clear and convincing evidence that he gave adequate consideration to support the 50% interest he received in the patent. Monco has not directly appealed this finding and, in any event, it is supported by the manifest weight of the evidence. Even when all of the benefits Monco conferred are taken together, we believe they are out of all proportion to the 50% interest he received and the corresponding rights associated with a shareholder holding such interest. Accordingly, for these reasons, the circuit court erred in dismissing Janus' counterclaim.

[The court remanded the case to the trial court for consideration of remedy under Janus' counterclaim.]

NOTES ON BUSINESS TRANSACTIONS WITH CLIENTS

1. Compare the three part analysis used by the court for judging business transactions with the requirements of Model Rule 1.8(a). While the Model Rules do not speak to the *Monco* court's requirement of clear and convincing proof, the Model Rule requirements are actually stiffer than those required by the court. To justify a business transaction with the client in which the lawyer is going to be both a business partner and a lawyer in the transaction,

a. The transaction must be fair to the client;

b. It must be communicated to the client in writing;

c. The writing must "fully disclose" the terms whereby the lawyer acquires an interest;

d. The client must be advised in writing of the "desirability" of obtaining independent counsel;

e. The client must be given an opportunity to obtain that independent counsel;

f. The client must provide informed written consent to the transaction, including informed consent as to whether the lawyer is representing the client.

2. **Ongoing Business Transactions:** Continuing business relationships with clients, often resulting from the lawyer "taking a piece of the action" in lieu of a fee, can be particularly troublesome. In *In re Conway*, 409 S.E.2d 357 (S.C. 1991), a lawyer formed a joint venture with three other persons—including a young associate in his own firm—to purchase and develop real estate. The lawyer acted as both president of and attorney for the company. He was disbarred for receiving kickbacks from contractors and causing unauthorized payments to be made to himself by the company, all without adequate disclosure to and consent from the joint venturers. In *In re Jans*, 666 P.2d 830 (Or. 1983), an attorney was suspended after helping the client form a corporation. The attorney took shares and an office in the corporation, served as its general counsel, continued to represent the individual client, drafted an employment contract between client and corporation, and after the client left the company sued him to enforce the employment contract. Does Model Rule 1.8(a) adequately deal with such continuing relationships?

ABA Formal Ethics Opinion 00–418 (2000) deals comprehensively with the conflict issues presented by the acquisition of ownership in a client in connection with performing legal services. Specifically, it views such arrangements as "business transaction[s] with a client," governed by Model Rule

1.8(a), with the standard of reasonableness of Model Rule 1.5(a) applicable if the acquisition is in lieu of a fee, and Model Rule 1.7 applicable to other conflicts. It also reminds lawyers that ownership interest in the client does not give them a right to be retained as counsel, if the client chooses to discharge them.

Occasionally, of course, the picture may show a predatory or unruly client taking advantage of a scrupulous lawyer, perhaps further reinforcing the message of caution. In *McRentals, Inc. v. Barber*, 62 S.W.3d 684 (Mo.Ct.App. 2001), a client sought unsuccessfully to sell his business, first without and then with the assistance of his lawyer. He then sought to persuade the lawyer to buy the business, and at the insistence of the lawyer hired other counsel to represent him in the negotiations. The client rejected various forms of direct stock purchase by the lawyer, and they eventually agreed on a plan whereby the lawyer would be employed as president of the company with salary, benefits, and bonuses, with the option to purchase stock over a period of time, and ownership and control of the company being transferred to the lawyer only after he had acquired 100% of the stock. The client insisted on a 20–year period of employment to ensure long-term commitment from him, and on setting the option price for purchase of the shares at an unusually high multiple of earnings. After four years of highly successful company perform-ance and growth under the lawyer's leadership, the client demanded major changes in the agreement making it substantially more difficult for stock options to be exercised, giving the client final say over all management decisions, forbidding further growth, and requiring all book earnings of the company to be distributed to shareholders every month. When the lawyer did not immediately consent to these changes, the client locked him out, termi-nated his employment and sued him for rescission and damages for breach of fiduciary duty. The client lost on his claims, while the defendant was awarded nearly $1 million in damages on his counterclaims for breach of contract.

3. **"Full Disclosure":** How complete must the lawyer's disclosure be in such cases? Consider Model Rule 1.8(a)(1) ("the transaction and terms on which the lawyer acquires the interest * * * are fully disclosed * * * in writing in a manner that can be reasonably understood by the client") in conjunction with Model Rule 1.0(e) defining "informed consent" as "agree-ment * * * to a proposed course of conduct after the lawyer has communicat-ed adequate information and explanation about the material risks * * * and reasonably available alternatives."

Does this standard take into account the level of sophistication of the particular client in relation to the particular transaction, who may need more or less disclosure from the attorney in order to achieve the understanding required for an "informed" decision? Does it imply individualization to the particular client? The comments to Model Rule 1.8 do not address this question directly.

At least one court has taken the level of sophistication of the client into account in determining the appropriate sanction for an otherwise relatively clear violation. In *Florida Bar v. Ticktin*, 14 So.3d 928 (Fla. 2009), a lawyer represented a businessman on various personal and business matters, includ-ing a number of issues concerning three companies that the client founded. In anticipation of the client's impending arrest, he and lawyer agreed that the latter, with his law partner, would take over one of the companies, but the lawyer failed to reduce this agreement to writing for the client to sign after full disclosure. Instead, the transition was merely disclosed in a public relations release from the company. Later, after client's conviction and incarceration, the lawyer acted against the client's interest on behalf of the company, and a disciplinary complaint was filed. The court held that the lawyer violated Model Rule 1.8 with respect to the agreement and the writing requirement, but refused to treat the fact that the client was in jail when the harmful action took place as an aggravating factor, noting that the client "was a 'very sophisticated client who was the CEO of publicly traded corporations' who received a twenty-year sentence in a federal prison for defrauding investors of $20 million." *Id.* at 938.

4. **Independent Legal Advice:** Must the lawyer always explicitly recommend that the client seek independent legal advice concerning the transaction? *Pollock v. Marshall*, 462 N.E.2d 312 (Mass. 1984), was an action for attorneys' fees in which the defendants (a corporation and the estate of its founding president) counterclaimed for rescission of certain transactions between the plaintiff attorneys, the corporation, and its deceased president. The trial court found that the transactions were not unfair, that on the basis of full disclosure by the attorneys, the president and other corporate officers involved fully understood the nature and consequences of the transactions, and that there was no actual overreaching or improper influence on the part of the attorneys. It was held on appeal that the mere fact that the attorney had not recommended independent legal advice was insufficient to support rescission. The opinion rested on the general law of fiduciaries, but also referred to the predecessor to Model Rule 1.8(a), which did not explicitly refer to obtaining independent legal advice concerning a lawyer-client business transaction.

Would the decision have been different, if Model Rule 1.8(a) had been the applicable law? Note how the current version of the rule stresses the writing requirement, while prior versions do not. *See also* RESTATEMENT, § 126(3) (requiring, *inter alia*, that the client's consent to the lawyer's role in a transaction with the client be given "after being encouraged, and given a reasonable opportunity, to seek independent legal advice concerning the transaction").

5. **Literary Rights:** Model Rule 1.8(d) singles out one particular form of attorney-client business transaction, the literary rights agreement exploiting the media value of the client's matter, for special treatment. Unlike the general rule on attorney-client transactions, Model Rule 1.8(d) absolutely prohibits literary rights agreements during the representation, regardless of disclosure and client consent. What is it about such agreements that justifies the absolute prohibition? In *Maxwell v. Superior Court*, 639 P.2d 248 (Cal. 1982), the court sustained such an agreement in a criminal case against challenge by the prosecution, on the ground that the defendant is entitled to make his own choice of counsel. This was done after a complex pretrial procedure resulted in a finding that the defendant fully understood the agreement's terms. However, California's Code of Professional Responsibility did not contain a provision comparable to Model Rule 1.8(d). For a case from

the same state in which a client's conviction was overturned in part because his lawyer's literary rights agreement represented a conflict of interest in respect to the client's defense, see *People v. Corona*, 145 Cal.Rptr. 894 (Ct.App. 1978). Is there any legitimate interest to protect other than that of the client? *See* 1 Geoffrey C. Hazard, Jr. & W. William Hodes, The Law of Lawyering, § 12.10 at 28–29 (Supp. 2004) (citing only the risk of "less than vigorous representation").

Would it make a difference if the lawyer signs a media contract, the primary purpose of which is to get the lawyer's own story, of which her perspective on the particular case would be only a part? In D.C. Bar Ethics Opinion 334 (2006), the committee addressed a proposed agreement between media representatives and a lawyer representing a pro bono client in litigation, contemplating books and a possible movie with primary focus on the lawyer rather than the client, although the client's life story would also be secondarily involved. As the facts were posed to the committee, the lawyer would not disclose any confidential information without the client's consent. The lawyer would be compensated for his cooperation and the rights to his story, and the client would be compensated as well. The opinion takes the position that D.C. Rule 1.8(c), identical to Model Rule 1.8(d), does not apply to such a situation, because the lawyer is not acquiring rights from the client or otherwise with the intention to exercise them later, but is instead transferring his own rights, and that this kind of arrangement does not necessarily give the same incentive to the lawyer to sensationalize the case at the client's expense. Rather, the applicable rule is D.C. Rule 1.7(b)(4), essentially equivalent to Model Rule 1.7(a)(2), requiring the client's consent after full disclosure, the potential difficulties of which the opinion outlines. In *Harrison v. Mississippi Bar*, 637 So.2d 204, 223 (Miss. 1994), on the other hand, a similar arrangement (described in less detail than in the D.C. opinion) was taken to be a violation of Model Rule 1.8(d) without further discussion.

Even though the literary rights agreement entered into before the completion of the representation is a *per se* ethics violation, a criminal defendant who is convicted after such an agreement is entered into still must show prejudice in order to get relief from the conviction. *See Neelley v. Nagle*, 138 F.3d 917 (11th Cir. 1998), holding that such an agreement, formally entered into after trial, conviction, and the filing of a motion for new trial, was not shown in fact to have adversely affected the quality of defense counsel's representation, and therefore could not support post-conviction relief.

NOTES ON OTHER ATTORNEY SELF-INTEREST CONFLICTS

1. **Attorney's Self–Interest in Litigation:** A conflict of interest between lawyer and client can arise in the context of litigation. For example, lawyer A represents client C in a personal injury action against a third party, which results in an unsatisfactory judgment at trial. C discharges A and retains lawyer B to represent him on appeal, which is also unsuccessful because the appeal is not perfected in a timely fashion. B now files an action against A on C's behalf for legal malpractice in conducting the trial and failing to perfect an appeal. A asserts a third-party claim against B, asserting that it was B as successor counsel, rather than A as original counsel, who was

responsible for perfecting the appeal in the underlying personal injury action. Can B properly continue to represent C in this malpractice action? In *Schenck v. Hill, Lent & Troescher (Freund v. Meiselman, Boland, Reilly & Pittoni)*, 530 N.Y.S.2d 486 (Sup.Ct. 1988), such a representation was held improper despite purported client consent, especially where the affidavits of consent on the part of the client (asserting, *inter alia*, that the client had no claim against B for malpractice) did not show a full understanding of the rights being waived.

A different type of attorney self-interest litigation conflict took place in *Rubin v. Gee*, 292 F.3d 396 (4th Cir. 2002), where a woman who had shot her estranged husband sought the assistance of her attorney and private investigators immediately afterward. The attorney observed that she had taken a lot of medication, and instructed the investigators (1) to take her to a hospital for a possible drug overdose, and (2) to register her under an assumed name. The lawyer disclosed to the police that the husband was dead, but did not disclose his client's identity or whereabouts. While she was still at large the day after the shooting, the lawyer took her to the bank so she could withdraw $105,000 to cover his and his partner's legal fees and expenses, and took possession of all the evidence the client had. At the end of that day, after learning that a warrant had been issued for her arrest, the lawyer turned her in to the police. The partners continued to advise her, in particular about whom to hire as trial counsel, and remained part of the defense team, collecting a fee from her for that service. At trial, the prosecution used the client's post-shooting behavior (fleeing from the scene and lying about her identity) to refute her claim of self-defense, but no evidence was offered by her trial counsel concerning the role that her lawyers had played in directing that behavior. After state courts refused to grant her relief after a post-conviction hearing at which such evidence was presented, the federal courts granted *habeas corpus* relief, finding that the lawyers were infected with a clear conflict of interest rendering the assistance of her counsel ineffective.

2. **Sexual Relationships with Clients:** Model Rule 1.8(j), which was added in 2002, prohibits sexual relationships between an attorney and a client, except when the sexual relationship preceded the attorney-client relationship. Interestingly, the portion of Model Rule 1.8 that imputes all of the other conflict of interest restrictions in Model Rule 1.8 to other attorneys associated with the conflicted lawyer does not apply to Model Rule 1.8(j). *See* Model Rule 1.8(k). Thus, it can be inferred that an attorney is not necessarily prohibited from engaging in a sexual relationship with a client of that attorney's partner or associate. Is this the correct resolution of this issue?

In the years before this amendment, ethics authorities and courts reached a variety of conclusions regarding the permissibility of consensual attorney-client sexual relationships. Most states have now adopted rules identical or similar to 1.8(j), with a few addressing specific ethical issues presented by such relationships without the general prohibition in formal rules, while a number still omit specific mention of the issue. *Cf. In re Bash*, 880 N.E.2d 1182 (Ind. 2008) (finding that a lawyer's attempts to have sexual relationships with an unwilling client violate both Model Rule 1.8(j) and Model Rule 8.4(a)).

B(2) USING CONFIDENTIAL CLIENT INFORMATION AND GIFTS FROM CLIENTS

IN RE CRARY

Supreme Court of North Dakota, 2002.
2002 ND 9, 638 N.W.2d 23.

PER CURIAM.

Disciplinary counsel filed a petition for discipline against Paul T. Crary. * * * The hearing panel issued its report * * * recommending that Crary be disbarred and that he be ordered to pay restitution to the victim. * * *

I

Paul Crary has been admitted to practice law in North Dakota since 1965. In 1997, Crary's wife became acquainted with 85–year–old Mary Harris. In August 1997, Harris asked to meet with Crary to prepare a new will. Crary drafted a will for Harris, and Harris also signed documents giving Crary power of attorney. Although Harris was not related to the Crarys, over the next two-and-one-half years Crary and his wife provided general assistance to Harris, including bringing her meals, taking her to medical appointments, and visiting her regularly.

In December 1997, Crary drafted a codicil to Harris's will. The codicil provided that Crary's wife would receive one-half of any funds which Harris's estate received from insurance companies, including annuities, life insurance policies, and other benefits. Crary's wife also was to receive a grandfather clock under the codicil to Harris's will.

Harris also asked Crary to help with her investments. In September 1997, Crary assisted Harris in purchasing a $42,000 annuity from the Independent Order of Foresters ("IOF"). In December 1997, Crary had Harris purchase a $10,000 annuity from IOF. In January 1998, Crary assisted Harris in cashing out an existing $100,000 annuity she had purchased just over a year earlier from Bankers Life and Casualty. Harris received approximately $92,000 in proceeds from the Bankers Life annuity, and used those funds to purchase a $90,000 annuity from IOF. Throughout this series of transactions Crary never told Harris he was an agent for IOF and received commissions on the annuities she purchased.

In September 1998, Harris gave Crary a check for $3,500. A note on the memo line of the check indicated it was a loan to Crary. Harris testified Crary promised to repay the loan within six months with eight percent interest. Crary never repaid the $3,500 to Harris.

The relationship between Harris and the Crarys eventually soured, and in January 2000 Harris terminated Crary's legal representation. In October 2000, disciplinary counsel filed a petition for discipline, and a hearing panel was appointed. Following a hearing, the hearing panel concluded that: (1) the $3,500 payment to Crary was a loan which constituted a prohibited transaction in violation of [Model Rule] 1.8(a); (2) the annuity purchases upon which Crary received commissions were prohibited transactions under [Model Rule] 1.8(b); and (3) Crary's drafting of the codicil devising property to his wife was a prohibited transaction under [Model Rule] 1.8(c). The hearing panel recommended that Crary be disbarred and ordered to pay restitution to Harris. * * *

III

[The court agreed with the hearing panel's finding that the $3,500 was a loan to Crary, and that Crary did not encourage Harris to seek the advice of an independent attorney before making the loan.]

IV

The hearing panel found that Crary, while acting as Harris's lawyer and with power of attorney, had Harris cash in other annuities and investments to purchase annuities from IOF without advising Harris that he was an agent for IOF and would receive commissions on those transactions, and without advising her to seek independent legal advice about the transactions. Disciplinary counsel argues Crary's conduct violated [Model Rule 1.8(b), which prohibits the lawyer from using "information relating to representation of a client to the disadvantage of the client" without client consent.]

Harris testified that Crary never told her he worked for IOF and received a commission on these transactions, and did not advise her to seek independent legal advice about the transactions. Crary testified Harris "must have known" he was an agent of IOF because he filled out the applications with her[.]

Crary's assertion that Harris "must have known" he was an agent of IOF and receiving commissions merely because he procured the applications and assisted Harris in filling them out is not plausible. It would be commonplace for a person acting as counsel, and with power of attorney, to provide such assistance without being an agent of the company from which the annuities were being purchased. We agree with the hearing panel's findings that Crary did not advise Harris he was an agent of IOF, did not advise her he received commissions on the transactions, and did not advise her to seek independent counsel. Crary's conduct violated [Model Rule] 1.8(b), because he used his knowledge of Harris's financial situation and her desire to find another investment to her disadvantage for his own personal profit.

V

The hearing panel concluded that Crary's drafting of the codicil to Harris's will violated [Model Rule 1.8(c) prohibiting the lawyer from soliciting or preparing an instrument that gives a gift to the lawyer or a member of the lawyer's immediate family].

There is no dispute that Crary drafted the codicil, and that the Crarys were not related to Harris. The codicil to Harris's will created a testamentary gift to Crary's wife of one-half of the value of "all moneys and funds which my estate shall receive from all insurance companies, including but not limited to, annuities, life insurance policies and any other benefits." Crary's wife was also to receive a "large Grandfather's Clock." At various times after Harris signed the codicil the values of her annuities ranged between $130,000 and $180,000. Crary conceded in his testimony at the hearing that his wife's one-half testamentary interest in the annuities was "substantial."

At the hearing, Crary suggested the codicil was prepared at Harris's request. When asked whether he told her she could consult another attorney, he responded, "I think I told her she could talk to someone else."

Unlike the prohibitions in [Model Rules 1.8(a) and 1.8(b), Model Rule 1.8(c)] creates a bright-line rule. * * * Disclosure of the conflict to the client and advising the client to consult independent counsel are immaterial to a violation of [Model Rule] 1.8(c). Courts interpreting other states' adoptions of [this Model Rule] have held that the rule creates a strict and explicit prohibition against attorneys drafting documents which result in a substantial gift to the attorney or the attorney's parent, child, sibling, or spouse. [Model Rule 1.8(c)] "flatly prohibits a lawyer from preparing an instrument giving the lawyer a testamentary gift from a client" and "does not include any disclosure or fairness provisions[."]

[T]he purpose of [Model Rule 1.8(c)] is to require that a client actually receive independent legal advice before executing a document giving the attorney, or close family member of the attorney, a substantial gift. * * *

We conclude Crary's conduct violated [Model Rule 1.8(c)].

VI

Our determination of the appropriate sanction for a lawyer's violation of the Rules of Professional Conduct is governed by the * * * Standards for Imposing Lawyer Sanctions. * * *

In this case, the presence of numerous aggravating circumstances tips the scales in favor of disbarment. * * *

Crary has a prior disciplinary offense. * * *

Crary has failed to file a brief with this Court, and has not called our attention to any mitigating factors. We have reviewed the mitigating factors * * * and find none which apply on the face of the record.

In light of the nature of Crary's conduct and the presence of significant aggravating factors, we order that Crary be disbarred. We further order that Crary pay restitution to Harris and pay the costs of the disciplinary proceedings * * *.

NOTES ON ATTORNEY AS BENEFICIARY OF CLIENT'S TRANSACTION AND USE OF CONFIDENTIAL INFORMATION

1. **Deference to the Client's Insistence?** In dealing with the bequest, was Crary disciplined for not trying hard enough? Suppose he had steadfastly "insisted" that Harris either leave his wife out of the will or get another lawyer to draft it, with full explanation of why he should not draft it, but Harris had clearly and firmly refused to do either, "insisting" that she did not want anyone else to know what her testamentary intentions were until after she died? In *In re Barrick*, 429 N.E.2d 842, 846 (Ill. 1981), the Illinois Supreme Court held that under such circumstances it was not improper for the lawyer ultimately to agree to draft the instrument.

> We cannot quarrel with her conclusion that she would be better served by the respondent. We cannot fault the respondent for agreeing that if that was what she wanted she should have it. He was not required to resist to the point of offensiveness. The choice was hers to make, and [respondent] would not have served his client properly had he persisted in frustrating her wishes.

Even if the same dialog had taken place in *Crary*, does the court think it would matter under Model Rule 1.8(c)? Should it? Why?

2. **Common Law Rebuttable Presumption:** In *Franciscan Sisters Health Care Corp. v. Dean*, 448 N.E.2d 872 (Ill. 1983), will contestants invoked the common law rule that a will giving a substantial gift to the lawyer who drafted it is subject to a rebuttable presumption of undue influence affecting the validity of the will in its entirety. The beneficiary attorney had known the decedent for twenty years socially, and for several years professionally, when he drafted the will making himself and the contestants equal residual legatees. The attorney took the will to an independent lawyer's office in the same building, explained the circumstances, and asked the other lawyer and his secretary to witness the will and talk to the testator about it. He then went back to his office, brought the client and the will to the other lawyer, and left them alone while the other lawyer questioned the client about her intentions and understanding concerning the will and her attorney's interest in it. After twenty minutes the other lawyer was satisfied that the testator understood what she was doing, and witnessed the will. The court held that this independent consultation and evaluation was sufficient to rebut the presumption of undue influence, though the trial court still had to decide as a fact, without the aid of the presumption, whether the attorney had exercised undue influence.

In *Sandford v. Metcalfe*, 954 A.2d 188 (Conn.App.Ct. 2008), a drafter-as-beneficiary situation on stipulated facts similar to *Barrick* (previous note) was presented to a Connecticut court in a post-probate proceeding. The probate court rejected the argument of the heirs at law that probate of the decedent's will that left half her estate to the lawyer friend who drafted it would be contrary to public policy. The heirs' appeal to the superior court (court of general jurisdiction) from that ruling was dismissed as untimely. The heirs then attacked the executrix's proposed distribution to the lawyer, and the probate court sustained their objection, but the superior court reversed, finding no violation of public policy at that stage. The Appellate Court sustained the superior court's ruling, holding that, although the lawyer was "ill-advised, as a matter of public policy" to draft the will, the courts lacked an equitable power to prevent the distribution, in the absence of a statute specifically barring such. *Id.* at 193.

3. **Lawyer Named as Executor or Other Fiduciary by a Client Document:** Is the situation different when the attorney is named as executor or recommended as attorney for the estate? Some jurisdictions have held that preparing a document requiring or implying the attorney's future services is presumed to be improper, in the absence of special reasons such as a close relationship to the client or unusual familiarity with their affairs. *See In re Felli*, 718 N.W.2d 70 (Wis. 2006) (disciplining attorney for targeting vulnerable elderly estate planning clients, after distinguishing *State v. Gulbankian*, 196 N.W.2d 733 (Wis. 1972), which refrained from disciplining a lawyer whose clients were fellow members of a distinctive ethnic and linguistic community); *see also In re Estate of Peterson*, 565 S.E.2d 524 (Ga.Ct.App. 2002) (holding that a lawyer who had fully disclosed all relevant factors to the client before the will was executed that named him as executor was disqualified from serving as such, due to failure to obtain written consent or provide written notice, thereby rejecting counsel's argument that the client's signature on the will after full disclosure satisfied this requirement).

The original version of the Model Rules did not address the question. This omission drew criticism. *See, e.g.*, Joseph W. deFuria, Jr., *A Matter of Ethics Ignored: The Attorney–Draftsman as Testamentary Fiduciary*, 36 U.Kan.L.Rev. 275 (1988). Model Rule 1.8 Comment [8] (under the heading "Gifts to Lawyers") (added in 2002), now states that the Model Rule does not prohibit a lawyer from seeking to be named as executor of the client's estate, but that Model Rule 1.7's general conflict of interest provisions apply and may require informed consent of the client if "there is a significant risk that the lawyer's interest in obtaining the appointment will materially limit the lawyer's independent professional judgment" concerning the choice of the fiduciary. ABA Formal Opinion 02–426 (2002) emphasizes that this is the client's decision, and that Model Rule 1.4(b) requires frank discussion of the client's options:

> This discussion should cover information reasonably adequate to permit the client to understand the tasks to be performed by the fiduciary; the fiduciary's desired skills; the kinds of individuals or entities likely to serve most effectively, such as professionals, corporate fiduciaries, and family members; and the benefits and detriments of using each, including relative costs.

Id., part I. The opinion then notes and affirms the potential application of Model Rule 1.7(b), but does not indicate a presumption as to when it applies. How is the attorney to assess the risk of personal interest limiting professional judgment? Is the opinion's position inconsistent with the Wisconsin and Georgia decisions above, or does it implicitly counsel following Model Rule 1.7(b) whenever the client decides to ask that the drafting lawyer be appointed or recommended?

4. **Use of Confidential Information:** When the lawyer makes personal use of client confidential information, it is a violation of the lawyer's duty of loyalty. In addition to discipline, as in *Crary*, the RESTATEMENT notes that the lawyer who uses confidential information and personally gains therefrom "must account to the client for any profits made." RESTATEMENT, § 60(2).

C. "SWITCHING SIDES": DUTIES TO FORMER CLIENTS

PROBLEM

Following your graduation from law school, you became an associate in the Chicago firm of Patterson & Cooper. Your primary responsibility over several years as an associate was to work with the partner in charge of the Bramco Steel account. Bramco supplies steel for bridge construction throughout the United States. P & C handles virtually all of their legal work. Your position was to help the general partner negotiate contracts and advise on suits against Bramco, which self-insures. Although you rarely met a principal in Bramco, your work necessitated that you read most of the company's correspondence with the P & C partner.

One of the suits you worked on arose out of a bridge collapse in Massachusetts, which injured a number of people who happened to be on the bridge in automobiles when the collapse occurred. Several of them joined in a suit against the city that built the bridge, the architect who designed it, the general contractor, the subcontractor supplying steel workers, and Bramco as supplier of the steel. The allegation against Bramco is that the steel supplied was defective. After extensive discovery and settlement negotiations, during which you had numerous contacts and exchanges with counsel for the other co-defendants, the claims are finally settled.

You have now left P & C and have established your own law office, leaving behind all of your work for Bramco. Into your office comes Hank Orbison, an independent truck owner/driver who suffered personal injury and property damage in another bridge collapse in Illinois, this one built and maintained by the State of Illinois.

QUESTIONS

(a) You determine that the appropriate defendants for a lawsuit by Orbison include Bramco as the supplier of steel, which appears to have been defective. Assuming that you did no work on and acquired no information directly concerning the Illinois bridge during your tenure at P & C, may you properly accept Orbison's case?

(b) You determine instead that the appropriate defendants for Orbison's lawsuit include all of the contractor defendants in the Massachusetts bridge case *except* Bramco, which had lost the bid on the Illinois bridge to another steel supplier. You file suit on his behalf against all appropriate defendants, and the general contractor defendant moves to disqualify you as counsel for Orbison on the ground of your prior representation of Bramco in the Massachusetts case. On what theory would such a motion be based? Should it succeed?

RULE REFERENCES

Model Rule 1.9

RESTATEMENT § 132

KANAGA v. GANNETT COMPANY

Superior Court of Delaware, 1993.
1993 WL 485926.

BIFFERATO, JUDGE. * * *

Dr. Kanaga filed a complaint in this Court, alleging that she was defamed by an article printed in *The Sunday News Journal* * * *. The article contained information provided by Pamela Kane, a former patient of Dr. Kanaga. It was authored by Jane Harriman. *The Sunday News Journal* is * * * owned by Gannett Co., Inc.

Essentially, the article alleged that Dr. Kanaga recommended that Ms. Kane undergo a hysterectomy which later was determined to be unnecessary by another physician. The complaint alleged that the article wrongly criticized Dr. Kanaga's skill and ethics as a practicing obstetrician and gynecologist and caused severe damage to her reputation and medical practice. * * *

Gannett Co., Inc. and Ms. Harriman (collectively referred to as "Respondents") filed an Answer through counsel of the law firm, Richards, Layton and Finger. Subsequently, Dr. Kanaga filed this motion to disqualify Respondents' counsel on the grounds that Dr. Kanaga was a former client of the firm. * * *

It is undisputed that John A. Parkins, Jr., a member of the law firm Richards, Layton and Finger, represented Dr. Kanaga in a prior action brought against her * * *. Dr. Kanaga argues that this prior representation by Mr. Parkins has created a conflict of interest and [that] counsel from his firm should be disqualified from representing Respondents in this present action. * * *

In arguing that there is a conflict of interest in this case, Dr. Kanaga cites the [Delaware version of Rule 1.9(a)].

It is undisputed that Richards, Layton and Finger currently represents new clients, other than Dr. Kanaga; that this action is materially adverse to Dr. Kanaga's interests; that Dr. Kanaga has not consented to this representation; and that this action is not the "same matter". The issue, therefore, is whether the matter presently before this Court is "substantially related" to the former matter.

Essentially, Dr. Kanaga argues that the two matters are "substantially related" because both actions involve allegations of improper medical treatment. Respondents argue that the matters are not "substantially related" because this action is a defamation action which involves different defenses and a different standard of proof than the former medical malpractice action. * * *

In determining whether a "substantial relationship" exists between the two representations, three questions are to be considered. They are:

1) What is the nature and scope of the prior representation at issue?

2) What is the nature of the present lawsuit against the former client?

3) In the course of the prior representation, might the client have disclosed to his attorney confidences which could be relevant to the present action? In particular, could any such confidences be detrimental to the former client in the current litigation? * * *

The first factor is the nature and scope of the prior representation of Dr. Kanaga by Mr. Parkins. He defended her against serious allegations of medical malpractice arising from the performance of a hysterectomy. Dr. Kanaga strongly contested these allegations. The case lasted seven years. It went to trial and the jury returned a verdict in favor of Dr. Kanaga. Ultimately, the Delaware Supreme Court held that a verdict should have been directed in favor of Dr. Kanaga because there was no expert testimony presented against her at trial. *Russell v. Kanaga*, Del. Supr., 571 A.2d 724 (1990).

The second factor is the nature of the present lawsuit involving * * * Dr. Kanaga. Respondents have been sued for their participation in the publication of the article which allegedly defamed Dr. Kanaga by suggesting that she recommended the performance of an unnecessary hysterectomy.

The third factor is the possibility that Dr. Kanaga may have disclosed confidential matter during the first representation by Mr. Parkins which could be relevant and detrimental to Dr. Kanaga's subsequent action for defamation. In order to determine whether counsel may have acquired potentially detrimental confidential information during a former representation, "[t]he court should not allow its imagination to run free with a view to hypothesizing conceivable but unlikely situations in which confidential information 'might' have been disclosed which would be relevant to the present suit." *Satellite Fin. Planning Corp.* [v. *First Nat'l Bank of Wilmington*], 652 F.Supp. [1281,] 1283 [(D.Del. 1987).] Rather, "[t]he Court should consider whether a client ought to have discussed the relevant facts or whether it would not have been unusual for the lawyer and client to have discussed the relevant facts." * * *

Dr. Kanaga contends that she shared confidential information during consultations with Mr. Parkins on the *Russell* case. She asserts that in discussing the specific facts of the *Russell* case, she disclosed, to Mr. Parkins, her medical practices and procedures as well as her skill as a physician and her reputation and standing in the medical community. She alleges that these facts are critical to the defense in this action and therefore detrimental to her case.

Respondents argue that Dr. Kanaga has failed to demonstrate that potentially detrimental confidential information was gained. Respondents argue that Dr. Kanaga's professional abilities are not confidential because they are held out to the public and that standards of care are not confidential because they are determined by the medical community. In addition, Respondents argue that Dr. Kanaga's professional standing and reputation in the medical community are not confidential because such are based upon other's opinions. By affidavit, Mr. Parkins asserts that he has no recollection of a discussion with Dr. Kanaga on her standing and reputation. Respondents argue that such a conversation is unlikely because it would be irrelevant to medical malpractice cases.

This Court finds Dr. Kanaga's arguments to be more persuasive. It is reasonable to assume that a medical malpractice lawsuit would be potentially traumatic for a physician. It would be likely that Dr. Kanaga would engage in open discussion with her attorney on many issues connected with the lawsuit. Her counsel may not have initiated discussion on issues not specifically relevant to a defense in a medical malpractice case. However, it is conceivable that Dr. Kanaga may have volunteered information which fell outside such a scope. Although Dr. Kanaga has not delineated an exact dialogue which could be deemed confidential and explained how it would negatively impact the present action, she is not required to do so. * * * It is enough to demonstrate that such information could have been acquired, * * * and Dr. Kanaga has proven that this possibility exists. * * *

The Motion to Disqualify Counsel is Granted.

WILSON P. ABRAHAM CONSTRUCTION CORPORATION v. ARMCO STEEL CORPORATION

United States Court of Appeals, Fifth Circuit, 1977.
559 F.2d 250.

PER CURIAM: * * *

This dispute centers around exactly what relationship co[-]counsel for the plaintiff, a Mr. Stephen D. Susman, had with the various defendants in this suit in a prior legal matter. The factual background which leads up to this current dispute is somewhat detailed and complicated. It begins * * * when Mr. Susman was associated with the firm of Fulbright and Jaworski in Houston, Texas. At that time, he undertook to represent Whitlow Steel Company, Inc., an independent rebar [steel reinforcement bar] fabricator in Houston. This representation was in connection with a Federal Grand Jury investigation of the rebar steel industry in Texas. In August 1973, charges of antitrust violations were levied against Whitlow, Armco Steel Corp., The Ceco Corp., and Laclede Steel Company. Armco, Ceco, and Laclede are the defendants in the present action before this court. As counsel for Whitlow, Mr. Susman met on more than one occasion with the representatives of Armco, Ceco, and Laclede. At these meetings some efforts allegedly were made to develop a cooperative defense. Exactly what information was exchanged, and the importance of that information, is hotly disputed. Mr. Susman contends that the meetings were disorganized and nothing of substance was ever discussed. The defendants contend that documents were in fact discussed and disseminated, grand jury witness lists were prepared, and reports were given as to exactly what testimony was being presented before the grand jury by the various witnesses. The gist of the defendants' argument is that Mr. Susman was privy to a substantial amount of confidential information. Mr. Susman flatly denies this.

[At about the same time these same defendants, but not Whitlow, were indicted by a grand jury in Louisiana for similar antitrust violations, and pleaded nolo contendere. After unsuccessfully pleading double jeopardy in the Texas criminal proceedings, they also pleaded nolo contendere to those charges.]

The final fact which needs to be brought out to fully understand the controversy before this Court is that some time after the Texas grand jury investigation, a civil suit was filed in Texas against Whitlow and the defendants in this suit. The counsel for the plaintiff in that suit was a Mr. William E. Wright. That civil suit is still pending, but at the time it was filed Mr. Susman was still counsel for Whitlow. Mr. Susman, however, denies that anything of substance was done in connection with the defense of that case where he represented Whitlow.

We are now in a position to set forth exactly what the present controversy involves. The plaintiff in the present suit, Wilson P. Abraham Construction Corporation, has filed a civil suit in Louisiana based primarily upon some facts which led to the Louisiana indictments. Counsel for the plaintiff in this suit is William E. Wright, the same person who had been counsel for another party in the Texas civil suit in which Mr. Susman represented Whitlow Steel Company. The defendants allege that the complaint in this case is virtually identical to the Texas complaint in which they were also party defendants. In any event, Mr. Wright has sought to engage Mr. Susman as co-counsel in this case. The defendants are challenging this alleging basically that Mr. Susman has a conflict of interest because of his previous relationship with them when he represented Whitlow Steel Company.

The law in this Circuit is fairly straightforward. This Court has recently reaffirmed with regards to attorney disqualification that a former client seeking to disqualify an attorney who appears on behalf of his adversary, need only to show that the matters embraced within the pending suit are *substantially related* to the matters or cause of action wherein the attorney previously represented him. * * * This rule rests upon the presumption that confidences potentially damaging to the client have been disclosed to the attorney during the former period of representation. The Court may not even inquire as to whether such disclosures were in fact made or whether the attorney in fact is likely to use the damaging disclosures to the detriment of his former client. * * * The inquiry is limited solely to whether the matters of the present suit are substantially related to matters of the prior representation, and this is because this Court recognizes that in order to aid the frank exchange between attorney and client, it is necessary to preclude even a possibility that information given in confidence by a former client will ever be used without that client's consent. * * *

The case before us, however, presents somewhat of a twist to the usual attorney-client controversy. It is not a former client of Mr. Susman who seeks to disqualify him, but rather co-defendants of a former client. The defendants here contend that in a case alleging conspiracy, such as the case at bar, the defendants have a right to consult together about the case, and that all information derived by any of the counsel from such consultation is necessarily privileged. The defendants persuasively argue that in a joint defense of a conspiracy charge, the counsel of each defendant is, in effect, the counsel of all for the purposes of invoking the attorney-client privilege in order to shield mutually shared confidences. We agree, and hold that when information is exchanged between various co-defendants and their attorneys that this exchange is not made for the purpose of allowing unlimited publication and use, but rather, the exchange is made for the limited purpose of assisting in their common cause. In such a situation, an attorney who is the recipient of such information breaches his fiduciary duty if he later, in his representation of another client, is able to use this information to the detriment of one of the co-defendants. Just as an attorney would not be allowed to proceed against his former client in a cause of action substantially related to the matters in which he previously represented that client, an attorney should also not be allowed to proceed against a co-defendant of a former client wherein the subject matter of the present controversy is substantially related to the matters in which the attorney was previously involved, and wherein confidential exchanges of information took place between the various co-defendants in preparation of a joint defense.

Having stated the bare facts of this rather complicated dispute, and having set forth the law, we unfortunately are unable to presently resolve the controversy. Exactly what information was exchanged between Mr. Susman when he represented Whitlow Steel Company and worked with counsel for the various defendants is greatly contested. Here there is no presumption that confidential information was exchanged as there was no direct attorney-client relationship. Mr. Susman should not be disqualified unless the trial court should determine that Mr. Susman was actually privy to confidential information. The parties also have a completely different version as to the similarity of the Texas grand jury investigation and the Louisiana investigation, and whether or not these investigations are substantially related to the present case.

Under these circumstances it is impossible for us to resolve this matter without some specific factual findings by the trial judge * * *. [There being none, the case was remanded for further proceedings.]

[On remand, the trial court ordered a hearing before a magistrate to determine whether confidential information had been exchanged between Susman and counsel for the other defendants in the prior action. The magistrate found (1) that although Susman had initiated the idea of a common defense, only two meetings had been held involving the present defendants, during which it was concluded that their interests conflicted and the common defense could not be pursued, (2) that no confidential information had been given by the present defendants to Susman, and (3) that in any event the prior litigation was so dissimilar to the present one in terms of the party configurations, as well as the markets and locations involved in the alleged conspiracies, that there was no "substantial relationship" between the representations. Disqualification was denied. 1979 WL 1614, 1979–1 Trade Cases P 62,569.]

NOTES ON SUBSTANTIAL RELATIONSHIP AND SAME MATTER

1. **Substantial Relationship—Other Cases:** In 2003 and 2004, an attorney represented a corporation in the sale of two of its divisions to a newly created independent company, which resulted in a number of the corporation's employees moving to the new entity. In the course of this sale, it was agreed that the corporation would remain responsible for a pension plan for key employees who moved to the new entity. The attorney did no further work for the corporation. Four years later, in 2008, the corporation announced the termination of the retirement plan, and a dispute arose between the beneficiaries of the plan and the corporation concerning the calculation of the beneficiaries' vested rights under the plan. A settlement was reached giving the beneficiaries 50% of what they would have been entitled to under the plan as of 2010. In 2009 the beneficiaries sued the corporation to have the settlement declared invalid due to alleged coercion, and to have the court determine what they were entitled to under the plan. The corporation moved to disqualify the attorney's firm, based on his prior representation of the corporation in the sale. How should the court rule on the motion? *See Edelstein v. Optimus Corp.*, No. 8:10–cv–00061–JFB–FG3, 2010 WL 3843595 (D.Neb. Sept. 24, 2010) (relying on Model Rule 1.9, as adopted in Nebraska).

In a two-person firm, one lawyer prepared an agreement between two solid waste management districts in adjacent states, establishing a bi-state solid waste management project. Representatives of the two districts sat on the managing board of the project, but it was a distinct legal entity. The firm did no further work for the project or the districts. Two years later, a member of the managing board sued the project and its director under one of the states' "Right-to-Know" laws, seeking information about all legal bills paid by the project during a particular year, for the purpose of challenging the propriety under the agreement of some of the payments. The other lawyer in the firm was asked to represent the plaintiff. Assuming that the firm's bills for the drafting work are not involved in the challenge, would this representation be proper? *See Franklin v. Callum*, 782 A.2d 884 (N.H. 2001) (applying Model Rule 1.9); RESTATEMENT, § 132, Comment *d(ii)*.

2. **Playbook Knowledge:** *Kanaga* indicates that even if a prior representation of a client dealt with matters factually distinct from the present representation of that client's opponent, it may give the lawyer knowledge about how the former client normally behaves in similar factual settings or how it responds to legal challenges. This can be useful to the opponent in the current case. It is often referred to as "playbook knowledge." Some other cases suggest the nature of the inquiry.

In *Franzoni v. Hart Schaffner & Marx*, 726 N.E.2d 719 (Ill.App.Ct. 2000), an employee sued his employer under the workers' compensation statute for damages due to retaliatory discharge. The employee was represented by an attorney who had been house counsel for the employer and its parent corporation for fourteen years, had in-house responsibility for many litigated employment cases, had participated in the company's employment practices policy-making, and had eventually become general counsel for the parent corporation, before leaving for private practice. The court held that, although four years had elapsed since the attorney left the company, the prior representation was "substantially related" to the present case, so he was disqualified.

In *State* ex rel. *Wal–Mart Stores, Inc. v. Kortum*, 559 N.W.2d 496 (Neb. 1997), a suit brought by a customer for injuries allegedly suffered in a fall in the defendant's parking lot due to failure to repair a pothole, the court held that plaintiff's counsel was not disqualified by reason of having represented the defendant in four previous tort cases from the same store. Two of the cases involved claims of false arrest and malicious prosecution, one involved an assault inside the store, and one involved a slip-and-fall on a wet floor inside the store.

In *Niemi v. Girl Scouts*, 768 N.W.2d 385 (Minn.Ct.App. 2009), Niemi asserted an employment discrimination claim against a regional scouting organization. Attorney Roby appeared on behalf of the defendant. More than 25 years earlier, Roby had represented Niemi in her employment discrimination claim against her then employer, the City of Duluth. In the Duluth suit, Niemi had asserted gender discrimination and retaliation, and in the Girl Scouts suit she alleged age discrimination and retaliation. Niemi moved to disqualify Roby and his firm, alleging that Roby in the prior representation had learned about her "job experience, qualifications, supervisory skills, relationship with peers and staff, and approach to litigation." The court held that the "approach to litigation" information was not sufficiently factual, and that the employment-related information was too old to be substantially related to the current claim.

Comment [3] to Model Rule 1.9, added by the ABA in 2002, states that "general knowledge of the client's policies and practices ordinarily will not preclude a subsequent representation; on the other hand, knowledge of specific facts gained in a prior representation that are relevant to the matter in question ordinarily will preclude such a representation." Does this explain the differences among the above "playbook" decisions, since only *Niemi* applied the 2002 version of the comments?

3. **Conflicts Among Co–Parties:** The mutual obligation of confidentiality among co-parties, which the defendants in *Abraham* sought unsuccessfully to invoke, is often called the "joint defense privilege." For a case where the claim was successful, see *Meza v. H. Muehlstein & Co.*, 98 Cal.Rptr.3d 422 (Ct.App. 2009), where a plaintiff sued a total of 17 mostly corporate defendants for personal injuries resulting from exposure to toxic chemicals in her workplace. The defendants entered into a case management agreement, approved by court order, pursuant to which they agreed to share confidential information without waiving either work product protection or attorney-client privilege. Drouet, a lawyer for one of the defendants, participated in the agreements and in numerous conferences during which such information about the plaintiff's claim and their respective defenses were shared. While the case was being litigated, Drouet left the firm representing that defendant and joined the firm representing the plaintiff, staying there for several months before leaving that firm as well. The plaintiff then dismissed the defendant Drouet had represented from the lawsuit. Shortly thereafter several other defendants moved to dismiss the plaintiff's firm because of Drouet's association with the firm. The appellate court sustained the trial court's disqualification of the firm, holding that the movants were entitled to the joint defense privilege, and that Drouet's knowledge was imputed to the plaintiff firm.

In *Trinity Ambulance Service, Inc. v. G & L Ambulance Services, Inc.*, 578 F.Supp. 1280 (D.Conn. 1984), it was held that when a co-plaintiff unforeseeably switches sides and becomes a defendant, that party's counsel must be disqualified on a showing that the co-plaintiffs had shared planning and strategy with an expectation of confidentiality. The remaining plaintiff's counsel, however, need not be disqualified, because there was no risk of disclosure of the switching plaintiff's confidences to unintended parties.

4. **"Same Matter" in Model Rule 1.9:** Model Rule 1.9(a) prohibits representation of a client whose interests are adverse to a former client without the latter's informed consent, if the matters involved in the successive representations are either "the same or * * * substantially related." There is no definition of "matter" or "same matter" in this Rule or in the Model Rule 1.0 definitions. While the most frequently litigated criterion, as evidenced by the cases above, is substantial relationship, occasionally parties or lower courts have to be reminded that the "same matter" criterion is an independent and sufficient ground for disqualification. In *Twenty–First Century Rail Corp. v. New Jersey Transit Corp.*, 44 A.3d 592 (N.J. 2012), three companies were contractors on a substantial light rail construction project for New Jersey Transit (NJT). Company A, the primary contractor, subcontracted with Company B for civil, electrical, mechanical, and emergency system work, while Company C was NJT's overall project engineer responsible for design and engineering matters. When Company B experienced substantial delays in completing its work, it consulted a partner in Law Firm X on its responsibility for such delays in relation to Company A's demands, asking the lawyer for an opinion taking into consideration potential design issues (for which Company C might be responsible). After submitting his opinion, neither the partner nor the firm did further work for Company B. Later, Company A and Company B sued Company C and NJT, alleging that faulty design by Company C was the

sole cause of the delays. Company C retained Law Firm X to defend against this claim. Company B moved to disqualify the firm. The lower courts denied the motion, on the basis of a state supreme court precedent defining "substantially related" in terms of the information acquired in the prior representation and its relevance and materiality to the new one. The New Jersey Supreme Court reversed and remanded, holding that the successive representations involved the same matter, and that the other precedent was thus inapplicable. The court held:

> Both matters involve the same discrete phase of that overall project, the same contracts, the same parties and, based upon our evaluation of the documents that the parties have provided concerning the matters on which [Company B] consulted the lawyers in the first instance, the same dispute.

44 A.3d at 599.

D. IMPUTED DISQUALIFICATION

PROBLEM

Return to the previous problem, in which Patterson & Cooper of Chicago represent Bramco Steel Co., a company that supplied structural steel for a bridge that has collapsed in Massachusetts. Patterson & Cooper is a large law firm that also has offices in Boston, New York and Topeka. Each office operates as a separate management entity, with authority to hire and fire attorneys, set the salaries of employees and the equity percentage of partners within the office, set billing rates for its clients, and so on. However, all partners generally share in the fees generated by each office, with each office assigned a percentage of the total. Also, no one can become a partner without approval of all existing partners at their annual meeting. Each office practices under the name Patterson & Cooper and uses letterhead, cards, notices, yellow pages entries, and other communications that identify the location of all offices of the firm.

After the Massachusetts bridge matter has become an active file in the Chicago office, Paul Petty comes to the Boston office of P & C with a claim for personal injury and property damage resulting from that bridge collapse, which occurred just after he entered it with his truck. The Boston office has never worked on any matter for Bramco.

QUESTIONS

(a) The Boston partner whom Petty consults agrees to take his case, pending a conflict check. The partner gets a list of all the parties responsible for construction and maintenance of the bridge, and recognizes Bramco as a client of the Chicago office. May he nonetheless continue with the representation?

(b) Assume that the Boston partner, on determining that one of the proper defendants in Petty's suit is a client of the Chicago office, arranges with the responsible Chicago partners that there will be no communication of any confidential information between the two offices on the Petty claim, that the fees earned by each office from its client on the matter will not be shared by the other office, and that in respect of that matter they will deal with each other as adversaries. This arrangement is put into writing and disclosed to each client. Can the respective representations continue? If so, under what further conditions?

RULE REFERENCES

Model Rule 1.10, 1.0(c) & (k), 1.8(k), and 1.18(c)–(d)

RESTATEMENT §§ 123–24

D(1) IMPUTATION GENERALLY

IN RE SEXSON

Supreme Court of Indiana, 1993.
613 N.E.2d 841.

PER CURIAM.

The Respondent in this case, David B. Sexson, has been charged with engaging in the representation of a client that was directly adverse to the interests of another client and thereby violating Rules 1.7(a) and 1.10(a) of the *Rules of Professional Conduct for Attorneys at Law*. * * *

Respondent, an attorney subject to the disciplinary jurisdiction of this Court, at all times relevant to this proceeding, maintained an office in a remodeled home at 3035 South Keystone Avenue in Indianapolis, Indiana. Another attorney, Rollin E. Thompson, Respondent, and four other attorneys maintained offices at this location. All attorneys shared office space, shared one secretary, used a common letterhead as stationery, and used three common telephone lines. As a routine practice, the attorneys left their offices unlocked and the doors open. Attorney file cabinets could be observed by the clients of the other attorneys from a common hallway and conversations in the individual offices could be heard in this hallway.

In November 1987, Thompson was retained by the Zimmermans to handle a personal injury claim in which they were the plaintiffs. On February 25, 1991, while the personal injury claim was still pending, Mr. Zimmerman filed an action for dissolution of marriage; he was represented by an attorney unrelated to either Thompson or Respondent. At that time, Mrs. Zimmerman's mother was employed as a secretary for both Thompson and Respondent. Mrs. Zimmerman retained Respondent for the dissolution proceeding and on March 29, 1991, Respondent appeared for Mrs. Zimmerman and filed a cross-petition for dissolution of the marriage.

On July 15, 1991, Thompson settled the personal injury case for the Zimmermans. On July 18, 1991, Respondent filed, on behalf of Mrs. Zimmerman, a Petition for Contempt and a Restraining Order, seeking an order restraining Mr. Zimmerman from negotiating his settlement check. An order was issued *ex parte* to that effect on the date of filing. At approximately 11:00 a.m. on July 19, 1991, Mr. Zimmerman called Thompson to set a time to pick up his settlement check from the personal injury case. Upon arriving at the office one hour after making the call, Mr. Zimmerman was met by Respondent and served with the restraining order issued on July 18, 1991. * * *

As found above, the Respondent did not represent Mr. Zimmerman; Mr. and Mrs. Zimmerman were represented by Thompson in the personal injury matter. Respondent represented Mrs. Zimmerman in a separate domestic relations proceeding. Thus, in order to find misconduct on the part of the Respondent, we must conclude that Thompson was disqualified from representing Mrs. Zimmerman in the domestic relations proceeding and such disqualification can be imputed to Respondent.

Under [Rule 1.7(a)(1)], absent disclosure and consent, Thompson could not have represented Mrs. Zimmerman if such representation would have been directly adverse to Mr. Zimmerman. This Court has previously held that the representation of one marital party in a dissolution proceeding and the joint representation of the marital parties in other legal proceedings can constitute representation of adverse interests. * * * In the present case, Thompson was still representing the interests of Mr. and Mrs. Zimmerman when the dissolution was commenced and Respondent appeared and counter-petitioned. Mrs. Zimmerman's interests were adverse to Mr. Zimmerman. Thompson could not have represented Mrs. Zimmerman in the dissolution proceeding.

As to whether Thompson's disqualification can be imputed to Respondent, the issue is whether the office sharing arrangement of Respondent, Thompson, and the other attorneys constituted a "firm" under [Rule] 1.10(a). This case presents our first opportunity to address an issue of this nature.

[Comment [1]] to Rule 1.10 notes that within the context of the professional disciplinary rules, the definition of "firm" is a question of fact. In such analysis, it is crucial to look at the level of association, the appearance of the association to the public, any specific agreements, access to confidential information, and the purpose of the rule. * * *

In the present case, Respondent, Thompson, and the other attorneys used common letterhead, shared phone lines, had apparent access to each other's confidential information, and shared office personnel. When Mr. Zimmerman made arrangements to get his settlement check, he was greeted by Respondent with a restraining order prohibiting him from negotiating the check. It was reasonable for Mr. Zimmerman to assume that Thompson and Respondent were part of a "firm", and it was equally reasonable for Mr. Zimmerman to conclude, that under these circumstances, Respondent engaged in adverse representation.

In view of the above analysis, we conclude that Respondent violated [Rules] 1.7(a) and 1.10(a) as charged.

NOTES ON IMPUTATION GENERALLY

1. In *In re Recker*, 902 N.E.2d 225 (Ind. 2009), the issue was the relationship between two public defenders in an Indiana county where each defender was employed individually on a part-time basis by either of two courts hearing criminal cases. The two public defenders had separate private practices. In the old county court library, they had separate cubicles, with a single incoming telephone line and no doors on the cubicles, but normally conversations in one cubicle could not be overheard in the next. The county provided generic letterhead stationery, "Office of the Public Defender," which listed the two courts but not the individual attorneys. Court secretaries provided secretarial help. One of the secretaries kept all the defender files, but these files could only be accessed by a lawyer assigned to the particular case.

Recker was assigned by the circuit court to represent client A in a criminal case as well as in a child welfare case involving his child. The other public defender, Paul, was assigned to represent client B in a criminal case before the superior court. The two clients were being held in the same cell in the county jail. Client A then hired a private attorney to represent him in the criminal case, but kept Recker on the child welfare matter.

Client B passed a note to the sheriff indicating Client A had told him some details about the battery homicide for which he was being held. The prosecutor believed Client B wanted to make a deal before disclosing, so the prosecutor had a conversation with Paul about this possibility when Recker was not in the office. When Recker came back to the office, Paul told him about her client's message without identifying Client B, then asked what she should do. At the time, Paul did not know that Recker was representing Client A, and Recker thought Paul's client B was a private client. Recker then told the lawyer representing Client A in the criminal case about the situation. The private lawyer told A, who suspected B was the informant. When Client A was tried for murder, B testified against him. Client A was convicted.

Recker was then charged in disciplinary proceedings with violating Client B's confidences and using confidential information to Client B's disadvantage. The disciplinary charges alleged that Client B was a client of Paul and that Paul and Recker were associated in the same firm, within the meaning of Model Rule 1.8(k). The primary authority relied on in imputing Paul's obligation to Recker was *Sexson*. The Indiana court found for Recker, distinguishing *Sexton* and rejecting the imputation argument. Can you identify what was missing in *Recker* that made it distinguishable from *Sexson*?

2. **Common Letterhead and Phones as "Firm":** The use of common letterhead and common phone lines by the lawyers in *Sexson*, as well as the open atmosphere within the office, can be seen as the equivalent of the lawyers holding themselves out as a firm. Would the result have been different if they had used separate letterhead and maintained separate phone lines, sharing only secretarial services, library, and entryway, or does an inference of confidence-sharing arise merely from the sharing of office space and facilities? Section 123(3) and Comment *e* of the RESTATEMENT place the

burden on lawyers in office-sharing arrangements to take adequate measures to ensure the confidentiality of each lawyer's communications with clients.

3. **Waiver of Imputed Conflicts:** Under Model Rule 1.10(c), an attorney who would otherwise be disqualified due to another firm attorney's conflict is allowed to represent a client, if the affected clients waive the conflict under circumstances where waiver is allowed by Model Rule 1.7.

D(2) IMPUTATION AND
PUBLIC INTEREST ORGANIZATIONS

PEOPLE v. CHRISTIAN

California Court of Appeal, First District, Division 2, 1996.
48 Cal.Rptr.2d 867.

KLINE, PRESIDING JUSTICE.

Ron Dupries Christian and Dishon Jackson appeal their convictions, following a joint jury trial, of several offenses related to the robbery of a Taco Bell restaurant. * * * Jackson contends the trial court erred in permitting the Contra Costa County Public Defender's Office (PD) to represent codefendant Christian and the Alternate Defender Office (ADO) to represent Jackson. According to Jackson, because both offices are under the supervision of Public Defender Charles James, they are not separate entities for conflict of interest purposes, and the joint representation of Jackson and his codefendant denied Jackson the right to conflict-free and independent counsel.

STATEMENT OF THE CASE AND FACTS

On March 10, 1994, Jackson and Christian approached the counter at a Taco Bell restaurant in Richmond, California. As Jackson ordered some food, Christian pulled a gun on Rudolfo Gomez, who was working behind the counter. Jackson demanded money from Gomez, who gave him money from the cash register. Jackson then jumped over the counter, followed by Christian. Jackson attempted to open another cash register, but was unsuccessful; the clerk opened the register and Jackson took money from it.

Christian went to the back of the restaurant where he demanded that Melvin Lopez, the shift manager, give him money from the safe. Lopez opened the safe and Christian took the money. Jackson also went to the back of the restaurant, where he tried to exit through a back door, but he stopped when Lopez told him an alarm would ring. Jackson then returned to the front of the restaurant, jumped over the counter, and told Christian to "[h]urry up." Christian joined him and they left out the front of the restaurant.

Richmond police officers responded to reports of the robbery. Officer Mark Granko noticed two men fitting the robbers' descriptions walking through a parking lot. He approached the two men and ordered them to stop, at which point Jackson pulled a handgun from his waistband and dropped it on the ground. Jackson then ran in the direction of a Home Depot store, where he was apprehended. Christian attempted to hide under some shrubbery, but was arrested by Granko.

[Christian was charged with two counts of robbery enhanced by personal use of a firearm, making him ineligible for probation; Jackson was charged with two counts of armed robbery and possession of a firearm by a felon, and his prior felony convictions made him ineligible for probation.]

After his arrest, Christian gave a statement to the police in which he implicated Jackson in the robbery. He told police he had handed Jackson some money and the gun after they had left Taco Bell. Based on this statement, Jackson moved to sever his trial from Christian's. However, the prosecutor stated that he would not use Christian's statement at trial unless Christian testified. Neither appellant testified during trial, and the statement was not introduced into evidence.

Christian was represented in the trial court by Deputy Public Defender Jonathan Cooper and Jackson was represented by William Veale of the ADO. Before trial, Jackson moved for substitute counsel * * *, saying that he wanted a court-appointed attorney. The motion was denied. On the second day of trial Jackson [renewed his] motion, generally asserting that "there is a conflict of interest here that is involving my case." This motion also was denied.

[A jury found Christian guilty on all counts and Jackson guilty on all counts except the second robbery, and they were sentenced to seven and three years in prison respectively. Both appealed, but Christian requested only an independent review of the record on the basis of which his conviction was affirmed.]

DISCUSSION * * *

II.   * * *

Jackson argues that in this case there existed both a potential conflict of interest (had either defendant testified, he would have incriminated his codefendant) and an actual conflict of interest (both defendants attempted to show that the other defendant dropped the gun in front of Officer Granko). Since, according to Jackson, the Public Defender in effect represented both him and his codefendant without first obtaining their informed consent, the conflicting loyalties that ensued undermined his right to effective assistance of counsel, requiring reversal of the judgment.

III.

In November 1991, in response to the escalating cost of obtaining legal representation for indigent criminal defendants in conflict of interest cases, the Contra Costa County Board of Supervisors authorized establishment of the ADO. The ADO serves indigent clients who would otherwise be represented by private attorneys appointed through the Conflicts Panel of the Contra Costa County Bar Association.

At the ADO's inception, the Public Defender promulgated a policy statement that articulated the nature of the ADO and its relationship to the PD. The policy was disseminated to all staff at both the PD and the ADO. The structure and functioning of the ADO, as explained in the 1991 policy statement, are as follows. Although the ADO is formally a branch of the PD, it operates autonomously, with a separate supervising attorney who is responsible for directing, coordinating, and evaluating the work of attorneys employed by the ADO. This supervising attorney is solely responsible for providing guidance to and determining litigation strategy of ADO attorneys. The Public Defender exercises no control or influence over the handling of cases by the ADO. Nor does he have access to the client files or other client confidences of the ADO. Only upon the specific recommendation of the ADO supervising attorney may the Public Defender make changes in the salary or working conditions of persons working for the ADO.

Individual cases in the ADO are opened, litigated, and closed under separate ADO file numbers. The ADO generates calendars listing appearances only for attorneys in the ADO. The ADO has its own clerical support staff and investigators, independent of those employed by the PD. The ADO offices are physically separate from those of the Public Defender. The keys to the offices of the ADO are different from the keys to the PD offices, and ADO keys are not available to attorneys or support staff not employed by the ADO. The Public Defender does not personally possess a key to the ADO offices, nor does the ADO supervisor possess keys to the PD offices. The ADO maintains a separate communications network, with its own telephone number, computer hookups to the Law & Justice computer system, facsimile machine, and computer equipment. The ADO also uses independent library facilities.

The files of ADO clients are housed separately from those of the PD to insure that only ADO attorneys have access to the confidential files of the ADO. In turn, files of the primary branches of the PD are protected as separate and likewise inaccessible to ADO attorneys or staff. Every employee of the PD and ADO has been specifically advised to maintain the confidences of individual clients and to be sensitive to the required degree of separation between the ADO and the PD. * * *

IV.

Castro v. Los Angeles County Board of Supervisors, [284 Cal.Rptr. 154 (Ct.App. 1991)], addressed a question similar to that raised here, regarding alleged conflicts of interest in the context of the juvenile dependency court system. Los Angeles County, in order to save money, had replaced its dependency court conflicts panel system with Dependency Court Legal Services, Inc. (DCLS), a nonprofit organization, which was to represent all parties in dependency proceedings. * * * Under its operating rules, DCLS had three separate groups, each of which reported, through its individual chain of command, to a common executive director. All three groups received funding through a single administrative unit that handled certain common administrative functions, unrelated to providing legal representation. * * *

However, each group was otherwise autonomous, with attorneys from each group making all decisions regarding the handling of cases within that group; with separate offices, including different addresses and telephone numbers; separate staff and attorneys; separate files, secure from both the other two groups and from the administrative unit; and separate computers. * * * DCLS represented up to three separate indigent parties in a dependency proceeding, including proceedings where a conflict existed between the parties. * * * The plaintiffs, panel attorneys whose services were being displaced by DCLS, sued for declaratory and injunctive relief, claiming that the new system was irreparably flawed because of an inherent conflict of interest between attorneys in the three groups. * * *

The Court of Appeal upheld the trial court's denial of a preliminary injunction, finding the doctrine of "vicarious" or firm disqualification inapplicable to DCLS's situation. * * *

First, the court rejected plaintiffs' analogy of DCLS to a private law firm; since DCLS did not charge clients and received its funding from the county, no DCLS attorney had any financial incentive to favor one client over any other. "Quite the opposite is true; because a third party pays, the attorney has every incentive to devote his or her entire efforts on behalf of the client." * * * The court further noted that the trial court had credited DCLS's evidence of screening measures and "Chinese walls." * * *

The court also rejected the plaintiffs' characterization of DCLS as a single "firm" for conflict of interest purposes[, while citing ABA Model Rule 1.10.] The court found that DCLS was not analogous to the conventional definition of a "firm," in that it was a nonprofit corporation, was a creation of a public entity, did not present itself to the public as a law firm, had only one source of clients in a single kind of legal proceeding, did not solicit clients or accept referrals from the public, and had been structured so its attorneys and three groups had no contact with one another. * * * "It is not to be assumed hypothetically, in the absence of facts, that DCLS attorneys will act to violate their client's confidence or to compromise their legal interests. The structures of the organization reinforce this ethical duty, which is well known to all attorneys." * * * The court also found the plaintiffs' many examples of situations in which DCLS attorneys *might* find themselves with divided loyalties—such as possible disinclination to pursue a costly appeal or reluctance to charge an opposing counsel with unethical conduct—to be "[s]peculative contentions of conflict of interest [that] cannot justify disqualification of counsel." * * *

Finally, the court rejected the plaintiffs' argument that DCLS's representation of opposing parties in a single proceeding would create the "appearance of impropriety." * * *

V.

[W]e find unpersuasive Jackson's attempts to distinguish the present situation from that at issue in *Castro*. The differences between the juvenile dependency proceedings at issue in *Castro* and the criminal proceedings with which we are here concerned are not material. Although a juvenile dependency proceeding is not one which can result in deprivation of liberty, it is one in which highly protected interests are at stake and in which those interests could be seriously prejudiced by a conflict of interest between parents or between a parent and a child. In our view, the reasoning of the *Castro* opinion is largely applicable to the question we confront: whether the PD/ADO system provides representation to indigent criminal defendants that is free from inherent conflicts of interest.

VI.

Although conflict rules clearly apply both to private and public sector attorneys, they appear to have been drafted with private attorneys primarily in mind. * * * There are certain distinctions between these two types of practices—public and private—that are relevant to our analysis. In particular, the financial incentive, often present in private practice, to favor a more important client over a lesser one is not an issue for the PD or ADO, given that they are government-funded offices performing services for indigent clients.

[D]isqualification of public sector attorneys should proceed with caution since such disqualifications can result in increased public expenditures for legal representation. "Where only speculative or minimal benefit would be obtained by disqualification of public counsel, the 'dislocation and increased expense of government' is not justified.["]

Thus, in the public sector, in light of the somewhat lessened potential for conflicts of interest and the high public price paid for disqualifying whole offices of government-funded attorneys, use of internal screening procedures or "ethical walls" to avoid conflicts within government offices, such as those found acceptable in *Castro*, have been permitted. * * *

In the present case, the record shows that the PD and ADO not only claim to have an ethical separation, but that such a separation in fact exists. As was the case with the executive director of DCLS in *Castro*, the Public Defender of Contra Costa County is nominally in charge of both offices, but in a strictly administrative sense. He is not involved in any way in the day-to-day operation of the ADO. He may not initiate any promotional or disciplinary actions; rather his role is limited to reviewing and acting upon the recommendations of the ADO supervising attorney. In addition, like the three DCLS groups discussed in *Castro*, attorneys from the two offices remain physically apart, have no access to each other's files, and adhere to a well-known policy of keeping all legal activities completely separate. There is no evidence that use of these "ethical walls" have been ineffective in avoiding conflicts of interest between the PD and the ADO. * * *

VII.

We also find that the PD and ADO are separate "firms" for purposes of conflict analysis. Again, their structure is remarkably similar to that of the three groups that constituted DCLS and that were found to be distinct firms by the court of appeal in *Castro, supra* * * *. Like DCLS, the PD and ADO are nonprofit organizations, with a single source of clients in a single type of legal proceeding, and their attorneys practice only in a specific area of law. The PD and ADO are also funded by the county, not by clients, thus eliminating any financial incentive to favor one client over another. Like DCLS, neither the PD nor the ADO solicits clients, nor do they accept referrals from the public. The two offices also have been structured to have minimal contact with each other. * * *

Furthermore, as with DCLS, when analyzed under the criteria set forth in the comment to ABA rule 1.10 the PD and ADO do not constitute a single "firm" in that they present themselves to the public as separate entities with separate offices, phone numbers, letterhead, pleading paper, and distinct business cards. The two offices likewise conduct themselves as separate firms. They keep separate confidential files, none of which are cross-accessible, and each office has its own support staff and keeps separate computers, as well as copying and facsimile machines. Importantly supervision of ADO attorneys is the responsibility of the ADO supervising attorney, not the Public Defender, and neither office consults with the other on general litigation strategy or the handling of individual cases. These rules are reflected in the Public Defender's Policy Statement, disseminated to all staff in the PD and ADO. In sum, the two offices are separate "firms," coinciding only for matters of administrative convenience and only at the top administrative level.

VIII.

Finally, * * * [t]he purpose of the careful separation between the ADO and the PD is to avoid either the appearance of any conflict of interest or any actual ethical impropriety. * * * We conclude that these efforts have been successful.

In addition, we have found no evidence of impropriety in the particular circumstances of this case. The record shows that, as Jackson claims, there *was* a potential and actual conflict of interest between him and his codefendant. However, the record also shows that each of the two trial attorneys vigorously defended his client, objecting to the admission of evidence when appropriate and even attempting to implicate each other's client through argument and cross-examination. Both attorneys focused their defense on negating the second robbery charge (from the safe in the back of the restaurant) by alluding to possible embezzlement by Lopez and suggesting the entire incident could not have constituted more than a single robbery; Jackson was in fact acquitted of the second robbery count.

Furthermore, although there was no question as to the identities of the robbers, since the incident had been captured on videotape and was shown to the jury, each attorney attempted to portray the other defendant as the instigator of the crime and to prove that it was the other defendant, and not his client, who had dropped the gun in front of Granko. There is simply no evidence that either attorney represented conflicting interests in his defense of this case. * * *

We thus conclude that Jackson's concerns about an inherent conflict of interest between the Contra Costa County PD and ADO in general, and between the two attorneys in this case in particular, are unfounded. * * *

The judgments are affirmed as to both appellants.

NOTES ON IMPUTED DISQUALIFICATION IN NONPROFIT LEGAL AID AGENCIES

1. **Imputed Disqualification and Civil Legal Services Offices:** Should the same principles apply to a nonprofit agency (whether or not publicly funded) for providing legal services to low-income persons, as apply to a private law firm? Consider the situation of a woman who files for divorce on the ground of adultery, and is represented by the local Legal Aid Society. If her husband is also unable to pay for his own attorney, can the court properly appoint another Legal Aid attorney to represent him? In *Borden v. Borden*, 277 A.2d 89 (D.C. 1971), such an appointment was objected to by both counsel and held improper. The court rejected the argument that the absence of an *economic* conflict of interest protected against prejudice to either party from being represented by members of the same organization.

> We are not persuaded that the possibility of conflict of interest which appellee's attorney proferred as his reason for wishing to withdraw from participation in this case is remote. While the NLSP [Neighborhood Legal Services Program] is not a law firm it is a group of attorneys practicing law together in an organizational structure much like a law firm. It has a Board of Directors and an Executive Director who are analogous to a firm's managing partners. ABA Formal Opinion 324, [at] 6 (August 9, 1970). It has one attorney in each of its branch offices whose responsibility is to supervise the junior attorneys, much like a firm's senior partner working with his associates. All NLSP attorneys participate in office meetings and receive intra-office communications on substantive law, litigation techniques and tactics and office policy. Lawyers who practice their profession side-by-side, literally and figuratively, are subject to subtle influences that may well affect their professional judgment and loyalty to their clients, even though they are not faced with the more easily recognized economic conflict of interest. In addition, the appointment of attorneys who work together presents an impression scarcely consistent with the bar's efforts to maintain public confidence in the law and lawyers.
>
> Also we fail to find in this case the extraordinary circumstances present in *N.A.A.C.P. v. Button*, [371 U.S. 415, 83 S.Ct. 328, 9 L.Ed.2d 405 (1963)], where legal representation to vindicate constitutional rights of a group of citizens was simply unavailable except in the form of group legal services which the State contended amounted to barratry, maintenance and champerty. With all deference to the trial court's efforts to

date to assure full representation of all who seek access to the Domestic Relations Court we are not persuaded that the supply of attorneys available in the District of Columbia has been exhausted so that NLSP attorneys must now represent *both* sides of a divorce action.

277 A.2d at 91–92. The ABA Committee on Ethics and Professional Responsibility adopted the *Borden* position in two informal opinions. *See* ABA Comm. on Ethics and Prof'l Resp., Informal Op. 1309 (1975); ABA Comm. on Ethics and Prof'l Resp., Informal Op. 1233 (1972). On the other hand, the Maryland Court of Appeals held that "at a minimum, each district office of the public defender should be treated as a private law firm for conflict of interest purposes" and therefore imputed the conflict of one public defender to another public defender in the same office. *Duvall v. State*, 923 A.2d 81, 95 (Md.Ct.App. 2007).

In the 2002 revisions to the Model Rules, the ABA added a provision designed to make it easier for attorneys to volunteer to provide short-term legal services despite some other potential conflicts of interest from the regular clients of the attorney or the attorney's firm. Under Model Rule 6.5(a), when an attorney participates in a short-term program sponsored by a nonprofit organization or a court, the only conflicts that limit the attorney's provision of services are those that the attorney knows about at the time. In addition, the conflicts that arise from the attorney's short-term services are not imputed to members of the attorney's firm. *See* Model Rule 6.5(b).

2. **Imputation of Conflicts from Legal Services Offices:** Where a private attorney is an officer or a member of the board of directors of a legal aid agency, are that attorney's clients' interests imputed to the agency for conflict purposes? See Model Rule 6.3, which denies any *per se* imputation based upon the attorney's service as an officer, director, or member of a legal services organization, but precludes the attorney from participating in decisions of the organization that would either conflict with obligations owed to private clients or have an adverse effect on organization clients whose interests are adverse to those of the attorney. For an argument that this is too narrow a reading of potential conflicts in such a situation, see John S. Dzienkowski, *Positional Conflicts of Interest*, 71 Tex.L.Rev. 457, 531–33 (1993).

The Model Rules are even less restrictive regarding law reform activities. Model Rule 6.4 allows an attorney to be a "director, officer, or member of an organization" that participates in administration or reform of the law, even if that reform might affect the attorney's clients. The rule does require the attorney to disclose the fact that the organization's decisions might benefit a client, but does not require the attorney to disclose the identity of the affected client.

D(3) IMPUTATION AND SCREENING IN THE PRIVATE FIRM

SILICON GRAPHICS, INC. v. ATI TECHNOLOGIES, INC.

United States District Court, Western District of Wisconsin, 2010.
741 F.Supp.2d 970.

BARBARA B. CRABB, DISTRICT JUDGE.

[This is a patent case involving infringement claims with respect to three graphics processing technology patents. Two claims were eliminated without trial, but the third was tried to a jury, which found for the plaintiff. On appeal, the court held that the trial judge had misconstrued the patent and remanded for reconsideration under the new construction of the patent. After the ruling on appeal, the plaintiff filed a motion to disqualify the defendants' law firm.]

The lawyer at the center of plaintiff's motion for disqualification is David Leichtman. Between December 2006 and October 2007, Leichtman performed legal work in this case for plaintiff in his capacity as a partner at Morgan, Lewis and Brockius, one of the law firms representing plaintiff. Leichtman left Morgan Lewis in October 2007 to become a partner at Lovells (now Hogan Lovells). In February 2010, while this case was on appeal and after oral argument, Leichtman took a job as a partner at [defendants' law firm] Robins Kaplan's New York office.

The parties agree that Leichtman may not perform any work for defendants in this case. The question is whether Robins Kaplan must be disqualified as well. Defendants say that disqualification is not required or appropriate because Leichtman performed a relatively small amount of work for plaintiff and because Robins Kaplan has employed a screening protocol in this case to prevent Leichtman, who works in New York, from disclosing any information he might have to the lawyers in this case, who work in Minneapolis. For its part, plaintiff has few qualms about Robins Kaplan's screening mechanism. Instead, plaintiff says that Leichtman performed so much work on the case that screening cannot be used to rebut the presumption that Leichtman has shared confidential information with defendants' lawyers working on this case or will do so in the future. * * *

With respect to plaintiff's motion for disqualification, I conclude that screening is an appropriate method to address concerns about confidentiality when a lawyer changes law firms in the middle of a case, even if the lawyer performed a substantial amount of work for the former client. This conclusion is required by *Cromley v. Board of Education of Lockport Township High School District 205,* 17 F.3d 1059 (7th Cir. 1994), and other cases decided by the Court of Appeals for the Seventh Circuit in which the court has held that law firms may avoid imputation through appropriate screening mechanisms regardless of the scope of the work performed for the former client by the disqualified lawyer. Because plaintiff does not raise any serious challenges to the screening conducted in this case, plaintiff's motion to disqualify Robins Kaplan will be denied. * * *

UNDISPUTED FACTS

A. *David Leichtman's Work for Plaintiff*

Plaintiff Silicon Graphics filed this lawsuit on October 23, 2006. At the time, David Leichtman was a partner for Morgan, Lewis and Brockius, one of the law firms representing plaintiff. Robins, Kaplan, Miller & Ciresi LLP represented defendants at the time and still represents them.

Leichtman began working on the case on December 7, 2006; he did not participate in any pre-suit investigation of plaintiff's claims. On December 12, 2006, defendants filed a motion in which they asked for pro hac vice status for Leichtman, along with five other lawyers. The court granted the motion the following day.

The scope of the lawsuit was extensive, including 306 document requests, 37 interrogatories, 33 depositions, 10,000,000 pages of documents, 24 third-party subpoenas and approximately 100 motions. Leichtman was involved in three areas of the lawsuit: (1) third party discovery; (2) inequitable conduct; and (3) damages. Between December 7, 2006 and October 2, 2007, Leichtman billed plaintiff for 186 hours, for a total of $111,273.88. This represents approximately 8% of his billable time during that time period. Leichtman left Morgan Lewis in October 2007 to become a partner at Lovells.

B. *Leichtman's Job with Robins Kaplan*

In the fall of 2009 Leichtman interviewed with Robins, Kaplan, Miller & Ciresi LLP for a position in a new office to be opened in New York City. To identify potential conflicts of interest, Leichtman filled out a questionnaire identifying all of the clients for which he had performed services in the last five years. He listed plaintiff as one such client.

At the request of the ethics partner for Robins Kaplan, Leichtman wrote a letter asking plaintiff to waive any potential conflicts:

> The Rules of Professional Conduct require that I maintain client confidences or confidential information which I may have learned about Silicon Graphics, Inc. and I will of course maintain such confidences. But because of my former representation of Silicon Graphics, Inc., Robins, Kaplan, Miller & Ciresi LLP believes it appropriate to request waivers of the conflict of interest that would otherwise arise from me becoming a partner there. Robins is also in the process of obtaining AMD and ATI's consent, and have asked me to obtain Silicon Graphics, Inc.'s consent.

Leichtman described Robins Kaplan's screening procedures in the letter:

As part of the consent, Robins, Kaplan, Miller & Ciresi LLP will create an ethical wall. This ethical wall will prohibit any access to the files or communication between me and anyone working on the matter or any future litigation involving Silicon Graphics, Inc. as an adverse party. This includes not only the physical hardcopy files but the electronic document management system.

When Leichtman did not receive a response from plaintiff, the ethics partner conducted additional research regarding the ethical rules and talked to Leichtman about "the timing and general scope" of Leichtman's work for plaintiff. They agreed that Leichtman's work was minor and isolated. The ethics partner concluded that Leichtman would not receive any compensation for this lawsuit and that it would not be necessary to obtain consent from plaintiff.

In a letter dated December 28, 2009 Leichtman gave plaintiff notice that he was joining Robins Kaplan. He wrote:

I wanted to advise you that Robins Kaplan has determined that the applicable rules of professional responsibility do not require that we obtain consent from either party in order for me to join the firm. . . .

[M]y minor previous work for Silicon Graphics in the Matter was isolated. I did not learn confidential information and did not have contact with Silicon Graphics. I am no longer associated with the firm where that minor work was done, and have not been for over two years.

In addition, I have been screened from any participation in the matter and will be apportioned no part of the fee from the matter.

Counsel for plaintiff responded in a letter dated January 29, 2010:

I have received your correspondence (i) requesting a waiver from SGI and later (ii) withdrawing this request. As we discussed, I passed on your initial request to Barry Weinert. [Plaintiff] was not inclined to grant any waiver, and so I guess in a sense, your withdrawal of the request is fine.

Once a decision is made in the *SGI v. ATI* appeal, I'm sure [plaintiff] will consider the issue of your waiver request and "notice." We note that your second letter seems to suggest that no waiver is required because you "performed no more than minor and isolated services" for SGI at Morgan Lewis. [Plaintiff] does not believe that this provision applies and therefore reserves all of its rights with respect to this matter.

On January 11, 2010 Robins Kaplan sent an "ethical wall memorandum" to Leichtman and all the members of the litigation team for this case. The memorandum instructed team members not to discuss the case with Leichtman or in his presence. Under the memorandum, Leichtman is denied access to any records relating to this case and may not provide team members any information he knows about the case.

Leichtman joined Robins Kaplan on February 1. The firm employs 242 lawyers nation-wide; 100 of these practice "in the intellectual property field." All of the Robins Kaplan lawyers working on this case and defendants' physical records related to the case are in the Minneapolis office. All of the electronic records are protected by a computer security protocol that prevents Leichtman from viewing or searching those records. Leichtman has never spoken to anyone at Robins Kaplan about this case and no staff members have had a discussion about the case in his presence. He has not viewed any of the records relevant to this case or attempted to do so.

Robins Kaplan has represented defendants from the beginning of the lawsuit.

OPINION * * *

When a lawyer "switches sides," it implicates a number of competing interests. First, the former client may be understandably concerned about confidential information that could be shared with the opposing party. In addition, "[t]he bar and this court have an interest in maintaining the integrity and favorable public image of both the legal profession and the judicial system by preventing even the 'appearance of professional impropriety.' " * * * On the other side, the client of the law firm that hired the lawyer has an interest in keeping the law firm that it has chosen and that is familiar with the case. Particularly in a case like this one that has lasted for several years, a requirement to choose a new law firm is potentially devastating to defendants and could lead to substantial delays in the final resolution of this case. * * * In the middle is the individual lawyer who has an interest in finding fulfilling employment. *In re County of Los Angeles*, 223 F.3d 990, 996 (9th Cir. 2000) ("An automatic disqualification rule would make firms be understandably more reluctant to hire mid-career lawyers, who would find themselves cast adrift as 'Typhoid Marys.' "). * * *

At the center of these considerations is a desire to prevent *either* side from using the switch to obtain a tactical advantage in the lawsuit. Former clients should not be exposed to unfair risks that a lawyer will use confidential information to aid her new employer at the expense of the former client. At the same time, former clients should not be permitted to use ethical rules as a weapon to cripple their opponent when there is no legitimate concern about potential harm. * * *

Under the previous version of Model Rule 1.10 of the Model Rules of Professional Conduct, law firms could not use screening as a method for avoiding imputation. * * * This changed in 2009, when the ABA adopted a new version of Model Rule 1.10 * * *. Under the new rule, screening is generally permitted so long as the notice requirements are met.

The ABA considered and rejected a rule that disqualified a law firm, regardless of screening, in any case involving a lawyer's "substantial involvement" with a former client or in which the lawyer had "substantial material information" about a former client. One of the reasons for the rejection was that the proposed standards were too vague. ABA Standing Committee on Ethics & Professional Responsibility, Report to the House of Delegates, at 14 (Feb. 2009), *available at* www.abanet.org ("Clarity is required when a lawyer and a firm decide whether to consider associating with each other, at which time no tribunal is available to decide the 'substantial involvement' question.") * * * In concluding that screening was appropriate as a general matter, the ABA rejected the view that "client protection and lawyer mobility" are mutually exclusive goals. *Id.* at 10. It noted that a

> confidentiality duty continues after termination of the client-lawyer relationship. If a lawyer breaches that duty, she is subject to discipline, whether she has changed firms or not. Screening is a mechanism to give effect to the duty of confidentiality, not a tool to undermine it[.] Screening does not solve all ... problems, but reduces them to situations where the interests of the former clients cannot adequately be addressed by the screening mechanism.

Id. at 11–12.

At least 12 states have a rule of imputed disqualification similar to th[e] ABA model rule that allows for screening regardless of the scope of the work conducted by the lawyer for the former client. * * * About the same number of states allow for screening under more limited circumstances. * * * In adopting the new rule, the ABA relied on the experience of these states, concluding that history has "established [that] screens are effective to protect confidentiality" and "that courts have exhibited no difficulty in reviewing and, where screening was found to have been effective, approving screening mechanisms." * * *

This leaves about half of the states that require automatic disqualification. However, some predict that, "[w]ith the passage of amended Model Rule 1.10, more states will likely follow suit" to allow screening under more circumstances. * * *

A. *Choice of Law*

In this case, the parties point to different sources of law that they say should guide the court's decision on the question whether Robins Kaplan should be disqualified from representing defendants in this case. [Plaintiff argued for application of Wisconsin's version of Model Rule 1.10(a)(2), which permits removal of imputation by screening only if the migrating lawyer "performed no more than minor and isolated services in the disqualifying representation."]

Plaintiff says that * * * screening is not sufficient in this case because Leichtman's work was not "minor" and "isolated" within the meaning of the rule.

Defendants point to a standard that the Court of Appeals for the Seventh Circuit has applied in the past:

First, we must determine whether a substantial relationship exists between the subject matter of the prior and present representations. If we conclude a substantial relationship does exist, we must next ascertain whether the presumption of shared confidences with respect to the prior representation has been rebutted. If we conclude this presumption has not been rebutted, we must then determine whether the presumption of shared confidences has been rebutted with respect to the present representation. Failure to rebut this presumption would also make disqualification proper.

Schiessle v. Stephens, 717 F.2d 417, 420 (7th Cir.1983) (footnote omitted). *See also Cromley v. Board of Education of Lockport Township High School District 205,* 17 F.3d 1059, 1064 (7th Cir.1994) (applying same standard). Defendants do not deny that the first two parts of this standard are met, but they argue that "the presumption of shared confidences has been rebutted with respect to the present representation." * * *

The court of appeals has stated explicitly that a law firm can rebut the presumption through "proof that screening procedures were timely employed in the new law firm to prevent the disclosure of information and secrets." *Cromley,* 17 F.3d at 1065. * * *

Despite the lack of a clear holding in this circuit, I agree with defendants that federal law is controlling. * * *

The natural inference to be drawn from the court's silence regarding state rules of professional conduct is that the federal standard does not incorporate state rules and that district courts should not use those rules as supplemental authority, at least when there is a conflict between the two. * * *

Even if there were authority suggesting that the court of appeals looked to state ethical rules for guidance as a general matter, I do not believe the court would do so in this case for two reasons. First, although the court has not relied on state rules in previous decisions, it *has* suggested that previous versions of the ABA model rules influenced its decisions. * * *

A second reason for exercising caution before following the Wisconsin rules is their internal inconsistency. The prohibition on screening for lawyers who performed more than "minor and isolated" work for a former client is limited to lawyers moving from one private firm to another private firm. Under SCR 20:1.11, if a government lawyer "switches sides" and joins a private firm representing a client with interests adverse to the former employer, the firm is not disqualified if the lawyer is timely screened from any participation in the matter and is apportioned no part of the fee therefrom. SCR 20:1.11(b)(1), (c). * * *

The commentary to the Wisconsin rules do not provide a rationale for the different standards and none is apparent, unless one assumes that private lawyers as a group are less trustworthy than former government lawyers. * * *

B. *Application of the Federal Standard*

There is no serious dispute that defendants have rebutted the presumption of shared confidences under the Seventh Circuit standard. In *LaSalle National Bank* [*v. County of Lake,* 703 F.2d 252, 258–259 (7th Cir.1983)], the court of appeals identified various factors that a court may consider in assessing the adequacy of a firm's screening procedures: (1) whether the disqualified lawyer is denied access to relevant files; (2) whether the lawyer is excluded from profits or fees derived from the representation in question; (3) whether discussion of the suit is prohibited in the lawyer's presence; (4) whether members of the firm are prohibited from showing the lawyer any documents relating to the case; (5) whether the disqualified lawyer and others in his firm have affirmed under oath that they have not discussed the case with each other and will not do so in the future; (6) whether the screening arrangement was set up at the time the potentially disqualifying event occurred, either when the attorney first joined the firm or when the firm accepted a case presenting an ethical problem.

Plaintiff does not deny that defendants' screening procedures comply with each of these factors. Three weeks before Leichtman joined Robins Kaplan, the firm sent a memorandum to Leichtman and all the members of the litigation team for this case. The memorandum instructed team members not to discuss the case with Leichtman or in his presence. Under the memorandum, Leichtman is denied access to any records relating to this case and is prohibited from providing team members any information he knows about the case. All of the electronic records are protected by a computer security protocol that prevents Leichtman from viewing or searching those records. Leichtman and each of the lawyers for Robins Kaplan working on this case have filed declarations in which they aver that Leichtman and the others have not spoken with each other about the case, that none of the lawyers has had a discussion about the case in Leichtman's presence and that Leichtman has not viewed any of the records relevant to this case or attempted to do so. An analysis conducted by Robins Kaplan's computer support group shows that Leichtman has not attempted to view the electronic files. Leichtman will not receive any fees related to this case.

[The opinion went on to conclude that even if the Wisconsin rule were applied, it should be interpreted in light of policy considerations and not require disqualification in this case. As indicated at the outset, the motion to disqualify was denied.]

NOTES ON THE MIGRATING LAWYER, DISQUALIFICATION, AND SCREENING

1. **The Developing Trend Toward Allowing Nonconsensual Screening**: Note the passage in the *Silicon Graphics* opinion that summarized a trend toward allowing screening to remove imputation of conflicts in cases of attorney migration from one private firm to another. The omitted reference was to a passage in *Kirk v. First American Title Insurance Co.,* 108

Cal.Rptr.3d 620 (Ct.App. 2010) containing an enumeration of 24 states with such rules, evenly split between those allowing screening without reference to the level of the migrant's prior involvement or the significance of the confidential information brought with her, and those that do attach some limitation based on one or more such factors. By early 2012, perhaps vindicating Judge Crabb's prediction, at least two more states had joined the ranks, both in the first category. The common requirement is that the newly associated lawyer's personal disqualification be based on a relationship with a former client under Model Rule 1.9, rather than a current conflict based on Model Rule 1.7. In the following notes offering a somewhat more up-to-date enumeration, the more restrictive group will be referred to as "the Restatement position and its analogues," and the less restrictive group will be referred to as the ABA position.

2. **The Restatement Position and its Analogues:** RESTATEMENT § 124(2) contemplates screening as a means of "removing imputation" of one lawyer's prohibition against a particular representation to all affiliated lawyers only if the prohibition is based on a former-client conflict. The provision, which purports to cover the remedy of judge-ordered disqualification as well as lawyer disciplinary rules, is not limited to the migratory lawyer situation, but applies by its terms to any affiliated-lawyer imputation—a position that does not appear to have been adopted by any jurisdiction in its disciplinary rules. It does adopt another kind of limitation, based on the level of risk that confidential information acquired from the former client would be used to that client's material disadvantage in the new representation—i.e., that any such information "is unlikely to be significant in the subsequent matter."

At least twelve jurisdictions have adopted risk-to-the-former-client criteria similar to the Restatement criteria in their versions of Model Rule 1.10, expressly limited to the migrating lawyer situation on the model of the 2001 proposal rejected by the ABA. *See infra* note 3. Their criteria reflect the two ways in which Model Rule 1.9 disqualifies a lawyer based on a relationship with a former client now in an adverse position in the same or a substantially related matter: (a) *representation* of the former client, and (b) *association in a firm* with a lawyer representing the client, which only disqualifies if the nonrepresenting lawyer acquired material confidential information about the prior matter. Two states have adopted the Restatement's significance-in-the-matter criterion. *See* Minn. Rule 1.10(b)(1) (2000); N.D. Rule 1.10(b) (2006) (adding, as a cumulative requirement, that "there is no reasonably apparent risk that any use of confidential information of the former client will have a material adverse effect on the client").

A second risk-related criterion that other states have adopted as potentially precluding cure via screening is the level of the migrant's involvement with the prior representation. This criterion gets somewhat varied formulation: "substantially participated" (Colorado Rule 1.10(e)(1) (2008)); "have primary responsibility for" (Indiana Rule 1.10(c)(1) (2005)); "did not have a substantial role" (New Mexico Rule 16–110(C)(2) (2011, adopted 2008)); "substantial role in or primary responsibility" (Nevada Rule 1.10(e)(1) (2011, adopted 2006)); "substantial responsibility" (Ohio Rule 1.10(c) (2007)); "more than minor and isolated service" (Wisconsin Rule 1.10(a)(2)). Two states have adopted combinations of these criteria, one with an additional twist: "sub-

stantial involvement [or] substantial material information" (Massachusetts
Rule 1.10(d)(2)(i) (2011, first adopted 1998)); and no screening if "substantial
involvement in, or received substantial material information about, a matter
that is ongoing at the time of the firm transfer and that would be the focus of
the screening procedures" (New Hampshire Rule 1.10(c)(3) (2008)). Finally,
two states impose another kind of same-matter exclusion from screening: that
the matter "in which [the migrating] lawyer is disqualified" (i.e., the current
matter) "involve[s] a proceeding before a tribunal in which the personally
disqualified lawyer had a substantial role" (Arizona Rule 1.10(d)(1) (2003)
and New Jersey Rule 1.10(c)(1)(2004) (similar, but using "primary responsibility" instead of "a substantial role")).

3. **The Evolution of the ABA Position:** As the *Silicon Graphics*
opinion indicates, the Model Rules themselves did not allow screening in the
situation of the private practitioner migrating to another practice until
amendment of Model Rule 1.10 in 2009. Although the ABA's Ethics 2000
Commission proposed a screening rule in 2001, the ABA House of Delegates
rejected this proposal. *See* Robert A. Creamer, *Lateral Screening After Ethics
2000*, 2006 Prof.Law. 85, 85–86. The Commission's rejected draft, applying
only "when a lawyer becomes associated with a firm," would have permitted
removal of imputation if the affected lawyer was screened from any participation in the case and received no portion of the fee generated from the case,
and if prompt written notice were given to any affected former client. *See*
Report of the Ethics 2000 Commission, Proposed Model Rule 1.10(c) (2002).
As did the 2001 proposal, the newly adopted version requires only that the
newly associated lawyer be disqualified under Model Rule 1.9, and attaches no
conditions on the availability of screening based on the specific degree or
other circumstances of the prior involvement.

In the meantime, twelve states had adopted versions of Model Rule 1.10
allowing for screening more or less on the model of the rejected 2001 ABA
proposal without further restrictions: Delaware Rule 1.10(c); Illinois Rule
1.10(e); Kentucky Rule 1.10(d); Maryland Rule 1.10(c); Michigan Rule 1.10(b);
Montana Rule 1.10(c); North Carolina Rule 1.10(c); Oregon Rule 1.10(c);
Pennsylvania Rule 1.10(b); Rhode Island Rule 1.10(c); Tennessee Rule 1.10(b);
and Utah Rule 1.10(c). Two states have adopted most or all of the language of
the 2009 ABA amendment. *See* Idaho Rule 1.10(a)(2); Washington Rule
1.10(e).

Finally, one state that has not adopted the Model Rules or any other
formal rule dealing with imputed disqualification of associated lawyers in the
private-to-private migration situation has begun to allow screening by judicial
decision. *See Kirk v. First Am. Title Ins. Co.*, 108 Cal.Rptr.3d 620 (Ct.App.
2010). The logic of the court's opinion, with which the *Silicon Graphics*
opinion agrees, is based on the established screening exception for former
government attorneys moving to private practice (see *infra* Ch. 5(E)):

> [I]f ethical screening can, in any given case, be considered effective to
> screen a former government attorney in a private law firm, it gives rise to
> the question why screening cannot be equally effective to screen a private
> attorney in the same private law firm. The effectiveness of the screening

process depends on the policies implemented by the law firm, not on the former employment of the screened attorney.

108 Cal.Rptr.3d at 642.

4. **Screening Measures Under the New Model Rule:** The *Silicon Graphics* opinion helpfully discussed the general criteria for effective screening in this context. The 2009 version of Model Rule 1.10(a)(2) does not precisely define the measures to be taken, but it provides more detail for the obligations of the screening firm: more specific requirements for the written notice to be sent to affected former clients and an additional requirement to provide certifications of compliance by the firm and the screened lawyer (1) at reasonable intervals on request of the affected former client and (2) upon termination of the screening. This is supplemented by Model Rule 1.0(k), added in 2002, providing a generic definition of the term "screened" as "denot[ing] the isolation of a lawyer from any participation in a matter through the timely imposition of procedures within a firm that are reasonably adequate under the circumstances to protect information that the isolated lawyer is obligated to protect under these Rules or other law." It is clear from these rules that the determination of the sufficiency of screening measures is strongly fact-driven and tailored to the particular circumstances.

For further guidance about the measures to implement, comparing the provisions of Model Rule 1.10 with other Model Rules contemplating screening (1.11 for the former government attorney, 1.12 for prior involvement as a judge or other neutral, and 1.18 for prospective but declined clients), see Michael Downey, *Conflicts of Interest: Elements of an Effective Ethics Screen*, 27 Laws.Man. on Prof. Conduct (ABA/BNA) 587 (2011), with references to recent cases.

5. **Conflict Checks and Confidentiality:** Notice that the hiring firm in *Silicon Graphics* sought disclosure from the migrant of his prior clients, before the decision to hire was final. For elaboration of their mutual duty to disclose, with discussion of how to balance the competing goals of protecting confidentiality and enabling both to avoid unexpected imputed disqualification, see ABA Standing Committee on Ethics & Professional Responsibility, Formal Opinion 09–455 (2009). It summarizes its conclusions as follows:

> When a lawyer moves between law firms, both the moving lawyer and the prospective new firm have a duty to detect and resolve conflicts of interest. Although Rule 1.6(a) generally protects conflicts information (typically the "persons and issues involved" in a matter), disclosure of conflicts information during the process of lawyers moving between firms is ordinarily permissible, subject to limitations. Any disclosure of conflicts information should be no greater than reasonably necessary to accomplish the purpose of detecting and resolving conflicts and must not compromise the attorney-client privilege or otherwise prejudice a client or former client. A lawyer or law firm receiving conflicts information may not reveal such information or use it for purposes other than detecting and resolving conflicts of interest. Disclosure normally should not occur until the moving lawyer and the prospective new firm have engaged in substantive discussions regarding a possible new association.

6. **"Prior Firm" in ABA Model Rule 1.10(a)(2):** Suppose a lawyer has been engaged in solo practice (*i.e.*, all by himself without partners or associates), and then joins a 100–lawyer firm in his city. If a matter comes into the firm that is substantially related to a matter that the migrant handled as a sole practitioner, disqualifying him personally from acting in that matter under 1.9(a), would Model Rule 1.10(a)(2) allow the other members of the firm to avoid imputation of that disqualification to them by screening? Does the migrant's disqualification "arise out of [his] association with a prior firm"? Comment [1] to Model Rule 1.10 defines "firm" as "lawyers in a law partnership, professional corporation, sole proprietorship or other *association* authorized to practice law" (emphasis added). Even Model Rule 1.0(c), to which the Comment refers, while it starts with "a lawyer or lawyers," defines "firm" as an "association," and Comments [2] and [3] both discuss only multiple-lawyer groups. There is, however, a good indication that the ABA Standing Committee on Professional Ethics and Responsibility recommending the addition of the clause "and arises out of the disqualified lawyer's association with a prior firm" in August of 2009 did not have this interpretational issue in mind. In its "General Information Form" attached to the recommendation, it summarized this recommendation as one to amend the Model Rule "to explicitly state that the screening procedures permitted under the Rule apply only when a lawyer has moved laterally from one practice situation to another." ABA Standing Comm. on Ethics & Prof'l Resp., Section of Litig., Standing Comm. on Professionalism, Report 109, at 5 (August 2009). Further, to the question of whether this or a similar recommendation had been submitted previously, the committee chair answered that, in presenting the original amended Model Rule 1.10 to the ABA at an earlier meeting in 2009, he had stated "this Rule applies only where a lawyer moves from one private practice or corporate practice to another private practice or corporate practice," but the language at that time did not explicitly so state. *Id.*

The ambiguity was reflected in the format of the 2009 version of Model Rule 1.10 adopted in February, which can be found at Rick Valliere, *ABA Delegates Modify Conflicts Rule, Allow Screens When Lawyers Change Firms*, 25 Laws.Man. on Prof. Conduct (ABA/BNA) 88 (2009). Whereas the rejected 2001 proposal addressed screening for the migrating lawyer in a separate paragraph (b), beginning with the phrase "When a lawyer becomes associated with a firm," the 2009 version authorizing screening is a second exception, paragraph (a)(2), attached to the main prohibition, which begins "While lawyers are associated in a firm." That second "unless" by its original terms applied not only in the migration situation, but whenever a lawyer "associated in a firm" was individually disqualified by Model Rules 1.9(a) or 1.9(b). The "fix" adopted in August, simply adding the phrase "and arises out of the disqualified lawyer's association with a prior firm" after the enumeration of the disqualifying rules, did explicitly limit screening to the migrating lawyer situation. However, drafters failed to notice that the Model Rule also does not explicitly state that the term "firm" includes a sole practitioner.

Note, however, that a majority of the state rules applying risk-to-the-client restrictions similar to the Restatement model would probably preclude screening in such a situation, because the sole practitioner's involvement would by definition have been "primary" or "substantial," *see supra* note 2. On the other hand, almost all of the state rules more analogous to the ABA version would allow screening here because they lack that clause added to the ABA version in late 2009, *see supra* note 3.

7. **Screening as an Inducement to Consent by the Former Client:** In those twenty-odd states that have not adopted formal rules or case law supporting it, screening alone (i.e., without client consent) does not overcome an imputed conflict arising from a new lawyer's former employment in a different private law firm. However, screening sometimes can be used to gain the necessary informed consent to a conflict, in circumstances where Model Rule 1.9(b) would allow consent. In such circumstances, both the client of the new lawyer's old firm and the client of the lawyer's new firm must give informed consent to the conflict in writing. The same may be true with concurrent conflicts under Model Rule 1.7(b).

8. **Duties to Prospective Clients:** The conflict of interest provisions of Model Rule 1.18, the rule that outlines duties to prospective clients, ordinarily prevent an attorney or others in the attorney's firm from representing someone with interests materially adverse to the prospective client if the prospective client provided the attorney with significant information that could harm the prospective client. *See* Model Rule 1.18(c). However, Model Rule 1.18(d)(1) allows the attorney who received the information to represent someone with adverse interests if both the prospective client and the ultimately represented client give written informed consent. Model Rule 1.18(d)(2) allows the other attorneys associated with the lawyer who received disqualifying information to represent someone with materially adverse interests if: the lawyer took reasonable steps to avoid exposure to information from the prospective client beyond that necessary to determine whether to represent him; the disqualified lawyer is screened from the matter and given no portion of the fees generated from it; and the firm promptly gives the prospective client written notice. The latter provision is presumably designed to avoid the problem of the "prospective client" who is not actually seeking representation when talking to the lawyer, but is simply trying to render that lawyer ineligible to represent an opposing party.

E. THE FORMER GOVERNMENT ATTORNEY

PROBLEM

The Office of Attorney General of the State of Jefferson has a Securities Division that employs twenty lawyers. It is responsible for investigation and enforcement under the state's securities laws. Among the hundreds of matters under investigation or review in the division is the activity of Jack Armstrong, a real estate developer. Armstrong has been selling limited partnerships in a proposed resort development in a remote area of the state, without disclosing known geological information that makes the investment essentially worthless. Two junior lawyers in the division conduct the investigation and institute an action on behalf of the division against Armstrong, seeking to enjoin further sale of the partnerships on the ground of fraud.

Mary Croft has been Assistant Attorney General in charge of the Securities Division for a number of years. During the investigation of the Armstrong matter she receives periodic progress reports, as is routine with all matters. She gives occasional advice on techniques of investigation, but does not get involved with the day-to-day conduct of the matter. Shortly before the junior lawyers are ready to recommend the injunctive action, Croft leaves her position and joins the private law firm of Knight & Day, which is engaged in general practice in the capital city.

QUESTIONS

(a) The division's suit against Armstrong is settled by consent decree whereby Armstrong agrees to stop selling the partnerships. Wilma Williams, who had bought a limited partnership from Armstrong, now comes into Croft's office at Knight & Day wanting to sue Armstrong for damages for fraud. She would like Croft to represent her. May Croft properly take Williams' case?

(b) Assume instead that Williams talks to Daniel Day, one of Croft's partners. Under what conditions, if any, can Day properly accept the case on behalf of the firm?

RULE REFERENCES

Model Rule 1.11
RESTATEMENT § 133

INTRODUCTORY NOTE

Model Rules 1.10(d) and 1.11 were amended in 2002 by the ABA as part of its Ethics 2000 effort primarily to incorporate the conclusions of the ABA's Ethics Committee expressed in the following opinion, which sought to resolve ambiguities in the texts of former Model Rules 1.9, 1.10, and 1.11.

CONFLICTS OF INTEREST: SUCCESSIVE GOVERNMENT AND PRIVATE EMPLOYMENT FORMAL ETHICS OPINION 97–409

American Bar Association Standing Committee on
Ethics and Professional Responsibility, 1997.*

The Committee has been asked to advise on the applicability of the Model Rules of Professional Conduct where a lawyer formerly employed by a government claims administration agency wishes to represent private claimants before her old agency in connection with the same general kinds of claims she handled while in government service. The lawyer has also asked whether she may bring a suit against her old agency on behalf of a private client challenging agency rules in whose development and implementation she was herself involved. This inquiry requires the Committee to consider whether Model Rule 1.11 is the sole source of a former government lawyer's postemployment obligations, or whether Model Rule 1.9 also applies, in whole or in part, to a lawyer who leaves government service.

---

* Formal Opinion 97–409 ©Copyright 1997 by the American Bar Association. Reprinted with permission. Copies of ABA Formal Ethic Opinions are available from Service Center, American Bar Association, 321 North Clark Street, Chicago, IL 60654, 1–800–285–2221.

The Committee concludes that Rule 1.11 alone determines the conflict of interest obligations of a former government lawyer, and that the provisions of Rule 1.9(a) and (b) do not apply. This conclusion is grounded in inconsistencies in the text of the two rules, and finds support in their commentary and legislative history. A former government lawyer is therefore disqualified only from particular matters, involving identifiable parties, in which she personally and substantially participated while in government service, and her disability does not depend upon whether or not she would be adverse to her former government client in the successive private representation. *See* Rule 1.11(a). Disqualification under Rule 1.11 may also be triggered by her possession of confidential government information about an adverse third party. *See* Rule 1.11(b). In addition, the former government lawyer may be barred by Rule 1.9(c) from representing a private client, against her former agency or otherwise, if she would be required to use or disclose in the private representation information relating to her representation of the government. A former government lawyer's personal disqualification is not imputed to other lawyers in her firm, whether its source is Rule 1.11(a) or Rule 1.9(c), as long as she is screened in accordance with Rule 1.11(a).

Accordingly, the former government lawyer in this case is barred from representing private claimants before her old agency only in connection with particular claims she personally handled. Although the provisions of Rule 1.11(b) barring use of confidential information against adverse third parties appear to have no applicability in this situation, the lawyer has confidentiality obligations to her former government client by virtue of Rule 1.9(c) that could effectively preclude her from representing private claimants against her old agency, even where the representation involves general agency rules or policies and not a "particular matter." Even if she is personally disqualified, however, other members of her new firm may undertake the representation as long as she is appropriately screened.

1. *Conflict of Interest Rules for Former Government Lawyers * * ***

While Rule 1.9 applies on its face to all lawyers, and does not specifically exempt former government lawyers from its coverage, in most situations Rule 1.9 and Rule 1.11 cannot both be given full effect. Quite apart from the difference between the two rules in connection with imputation and screening, the standard of personal disqualification under the two rules is not the same. This means that applying both rules to the same situation will not always produce the same result, and indeed these results will often be inconsistent with one another. While compliance with the personal disqualification standard of both rules is theoretically possible, the resulting disability for former government lawyers is considerably broader than would be produced by application of either rule standing alone.

For example, in adverse representations, to which both rules apply, a former government lawyer would be subject under Rule 1.9 to disqualification from any matter in which she was deemed to have "represented" the government, while under Rule 1.11(a) she would be disqualified only if her prior involvement in the matter amounted to "personal and substantial participation." The concept of "representation" is broader than "personal and substantial participation," and the range of matters from which the lawyer would be disqualified under Rule 1.9(a) is correspondingly broader than under Rule 1.11(a) in this important respect.[8]

In addition, quite apart from the "representation v. participation" issue, the range of adverse "matters" from which a former government lawyer would be disqualified under Rule 1.9, if it applied, would be considerably broader ("same or a substantially related matter") than the range of adverse matters subject to disqualification under Rule 1.11(a) ("particular matter involving a specific party or parties"). Under Rule 1.11, a "matter" must involve "discrete transactions" and "identifiable parties," * * * while no such limits on the definition of a "matter" obtain under Rule 1.9. Thus, for example, Rule 1.11 would permit a lawyer who had participated on behalf of the government in a rulemaking to later represent a private party in a matter closely related to that rulemaking, while Rule 1.9 would not.

Finally, Rule 1.9(b), if applicable to a former government lawyer, would prohibit her undertaking a private representation adverse to her former government client if she had acquired during her government service "information relating to [her] representation" of the government that was material to the subsequent representation. In contrast, disqualification under Rule 1.11(a) does not depend upon what client information the lawyer acquired during government service. Moreover, Rule 1.11(b) comes into play only if the lawyer acquired "confidential government information" about an adverse third party while in government service, and offers no protection to the former government client respecting its confidences. * * *

In sum, Rule 1.9 sweeps more broadly than Rule 1.11 in the matters to which it applies; does not apply at all in some matters to which Rule 1.11 does apply; and extends to all members of a lawyer's new firm by virtue of Rule 1.10, while Rule 1.11(a) allows screening. * * *

Rule 1.11 is [designed] 1) to limit the possibility that a lawyer might be tempted to use the power of public office to secure for herself lucrative private employment after leaving government service, and be distracted from her current public duties by the prospect of eventually going to work for the other side; and 2) to ensure against the possibility that "substantial unfair advantage could accrue to the private client by reason of access

---

8. *See* Violet v. Brown, 9 Vet. App. 530 (Vet. App. 1996) (lawyer who entered an appearance on behalf of the Secretary of Veterans Affairs by signing and filing the decision of the Board of Veterans' Appeal deemed to have "represented" the government for purposes of applying Rule 1.9(a); this limited role did not, however, amount to "personal and substantial participation" under Rule 1.11(a)). * * * As a general matter, whether there is a "representation" under Rule 1.9(a) depends upon whether a lawyer received client confidences material to the subsequent representation. * * * The test of "personal and substantial participation" does not depend upon whether a lawyer has received client confidences (which will generally be presumed from the fact of personal and substantial participation). * * *

to information about the client's adversary obtainable only through the use of public resources available during the lawyer's government service." While Rule 1.11 does to some extent reflect the more general "side-switching" and related client loyalty concerns that underpin the conflict of interest provisions of Rule 1.9, Rule 1.11 is animated by a specific desire to limit the use of government authority to benefit any private person (either the lawyer herself or her future private client), as opposed to the concern to protect the interests of the former client that is the focus of Rule 1.9. This explains why the disqualification standard of Rule 1.11 does not depend upon adverseness towards the former government client, or upon the possibility that a lawyer might in a subsequent related private representation breach her government client's confidences. It is narrowly and precisely drawn to address the particular dangers associated with the use of public office to further private ends.

A third purpose for Rule 1.11 emerges from the commentary, however, which even more strongly supports the conclusion that Rule 1.11 was intended to supplant and not supplement Rule 1.9: *viz.*, the conflict of interest rules should not "impos[e] too severe a deterrent against entering public service" or "inhibit transfer of employment to and from the government." Rule 1.11 Comment [3]. *See also* Model Rule 1.10 Comment [4] and [5]. Subjecting government lawyers to the broader personal disqualification standard of Rule 1.9(a) and (b), coupled with the "no adverseness" requirement of Rule 1.11(a) and the "adverse third party" constraints of Rule 1.11(b), would inevitably act as a deterrent to lawyers entering (or leaving) public service even with the availability of screening. * * *

2. Use and Disclosure of Client Information after the Termination of Government Service

[The opinion concludes that Rule 1.9(c), prohibiting the use of confidential information about a former client to the disadvantage of that client without consent, should and does apply to government lawyers, in addition to private lawyers.]

3. Application of Rules 1.11(a) and 1.9(c) to the Instant Inquiry

Applying the conclusions reached in the foregoing sections to the instant inquiry, we conclude that the former government lawyer is not disqualified under Rule 1.11 from representing private claimants before her old agency unless, based on all of the facts and circumstances, their claims are deemed to be the same "particular matters" as the cases in which she participated while in government service. Similarly, Rule 1.11 would not appear to bar her representation of a private client in a challenge to agency rules even where she was personally involved in their development and implementation while working for the government, since rulemaking is generally not deemed to be a "particular matter." (Both of these conclusions assume that the lawyer will not be adverse in the successive representation to a private third party about whom she has acquired confidential government information.)

At the same time, if zealous and competent representation of her new private claimants would require the lawyer to use or reveal nonpublic information relating to her representation of the government to the government's disadvantage, she would be unable to undertake those representations without violating either her obligation of confidentiality to her former government client under Rule 1.9(c), or her obligations toward her new private clients under Rule 1.7([a]), without the government's consent. However, even if the former government lawyer were therefore personally disqualified from the matter, other members of her new firm could undertake the representation as long as the former government lawyer was screened from participation in accordance with Rule 1.11(a).

NOTES ON PERSONAL DISQUALIFICATION OF THE FORMER GOVERNMENT ATTORNEY

1. **Should the Model Rule 1.9 Definition of Disqualifying Matter Still Apply?** The District of Columbia is one jurisdiction that has resisted the argument of Formal Opinion 97–409 and the revised Model Rule 1.11(a), and still extends the former government attorney's disqualification from private employment under its Rule 1.11(a) to a matter that is "the same as, or substantially related to" one in which he "participated personally and substantially" in government service. This formulation was explicitly derived from judicial interpretation of the term "matter" under the Code of Professional Responsibility as applied to migration from one private firm to another. *See Brown v. D.C. Bd. of Zoning Adjustment*, 486 A.2d 37 (D.C. 1984). Perhaps the unique position of former government lawyers in the D.C. Bar gives rise to a special sensitivity to appearances.

For a high profile disciplinary case applying this rule, see *In re Sofaer*, 728 A.2d 625 (D.C. 1999). Sofaer was the Legal Adviser to the State Department when a Pan American flight was blown up over Lockerbie, Scotland, giving rise to an extensive investigation (largely conducted by the Department of Justice) resulting in indictments of two Libyan nationals and implication of the Libyan government. For a year and half after the incident, he regularly attended briefings on the criminal investigation and oversaw the State Department's response to civil third-party subpoenas relating to the incident. Before the indictments Sofaer left the Department and joined a private firm. He and his firm were hired three years later to represent Libya in negotiating settlements with the victims and agreements with the U.S. and the U.K. to surrender the indicted Libyans for trial at a mutually agreeable venue. Despite his sincere belief that this representation would be "insulated, factually and ethically" from his prior involvement, he was held to have violated D.C. Rule 1.11(a) and informally admonished. The court found that "[t]he 'substantially related' test by its terms * * * is meant to induce a former government lawyer considering a representation to err well on the side of caution[, and] [r]espondent did not do so." *Id.* at 628.

Some other jurisdictions continue to adhere to the position, also rejected in Formal Opinion 97–409 and by the Model Rule, that Model Rule 1.9(a) applies to the former government attorney's disqualification from private representation in direct opposition to the former government employer. *See, e.g., State v. Craddock*, 2010–1473 (La.App. 1 Cir. 3/25/11); 62 So.3d 791 (applying both, but finding no violation of either Rule 1.9 or 1.11 on the particular facts).

2.   **Same "Matter" Under Model Rule 1.11(e):** Assume that two cars collide on city streets. The police are called to investigate. They arrest one of the drivers, who appears to be under the influence. While they are still at the scene, the arrested driver pulls out a pistol and starts firing, injuring two officers and killing the other driver. The shooter is prosecuted alone for the shootings, and the parents of the deceased driver bring a civil action against the shooter for wrongful death, but they join the officers as well as the city as defendants, alleging they failed to prevent the shootings. Are these two proceedings "the same matter"? In *Olivier v. Town of Cumberland*, 540 A.2d 23 (R.I. 1988), involving essentially these facts, attorney Violet represented the plaintiffs in filing the civil action. While both cases were pending, Violet was elected state attorney general, and another lawyer was substituted for the plaintiff parents. As attorney general she recused herself from any involvement in the criminal prosecution and insulated herself from any information concerning it, delegating responsibility to a deputy. When she lost her reelection bid she returned to private practice and reassumed her prior role as lead counsel for the parents in the civil suit. The defendants moved to disqualify her from this representation on the ground of her having been attorney general while the prosecution was pending. Violet did not dispute, and the court held, that the criminal prosecution and the civil case were sufficiently related to one another to constitute a single "matter" under the applicable Code of Professional Responsibility. (The court held, however, that her participation in the criminal proceeding while Attorney General was not substantial within the meaning of that Code's "substantial responsibility" criterion.)

Is the decision consistent with either Model Rule 1.11(e) or Formal Opinion 97–409 on the definition of "matter"? Did the criminal and civil cases involve the same "particular matter involving a specific party or parties"? Is Comment [10] to Model Rule 1.11 helpful, in noting that the same matter can continue in a different form, and counseling the migrating lawyer to "consider the extent to which the matters involve the same basic facts, the same or related parties, and the time elapsed"? For an example of the same matter continuing in a different form, see *Essex Equity Holdings USA, LLC v. Lehman Bros. Inc.*, 909 N.Y.S.2d 285 (Sup.Ct. 2010), where a member of the U.S. Attorney's office in New York led an investigation into alleged securities fraud in sales by Lehman Bros. of "auction rate[d] securities" to various investors. The lawyer then left the U.S. Attorney's office to join a firm that was representing certain of those investors in an arbitration proceeding against Lehman and individual managers before the Financial Industry Regulatory Authority (a non-governmental organization combining the enforcement functions of the major stock exchanges in the U.S.). The managers moved to disqualify the investors' firm under Model Rule 1.11, and the arbitrators referred the issue to the court, which held that since the same transactions that were the subject of the arbitration had been among those investigated by the migrating lawyer, the "same matter" requirement was met. (The motion was granted because the screening efforts of the firm were inadequate.)

Note that attorney Violet in the *Olivier* case, in recusing herself from the case while she was attorney general, conformed to the explicit requirement of Model Rule 1.11(d). This provision requires disqualification when a current government attorney participated "personally and substantially" in the matter as a private attorney.

In *Hitchens v. State*, 931 A.2d 437 (Del. 2007), an unpublished opinion, a deputy Attorney General participated in the prosecution of a defendant for burglary, signing the charging documents and the plea agreements that resulted in the defendant's being sentenced to probation. The deputy AG then left that office and joined the Public Defender's office. When the defendant later came up before the trial court for hearing on a charge of violating the conditions of his probation, he was first represented by one assistant PD, and then at a second hearing on that charge was represented by the former assistant AG. Upon having his probation revoked for these violations, the defendant appealed on the ground that his lawyer had been under a conflict of interest that denied him the right to effective counsel. The state supreme court held, applying Model Rule 1.11 as adopted in Delaware and specifically invoking Comment [10], that the original prosecution and the probation violation proceedings were not the same matter, since they were based on different conduct by the defendant and the only common element was that the parties were the same.

3. **Appearance of Impropriety and "Substantial Responsibility":** Some jurisdictions have explicitly rejected the pragmatic approach of Formal Opinion 97–409 and have retained a more rigid "appearance of impropriety" standard. In *Rennie v. Hess Oil Virgin Islands Corp.*, 981 F.Supp. 374 (D.V.I. 1997), a former Virgin Islands Commissioner of Labor was held, under a Rule 1.11(a) identical to the Model Rule, to be disqualified from representing private clients in matters related to some that had been before the Commission during his tenure there, not because he had "personally and substantially participated" in those related matters (the court found this requirement not satisfied), but because the lawyer's having been the leader of the Commission at a time during which related matters were being processed in the office created an "appearance of impropriety": "[T]he mere suggestion of misconduct alleged here may seriously undermine the public confidence in the integrity of this government and the legal profession." *Id.* at 377. An "appearance of impropriety" standard was rejected generally for determining disqualification questions by the comments to former Model Rule 1.9. *See* Model Rule 1.9, Comment [5] (2001). Former Comment [5] is excised from the current version of Model Rule 1.9.

Some jurisdictions, while abandoning an explicit "appearance of impropriety" criterion, retain another related criterion from the Code: "substantial responsibility" in addition to the "personal and substantial participation" of Model Rule 1.11. *See* New Jersey Rule 1.11(a)(2).

4. **Former Judges and Other Adjudicative Officers:** Model Rule 1.12 is similar to Model Rule 1.11. However, it applies to former judges, other adjudicative officers, and their law clerks as well as to arbitrators, mediators, and other third-party neutrals. Model Rule 1.12(a) prohibits a lawyer, in the absence of "informed consent" in writing, from representing a party in the same "matter" in which he "participated personally and substantially as a judge or other adjudicative officer or law clerk to such a person." *See, e.g., In re Hoffman*, 2003 ND 161, ¶ 12, 670 N.W.2d 500, 503 (holding that "presiding as a judge in a divorce proceeding, whether by default or trial, constitutes personal and substantial involvement" that prevents a former judge from representing one of the parties to the divorce in the same case); *James v. Miss. Bar*, 2005–BA–01622–SCT, ¶ 1, 962 So.2d 528, 530 (Miss. 2007) (publicly reprimanding a former judge for representing "a party in a case related to one over which she formerly presided"); *J.N.W.E. v. W.D.W.*, 2004–CA–0166–COA, ¶ 20, 922 So.2d 12, 16 (Miss.Ct.App. 2005) (affirming finding that youth court judge who had access to records in prior case was not disqualified from serving as an attorney in a matter because "there was no evidence presented that [he] ever acted as a judge in the case" and therefore no basis for finding that he participated personally and substantially in it). "Other adjudicative officers" includes "referees, special masters, hearing officers and other parajudicial officers." Model Rule 1.12, Comment [1]. As to law clerks, see, *e.g., Bradley v. State*, 16 P.3d 187, 190 (Alaska Ct.App. 2001), which found that the law clerk in question had not participated personally or substantially in the matter in that capacity.

Model Rule 1.12(b) prohibits the adjudicatory officer from negotiating for future employment with a party or lawyer for a party in a matter in which the officer has served personally and substantially. The New Jersey Supreme Court emphasized this point:

> [J]udges may not discuss or negotiate for employment with any parties or attorneys involved in a matter in which the judge is participating personally and substantially. Similarly, lawyers may not approach a judge to discuss post-retirement employment while such a matter is pending. If the subject is raised in any fashion, judges should put a halt to the conversation at once, rebuff any offer, and disclose what occurred on the record. The judge and all parties can then evaluate objectively whether any further relief is needed.

DeNike v. Cupo, 958 A.2d 446, 456–57 (N.J. 2008). A law clerk for such an officer may negotiate for post-clerkship employment with firms involved in cases in which the law clerk is participating, but only after notifying the judge or other adjudicatory officer that the law clerk is so doing.

5. **Government Statute Conflicts:** Statutes, often called "ethics in government" laws, often impose similar and perhaps more stringent restrictions on former public servants, including lawyers. Consider, for example, 18 U.S.C. § 207(a) (2006):

§ 207. Restrictions on former officers, employees, and elected officials of the executive and legislative branches

(a) RESTRICTIONS ON ALL OFFICERS AND EMPLOYEES OF THE EXECUTIVE BRANCH AND CERTAIN OTHER AGENCIES.—

(1) PERMANENT RESTRICTIONS ON REPRESENTATION ON PARTICULAR MATTERS.—Any person who is an officer or employee (including any special Government employee) of the executive branch of the United States (including any independent agency of the United States), or of the District of Columbia, and who, after the termination of his or her service or employment with the United States or the District of Columbia, knowingly makes, with the intent to influence, any communication to or appearance before any officer or employee of any department, agency, court, or court-martial of the United States or the District of Columbia, on behalf of any other person (except the United States or the District of Columbia) in connection with a particular matter—

> (A) in which the United States or the District of Columbia is a party or has a direct and substantial interest,
>
> (B) in which the person participated personally and substantially as such officer or employee, and
>
> (C) which involved a specific party or specific parties at the time of such participation,

shall be punished as provided in section 216 of this title.

(2) TWO-YEAR RESTRICTIONS CONCERNING PARTICULAR MATTERS UNDER OFFICIAL RESPONSIBILITY.—Any person subject to the restrictions contained in paragraph (1) who, within 2 years after the termination of his or her service or employment with the United States or the District of Columbia, knowingly makes, with the intent to influence, any communication to or appearance before any officer or employee of any department, agency, court, or court-martial of the United States or the District of Columbia, on behalf of any other person (except the United States or the District of Columbia), in connection with a particular matter—

> (A) in which the United States or the District of Columbia is a party or has a direct and substantial interest,
>
> (B) which such person knows or reasonably should know was actually pending under his or her official responsibility as such officer or employee within a period of 1 year before the termination of his or her service or employment with the United States or the District of Columbia, and
>
> (C) which involved a specific party or specific parties at the time it was so pending,

shall be punished as provided in section 216 of this title.

(3) CLARIFICATION OF RESTRICTIONS.—The restrictions contained in paragraphs (1) and (2) shall apply—

> (A) in the case of an officer or employee of the executive branch of the United States (including any independent agency), only with respect to communications to or appearances before any officer or employee of any department, agency, court, or court-martial of the United States on behalf of any other person (except the United States), and only with respect to a matter in which the United States is a party or has a direct and substantial interest; and

(B) in the case of an officer or employee of the District of Columbia, only with respect to communications to or appearances before any officer or employee of any department, agency, or court of the District of Columbia on behalf of any other person (except the District of Columbia), and only with respect to a matter in which the District of Columbia is a party or has a direct and substantial interest.

The section goes on to specify a number of other similar restrictions specific to certain offices and functions. It is part of a chapter of the criminal statutes entitled "Bribery, Graft, and Conflicts of Interest."

Most states have statutes of similar import, although the specific provisions vary considerably. How do these statutes relate to Model Rule 1.11(a), if adopted in the particular jurisdiction? If the relevant statute expressly permits conduct otherwise prohibited by the Model Rule, the latter expressly yields in its introductory clause: "[e]xcept as law may otherwise expressly permit." If the relevant statute prohibits conduct that is not prohibited by Model Rule 1.11(a), Comment [1] suggests that the Model Rule yields here as well, by noting that lawyers "may be subject to statutes * * * regarding conflict of interest." A more restrictive statute may, however, be subject to the particular state's "inherent power" doctrine, and may be struck down, in so far as it purports to apply to lawyers who have left government service, as an unconstitutional legislative regulation of the practice of law. *See, e.g., In re Petition for Review of Op. No. 569 of Advisory Comm. on Prof'l Ethics*, 511 A.2d 119 (N.J. 1986); *Shaulis v. Pennsylvania State Ethics Comm'n*, 739 A.2d 1091 (Pa.Commw.Ct. 1999); *supra* section 2(A).

NOTES ON THE FORMER GOVERNMENT ATTORNEY'S CURRENT FIRM

1. **Screening:** In *Kovacevic v. Fair Automotive Repair, Inc.*, 641 F.Supp. 237, 242–44 (N.D.Ill. 1986), Kurylak was an Associate Attorney General who worked with franchises. While an Associate Attorney General, Kurylak received a number of complaints from Fair Automotive Repair franchisees. Kurylak caused an investigative file to be opened and received pleadings from the present action. Kurylak also communicated with Fair Automotive Repair and its counsel and received information from them. Kurylak then left the attorney general's office and went into private practice with a firm that was asked to represent some of the same franchisees. The firm attempted to build a "Chinese Wall" around Kurylak as a former government lawyer. The court discusses both the type of notice required to the government and what is required for effective screening:

> [Earlier Rules of Professional Conduct appeared to impute the disqualification of Kurylak to all members of his new firm]. However, many courts and commentators, including * * * the ABA itself, have "espoused a less Draconian approach" to [the former government attorney problem]. Some earlier authority adopted the position that, if the government waives a firm's vicarious disqualification, and the firm "effectively screens" the disqualified individual lawyer, the firm can thereby avert vicarious disqualification. * * * However, more recent authority elimi-

nates the requirement of governmental consent, holding that effective screening alone may prevent vicarious or imputed disqualification. * * *

The ABA Rules adopt such a position in Rule 1.11 * * *. Under [Rules 1.11(a) & (b)], governmental consent is required only when the former government attorney wishes to represent a private litigant. Should the attorney's firm wish to represent the private litigant, it need only notify the appropriate government agency, in addition to screening. * * *

This court now holds * * * that effective screening of a former government attorney from participation in a case concerning a matter in which he participated personally while working for the government may avert the vicarious disqualification of the attorney's law firm. To be "effective," the screen should prevent the former government lawyer from: (1) gaining access to the case files; (2) sharing in the profits or fees derived from the representation; (3) discussing the suit with any of his firm's attorneys or staff members; and (4) reviewing any of the case documents. * * * In addition, under ABA Rule 1.11, the law firm should promptly give written notice to the appropriate government agency to enable it to ascertain compliance with the ABA Rules. Furthermore, the law firm should institute all of these measures as soon as the potentially disqualifying event occurs, whether it be when the attorney first joins the firm or when the firm accepts a case in which the attorney was involved previously.

For a screening attempt that failed, see *In re Essex Equity Holdings USA, LLC v. Lehman Bros. Inc.*, 909 N.Y.S.2d 285 (Sup.Ct. 2010), mentioned in *supra* note 2 of Notes on Personal Disqualification of the Former Government Attorney for its "same matter" dimension. After rejecting the argument that a "small firm" cannot reliably screen any one lawyer from the others—noting that there were at least 20 other lawyers on the same floor with the disqualified lawyer, and that the New York rule has a specific comment [10] cautioning "small firms" to exercise "special care and vigilance" but stating that it can be done—the court proceeded to analyze the measures taken as disclosed by the record. The managing partners knew in advance of the former District Attorney's hiring that there would be screening issues, but decided not to send out instructions to the rest of the firm right away, because the firm was structured in "silos" or teams to one of which the case was assigned, and lawyers not in the assigned team would have nothing to do with the case anyway. A professional staff person met with the migrant before he started work to discuss possible situations on which he would have to be screened, and the managing partners did so within days after he started work, but it was not until 3 months after he started that a memorandum was circulated to the whole firm identifying the matters about which they should not have any contact with him. The court held that this did not constitute "timely" implementation, and that early informal instruction to the migrant combined with the compartmentalized structure of the firm was not enough. Moreover, it was still a month later before notice was given to the District Attorney's office with whom the migrant had worked, which failed the Model Rule's requirement of "prompt" notice. The firm was disqualified from participating in the arbitration.

2. **Former Judges, Arbitrators, Mediators or Other Neutrals:**
Model Rule 1.12(c) closely mirrors Model Rule 1.11(b) on imputed disqualification. The law firm with which the former adjudicatory officer is associated is not disqualified if the firm adequately screens the former officer and provides written notice to allow the parties and the tribunal to determine compliance with the rule. *See In re Cnty. of L.A.*, 223 F.3d 990, 993 (9th Cir. 2000); *Cho v. Superior Court*, 45 Cal.Rptr.2d 863, 867 (Ct.App. 1995).

3. **"Confidential Government Information":** Under Model Rule 1.11(c), if a former government attorney obtained information about a person through the use of governmental authority, the attorney cannot "represent a private client whose interests are adverse to that person in a matter" where the information could materially disadvantage that person. The former government attorney's partners and associates can engage in such a representation, if the firm screens the former government attorney from the case.

F. JUDICIAL DISQUALIFICATION AND RECUSAL

PROBLEM

As part of its obligation to the community, your law firm regularly accepts appointments in criminal cases. One such appointment resulted in you being assigned to represent Jimmy Bolte, an active member of the Gray Panthers, a senior citizen advocacy group. Bolte has been charged with two counts of conspiracy to steal confidential government documents. U.S. District Court Judge Alice Whynne has been assigned to the case.

The file provided to you by the U.S. Attorney's Office reveals that Bolte allegedly took the government documents intending to publish them in his newspaper, "Gray Power," in an exposé of Senator "Big John" Thompson, a vigorous opponent of special legislation for senior citizens. The issues you might wish to pursue include:

1. The government used electronic surveillance to obtain evidence, possibly in violation of Bolte's Fourth Amendment rights.

2. The conspiracy statute under which Bolte is charged is unconstitutionally vague. It vests total discretion in the Secretary of Defense to classify material as "confidential," and the standard has frequently changed with no notice to the public.

3. Bolte is being discriminatorily prosecuted in that seven others were involved in the alleged conspiracy, none of whom were prosecuted. You are considering trying to show that the U.S. Attorney's Office was "out to get Jimmy" because of his frequent attacks on corruption in government.

Judge Whynne recently gave the First Annual Justice Harlan Lecture at the local law school on the subject of criminal law reform, during which she said: "There is no such thing as 'discriminatory prosecution.' Either a defendant has broken the law or not. If he has, then he should be convicted, whatever the government's motives in bringing the prosecution."

Judge Whynne had been "Big John" Thompson's law partner before her election to a state court judgeship, and was his campaign manager for his successful elections to local and state office. After she lost her bid for reelection to the state bench, she managed Thompson's successful campaign for the U.S. Senate. Several years later she was appointed to the federal bench with the open support of Senator Thompson.

As a state judge Whynne tried a libel action against Bolte. The suit was filed by a candidate for office that Bolte had accused of bribery. Judge Whynne entered judgment against Bolte, finding that his accusation was "wholly without foundation" and "obviously animated by malicious intent to injure the plaintiff."

Your firm has always had excellent interaction with Judge Whynne. Indeed your firm hired Judge Whynne's law clerk at the end of the last court term, and it is currently negotiating with another one of her clerks to start with your firm next fall.

QUESTIONS

(a) Should Judge Whynne be disqualified from this case, on the basis of any of the above facts? If so, what procedure should be followed (i) by you and/or (ii) by the judge? Is any such disqualification subject to cure by consent of the parties?

(b) Do you or your firm have conflicts of interest based on the above facts, which would require you and/or it either to withdraw or to take some other protective action?

RULE REFERENCES

ABA Model Code of Judicial Conduct, Rules 2.11(A–B), 2.10, and 2.11(C) (formerly Canons 3E, 3B(9), and 3F), plus definitions of "Impartiality" and "Third degree of relationship" from Terminology section

Federal Judicial Disqualification Statutes, 28 U.S.C. §§ 144 & 455 (2006)

F(1) GENERAL STANDARDS OF DISQUALIFICATION

LITEKY v. UNITED STATES

Supreme Court of the United States, 1994.
510 U.S. 540.

JUSTICE SCALIA delivered the opinion of the Court.

Section 455(a) of Title 28 of the United States Code[, which is almost identical in this regard to Rule 2.11(A) (formerly Canon 3E(1)) of the ABA Model Code of Judicial Conduct,] requires a federal judge to "disqualify himself in any proceeding in which his impartiality might reasonably be questioned." This case presents the question whether required recusal under this provision is subject to the limitation that has come to be known as the "extrajudicial source" doctrine.

I

In the 1991 trial at issue here, petitioners were charged with willful destruction of property of the United States in violation of 18 U.S.C. § 1361. The indictment alleged that they had committed acts of vandalism, including the spilling of human blood on walls and various objects, at the Fort Benning Military Reservation. Before trial[,] petitioners moved to disqualify the District Judge pursuant to 28 U.S.C. § 455(a). The motion relied on events that had occurred during and immediately after an earlier trial, involving petitioner Bourgeois, before the same District Judge.

In the 1983 bench trial, Bourgeois, a Catholic priest of the Maryknoll order, had been tried and convicted of various misdemeanors committed during a protest action, also on the federal enclave of Fort Benning. Petitioners claimed that recusal was required in the present case because the judge had displayed "impatience, disregard for the defense and animosity" toward Bourgeois, Bourgeois' codefendants, and their beliefs. The alleged evidence of that included the following words and acts by the judge: stating at the outset of the trial that its purpose was to try a criminal case and not to provide a political forum; observing after Bourgeois' opening statement (which described the purpose of his protest) that the statement ought to have been directed toward the anticipated evidentiary showing; limiting defense counsel's cross-examination; questioning witnesses; periodically cautioning defense counsel to confine his questions to issues material to trial; similarly admonishing witnesses to keep answers responsive to actual questions directed to material issues; admonishing Bourgeois that closing argument was not a time for "making a speech" in a "political forum"; and giving Bourgeois what petitioners considered to be an excessive sentence. The final asserted ground for disqualification—and the one that counsel for petitioners described at oral argument as the most serious—was the judge's interruption of the closing argument of one of Bourgeois' codefendants, instructing him to cease the introduction of new facts, and to restrict himself to discussion of evidence already presented.

The District Judge denied petitioners' disqualification motion, stating that matters arising from judicial proceedings were not a proper basis for recusal. At the outset of the trial, Bourgeois' counsel informed the judge that he intended to focus his defense on the political motivation for petitioners' actions, which was to protest United States Government involvement in El Salvador. The judge said that he would allow petitioners to state their political purposes in opening argument and to testify about them as well, but that he would not allow long speeches or discussions concerning Government policy. When, in the course of opening argument, Bourgeois' counsel began to explain the circumstances surrounding certain events in El Salvador, the prosecutor objected, and the judge stated that he would not allow discussion about events in El Salvador. He then instructed defense counsel to limit his remarks to what he expected the evidence to show. At the close of the prosecution's case, Bourgeois renewed his disqualification motion, adding as grounds for it the District

Judge's "admonishing [him] in front of the jury" regarding the opening statement, and the District Judge's unspecified "admonishing [of] others," in particular Bourgeois' two *pro se* codefendants. The motion was again denied. Petitioners were convicted of the offense charged.

Petitioners appealed, claiming that the District Judge violated 28 U.S.C. § 455(a) in refusing to recuse himself. The Eleventh Circuit affirmed the convictions, agreeing with the District Court that "matters arising out of the course of judicial proceedings are not a proper basis for recusal." * * * We granted certiorari. * * *

II

Required judicial recusal for bias did not exist in England at the time of Blackstone. * * * Since 1792, federal statutes have compelled district judges to recuse themselves when they have an interest in the suit, or have been counsel to a party. * * * In 1821, the basis of recusal was expanded to include [any] judicial relationship or connection with a party that would in the judge's opinion make it improper to sit. * * * Not until 1911, however, was a provision enacted requiring district-judge recusal for bias *in general*. In its current form, codified at 28 U.S.C. § 144, that provision reads as follows:

> "Whenever a party to any proceeding in a district court makes and files a timely and sufficient affidavit that the judge before whom the matter is pending has a personal bias or prejudice either against him or in favor of any adverse party, such judge shall proceed no further therein, but another judge shall be assigned to hear such proceeding.

> "The affidavit shall state the facts and the reasons for the belief that bias or prejudice exists, and shall be filed not less than ten days before the beginning of the term at which the proceeding is to be heard, or good cause shall be shown for failure to file it within such time. A party may file only one such affidavit in any case. It shall be accompanied by a certificate of counsel of record stating that it is made in good faith."

Under § 144 and its predecessor, there came to be generally applied in the courts of appeals a doctrine, more standard in its formulation than clear in its application, requiring—to take its classic formulation found in an oft-cited opinion by Justice Douglas for this Court—that "[t]he alleged bias and prejudice to be disqualifying [under § 144] must stem from an extrajudicial source." *United States v. Grinnell Corp.*, 384 U.S. 563, 583 (1966). * * *

Whatever the precise contours of the "extrajudicial source" doctrine (a subject to which we will revert shortly), it is the contention of petitioners that the doctrine has no application to § 455(a). Most Courts of Appeals to consider the matter have rejected this contention * * *. Some, however, have agreed with it * * *. To understand the arguments pro and con it is necessary to appreciate the major changes in prior law effected by the revision of § 455 in 1974.

Before 1974, § 455 was nothing more than the then-current version of the 1821 prohibition against a judge's presiding who has an interest in the case or a relationship to a party. It read, quite simply:

"Any justice or judge of the United States shall disqualify himself in any case in which he has a substantial interest, has been of counsel, is or has been a material witness, or is so related to or connected with any party or his attorney as to render it improper, in his opinion, for him to sit on the trial, appeal, or other proceeding therein." 28 U.S.C. § 455 (1970 ed.).

The 1974 revision made massive changes, so that § 455 now reads as follows:

"(a) Any justice, judge, or magistrate of the United States shall disqualify himself in any proceeding in which his impartiality might reasonably be questioned.

"(b) He shall also disqualify himself in the following circumstances:

"(1) Where he has a personal bias or prejudice concerning a party, or personal knowledge of disputed evidentiary facts concerning the proceeding;

"(2) Where in private practice he served as lawyer in the matter in controversy, or a lawyer with whom he previously practiced law served during such association as a lawyer concerning the matter, or the judge or such lawyer has been a material witness concerning it;

"(3) Where he has served in governmental employment and in such capacity participated as counsel, adviser or material witness concerning the proceeding or expressed an opinion concerning the merits of the particular case in controversy;

"(4) He knows that he, individually or as a fiduciary, or his spouse or minor child residing in his household, has a financial interest in the subject matter in controversy or in a party to the proceeding, or any other interest that could be substantially affected by the outcome of the proceeding;

"(5) He or his spouse, or a person within the third degree of relationship to either of them, or the spouse of such a person:

"(i) Is a party to the proceeding, or an officer, director, or trustee of a party;

"(ii) Is acting as a lawyer in the proceeding;

"(iii) Is known by the judge to have an interest that could be substantially affected by the outcome of the proceeding;

"(iv) Is to the judge's knowledge likely to be a material witness in the proceeding."

Almost all of the revision (paragraphs (b)(2) through (b)(5)) merely rendered objective and spelled out in detail the "interest" and "relationship" grounds of recusal that had previously been covered by § 455. But the other two paragraphs of the revision brought into § 455 elements of general "bias and prejudice" recusal that had previously been addressed only by § 144. Specifically, paragraph (b)(1) entirely duplicated the grounds of recusal set forth in § 144 ("bias or prejudice"), but (1) made them applicable to *all* justices, judges, and magistrates (and not just district judges), and (2) placed the obligation to identify the existence of those grounds upon the judge himself, rather than requiring recusal only in response to a party affidavit.

Subsection (a), the provision at issue here, was an entirely new "catch all" recusal provision, covering both "interest or relationship" and "bias or prejudice" grounds * * *—but requiring them *all* to be evaluated on an *objective* basis, so that what matters is not the reality of bias or prejudice but its appearance. Quite simply and quite universally, recusal was required whenever "impartiality might reasonably be questioned."

What effect these changes had upon the "extrajudicial source" doctrine—whether they in effect render it obsolete, of continuing relevance only to § 144, which seems to be properly invocable only when § 455(a) can be invoked anyway—depends upon what the basis for that doctrine was. Petitioners suggest that it consisted of the limitation of § 144 to "*personal* bias or prejudice," bias or prejudice officially acquired being different from "personal" bias or prejudice. And, petitioners point out, while § 455(b)(1) retains the phrase "personal bias or prejudice," § 455(a) proscribes all partiality, not merely the "personal" sort.

It is true that a number of Courts of Appeals have relied upon the word "personal" in restricting § 144 to extrajudicial sources * * *. And several cases have cited the absence of that word as a reason for excluding that restriction from § 455(a) * * *. It seems to us, however, that that mistakes the basis for the "extrajudicial source" doctrine. * * *

In our view, the proper (though unexpressed) rationale for *Grinnell*, and the basis of the modern "extrajudicial source" doctrine, is not the statutory term "personal"—for several reasons. First and foremost, that explanation is simply not the semantic success it pretends to be. Bias and prejudice seem to us not divided into the "personal" kind, which is offensive, and the official kind, which is perfectly all right. As generally used, these are pejorative terms, describing dispositions that are *never* appropriate. It is common to speak of "personal bias" or "personal prejudice" without meaning the adjective to do anything except emphasize the idiosyncratic nature of bias and prejudice, and certainly without implying that there is some other "nonpersonal," benign category of those mental states. In a similar vein, one speaks of an individual's "personal preference," without implying that he could also have a "nonpersonal preference." Secondly, interpreting the term "personal" to create a complete dichotomy between court-acquired and extrinsically acquired bias produces results so intolerable as to be absurd. Imagine, for example, a lengthy trial in which the presiding judge for the first time learns of an obscure religious sect, and acquires a passionate hatred for all its adherents. This would be "official" rather than "personal" bias, and would provide no basis for the judge's recusing himself.

It seems to us that the origin of the "extrajudicial source" doctrine, and the key to understanding its flexible scope (or the so-called "exceptions" to it), is simply the pejorative connotation of the words "bias or prejudice." Not *all* unfavorable disposition towards an individual (or his case) is properly described by those terms. One would not say, for example, that world opinion is biased or prejudiced against Adolf Hitler. The words connote a favorable or unfavorable disposition or opinion that is somehow *wrongful* or *inappropriate*, either because it is undeserved, or because it rests upon knowledge that the subject ought not to possess (for example, a criminal juror who has been biased or prejudiced by receipt of inadmissible evidence concerning the defendant's prior criminal activities), or because it is excessive in degree (for example, a criminal juror who is so inflamed by properly admitted evidence of a defendant's prior criminal activities that he will vote guilty regardless of the facts). The "extrajudicial source" doctrine is one application of this pejorativeness requirement to the terms "bias" and "prejudice" as they are used in §§ 144 and 455(b)(1) with specific reference to the work of judges.

The judge who presides at a trial may, upon completion of the evidence, be exceedingly ill disposed towards the defendant, who has been shown to be a thoroughly reprehensible person. But the judge is not thereby recusable for bias or prejudice, since his knowledge and the opinion it produced were properly and necessarily acquired in the course of the proceedings, and are indeed sometimes (as in a bench trial) necessary to completion of the judge's task. As Judge Jerome Frank pithily put it: "Impartiality is not gullibility. Disinterestedness does not mean child-like innocence. If the judge did not form judgments of the actors in those courthouse dramas called trials, he could never render decisions." * * * Also not subject to deprecatory characterization as "bias" or "prejudice" are opinions held by judges as a result of what they learned in earlier proceedings. It has long been regarded as normal and proper for a judge to sit in the same case upon its remand, and to sit in successive trials involving the same defendant.

It is wrong in theory, though it may not be too far off the mark as a practical matter, to suggest, as many opinions have, that "extrajudicial source" is the *only* basis for establishing disqualifying bias or prejudice. It is the only *common* basis, but not the exclusive one, since it is not the *exclusive* reason a predisposition can be wrongful or inappropriate. A favorable or unfavorable predisposition can also deserve to be characterized as "bias" or "prejudice" because, even though it springs from the facts adduced or the events occurring at trial, it is so extreme as to display clear inability to render fair judgment. * * *

As we have described, * * * the pejorative connotation of the terms "bias" and "prejudice" demands that they be applied only to judicial predispositions that go beyond what is normal and acceptable. We think there is an equivalent pejorative connotation, with equivalent consequences, to the term "partiality" [in § 455(a)]. See American Heritage Dictionary 1319 (3d ed. 1992) ("partiality" defined as "[f]avorable prejudice or bias"). A prospective juror in an insurance-claim case may be stricken as partial if he always votes for insurance companies; but not if he always votes for the party whom the terms of the contract support. "Partiality" does not refer to all favoritism, but only to such as is, for some reason, wrongful or inappropriate. Impartiality is not gullibility. Moreover, even if the pejorative connotation of "partiality" were not enough to import the "extrajudicial source" doctrine into § 455(a), the "reasonableness" limitation (recusal is required only if the judge's impartiality "might *reasonably* be questioned") would have the same effect. To demand the sort of "child-like innocence" that elimination of the "extrajudicial source" limitation would require is not reasonable. * * *

For all these reasons, we think that the "extrajudicial source" doctrine, as we have described it, applies to § 455(a). As we have described it, however, there is not much doctrine to the doctrine. The fact that an opinion held by a judge derives from a source outside judicial proceedings is not a *necessary* condition for "bias or prejudice" recusal, since predispositions developed during the course of a trial will sometimes (albeit rarely) suffice. Nor is it a *sufficient* condition for "bias or prejudice" recusal, since *some* opinions acquired outside the context of judicial proceedings (for example, the judge's view of the law acquired in scholarly reading) will *not* suffice. Since neither the presence of an extrajudicial source necessarily establishes bias, nor the absence of an extrajudicial source necessarily precludes bias, it would be better to speak of the existence of a significant (and often determinative) "extrajudicial source" *factor*, than of an "extrajudicial source" *doctrine*, in recusal jurisprudence.

The facts of the present case do not require us to describe the consequences of that factor in complete detail. It is enough for present purposes to say the following: First, judicial rulings alone almost never constitute valid basis for a bias or partiality motion. * * * In and of themselves (*i.e.*, apart from surrounding comments or accompanying opinion), they cannot possibly show reliance upon an extrajudicial source; and can only in the rarest circumstances evidence the degree of favoritism or antagonism required (as discussed below) when no extrajudicial source is involved. Almost invariably, they are proper grounds for appeal, not for recusal. Second, opinions formed by the judge on the basis of facts introduced or events occurring in the course of the current proceedings, or of prior proceedings, do not constitute a basis for a bias or partiality motion unless they display a deep-seated favoritism or antagonism that would make fair judgment impossible. Thus, judicial remarks during the course of a trial that are critical or disapproving of, or even hostile to, counsel, the parties, or their cases, ordinarily do not support a bias or partiality challenge. They *may* do so if they reveal an opinion that derives from an extrajudicial source; and they *will* do so if they reveal such a high degree of favoritism or antagonism as to make fair judgment impossible. * * * *Not* establishing bias or partiality, however, are expressions of impatience, dissatisfaction, annoyance, and even anger, that are within the bounds of what imperfect men and women, even after having been confirmed as federal judges, sometimes display. A judge's ordinary efforts at courtroom administration—even a stern and short-tempered judge's ordinary efforts at courtroom administration—remain immune.

III

[The court proceeded to find that none of the actions complained of warranted disqualification, and affirmed the judgment below.]

JUSTICE KENNEDY, with whom JUSTICE BLACKMUN, JUSTICE STEVENS, and JUSTICE SOUTER join, concurring in the judgment. * * *

I must part * * * from the Court's adoption of a standard that places all but dispositive weight upon the source of the alleged disqualification. The Court holds that opinions arising during the course of judicial proceedings require disqualification under § 455(a) only if they "display a deep-seated favoritism or antagonism that would make fair judgment impossible." * * * That standard is not a fair interpretation of the statute, and is quite insufficient to serve and protect the integrity of the courts. In practical effect, the Court's standard will be difficult to distinguish from a *per se* extrajudicial source rule, the very result the Court professes to reject.

The Court's "impossibility of fair judgment" test bears little resemblance to the objective standard Congress adopted in § 455(a): whether a judge's "impartiality might reasonably be questioned." The statutory standard, which the Court preserves for allegations of an extrajudicial nature, asks whether there is an appearance of partiality. * * * The Court's standard, in contrast, asks whether fair judgment is impossible, and if this test demands some direct inquiry to the judge's actual, rather than apparent, state of mind, it defeats the underlying goal of § 455(a): to avoid the appearance of partiality even when no partiality exists.

And in all events, the "impossibility of fair judgment" standard remains troubling due to its limited, almost preclusive character. As I interpret it, a § 455(a) challenge would fail even if it were shown that an unfair hearing were likely, for it could be argued that a fair hearing would be possible nonetheless. The integrity of the courts, as well as the interests of the parties and the public, are ill served by this rule. There are bound to be circumstances where a judge's demeanor or attitude would raise reasonable questions concerning impartiality but would not devolve to the point where one would think fair judgment impossible. * * *

The standard that ought to be adopted for all allegations of an apparent fixed predisposition, extrajudicial or otherwise, follows from the statute itself: Disqualification is required if an objective observer would entertain reasonable questions about the judge's impartiality. If a judge's attitude or state of mind leads a detached observer to conclude that a fair and impartial hearing is unlikely, the judge must be disqualified. Indeed, in such circumstances, I should think that any judge who understands the judicial office and oath would be the first to insist that another judge hear the case. * * *

Although the source of an alleged disqualification may be relevant in determining whether there is a reasonable appearance of impartiality, that determination can be explained in a straightforward manner without resort to a nearly dispositive extrajudicial source factor. I would apply the statute as written to all charges of partiality, extrajudicial or otherwise, secure in my view that district and appellate judges possess the wisdom and good sense to distinguish substantial from insufficient allegations and that our rules, as so interpreted, are sufficient to correct the occasional departure.

NOTES ON BASES OF DISQUALIFICATION

1. **When Does the Appearance of Judicial Partiality Become a Constitutional Problem?** In *Caperton v. A.T. Massey Coal Co., Inc.*, 556 U.S. 868 (2009), the court had before it a decision of the West Virginia Supreme Court of Appeals that reversed a trial court verdict and judgment against Massey and affiliated companies, awarding Caperton and affiliated companies $50 million in compensatory and punitive damages for fraud and tortious interference with contract. After the trial court's judgment was entered and post-trial motions denied, but before Massey filed its appeal, an election was held, in which one incumbent justice of the appellate court was challenged by a lawyer named Benjamin. Massey's chairman and principal officer donated $2.5 million to a political action committee supporting Benjamin and independently spent another $500k in Benjamin's favor—totaling more than half of all the funds expended in favor of Benjamin. Benjamin won the election and took office on the court.

Before Massey's appeal was filed, the Caperton plaintiffs moved to disqualify Benjamin from sitting on the appeal, but he refused to recuse himself, finding no objective evidence to show bias. The appeal was heard and the court voted—by a 3–2 vote with Benjamin in the majority—to reverse the judgment, on the grounds that the suit was barred by a contractual provision and by the res judicata effect of an out-of-state judgment. In their motion for rehearing, the plaintiffs renewed their recusal motion with respect to Benjamin and added a motion to recuse another justice because of his public friendship with Massey's chairman, while the defendants countered with a motion to recuse a third justice who had made public remarks critical of the chairman. The other two did recuse, but Benjamin did not. Benjamin then became acting chief justice and appointed replacements for the two recused members of the court. With Benjamin voting in the majority, the court again decided 3–2 to reverse the trial court judgment. The dissenters challenged not only the merits of the decision but also the refusal of Benjamin to recuse, citing due process.

After the plaintiffs filed their petition for certiorari with the U.S. Supreme Court on due process grounds, Benjamin filed a concurring opinion in the state court, justifying his refusal to recuse on the ground that he was not objectively biased and that a recusal based on an "appearance" standard would open the court to partisan manipulation. The Supreme Court granted certiorari and ultimately decided, on a 5–4 vote, to reverse the state supreme court's judgment on the ground that Benjamin's participation denied due process to the plaintiffs under the 14th Amendment.

Noting that only two types of conflict of interest on the part of a non-recusing judge had been held to create a denial of due process (direct financial interest in the outcome and trying criminal contempt charges based on personal attacks against the judge himself), and rejecting a standard of "actual bias" as too subjective when it is the conflicted judge alone who is deciding whether or not to recuse, Justice Kennedy's opinion for the majority applied an "objective" standard:

> Due process requires an objective inquiry into whether the contributor's influence on the election under all the circumstances "would offer a possible temptation to the average ... judge to ... lead him not to hold the balance nice, clear and true." * * * In an election decided by fewer than 50,000 votes (382,036 to 334,301), * * * Blankenship's campaign contributions—in comparison to the total amount contributed to the campaign, as well as the total amount spent in the election—had a significant and disproportionate influence on the electoral outcome. And the risk that Blankenship's influence engendered actual bias is sufficiently substantial that it "must be forbidden if the guarantee of due process is to be adequately implemented."

556 U.S. at 885. Justice Kennedy emphasized that this, like the other cases where due process had been held to require recusal, was extraordinary, "extreme by any measure." *Id.* at 887.

Chief Justice Roberts' dissenting opinion, on the other hand, saw the majority's rationale as infusing the issue with uncertainty. After listing forty "fundamental questions" that courts will now have to decide in applying the majority's rationale, Chief Justice Roberts said:

> The Court's inability to formulate a "judicially discernible and manageable standard" strongly counsels against the recognition of a novel constitutional right. * * * The need to consider these and countless other questions helps explain why the common law and this Court's constitutional jurisprudence have never required disqualification on such vague grounds as "probability" or "appearance" of bias. * * *

> It is an old cliché, but sometimes the cure is worse than the disease. I am sure there are cases where a "probability of bias" should lead the prudent judge to step aside, but the judge fails to do so. Maybe this is one of them. But I believe that opening the door to recusal claims under the Due Process Clause, for an amorphous "probability of bias," will itself

bring our judicial system into undeserved disrepute, and diminish the confidence of the American people in the fairness and integrity of their courts. I hope I am wrong.

Id. at 898–99 and 902. For discussions of this case and its potential ramifications, see Ronald D. Rotunda, *Judicial Disqualification in the Aftermath of Caperton v. A.T. Massey Coal Co.*, 60 Syracuse L.Rev. 247 (2010), and Molly McLucas, Comment, *The Need for Effective Recusal Standards for an Elected Judiciary*, 42 Loy.L.A.L.Rev. 671 (2009).

2. **Bias Demonstrated by Conduct During Proceedings:** When would the limits of the extrajudicial source rule as outlined by Justice Scalia in *Liteky* be met? In *Sentis Group, Inc. v. Shell Oil Co.*, 559 F.3d 888 (8th Cir. 2009), a breach of business contract case, the trial judge dismissed the plaintiffs' case before trial as a sanction for "systematic abuse of the discovery process," after denying the plaintiffs' motion to recuse himself for appearance of partiality. *Id.* at 906. On appeal, a panel of the Eighth Circuit held the bases for the trial judge's ruling to be inadequately supported, and remanded the case for reconsideration of the dismissal, but directed that the case be reassigned to another judge. In doing so, the court acknowledged that there was no extrajudicial source for the trial judge's appearance of partiality, but concluded it was a case of circumstances that "reflect a sufficiently high degree of antagonism to require reassignment," citing *Liteky* as "rejecting strict application of the extrajudicial source doctrine." *Id.* at 904. The court summarized the circumstances leading up to and surrounding the judge's ruling as follows:

> In the course of numerous in-person and telephone conferences and hearings, the court directed profanities at Plaintiffs or Plaintiffs' counsel over fifteen times. In addition, at the December 15 sanctions hearing, the court denied Plaintiffs a meaningful opportunity to respond following Defendants' lengthy presentation, and in doing so, misconstrued the language of its own discovery orders and dismissed Plaintiffs' attempt to explain those orders. The court adopted Defendants' characterization of the four discovery orders as all having required production of the same "Walls documents." This was the case even though the first three orders had temporal or qualitative limitations on the documents subject to the order, and the third order demanded only the production of one document. When Plaintiffs attempted to explain at the sanction hearing "that you have not ruled four times to give them those 58 documents," the district court cut off Plaintiffs and moved toward dismissal.

Id. at 904–05. A dissent would have sustained the trial judge's ruling, not only finding no clear error in determining or articulating the grounds for the sanction but also disagreeing that the judge's behavior met the *Liteky* standard for disqualifying a judge absent extrajudicial sources.

In other cases the influence of an extrajudicial source is not entirely clear. In *Valdes–Fauli v. Valdes–Fauli*, 903 So.2d 214 (Fla.Dist.Ct.App. 2005), a marriage dissolution case involving a wealthy husband and a civically active wife married for 32 years, the following dialogue between judge and wife was held to demonstrate a disqualifying appearance of impartiality:

> The Court: What do you want to do with your life?

Mrs. Valdes–Fauli: I have been involved with a number of charitable organizations over the last several years. I'm at present the chairman of the Miami Museum of Science, the Planetarium.

The Court: Awesome. A wonderful facility, wonderful program.

Mrs. Valdes–Fauli: Thank you. I'm very, very enthusiastic.

The Court: You are a volunteer without being paid?

Mrs. Valdes–Fauli: I'm not paid, no sir.

The Court: So if you want to continue those charitable pursuits in a voluntary position as opposed to being paid—

Mrs. Valdes–Fauli: Yes.

The Court: So then you are seeking alimony from your husband.

Mrs. Valdes–Fauli: Yes.

The Court: So that you could pursue that?

Mrs. Valdes–Fauli: So that I can continue to live the life that I've lived for the last many years.

The Court: Right, which is what your lawyers have been telling you, is that right? I'm not asking specifically what they told you, but that is the standard that's in all of these books I've read. **So do you think you're going to end up being an alimony drone?**

Mrs. Valdes–Fauli: **I'm not sure what that means, sir.**

The Court: **Drone. Do you know what a drone is? A queen in a hive is a drone.**

Mrs. Valdes–Fauli: **You mean a worker?**

The Court: **No, because you don't want to be a worker, right?**

Mrs. Valdes–Fauli: **Sir, I don't want to have to go and get a job. I don't want to.**

Later in the hearing, when the wife expressed her feelings regarding the demise of her marriage, the trial court judge referred to her as a "woman scorned." When the wife agreed with the judge that she "need[ed] some closure," the trial court judge remarked that "closure" was the last thing she was going to get if she persisted with her claims:

The Court: And the way to get that closure is once I rule you'll take all your appeals, spend another couple of hundred thousand dollars, the Third DCA will say I'm right or not, in all probability they'll say I was right. I have a lot of discretion as long as I make specific findings.

Id. at 215–16 (emphasis added by the appellate court). The appellate court granted Ms. Valdes–Fauli's petition for disqualification of the trial judge after finding that "taken separately or all together, the trial court's words and actions reasonably gave the wife a legitimate fear that she would not receive a fair trial in this matter." *Id.* at 218.

Consider also *State v. Perez*, 813 A.2d 597 (N.J.Super.Ct.App.Div. 2003), where the following dialogue occurred:

[DEFENSE COUNSEL]: My client says he wants an interpreter.

THE COURT: For what language?

MR. PEREZ: Spanish.

THE COURT: How do you know what I just said?

(No audible response.)

THE COURT: You speak English.

[DEFENSE COUNSEL]: He—he understands English. It's not his first language.

THE COURT: When are we going to stop this.

[DEFENSE COUNSEL]: I'm just telling you—

THE COURT: Can I go into court and say, I want a Celtic interpreter?

[DEFENSE COUNSEL]: I'm just telling you what he told me, Judge.

THE COURT: Hey, I'm Irish. I want somebody who speaks Irish. That's it. The fact that I speak English, too, too bad. I want somebody who speaks Irish. These Spanish people coming in here and saying, I want an interpreter. Well, you speak English.

So what? I want an interpreter. Somewhere, this has got to stop. So, somebody racks up $200.00 an hour for interpreting and the guy speaks perfect English, proved by the fact that he understood exactly what you and I just said.

Why don't you speak English, sir?

(No audible response.)

THE COURT: Why do you want an interpreter?

(No audible response.)

THE COURT: You did learn in a hurry, didn't you?

(Laughter)

THE COURT: You've got to give them credit. They just—he picked up on that quick.

Well, I guess I better do it. I'd have the ACLU and the people marching outside with signs and so forth.

Id. at 598–99. The appellate court noted that while the judge granted the request, he did so in a manner that reflected bias, and not simply based on evidence that the particular defendant was misrepresenting his need, but on an imputed characteristic of the ethnic group to which he belongs. It ordered a new trial before a different judge. While the bias could have been simple prejudice brought into the courtroom, it could easily have been one formed on the basis of judicial experience. In any event, the bias in question is clearly prohibited by Model Code of Judicial Conduct Rule 2.3 (formerly Canon 3B(5) & (6)).

3. **Pre–Appointment Statements of Opinion on Issues in the Case:** In *Laird v. Tatum*, 409 U.S. 824 (1972) (memorandum by Justice Rehnquist), surveillance targets brought a civil suit against the Department of Defense. The case was defended by lawyers in the Justice Department while Mr. Rehnquist was head of the Department's Office of Legal Counsel. The

case had reached the appellate level when Mr. Rehnquist was appointed to the Court. When the case came to the Court on appeal, Justice Rehnquist voted with the majority overturning the plaintiffs' claims, and they sought *nunc pro tunc* to have him recuse himself because of his prior involvement in the case. As he described it in his memorandum refusing to recuse himself, his involvement consisted in having referred to an aspect of the case, on the basis of a briefing by Department attorneys responsible for defending it, in testimony before a congressional committee concerned with surveillance generally. His memorandum also indicated that he had expressed his opinion, both in this testimony and in other speeches, that government surveillance of the sort complained of in the case was constitutional. With respect to the public statements of opinion, Justice Rehnquist said:

> I do not doubt that a litigant in the position of respondents would much prefer to argue his case before a Court none of whose members had expressed the views that I expressed about the relationship between surveillance and First Amendment rights while serving as an Assistant Attorney General. * * *

> Since most Justices come to this bench no earlier than their middle years, it would be unusual if they had not by that time formulated at least some tentative notions which would influence them in their interpretation of the sweeping clauses of the Constitution and their interaction with one another. It would be not merely unusual, but extraordinary, if they had not at least given opinions as to constitutional issues in their previous legal careers. Proof that a Justice's mind at the time he joined the Court was a complete *tabula rasa* in the area of constitutional adjudication would be evidence of lack of qualification, not lack of bias.

> Yet whether these opinions have become at all widely known may depend entirely on happenstance. With respect to those who come here directly from private life, such comments or opinions may never have been publicly uttered. But it would be unusual if those coming from policy making divisions in the Executive Branch, from the Senate or House of Representatives, or from positions in state government had not divulged at least some hint of their general approach to public affairs, if not as to particular issues of law. Indeed, the clearest case of all is that of a Justice who comes to this Court from a lower court, and has, while sitting as a judge of the lower court, had occasion to pass on an issue which later comes before this Court. No more compelling example could be found of a situation in which a Justice had previously committed himself. Yet it is not and could not rationally be suggested that, so long as the cases be different, a Justice of this Court should disqualify himself for that reason. * * *

> The fact that some aspect of these propensities may have been publicly articulated prior to coming to this Court cannot, in my opinion, be regarded as anything more than a random circumstance which should not by itself form a basis for disqualification.

409 U.S. at 833–36.

Justice Rehnquist relied primarily on the pre–1974 version of 28 U.S.C. § 455, quoted in *Liteky* (immediately before the text of the 1974 version).

Would the decision have been otherwise, if the present version of § 455 had governed? *See* 28 U.S.C. § 455(b)(3), as set forth in *Liteky* and still in force in 2012, which requires recusal if a justice or judge "expressed an opinion concerning the merits of the particular case in controversy" as a government employee. For an argument to the effect that the ABA's Model Code of Judicial Conduct (1972)—which eventually formed a large part of the basis for the 1974 amendment of § 455—would have called for a different result in *Laird*, see Robert H. Aronson, Note, *Disqualification of Judges for Bias or Prejudice—A New Approach*, 1972 Utah L.Rev. 448, 462.

It appears that disqualification or recusal of federal judges solely on the basis of prior public statements on general issues of law has not occurred since *Laird* and the 1974 revision. *See* James J. Alfini, Jeffrey M. Shaman & Steven Lubet, Judicial Conduct and Ethics § 12.07C (4th ed. 2010).

4. **Public Statements by a Sitting Judge Concerning Pending or Impending Cases:** Quite a different matter are public statements regarding the merits of cases that are pending before the judge's court or before lower courts whose judgments may be subject to review in her court. In *Elk Grove Unified School District v. Newdow,* 540 U.S. 945 (2003), certiorari was granted to review a judgment of the Ninth Circuit holding in *Newdow v. United States Congress*, 328 F.3d 466 (9th Cir. 2003), that a public school's policy requiring teachers to lead recitation of the Pledge of Allegiance is a violation of the Establishment Clause of the First Amendment, because of the presence of the phrase "under God" in the Pledge. After the petition for certiorari was filed, the respondent Newdow requested that Justice Scalia recuse himself because of remarks made at a public speaking engagement after the Ninth Circuit's judgment had been handed down, in which he was reported to have referred to that decision as an example of mistaken attempts to "exclude God from the public forums and from political life." Newdow alleged that such remarks violated the Code of Conduct for United States Judges, Canon 3A(6), directing that judges should avoid public comment on the merits of a pending or impending action. *See* Charles Lane, *High Court to Consider Pledge in Schools: Scalia Recuses Himself from California Case*, Wash. Post, Oct. 15, 2003, at A1. Justice Scalia recused himself from all participation in the case, without comment. Rule 2.10(A) (formerly Canon 3B(9)) of the ABA's Model Code of Judicial Conduct uses the more categorical "shall not" form, but a much broader and vaguer definition prohibiting "any public statement that might reasonably be expected to affect the outcome or impair the fairness of a matter." Would the remarks attributed to Justice Scalia violate that provision?

In a particularly highly publicized case, *United States v. Microsoft Corp.*, 253 F.3d 34 (D.C.Cir. 2001), the trial judge in a major antitrust matter was found to have engaged in extensive interviews with reporters (under a pledge of secrecy until after judgment) throughout the trial. He also participated in interviews and public speaking engagements after he handed down his judgment, concerning the course of the trial, the merits of particular defenses asserted by Microsoft, the credibility of its witnesses, its overall behavior in the marketplace, and the appropriateness of particular remedies. On appeal from his judgment against Microsoft, the Court of Appeals held that these repeated violations of Canons 3A(6) and 3A(4) of the Code of Conduct for

United States Judges required disqualification of the judge on remand for further proceedings. *See also In re Boston's Children First*, 244 F.3d 164 (1st Cir. 2001).

On the other hand, Rule 2.10(D) (formerly Canon 3B(9)) of the ABA's Model Code of Judicial Conduct, like its earlier ABA and federal counterparts, specifically allows judges to "explain court procedures." For an application of this exception, see *Ex parte Monsanto Co.*, 862 So.2d 595 (Ala. 2003), a mass toxic tort case that also received extensive publicity, in which the judge gave frequent media interviews, where the Alabama Supreme Court (after a comprehensive review of the case law) held that Monsanto's petition for disqualification did not disclose any public statements that did not fit within the concept of unbiased public explanation of procedures.

5. **Consequences of Recusal in the U.S. Supreme Court:** Justice Rehnquist added, as a final point in his *Laird* memorandum, that the situation with disqualification or recusal of Supreme Court Justices is different from that of other federal judges, because there is no substitution of judges allowed on the Court. Thus, his recusal would have meant that the Court would decide with eight Justices rather than nine. (Indeed, since his vote was part of a 5–4 majority to reverse the Court of Appeals, his recusal would have changed the outcome by leaving the Court in a 4–4 division, preventing reversal.) Is this a sufficient reason for denying recusal, even when the criteria for recusal under section 455 are met? Note that Justice Scalia did not invoke any such consideration. For discussion of the issue, see James J. Alfini, et al., *supra* note 3. Also see the 2011 annual report by Chief Justice Roberts, devoted to questions of application of principles of judicial ethics to the Supreme Court, which noted there is no higher court to review U.S. Supreme Court recusal decisions and that there are no substitutes for recused U.S. Supreme Court justices. Chief Justice Roberts then concluded that a justice "cannot withdraw from a case as a matter of convenience or simply to avoid controversy" but instead "has an obligation to the Court to be sure of the need to recuse before deciding to withdraw." 2011 Year–End Report on the Federal Judiciary, http://www.supremecourt.gov/publicinfo/year-end/2011 year-endreport.pdf, at 9. The Chief Justice also noted that while the Code of Conduct for United States Judges does not by its terms apply to Supreme Court justices, they do treat it as a source of guidance. *Id.* at 3–4.

6. **Prior Judicial Involvement with Matter or Party:** The 2007 revision of the Model Code of Judicial Conduct Rule 2.11 added, as a disqualifying criterion, that the judge "previously presided as a judge over the matter in another court." Rule 2.11(A)(6)(d). This presumably would not apply when a member of a panel of an appellate court participates in an *en banc* hearing in the same court. Previous versions of the Code contained no such provision, and under them such prior judicial involvement normally did not satisfy the general standard for disqualification. In *State v. Reeter*, 848 S.W.2d 560 (Mo.Ct.App. 1993), the defendant was charged with assault and burglary. The trial judge had, three days after the alleged assault on the defendant's wife and another person, presided over the wife's dissolution proceeding against the defendant, ruled in favor of the wife on her claim, and observed the wife's cuts and bruises. It was held that neither the ruling nor the observation constituted proper bases for disqualification of the judge from

the criminal trial. Notably, the Missouri Supreme Court, in its revision of its Code of Judicial Conduct after the 2007 ABA revision, did not adopt Rule 2.11(A)(6)(d).

7. **Prior Service as Counsel:** Model Code of Judicial Conduct Rule 2.11(A)(6)(a) (formerly Canon 3E(1)(b)) requires recusal if the judge "served as a lawyer in the matter in controversy," and Rule 2.11(A)(1) (formerly Canon 3E(1)(a)) requires it if "the judge has personal knowledge of facts that are in dispute in the proceeding." Defendants in criminal cases are generally unsuccessful in seeking to disqualify judges who have previously acted as prosecutors against the defendant in unrelated cases. *See, e.g., Smith v. State*, 795 So.2d 788 (Ala.Crim.App. 2000); *People v. Mitchell*, 734 N.Y.S.2d 252 (App.Div. 2001). However, Alaska has adopted a modification of the Code of Judicial Conduct that disqualifies a judge who has prosecuted the defendant within two years prior to the present case, regardless of the relationship between the matters. *See Mustafoski v. State*, 867 P.2d 824 (Alaska Ct.App. 1994).

If the matters are related, however, disqualification may be required. In *Collins v. Joshi*, 611 So.2d 898 (Miss. 1992), and *Davis v. Neshoba County General Hospital*, 611 So.2d 904 (Miss. 1992), a trial judge presided over four medical malpractice cases against a hospital for which he had been general attorney and against a staff physician who was hired during that representation. In each case, the plaintiff's attorney and the principal plaintiff's expert witness were also the same. In one such case he recused himself, but he refused recusal in the two cited cases on the ground of inconvenience to the parties. The Mississippi Supreme Court held that the judge's impartiality might reasonably be questioned under the circumstances, and the general standard required recusal. It further held that inconvenience was not a sufficient reason for refusing recusal.

Some jurisdictions have added across-the-board party- or counsel-bound rules such as that of Illinois Supreme Court Rule 63C(1)(c) (2007), where disqualification is automatic if the judge has been associated in private practice within the last three years with an attorney representing a party in the case, or has represented a present party within the last seven years.

8. **Extrajudicial Relationship with Parties, Lawyers, or Witnesses:** Model Code of Judicial Conduct Rule 2.11(A)(2) (formerly Canon 3E(1)(d)) addresses the issue of disqualification when a judge is or is related to a party, a lawyer, or a material witness in the proceeding. In *Pannell v. State*, 71 S.W.3d 720 (Tenn.Crim.App. 2001), the judge was the stepfather of the victim, who had lived in the judge's home until the judge and the victim's mother divorced eight years before the case. Even though the judge had not maintained a relationship with the victim since the divorce, the court held this to be a disqualifying relationship, although cured by the defendant's consent. In *Bethesda Memorial Hospital, Inc. v. Cassone*, 807 So.2d 142 (Fla.Dist.Ct.App. 2002), a debt collection case, it was held that the judge ought to have granted a motion to disqualify submitted by the plaintiff, which alleged that the judge was currently involved in a debt collection matter concerning his late wife's estate, and that he and his wife had previously been involved with a collection matter in which they had claimed harassment of the

same kind as the debtor was claiming in the present case. In both matters, the collection agency was an affiliate of the present plaintiff. On the other hand, in *United States v. Cole*, 293 F.3d 153 (4th Cir. 2002), it was proper to deny the defendant's motion to disqualify where an important prosecution witness was the son of the judge's godparents, but the judge had not seen the witness for ten years prior to his appearance and insisted that he could be impartial in the matter.

F(2) PROCEDURES FOR DISQUALIFICATION

UNITED STATES v. SYKES

United States Court of Appeals, Seventh Circuit, 1993.
7 F.3d 1331.

DIAMOND ROVNER, CIRCUIT JUDGE.

[Lydia Sykes pled guilty to one count of using a false social security number to obtain credit. Other counts were dismissed, but were taken into account in determining sentence. She appealed from her sentence. One of the grounds for her appeal was that the judge should have recused himself from the sentencing phase.]

Sykes also argues that the district court should have recused itself because the court's comments at Sykes' plea hearing evidenced actual prejudice that affected her sentence. Because we are remanding the case for resentencing, it is incumbent on us to consider this argument.

The allegations of prejudice stem from the district court's response to a question raised by Sykes' former counsel about the particular section of the Sentencing Guidelines that would be used to calculate Sykes' base offense level. The district court warned that it would not accept the plea if the parties had stipulated to a particular Guidelines application. * * * After the government attorney assured the district court that no such agreement had been made, the court stated:

> Well, I've made it clear, never as clear as I've had to make at this—as I have at this time, but I think that the best way to proceed at this time is not to accept the plea agreement because I do know the concerns—in fact, I read an article written by someone I believe from Mr. Feingold's [Sykes' attorney at the time] office by the name of Bates who suggested the concerns he had with the manner in which the sentencing guidelines operate in the Western District of Wisconsin, and I take judicial notice of that. And I do see that this is an attempt to get around the sentencing guidelines, and I'm not going to accept it. * * *

The district court ultimately accepted Sykes' plea, after satisfying itself that the plea was not based on a representation that a particular section of the Guidelines would apply. The court sentenced Sykes approximately two months later. Sykes' counsel then moved to withdraw, and Sykes submitted her affidavit suggesting that the district court was biased because of the comments the court made at the guilty plea hearing. * * *

The district court construed Sykes' affidavit as a request for recusal under 28 U.S.C. § 144, which requires recusal "if a party files a timely and sufficient affidavit that the judge has 'a personal bias or prejudice' against [her]." *United States v. Balistrieri*, 779 F.2d 1191, 1199 (7th Cir. 1985). The district court denied the motion on the grounds that it was untimely, that it was not accompanied by a certificate of counsel as required by the statute, and that the court was not prejudiced against Sykes. * * * We review that determination de novo. * * *

Recusal under section 144 is mandatory once a party submits a timely and sufficient affidavit and her counsel presents a certificate stating that the affidavit is made in good faith. * * * A section 144 affidavit is not timely unless filed " 'at the earliest moment after [the movant acquires] knowledge of the facts demonstrating the basis for such disqualification.' " *United States v. Barnes*, 909 F.2d 1059, 1071 (7th Cir.1990) (quoting *United States v. Patrick*, 542 F.2d 381, 390 (7th Cir.1976), *cert. denied*, 430 U.S. 931, 97 S.Ct. 1551, 51 L.Ed.2d 775 (1977)). In passing on the legal sufficiency of the affidavit, the court must assume the truth of its factual assertions even if it "knows them to be false." * * * At the same time, the facts averred must be sufficiently definite and particular to convince a reasonable person that bias exists; simple conclusions, opinions, or rumors are insufficient. * * * Because the statute "is heavily weighed in favor of recusal," its requirements are to be strictly construed to prevent abuse. *Balistrieri*, 779 F.2d at 1199.

Sykes' affidavit fails to satisfy the stringent requirements of section 144 in a number of respects. First, the affidavit was untimely. Sykes' claim was based on the district court's remarks at the June 12, 1992 change of plea hearing. Yet the affidavit was not filed until August 19, after Sykes already had been sentenced. Two months after the allegedly prejudicial statement is certainly not "at the earliest possible moment" after discovery of the prejudice. * * *

Moreover, the averments in Sykes' affidavit focused more on the district court's alleged bias against her counsel and his law firm than against Sykes herself. Indeed, Sykes acknowledges that she repeatedly "expressed her belief to counsel and others * * * that the Trial Judge was prejudiced against her as expressed in the Court's statements about opinions expressed by members of the law firm of her counsel." * * * The prejudice alleged is therefore derivative of a purported bias against counsel and his law firm. Although we have not yet considered the question, other circuits have held that bias against counsel alone is insufficient because "section 144 makes clear on its face * * * that '[a]ntipathy to an attorney is insufficient grounds for disqualification of a judge because it is not indicative of extrajudicial bias against a "party." ' " *Souder v. Owens–Corning Fiberglas Corp.*, 939 F.2d 647, 653 (8th Cir.1991) (quoting *Gilbert v. City of Little Rock*, 722 F.2d 1390, 1398 (8th Cir.1983), *cert. denied*, 466 U.S. 972, 104 S.Ct. 2347, 80 L.Ed.2d 820 (1984)) * * *. *Souder* acknowledged, however, that in some circumstances, "bias against an attorney can reasonably be imputed to a party" (939 F.2d at 653), and we agree. But the party seeking recusal on that theory must allege facts suggesting that the alleged bias against counsel might extend to the party. * * * The allegations to that effect here are merely conclusory and insufficient to require recusal under section 144.

In any event, any prejudice here would presumably have been alleviated by the appointment of new counsel. This may explain why the affidavit was not submitted in connection with a motion for recusal under section 144, but rather a motion for the withdrawal of Sykes' former counsel. It is apparently for this reason that the affidavit was not accompanied by "a certificate of counsel of record stating that it is made in good faith," as required by the statute.

Given the procedural and substantive shortcomings of Sykes' affidavit, recusal was not required. The case will be remanded to Judge Shabaz for resentencing in accordance with this opinion. * * *

UNITED STATES v. COOLEY

United States Court of Appeals, Tenth Circuit, 1993.
1 F.3d 985.

STEPHEN H. ANDERSON, CIRCUIT JUDGE.

[The anti-abortion group Operation Rescue held a summer-long protest at clinics in Wichita, Kansas, in 1991. The clinics obtained a preliminary injunction against blocking access to their facilities, which the protesters openly vowed to disobey. In August, about forty protesters stormed the fences and walls around a clinic and closed it from the inside, after which they were arrested and charged with obstructing the federal marshals in the performance of their duty to enforce the injunction. A number of the defendants moved, under 28 U.S.C. § 455(a) or (b)(1), to disqualify the federal judge who issued the preliminary injunction and who would be trying the criminal charges, on the ground that various public statements by him, both in court and in local and national media, showed bias or partiality. The remarks generally showed anger at the open defiance of his injunction and threatened harsh penalties for those who violate it. The judge had been subjected to threats of death or violence, and even excommunication from his church, throughout the summer.

The judge denied the motions on the ground that he was not biased against the defendants, because previous actions by him to secure compliance with the injunction were irrelevant to the defendants' guilt or innocence. Although the defendants' motions were also based on section 144, the Court of Appeals dealt with them under section 455.]

II.

DISCUSSION

A. *Disqualification.*

Title 28 U.S.C. § 455(a) * * * is part of a 1974 amendment to the statute, enacted for the purpose of clarifying and broadening the grounds for judicial disqualification. "The general language of subsection (a) was designed to promote public confidence in the integrity of the judicial process by replacing the subjective ['in the opinion of the judge'] standard with an objective test." *Liljeberg v. Health Servs. Acquisition Corp.*, 486 U.S. 847, 858 n.7, 108 S.Ct. 2194, 2202, n.7, 100 L.Ed.2d 855 (1988). * * * The subsection "applies to the varied and unpredictable situations not subject to reasonable legislative definition in which judges must act to protect the very appearance of impartiality." *United States v. Gipson*, 835 F.2d 1323, 1325 (10th Cir. 1988). Under it a judge has a continuing duty to recuse before, during, or, in some circumstances, after a proceeding, if the judge concludes that sufficient factual grounds exist to cause an objective observer reasonably to question the judge's impartiality. * * * However, this court has held that "[a] motion to recuse under section 455(a) must be timely filed." * * *

In applying § 455(a), the judge's actual state of mind, purity of heart, incorruptibility, or lack of partiality are not the issue. * * * The test in this circuit is " 'whether a reasonable person, knowing all the relevant facts, would harbor doubts about the judge's impartiality.' " * * * The standard is purely objective. The inquiry is limited to outward manifestations and reasonable inferences drawn therefrom. In applying the test, the initial inquiry is whether a reasonable *factual* basis exists for calling the judge's impartiality into question. * * *

Judicial gloss on the statute by way of various limitations stems from a necessary emphasis on the term "reasonably" in section 455(a). We have stressed that "section 455(a) must not be so broadly construed that it becomes, in effect, presumptive, so that recusal is mandated upon the merest unsubstantiated suggestion of personal bias or prejudice." * * * The statute is not intended to give litigants a veto power over sitting judges, or a vehicle for obtaining a judge of their choice. * * *

We review the denial of a motion to recuse under § 455(a) for abuse of discretion. * * * Applying the factors outlined above, we have no difficulty concluding in this case that the district judge did not abuse his discretion by denying the defendants' motions to recuse based on every ground except one: the judge's appearance and statements on the network news program "Nightline." Because of insufficient facts in the record we do not address the effect of other interviews which the judge may have granted the "media" regarding the abortion protests and his order.

Except for the one television appearance, the defendants' general allegations of impropriety either state no reasonable basis for recusal, or are so lacking in particularity and substantiation as to fall short of establishing the necessary factual predicate for any meaningful review. The judge's appearance on Nightline is another matter, however. The program and interviewer, Barbara Walters, were identified and the subject was repeatedly brought to the court's attention. The court not only did not deny either the television appearance or its subject matter—the abortion protests taking place at Wichita clinics, including the Tiller clinic—it tacitly acknowledged the point. * * * In its comments at one point, the court acknowledged seeing to it, both in and out of court, that "these people whose purpose it is to close these clinics by illegal means ... understood fairly so, firmly so, that this order [the court's injunction prohibiting obstruction of access to the clinics] would be honored." * * *

The court made no analysis under § 455(a) of its television appearance except to state that the only relevant consideration was the specific charge against these defendants, and that the court knew nothing about the facts of their cases, and had no predisposition as to their guilt or innocence of the charges. But § 455(a) asks a broader question which, on these facts, makes it impossible to take these cases out of context. The protests and tactics of the protesters at the Wichita clinics, and the court's order forbidding obstruction of ingress and egress, are subjects and events with which these cases are inextricably intertwined.

Two messages were conveyed by the judge's appearance on national television in the midst of these events. One message consisted of the words actually spoken regarding the protesters' apparent plan to bar access to the clinics, and the judge's resolve to see his order prohibiting such actions enforced. The other was the judge's expressive conduct in deliberately making the choice to appear in such a forum at a sensitive time to deliver strong views on matters which were likely to be ongoing before him. Together, these messages unmistakenly conveyed an uncommon interest and degree of personal involvement in the subject matter. It was an unusual thing for a judge to do, and it unavoidably created the appearance that the judge had become an active participant in bringing law and order to bear on the protesters, rather than remaining as a detached adjudicator.

We conclude that at least after the judge's volunteer appearance on national television to state his views regarding the ongoing protests, the protesters, and his determination that his injunction was going to be obeyed, a reasonable person would harbor a justified doubt as to his impartiality in the case involving these defendants. Accordingly, we hold that the district judge abused his discretion when he denied the defendants' motions under § 455(a) to disqualify himself from sitting on these cases.

Because of this holding it is unnecessary for us to address the allegations under § 144 or § 455(b)(1) of actual bias against the defendants. We do note, however, that the record of the proceedings below, including the sentences imposed, discloses no bias. To the contrary, it appears that the district judge was courteous to the defendants and sedulously protected their rights.

NOTES ON PROCEDURES FOR DISQUALIFYING JUDGES AND REMITTAL OF DISQUALIFICATION

1. **Requirement of an Affidavit with Specific Allegations:** 28 U.S.C. § 144 (2006) is a mandatory disqualification provision, conditioned

only by the filing of a timely and sufficient affidavit by a party to the proceeding. However, it requires specific allegations of bias or prejudice against the party or in favor of an adverse party—only one of the grounds available under section 455 for recusal—and (as the cases indicate) the requirement of "sufficiency" leaves the judge room to determine that the allegations in the affidavit do not establish a disqualifying bias, even if taken as true. A number of states have similar provisions. *See, e.g.*, Cal.Civ.Proc. Code § 170.6 (West 2004) (prescribing a form entitled "peremptory challenge"); Fla.Stat. § 38.10 (2012); 725 Ill.Comp.Stat. 5/114–5(a) (2003) (criminal cases); Wash.Rev. Code §§ 4.12.040 (1988) (first adopted in 1911).

2. **State Change-of-Judge Rules Without Affidavit Requirements:** In order to avoid the discomfort of explicit allegations of bias or prejudice, a number of states have adopted provisions allowing for a change of judge without requiring a statement of reasons. As long as the application is timely filed and in proper form, the motion is automatically granted, although typically no one party can make more than one such application, and the application must be filed within a short period after commencement of the proceedings. *See, e.g.*, Alaska R.Civ.P. 42(c)(3) (five days from moving party's first appearance); Ariz.R.Civ.P. 42(f); 735 Ill.Comp.Stat. 5/2–1001(a)(2) (2003) (civil cases); Mo.Sup.Ct.R. 32.07 (criminal cases) & 51.05 (civil cases); Wis. Stat. §§ 801.58 (1994) (civil) & 971.20 (1998) (criminal). Under the Missouri rule, for example, no judge can take any action to prejudice a party seeking the automatic disqualification, even though the judge may feel slighted, and even when a particular attorney regularly disqualifies the same judge. *In re Buford*, 577 S.W.2d 809, 828 (Mo. 1979).

There is some concern about what is often perceived as overuse of automatic change-of-judge rules. An originally "experimental" amendment to Rule 10.2 of the Arizona Rules of Criminal Procedure, for example (adopted 2001, made permanent 2004), requires the attorney submitting such a request to include an "avowal" that the request is made in good faith and not:

1. For the purpose of delay;

2. To obtain a severance;

3. To interfere with the reasonable case management practices of a judge;

4. To remove a judge for reasons of race, gender or religious affiliation;

5. For the purpose of using the rule against a particular judge in a blanket fashion by a prosecuting agency, defender group or law firm * * *;

6. To obtain a more convenient geographical location; or

7. To obtain advantage or avoid disadvantage in connection with a plea bargain or at sentencing * * *.

3. **Who Decides the Motion to Disqualify?** As in the federal courts, in most states party motions to disqualify are addressed to the affected judge, who is expected to rule on the motion. However, the general California statute on judicial disqualification, Cal.Civ.Proc. Code § 170.3(c)(1) (West 2012), provides that requests by parties for disqualification of judges who do not

recuse themselves *sua sponte* must be filed with the clerk of the court and served on the judge and all interested parties, and that if a judge against whom such a request has been filed does not recuse herself the issue must be decided by another judge. The judge nonetheless has jurisdiction to strike the request for untimeliness or insufficiency within ten days after it is filed, even if he has already filed an answer to it. *See PBA, LLC v. KPOD, Ltd.*, 5 Cal.Rptr.3d 532 (Ct.App. 2003).

4. **Residual Jurisdiction of the Disqualified Judge:** Once a judge is disqualified, the judge generally loses subject matter jurisdiction over the matter and any subsequent action taken by the judge is void. *See Harbor Enters., Inc. v. Gudjonsson*, 803 P.2d 798 (Wash. 1991). However, where the disqualification or recusal occurs after rulings have been made, which are not affected by the ground for disqualification, the judge will have authority to perform purely ministerial actions such as reducing oral rulings to writing. *See Fernwoods Condo. Ass'n #2, Inc. v. Alonso*, 26 So.3d 27 (Fla.Dist.Ct.App. 2009). In the case of a judge who was a member of a three-judge panel deciding unanimously, it was held that invalidating all prior acts of the panel was unnecessarily burdensome, so that the appropriate remedy was disqualification from all future participation in the matter coupled with review of prior panel rulings. *See Harris v. Champion*, 15 F.3d 1538 (10th Cir. 1994). Even in the case of an individual judge, where she has already taken permissible action in the matter, she may retain jurisdiction to enter further orders in the permitted area. *See Schwartz v. Schwartz*, 431 So.2d 716, 717 (Fla.Dist.Ct. App. 1983).

The California statute, recognizing the need to minimize the impact of a disqualification on the efficient management of a case, provides:

(a) A disqualified judge, notwithstanding his or her disqualification[,] may do any of the following:

(1) Take any action or issue any order necessary to maintain the jurisdiction of the court pending the assignment of a judge not disqualified.

(2) Request any other judge agreed upon by the parties to sit and act in his or her place.

(3) Hear and determine purely default matters.

(4) Issue an order for possession prior to judgment in eminent domain proceedings.

(5) Set proceedings for trial or hearing.

(6) Conduct settlement conferences.

Cal.Civ.Proc. Code § 170.4(a) (West 2006).

5. **Waiver or Remittal of Disqualification by Express Consent:** Both the federal statute, 28 U.S.C. § 455(e) (2006), and Rule 2.11(C) (formerly Canon 3F) of the Model Code of Judicial Conduct contemplate the possibility of explicit party agreement that an otherwise disqualified judge be permitted to continue in the case. Under either provision, such remittal or waiver by agreement must be preceded by full disclosure by the judge on the record of the ground(s) of disqualification. They differ dramatically, however, in the

definition of grounds that are subject to remittal. Under the Code, all grounds are remittable except that of personal bias or prejudice. Under the federal statute, only the general standard—not any of the specific grounds enumerated in section 455(b)—is remittable. Moreover, while the Code expressly permits the judge, after laying out the grounds of disqualification on the record, to ask the parties to consider (outside the judge's presence) whether they would remit, the statute simply addresses whether the judge may "accept * * * a waiver" from the parties. What arguments support these differing positions with respect to remittability?

6. **Waiver or Remittal of Disqualification by Procedural Waiver of Objection:** Whatever the statutory or rule limitations on the scope of explicit agreement, most jurisdictions require that a party assert known grounds for disqualification in a timely fashion, on pain of waiver. Some states have statutory timeliness requirements, *e.g.*, Fla.Stat. § 38.02 (1999), *Steinhorst v. State*, 636 So.2d 498 (Fla. 1994), but in others the timeliness rule is imposed by case law, *see, e.g.*, *Campbell v. State*, 660 S.W.2d 926 (Ark. 1983). Thus at least where the claim is that of bias against a defendant's counsel, it will be waived by participation in pretrial proceedings after the basis for the claim is known, *State v. Hollingsworth*, 467 N.W.2d 555 (Wis.Ct.App. 1991), and when a prior association between prosecutor and judge is known prior to trial, objection is untimely when asserted for the first time on appeal, *Commonwealth v. Edmiston*, 634 A.2d 1078 (Pa. 1993). Texas courts appear to distinguish between grounds for disqualification and grounds for recusal, treating the latter as waivable but the former not—though the distinction is admittedly less than clear in its applicability. *See Gulf Mar. Warehouse Co. v. Towers*, 858 S.W.2d 556, 559–60 (Tex.App. 1993).

It appears that the majority of federal circuits have adopted judge-made timeliness requirements for all motions to disqualify, keyed to the moving party's knowledge or imputed knowledge of the facts on which it is based, despite the failure to retain an explicit requirement in the 1974 revision of section 455. The decision most often cited is *Delesdernier v. Porterie*, 666 F.2d 116 (5th Cir. 1982). *See also United States v. Murphy*, 768 F.2d 1518, 1539 (7th Cir. 1985) (characterizing the same court's earlier decision requiring formal waiver on the record as standing alone and indicating an inclination to abandon it). Some decisions purport to distinguish between sections 455(a) and 455(b) in this respect. *See United States v. Slay*, 714 F.2d 1093 (11th Cir. 1983). This restriction results from concern about potential tactical abuse of such motions, particularly by a party attempting to wait and see whether a judge will make favorable substantive rulings before deciding to raise the disqualification issue. *See United States v. Alabama*, 828 F.2d 1532, 1544 n.49 (11th Cir. 1987).

CHAPTER 6

PARTICULAR LAWYER ROLES AND RESPONSIBILITIES

■ ■ ■

INTRODUCTION

In this chapter we examine further aspects of particular lawyer roles—many of which have already been illustrated in earlier materials dealing with issues common to all roles.

Although relatively few cases actually go to trial, the lawyer's most visible role is that of advocate, before, during, and after trial, in both civil and criminal litigation. Litigation is not, however, the only role in which lawyers operate. The traditional term counselor-at-law reflects the lawyer's long standing duty to advise clients, and lawyers also sometimes conduct evaluations for parties other than clients. The recent meteoric rise of alternative dispute resolution has placed lawyers in the new roles of mediator and arbitrator and has put advocates into new arenas. The Model Rules seek to address these functions.

This chapter begins with some special problems of advocacy—a role that varies according to the type of litigation, as well as the position of the client—and follows with consideration of some of the issues presented by other roles, including advisor, evaluator, alternative dispute resolution participant, and alternative dispute resolution neutral. It then briefly reviews ethical issues faced by lawyers in one particularly important role—judge. It concludes with a discussion of the issues faced by lawyers as they pursue, and attempt to balance, their careers and lives.

A. ADVOCATE

A(1) THE LAWYER IN CIVIL LITIGATION

A(1)(a) Procedural and Disciplinary Sanctions for Frivolous Claims and Defenses

PROBLEM

Bill Amsterdam was not sure if he had a medical malpractice claim. Sharon Stevens, who practiced at the Midtown Clinic, a prestigious osteopathic research center, had been Bill's doctor. According to Bill, he consulted Stevens two years ago about a sore shoulder. She took an x-ray and told him to go home, take some aspirin, and exercise more frequently. Another doctor from Midtown Clinic called Bill the next day and told him that nothing showed up on the x-ray. Stevens did not charge for Bill's visit, because Bill was the coach of her son Timmy's soccer team, and he had spent a lot of extra hours with Timmy on his skills.

The soreness got better for a while, then flared up, and Bill went to another doctor who found cancer that required surgery, radiation, and chemotherapy. This doctor casually mentioned, in explaining his diagnosis and recommendations to Bill, that he was surprised the earlier examination had not detected the cancer, and that if it had been caught earlier it might have been treated by less drastic means. The treatments were successful, but they left his arm partially disabled.

Not sure he had a claim, Bill consulted attorney Roger Lincoln about a malpractice complaint and gave Lincoln a sheaf of medical bills adding up to over $200,000 in actual expenses. Lincoln called a friend now in his second year of medical school, outlined the facts as they had been related to him, and asked if a case could be made out for Stevens' negligence. The friend said, "Maybe, but I really do not know that much about cancer detection yet." On this basis, Lincoln filed a medical malpractice suit on Bill's behalf, naming Stevens as the defendant.

Stevens' attorney, Jerry Davis, filed an answer that denied each allegation in the complaint, including those alleging that Stevens was a resident of Midtown, that Stevens treated Bill, and that another Midtown Clinic doctor reviewed the x-ray and discussed it with Bill. In his work on the case after filing the answer, Davis learned that each of these allegations was true, but he never filed an amended answer admitting these allegations.

In Stevens' deposition, she stated that she had indeed found nothing significant in her examination of Bill, but had recommended to him that further tests be undertaken for the possibility of cancer "just in case." Bill then conceded in his own deposition that he had dismissed this possibility out of hand and had forgotten it. Stevens moved successfully for summary judgment on the claim and it was dismissed.

QUESTIONS

(a) Did Lincoln have a duty to investigate Bill's story before filing the action? If so, was his investigation adequate?

(b) Did Davis have a duty to investigate the allegations in the complaint before he filed the answer on behalf of Stevens? If so, was his investigation adequate? Did he have a duty to amend the answer?

(c) What remedies, if any, should be available to parties who are wrongfully sued? What sanctions, if any, should be imposed on attorneys who bring or defend actions on grounds not soundly based in law or in fact? Should it matter whether the particular deficiency is legal or factual? Do the standards differ according to the remedy or sanction sought? Consider procedural sanctions in the original proceeding, disciplinary action, and a civil lawsuit for damages.

RULE REFERENCES

Model Rules Preamble ¶¶ [2], [8], and [9] and Model Rules 1.1, 1.3, 3.1, 3.2, and 3.4(c)

RESTATEMENT § 110

Rule 11 of Federal Rules of Civil Procedure

GIANGRASSO v. KITTATINNY REGIONAL HIGH SCHOOL BOARD OF EDUCATION

United States District Court, District of New Jersey, 1994.
865 F.Supp. 1133.

SAROKIN, DISTRICT JUDGE.

IT IS * * * ORDERED that the Report and Recommendation [of the United States Magistrate Judge that appears below is affirmed.]

REPORT AND RECOMMENDATION

PISANO, UNITED STATES MAGISTRATE JUDGE.

INTRODUCTION

This matter comes before the court upon defendants' motion for the imposition of sanctions on Edward J. Gaffney, Jr., Esq., counsel for plaintiff, pursuant to Rule 11 of the Federal Rules of Civil Procedure. * * *

Mr. Gaffney filed the complaint in the present matter * * * naming as defendants the Kittatinny Regional High School Board of Education; [Assistant Principal Susan] Kappler; [teacher Harriet] Kesselman; Superintendent Robert Walker; Child Study Team Supervisor Donna Greene; and school psychologist Robert Ferrari. Plaintiff[, a student at the defendant school,] claimed that he had been suspended prior to receiving oral notice of the charges and evidence against him and was not presented with an opportunity to rebut the evidence, contrary to *Goss v. Lopez*, 419

U.S. 565, 95 S.Ct. 729, 42 L.Ed.2d 725 (1975). Plaintiff alleged that certain defendants conspired to fraudulently convince his mother to place him in a school for the emotionally disturbed.

[After the filing of the complaint,] defendants filed for summary judgment and for Rule 11 sanctions against Mr. Gaffney. * * * Defendants' version of the facts, which is deemed admitted because plaintiff did not oppose the motion, revealed that: (1) * * * plaintiff admitted that he was sleeping in class and that he threatened to punch his teacher and (2) plaintiff was afforded two hearings * * * both of which were more than sufficient under *Goss*. Moreover, the facts established that plaintiff never attended a school for the emotionally disturbed, thus rendering him unable to prove the necessary element of damages in his civil rights conspiracy claim. Accordingly, [the trial judge] granted defendants' motion for summary judgment and imposed Rule 11 sanctions on Mr. Gaffney.

DISCUSSION * * *

Rule 11[3] "imposes on counsel a duty to look before leaping and may be seen as a litigation version of the familiar railroad crossing admonition to 'stop, look, and listen.'" * * * When deciding whether to impose sanctions under Rule 11, a district court must evaluate the reasonableness of the signer's conduct at the time the pleading, motion, or other paper was submitted.

[T]he primary purpose of Rule 11 is to deter abuses of the legal system. Although a court may not impose a sanction that is punitive or that might drive an attorney out of practice, * * * the sanction imposed should be " 'the minimum that will serve to adequately deter the undesired behavior[ ]' " * * *. [T]he Third Circuit [has] emphasized the discretion of the district court in tailoring an appropriate sanction * * *.

The recently amended Rule 11 incorporates these holdings and provides in pertinent part * * *:

(b) **Representations to Court**. By presenting to the court (whether by signing, filing, submitting, or later advocating) a pleading, written motion, or other paper, an attorney or unrepresented party is certifying that to the best of the person's knowledge, information, and belief, formed after an inquiry reasonable under the circumstances,—

(1) it is not being presented for any improper purpose, such as to harass or to cause unnecessary delay or needless increase in the cost of litigation;

(2) the claims, defenses, and other legal contentions therein are warranted by existing law or by a nonfrivolous argument for the extension, modification, or reversal of existing law or the establishment of new law;

(3) the allegations and other factual contentions have evidentiary support or, if specifically so identified, are likely to have evidentiary

---

3. [Sanctions were ordered] against Mr. Gaffney prior to December 1, 1993, the effective date of the amendments to Rule 11. Thus, the new requirements [offering] a "safe haven" period in which the challenged paper may be withdrawn to avoid sanctions * * * do not apply.

support after a reasonable opportunity for further investigation or discovery; and

(4) the denials of factual contentions are warranted on the evidence or, if specifically so identified, are reasonably based on a lack of information or belief.

(c) **Sanctions**. If, after notice and a reasonable opportunity to respond, the court determines that subdivision (b) has been violated, the court may, subject to the conditions state[d] below, impose an appropriate sanction upon the attorneys ... that have violated subdivision (b)....

(2) **Nature of Sanction; Limitations**. A sanction imposed for a violation of this rule shall be limited to what is sufficient to deter repetition of such conduct or comparable conduct by others similarly situated.... [T]he sanction may consist of, or include, directives of a nonmonetary nature, an order to pay a penalty into court, or, if imposed on motion and warranted for effective deterrence, an order directing payment to the movant of some or all of the reasonable attorneys' fees and other expenses incurred as a direct result of the violation. * * *a

MR. GAFFNEY'S CONDUCT IN THE PRESENT LITIGATION

The bulk of the claims in the instant case arise from plaintiff's one day suspension and ensuing mandatory homebound instruction. Plaintiff

---

a. [In 2007, after this opinion, all of the Federal Rules of Civil Procedure were amended in a set of stylistic amendments that were designed to improve the language and format of the Rules, without making any substantive changes. The post–2007 versions of the provisions of Rule 11 quoted in the opinion provide:

(b) Representations to the Court. By presenting to the court a pleading, written motion, or other paper—whether by signing, filing, submitting, or later advocating it—an attorney or unrepresented party certifies that to the best of the person's knowledge, information, and belief, formed after an inquiry reasonable under the circumstances:

(1) it is not being presented for any improper purpose, such as to harass, cause unnecessary delay, or needlessly increase the cost of litigation;

(2) the claims, defenses, and other legal contentions are warranted by existing law or by a nonfrivolous argument for extending, modifying, or reversing existing law or for establishing new law;

(3) the factual contentions have evidentiary support or, if specifically so identified, will likely have evidentiary support after a reasonable opportunity for further investigation or discovery; and

(4) the denials of factual contentions are warranted on the evidence or, if specifically so identified, are reasonably based on belief or a lack of information.

(c) Sanctions.

(1) *In General.* If, after notice and a reasonable opportunity to respond, the court determines that Rule 11(b) has been violated, the court may impose an appropriate sanction on any attorney, law firm, or party that violated the rule or is responsible for the violation. * * *

(4) *Nature of a Sanction.* A sanction imposed under this rule must be limited to what suffices to deter repetition of the conduct or comparable conduct by others similarly situated. The sanction may include nonmonetary directives; an order to pay a penalty into court; or, if imposed on motion and warranted for effective deterrence, an order directing payment to the movant of part or all of the reasonable attorney's fees and other expenses directly resulting from the violation.

Ed.]

incurred the suspension for threatening to punch his teacher in her head. * * * *Goss* set forth the minimum due process requirements to be afforded a [student] who is suspended for ten days or less: (1) the student must be given oral or written notice of the charges against him; (2) if the student denies those charges, he is entitled to an explanation of the evidence which forms the basis for those charges; and (3) the student is to be given an opportunity to present his or her side of the story. *Goss*, 419 U.S. at 581, 95 S.Ct. at 740.

The last two requirements apply only where a student denies the charges against him. In the instant case, * * * plaintiff did not deny that he had been sleeping in class or that he threatened to hit his teacher. Therefore, defendants were not required to explain the evidence to plaintiff and give him an opportunity to present his side of the story. However, on at least two occasions [on] the date of the incident, plaintiff was afforded an opportunity to present his version of the facts. The undisputed facts reveal that defendants more than met the procedural due process requirements of *Goss*.

Mr. Gaffney had previously represented both Adrien King and Richard Williams in *Goss* cases against the same school district. As Judge Debevoise noted, *Goss* is not a complicated case. It is not unreasonable to expect Mr. Gaffney to have understood *Goss* prior to filing the complaint in this matter. However, even the fact that he was sanctioned in *Williams* for filing a frivolous [claim] under *Goss* did not deter Mr. Gaffney from continuing the instant action and from filing papers in support of it.

Mr. Gaffney must also have realized that Count VII of plaintiff's complaint was not well-grounded in law or fact. Count VII alleged that defendants Robert Walker, Robert Ferrari, and Donna Greene conspired to fraudulently convince plaintiff's mother to place plaintiff in a school for the emotionally disturbed, in violation of various federal rights.

Plaintiff never attended a school for the emotionally disturbed. * * * Damages are a necessary element of a civil rights conspiracy claim. * * * At oral argument on [the defendants' motion,] Mr. Gaffney described himself as a "civil rights attorney." Surely Mr. Gaffney must have realized that the civil rights conspiracy claim was baseless because the alleged conspiracy did not result in an * * * injury to plaintiff. * * *

Mr. Gaffney never filed any opposition to defendants' motion for summary judgment, and * * * filed opposition to the accompanying motion for Rule 11 sanctions only after such sanctions had been granted. Mr. Gaffney's behavior is especially inexcusable given that Judge Sarokin granted his request for an extension of almost a month in which to file opposition papers. Mr. Gaffney's failure to file opposition to defendants' summary judgment motion is but one occasion in this litigation during which he exhibited an unwillingness to comply with fundamental rules of practice, thus violating his obligation to act in the best interests of his client. Mr. Gaffney has repeatedly failed to comply with discovery deadlines, has failed to provide counsel with copies of necessary documents, and has failed to appear or was late for conferences and oral arguments. * * *

Defendants * * * assert that Mr. Gaffney's conduct is spurred by a "personal vendetta" against Kittatinny Regional High School. In connection with a reprimand for various violations of the Rules of Professional Conduct, Mr. Gaffney was ordered by the Supreme Court of the State of New Jersey to undergo psychiatric evaluation. * * * Mr. Gaffney represented to this court that he had undergone the ordered evaluation which revealed that he does not have a disorder. I must therefore conclude that he filed the instant case willfully and intentionally, and because the case is without merit, that he did it for his own purposes, whatever they might be.

This court is not called upon to examine Mr. Gaffney's psyche to determine the cause of his hostility toward defendants. However, this court is required to make factual findings as to whether plaintiff's filing of frivolous claims was for an improper motive. Mr. Gaffney's relentless history of unprofessional behavior toward defendants, including the repeated filing of frivolous claims, confirms that he bears them an obvious animosity. The manner in which Mr. Gaffney has conducted this litigation demonstrates that he has committed every transgression Rule 11 is intended to deter. Mr. Gaffney has abused the legal system to harass defendants. Previous attempts at deterrence having been unsuccessful, I conclude that extreme sanctions are justified and required in this case.

RECOMMENDATIONS AS TO THE APPROPRIATE SANCTIONS

Attorneys' Fees

As discussed, both the case law interpreting Rule 11 and the amendments make clear that the purpose of sanctions is to deter future violations, and that monetary sanctions should not be more severe than those necessary to deter repeated violations of the rule. [S]anctions should not be so severe as to put an attorney out of practice. * * *

I recommend that monetary sanctions of $100,000 be imposed * * *. The sanctions of $5000 [previously] imposed [against Mr. Gaffney] by Judge Debevoise * * *, as well as the Judge's stern admonishment, have not deterred Mr. Gaffney from repeating to violate Rule 11. Indeed, Mr. Gaffney persisted to litigate the frivolous *Goss* claims in the instant matter well after receiving Judge Debevoise's painstaking explanation of *Goss* and why [the prior] *Goss* claims were frivolous. Therefore, a greater sanction is required to deter Mr. Gaffney from committing another violation of Rule 11.

I recommend that the court order the monetary sanctions to be paid to defendants, rather than to the court. The amended Rule 11 indicates that attorneys fees are to be paid to the moving party if "warranted for effective deterrence." Fed.R.Civ.P. 11(c)(2). Mr. Gaffney's strong animosity toward defendants apparently prompted this frivolous suit. Requiring him to bear the costs of this litigation will likely deter him from filing further frivolous suits against those to whom he may be similarly hostile.

Additional Sanctions

[Under] the new Rule 11(c)(2), the court may impose non-monetary sanctions where appropriate to deter future violation[s] of Rule 11. Therefore, to ensure that Mr. Gaffney will not continue to file frivolous suits against defendants, I recommend that the court permanently enjoin Mr. Gaffney from filing, as an attorney, any complaint in this court involving Kittatinny Regional High School. To protect other parties from similar abuse, I also recommend that the court direct the Clerk to refuse to accept any other complaint Mr. Gaffney attempts to file, unless and until the complaint is approved for filing by the duty judge sitting on the day of the attempted filing.

The Committee Notes on the revision of Rule 11 recognize that "the court has available a variety of possible sanctions to impose for violations, such as . . . referring the matter to disciplinary authorities." * * * Moreover, Local [Court Rules provide] that: [w]hen misconduct or allegations of misconduct which, if substantiated, would warrant discipline of an attorney, shall come to the attention of a Judge of this Court, and the applicable procedure is not otherwise mandated by these Rules, that Judge shall refer the matter in writing to the Chief Judge.

During the course of this litigation, Mr. Gaffney has violated several Rules of Professional Conduct. By filing this lawsuit, Mr. Gaffney violated [Rule] 3.1, which prohibits an attorney from bringing a frivolous proceeding. Mr. Gaffney repeatedly failed to meet case management deadlines, therefore violating [Rule] 3.2. Rule 3.2 directs attorneys to make reasonable efforts to expedite litigation. In failing to file opposition to a dispositive motion, Mr. Gaffney appears to have violated [Rule] 1.3, which requires that an attorney act with reasonable diligence and promptness in representing a client. * * *

Based on the foregoing examples of Mr. Gaffney's misconduct in this litigation, I recommend that the court refer the matter to Chief Judge Gerry, pursuant to Rule 11 * * * for such investigation and further proceedings as may be deemed appropriate. * * *

NOTES ON PROCEDURAL AND DISCIPLINARY SANCTIONS FOR ASSERTING FRIVOLOUS POSITIONS

1. **Rule 11 and Its Safe Harbor:** Rule 11(a) of the Federal Rules of Civil Procedure provides that "[e]very pleading, written motion, and other paper must be signed by at least one attorney of record in the attorney's name." As noted in *Giangrasso*, by signing and presenting a document to the court, an attorney represents that it has merit.

As the *Giangrasso* court noted in footnote 3, the post–1993 versions of Rule 11 contain a "safe harbor" provision allowing an attorney to avoid sanctions by withdrawing a meritless document in response to the opposing party's notice of an intention to seek sanctions. Following the 2007 restyling amendments to Rule 11, which were designed to improve the language but not change the substance of the Federal Rules of Civil Procedure, this provision giving an attorney twenty-one days to withdraw the offending claim or document is in Rule 11(c)(2). Some believe the 21–day safe harbor provision should be eliminated and Rule 11 sanctions should once again become mandatory upon a finding by the court that Rule 11 was violated, as the 1983 to 1993 version of Rule 11 required. *See, e.g.*, Gregory P. Joseph, *Sanctions: The Lawsuit Abuse Reduction Act of 2011*, Litig., Fall 2011, at 8 (opposing these proposed changes); Sandra Davidson, *FRCP 11: A Wounded Remedy for Unethical Behavior*, J.Mo.B., Jan.–Feb. 2006, at 16 (describing debate regarding Rule 11).

2. ***Sua Sponte* Rule 11 Court Action:** Under Rule 11(c)(3), the court can, by order to show cause, act *sua sponte* to sanction without providing the offending attorney a chance to withdraw a meritless document. Because the court has this power to act on its own motion, one court has held that such sanctions should be entered only when the attorney has acted in subjective bad faith, not when there is only objectively unreasonable attorney conduct. *In re Pennie & Edmonds LLP*, 323 F.3d 86 (2d Cir. 2003); *see also* Rule 11(c)(5)(B) (establishing limitations on *sua sponte* monetary sanctions).

3. **Rule 11 and Innovative Claims:** Does rigorous application of Rule 11 threaten the ability of lawyers and parties to obtain a hearing on legally innovative claims? Critics of Rule 11's objective standard contend that sanctions that deter truly meritless claims may deter innovative claims as well. In other words, today's frivolous claim may be tomorrow's law. Consider the lawyer in *MacPherson v. Buick Motor Co.*, 111 N.E. 1050 (N.Y. 1916), who, despite the long established rule denying damages against a manufacturer of a vehicle where the car was purchased from a dealer, nevertheless brought the suit. Given the well established requirement of privity at that time, could he have been sanctioned had Judge Cardozo not chosen to use this case to overturn long standing precedent? Does Rule 11(b)(2), under which a lawyer certifies that all claims are either warranted by existing law or by a non-frivolous argument for extending existing law, adequately address this issue?

To the extent that law is culturally determined and thus continually changing, it may be difficult to reach any agreement on whether a given claim is frivolous. *See* Melissa L. Nelken, *Has the Chancellor Shot Himself in the Foot? Looking for a Middle Ground on Rule 11 Sanctions*, 41 Hastings L.J. 383 (1990). Considering these arguments, is there any reason for treating civil rights cases more leniently? *See* Carl Tobias, *Rule 11 and Civil Rights Litigation*, 37 Buff.L.Rev. 485 (1988–1989) (arguing that the difficulties civil rights attorneys face in obtaining information prior to discovery make them particularly susceptible to Rule 11's chilling effect).

Those concerned about Rule 11's potential to discourage plaintiffs from bringing innovative claims have also expressed concern about two U.S. Supreme Court decisions regarding pleading in federal civil cases. In *Bell Atlantic Corp. v. Twombly*, 550 U.S. 544 (2007), the plaintiffs alleged that the "BabyBell" companies failed to compete. The Supreme Court held that the complaint should be dismissed for failure to state a claim because it did not allege that the defendants had entered into an agreement not to compete and therefore did not plead "enough facts to state a claim to relief that is plausible on its face." *Id.* at 570. In *Ashcroft v. Iqbal*, 556 U.S. 662 (2009), the plaintiff, a pretrial detainee, alleged that government officials engaged in activities that violated his constitutional and statutory civil rights. The Supreme Court held that his complaint failed to plead sufficient facts to state a claim, because its allegations were conclusory rather than specific. Does the combination of the *Twombly/Iqbal* specific plausibility pleading standard and Rule 11's requirement of a non-frivolous factual and legal basis raise too high a barrier for civil complaints? For discussions of the relationship between the *Twombly/Iqbal* plausibility pleading standard and Rule 11, see Bradley Scott Shannon, *I Have Federal Pleading All Figured Out,* 61 Case W.Res.L.Rev. 453 (2010), and Benjamin Grossberg, Comment, *Uniformity, Federalism, and Tort Reform: The* Erie *Implications of Medical Malpractice Certificate of Merit Statutes,* 159 U.Pa.L.Rev. 217, 247–57 (2010).

4. **Identification of Innovative Claims:** Should a lawyer be required to identify a specific allegation or contention as an extension of the law?

> Arguments for extensions, modifications, or reversals of existing law or for creation of new law do not violate subdivision (b)(2) provided they are "nonfrivolous." This establishes an objective standard, intended to eliminate any "empty-head pure-heart" justification for patently frivolous arguments. However, the extent to which a litigant has researched the issues and found some support for its theories even in minority opinions, in law review articles, or through consultation with other attorneys should certainly be taken into account in determining whether paragraph (2) has been violated. Although arguments for a change of law are not required to be specifically so identified, a contention that is so identified should be viewed with greater tolerance under the rule.

Fed.R.Civ.P. 11 advisory committee's note (1993 amendment).

5. **Client Representation of Facts:** To what extent may an attorney rely on his client's representation of the facts? It is generally inappropriate for a lawyer to rely on the client's version of the events when there are other sources of information available to verify, or disprove, the client's story. Lawyers should be skeptical of their client's statements of facts and should seek independent verification of these facts when possible. *See Nassau–Suffolk Ice Cream, Inc. v. Integrated Res., Inc.,* 114 F.R.D. 684 (S.D.N.Y. 1987). This is especially so for a lawyer who blindly relies on a lay client's opinion on a point of law. In *Hendrix v. Naphtal*, 971 F.2d 398 (9th Cir. 1992), the court found that the lawyer had violated Rule 11 by relying on the client's own conclusion about where he was legally domiciled as the basis for diversity jurisdiction.

The situation is different, however, when other sources of information are not readily available. In *Kraemer v. Grant County*, 892 F.2d 686 (7th Cir. 1990), the court recognized that the lawyer had little choice but to accept his client's version of the facts as the basis for filing suit, where other efforts at investigation were unavailing and the prospective defendants had "stone-walled" the lawyer. The court found that, under the circumstances, the lawyer needed access to discovery in order to flesh out the client's case. Additionally, it appears that a lawyer may rely on a client and the attorney who forwards the case for information where time prevents further inquiry. *CTC Imps. & Exps. v. Nigerian Petroleum Corp.*, 951 F.2d 573 (3d Cir. 1991); *see also Cont'l Ins. Co. v. Constr. Indus. Servs. Corp.*, 149 F.R.D. 451 (E.D.N.Y. 1993) (finding that a lawyer's reliance upon erroneous jurisdictional information supplied by the client's in-house counsel was reasonable under the circumstances).

However, lawyers can violate Rule 11 by trusting blindly, or failing to expand, another lawyer's investigation. *Unioil Inc. v. E.F. Hutton & Co.*, 809 F.2d 548 (9th Cir. 1986) (holding that a lawyer improperly relied on forwarding co-counsel). Similarly, a court faulted a lawyer for relying upon a newspaper article that itself relied upon anonymous sources. *Walker v. S.W.I.F.T. SCRL*, 517 F.Supp.2d 801, 804–07 (E.D.Va. 2007).

6. **Rule 11 and the Offending Lawyer's Firm:** When an individual lawyer signs a frivolous complaint or other paper governed by Rule 11 on behalf of a law firm of which he is a member, is the firm subject to sanctions as well as the individual signer? Under Rule 11(c)(1), "Absent exceptional circumstances, a law firm must be held jointly responsible for a violation committed by its partner, associate, or employee." In part, this is because the twenty-one day safe harbor provision allows lawyers in the firm to investigate the potentially offending document.

7. **Rule 11 and Discovery:** Rule 11 "does not apply to disclosures and discovery requests, responses, objections, and motions." Rule 11(d). However, Rule 26(c) permits the entry of a protective order to thwart abusive discovery requests, and Rule 37 provides for sanctions for parties and attorneys who fail to properly respond to discovery requests or file frivolous discovery motions. *See infra* section 6(A)(1)(c).

8. **Rule 11 in State Court:** Following the federal adoption of Rule 11, some, but not all, states have adopted civil procedure rules or statutes containing provisions designed to deter the filing of frivolous claims or defenses. Though some states have adopted provisions similar to Rule 11, others have adopted only some (or none) of its sanctions framework.

9. **Zealous Advocacy and the Model Rules:** Practicing attorneys, especially litigators, are fond of asserting that their primary duty is to "zealously" represent their clients. This frequently asserted claim is based largely upon the old Model Code of Professional Responsibility. In the current Model Rules, outside of several comments, the word "zealously" appears only in the Preamble. *See* Model Rules Preamble ¶¶ [2], [8] & [9]. In the Model Rules themselves, references to zealousness have been replaced by several duties owed by the lawyer to the client. Model Rule 1.1 requires "competent representation," including "the legal knowledge, skill, thoroughness and preparation reasonably necessary." Model Rule 1.3 mandates "reasonable diligence and promptness." Model Rules 1.7 through 1.11 reinforce the duty of loyalty to the client by prohibiting conflicts of interest that would interfere with or lessen this loyalty. The concept of zealousness is retained in Comment [1] to Model Rule 1.3, which states that a lawyer must "act with commitment and dedication to the interests of the client and with zeal in advocacy upon

the client's behalf." However, this Comment then says that a lawyer need not "press for every advantage" on behalf of a client.

10. **Frivolousness and Criminal v. Civil Cases:** Model Rule 3.1 was briefly discussed by the court in *Giangrasso.* Unless the lawyer is serving as a criminal defense attorney, Model Rule 3.1 prohibits her from asserting or controverting an allegation unless there is a non-frivolous basis in law and fact for doing so. *See also* RESTATEMENT, § 110(1). When existing law does not support a claim or defense, a lawyer can assert the claim or defense only when there is a "good faith" basis for arguing that the law should be modified. Model Rule 3.1. The rule draws an important distinction between criminal defense attorneys and other litigators (i.e., civil defense attorneys, plaintiffs' attorneys, and prosecutors). A criminal defense attorney is allowed to force the prosecutor to prove any element of a crime, even if there is no good faith basis for disputing an element. Model Rule 3.1; *see also* RESTATEMENT, § 110(2). In contrast, a plaintiff's attorney, a prosecutor, or a civil defense attorney can dispute a claim only when there is a non-frivolous basis for doing so. In any jurisdiction with a provision like Rule 11 of the Federal Rules of Civil Procedure, violating such a rule would run afoul of Model Rule 3.4(c)'s prohibition of knowingly disobeying "an obligation under the rules of a tribunal."

11. **Discipline v. Procedural Sanction or Civil Claim:** Among the three principal sanctions for filing frivolous claims, it appears that formal discipline is relatively unusual, by comparison with procedural sanctions and civil actions for abuse of process, described in the next subsection. Does this fact demonstrate a lack of concern on the part of the profession for the problem? Does it simply indicate that disciplinary action is less effective and therefore less attractive to the courts and to the lawyers representing the victims of such conduct? For a discussion of the interplay between Rule 11 sanctions and discipline under the Model Rules, see Peter A. Joy, *The Relationship Between Civil Rule 11 and Lawyer Discipline: An Empirical Analysis Suggesting Institutional Choices in the Regulation of Lawyers,* 37 Loy.L.A.L.Rev. 765 (2004); *see also Fla. Bar v. Committe,* 916 So.2d 741 (Fla. 2005) (suspending a lawyer who also was sanctioned under Rule 11).

A(1)(b) Civil Liability for Unwarranted Litigation

D'ANGELO v. MUSSLER

Court of Appeals of Kentucky, 2009.
290 S.W.3d 75.

MOORE, JUDGE.

This case against attorney Theodore Mussler and his law firm is the result of the filing and subsequent dismissal of a prior malpractice action against Gregory D'Angelo, M.D., which Mussler brought on behalf of one of D'Angelo's former patients, Austin Jacobs. In the prior malpractice action, Mussler voluntarily dismissed the malpractice action with prejudice on May 30, 2006. Exactly one year after the dismissal, Dr. D'Angelo filed his action against Mussler and his firm alleging wrongful use of civil proceedings. Mussler moved for summary judgment contending that Dr. D'Angelo had not produced evidence sufficient to establish the element of lack of probable cause. The circuit court granted summary judgment. Upon review, we affirm.

STATEMENT OF FACTS

On June 24, 1999, Austin Jacobs suffered a fracture of his right elbow while riding a go-cart on his family farm in Winchester, Kentucky. * * * On June 25, Austin was seen in the office of Dr. D'Angelo, an orthopaedic surgeon, who evaluated the injury. The examination revealed that Austin's arm was neurovascularly intact. Dr. D'Angelo determined that Austin had a displaced, extended fracture of the elbow. The next day, Dr. D'Angelo performed an orthopaedic procedure wherein he externally pinned Austin's elbow fracture. This involved placing pins through the skin and into the bones without opening up Austin's arm. Immediately following surgery, Austin complained, for the first time, of pain and a cold sensation in his right arm. Austin was then seen by another orthopedist, Dr. Mary Ireland, who referred Austin to Dr. Walter Badenhausen.

On December 7, 1999, Dr. Badenhausen performed surgery to explore the path of Austin's ulnar nerve. During the surgery, Dr. Badenhausen performed neurolysis and anterior transposition of the ulnar nerve, which allowed Dr. Badenhausen to see the condition of the ulnar nerve. Dr. Badenhausen noticed localized scar tissue on the ulnar nerve and believed that a pin had gone through the nerve. Austin remained under Dr. Badenhausen's care through July 10, 2002.

In May of 2004, Austin's mother, Audeen Jacobs, contacted Mussler about a possible malpractice suit against Dr. D'Angelo because of the permanent damage to Austin's elbow following the June 26, 1999 surgery performed by Dr. D'Angelo. Mussler agreed to investigate a potential malpractice lawsuit against Dr. D'Angelo.

On May 13, 2004, Mussler met with Dr. Badenhausen. Dr. Badenhausen was in possession of 111 pages of medical records regarding Austin's treatment. Of these records, the only record describing Austin's June 26, 1999 surgery was Dr. D'Angelo's operating note. The operating note did not document the types of precautions employed by Dr. D'Angelo to avoid injury to the nerve. In an affidavit, Mussler stated that during that meeting, Dr. Badenhausen expressed the opinion to Mussler that Dr. D'Angelo's care of Austin during the June 26, 1999 surgery was below the acceptable standard of medical care under like or similar circumstances and caused Austin permanent injury. On May 14, 2004, Dr. Badenhausen provided Mussler a copy of Austin Jacobs' medical records in his possession.

On October 4, 2004, based upon his review of the medical records and his consultation with Dr. Badenhausen, Mussler filed a malpractice suit against Dr. D'Angelo in Fayette Circuit Court. * * * On July 13, 2005, Dr. D'Angelo moved for summary judgment claiming that the plaintiffs would be unable to support their claim with expert testimony. On July 29, 2005, Dr. D'Angelo's motion for summary judgment was denied. * * * On March 17, 2006, counsel for Dr. D'Angelo took Dr. Badenhausen's deposition. At this deposition, and for the first time, Dr. Badenhausen's criticism of Dr. D'Angelo was equivocal and uncertain. On May 30, 2006, Mussler voluntarily dismissed the suit against Dr. D'Angelo.

On May 30, 2007, Dr. D'Angelo filed this action against Mussler alleging that Mussler filed the Jacobs litigation without probable cause and for improper purpose. Dr. D'Angelo also alleged that Mussler did not conduct a reasonable investigation of the facts before filing suit against Dr. D'Angelo. * * *

On April 29, 2008, the court granted Mussler's motion for summary judgment on the following bases: (1) in light of the fact that Dr. Badenhausen's deposition reaffirmed the existence of a pre-litigation consultation, Mussler held a reasonable belief that Dr. Badenhausen's criticisms of the care rendered by Dr. D'Angelo gave Austin's claim viability; (2) D'Angelo did not offer any evidence to place these facts in controversy, or suggest how further discovery might create an issue of fact on this question; and (3) the denial of Dr. D'Angelo's motion for summary judgment in the Jacobs litigation supports the position that Mussler had probable cause to file the underlying claim.

Dr. D'Angelo filed a timely appeal, arguing that the circuit court ruled incorrectly that Mussler was not liable as a matter of law for wrongful use of civil proceedings. Upon review, we affirm.

ANALYSIS * * *

"Public policy requires that all persons be able to freely resort to the courts for redress of a wrong, and the law should and does protect them when they commence a civil or criminal action in good faith and upon reasonable grounds." *Prewitt v. Sexton*, 777 S.W.2d 891, 895 (Ky.1989) (paraphrasing *Davis v. Brady*, 218 Ky. 384, 291 S.W. 412 (1927)). It is for this reason that one must strictly comply with the prerequisites of maintaining an action for wrongful use of civil proceedings. The elements of this cause of action are: (1) the institution or continuation of original judicial proceedings, either civil or criminal, or of administrative or disciplinary proceedings, (2) by, or at the instance, of the plaintiff, (3) the termination of such proceedings in defendant's favor, (4) malice in the institution of such proceeding, (5) want or lack of probable cause for the proceeding, and (6) the suffering of damage as a result of the proceeding. *Smith v. Smith*, 296 Ky. 785, 178 S.W.2d 613 (Ky.1944); *Cravens v. Long*, 257 S.W.2d 548 (Ky.1953); *Blankenship v. Staton*, 348 S.W.2d 925 (Ky. 1961); *H.S. Leyman Co. v. Short*, 214 Ky. 272, 283 S.W. 96 (1926); Restatement (Second) of Torts § 674, (1977), *et seq.*

The trial court ruled only on the element of lack of probable cause. Having decided that Dr. D'Angelo did not establish this element with affirmative evidence, the court granted Mussler's motion for summary judgment without discussing the other elements. If the trial court was correct, there is no need for a discussion of the other elements at this level.

Present law in Kentucky regarding the ramifications of wrongful use of civil proceedings is set out by our Supreme Court in *Mapother and Mapother, P.S.C. v. Douglas,* 750 S.W.2d 430 (Ky.1988), and *Prewitt v. Sexton,* 777 S.W.2d 891 (Ky.1989), wherein the Court adopted Restatement (Second) of Torts §§ 674–681B (1977).

In an action for wrongful civil proceedings, [a] plaintiff must prove that the proceeding was initiated or continued without probable cause. Restatement (Second) of Torts § [662], comment (f) states:

> The question of probable cause is to be determined in the light of those facts that the accuser knows or reasonably believes to exist at the time when he acts. His subsequent discovery of exculpatory facts does not indicate a lack of probable cause for initiating the proceedings, although he may make himself liable by subsequently taking an active part in pressing the proceedings.

See also id. at § 675, comment (c) (adapting this comment to wrongful civil proceedings).

In a civil proceeding, the quantum of necessary probable cause is less than that required in a criminal action:

> [W]hen the proceedings are civil, while the person initiating them cannot have a reasonable belief in the existence of the facts on which the proceedings are based if he knows that the alleged facts are not true and his claim is based on false testimony, it is enough if their existence is not certain but he believes that he can establish their existence to the satisfaction of court and jury. In a word, the initiator of private civil proceedings need not have the same degree of certainty as to the relevant facts that is required of a private prosecutor or criminal proceedings. In many cases civil proceedings, to be effective, must be begun before all of the relevant facts can be ascertained to a reasonable degree of certainty. To put the initiator of civil proceedings to a greater risk of liability would put an undesirable burden upon those whose rights cannot be otherwise effectively enforced.

Id. § 675, comment (d).

The evidence before the Court shows that Mussler had probable cause to bring the underlying suit on behalf of his client against Dr. D'Angelo. As we indicated above, "[t]he moving party bears the initial burden of showing that no genuine issue of material fact exists, and then the burden shifts to the party opposing summary judgment to present 'at least some affirmative evidence showing that there is a genuine issue of material fact for trial.'" *Lewis* [*v. B & R Corp.,* 56 S.W.3d 432, 436 (Ky.Ct.App. 2001).]

Relying on Restatement (Second) of Torts § 675, comment (d), we conclude that Dr. D'Angelo failed to provide any affirmative evidence demonstrating that Mussler knew that the averments stated in the Jacobs litigation complaint were not true, or that the claims were based on false testimony. At worst, Dr. D'Angelo may argue that Mussler began the Jacobs litigation before all of the relevant facts could be ascertained to a reasonable degree of certainty (*i.e.*, whether, in fact, circumstances existed demonstrating that the injury caused by pinning the ulnar nerve could have been avoided). However, it is enough if the existence of the relevant facts is not certain, but Mussler believed that he could establish their existence to the satisfaction of court. Here, under the investigation and facts as Mussler knew them when he filed the Jacobs litigation, we cannot find that he lacked probable cause for the basis of the action. Having so found, we cannot find error in the trial court's decision.

For the reasons stated, we affirm the decision of the circuit court.

NOTES ON CIVIL LIABILITY AND THREATENING CRIMINAL PROSECUTION

1. **Wrongful Use of Civil Proceedings:** In *Prewitt v. Sexton*, 777 S.W.2d 891 (Ky. 1989), which was cited in *D'Angelo*, the court pointed out that, although suits claiming that prior civil suits were improper were once called "malicious prosecution" cases, this terminology, which comes from wrongful assertion by alleged victims leading to prosecution of criminal cases, is now outdated. As the *Prewitt* court noted, 777 S.W.2d at 893, the RESTATEMENT (2D) OF TORTS, § 653–73 (1977), now refers to suits alleging that prior civil suits were improper as suits for "wrongful use of civil proceedings." Sections 674 to 681B of the RESTATEMENT (2D) OF TORTS outline the elements of these suits. The *D'Angelo* decision lists these elements of this disfavored tort.

2. **Improper Purpose:** The "improper purpose" standard of the RESTATEMENT OF TORTS was also applied in *Wilson v. Hayes*, 464 N.W.2d 250 (Iowa 1990). A similar standard, drawing on professional standards as well as the general principle that the courts should be fully available to persons seeking peaceful redress of grievances asserted in good faith, was applied in *Spencer v. Burglass*, 337 So.2d 596 (La.Ct.App. 1976) (on which our problem is based), rejecting a malicious prosecution claim in a medical malpractice case even where the plaintiff's lawyer failed to (i) interview witnesses, (ii) obtain medical opinions, or (iii) verify the client's allegations in any other way before suing, and failed to withdraw or dismiss the action when it appeared, before trial, that the evidence would be insufficient to sustain the client's claim.

Bringing a civil suit while hoping to force the defendant to settle is ordinarily not held to be an improper purpose. *See Rusakiewicz v. Lowe*, 556 F.3d 1095, 1107–08 (10th Cir. 2009). On the other hand, one court has held that suing one party in an effort to coerce settlement of unrelated claims by a non-party can be an improper purpose. *See Ciolli v. Iravani*, 625 F.Supp.2d 276, 295 (E.D.Pa. 2009).

3. **Reasonable Investigation:** In *Prewitt, supra* note 1, the court held that "[t]here was no evidence to show that Attorney Prewitt failed to make a reasonable effort to investigate the basis of his client's claim before filing suit," 777 S.W.2d at 896, thereby emphasizing that such evidence could lead to a successful wrongful use of civil proceedings suit. If further inquiry before suing were required beyond the client's story in the problem at the beginning

of this section, what should Lincoln have done? Would it be sufficient to write a letter to the physician outlining the client/patient's claim and asking for a response? For a suggestion that this might be appropriate, see *Nelson v. Miller*, 607 P.2d 438 (Kan. 1980). What would you think the response of the physician to such a letter would be? Would such a scenario further the interest of assuring that the courts not be burdened with frivolous lawsuits, if the plaintiff's lawyer would be insulated from liability merely by having given the defendant a prelitigation chance to defend against the claim? Note that, even if a suit is proper at the outset, perhaps due to practical limitations on pre-suit investigation, it can become improper, because "*continuing* to prosecute a lawsuit discovered to lack probable cause" is actionable. *See Zamos v. Stroud*, 87 P.3d 802, 807 (Cal. 2004).

4. **Threatening Criminal Prosecution:** Under prior disciplinary rules, a lawyer could not threaten to bring about criminal prosecution of the opposing party in order to gain advantage in a civil action. There is no such counterpart in the current Model Rules, and it appears that the omission represented a conscious decision to rely on other provisions to define improper conduct, while avoiding the apparent prohibition of "legitimate pressure tactics and negotiation strategies." *See* 2 Geoffrey Hazard, Jr. & W. William Hodes, The Law of Lawyering § 4.4:103 (2d ed. 1990); *see also* J. Nick Badgerow, *Rattling the Saber: The Ethics of Threatening Criminal and Disciplinary Prosecution*, J.Mo.B., Jan.–Feb. 2005, at 13 (outlining the history of Model Code and Model Rules provisions). The ABA Standing Committee on Ethics and Professional Responsibility, in Formal Opinion 92–363 (1992), confirmed that there is no general prohibition in the Model Rules against using the possibility of a criminal prosecution to gain advantage in a civil matter:

> The deliberate omission of [the prior] language or any counterpart from the Model Rules rested on the drafters' position that "extortionate, fraudulent, or otherwise abusive threats were covered by other, more general prohibitions in the Model Rules and thus that there was no need to outlaw such threats specifically."

Charles W. Wolfram, Modern Legal Ethics § 13.5.5, at 718 (1986) (citing Model Rule 8.4 legal background note (Proposed Final Draft, May 30, 1981) (last paragraph)).

What other rules might come into play? The ABA Committee mentioned: Model Rules 3.1 (frivolous claims), 4.1 (untruthfulness in statements to others), 4.4 (actions having no substantial purpose other than harassment, delay, or burden to another), 8.4(b) (criminal acts reflecting on the lawyer's fitness to practice law), 8.4(d) (conduct prejudicial to the administration of justice), and 8.4(e) (implying an ability to influence improperly a government agency or official). The opinion says a threat to prosecute doesn't *necessarily* violate any of these prohibitions:

> [A] threat to bring criminal charges for the purpose of advancing a civil claim would violate the Model Rules if the criminal wrongdoing were unrelated to the client's civil claim, if the lawyer did not believe both the civil claim and the potential criminal charges to be well-founded, or if the threat constituted an attempt to exert or suggest improper influence over

the criminal process. If none of these circumstances was present, however, the threat would be ethically permissible under the Model Rules.

On the distinction for a lawyer between extortion and legitimate negotiating strategy, see *Committee on Legal Ethics v. Printz*, 416 S.E.2d 720, 727 n.4 (W.Va. 1992): "Receiving repayment of money taken from a victim is not extortion; however, asking a higher price (i.e., 'Give my money back and $20,000 or I'll call the cops!') in return for the victim's silence is extortion."

5. **Threatening Discipline:** Do the same principles apply to a lawyer's threatening disciplinary action for alleged unprofessional conduct of the opposing counsel, in order to obtain advantage in a civil matter? In ABA Standing Committee on Ethics and Professional Responsibility, Formal Opinion 94–383 (1994), the ABA Committee held that they do, but pointed out that if the professional misconduct at issue raises a substantial question as to the opposing lawyer's honesty, trustworthiness, or fitness as a lawyer, the threatening lawyer has a duty to report under Model Rule 8.3(a) that would be violated by an agreement to keep the disciplinary misconduct of the adversary silent.

A(1)(c) Pretrial Delay and Discovery and Disclosure Abuse

PROBLEM

After Dr. Mascarenas treated four-year-old Jill Olson's asthma attack with Fisons Corporation's Somophyllin Oral Liquid (the brand name for one form of its drug theophylline), she suffered a seizure, went into a coma, and eventually died. Jill's parents sued Dr. Mascarenas and Fisons, alleging that the drug was dangerous to children with asthma and that Dr. Mascarenas' use of it was negligent. Dr. Mascarenas filed a cross-claim against Fisons alleging that it was negligent either in the manufacture of the drug or in failing to advise doctors of its adverse side effects.

Fisons' files contain numerous documents outlining the development and marketing of theophylline and Somophyllin Oral Liquid, including many documents praising them. In addition, Fisons' files for its product Intal, an alternative asthma drug, contain a few "smoking gun" documents written several years before Jill's death by one of its physicians and others. These documents criticize theophylline and contend that it might cause dangerous side effects when used by children with asthma. Each of them discusses "theophylline." None of the critical documents explicitly refers to or discusses Somophyllin Oral Liquid.

QUESTIONS

(a) In the absence of a discovery request, must Fisons and its attorneys disclose the existence of the smoking gun theophylline documents to the Olsons, Dr. Mascarenas, and their attorneys?

(b) Assume that the attorneys for the Olsons and Dr. Mascarenas issued interrogatories and requests for production that asked Fisons to identify and produce any documents discussing theophylline. Assume that the law firm representing Fisons responded by objecting to the scope and burden of these discovery requests and by stating, "Without prejudice to the above objections, documents responsive to this request concerning Somophyllin Oral Liquid will be produced at the office of the company's general counsel at a time convenient to the company." Assume that Fisons then produced large numbers of documents, but that the smoking gun documents were not produced. Finally, assume that the attorneys for the Olsons and Dr. Mascarenas somehow became aware of the smoking gun documents and moved for sanctions against Fisons, its in-house counsel, and its law firm for failing to identify and produce them in response to the discovery requests.

If you assume that the law firm relied upon Fisons to forward all documents to it for production to the Olsons and Dr. Mascarenas and that Fisons did not forward the smoking gun documents, should the firm be sanctioned or disciplined? If Fisons' in-house counsel knew about the smoking gun documents, but did not send them to the firm because they did not explicitly discuss Somophyllin Oral Liquid, should he be sanctioned or disciplined? Should Fisons be sanctioned?

(c) Now assume that Fisons and its in-house counsel did forward the smoking gun documents to the law firm, but the firm chose on its own initiative to respond to the discovery requests in the manner described in question (b). Should the firm be sanctioned or disciplined? Should Fisons' in-house counsel be sanctioned or disciplined? Should Fisons be sanctioned?

(d) Now assume that Fisons and its in-house counsel sent the smoking gun documents to the law firm, but demanded that it refrain from identifying or producing them and that it come up with some basis for this action. Assume that the firm then responded to the discovery requests in the manner described in question (b). Under these circumstances, should the firm be sanctioned or disciplined? What should the firm have done in response to this client demand? Should Fisons' in-house counsel be sanctioned or disciplined? Should Fisons be sanctioned?

(e) Now assume a different, broader set of interrogatories and requests for production in which the attorneys for the Olsons and Dr. Mascarenas asked Fisons to identify and produce "any document that in any way discusses any drug containing any ingredient found in theophylline and/or Somophyllin Oral Liquid." Assume that Fisons objected, claiming that these discovery requests were overly broad and burdensome because they would require production of documents about hundreds of drugs, including many that had little in common with theophylline and/or Somophyllin Oral Liquid other than the insignificant sharing of inactive ingredients. Assume that Fisons, through its law firm, offered to provide documents regarding theophylline, Somophyllin Oral Liquid, and any drug that contained the "active ingredients" of theophylline and Somophyllin Oral Liquid, but that the attorneys for the Olsons and Dr. Mascarenas refused to agree to this limitation. Should the attorneys for the Olsons and Dr. Mascarenas be sanctioned or disciplined? Should Fisons or its attorneys be sanctioned or disciplined? If the Olsons and Dr. Mascarenas file a motion to compel Fisons to identify and produce documents regarding any drug containing any ingredient found in theophylline and/or Somophyllin Oral Liquid, how should the court respond?

RULE REFERENCES

Model Rules 3.1, 3.4(b)–(d), and 3.3

RESTATEMENT §§ 105, 106, 110(3) & 118

Rules 26 and 37 of Federal Rules of Civil Procedure

NOTES ON DISCOVERY ABUSES AND DELAY

1. The problem and questions (b), (c), and (d) are loosely based upon, but not identical to, the facts described in *Washington State Physicians Insurance Exchange and Association v. Fisons Corp.*, 858 P.2d 1054 (Wash. 1993); *see also* Barbara J. Gorham, Note, Fisons: *Will It Tame the Beast of Discovery Abuse?*, 69 Wash.L.Rev. 765 (1994). In *Fisons*, twelve experts filed affidavits supporting Fisons. Fisons argued that "the affidavits * * * confirm that no *reasonable* attorney would believe that Fisons was agreeing to produce all letters referencing 'theophylline,' when Fisons specifically limited its response to letters 'regarding Somophyllin Oral Liquid.' If opposing counsel disagreed with this limitation, he was obligated under the rules of discovery to bring a motion to compel * * *."

However, the Washington Supreme Court found that the drug company and its attorneys' discovery responses failed to "comply with either the spirit or the letter of the discovery rules" and thus violated Washington Civil Rule 26(g). *Fisons*, 858 P.2d at 1083. The court specifically rejected Fisons' arguments based upon the adversary nature of the civil discovery rules:

> First, neither the child nor the doctor limited the scope of discovery in this case. Attorneys for the child, the doctor and the drug company repeatedly referred to both theophylline and Somophyllin Oral Liquid. * * *

> Second, [n]o matter what its initial purpose, and regardless of where it had been filed, under the facts of this case, a document that warned of the serious dangers of the primary ingredient of Somophyllin Oral Liquid is a document *regarding* Somophyllin Oral Liquid.

> Third, the discovery rules do not require the drug company to produce only what it agreed to produce or what it was ordered to produce. The rules are clear that a party must *fully* answer all interrogatories and all requests for production, unless a specific and clear objection is made. If the drug company did not agree with the scope of production or did not want to respond, then it was required to move for a protective order. * * *

> Fourth, the drug company further attempts to justify its failure to produce the smoking guns by saying that the requests were not specific enough. Having read the record herein, we cannot perceive of *any* request that would have produced the smoking gun documents. * * *

> Fifth, the drug company's attorneys claim they were just doing their job, that is, they were vigorously representing their client. The conflict here is between the attorney's duty to represent the client's interest and

the attorney's duty as an officer of the court to use, but not abuse[,] the judicial process.

Id. at 1083–84.

Upon remand to determine the appropriate sanctions, the trial court approved a settlement in which the drug company and the firm agreed to pay the plaintiff $325,000. Order Imposing Sanctions, *Fisons*, No. 86–2–06254–6, 1990 WL 640794 (Wash.Super.Ct. Apr. 27, 1990). In the settlement, the law firm admitted that its attorneys had advised Fisons that the rules did not require the drug company to produce the documents. All Parties' Joint Recommendation of Award of Sanctions at 2, *Fisons* (No. 86–2–06254–6).

2. *Fisons* held that the law firm violated Washington Civil Rule 26(g), which was similar to Fed.R.Civ.P. 26(g). In language paralleling Rule 11, Federal Rule 26(g)(1) now provides:

> **Signature Required; Effect of Signature.** Every disclosure * * * and every discovery request, response, or objection must be signed by at least one attorney of record in the attorney's own name—or by the party personally, if unrepresented—and must state the signer's address, e-mail address, and telephone number. By signing, an attorney or party certifies that to the best of the person's knowledge, information, and belief formed after a reasonable inquiry:

> (A) with respect to a disclosure, it is complete and correct as of the time it is made; and

> (B) with respect to a discovery request, response, or objection, it is:

> (i) consistent with these rules and warranted by existing law or by a nonfrivolous argument for extending, modifying, or reversing existing law, or for establishing new law;

> (ii) not interposed for any improper purpose, such as to harass, cause unnecessary delay, or needlessly increase the cost of litigation; and

> (iii) neither unreasonable nor unduly burdensome or expensive, considering the needs of the case, prior discovery in the case, the amount in controversy, and the importance of the issues at stake in the action.

3. **Reasonable Inquiry:** What constitutes a reasonable inquiry within the meaning of Rule 26(g)? As a defense to sanctions, may an attorney claim a lack of intent to impede discovery? Should it matter that an attorney's actions fit within the legal community's practice norms? The *Fisons* court found that a reasonable inquiry is to be "judged by an objective standard. Subjective belief or good faith alone no longer shields an attorney from sanctions under the rules." *Fisons*, 858 P.2d at 1078.

May an attorney rely on a client's assertion that the relevant documents do not exist? In *Miller v. Badgley*, 753 P.2d 530 (Wash.Ct.App. 1988) (interpreting the similar standard in Rule 11), the court found that an attorney's "blind reliance" on a client's representations would rarely constitute a reasonable inquiry. But what if an attorney reads every document provided by the client and still does not discover the "smoking gun"?

The authors of Rule 26(g) provide little, if any, definitive guidance. The Advisory Committee notes that accompanied the original adoption of Rule 26(g) state:

> The duty to make a "reasonable inquiry" is satisfied if the investigation undertaken by the attorney and the conclusions drawn therefrom are reasonable under the circumstances. It is an objective standard similar to the one imposed by Rule 11. * * * In making the inquiry, the attorney may rely on assertions by the client and on communications with other counsel in the case as long as that reliance is appropriate under the circumstances. Ultimately, what is reasonable is a matter for the court to decide on the totality of the circumstances.

> Rule 26(g) does not require the signing attorney to certify the truthfulness of the client's factual responses to a discovery request. Rather, the signature certifies that the lawyer has made a reasonable effort to assure that the client has provided all the information and documents available to him that are responsive to the discovery demand.

Fed.R.Civ.P. 26(g) advisory committee's note (1983 amendment).

One court held that a reasonable inquiry into the facts ordinarily requires more than exclusive reliance on the client. If an attorney uncovers facts during the investigation that conflict with those provided by the client, the attorney must either convince the client to provide the true facts or withdraw. *Bergeson v. Dilworth*, 132 F.R.D. 277 (D.Kan. 1990), *vacated and remanded for determination of appropriate sanctions*, 749 F.Supp. 1555 (D.Kan. 1990).

4. **Nature of Discovery and Discovery Disputes:** Perhaps nothing in modern civil litigation is so frequently contentious as discovery and its recently created complement, mandatory disclosure. Several factors combine to create the conditions that lead to so many contentious disputes among lawyers over discovery. First, very few civil cases actually go to trial, but many of them languish in the pretrial world of disclosure and discovery for several years. *See* Marc Galanter & Mia Cahill, *"Most Cases Settle": Judicial Promotion and Regulation of Settlements*, 46 Stan.L.Rev. 1339, 1342 (1994). When lawyers who are trained to fight for their clients find little opportunity to do so in front of juries, some of them turn to discovery for opportunities to zealously represent their clients. Second, an attorney receives data and documents from the opposing party and counsel through disclosure and discovery only when the opposing party and counsel locate and provide these items, including data and documents that hurt the litigation position of the party and attorney who must find and provide them. Any system that depends upon a party and its counsel's efforts to find and produce damaging information is bound to breed a certain amount of distrust.

In addition, parties often have vastly different views about the proper scope of discovery. Some parties, often individual plaintiffs, have relatively little data that could be provided to their opponents even under the most expansive scope of discovery. Other parties, often including corporate and other institutional defendants in employment, products liability, medical malpractice, and other personal injury litigation, have large amounts of data and many thousands of documents spread among dozens or even hundreds of employees. It is not surprising that many plaintiffs' attorneys push for extensive, widespread discovery in the hopes of being provided with "smoking gun" data or documents and accuse their institutional opponents of hiding these items through dishonest and incomplete discovery responses, overly narrow interpretations of discovery requests and disclosure rules, incomplete searches for data and documents, and other forms of fraud and discovery abuse. At the same time, attorneys representing institutional defendants often accuse their opponents of conducting undirected "fishing expeditions" that are essentially cost-free to plaintiffs but expensive for defendants. In such cases, defendants must engage in costly and time-consuming searches for marginally relevant or irrelevant data and documents. Plaintiffs' attorneys who are seeking sanctions often accuse institutional defendants of evasive discovery responses, while defense attorneys frequently allege that plaintiffs' attorneys use such motions to create pressure not for discovery, but for settlement. In summary, both plaintiffs' and defense attorneys charge that their opponents abuse the discovery process, in part by attempting to raise the expense and risk of litigation to levels that will force favorable settlement offers.

Interestingly, though there are many complaints about discovery abuse, some commentators believe that actual discovery abuse is relatively rare. *Compare, e.g.*, John S. Beckerman, *Confronting Civil Discovery's Fatal Flaws*, 84 Minn.L.Rev. 505 (2000); Harrison Sheppard, *American Principles & the Evolving* Ethos *of American Legal Practice*, 28 Loy.U.Chi.L.J. 237, 241 n.7 (1996); Charles W. Sorenson, Jr., *Disclosure Under Federal Rule of Civil Procedure 26(a)—"Much Ado About Nothing?"*, 46 Hastings L.J. 679, 699–700 (1995) ("Among the more commonly mentioned activities used to resist legitimate discovery are refusing to provide information, hiding information, raising frivolous privilege claims, disingenuously construing discovery requests narrowly, destroying documents, assisting in perjury, coaching witnesses to avoid disclosing information, and providing deliberately evasive answers to discovery requests.") *with* Linda S. Mullenix, *Discovery in Disarray: The Pervasive Myth of Pervasive Discovery Abuse and the Consequences for Unfounded Rulemaking*, 46 Stan.L.Rev. 1393 (1994).

As stated in *Fisons*, the problems of discovery abuse reveal the tension between a lawyer's duties of loyalty and zealous representation to the client, on the one hand, and the attorney's duty of candor to the public, the court, and the opposing party, on the other. Which duty should be given priority? To what degree should an attorney's personal morality affect her conduct?

In *Malautea v. Suzuki Motor Co.*, 987 F.2d 1536 (11th Cir. 1993), the court found that the defendant had "stubbornly withheld discoverable information" by (1) improperly refusing to answer interrogatories on the ground that certain words and phrases were not defined; (2) improperly refusing to answer general questions by limiting the response to a narrow field; (3) delaying the production of deposition transcripts; and (4) deliberately covering up damaging evidence by objecting to questions as vague and overly broad. *Id.* at 1540. The court upheld sanctions that included a default judgment, fines against the clients and attorneys, and costs and attorneys' fees associated with the abuse. The court concluded, "An attorney's duty to a client can never outweigh his or her responsibility to see that our system of justice functions smoothly. * * * Too many attorneys, like defense counsel in this case, have allowed the objectives of the client [and their zealousness] to override their ancient duties as officers of the court. In short, they have sold out to the client." *Id.* at 1546–47. See *supra* section 1(C) for a discussion of the philosophical justifications and limits on adversarial ethics.

5. **Sanction Through Procedural Rather Than Disciplinary Process:** As with frivolous claims and defenses, *see supra* section 6(A)(1)(a), note 11, most parties who believe they have been harmed by abusive discovery and disclosure practices eschew disciplinary action in favor of motions for sanctions filed under procedural rules, including Rule 37 of the Federal Rules of Civil Procedure and similar state rules. Nonetheless, the Model Rules are not silent regarding an attorney's discovery and disclosure obligations. Model Rule 3.4(b)'s prohibition of falsification of evidence proscribes false disclosures and discovery responses. *See also* RESTATEMENT, § 118 (2000). Model Rule 3.4(d) outlaws "frivolous" discovery requests and requires an attorney to engage in a "reasonably diligent effort to comply with a legally proper discovery request." *See Fla. Bar v. Hmielewski,* 702 So.2d 218 (Fla. 1997) (suspending plaintiff's attorney who failed to provide documents covered by defendant's request for production); *see also* RESTATEMENT, § 110(3). Perhaps most significantly, Model Rule 3.4(c) forbids an attorney from "knowingly disobey[ing] an obligation under the rules of a tribunal," unless the attorney does so openly based upon an argument that there is no valid obligation. *See also* RESTATEMENT, § 105. Because most violations of procedural rules are therefore also misconduct under the Rules of Professional Conduct, an understanding of the procedural rules is critical.

6. **Obligation to Reveal Damaging Evidence Under Federal and State Rules:** The Model Rules contain no provision that itself explicitly requires an attorney to reveal evidence that is damaging to the attorney's client, except in the unusual circumstances of ex parte proceedings or disclosure to prevent fraud, *see* Model Rules 3.3(b) & (d). Reacting to a belief that such an obligation may have existed under Federal Rule of Civil Procedure 26 from 1993 to 2000, a reading of which might have required disclosure of the smoking gun theophylline documents in the circumstances of question (a), the mandatory pre-discovery disclosure obligations of Rule 26(a)(1)(B) were modified in 2000 (and again modified, though for stylistic purposes only, in 2007, including a slight change in the subsection numbering). Now a party is required to disclose only the documents and items "that the disclosing party ... may use to support its claims or defenses." Fed.R.Civ.P. 26(a)(1)(A)(ii). Because Fisons would not have used the smoking gun theophylline documents in its defense, presumably there would be no obligation to disclose these documents under the current rules before opposing counsel issued a discovery request.

Following the 1993 federal creation of mandatory disclosure, several states adopted similar provisions in their civil procedure rules. *See* John B. Oakley, *A Fresh Look at the Federal Rules in State Courts,* 3 Nev.L.J. 354 (2002–2003). If a particular state has not modified their rules after 2000 to adopt the federal limiting of the disclosure obligation to documents to be used in support of a party's case, attorneys in these states might have an obligation to provide documents like the smoking gun theophylline documents before receiving any discovery request from their opponents. *See* Alaska R.Civ.P.

26(a)(1)(D) (requiring disclosure of documents "that are relevant to disputed facts"); Colo.R.Civ.P. 26(a)(1)(B) (similar).

As a practical matter, rules providing for mandatory pre-discovery disclosure of documents and identification of witnesses, *see* Fed.R.Civ.P. 26(a)(1)(A), outline only the parameters of initial disclosures. Except with regard to expert witnesses, mandatory disclosure rules have little practical effect in outlining the ultimate scope of discovery. Attorneys who litigate are well aware of the limits of mandatory disclosure and of their ability to expand the scope of information their opponents must provide through the simple expedient of serving interrogatories and requests for production of documents. In other words, it is almost unimaginable that the attorneys representing the Olsons and Dr. Mascarenas would not have served Fisons with the interrogatories and requests for production of documents described in question (b).

7. **Overly Broad Discovery:** As suggested by question (e), attorneys can also abuse the discovery process by issuing overly broad discovery requests. The Federal Rules of Civil Procedure contain provisions designed to curb such practices. Rule 26(b)(2)(C) allows a court to limit otherwise available discovery when the desired discovery would be cumulative, unnecessarily burdensome, unneeded due to alternative means for acquiring information, or disproportionately expensive when compared to the issues at stake in the litigation. Rule 26(c)(1) allows a court to enter a protective order to limit, modify, or disallow discovery "to protect a party or person from annoyance, embarrassment, oppression, or undue burden or expense." Rule 33(a) limits a party to 25 interrogatories, including subparts, absent leave of the court or written stipulation. Following a substantive amendment in 2000 that narrowed the scope of automatically allowed discovery and a stylistic amendment in 2007, Rule 26(b)(1) now provides that parties "may obtain discovery regarding any nonprivileged matter that is relevant to any party's claim or defense." As a result of these changes, courts may be required to rule more frequently on the permissible scope of discovery.

8. **Electronic Discovery:** In modern litigation, many of the "documents" that parties and their attorneys seek to obtain from their opponents are actually stored in electronic form, including e-mails, text messages, and other communications. In the early days of electronic discovery, courts had to apply rules written for paper discovery to electronic communications and electronic storage. The Federal Rules of Civil Procedure have now been revised to explicitly cover what is now often referred to as e-discovery. *See, e.g.*, F.R.Civ.P., Rules 26(a)(1)(A)(ii) (regarding automatic disclosure of electronically stored information), 26(b)(2)(B), 26(f)(3)(C), 34 & 37(e). Although the basic principles of e-discovery do not differ from those applicable to other discovery, often there is much more information potentially available via e-discovery, due to the reality that massive amounts of information can be stored, and potentially retrieved, electronically. Perhaps as a result of this reality, combined with the potential for e-discovery costs to also become substantial, modern litigation seems to spawn many disputes about cost, proportionality, evidence retention (and destruction), and the mechanics of e-discovery. For further discussion of e-discovery issues, see, e.g., *Zubulake v. UBS Warburg LLC*, 229 F.R.D. 422 (S.D.N.Y. 2004); *Coleman (Parent) Holdings, Inc. v. Morgan Stanley & Co.*, No. 502003CA005045XXOCAI, 2005 WL

679071 (Fla.Cir.Ct. Mar. 1, 2005) (reversing the burden of proof as a sanction for party's failure to produce e-mails), *described in* Mary S. Diemer, *E–Discovery Sanctions Precede $1.45 Billion Verdict*, Litig. News, Sept. 2005, at 1; Michael W. Deyo, *Deconstructing* Pension Committee*: The Evolving Rules of Evidence Spoliation and Sanctions in the Electronic Discovery Era*, 75 Alb.L.Rev. 305 (2011–2012); Alberto G. Araiza, Note, *Electronic Discovery in the Cloud*, 2011 Duke L. & Tech.Rev. 8 (2011).

9. **Deposition Abuse:** Return to the problem. Assume that the smoking gun documents were never produced and that the attorneys for the Olsons and Dr. Mascarenas had not found out about them before the Olsons' attorney scheduled the deposition of the Fisons doctor who wrote some of them. When the plaintiffs' attorney asked the doctor whether he "was aware of any Fisons documents discussing potential problems with Somophyllin Oral Liquid or its ingredients," Dee Rayle, the attorney from the firm representing Fisons, reacted by saying, "I object to the form of the question. Though I will allow the doctor to answer the question, I remind him that he is to limit his answer to documents that explicitly address Somophyllin Oral Liquid and not any other drug." Later in the deposition, the Olsons' attorney asked the Fisons' doctor whether he "was aware of any Fisons documents discussing potential problems with theophylline or any drug containing theophylline's active ingredients." Rayle responded by saying, "Objection. Irrelevant. There is no way you are entitled to discovery about all forms of theophylline. I instruct the witness not to answer the question." When the doctor started to respond to the question despite Rayle's instruction, Rayle said, "I call for an immediate recess, so that I can confer with my client." The Olsons' attorney responded, "We can take a recess right after this question is answered." Rayle said "no way," stood up, grabbed the doctor by the elbow, and led him out of the room, where she told him that he was required, as an employee of Fisons, to follow any instruction by her to refrain from answering a question. Should Rayle be sanctioned or disciplined?

Depositions present the opportunity for discovery (or hiding) of significant information in an environment that is usually not supervised actively by judges or magistrates. Some attorneys engage in deposition practices that others consider obstructionist, unprofessional, and abusive. *See In re Fletcher*, 424 F.3d 783 (8th Cir. 2005) (suspending attorney for repeated misconduct during depositions); James A. George, *The "Rambo" Problem: Is Mandatory CLE the Way Back to Atticus?*, 62 La.L.Rev. 467, 475–81 (2002) (excerpting deposition transcripts); Robert B. Sykes, *Abusive Deposition Objections and Tactics—In Search of a Standing Order*, Utah B.J., Aug. 1998, at 8; J. Stratton Shartel, *Abuses in Depositions: Litigators Describe Response Strategies*, Inside Litig., July 1994, at 1.

In an effort to limit controversial deposition tactics, the Federal Rules of Civil Procedure have been amended to: provide that depositions generally should continue despite objections; allow attorneys to instruct witnesses not to answer only when protecting privileged matters, when enforcing previous court orders, or when thwarting another attorney's bad faith or attempt to annoy, embarrass, or oppress the deponent or a party; limit a deposition to seven hours on a single day, absent a court order or stipulation; and explicitly allow sanctions for abusive deposition conduct. Fed.R.Civ.P. 30(c) & (d). Some states have adopted similar or even more expansive rules designed to thwart not only attorney instructions to witnesses to not answer, but also "speaking objections" whereby an attorney coaches a witness while ostensibly objecting, interruption of examinations for off-the-record attorney-witness conferences, and other controversial deposition tactics. *See, e.g.,* Mass.R.Civ.P. 30(c); S.C.R.Civ.P. 30(j). In addition, Comment [5] to Model Rule 3.5 states that Model Rule 3.5(d)'s prohibition of disruptive conduct applies to depositions. Also, an attorney's Model Rule 3.3 obligation to take reasonable remedial measures after learning that prior evidence was false applies to deposition testimony, so an attorney who learns that a client lied at the deposition might have to disclose this to the court. *See* N.Y. Cnty. Bar Ass'n Comm. on Prof'l Ethics, Op. 741 (2010).

10. **Delay:** Frivolous maneuvers, such as an insubstantial counterclaim or an unjustified attempt to remove a case from state to federal court, may lead to an award of fees against the offending party. In *Grinnell Bros., Inc. v. Touche Ross & Co.,* 655 F.2d 725 (6th Cir. 1981), the court penalized an improper removal attempt by affirming the trial court's assessment of fees and costs "in the interest of justice," without considering whether the attempt was in "bad faith." *See also Howard v. Grp. Hosp. Serv.,* 618 F.Supp. 38 (W.D.Okla. 1984) (using a bad faith standard). In assessing fees and costs, the federal courts can also use the provisions of 28 U.S.C. § 1927 (2006), which provides that "[a]ny attorney or other person admitted to conduct cases in any court of the United States * * * who so multiplies the proceedings in any case unreasonably and vexatiously may be required by the court to satisfy personally the excess costs, expenses, and attorneys' fees reasonably incurred because of such conduct." *See also Claiborne v. Wisdom,* 414 F.3d 715 (7th Cir. 2005) (finding that 28 U.S.C. § 1927 did not authorize sanctions against the offending attorney's law firm); *Benson v. Giant Food Stores, LLC,* No. 09–cv–3194, 2011 WL 6747421 (E.D.Pa. Dec. 22, 2011) (applying 28 U.S.C. § 1927); James F. Holderman, *Section 1927 Sanctions and the Split Among the Circuits,* Litig., Fall. 2005, at 44.

11. **Duty to Expedite:** As noted by the *Giangrasso* court, *see supra* section 6(A)(1)(a), Model Rule 3.2 requires attorneys to make reasonable efforts to expedite litigation. When is delay an appropriate tactic? In the comments, the test is stated as "whether a competent lawyer acting in good faith would regard the course of action as having some substantial purpose other than delay. Realizing financial or other benefit from otherwise improper delay in litigation is not a legitimate interest of the client." Model Rule 3.2, Comment [1].

A(2) THE LAWYER IN CIVIL OR CRIMINAL LITIGATION

A(2)(a) Communications with Parties and Witnesses

PROBLEM

While shopping at one of the five grocery stores owned by Ashton Foods, Inc., Mr. Ted Downs slipped and fell, hurting his hip. Downs retained attorney Sue Thatcher, who filed suit against Ashton Foods, alleging that Downs slipped on grapes that had fallen from a produce stand in the store. Witnesses to the accident, to the store's policies regarding monitoring and cleaning of floors, and to the arguments between Downs and store officials following the accident include:

Ann Otherton, who was shopping for tomatoes nearby;

Loretta Green, who serves as the store's produce department manager;

Justin Kidd, a college student who works part-time stocking shelves at the store; and

Harold Eberly, who was Ashton Foods Vice President before quitting a month ago.

QUESTIONS

(a) Ashton Foods has retained Lester Minard to defend the suit. He would like to ask each of these witnesses to refrain from talking to Sue Thatcher or anyone working on her behalf. Can he do so?

(b) Sue Thatcher would like to interview each of these witnesses (without advising Minard or inviting him to participate). Can she do so?

(c) Now assume that Thatcher is afraid the witnesses will not be cooperative if she interviews them, because she is an attorney. Therefore, she hires John Guerney to conduct the interviews on her behalf. Last month, Guerney quit his job as an investigative reporter for the local newspaper, just after writing several stories about unsafe conditions in local businesses, including grocery stores. The day after he quit, he acquired his license as a private investigator. During Thatcher's briefing of Guerney about the case, Guerney indicates that it is his "standard operating procedure" as a private investigator to never reveal the identity of his client, unless explicitly instructed to do so by the client. With a smirk, he adds, "Not that any of these folks are likely to ask. They will probably think I am still working for the paper doing stories about unsafe floors." How should Thatcher respond? Can Guerney interview the witnesses, as long as he does not reveal his client's identity? Can he interview them if he does reveal his client's identity? Can he interview them if the subject of his client's identity never comes up in his interviews?

RULE REFERENCES

Model Rules 4.2, 4.4(a), 3.4(f), 4.1(a), 4.3, 8.4(a), and 5.3

RESTATEMENT §§ 99, 100, 101, 102 & 116

IN RE AIR CRASH DISASTER NEAR ROSELAWN, INDIANA

United States District Court for the Northern District of Illinois, 1995.
909 F.Supp. 1116.

CASTILLO, DISTRICT JUDGE.

* * * This opinion * * * involves serious ethical issue[s] which will often be confronted by plaintiffs' attorneys who seek to aggressively represent their clients. * * *

BACKGROUND

* * * The aircraft involved in this crash was an ATR 72–212, manufactured by Avions de Transport Regional ("ATR") and flown by Simmons Airlines, Inc. ("Simmons"). ATR, Simmons, and various corporations related to them are defendants in the consolidated lawsuits pending before this Court. [The Court] allowed damages discovery to proceed but deferred liability discovery * * *.

The Disputed Questionnaire

[T]he Airline Defendants learned that several Simmons pilots had received a letter and questionnaire ("the ATR Questionnaire") from Robert Rendzio, who is the president of a consulting firm named Safety Research Corporation of America ("SRCA"). * * * The main focus of the ATR Questionnaire pertained to the training and experience of ATR pilots in icing conditions. In light of the fact that the NTSB [(National Transportation Safety Board)] was investigating whether icing conditions played a significant role in causing the accident, the Airline Defendants became suspicious that the ATR Questionnaire was in some way linked to the pending litigation. * * *

Because the Airline Defendants were unable to determine the identity of those persons who had commissioned the survey and more ATR Questionnaires were about to be sent, the Airline Defendants prepared to file a motion for leave to take limited discovery in order to determine whether Plaintiffs' Counsel were involved in the distribution of the ATR Questionnaire.[4] * * *

However, * * * the day before the hearing on this motion * * *, Robert A. Clifford, representing certain plaintiffs in these cases, telephoned the Airline Defendants' Counsel and admitted that he and his co-counsel, Corboy & Demetrio P.C., were the "undisclosed clients" who had commissioned the ATR Questionnaire. * * * In addition, Mr. Clifford admitted that the "intermediary" was a consulting expert whom Mr. Clifford had retained to work on the litigation arising out of the Roselawn accident. * * * The next morning, * * * Mr. Clifford made these same admissions to the Court. Following such disclosure, the Airline Defendants converted their discovery motion into a motion for sanctions. * * *

The Clifford Affidavit

To his credit, Mr. Robert A. Clifford has filed an affidavit which takes full responsibility for his actions and which seeks to explain the context in

---

4. Mr. Rendzio allegedly informed one of the Airline Defendants' Counsel that he sent the ATR Questionnaire at the request of an "undisclosed client," whose identity he did not know. He further stated that he had received instructions concerning the ATR Questionnaire from an "intermediary" who refused to permit disclosure of his/her identity. * * * Subsequent attempts to ascertain the identities of the "undisclosed client" and "intermediary" were unsuccessful. * * *

which he commissioned the disputed questionnaire. This affidavit makes it clear that Mr. Clifford was "the only attorney * * * to have worked on this matter" and "the only lawyer responsible for all of the complained of activity." * * *

This Court has closely reviewed Mr. Clifford's affidavit and concluded that it establishes his good faith and intentions. This affidavit candidly acknowledges that "[i]n hindsight—a logical extension of the completed survey process could possibly result in a managerial or supervisory person's receipt of the survey." * * * In his apology to the Court, counsel, and the Airline Defendants, Mr. Clifford admits that "[c]ontact with a 'represented party' under [the] circumstances may well be criticized." * * * However, he notes that "it is a far cry from something that occurred intentionally or with the inappropriate scheme erroneously outlined by Defendants." * * * In his defense, Mr. Clifford asserts that "[i]t was not until after finding out about the [defendants'] motion that [he] knew the identity of the survey company, the fact that the survey indeed has been started on a phased process and the format of the survey." * * * Mr. Clifford also generally asserts that it was his "understanding that similar surveys had been conducted in other commercial air crash disaster litigation." * * * However, no specific cases are detailed.

DISCUSSION * * *

I. VIOLATIONS OF THE RULES OF PROFESSIONAL CONDUCT * * *

A. RULE 4.2 VIOLATION

The Airline Defendants claim that sending the cover letter and questionnaire to the Airline Defendants' ATR pilots was an *ex parte* contact in violation of Rule 4.2. * * * Rule 4.2 serves two distinct but related purposes. It preserves the integrity of the lawyer-client relationship by prohibiting contact, absent consent or legal authorization, with the represented party. * * * It also recognizes that without such a Rule "the professionally trained lawyer may, in many cases, be able to win, or in the extreme case coerce, damaging concessions from the unshielded layman." * * *

In those cases where the parties are individuals, Rule 4.2 is easily enforced because it is easy to identify the "represented parties" protected. However, when the named party is a corporation, * * * it is more difficult to delineate the parameters and scope of the protected class. Corporations can only act through individuals; but it can be troublesome to determine which individuals are the "represented parties" protected by the rule. The Official Comment to Rule 4.2 [prohibits contact] "with persons having a managerial responsibility on behalf of the organization, and with any person whose act or omission * * * may be imputed to the organization for purposes of civil or criminal liability or whose statement may constitute an admission on the part of the organization." * * *

Particularly in cases involving corporate defendants, Rule 4.2 unquestionably restricts a party's ability to conduct low cost, informal discovery. However, such a restriction is necessary because the provisions of Fed. R.Evid. 801(d)(2)(D) allow an employee's statement to be used against the employer as an admission so long as it is made during the existence of the relationship and concerns a matter within his agency or employment. * * *

Since an employee could potentially bind the corporation pursuant to Fed.R.Evid. 801(d)(2)(D), it is fair to require that the employer's attorney be present. Nevertheless, this Court recognizes that it may be difficult to determine which employees fit into the category prior to attempting discovery. This difficulty, however, does not justify an aggressive approach that results in ethical violations. Instead, counsel, when confronted with a need to obtain information from witnesses that might reasonably lead to ethical problems, must take a conservative rather than aggressive approach. * * *

In particular, this Court finds the Court's solution in *McCallum v. CSX Transp., Inc.*, 149 F.R.D. 104 (M.D.N.C. 1993) to be well reasoned and compelling. [That court] noted that an attorney seeking to ascertain an appropriate course of conduct need only request permission from the company's attorney *or* seek permission from the court[ ] prior to making any informal contacts. * * * "[T]he attorney who seeks court approval before contact does not risk an ethical violation, but one who does not acts at his or her own peril." * * *

As the Rule applies to the instant case, this Court finds the sending of the ATR Questionnaire and its receipt by the Simmons pilots to be an *ex parte* contact in violation of Rule 4.2. First, the ATR Questionnaire clearly sought information that is at the core of "the matter in representation" as outlined by the [Rule's] Official Comment. * * * Second, the Simmons pilots are persons whose statements "may constitute admissions on the part of the organization." * * * Flying ATR planes, even in icing conditions, is well within the scope of the Simmons pilots' employment. Therefore, any statements they might have made with regard to inadequate training or problems with the plane within that scope could be deemed admissions of the Airline Defendants. * * *

Plaintiffs' Counsel's argument that this issue involves a "gray area" or at least "an area that lacks precise and simple definition," thereby excusing their conduct, is simply unpersuasive. The Official Comment to Rule 4.2 provides an explicit interpretation regarding the meaning of "represented parties" in the corporate context. Moreover, even if the experienced Plaintiffs' Counsel found that the rule was unclear, they had a duty to ask the opposing counsel's permission *or* obtain this Court's approval prior to distributing the ATR Questionnaire. In conclusion, if Plaintiffs' Counsel thought there truly was a disparity between possible interpretations of the rule, counsel had three courses of action available:

(1) follow the more restrictive interpretation of the Rule; (2) contact opposing counsel; or (3) seek guidance from the Court. * * *

B. RULE 4.3 VIOLATION

The Airline Defendants also allege that Plaintiffs' Counsel violated Rule 4.3 by sending the ATR Questionnaire under a "deceptive cover letter that concealed that the questionnaire was being done at the direction of counsel for use in pending litigation."

[T]he ATR pilots, other than those employed by the Airline Defendants, are "unrepresented persons" under Rule 4.3, and any contacts with them are governed by that rule. Therefore, this Court will examine whether Plaintiffs' Counsel did in fact violate Rule 4.3.

The Court finds that the cover letter accompanying the ATR Questionnaire contained misleading information regarding the true purpose underlying the distribution of the questionnaire. The cover letter does not disclose on its face the fact that the ATR Questionnaire was prepared at the request of an attorney on behalf of plaintiffs who have sued the Airline Defendants. Moreover, the letter goes to great lengths to persuade the recipient of its neutral and unbiased character. For example, the letter describes the questionnaire as an "independent survey," thereby implying that there is no underlying motive in obtaining the information and that the parties seeking such information are "disinterested," even though Rule 4.3 explicitly states that a lawyer shall not imply that he or she is disinterested. Furthermore, the letter explains that the pilots' names were "provided to us by the FAA," strongly implying that the FAA was participating or, at least, had endorsed the survey. Finally, the letter states that the questionnaire focused on icing conditions and the ATR aircraft solely "[i]n our attempt to keep the questions to an absolute minimum" rather than because that is the nature of the litigation. * * *

Such deception, which is undertaken or at least condoned by Plaintiffs' Counsel through their intermediary, is a paradigm example of conduct prohibited by Rule 4.3. The ATR pilots who received the questionnaire may have been led to believe that they were dealing with a disinterested third party. Since Plaintiffs' Counsel are not disinterested parties, attempting to mislead the ATR pilots into so believing is a clear violation of Rule 4.3.

The Court specifically finds that Plaintiffs' Counsel not only failed to take precautions to prohibit any misunderstandings associated with the cover letter and ATR Questionnaire, but also affirmatively violated the rule by not fully disclosing their representative capacity and the true motive behind obtaining such information. In light of the numerous airline incidents that have occurred in recent years, with ATR planes in particular, it is not illogical to suspect that the ATR pilots might respond overzealously in an attempt to generate a quick favorable response by the FAA. The illusive language used in the cover letter may have ultimately led the ATR pilots to make exaggerated or untrue statements in order to protect their own livelihoods.

The fact that Plaintiffs' Counsel, themselves, did not actually develop the ATR Questionnaire and cover letter is irrelevant with regard to their accountability for such actions. According to Rule 8.4(a)(2), "[a] lawyer shall not induce another to engage in conduct, or give assistance to another's conduct, when the lawyer knows that conduct will violate these Rules." Therefore, Plaintiffs' Counsel are legally responsible for the violation of Rule 4.3 since they hired the intermediary and Mr. Rendzio, thereby "inducing" them to formulate the ATR Questionnaire and misleading cover letter. An attorney [cannot] evade his professional and ethical obligations by delegating the job of developing and distributing deceptive materials to a paid expert or consultant. * * *

II. SANCTIONS

[T]his Court grants the Airline Defendants' Motion for sanctions and orders that: (1) all questionnaires be returned to the Airline Defendants' counsel within fourteen days of this order; (2) the current order barring Plaintiffs' Counsel from any further distribution of the questionnaires be extended until such time as the Court approves a questionnaire procedure, if and when requested by the parties; and (3) this Court will bar the questionnaires from being offered as evidence in this case.

NOTES ON COMMUNICATING WITH ADVERSE PARTIES AND WITNESSES

1. **Model Rule 4.2:** In the Ethics 2000 Commission changes, which occurred after *Air Crash*, the circumstances under which an attorney could communicate with a represented person without permission of the attorney representing that person were expanded from those when "authorized by law" to those when "authorized to do so by law or a court order." *But see* RESTATEMENT, § 99 (2000) (not including the "or a court order" exception).

Model Rule 4.2 does not state that an intent to violate the rule or take advantage of the contacted individual is an element of misconduct. As a result, an attorney violates Model Rule 4.2 by sending a letter to a represented person, even when she sends a copy of the letter to the represented person's attorney. *See In re Uttermohlen*, 768 N.E.2d 449 (Ind. 2002). Also, a lawyer can violate Model Rule 4.2 by "friending" a represented person on a social media site. *See* Mo. Legal Ethics Counsel, Op. 2009–0003; San Diego Cnty. Bar Ass'n, Op. 2011–2.

Formal litigation is not a prerequisite to a Model Rule 4.2 violation. Instead, an attorney who contacts a represented person before litigation is formally filed still violates the no contact rule. *See Penda Corp. v. STK, LLC*, Nos. Civ.A. 03–5578 & 03–6240, 2004 WL 1628907 (E.D.Pa. July 16, 2004) (pointing to the ABA's 1995 change from "party" to "person" in the language of Model Rule 4.2 as support for the conclusion that formal litigation is not a required element of a violation).

2. **Contact by Non–Lawyers:** As in *Air Crash*, some lawyers refrain from directly contacting witnesses and instead ask legal assistants, private investigators, experts, or others to interview them. The Model Rules regulate such communications, by providing that relevant Model Rules provisions apply not only to actions taken by lawyers, but also to actions taken on behalf of lawyers. Pursuant to Model Rule 5.3(c), discussed in *supra* section 2(F)(3), a lawyer who orders or ratifies the conduct of a non-lawyer employee is responsible for that conduct, as is one who learns of a non-lawyer subordinate's conduct when its consequences can be mitigated or avoided, but fails to engage in remedial action. Under Model Rule 8.4(a), whose local equivalent was discussed in *Air Crash*, a lawyer who knowingly induces or assists

another in a violation of the Model Rules has thereby engaged in misconduct. These Model Rules apply to all of the restrictions on attorney conduct, of course, but they often become relevant in the context of contact with witnesses and represented persons due to the tendency of some lawyers to make these contacts through their employees and agents. *See Bd. of Prof'l Resp. v. Jenkins*, 2011 WY 89, 260 P.3d 264, 265 (finding a Model Rule 4.2 violation where attorney "attempted to utilize a third person to communicate information to and/or obtain information from a person who was represented by counsel").

3. **Contact by Parties:** Though a lawyer cannot circumvent the anti-contact rule by having a third party communicate with the adverse party, there is no prohibition against opposing parties communicating with each other directly. Comment [4] to Model Rule 4.2 notes, "Parties to a matter may communicate directly with each other, and a lawyer is not prohibited from advising a client concerning a communication that the client is legally entitled to make." Can an attorney circumvent the rule prohibiting contact with a represented party by having his or her client communicate with the adverse party? This issue often arises when a lawyer suspects that the opposing counsel is not communicating settlement offers to his or her client.* In Formal Opinion 92–362 (1992), the ABA's Standing Committee on Ethics and Professional Responsibility concluded that, while the lawyer may not communicate with the party, the lawyer for the offeror-party should:

> advise that party with respect to the lawyer's belief as to whether the offers are in fact being communicated to the offeree-party. Likewise the offeror-party's lawyer has a duty to that party to discuss not only the limits on the lawyer's ability to communicate with the offeree-party, but also the freedom of the offeror-party to communicate with the opposing offeree-party.**

In some contexts, however, it may be improper to advise one's client to contact an adverse party, if the contact would essentially be one made on behalf of the lawyer. *See, e.g., In re Anonymous*, 819 N.E.2d 376 (Ind. 2004) (disciplining an attorney who gave a copy of an affidavit to his employer client, knowing that the employer would give it to the represented employee, then watched the employee sign the affidavit, despite the attorney's refusal to speak with the employee); *In re Marietta*, 569 P.2d 921 (Kan. 1977) (publicly censuring a lawyer for causing a client to communicate with his ex-wife and deliver a release of child support payments without the consent of the ex-wife's attorney); *Bd. of Prof'l Resp. v. Melchior*, 2012 WY 8, 269 P.3d 1088, 1091 (publicly censuring an attorney who "created and gave to his client a divorce settlement agreement and a confidential financial statement at a time when [he] knew or reasonably should have known that there was a substantial risk that she would deliver them to the husband, whom [he] knew was being represented by counsel").

Also, it is important to note that a represented person's initiation of contact with adverse counsel (as opposed to an adverse party) does not serve as a waiver of the anti-contact provisions of Model Rule 4.2. Instead, even if the represented person first contacts the adverse attorney, that adverse attorney still cannot communicate with the represented person without permission from the adverse party or via law or court order. *See Am. Plastic Equip., Inc. v. Toytrackerz, LLC*, No. 07–2253–DJW, 2009 WL 902424, at *8 (D.Kan. Mar. 31, 2009).

4. **Contacts with Current Corporate or Entity Employees:** As *Air Crash* notes, the no contact rule becomes challenging to apply when the represented party is a corporation or other institutional entity. *Air Crash* quotes the pre–2002 Comment on this issue. Comment [7] to Model Rule 4.2 now states that the restriction against contact applies to those who regularly oversee or consult with the entity's lawyer, or have the authority to bind the entity regarding the matter in dispute. *See also* RESTATEMENT, § 100(2)(a). This presumably would be a smaller group than the former no-contact group of managers, which included all employees with managerial responsibility.

With respect to other employees, Comment [7] to Model Rule 4.2 now limits the no-contact group to those whose actions or omissions could be imputed to the entity. *See also* RESTATEMENT, § 100(2)(b). The ABA deleted the comment language quoted in *Air Crash* that applied the no-contact rule to anyone who could make a statement that could constitute an admission by the entity, which effectively placed all or almost all employees in the no contact group. *See also* RESTATEMENT, § 100(2)(c) (prohibiting contact if the employee's statements "would have the effect of binding the organization with respect to proof of the matter"). Thus, if a state has adopted the 2002 changes to Comment [7], it presumably would reject *Air Crash*'s holding that an attorney cannot contact anyone who could make a statement that would be considered a non-hearsay admission under Rule 801(d)(2) of the Federal Rules of Evidence or a similar state provision. *See Paris v. Union Pac. R.R.*, 450 F.Supp.2d 913 (E.D.Ark. 2006) (holding that the post-Ethics 2000 Comment [7] to Model Rule 4.2 allows a plaintiff's attorney to contact a defendant railroad's engineer and brakeman). However, at least one court, apparently reluctant to adopt this Ethics 2000 Commission reduction in the set of entity employees covered Model Rule 4.2, found, like the *Air Crash* court, that employees who might make admissions cannot be contacted. *See Microsoft Corp. v. Alcatel Bus. Sys.*, No. 07–090–SLB, 2007 WL 4480632 (D.Del. Dec. 18, 2007) (finding a Model Rule 4.2 violation when plaintiff's attorneys in a patent case purchased the communication system at issue from defendant, then received training about that system from a technician employed by defendant). For a discussion of the extent to which corporate employees are covered by the no contact rule, including a review of the evolution of several iterations of professional responsibility provisions, see Bran C. Noonan, *The Nieseg and NLRA Union: A Revised Standard for Identifying High–Level Employees for Ex Parte Interviews*, 54 N.Y.L.Sch.L.Rev. 261 (2009–2010).

5. **Contacts with Former Corporate or Entity Employees:** Former employees of represented entities have also generated inconsistent applications of Model Rule 4.2. *Compare Chancellor v. Boeing Co.*, 678 F.Supp. 250 (D.Kan. 1988) (preventing contact with former employees who held "confidential" positions or whose conduct was the subject of the litigation), *with* ABA Standing Comm. on Ethics and Prof'l Resp., Formal Op. 91–359 (1991) (allowing contact with former employees due to the absence of any language in Model Rule 4.2 regarding former employees). A 2002 addition to Model Rule 4.2's Comment [7] attempts to eliminate confusion by stating that ex parte contact with former employees is permissible. As in *supra* note 4 regarding contact with current employees, though, some seem reluctant to allow contact with former employees of represented organizations. *See Arnold v. Cargill Inc.*, No. 01–2086 (DWF/AJB), 2004 WL 2203410, at *8–10 (D.Minn. Sept. 24, 2004) (finding a Model Rule 4.2 violation when plaintiff's attorney contacted a former manager of a represented defendant corporation, due to concerns about disclosure of confidential and privileged communications and documents).

6. **Contacts "Authorized by Law":** Which communications with represented parties are authorized by law? When the other party is the government, does the client's First Amendment right to petition for grievances allow direct communication with the government itself? *Compare Vega v. Bloomsburgh*, 427 F.Supp. 593, 595 (D.Mass. 1977) (allowing such contact), *with Hammond v. Junction City*, No. 00–2146–JWL, 2002 WL 169370, at *6 (D.Kan. Jan. 23, 2002) (quoting ABA Formal Op. 97–408 in stating that contact with officials of represented government agencies is generally forbidden). *See also* RESTATEMENT, § 101 (2000) (allowing contact with government officials except when the lawyer is negotiating or litigating a claim against the government). Following its amendment in 2002, Comment [5] to Model Rule 4.2 now states, "Communications authorized by law may include communications by a lawyer on behalf of a client who is exercising a constitutional or other legal right to communicate with the government." Given the disagreement about ex parte communications with represented governmental entities, the choice of the vague verb "may" might have been intentional. *See* Carl A. Pierce, *Variations on a Basic Theme: Revisiting the ABA's Revision of Model Rule 4.2 (Part I)*, 70 Tenn.L.Rev. 121, 192 (2002) (reporting that the Ethics 2000 Commission "concluded that the relevant law was too complex and variegated to be described usefully in a Comment").

7. **Contacts by "Consent":** Model Rule 4.2 allows direct contact with a represented party where the opposing party's attorney has consented. Why is the power to consent in the attorney's hands? Should the client be able to consent without advice from counsel? What if it is the adverse party who approaches the opposing lawyer?

Attempts by clients to waive the protections of Model Rule 4.2 and speak directly to opposing counsel probably arise most frequently in criminal cases. Represented criminal defendants sometimes attempt to contact prosecutors in an effort to cooperate and provide information and testimony against others involved in criminal activity. When an attorney has advised (or, in the defendant's opinion, will advise) against seeking a favorable plea agreement or immunity in exchange for testimony, the defendant may attempt to contact a prosecutor directly.

Indeed, Model Rule 4.2 has proven to be particularly controversial when applied to prosecutors. Some prosecutors argue that the anti-contact rule should not apply when a represented person initiates contact, but defense attorneys counter that such a restriction will lead to creative efforts by law enforcement officials to convince defendants to initiate such contacts. Prosecutors also argue that contacts initiated by police officers should not subject prosecutors to possible Model Rule 4.2 discipline, because they do not have the same type of supervisory authority over police officers that lawyers in private practice exercise over their non-lawyer employees. Prosecutors also argue that many law enforcement contacts with suspects and witnesses are authorized by law. *Compare United States v. Lopez*, 4 F.3d 1455 (9th Cir. 1993) (applying the no-contact restriction even though the defendant initiated the contact), *with United States v. Powe*, 9 F.3d 68 (9th Cir. 1993) (allowing contact with a suspect who had not yet been charged).

Neither Model Rule 4.2 nor its comments explicitly resolve this issue. Current Comment [5] notes only that such communications "may" be authorized. The same Comment, however, asserts that a prosecutor must comply with both Model Rule 4.2 and the state and federal constitutions in communicating with "the accused" and that communications that are allowed under the state and federal constitutions might nonetheless violate Model Rule 4.2. The controversy over the application of Model Rule 4.2's no-contact provisions to prosecutors has been most hotly debated in the context of federal prosecutors. For a brief review of the history of this debate, see *infra* section 6(A)(4)(a), notes 7 and 8.

8. **Unrepresented Persons:** Model Rule 4.3, which governs an attorney's contact with an unrepresented person (including, but not limited to, a non-party witness) prohibits an attorney from stating or implying that the attorney is disinterested. *See* San Diego Cnty. Bar Ass'n, Op. 2011–2 (concluding that a lawyer who sends a "friend" request in an effort to access a potential witness's social media pages must disclose the lawyer's purpose in making the request); *cf.* Philadelphia Bar Ass'n Prof'l Guidance Comm., Op. 2009–2 (finding that all "friend" requests by attorneys to non-party adverse witnesses to gather impeachment material are improper, because they are inherently deceptive). It also requires an attorney who knows or should know that the unrepresented person "misunderstands" the attorney's role to correct this misunderstanding. Failure to do so can result in discipline. *See In re Millett*, 241 P.3d 35, 42–43 (Kan. 2010) (suspending attorney for, inter alia, failing to correct his client's brother's belief that the attorney was representing the brother's, in addition to the client's, interests). Model Rule 4.3 also prohibits an attorney from giving legal advice to unrepresented persons whose interests are adverse to the attorney's client, "other than the advice to secure counsel."

Model Rule 4.4(a) also regulates an attorney's contact with unrepresented persons, including witnesses, although it applies to all "third persons." It prohibits an attorney from using means "that have no substantial purpose other than to embarrass, delay, or burden a third person, or use methods of obtaining evidence that violate the legal rights of such a person." Courts are not reluctant to discipline attorneys who violate this rule. *See In re Campbell*, 199 P.3d 776 (Kan. 2009) (suspending prosecutor for six months for violation of state's version of Model Rule 4.4(a) by embarrassing underage drinker); *In re Wells*, 2009–2343 (La. 5/11/10); 36 So.3d 198, 206 (disbarring attorney for, inter alia, violation of state's version of Model Rule 4.4(a)); *In re White*, 707 S.E.2d 411 (S.C. 2011) (suspending attorney who sent a letter stating that its recipients had no soul and no brain and were "insane" and "pigheaded"); *Flowers v. Bd. of Prof'l Resp.*, 314 S.W.3d 882, 896–98 (Tenn. 2010) (suspending attorney for one year for violation of state's version of Model Rule 4.4(a)).

9. **Model Rule 3.4(f) and Requests to Refrain from Giving Information or Testimony:** In a portion of the *Air Crash* decision not reprinted here, the court found that the lawyer did not violate Model Rule 3.4(f). Model Rule 3.4(f) prohibits an attorney from asking a witness to refrain from voluntarily communicating with opposing counsel, unless the witness is the lawyer's client or a relative, employee, or other agent of the client. *See also In re Walsh*, 182 P.3d 1218, 1230 (Kan. 2008) (suspending attorney who asked a potential witness not to testify in a disciplinary hearing); *In re Alcantara*, 676 A.2d 1030 (N.J. 1995) (disciplining a criminal defense attorney who attempted to persuade his client's co-defendants to refrain from testifying against him); Utah St.B. Ethics Comm., Op. 04–06 (2004) (concluding that an attorney for a corporation could not prevent opposing counsel from interviewing corporate employees who were mere fact witnesses to an alleged tort). This anti-sequestration provision reflects the view that the truth-seeking process is usually enhanced when all attorneys have access to all witnesses. *See State ex rel. Okla. Bar Ass'n v. Cox*, 2002 OK 23, ¶ 14, 48 P.3d 780, 786 (suspending attorney for "attempt[ing] to dissuade his friend ... from giving expert testimony" and thereby engaging in "a grievous assault upon the truth-seeking function of the judicial process"); *see also* RESTATEMENT, § 116(4).

An Oregon ethics opinion prevents an attorney from attempting to persuade either a fact or expert witness not to testify. The opinion reasoned that such action "would be prejudicial to the administration of justice, because, if successful, it would obviously constitute substantial harm to the functioning of the proceeding as well as to the substantive interest of a party." Or. St. Bar Ass'n, Formal Op. 2005–132. Many jurisdictions have criminal or other statutes or rules that outlaw or at least discourage "payments to a potential witness to keep her from testifying, hiding of potential witnesses, persuading potential witnesses to avoid the subpoena power of a particular court or to fail to testify when subpoenaed, and threatening or discouraging potential witnesses from testifying." Stephen D. Easton, *"Red Rover, Red Rover, Send that Expert Right Over": Clearing the Way for Parties to Introduce the Testimony of Their Opponents' Expert Witnesses*, 55 SMU L.Rev. 1427, 1476–77 (2002); *see also* RESTATEMENT, § 116(2) & (3). The Oregon opinion does permit a lawyer to persuade a witness that her opinion, observation, or recollection is in error, if the lawyer avoids improper means of persuasion.

10. **Treating Physicians:** Assume that a plaintiff, who was injured in an accident, received treatment for those injuries from an emergency room or

other physician. Months or years later, he sues a person or entity in a tort action to recover for his injuries. Can the attorney representing the defendant make direct contact with the treating physician, without notifying the attorney for the plaintiff, to conduct an interview about the doctor's treatment of the plaintiff? Due perhaps to the predominance of personal injury litigation, this question commanded the attention of litigators, courts, ethics committees, and professional responsibility commentators for many years. The experts disagreed, with gusto. Some contended that patient privacy concerns and the physician-patient privilege prohibited direct defense attorney contact with treating physicians. Others contended that such contact was permissible, because a plaintiff waived privacy and physician-patient privilege rights by filing suit and placing her medical condition in issue. In addition, some argued that a treating physician was not a client of the plaintiff's attorney covered by Model Rule 4.2, and that the treating physician was also not an agent of the client under Model Rule 3.4(f).

To a significant extent, this once interesting question is now mostly, but perhaps not completely, dead. The federal Health Insurance Portability and Accountability Act of 1996, commonly referred to as "HIPAA," led to Department of Health and Human Services regulations that provide substantial privacy protection regarding health records. *See* 45 C.F.R. § 164.500 et seq. Generally (i.e., ignoring nuances and exceptions in the regulations), HIPAA regulations forbid a health care agency from disclosing patient information, absent a court order or a special "HIPAA release" whereby a patient grants permission for the health care agency to release these records to specified persons. Plaintiffs in personal injury cases often sign such releases for their own attorneys, but they are unlikely to sign HIPAA releases to allow opposing counsel direct access to their health care information. In the absence of a HIPAA release, a physician would almost certainly be violating federal law by talking directly to a defense attorney. Now that most doctors are aware of HIPAA privacy protection, most will presumably not violate HIPAA regulations by communicating ex parte with defense attorneys.

Therefore, while HIPAA does not directly regulate the conduct of defense attorneys in personal injury litigation, it has effectively foreclosed the possibility of ex parte contact by defense attorneys with treating physicians in most instances. Interestingly, though, at least one influential court has required plaintiffs in medical malpractice actions to sign HIPAA releases allowing defense attorneys to conduct ex parte interviews with non-party treating physicians. *Arons v. Jutkowitz*, 880 N.E.2d 831 (N.Y. 2007). Thus, issues surrounding defense attorney contact with treating physicians have not completely disappeared from the personal injury litigation landscape. However, informal defense attorney access to treating physicians, without court intervention and the litigated disputes it will often generate, has probably disappeared.

For discussions of HIPAA issues in personal injury litigation, see Ted Agniel et al., *Ex Parte Communications with Treating Health Care Providers: Does HIPAA Change Missouri Law?*, 63 J.Mo.B. 296 (2007), Beverly Cohen, *Reconciling the HIPAA Privacy Rule with State Laws Regulating Ex Parte Interviews of Plaintiffs' Treating Physicians: A Guide to Performing HIPAA Preemption Analysis*, 43 Hous.L.Rev. 1091 (2006), David G. Wirtes, Jr., et al.,

An Important Consequence of HIPAA: No More Ex Parte Communications Between Defense Attorneys and Plantiffs' Treating Physicians, 27 Am.J. Trial Advoc. 1 (2003), Scott Airpoli, Comment, *Hungry Hungry HIPAA: Has the Regulation Bitten Off More Than It Can Chew by Prohibiting Ex Parte Communication with Treating Physicians?*, 75 UMKC L.Rev. 499 (2006), and Andrew King, Comment, *HIPAA: Its Impact on Ex Parte Disclosures with an Adverse Party's Treating Physician*, 34 Cap.U.L.Rev. 775 (2006).

11.   **A Final Note on *Air Crash*:** In the court's conclusion, which is not reprinted here, the trial judge went to extensive lengths to praise the lawyer the court was sanctioning. The court indicated that the mere filing of the motion, and the proceedings thereon, were "more than enough punishment for Mr. Clifford," and further noting the lawyer's "long and successful history of service to [his] clients and to Chicago's legal community." *Air Crash*, 909 F.Supp. at 1125. Why did the court make these statements?

12.   **A Fool for a Client?** Many are fond of saying that an attorney who represents himself or herself "has a fool for a client." Perhaps the wisdom of this cliché results, at least in part, from the tendency of attorneys to lose perspective when they represent themselves in litigation, then engage in conduct that runs afoul of the Model Rules regulating litigators. *See, e.g., In re Pelkey*, 962 A.2d 268, 280 & n.27 (D.C. 2008) (disbarring attorney for Model Rule 4.4 violations and other misconduct in arbitration); *In re Scanio*, 919 A.2d 1137 (D.C. 2007) (suspending attorney for making false factual claims while attempting to secure a settlement for himself from an insurance company); *In re Lucas*, 2010 ND 187, 789 N.W.2d 73 (suspending attorney who represented himself in a dispute with his condominium association and violated Model Rule 4.2 by sending letters to board members and officers suggesting settlement); *Medina Cnty. Bar Ass'n v. Cameron*, 2011–Ohio–5200, ¶ 9, 958 N.E.2d 138, 140–41 (suspending attorney for violating Model Rule 4.2 by contacting a represented party who sued him for non-payment, instead of the party's attorney, to discuss settlement); *In re Hammer*, 718 S.E.2d 442 (S.C. 2011) (suspending attorney for violating Model Rule 4.4's prohibition of harassment of third persons by subpoenaing a witness to a deposition in his *pro se* false arrest case, then asking him about his sexual orientation). Representation of relatives also seems to lead to problems for attorneys. *See Iowa Sup. Ct. Atty. Disc. Bd. v. Gailey*, 790 N.W.2d 801, 806 (Iowa 2010) (suspending attorney for violating state's version of Model Rule 4.2 by contacting his son's estranged wife outside the presence of her attorney); *In re Mertz*, 2006 ND 85, 712 N.W.2d 849 (disciplining attorney for violating Model Rule 4.4 by sending demeaning letter to victim who filed a vicious dog complaint against attorney's daughter).

A(2)(b)   Communications with Judges

PROBLEM

Juan Romero represents Shelly Mission, who has been charged with attempted murder in a case set for a jury trial in two months. While Romero is standing in line at a movie theater, he notices Judy Johnson, the judge assigned to the case. Although Juan tries to avoid eye contact, she walks up to him and says, "I am really having a tough time deciding that motion you filed, because I just don't understand the law on that issue. Without trying to convince me of anything, could you explain the law a bit?"

QUESTIONS

(a) How should Romero respond to Judge Johnson's question at the movie theater? Can he explain the law in question, as long as he is careful to refrain from advocating his position while doing so? If the motion in question is his request for a change of venue, can he explain the law and advocate his position? Can he say "Sorry, Your Honor, but I cannot say anything here," then send the judge a letter explaining the law, as long as he sends a copy of the letter to the prosecutor?

(b) Should Judge Johnson be disciplined?

RULE REFERENCES

Model Rules 3.5 and 3.3(d)

Model Code of Judicial Conduct, Rule 2.9 (formerly Canon 3B(7))

RESTATEMENT § 113

IN RE RAGATZ

Supreme Court of Wisconsin, 1988.
429 N.W.2d 488.

PER CURIAM.

* * * Attorney Ragatz, as a member of the Foley and Lardner law firm, undertook to represent the estate of Marie Swerig in a will contest filed * * * by the law firm of Clifford and Relles on behalf of the decedent's son. Soon thereafter, Attorney Ragatz filed an action, entitled *Bennin v. Swerig,* [an equitable adjustment action, the purpose of which was] to reduce the amount the son might receive in the event he prevailed in the will contest.

The Clifford and Relles law firm moved to dismiss the equitable adjustment action and have it declared frivolous, thereby entitling its client to payment of costs and attorney fees. Foley and Lardner agreed to dismiss the action but opposed the motion to hold the action frivolous. Oral argument on the frivolousness issue was made to the court, * * * and written briefs were then filed.

[The case was assigned to Judge Aulik who] met Attorney Ragatz by chance and in a brief conversation told him that the judge's law clerk had stated to the judge that *Bennin* might indeed be frivolous. Attorney Ragatz responded to the judge's remarks, maintaining that the law clerk was in error and that the action was not frivolous. Opposing counsel was not present during that conversation or thereafter advised that it had occurred.

Shortly after that conversation, Attorney Ragatz received by mail a document "in the form of a proposed decision in the *Bennin* case" indicating a ruling that the lawsuit was frivolous. Attorney Ragatz had not solicited that document and correctly assumed it had been sent by Judge Aulik.[1] * * *

After Attorney Ragatz ascertained the contents of the document he received from Judge Aulik, he met with Attorney David Reinecke, the attorney in his office who had been assigned to work on *Bennin* under his supervision, and directed him to prepare a response. Attorney Reinecke did so, citing authority and making legal arguments "intended to influence the Court in its decision." Attorney Ragatz reviewed and edited that letter, changing the salutation from "Dear Judge Aulik" to "Dear Jack" and signing it "Tom." Attorney Ragatz also added a paragraph stating that it was unlikely either side would appeal the judge's ruling on the frivolousness issue * * *. He wrote that, if successful in the will contest, he believed he could reach a compromise in *Bennin*. Attorney Ragatz then had the letter marked "Confidential" and sent to Judge Aulik, but he did not provide opposing counsel with a copy of it. Moreover, Attorney Ragatz did not intend that opposing counsel be aware of the existence or contents of it.

The related will contest was tried [before another judge and] the court ruled in favor of the will proponent, Foley and Lardner's client. [T]wo matters remained unresolved: the frivolousness issue in Judge Aulik's court and a determination of costs and fees in the will contest. The latter issue was scheduled for hearing[. In conjunction with that hearing,] Attorney Clifford examined the court file in *Bennin* and in it discovered the letter Attorney Ragatz had sent to the judge * * * setting forth legal arguments on the frivolousness issue. He asked the judge's clerk for a copy of the letter, but the clerk stated that she could not provide him one without the judge's authorization, as it had been marked "Confidential." The clerk took the letter to the judge, who was elsewhere in the courthouse, relaying Attorney Clifford's request for a copy. Judge Aulik retained the letter, and when the clerk returned to Attorney Clifford without either the letter or a copy, Attorney Clifford went to see the judge. When Attorney Clifford found him, the judge was engaged in a telephone conversation. Unbeknownst to Attorney Clifford, Judge Aulik was telling Attorney Ragatz that Attorney Clifford had found the letter. However, the judge did not tell Attorney Clifford to whom he had been talking or the subject of the conversation.

Attorney Clifford then returned to his office without having obtained a copy of the Ragatz letter, whereupon he called Attorney Ragatz. During the ensuing conversation, Attorney Ragatz did not reveal the fact that the judge had called him and he denied familiarity with the letter, stating that he would attempt to find a copy of it. The next morning, Attorney Ragatz

---

1. We considered the judge's conduct in this matter in *Disciplinary Proceedings Against Aulik*, 146 Wis.2d 57, 429 N.W.2d 759 (1988)[, in which the judge was suspended for 90 days for the ex parte communication in this case].

telephoned the judge and suggested that he schedule a conference with counsel. That request was not made through the judge's clerk, nor was it made in a telephone conference call with Attorney Clifford participating. Judge Aulik told Attorney Ragatz in that conversation that he had already determined to schedule such a conference for that morning.

That conference was held in the judge's chambers, at which time Judge Aulik signed and distributed copies of his decision on the frivolousness issue, which was in favor of Attorney Clifford's client. During the conference, Attorney Clifford renewed his request for a copy of the Ragatz letter, but Judge Aulik stated that he was no longer in possession of it and Attorney Ragatz said that he had not yet been able to locate a copy.

During the conference in the judge's chambers, both Attorney Ragatz and Judge Aulik urged Attorney Clifford to settle the pending litigation, as Judge Aulik's decision had not awarded a specific amount of attorney fees to the Clifford firm and that issue remained to be addressed. Attorney Clifford stated that he was not comfortable settling the matter until he had received a copy of the Ragatz letter. A file copy was later found in Attorney Ragatz's office and a copy of it was sent to Attorney Clifford.

* * * The referee considered Attorney Ragatz's letter to be "an advocacy piece" which "could have no possible intended purpose but to influence the outcome of litigation." In the referee's view, whether Attorney Ragatz was successful in having the judge decide the matter in favor of his client or in using his knowledge of the proposed decision to gain a favorable settlement did not alter the wrongfulness of the conduct. While on the basis of the character testimony presented on Attorney Ragatz's behalf the referee expressed a willingness to believe that his misconduct was "out of character," she considered it serious nonetheless.

The referee concluded that, by directing the preparation of the letter on the frivolousness issue and causing it to be sent to the judge without disclosing its contents to opposing counsel, Attorney Ragatz violated [Rule 3.5(b)], which prohibits a lawyer from engaging in ex parte communications on the merits of a case with a judge before whom that case is pending * * *.

We adopt the referee's findings of fact and conclusions of law and accept the recommendation for discipline. It is significant that in neither of the two instances of ex parte communication did Attorney Ragatz bring up the subject of the pending litigation. Rather, he was responding to communication from the judge: in one instance, to remarks concerning the judge's law clerk's conclusion on the frivolousness issue; in the other, to a proposed decision on that issue the judge had sent him, apparently without having sent a copy to opposing counsel. Nevertheless, the proscription against ex parte communications between a lawyer and a judge on the merits of a pending adversary proceeding applied here.

Attorney Ragatz had the duty to either refrain from participating in those communications or provide a copy of his response to opposing counsel. His refusal to do so was a serious breach of his professional responsibilities. He permitted ex parte information from the judge on a contested issue and additional ex parte argument to the judge on that issue to influence the outcome of litigation. In so doing, he acted contrary to the objectives of our court system, a system in which he, as attorney, serves an integral role. In effect, his actions denied one party to that litigation a full and fair hearing on the merits of the controversy.

As it violated a fundamental principle of our justice system, Attorney Ragatz's misconduct warrants severe discipline—a suspension of his license to practice law. In determining the appropriate length of that suspension, we take into account the fact that Attorney Ragatz did not initiate the ex parte communications but, rather, responded to communications initiated by the judge and the fact that this is the first time Attorney Ragatz has been the subject of a disciplinary proceeding.

IT IS ORDERED that the license of Thomas G. Ragatz to practice law in Wisconsin is suspended for a period of 60 days * * *.

NOTES ON EX PARTE CONTACT WITH JUDGES AND QUASI-JUDICIAL OFFICERS

1. **Ex Parte Contact "on the Merits" by Lawyers:** The *Ragatz* court notes that attorney Ragatz conducted ex parte communication with the court "on the merits" of the underlying action. Does that language exist in Model Rule 3.5? While language limiting the prohibition against ex parte communications to communications about the merits was included in the former Model Code of Professional Responsibility's Disciplinary Rule 7–110(B), it was eliminated with the adoption of Model Rule 3.5(b), which forbids *all* ex parte communications between attorneys and judges except those authorized by law or by court order. *See also* RESTATEMENT, § 113(1) (2000). Unfortunately, some attorneys cling to the incorrect belief that they can communicate with judges as long as they avoid "the merits."

Model Rule 3.5 does not prohibit all communications with a judge. Instead, it prohibits ex parte communications. Therefore, an attorney can send an otherwise appropriate letter to a judge, if the attorney also sends a copy of the letter to opposing counsel. *See In re Green*, 11 P.3d 1078 (Colo. 2000). But failure, even if inadvertent, to send a copy of written communications with the judge to opposing counsel is a prohibited ex parte communication. *See In re Cheatham*, 702 S.E.2d 559, 560 (S.C. 2010) (finding a violation when an attorney "did not serve opposing counsel with a copy of the proposed order when he submitted it to the family court"); *Bd. of Prof'l Resp. v. Dunn*, 2012 WY 25, 272 P.3d 941 (suspending attorney who submitted a proposed order to a trial judge without providing notice of doing so to opposing counsel).

Model Rule 3.5 also applies to communications with others beside the judge. In addition to contact with the judge, the rule bans contact with a juror, prospective juror, or "other official." Courts have applied this prohibition to attorney communications with a variety of officials, including clerks of court, judicial law clerks, and magistrates. *See, e.g., Kaufman v. Am. Fam. Mut. Ins. Co.*, No. 05–cv–02311–WDM–MEH, 2008 WL 4980360 (D.Colo. Nov. 19, 2008); *Randolph v. State*, 853 So.2d 1051, 1056–59 (Fla. 2003); *Miss. Bar v. Logan*, 726 So.2d 170 (Miss. 1998); *State v. Marcopolos*, 572 S.E.2d 820 (N.C.Ct.App. 2002).

2. **Ex Parte Contact by Judges:** In contrast to Model Rule 3.5's restriction on attorney contact with judges, the rule applied to judges does allow ex parte communications in some circumstances. Under Rule 2.9(A) (formerly Canon 3B(7)) of the Code of Judicial Conduct, a judge cannot "initiate, permit, or consider ex parte communications" about "pending or impending" matters with anyone, unless one of several exceptions applies. The first exception allows a judge to communicate ex parte regarding non-substantive administrative matters, scheduling, and emergencies, if no party thereby gains an advantage and the non-communicating parties are promptly advised of the ex parte communication and given a chance to respond. Rule 2.9(A)(1) (formerly Canon 3B(7)(a)). Other exceptions allow ex parte communications with persons other than parties and their attorneys, including disinterested experts (when the parties are advised and given the chance to respond) and court personnel. Rule 2.9(A)(2) & (3) (formerly Canon 3B(7)(b) & (c)). Judges are also permitted to meet separately with the parties and their attorneys in mediation, when the parties consent, and to engage in other ex parte communications that are "expressly authorized by law." Rule 2.9(A)(4) & (5) (formerly Canon 3B(7)(d) & (e)). Although *Ragatz* demonstrates that an attorney cannot justify an improper ex parte communication by asserting that the judge initiated it, if an attorney participates in an ex parte communication that a judge is permitted to initiate, has the attorney violated Model Rule 3.5? Does Model Rule 3.5's permission for attorneys to engage in ex parte communications authorized by law or court order apply to these situations?

Beyond the exceptions noted in the previous paragraph, Rule 2.9 (formerly Canon 3B(7)) of the Code of Judicial Conduct forbids ex parte communication by a judge with a lawyer or party in the vast majority of circumstances. Like attorneys, judges sometimes ignore this prohibition. Ex parte communications are among the most common violations that result in sanctions and discipline against judges. Allegations of prohibited communications by judges often occur in the context of domestic violence, custody, child support, and other family law cases. *See, e.g., Connor v. N.Y. State Comm'n on Judicial Conduct*, 260 F.Supp.2d 517 (N.D.N.Y. 2003); *In re Danikolas*, 783 N.E.2d 687 (Ind. 2003); *In re White*, 651 N.W.2d 551 (Neb. 2002); *cf. In re Cotton*, 939 N.E.2d 619 (Ind. 2010) (finding that an attorney in a divorce and protection order case engaged in a prohibited ex parte contact with a judge). Why do these cases generate ex parte communications?

3. **Ex Parte Proceedings:** Some proceedings are designed to be ex parte. When one party applies for a temporary restraining order, for example, that party will have contact with the judge without the knowledge of the other party. In that situation, Model Rule 3.5(b) permits the contact, but Model Rule 3.3(d) requires the participating attorney to advise the court of all relevant facts, including those adverse to the participating attorney's position. *See In re Ferguson*, 246 P.3d 1236, 1248 (Wash. 2011) (suspending attorney for violating state's version of Model Rule 3.3(d) by failing to make court aware of a "certified funds notice," while knowing that this "notice was relevant").

A(2)(c) Contact with Jurors

PROBLEM

Return to the problem in the previous subsection. A month before the trial in the *Mission* case, attorney Juan Romero receives a list of the names and addresses of the potential jurors. Jerry Pickens, a psychologist Romero hired to assist him with jury selection, suggests sending each potential juror a questionnaire. According to Pickens, "They will not even know they are getting the questionnaire because they are potential jurors. It will look just like the polls I do for my political clients, with the return address of my polling firm, Election Estimator, Inc. But the answers to the questions about who they are going to vote for will tell us a lot about whether we want them as jurors." Romero approves this plan.

During a lunch break on the third trial day, Romero sits at a booth at a café three blocks from the courthouse. After he is seated, four of the jurors sit in the next booth. Ten minutes later, one of the jurors, heading back from the restroom, recognizes him, stops at his booth, and says, "Hello, Mr. Romero. How do you think it is going for you over there?" Because he does not want to appear to be rude, Romero responds by saying, "Very well, but, of course, I can't really talk about it with you."

Two days after the jury's guilty verdict, Romero asks his legal assistant to contact each juror to interview her or him about the trial. "In addition to our usual questions about what they thought of our trial strategy," Juan tells the legal assistant, "be sure to ask them about what happened during deliberation, just in case there was something inappropriate that could help us get a new trial."

QUESTION

Should Romero be disciplined for any of the actions he took or directed with respect to jurors and potential jurors?

RULE REFERENCES

Model Rule 3.5

RESTATEMENT § 115

STATE v. WASHINGTON

Louisiana Court of Appeal, Second Circuit, 1993.
626 So.2d 841.

MARVIN, CHIEF JUDGE. * * *

PROSECUTORIAL MISCONDUCT

In the courtroom with the jury venire present before voir dire began on the morning the trial was scheduled, * * * were the Webster Parish District Attorney, the Clerk of Court, the court reporter, and the Sheriff.

They were later joined by the assistant district attorney who tried Washington's case. Not present were Washington, his counsel, and the trial judge. The remarks then made to the jury venire by the clerk of court and the district attorney, which were transcribed by the court reporter, are the basis for Washington's motion for a mistrial, which was filed * * * after the jury was sworn.

We edit, emphasize, and reproduce the pertinent remarks:

[THE CLERK OF COURT]: Good morning. I'm ... the Parish Clerk of Court, and *we* appreciate your coming to jury service. I do not have any idea how many cases the DA has scheduled. Quite often when he summons a group like this, it puts pressure on individuals and they will plead guilty or plead to a lesser offense. And *we* send you home, without having to serve.... This is the District Attorney ... And he will have some words to say to you....

[THE DISTRICT ATTORNEY]: ... Here comes ... my assistant. *We're* glad to have you—I know y'all would be doing something else, and you wouldn't be up here normally, and I hope you find it a rewarding experience. You'll probably hear lawyers talk a lot more this week than you want to, but that's the nature of the bea[s]t. *We're* glad to have you, and *we* do appreciate you. You're the backbone of our system, and you make it work, and that's the truth. And like I say, I hope it's not too much of an inconvenience, and if you do feel you have genuine hardships, then you should talk to the judge about that, and *we* appreciate it. * * *

DISCUSSION

Washington contends that the DA's ex parte communications with the prospective jurors were improper because they appeared to seek to curry favor with the potential jurors. He argues that the DA was practically conducting voir dire without the judge or defense attorney present. He also contends that the comments made by the clerk of court were improper because they implied that all or many of the defendants set for trial before a jury panel chosen from that venire must be guilty.

* * * Rule 3.5(b) of the Rules of Professional Conduct generally states that a lawyer shall not communicate ex parte with a prospective juror. * * *

Where a district attorney mailed a questionnaire to each of 100 [venirepersons], to be completed and returned to him, before trial, for his exclusive use in jury selection, defendant's forcible rape conviction was reversed. * * * Our supreme court found [a contrary] view to be "squarely at odds with that of the federal courts and [other authorities]," explaining: ["U]nilateral *ex parte* juror contacts can only result in a skewing of the otherwise impartial administration of justice.[" *State v. Bates*, 508 So.2d 1346, 1350 (La. 1987)].

The Clerk's remarks * * *, coupled with the DA's immediately following remarks * * * serve as additions to the illustrations given in *Bates* why ex parte communications to jurors by *either* prosecution *or* defense counsel have been forbidden. * * *

Ex parte comments to prospective jurors more egregiously "trench upon the broad ground of fair trial," when, as here, they are personal and direct ["we"] comments made in a courtroom setting to a jury venire by one public official in the presence of other public officials. * * * We find that the quoted comments are clearly forbidden by Rule 3.5(b) of the Rules of Professional Conduct and Standard 5.4(a) of the ABA Standard Relating to the Prosecution Function.

DECREE

Defendant's conviction and sentence are REVERSED and VACATED and the case is REMANDED for a new trial.

NOTES ON CONTACT WITH JURORS

1. **Pretrial Contact with Jurors:** As *Washington* notes, courts have held that pretrial contact with prospective jurors is impermissible. *See In re Myers*, 584 S.E.2d 357, 358 (S.C. 2003) (disciplining an attorney for failing to prevent a member of his "jury selection team" from telephoning a prospective juror); *In re Barton*, 554 S.E.2d 680 (S.C. 2001) (disciplining an attorney who sent questionnaires to prospective jurors); *see also* RESTATEMENT, § 115(1) (2000) (prohibiting communication with members of a jury pool); N.Y. Cnty. Lawyers' Ass'n, Op. 743 (2011) (concluding that an attorney could passively monitor jurors' publicly available website postings, but not "friend" or "tweet" jurors).

2. **Mid–Trial Contact with Jurors:** During trial, other than in the courtroom, almost any ex parte communication by an attorney (or a person aligned with an attorney, including a party) with a juror is considered improper, regardless of how insignificant it might be. *See, e.g., Fla. Bar v. Peterson*, 418 So.2d 246 (Fla. 1982) (disciplining attorney who allowed himself to be seated at a deli table occupied by two jurors); *Metropolitan Dade Cnty. v. Frank J. Rooney, Inc.*, 627 So.2d 1248, 1251 (Fla.Dist.Ct.App. 1993) (granting new trial after an employee of a county that was a party "was observed in repeated contact with the jury prior to trial commencing in the mornings and during recesses and lunch breaks"); *Omaha Bank for Coops. v. Siouxland Cattle Coop.*, 305 N.W.2d 458 (Iowa 1981) (finding a lawyer's eventual acceptance of a drink following initial attempts to decline to be "clear misconduct," where a juror spotted attorneys in a restaurant and offered to buy them a drink, even though the pending trial was never discussed); *In re Delgado*, 306 S.E.2d 591 (S.C. 1983) (disciplining an attorney for allowing juror to ask him "some 'human interest' questions about his background, legal training, etc.," even though he told the juror he could not discuss the case being tried); *see also* RESTATEMENT, § 115(2).

3. **Post–Trial Contact with Jurors:** Judicial distaste for post-trial surveys of jurors is reflected in judicial decisions, local rules, and orders that prohibit or limit this practice. *See, e.g., Haeberle v. Tex. Int'l Airlines*, 739 F.2d 1019 (5th Cir. 1984) (determining that First Amendment interests of

both litigant and counsel to satisfy curiosity and to improve advocacy were outweighed by the juror's interest in privacy and by the public's interest in efficient justice); *United States v. Puleo*, 817 F.2d 702 (11th Cir. 1987) (contending that a post-trial jury survey "represents a serious breach of ethics," but did not justify dismissal of the indictment); *L.S. v. Miss. Bar*, 649 So.2d 810 (Miss. 1994) (describing trial judge's order prohibiting post-trial contact with jurors); RESTATEMENT, § 115, Comment *d* and Reporter's Note. Some courts allow post-trial surveys of jurors for purposes of lawyer self-evaluation, but disapprove of surveys that inquire into the jury's decision-making process. *See Diettrich v. Nw. Airlines, Inc.*, 168 F.3d 961 (7th Cir. 1999); *Koo v. State*, 640 N.E.2d 95 (Ind.Ct.App. 1994). The rules of professional conduct do not reflect the common judicial distaste about post-trial contact between attorneys and jurors. Model Rule 3.5(c) specifically allows non-coercive, veracious post-trial communications with a former juror who has not expressed a desire to avoid such communications, unless such communications are prohibited by law or court order. *See also* RESTATEMENT, § 115(3); *Adams v. Ford Motor Co.*, 653 F.3d 299, 306–07 (3d Cir. 2011) (reversing trial court's finding that attorney violated Model Rule 3.5 by calling a juror after the trial ended).

A(2)(d) Presentation of Evidence and Arguments

PROBLEM

Federal Public Defender Miranda Crites represented Olin D. Wahl, who was charged with escaping from a federal prison. Crites hoped to present a necessity defense based upon threats of physical violence against Wahl by another inmate, Jesse Hinson. She hoped to call Neil Mason, who resided in the cell next to Wahl's cell, as a witness.

When meeting with Crites to prepare his testimony, Mason assured her that "Hinson was always threatening to beat Wahl to a pulp." Crites responded, "That is not helpful, because Hinson never actually did beat him up. We need to establish that there was an imminent threat that forced Olin to leave that night." Mason replied, "You darn right it was serious. He threatened it over and over and over. I was beginning to think he just might carry through on that threat, even though I happen to know that Hinson is all bark and no bite."

"Listen carefully, Mr. Mason," Crites said, "I need imminence, so I have to prove he threatened him that night." Mason replied, "Oh, that's what 'imminent' means. Fine. He threatened to beat him up that night—got it." When Crites asked Mason if he thought Hinson would follow through, he said, "And I really thought Hinson would get him that night. I understand. You don't have to tell me twice." As she left, Crites said, "Be sure to tell the truth." Mason replied, "Yeah. Right."

At trial, Mason testified, "Hinson threatened to beat Olin up and kill him that night, and I knew he meant it." This was the first time Crites ever heard Mason refer to a threat to "kill" Wahl.

After Mason's testimony, Judge Jules Olena asked the attorneys to "brief" the issue of whether the defense had presented enough evidence to require her to instruct the jury on the necessity defense, saying, "The defense attorney should file first, followed by the Assistant U.S. Attorney. If it wants to, the defense can file a reply brief." While conducting legal research for her brief, Crites found *U.S. v. Lawton*, an unpublished decision on Westlaw written by Judge Stanford Leland fifteen years ago. Judges Olena and Leland are two of the fifteen active judges in the district court where the trial was held. Judge Leland's decision held that a defendant in a prison escape case who had "merely established threats of violence of the type typical in prisons" was not entitled to a jury instruction on the necessity defense. Crites did not cite or otherwise refer to *Lawton* in her first brief. That brief argued that "evidence of a threat of violence is clearly enough to require a jury instruction on necessity" and cited three decisions of U.S. circuit courts (none of them from the circuit in which the trial took place) in support of this argument. To her amazement, the Assistant U.S. Attorney also did not cite or otherwise refer to *Lawton* in his brief. Crites then decided not to file a reply brief.

QUESTIONS

(a) Did Crites commit professional misconduct when meeting with Mason? Was she allowed to call Mason to the stand after this meeting?

(b) After Mason's trial testimony, was Crites required to respond in any way? If she did nothing, should she be disciplined?

(c) Was Crites' brief acceptable? Was her failure to cite *Lawton* in the brief permissible? After the prosecutor failed to cite this decision, was she required to call it to the court's attention?

RULE REFERENCES

Model Rules 8.4(c), 3.3, 1.0(d), 3.4(b), and 1.2(d)

RESTATEMENT §§ 106, 111, 116, 117, 118 & 120

NOTES ON PRESENTATION OF EVIDENCE AND ARGUMENTS

1. **Statements of Fact:** In a statement of general application, Model Rule 8.4(c) prohibits an attorney from "engag[ing] in conduct involving dishonesty, fraud, deceit or misrepresentation." In litigation, attorneys sometimes violate this provision with the documents or statements they present to courts. *See Disciplinary Counsel v. Gerchak*, 2011–Ohio–5075, 956 N.E.2d 292 (suspending attorney who used a different attorney's electronic filing privileges to submit a bankruptcy petition and falsely told the bankruptcy court his client could only pay a filing fee in installments); *State* ex rel. *Okla. Bar Ass'n v. Gassaway*, 2008 OK 60, ¶¶ 17–24, 196 P.3d 495, 500–01 (disbarring attorney for, inter alia, falsely telling judge the opposing party had waived his substantive rights).

In language more precisely applicable to litigators, Model Rule 3.3(a)(1) forbids an attorney from knowingly making a false statement of fact or law to a court. *See also* RESTATEMENT, § 120(1)(b) (2000). An attorney can be disciplined for misstating a fact while communicating with a court about any matter. *See In re Roose*, 69 P.3d 43, 46 (Colo. 2003) (suspending attorney who falsely claimed that she was appointed counsel); *Ky. Bar Ass'n v. Rye*, 336 S.W.3d 462, 464 (Ky. 2011) (disciplining attorney for false statement to court that he was unaware of his client's move); *In re Bailey*, 2003–0839 (La. 6/6/03); 848 So.2d 530 (suspending attorney who lied about a nonexistent schedule conflict); *In re Stuart*, 803 N.Y.S.2d 577 (App.Div. 2005) (suspending prosecutor who falsely responded to judge's inquiry about whether a witness had been located). For a brief discussion and application of Model Rule 3.3(a)(1)'s prohibition of false statements of fact, see *In re Vincenti* in *infra* section 6(A)(2)(e).

The prohibition of false statements is sweeping. One court has held that an attorney can violate Model Rule 3.3(a)(1)'s prohibition of knowingly making false statements to a tribunal without having an intent to deceive the court. *In re Dodge*, 108 P.3d 362, 367 (Idaho 2005) (holding that the "knowingly" standard was met where a prosecutor overstated defendant's brandishing of gun, perhaps inadvertently) ("If an attorney does not know if an assertion is true or cannot point to a reasonably diligent inquiry to ascertain the truth of the statement, the attorney can remain silent, profess no knowledge, or couch the assertion in equivocal terms so the court can assess the assertion's probative value.") Also, the prohibition of false statements applies to appeals. *See In re Liotti*, 667 F.3d 419, 426–27 (4th Cir. 2011) (disciplining appellate attorney for combining two separate parts of the trial transcript in his quotation, "thereby creating the look of a fluid conversation," and for misstating the government's estimate of the length of the trial).

2. **Disclosure of Adverse Facts:** Although an attorney cannot affirmatively misstate a fact, an attorney generally has no obligation to disclose adverse facts in the absence of a valid discovery request requiring disclosure, *see supra* section 6(A)(1)(c), note 6, except when the attorney is appearing in a permitted ex parte proceeding, *see supra* section 6(A)(2)(b), note 3.

3. **False Evidence:** Several Model Rules provisions are designed to prevent attorneys from creating false evidence. Model Rule 3.4(b) makes it illegal for an attorney to "falsify" evidence or to advise or help a witness testify falsely. *See also* RESTATEMENT, §§ 118(1) & 120(1)(a). Attorneys tend to run afoul of this provision by fabricating false evidence to try to cover past mistakes or misconduct. *See, e.g., In re McDonald*, 2000 ND 87, ¶¶ 9–12, 609 N.W.2d 418, 422–23 (suspending attorney who doctored an envelope to cover up his office's failure to properly mail important documents); *Lawyer Disciplinary Bd. v. Scott*, 579 S.E.2d 550, 551–52 (W.Va. 2003) (suspending attorney who "falsified copies of a backdated check and certified mail receipt" in an attempt to convince the court that he paid his bar dues).

The limitation regarding false evidence that presumably comes into play most often for lawyers is not the limitation on its creation, but the Model Rule 3.3(a)(2) prohibition of knowingly offering it. Of course, sometimes attorneys violate Model Rule 3.3(a)(3) in two ways, by both preparing and presenting false evidence. *See Ky. Bar Ass'n v. Orr*, 350 S.W.3d 427 (Ky. 2011) (suspending attorney for preparing and filing false credit counseling certificates in bankruptcy cases); *In re Dedefo*, 752 N.W.2d 523, 529–30 (Minn. 2008) (suspending attorney who coerced his estranged wife into signing a false affidavit, then filed that affidavit in court); *In re Robinson*, 713 S.E.2d 294 (S.C. 2011) (finding that filing of affidavits falsely asserting that witnesses personally appeared before attorney as notary violated Model Rule 3.3).

Pursuant to Model Rule 3.3(a)(3), a lawyer must refuse to present the testimony of a witness who plans to testify falsely. *See Noel v. State*, 26 S.W.3d 123, 126–27 (Ark. 2000); RESTATEMENT, § 120(1). Model Rule 3.3(a)(3) also provides that a lawyer "may" refuse to present evidence that the lawyer "reasonably believes is false," even if the lawyer does not "know" the evidence is false. *See also* RESTATEMENT, § 120(3); *but see supra* section 4(C) (regarding testimony by a criminal defendant, which is subject to more complicated measures).

Sometimes lawyers present evidence to the court not knowing that it was false, then later become aware of its falsity. Model Rule 3.3(a)(3) requires a lawyer who learns of the falsity of previously presented evidence to "take reasonable remedial measures, including, if necessary, disclosure to the tribunal." *See supra* section 4(C), Notes on Anticipation of Client Perjury and Preventive Measures, notes 8–10; *see also* Model Rule 3.3(b); Md. State Bar Ass'n Comm. on Ethics, Op. 2005–15 (finding that an attorney has an obligation to take reasonable remedial measures when a client, while the case is on appeal, tells the attorney that a witness told the client that he committed perjury at trial, even if the witness later recants this confession). This might require disclosure of client confidences generally protected by Model Rule 1.6, because Model Rule 3.3 obligations trump the confidentiality protection of Model Rule 1.6. *See* Model Rule 3.3(c); *see also* N.Y. State Bar Ass'n, Comm. on Prof'l Ethics, Op. 781 (2004) (requiring withdrawal of previously presented client financial statement after attorney learned of its falsity, if attorney efforts to convince client to undo fraud are unsuccessful, despite exposure of client confidence).

4. **Assisting Fraudulent Conduct:** Model Rule 1.2(d), which forbids an attorney from counseling or assisting a client in fraudulent conduct, prevents an attorney from helping a client suborn another witness's perjury or otherwise create false evidence. In addition, Model Rule 3.3(b) would force an attorney to "take reasonable remedial measures" when the attorney "knows" that a witness has engaged in, is engaging in, or plans to engage in criminal or fraudulent conduct, including perjury or other presentation of false evidence. *See* Model Rule 1.0(d) (defining fraud to include purposeful deceit); *see also supra* section 4(C), Notes on Anticipation of Client Perjury and Preventive Measures, note 7 (discussing perjury by non-clients); *Erpenbeck v. Ky. Bar Ass'n*, 295 S.W.3d 435 (Ky. 2009) (suspending an attorney for allowing his brother to transfer stock to attorney's company without notifying the bankruptcy court, thereby allowing a fraud to be perpetrated on the court).

5. **Witness Preparation/Coaching:** The restrictions on the creation of false testimony limit, but do not prohibit, an attorney's efforts to meet with witnesses and prepare them to testify. *See* RESTATEMENT, § 116(1) ("A lawyer may interview a witness for the purpose of preparing the witness to testify.").

Depending upon one's viewpoint and residency, these practices are known colloquially as "coaching," "sand papering," "wood shedding," or even, most colorfully, "horseshedding" the witness. Regardless of the title one assigns to meetings between attorneys and witnesses, one should recognize that they are not without effect. As Professors Fred Zacharias and Shaun Martin observed, "To be realistic, lawyers inevitably affect witnesses' testimony, at least to some extent, when the lawyers speak to witnesses in the course of gathering evidence." Fred C. Zacharias & Shaun Martin, *Coaching Witnesses*, 87 Ky.L.J. 1001, 1009 n.37 (1999).

Many, if not most, trial attorneys believe that some degree of witness preparation is not only allowed, but actually required as a component of effective representation. *See* W. William Hodes, *The Professional Duty to Horseshed Witnesses—Zealously, Within the Bounds of the Law*, 30 Tex. Tech L.Rev. 1343, 1350 (1999); Richard H. Underwood, *The Professional and the Liar*, 87 Ky.L.J. 919, 954 & n.122 (1999). Courts have not prohibited all such practices. *See Musselman v. Phillips*, 176 F.R.D. 194, 201 (D.Md. 1997) (observing "it is not improper for an attorney to assist a retained expert in developing opinion testimony"); *see also United States v. Rhynes*, 218 F.3d 310, 320 (4th Cir. 2000) (stating that "thorough cross-examination" is the most effective response to coaching of a witness). Nonetheless, it is misconduct for an attorney to cross the line between permissible witness preparation and impermissible creation of false testimony. *See In re Harris*, 2003–0212 (La. 5/9/03); 847 So.2d 1185, 1194 (holding that "[r]espondent manufactured evidence and presented perjured testimony"); *State* ex rel. *Okla. Bar Ass'n v. Braswell*, 1998 OK 49, ¶ 52, 975 P.2d 401, 415–16 (noting allegations that an attorney "coached [a witness] to lie"). Witness preparation is constrained by Model Rule 3.3(a)(3), which prevents a lawyer from offering testimony the lawyer knows is false. As Professor Bruce Green noted, "Whether coaching a witness to give a particular account comprises sanctionable misconduct * * * depend[s] on the lawyer's belief about whether the ultimate testimony is true." Bruce A. Green, *The Ten Most Common Ethical Violations*, Litigation, Summer 1998, at 48, 51.

Lawyers do not always know that a witness will testify falsely until they hear the testimony, and sometimes they do not realize that testimony or other evidence is false until after they present it. In that circumstance, Model Rule 3.3(a)(3) requires the lawyer who "comes to know of" the falsity of previously presented evidence to "take reasonable remedial measures." The required responses may "includ[e], if necessary, disclosure to the tribunal." Model Rule 3.3(c) states that the duties to avoid knowingly presenting false evidence and to take remedial measures if the false nature of previously presented evidence manifests itself "continue to the conclusion of the proceeding" and apply even if otherwise confidential information must be disclosed. *See also* RESTATEMENT, § 120(2); *supra* section 4(C), Notes on Anticipation of Client Perjury and Preventive Measures, note 10.

6. **False or Incomplete Statements of Law:** Model Rule 3.3(a)(1)'s prohibition of knowingly false statements also applies to statements of law. *See also* RESTATEMENT, § 111(1). Therefore, attorneys must be honest in their arguments and citations of legal authority. *See Precision Specialty Metals, Inc. v. United States*, 315 F.3d 1346 (Fed.Cir. 2003) (sanctioning attorneys under

Rule 11 for selectively quoting, and thereby altering the meaning of, precedent); *Wash. State Physicians Ins. Exch. v. Fisons Corp.*, 858 P.2d 1054 (Wash. 1993) (Brachtenbach, J., dissenting) (in case discussed in connection with discovery abuse at *supra* section 6(A)(1)(c), dissenting justice observed that "none" of the cases cited by the defendant "holds what defendant claims").

However, the requirements regarding citation of legal authority do not end there. Although an attorney is often under no duty to disclose adverse facts, there is a general duty to disclose some adverse legal precedent. Model Rule 3.3(a)(2) requires an attorney to make the judge aware of "legal authority in the controlling jurisdiction known to the lawyer to be directly adverse to the position" advocated by the lawyer, if the attorney's opponent fails to disclose the authority. *See also State v. Cagle*, 641 S.E.2d 705, 709 (N.C.Ct.App. 2007) (noting that counsel engaged in misconduct by failing to cite a case that overruled the cases cited by counsel); *Broken Arrow v. Bass Pro Outdoor World, L.L.C.*, 2011 OK 1, ¶ 32, 250 P.3d 305, 317; RESTATEMENT, § 111(2). With some frequency, courts have expressed displeasure with attorneys who failed to cite authority that fell within this rule. *See, e.g., Amoco Oil Co. v. United States*, 234 F.3d 1374 (Fed.Cir. 2000); *United States v. Marks*, 209 F.3d 577 (6th Cir. 2000); *Schnelle v. Soo Line R.R. Co.*, 976 F.Supp. 849, 851 n.2 (D.Minn. 1997). Courts sometimes interpret the phrase "adverse authority" more expansively than attorneys. *See Tyler v. State*, 47 P.3d 1095, 1104 (Alaska Ct.App. 2001) (agreeing with attorney that an uncited previous decision was arguably distinguishable and therefore not controlling, but fining him nonetheless because " 'directly adverse' is not synonymous with 'controlling' or 'dispositive' ").

Some attorneys leave little room for sympathy, by failing to cite published cases that they are undoubtedly aware of, due to the representation of one of the parties in the previous case. *See In re Thonert*, 733 N.E.2d 932 (Ind. 2000). On the other hand, one court found that the lawyer who worked on previous litigation does not have to cite the reported decision resulting from that litigation, if the reported decision does not control the case at hand. *O'Neill v. Dunham*, 203 P.3d 68, 73 (Kan.Ct.App. 2009). Also, one court has held that Model Rule 3.3(a)(2) "does not require defense counsel to develop and advance potential legal claims for the plaintiff." *Gibson v. Car Zone*, 31 A.3d 76 (Del. 2011). For a discussion of this somewhat unsettled area of law, see J. Thomas Sullivan, *Ethical and Aggressive Appellate Advocacy: Confronting Adverse Authority*, 59 U. Miami L.Rev. 341, 352–54 (2005).

7. **What Constitutes "Knowing"?** Some attorneys believe that the "knowing" qualifier on any restriction against preparing or presenting false evidence applies in many, most, or perhaps even almost all instances, because it is the jury's job to determine the truth, not the attorney's job. Is this view correct? For an argument that a trial attorney must make determinations about the truthfulness of potential witnesses and that the duty to effectively represent the client should thwart the presentation of evidence the attorney doubts (due to the ineffectiveness of most attorneys when taking positions in court that they do not themselves believe), see Stephen D. Easton, *The Truth About Ethics and Ethics About the Truth: An Open Letter to Trial Attorneys*, 33 Gonz.L.Rev. 463 (1997/1998).

8. **Witness Fees:** Model Rule 3.4(b) prevents the payment or offering of an illegal "inducement to a witness," and Comment [3] makes clear that this applies to any fee for an "occurrence witness" and to a contingent fee to an "expert witness." Thus, witness payments are limited to the rather paltry witness fees outlined in statutes or court rules, and attorneys should avoid even minor favors to witnesses like providing extra meals or airplane flight arrangements that are not allowed by law. *See In re Bruno*, 2006–2791 (La. 5/11/07); 956 So.2d 577 (suspending attorney who paid a witness, then failed to be honest with the court about doing so); RESTATEMENT, § 117; *cf. In re Howes*, 39 A.3d 1 (D.C. 2012) (disbarring federal prosecutor who distributed witness vouchers to individuals not eligible to receive them); *In re Kronenberg*, 117 P.3d 1134 (Wash. 2005) (disbarring criminal defense attorney who offered to "settle" with a rape victim by paying her and providing a plane ticket if she left town and was therefore not available to testify). However, attorneys are allowed "to compensate an expert witness on terms permitted by law," Model Rule 3.4, Comment [3], which typically include hourly fees.

A(2)(e) Other Trial Conduct

PROBLEM

Justine Newton, a first-year associate, was assigned by a partner to defend Kay Knighton in a civil suit that every senior attorney in the firm was trying to avoid. Plaintiff Vera Sutton alleged that Knighton's dog bit her while she jogged on the sidewalk in front of Knighton's home. The key fact witness was Knighton's neighbor, Nat Nhorak, who immigrated from Blavobia twenty years ago.

At trial, Nhorak testified that he previously saw the dog "bark and act aggressively" toward other joggers and that he heard loud barking just before he came out of his house and saw Sutton bleeding on the sidewalk. Lacking much of a basis for impeachment but wanting to prove her zeal in court, Newton remembered that a friend once told her that he watched a public television documentary about Blavobia that showed some residents of that country eating meat from dogs. Newton conducted the following cross-examination:

Q. Mr. Nhorak, you were not born in the United States. Is that correct?

A. That's right.

Q. In fact, you were born in Blavobia and lived there until age thirty, right?

A. Right.

Q. So you come from a culture that despises dogs?

At that point, the judge told Newton to "move on or sit down, because that sort of stuff is not going to happen in my courtroom." When she chose the latter option, the judge asked both attorneys if the witness could be excused from the obligation to remain in the courthouse under the subpoenas issued by both attorneys. As a new attorney whose basic instinct was to never waive any right, and as someone who was upset with Nhorak's testimony and did not mind the prospect of him sitting in the courthouse for the three or four days that it would take to complete the trial, Newton responded, "No, Your Honor. We reserve the right to recall this witness in our case and ask that he remain constrained by the subpoena." Nhorak stayed in the court-house for the remainder of the trial, but Newton did not recall him to the stand.

While preparing her closing argument, Newton remembered her trial advocacy instructor's admonition to "show the jury that you really believe in your case." During closing, she said, "You saw Nhorak and you heard him, and so did I. You are entitled to base your beliefs on what you saw and heard. In your heart, you believe he was lying. To the bottom of my heart, I believe he was lying." When the judge told her to "stop it right now with that kind of argument," Newton slammed her fist into the podium, turned to him and shouted, "I have had enough of this kangaroo court. Right from the start, you have been doing everything you can to keep me from winning this case because I am a woman and because I am young. I am mad as hell and I am not going to take it anymore."

QUESTIONS

(a) Was Newton's cross-examination permissible?

(b) Was it permissible for Newton to refuse to release Nhorak from the subpoena?

(c) Assuming that Newton believed everything she said in her final argument and in her response to the judge's interruption of the argument, were those statements permissible?

RULE REFERENCES

Model Rules 3.4(c) & (e), 4.4(a), 8.4(d), 3.5(d), 1.0(m), 3.2, and 3.7
RESTATEMENT §§ 106, 107 & 108

IN RE VINCENTI

Supreme Court of New Jersey, 1998.
704 A.2d 927.

PER CURIAM

Over the past fourteen years, respondent, Lester T. Vincenti, has been the subject of no fewer than three reported decisions concerning violations of the Rules of Professional Conduct. Several themes run throughout respondent's unique disciplinary history. One is disrespect, even contempt, for judges, lawyers, parties, witnesses, and the judicial process. To characterize his conduct as unprofessional, irrational, intemperate, insolent, arrogant, abusive, insulting, harassing, scurrilous, and misleading— as it has been characterized in his various disciplinary proceedings—is to minimize its impact on the administration of justice. * * *

With sedulous dedication to detail, the Special Master and the Disciplinary Review Board (DRB) have documented respondent's transgressions. Both the Special Master and the DRB have recommended that respondent be disbarred. Our independent review of the record leads us to adopt the full opinion of the DRB as our own. * * *

This matter was before the Board based on a recommendation for disbarment filed by Special Master Melvin P. Antell, P.J.A.D. [R]espondent was charged with violations of [Rule] 3.1 (asserting a frivolous issue), [Rule] 3.2 (failure to expedite litigation), [Rule] 3.3(a)(1) (making false statement of material fact to a tribunal), [Rule] 3.4(c) (knowingly disobeying a court order), [Rule] 3.4(e) (alluding at trial to irrelevant matters and stating personal opinions as to the justness of a cause and the credibility of a witness), [Rule] 3.5([d]) (conduct intended to disrupt a tribunal), [Rule] 4.4[(a)] (using means that have no purpose other than to embarrass, delay, or burden a third person), * * * [Rule] 8.4(c) (conduct involving dishonesty, fraud, deceit or misrepresentation), and [Rule] 8.4(d) (conduct prejudicial to the administration of justice). * * *

I. THE *A.R.S.* MATTER * * *

The Division of Youth and Family Services ("DYFS") filed a petition in Superior Court to terminate the parental rights of J.D., the natural mother of A.R.S. The matter * * * was tried before Judge Gerald B. Hanifan. Barbara Einhorn, an attorney employed by Somerset–Sussex Legal Services, represented J.D., while a Deputy Attorney General ("DAG") represented DYFS. In addition, James Valenti was appointed and served as law guardian for the child, A.R.S.

On * * * the first day of the trial, respondent appeared as a "volunteer" to assist Einhorn in her defense of J.D. According to J.D., Einhorn, who was acquainted with respondent, mentioned the termination of parental rights litigation to respondent. He expressed interest in a potential federal lawsuit against DYFS for violating J.D.'s civil rights. Accordingly, respondent's agreed role at the trial was to observe the proceedings to assist him in representing J.D. in the federal litigation. * * * Although not counsel of record, respondent took over the defense, cross-examining the witnesses called by DYFS to testify. The *A.R.S.* matter consumed more than forty trial days * * *.

[While the trial was pending,] Judge Hanifan entered an order, on his own motion, removing respondent from participation in the case for all matters, including trial appearances, because respondent "ha[d] repeatedly been obstructive of the Judicial Process and violative of the Rules of Professional Conduct, and having caused unnecessary delay by his intrusion in this matter." Shortly thereafter, * * * Judge Hanifan referred the matter to the * * * Ethics Committee.

During the *A.R.S.* trial, respondent was repeatedly disrespectful to Judge Hanifan. He constantly interrupted the Judge, particularly when he was ruling on objections or motions. * * *

Furthermore, respondent accused Judge Hanifan of exhibiting bias and prejudice when the court ruled against respondent:

Mr. Vincenti: I object to your comments. It shows nothing but prejudice and bias.

The Court: Fine. Fine.

Mr. Vincenti: You make a ruling and then you decide that simply because [the DAG] doesn't like it, you're going to change your ruling. How many times do you think you—

The Court: That's that's—

Mr. Vincenti:—have to do tha[t]—

The Court: Counsel—

Mr. Vincenti:—in order to be shown on the record for the Appellate Courts in this State to be biased and prejudiced?

Respondent's defense in the termination of parental rights case was based, in part, on his ill-founded theory that Judge Hanifan, DYFS staff, the witnesses called by DYFS, and the DAG were engaged in a conspiracy to deprive respondent's client, J.D., of her civil and constitutional rights to custody of her child. In this regard, respondent continued his sarcastic and insulting remarks during another objection:

The Court: Counsel—hang on.

Mr. Vincenti: She doesn't want us to develop the line to prove it because she's involved in the conspiracy.

The Court: Couns—

Mr. Vincenti: I have every right in the world to prove it even to you, Judge.

The Court: Would you. Would you let me speak counsel, please.

Mr. Vincenti: In your bias and prejudice.

The Court: Would you please let me speak?

Mr. Vincenti: I'm done.

The Court: Thank you.

Mr. Vincenti: I have the right to make statements on the record.

During his questioning of witnesses, respondent often asked multi-part questions that the witnesses were not able to answer. When Judge Hanifan requested respondent to repeat the question, the following colloquy occurred:

Mr. Vincenti: I don't know. I think I'm using the English language.

The Court: Counsel, I asked you nicely. Don't argue with me please. Just break it apart.

Mr. Vincenti: I'm not arguing with you.

The Court: That's what it sounds like, counsel.

Mr. Vincenti: Well I'm sorry for that. But that's your misperception, not mine. * * *

Finally, the following excerpts from the *A.R.S.* trial transcripts demonstrate respondent's disrespect for the court:

The Court: Counsel, your tone is difficult for me to handle on a day to day basis.

Mr. Vincenti: I apologize for that, but your rulings in this case—

The Court: I, well I'm, I'm telling—

Mr. Vincenti:—are beyond belief.

The Court: Counsel, it's, it's those kind of comments that, that make it difficult for me to process this matter.

Mr. Vincenti: Well then you know what, what remedies you have.

* * *

Mr. Vincenti: Oh, I've had my chance?

The Court: You've had your chance, yes, you did.

Mr. Vincenti: Oh, you permitted her to cut me off to be discourteous—

The Court: Please sit down and be quiet, counsel.

Mr. Vincenti: Objection.

The Court: Fine. I note your objection. Please sit down and be quiet.

Mr. Vincenti: You're biased and prejudiced and you know it.

As stated above, Judge Hanifan was not the only target of respondent's venomous attacks. Respondent's obnoxious demeanor was also directed at opposing counsel, the DAG, and went far beyond aggressive advocacy. Respondent repeatedly accused the DAG of being a liar. For example, when the DAG objected to a statement made by respondent, the following exchange ensued:

Mr. Vincenti: You're a liar.

The Court: Hang on counsel, please.

Mr. Vincenti: She is nothing but a liar.

The Court: Counsel—

Mr. Vincenti: And if you don't stop it—

The Court: No, counsel, wait—

Mr. Vincenti: You're going to stop me, right?

The Court: No, counsel—

Mr. Vincenti: Very good.

The Court: I think, I think that that's inappropriate behavior which you're just exhibiting.

Mr. Vincenti: Fine, make a note of it.

The Court: I am making a note of it.

Mr. Vincenti: Good.

Respondent also told Judge Hanifan "[T]his woman [the DAG] is out of her mind, Judge." He also insulted her with the remark that "her ignorance is beyond repair, it's monumental." Respondent accused the DAG of having destroyed families in the Superior Court for seventeen years, apparently a reference to the fact that she had represented DYFS for that length of time. In describing respondent's conduct toward the DAG, the special master found that "he was invariably abusive, insulting and profoundly vulgar."

Respondent's treatment of the State's witnesses was equally obnoxious. He was abusive and tried to intimidate the witnesses, with some success. Respondent personally attacked the witnesses during his unreasonably long and confrontational cross-examinations. He called the witnesses insulting names and belittled the credentials of the expert witnesses.

Dr. Douglas Haymaker, a psychologist, treated J.D.'s son, A.R.S. * * * Respondent harassed Haymaker by asking him irrelevant questions, such as whether he was an aficionado of pornography, a militarist and whether he believed in military solutions to political problems. When Haymaker testified that a statement made by A.R.S. could not necessarily be attributed to his foster mother, respondent sarcastically asked, "Oh, it could have come from the froggies or the horsies or some other non-living thing, is that right?" Respondent also accused Haymaker of having a highly selective memory and of being "in cahoots" with the foster parents. * * *

During the trial, respondent referred to Haymaker as a "liar," "so-called psychologist," "busy body do-gooder" and "so-called therapist." He belittled Haymaker's therapy sessions with A.R.S. as "your so-called game therapy, play therapy so-called." Respondent accused Haymaker of condoning violence, insults to women, pornography and brutality.

Another witness called by DYFS was a social worker. At the request of James Valenti, law guardian for A.R.S., the social worker conducted a bonding evaluation to address the issue of where A.R.S. should reside permanently. The social worker, too, was the victim of harassment and intimidation by respondent. * * *

Respondent * * * made insinuations about the social worker's sexual orientation. He suggested that she inappropriately touched his client, J.D., during a bonding-evaluation session with J.D. and A.R.S. Respondent attached significance to the fact that the social worker used purple paper for taking notes in her office, despite her explanation that it was the easiest color for her eyes. Respondent even said that he would bring in an expert to talk about the meaning of using purple paper. Respondent also used sashaying and other body language to question her sexuality. As the social worker testified at the ethics hearing:

The Court: Did he imply what meaning he read into this? * * *

The Witness: Given his body language, given that it came on the heels of his suggesting that I had touched his client, that there was something about my sexual orientation that was revealed by the colors of the paper and the paper clip, as well. That's why I mentioned the body language, also, that on the heels of all of this and the context within which it was raised, certainly the implication was that there was something about my sexual orientation that he was alluding to.

The Court: Is that what came across to you?

The Witness: Yes absolutely, without question.

In addition, respondent took the social worker's notes from her during her testimony. He then toyed with her, refusing to return the notes. When she asked Judge Hanifan to instruct respondent to return the notes, respondent berated the judge for talking to the witness. * * *

The *A.R.S.* trial was concluded following four trial days subsequent to respondent's removal from the case. Judge Hanifan ruled in favor of DYFS, terminating J.D.'s parental rights. Although respondent did not represent J.D. and was barred from participating in the matter, he filed an emergent application * * *. Respondent's subsequent motions [and appeals] were denied * * *.

In support of his appeals and motions, respondent included certifications containing [several] false statements, all without any factual basis[.]

At the conclusion of the ethics hearing, the Special Master found that respondent had violated all of the *Rules of Professional Conduct* cited in the complaint. * * * The Special Master also found that respondent violated [Rule] 3.2 and [Rule] 8.4(d) by his courtroom behavior * * *. He concluded that respondent was "discourteous, disrespectful, and insulting toward the tribunal[ ], opposing counsel and witnesses." The Special Master also found that respondent's verbal attacks * * * went well beyond the bounds of trial advocacy and constituted intimidation of opposing counsel and witnesses.

Moreover, the Special Master determined that respondent's behavior during the *A.R.S.* trial violated [Rule] 3.5([d]) and [Rule] 4.4[(a)]. The Special Master noted respondent's allusion to irrelevant matters when he asked Haymaker whether he was an aficionado of pornography or a militarist and when he made an issue about the color of the social worker's notepaper and paper clips. According to the Special Master, respondent offered his personal opinions about the case by suggesting that DYFS had done everything it could to destroy the relationship between the child and his natural mother. The Special Master found that respondent gave his personal opinions about witnesses' testimony and the manner in which the DAG presented her case. The Special Master concluded that the above misconduct was contrary to [Rule] 3.4(e). The Special Master also found that respondent violated [Rule] 3.5([d]), in that his conduct, questions and motions had no purpose other than to prolong the trial and harass the court, witnesses and opposing counsel. According to the Special Master, respondent's harassment of witnesses, repetitive questioning, and "harangues" against the witnesses were "wantonly cruel and uncalled for[."] The special master found that respondent violated [Rule] 4.4[(a)] by such conduct.

Also, respondent's filing of motions and appeals contrary to two court orders removing him from the case violated [Rule] 3.1, [Rule] 3.4(c) and [Rule] 8.4(d), according to the Special Master's report. The Special Master commented that respondent could not credibly assert that he was not obligated to abide by the court orders entered by Judge Hanifan and the Appellate Division, which prohibited him from participating in the *A.R.S.* matter. Further, the Special Master found [that] respondent committed an additional violation of [Rule] 3.1 by requesting to have transcripts prepared at public expense after the Appellate Division had denied such relief. The Special Master determined that respondent's misrepresentations in his certifications in support of the motions * * * violated [Rule] 3.3(a)(1) and [Rule] 8.4(c). * * *

Respondent's courtroom behavior * * * was abominable. [R]espondent engaged in a prolonged course of misconduct by mistreating virtually every person associated with the proceedings. He was disrespectful and discourteous to Judge Hanifan; antagonistic and hostile to the DAG; intimidating and overbearing to DYFS's witnesses, particularly expert witnesses; and, in general, combative and sarcastic. All in all, respondent failed to observe common courtesy, let alone proper courtroom decorum. Respondent repeatedly used vile tactics in an attempt to verbally and physically bully all involved in the litigation: the judge, opposing counsel and witnesses. Respondent had no basis for attacking these individuals, although he seemed to be operating under the premise that there was some kind of conspiracy in which the judge, the DAG, DYFS staff and DYFS's witnesses were all colluding to deprive his client of custody of her son. Respondent asked repetitive questions, pursued irrelevant lines of inquiry and launched into lengthy diatribes when making objections and motions. And when Judge Hanifan ruled against him on motions or objections, he accused the court of bias and prejudice. Respondent's overall conduct was prejudicial to the administration of justice, in violation of [Rule] 8.4(d).

Respondent also violated [Rule] 3.4(e), which prohibits an attorney from alluding to irrelevant matters, asserting personal knowledge of facts in issue or stating a personal opinion as to the justness of a cause, the credibility of a witness or the culpability of a civil litigant. As mentioned above, respondent alluded to such irrelevant matters as Haymaker's views on pornography and the military, as well as the social worker's use of purple notepaper. Respondent offered personal knowledge of facts by insisting, for example, that the social worker's office was located in her home or that the DAG owned a time-share property in Maine.[10] Respondent expressed his personal opinion about the case by contending that

---

10. He was wrong on both scores. * * *

DYFS had done everything it could to destroy the bond between J.D. and A.R.S. He also commented on the testimony of witnesses, and even called Haymaker a liar. Respondent's courtroom antics also violated [Rule] 3.5([d]), which prohibits conduct intended to disrupt a tribunal, and [Rule] 4.4[(a)], which prohibits using means that have no purpose other than to embarrass, delay or burden a third person.

Respondent's repeated appeals and motions filed after he was removed from the case by two court orders, one issued by Judge Hanifan, the other by the Appellate Division, violated [Rule] 3.4(c), which prohibits knowingly disobeying an obligation under the rules of a tribunal, [Rule] 3.1, which prohibits bringing a proceeding or asserting an issue unless the attorney has a basis for doing so that is not frivolous, and [Rule] 8.4(d).

By asserting falsehoods and misrepresentations in his certifications filed with * * * the Appellate Division and the Supreme Court, respondent also violated [Rule] 3.3(a)(1), which prohibits making a false statement of a material fact or law to a tribunal, and [Rule] 8.4(c), which proscribes conduct involving dishonesty, fraud, deceit, or misrepresentation. Respondent's certifications were rife with misstatements, half-truths and outright lies, despite the fact that he knew the courts would be considering such assertions in ruling on his requests for relief. * * *

In assessing the appropriate quantum of discipline for respondent's numerous and troubling ethics violations, the Board considered that this matter represents respondent's fifth serious encounter with the attorney disciplinary system. Significantly, in this case, respondent has violated many of the same *Rules of Professional Conduct* violated in the prior disciplinary cases. Such recidivism is borne out of respondent's refusal to acknowledge his mistakes and to conform his conduct to the ethics standards applicable to all attorneys. * * *

In the instant matter, respondent has not shown any remorse or contrition * * *. He made only the most insincere of apologies, in which he cast blame on the recipient of his attacks, as, for example, when in response to Judge Hanifan's request that he cease arguing with him, respondent replied, "Well I'm sorry for that. But that's your misperception, not mine." * * *

[R]espondent has wreaked havoc on many individuals * * *. As a result of his obnoxious and unprofessional manner, respondent left a trail of injuries and wounds that may never heal. As remarked by the Court in *Vincenti I*, "[t]he record lays bare a shameful display of atrocious deportment calling for substantial discipline." *Vincenti I*, * * * 458 A.2d 1268 [(N.J. 1983)]. In this regard, respondent has shown himself to be * * * ethically bankrupt * * *.

At some point, a court is forced to conclude that it can no longer expose judges, lawyers, litigants, witnesses, and the public to the inexcusable conduct of a renegade attorney. We have passed that point. The only appropriate sanction for respondent's misconduct is disbarment.

So ordered. * * *

Notes on Trial Conduct

1.   *Vincenti* is a virtual outline for violating almost all of the Model Rules governing trial practice, except those associated with the presentation of false evidence previously discussed in *supra* section 6(a)(2)(d).

2.   **Irrelevant Matters:** Model Rule 3.4(e) prohibits a trial attorney from making reference to irrelevant matters or matters that are not supported by admissible evidence. *See also* Restatement, § 107(2) (2000). Trial attorneys and judges refer to a "good faith basis" requirement. Most classically, this restriction prevents a lawyer from improperly intimating ideas to the jury by asking questions, often during cross-examination, that suggest the existence of irrelevant, inadmissible, unprovable, speculative, or untrue "facts." *See Abramian v. President & Fellows of Harvard Coll.*, 731 N.E.2d 1075, 1088–89 (Mass. 2000) (citing state's version of Model Rule 3.4(e) in support of the proposition that "a lawyer must not pursue a line of questioning when there is no reasonable expectation of being able to prove the matters to which the line refers"); *see also, e.g., David v. State*, 28 P.3d 309 (Alaska Ct.App. 2001) (reversing conviction and admonishing trial judge for mistakenly letting a prosecutor ask the defendant's psychologist expert witness if he "had engaged in sexual abuse of his children"); *Commonwealth v. Wynter*, 770 N.E.2d 542 (Mass.App.Ct. 2002) (reversing conviction due to unfounded prosecutorial cross-examination questions, including a question that suggested the existence of an apparently nonexistent statement by a witness). Because a lawyer must have a good faith basis supporting each question or comment during a trial, no lawyer should attempt the common tactic among television, movie, and other fictional lawyers of asking a wildly improper question or making an inappropriate remark and simply stating "withdrawn" in response to the inevitable objection by the court or opposing counsel.

Trial lawyers are often aware of "evidence" supporting factual allegations that is not admitted at trial. They sometimes run afoul of the Model Rule 3.4(e) prohibition of making reference to matters unsupported by admissible evidence by discussing inadmissible evidence in their opening statements or referencing evidence that was never admitted in their closing arguments. *See Lasar v. Ford Motor Co.*, 399 F.3d 1101 (9th Cir. 2005) (affirming trial court's sanctioning of defense attorney and withdrawal of his *pro hac vice* admission for his opening statement reference to plaintiff's drinking and failure to wear his seat belt, after the court issued pretrial rulings excluding evidence of these facts).

3.   **Tactics Designed to Embarrass, Delay, or Burden:** Model Rule 4.4(a) prevents a lawyer from employing tactics designed solely to "embarrass, delay, or burden" a person. *See also* Restatement, § 106. It is perhaps not surprising, though still disappointing, that the competitive environment of litigation causes some attorneys to go overboard in their advocacy and thereby violate Model Rule 4.4(a). *See Ky. Bar Ass'n v. Lavit*, 351 S.W.3d 210, 213 (Ky. 2011) (finding a Model Rule 4.4(a) violation when an attorney "yelled at opposing counsel while opposing counsel questioned [his] client[,] upbraided opposing counsel, interrupted the trial court, and reduced his own client to

tears"); *In re Ulanowski*, 800 N.W.2d 785, 794–95 (Minn. 2011) (finding Model Rule 4.4(a) violation where attorney harassed opposing counsel and sent her letters questioning her intelligence).

Comment [3] to Model Rule 8.4(d)'s prohibition of conduct prejudicial to the administration of justice provides that, except for "[l]egitimate advocacy," a lawyer may violate this provision by "knowingly manifest[ing] by words or conduct, bias or prejudice based upon race, sex, religion, national origin, disability, age, sexual orientation or socioeconomic status." Model Rule 4.4(a)'s prohibition against tactics designed solely to embarrass also applies to discourteous conduct that might have an impact on the outcome on the case. In *Rojas v. Richardson*, 703 F.2d 186 (5th Cir. 1983), the court found that the defense's reference in closing arguments to the plaintiff's alleged status as an illegal alien, which was not supported in the record and was irrelevant to the negligence claim at issue, was plain error. *See also Tobler v. State*, 688 P.2d 350 (Okla.Crim.App. 1984) (finding that irrelevant allegations of defendant's homosexuality were improper); *State v. Monday*, 257 P.3d 551, 555 (Wash. 2011) (reversing conviction where prosecutor's closing argument referred to an alleged African–American anti-snitch code to discredit his own witnesses). In addition, a lawyer should consider how jurors perceive such behavior and whether it is in the client's best interests.

The extent to which trial lawyers can follow their biases and prejudices in exercising peremptory challenges against potential jurors is also limited after *Batson v. Kentucky*, 476 U.S. 79 (1986), and its progeny. Under these cases, an attorney cannot strike a potential juror from a criminal case solely because of that juror's race or sex. *See* Cheryl A. C. Brown, Comment, *Challenging the Challenge: Twelve Years After* Batson, *Courts Are Still Struggling to Fill in the Gaps Left by the Supreme Court*, 28 U.Balt.L.Rev. 379, 393–402 (1999). However, an attorney can strike a potential juror of a particular race or sex if the attorney can state a "discriminatory-neutral" basis for doing so. *See* Kirk Pittard, Comment, *Withstanding* Batson *Muster: What Constitutes a Neutral Explanation?*, 50 Baylor L.Rev. 985, 986 (1998); *see also* Leonard L. Cavise, *The* Batson *Doctrine: The Supreme Court's Utter Failure to Meet the Challenge of Discrimination in Jury Selection*, 1999 Wis.L.Rev. 501, 501 (contending that, due to court acceptance of questionable explanations for peremptory challenges, "[o]nly the most overtly discriminatory or impolitic lawyer can be caught in *Batson*'s toothless bite"). The exercise of peremptory challenges, by which an attorney can remove any potential juror without cause, is inherently an exercise in discrimination of some sort, because the attorney must discriminate between those potential jurors who are acceptable and those who are not. Litigants and courts continue to struggle over the extent to which this exercise in discrimination will be limited, including the parameters of acceptable and unacceptable bases for exercising peremptory challenges.

4. **Personal Opinion:** Model Rule 3.4(e) also prevents a lawyer from stating a "personal opinion" about a witness' credibility, the justness of a cause, a civil party's culpability, or a criminal defendant's guilt or innocence. *See also* RESTATEMENT, § 107(1). Though trial judges allow attorneys more leeway in final argument than in any other portion of the trial, Model Rule 3.4(e) limits this freedom. *See Gaby v. State*, 949 N.E.2d 870, 880 (Ind.Ct.App. 2011) (reversing conviction where prosecutor's final argument stated that

"she was 'confident' that the jury 'would come to the same conclusion' that she and the police detectives had come to" regarding the credibility of the state's witnesses and that " 'I cannot and would not bring charges that I believe were false' "); *State v. Morris*, 196 P.3d 422, 432 (Kan.Ct.App. 2008) (reversing conviction where the prosecutor "on four occasions commented in closing argument on her personal opinion of defense witnesses' credibility"); *Grosjean v. Imperial Palace, Inc.*, 212 P.3d 1068, 1078–79 (Nev. 2009) (citing state's version of Model Rule 3.4(e), which prohibits lawyers from offering personal opinions on justness of a cause or witness credibility, in finding that plaintiff's attorney committed misconduct in his final argument); *Lioce v. Cohen*, 174 P.3d 970, 984 (Nev. 2008) (finding ethical violation where defense attorney in civil case gave a final argument that articulated his "personal opinion about the justness of personal injury litigants' causes and the defendants' culpability"). Assuming that many trial attorneys believe it is important for the jury to see the strength of their conviction, how do they convey this to the jury without running afoul of the rule?

5. **Disruptive Courtroom Behavior:** As in *Vincenti*, courts and other disciplinary authorities responding to courtroom tirades commonly discipline attorneys pursuant to Model Rule 3.5(d)'s prohibition of conduct designed to disrupt a tribunal or Model Rule 8.4(d)'s prohibition of conduct "prejudicial to the administration of justice." Though these provisions are arguably too vague to be applied to some conduct that may be within their reach, there seems to be little dispute about their applicability to histrionics by trial attorneys.

Litigators have misbehaved toward opposing counsel and witnesses in a wide variety of ways, including profanity, threats to "rip [the] face off" of an opposing party and waiving "the finger" in the face of a witness and shouting "f__ you." See Douglas R. Richmond, *The Ethics of Zealous Advocacy: Civility, Candor and Parlor Tricks*, 34 Tex. Tech L.Rev. 3, 4–5 (2002). Despite the judge's admonishments, one trial attorney repeatedly editorialized about adverse witnesses' appearances and testimony in front of the jury, made facial expressions in response to the judge's rulings, and called opposing counsel "a 'f_____g weasel,' " "a 'pinche cabron,' " and " 'hijo de puta.' " *People v. Brennan*, 240 P.3d 887, 893 (Colo. Office of the Presiding Disciplinary J. 2009) (suspending attorney). After one attorney called the other a "jackass," the other responded that the first attorney's "mother is a jackass," then the first assaulted the second, with both falling to the floor. *In re Greenburg*, 2008–2878, pp. 1–2 (La. 5/5/09); 9 So.3d 802, 804 (disciplining both attorneys for disruptive behavior).

Sometimes the bad behavior that results in discipline of trial attorneys is directed toward the court or court personnel. A Kansas attorney appearing in a Missouri municipal court yelled at a court bailiff that the bailiff should "get out of his face," called the court a " 'kangaroo court,' " and asserted that " 'all you guys in Grandview you are all snakes, that's all you all are.' " *In re Romious*, 240 P.3d 945, 951 (Kan. 2010) (disbarring attorney). Another attorney called a judge a "lying incompetent asshole." *See* Douglas R. Richmond, *supra*, at 5. Still another, perturbed that a judge recused himself, told the judge in an ex parte communication that the judge "had 'little balls and when you get f* * *ing big balls you let me know.' " *In re Lee*, 2007–2061, p.

4 (La. 2/26/08); 977 So.2d 852, 854–55 (suspending attorney). During a telephone conversation with the judge's bailiff, another attorney evened out the gender-based vulgarity by "call[ing] the judge a lying, cheating bitch." *Akron Bar Ass'n v. DiCato*, 2011–Ohio–5796, ¶ 4, 958 N.E.2d 938, 939 (suspending attorney, but staying suspension, in part because attorney acknowledged that the statements were inappropriate).

6. **Lawyers as Trial Witnesses:** Under Model Rule 3.4(e), a trial attorney cannot assert personal knowledge of disputed facts, unless the lawyer is testifying. In addition, Model Rule 3.7 generally prohibits a lawyer from testifying in a trial where the lawyer also serves as trial counsel for a party.

This is an area where the law changed significantly when the Model Rules replaced the Model Code of Professional Responsibility, because the restrictions in Model Rule 3.7 against an attorney testifying and serving as counsel do not cover as many circumstances as the provisions of the old Model Code. The more limited restrictions on dual roles for attorneys in the Model Rules presumably stem from the public policy generally allowing persons to choose their own counsel, because disqualification of an attorney due to that attorney's possible testimony limits this right. *See Finkel v. Frattarelli Bros., Inc.*, 740 F.Supp.2d 368, 372 (E.D.N.Y. 2010); *In re Deans*, 939 N.Y.S.2d 493, 495 (App.Div. 2012) (pointing to the general right of a party to choose counsel in denying motion to disqualify counsel). The countervailing considerations supporting the rule against dual roles include eliminating potential juror confusion, eliminating juror discounting of testimony because of concern that the attorney colored testimony to help the attorney's case, relieving opposing counsel of the difficulties of cross-examining a trial adversary, and avoiding having an attorney argue the strength of the attorney's own testimony in closing. *See Murray v. Metro. Life Ins. Co.*, 583 F.3d 173, 178 (2d Cir. 2009); *Smaland Beach Ass'n v. Genova*, 959 N.E.2d 955, 962 (Mass. 2012).

Model Rule 3.7 prevents an attorney from serving as *trial* counsel in a case when the lawyer is "likely to be a necessary witness," subject to the exceptions outlined below. *See State v. Rogers*, 725 S.E.2d 342, 348–49 (N.C.Ct.App. 2012) (affirming trial court's disqualification of defense counsel in criminal case because "there is competent evidence in the record to support the trial court's conclusion that [disqualified counsel] was likely to be a necessary witness at defendant's trial"); *Jozefik v. Jozefik*, 934 N.Y.S.2d 274, 275 (App.Div. 2011) (similar); RESTATEMENT, § 108 (prohibiting most testimony by a lawyer who is representing a client in a hearing or trial and containing a broader set of qualifications and exceptions than Model Rule 3.7). If the attorney merely "might be called as a witness at trial," the court can withhold its decision on whether to disqualify the attorney as trial counsel. *Hunt Constr. Grp., Inc. v. Hun Sch. of Princeton*, No. 08–3550 (FLW), 2010 WL 1752198, at *5 (D.N.J. Apr. 29, 2010). Also, if the attorney's testimony is not "necessary," the court should deny the opposing party's motion to disqualify the attorney as trial counsel. *Finkel*, 740 F.Supp.2d at 375–77; *Damron v. CSX Transp., Inc.*, 2009–Ohio–3638, ¶¶ 34–44, 920 N.E.2d 169, 175–77 (Ct. App.).

In addition to the restrictions of Model Rule 3.7, loyalty concerns might prevent an attorney from testifying against a former client. *See Brand v. 20th Century Ins. Co.*, 21 Cal.Rptr.3d 380, 381 (Ct.App. 2004) (preventing an attorney from presenting expert witness testimony against his former client in a case twelve years later, because the new case involved "matters substantially related" to the old one, which meant the attorney "had access to confidential information material to" the new case).

Under Model Rule 3.7, a lawyer can serve as an advocate and a witness at trial if the lawyer's testimony concerns an uncontested matter or the value and nature of legal services, or if disqualifying the lawyer as trial counsel would cause the lawyer's client "substantial hardship." Model Rule 3.7(a). *See Fidelity Nat'l Title Ins. Co. v. Suburban W. Abstractors*, 852 A.2d 318, 322 (Pa.Super.Ct. 2004) (allowing trial attorney's partner to testify about the reasonableness of attorneys' fees); *D.J. Invest. Grp., L.L.C. v. DAE/Westbrook, L.L.C.*, 2006 UT 62, ¶¶ 18–38, 147 P.3d 414, 420–25 (affirming trial court's denial of motion to disqualify trial counsel due to its determination that disqualification would cause substantial hardship to a party). The substantial hardship provision was presumably added to limit the ability of the opposing party to cause problems by calling the lawyer as a witness.

Contrary to the Model Code and the positions advocated by some who are concerned about attorney testimony, Model Rule 3.7(b) usually allows an attorney to serve as trial counsel when another member of the attorney's firm is likely to be called as a witness. *See Fognani v. Young*, 115 P.3d 1268 (Colo. 2005) (disqualifying attorney who was likely to be called as a witness from serving as trial counsel, but remanding for determination, under Model Rule 1.7, of whether attorney's firm could continue as trial counsel). However, if the conflict of interest provisions of Model Rules 1.7 or 1.9 would prevent an attorney from serving as trial counsel when another attorney in the firm was a likely witness, she cannot serve in this role. Model Rule 3.7(b); *see supra* section 5(B)(1), Notes on Other Attorney Self–Interest Conflicts, note 1 (discussing a case where a firm should have withdrawn as trial counsel because its attorneys should have testified for the firm's client); *see also Crossroads Sys., Inc. v. Dot Hill Sys. Corp.*, No. A–03–CA–754–SS, 2006 WL 1544621, at *11 (W.D.Tex. May 31, 2006) (citing Model Rule 3.7(b) and more restrictive provisions, including Model Code, in disqualifying entire law firm from serving as trial counsel due to likely appearance of some firm attorneys as trial witnesses, because alternatives to firm disqualification were "cumbersome procedures to prevent the jury from being unduly influenced by [the law firm]'s acting in dual roles, each of which may or may not be effective"). The U.S. Court of Appeals for the Second Circuit has determined that "disqualification by imputation should be ordered sparingly," so that "a law firm can be disqualified by imputation only if the movant proves by clear and convincing evidence that [A] the witness will provide testimony prejudicial to the client, and [B] the integrity of the judicial system will suffer as a result." *Murray*, 583 F.3d at 178–79.

Nothing in Model Rule 3.7 prevents an attorney from serving as trial counsel when a non-lawyer member of the firm will be a witness. Many trial attorneys ask non-lawyer employees to accompany them to inspections, interviews, or other situations where facts may be observed, to reduce the risk that the attorneys will become "necessary" witnesses.

7. **Other Model Rules in the Trial Context:** Some Model Rules provisions discussed previously in the discovery and disclosure context, *see supra* section 6(A)(1)(c), also restrict attorney conduct in trial and related matters. For example, Model Rule 3.2 requires attorneys to expedite litigation. *See In re Beauchamp*, 2011–1144, pp. 6–7 (La. 9/23/11); 70 So.3d 781, 788 (disbarring attorney for, inter alia, violating Model Rule 3.2 by failing to appear for two hearings); *In re Longtin*, 713 S.E.2d 297, 301 (S.C. 2011) (suspending attorney for, inter alia, violating Model Rule 3.2 "by failing to prosecute cases adequately on behalf of his clients"). In addition, Model Rule 3.4(c) prohibits a knowing violation of court rules, except one done openly based upon an assertion that the rule requirement is invalid. *See In re Paul*, 809 N.W.2d 693, 700–01 (Minn. 2012) (suspending attorney for, inter alia, failing to follow procedural rules regarding service and filing of motion); *In re Kirschner*, 2011 ND 8, ¶ 12, 793 N.W.2d 196, 200 (finding that attorney's failure to appear for a scheduled trial was a violation of Model Rule 3.4(c)); *Lawyer Disciplinary Bd. v. Grafton*, 712 S.E.2d 488, 493 (W.Va. 2011) (holding that an attorney violated Model Rules 3.2 and 3.4 by not properly complying with the trial court's scheduling order and not complying with rules to perfect an appeal).

8. **Scope of "Tribunal":** Many of the Model Rules discussed in this section and the previous section restrict attorney conduct affecting a "tribunal." Model Rule 1.0(m) defines tribunal to mean not only courts, but also arbitrators and administrative and even legislative bodies "acting in an adjudicative capacity" by considering evidence and argument and then reaching a decision that binds the parties that appear before them. *See Int'l Paper Co. v. Wilson*, 805 S.W.2d 668, 671 (Ark.Ct.App. 1991) (finding that a workers' compensation hearing was covered by rules applicable to a tribunal, not those usually applicable to a legislative or administrative body, *see infra* section 6(B)(3), note 2, because the Workers' Compensation Commission "was clearly performing an adjudicative or quasi-judicial function: it was deciding an issue in a case properly before it").

9. **Mitigation of Sanction by "Apology":** Attorney Vincenti's failure to sincerely apologize for his misconduct was one of the critical factors that led to the maximum disciplinary penalty of disbarment. The value of an apology by a misbehaving attorney is underscored by the standard practice of courts and other disciplinary authorities to adopt less severe discipline after an attorney admits wrongdoing and demonstrates remorse. *See In re Mpaka*, 939 N.Y.S.2d 157, 157 (App.Div. 2012) (staying the suspension of an attorney who "expressed remorse for his misconduct"); *Lawyer Disciplinary Bd. v. Scott*, 579 S.E.2d 550, 559 (W.Va. 2003) (holding that a disciplined attorney's "complete willingness to accept total responsibility for his actions [and other mitigating factors] require that his punishment be slightly less than annulment"); *Bd. of Prof'l Resp. v. Jenkins*, 2011 WY 89, 260 P.3d 264, 265 (entering public censure for misconduct where attorney was "extremely embarrassed by this matter, has apologized for his actions and will take steps in his practice to assure that nothing like this ever happens again"); ABA Standards for Imposing Lawyer Sanctions § 9.32(e) & (l) (as amended 1992)

(listing "full and free disclosure to disciplinary board or cooperative attitude toward [disciplinary] proceedings" and "remorse" as mitigating factors in the determination of the appropriate sanction). Because judges recognize that trials are high stress events that sometimes result in mistakes by otherwise ethical attorneys, an attorney apology for relatively minor trial misconduct may even result in no further action by the court, including no referring of the matter to disciplinary authorities.

Is the "apology discount" wise public policy? Does it further the general aim of the disciplinary system, by promoting attorney recognition and correction of problematic behavior? Does the resultant lesser discipline adequately protect the public and the courts? Does an apology discount place the attorney who is accused of misconduct in an overly difficult dilemma of choosing between denying misconduct and admitting it and apologizing? Is the experience of the criminal justice system with plea bargaining, along with the criticism sometimes launched against this practice, instructive for the disciplinary process?

10. **Codes of "Civility" or "Professionalism":** Many who are troubled by a perceived growth in uncivil attorney behavior, especially in the litigation context, have advocated the adoption of "civility" or "professionalism" codes. Some jurisdictions have heeded this call by adopting voluntary codes. In addition, some groups of litigators have adopted voluntary codes designed, at least in part, to reign in inappropriate litigation behavior. *See* N. Lee Cooper & Stephen F. Humphreys, *Beyond the Rules: Lawyer Image and the Scope of Professionalism*, 26 Cumb.L.Rev. 923, 935 (1995–1996) ("Eighty-eight jurisdictions have tried to do something about [the breakdown of civility] by adopting codes of civility. These are roughly patterned after the ethics codes, but without enforceability by sanctions."); American College of Trial Lawyers, *Code of Pretrial Conduct and Code of Trial Conduct* (2002); American Inns of Court, *Professional Creed of American Inns of Court* (1993); *see also* American Bar Association, Compendium of Professional Responsibility Rules and Standards 393–98 (2003 ed.) (reprinting Young Lawyers Division pledge of professionalism, Section of Tort and Insurance Practice creed of professionalism, and Standing Committee on Professionalism recommendation and report).

Civility codes are not without their detractors. *See* Amy R. Mashburn, *Professionalism as Class Ideology: Civility Codes and Bar Hierarchy*, 28 Val.U.L.Rev. 657 (1994); Brenda Smith, Comment, *Civility Codes: The Newest Weapons in the "Civil" War over Proper Attorney Conduct Regulations Miss Their Mark*, 24 U. Dayton L.Rev. 151 (1998). Some believe that lawyers who are unwilling to act courteously and professionally in the absence of such a code are unlikely to alter their behavior in response to the adoption of a voluntary code.

Are civility codes wise? If not, what should be done to thwart or eliminate misconduct during the pressure cooker of trial, which has a tendency to bring out the worst in some attorneys? *See* Thomas E. Richard, *Professionalism: What Rules Do We Play By?*, 30 S.U.L.Rev. 15, 22–23 (2002) (reviewing assorted responses to perceived professionalism problems, including law school orientation programs on professionalism, mandatory continuing legal education on professionalism, and professionalism commissions and centers).

A(3) FAIR TRIAL AND FREE PRESS

PROBLEM

Joe Dukas, 20, is accused of the violent murders of Ted and Donna Murphy and their children Lisa, 19, and Seth, 15. The only surviving member of the family, 17–year–old Michael Murphy, was at a high school basketball game at the time of the killings. After discovering their bloody and badly beaten bodies when he arrived home, he told a radio reporter that he suspected Dukas committed the crimes. In televised interviews that Saturday, Michael said his father had persuaded Lisa to stop dating Dukas. Michael let television crews into the house to film the bloodied rooms where his family died. Media coverage continued intensely in the following weeks.

The judge, concerned that high local interest and national publicity could turn the trial into a circus, prohibited the public from attending the pretrial proceedings and the jury voir dire. The judge also banned television cameras from the courtroom.

A week before trial, prosecutor Wanda Geller met with Police Officer C.O. Powell, who wanted to call a press conference to discuss the three times he arrested Dukas as a juvenile for minor violent crimes. After Geller talked Officer Powell out of calling the press conference, he asked what he should do if a reporter ever asked him about Dukas' juvenile record. She responded by telling him that he would "just have to cross that bridge when you come to it, if you come to it."

Three days before trial, prosecutor Geller told a Hinkson Daily News reporter, "Dukas has had trouble before, but I can't get his juvenile record admitted at trial. But justice will be served. We are confident of victory." Then she added, "All of that is off the record, of course." The reporter responded, "Too late. You know the rules. At least you ought to know the rules. If you want something off the record, you have to say so and I have to agree to it before you give me the quote, not after." The reporter then asked Geller to elaborate on the defendant's juvenile record, but she told the reporter to "leave immediately if you are going to quote me on stuff I want off the record." The prosecutor's remarks were quoted in a front page Daily News story the next day.

Following his interview of the prosecutor, the Daily News reporter visited Officer Powell, because he knew that he handled most juvenile matters in Hinkson. His story the next day quoted Powell as saying, "I personally arrested him three times for violent crimes when he was in school."

After the Daily News story, Dukas' defense attorney, Les Bradley, agreed to be interviewed by a New York Times reporter, though he had not explicitly discussed this with his client. The New York Times story accurately quoted him as saying: "The whole town is talking about a few juvenile offenses, but I can tell you that these alleged 'crimes of violence' were minor scuffles in school parking lots. Dukas may have been a bit of a hot head in high school, like many of us were at that age, but he is no murderer. I have met with my client many times. This is not my first criminal case, so I know if someone is telling me the truth. I can assure you that he is not guilty."

The jury found Dukas guilty. In an interview with the New York Times reporter a month later, Bradley said: "Hey, I did the best I could do for the guy, but the deck was stacked against me. When I told you before trial that he was 'not guilty,' I did not mean that he did not do it. I am a defense attorney. To me, 'not guilty' means the state has not proven that he did it. Well, now they have, but don't blame me. When you beat people up all through school and then leave a trail of physical evidence a mile long, what do you expect?" These comments appeared in the Times the next day.

QUESTIONS

(a) Are any of the statements or actions of the prosecutor improper? If so, why?

(b) Are any of the statements or actions of the defense attorney improper? If so, why?

(c) What other problems are presented by highly publicized trials? Did the judge respond to them properly? Should the judge have done anything else?

RULE REFERENCES

Model Rules 3.6, 1.6, 1.8(b), 3.5, and 3.8(f)

Code of Judicial Conduct, Rule 2.10 (formerly Canon 3B(9))

RESTATEMENT § 109

ALBERTO BERNABE–RIEFKOHL, SILENCE IS GOLDEN: THE * * * RULES ON ATTORNEY EXTRAJUDICIAL SPEECH

33 Loyola University Chicago Law Journal 323 (2002).

I. INTRODUCTION

* * * The rules that limit attorneys' contact with the media were enacted in an effort to protect both defendants and the state from the effects that too much publicity could have on a trial, while balancing an attorney's right to free speech. [T]he rules also have to consider the right of the press to provide coverage of the judicial system, which is also constitutionally protected, because press coverage is a valuable component of our democratic form of government.

[Some argue that rules limiting attorney speech] create a chilling effect and may suppress speech of particular social importance, particularly in cases where the defendant is claiming governmental misconduct. Also, a defendant's lawyer is often his or her only spokesperson and the attorney's ability to speak out on behalf of the client is part of his or her professional duty. In cases like these, denying the attorney the chance to access the media may result in substantial injustice for the client.

[Further] some * * * have argued that the rules that limit extrajudicial speech should apply only to prosecutors[. The argument is that defense counsel needs to create pretrial publicity] "to counter adverse non-lawyer publicity about the accused * * * that is fomented by actions and statements of the police at the time of the report of the crime and the arrest of the accused[. In addition, it is argued that] the fair trial right implicated by the anti-comment rules should be waivable by the accused."
* * *

II. REGULATION OF SPEECH BY ATTORNEYS AND TRIAL PUBLICITY

There is no doubt that prejudicial publicity can threaten a defendant's Sixth Amendment right to a fair trial by creating the possibility that the jury may reach a decision not based on the information provided at trial but on the publicity itself. Prejudicial publicity can also taint the reputation of trial participants who do not have the opportunity to respond to it. The Sixth Amendment's right to a fair trial * * * includes the defendant's right to have his or her guilt determined solely on the basis of the evidence introduced at trial, to have a speedy and public trial by an impartial jury, * * * and to have effective assistance of counsel. * * *

The debate about freedom of the press and fair trials * * * receive[d] increased national attention in 1963, after the Report of the Warren Commission on the Assassination of President Kennedy ("the Warren Report") criticized the news media for its role in creating the publicity surrounding the allegations against Lee Harvey Oswald. In fact, the Warren Commission expressed doubts that Oswald could ever have received a fair trial and concluded: "The courtroom, not the newspaper or television screen, is the appropriate forum in our system for the trial of a man accused of a crime."

Among other things, the Warren Report specifically recommended the creation of ethical standards regarding trial publicity to avoid interference with criminal investigations and the rights of defendants. In response to this recommendation and the decisions of the Supreme Court, the Judicial Conference of the United States conducted a study and suggested three areas of concern for trial courts: release of information to the press by attorneys, release of information by other trial participants, and the regulation of trial proceedings to protect jurors from prejudicial influences. Likewise, the ABA appointed a committee to develop standards to regulate the criminal justice system.

While the work of the ABA committee was ongoing, the Supreme Court provided guidelines on how to balance the interests of the press and the rights of a criminal defendant in *Sheppard v. Maxwell*[, 384 U.S. 333 (1966)]. In *Sheppard*, the Court reversed a conviction for murder, holding that the publicity surrounding the trial had deprived the defendant of his right to a fair trial. Even before the defendant was arrested, the media published countless stories about him, which accentuated his alleged failure to cooperate with the investigation and called strongly for his arrest. Many articles and editorials insinuated that Sheppard was guilty and discussed incriminating evidence that was never introduced at trial. During the trial itself, the constant movement of reporters in the courtroom made it difficult for witnesses to be heard. Furthermore, because of the defendant's proximity to reporters in the courtroom, it was almost impossible for him to speak privately with his attorney during the proceedings. Despite these circumstances, the trial judge did not take steps to limit the effects of the publicity or the behavior of the press during the trial. The judge did not grant a continuance, change the venue of the trial, sequester the jury, insulate the jurors from reporters, or prevent reporters from disrupting the proceedings.

In criticizing the trial court for allowing a "carnival atmosphere" in the courtroom and for failing to control the flow of publicity, the Supreme Court ordered lower courts to take an affirmative role in protecting the rights of defendants from undue interference by the press:

> From the cases coming here we note that unfair and prejudicial news comment on pending trials has become increasingly prevalent. Due process requires that the accused receive a trial by an impartial jury free from outside influences. Given the pervasiveness of modern communications and the difficulty of effacing prejudicial publicity from the minds of the jurors, the trial courts must take strong measures to ensure that the balance is never weighed against the accused.

[384 U.S. at 362.]

The [decisions including] *Sheppard* * * * sent a clear message to trial courts that even in the absence of actual prejudice, pervasive pretrial publicity can affect a defendant's right to a fair trial and * * * courts have a duty to protect the defendant from the effects of prejudicial publicity. * * *

III.   JUDICIAL INTERPRETATION OF THE APPROACH OF THE ABA * * *

A.   *The Approach of the ABA Model Rules* * * *

[I]n 1983, the ABA House of Delegates adopted * * * the Model Rules of Professional Conduct. [T]he drafters included a new rule to regulate attorneys' conduct in relation to pre-trial publicity. [Comment [1] to Rule 3.6] explains the ABA's concern for the integrity of the trial process on one hand and the value of free expression on the other * * *.

B.   *Interpretation of the Supreme Court of the United States:* Gentile v. State Bar of Nevada

With this * * * history as a background, the Supreme Court * * * addressed the free speech rights of lawyers in the context of trial publicity in *Gentile v. State Bar of Nevada*, [501 U.S. 1030 (1991). P]etitioner

Dominic Gentile was an experienced Nevada criminal defense lawyer who held a press conference soon after his client was indicted. During the press conference, he read a short statement and answered a few questions. The client was the owner of a storage facility where a police safe deposit box was located. He was indicted in connection with the theft of a large quantity of cocaine and traveler's checks from that deposit box. At the time of the press conference, the client had been the subject of media attention for about a year. The media had been generally favorable to the police and portrayed the client as a suspect in previous thefts and as uncooperative during the investigation.

Gentile argued that the press conference was simply an attempt to respond to local press reports that were prejudicial to his client. In fact, the night before the press conference, Gentile and two other lawyers studied the applicable rule on trial publicity to make sure his statements complied with it. During the press conference, Gentile asserted that his client was innocent, that he was being used as a scapegoat by a corrupt police force, and that a certain police officer was the more likely suspect in the theft. He also gave a description of his defense strategy. The case proceeded to trial and the court did not have any problems impaneling a jury. Neither party requested a change of venue or a continuance. There was no claim of prejudice caused by publicity at any time. At voir dire, none of the potential jurors recalled Gentile's press conference. Gentile's client was eventually acquitted of all charges.

Ten months after the press conference and four months after a jury acquitted Gentile's client, the State Bar of Nevada filed a complaint against Gentile for allegedly violating [the Nevada Rule], which was virtually identical to ABA Model Rule 3.6. At the time, the rule in Nevada prohibited an attorney from making a statement if the lawyer "knows or reasonably should know that it will have a substantial likelihood of materially prejudicing an adjudicative proceeding." However, the rule [went] on to list certain types of statements that attorneys could make "notwithstanding" the general ban. Gentile argued that he made an effort to ensure that his statements fell within this "safe harbor" provision of the rule. However, the southern Nevada disciplinary board held that Gentile knew or should have known that there was a substantial likelihood that his comments would materially prejudice the proceeding. The Nevada Supreme Court later affirmed the board's decision, finding that Gentile had violated the rule and imposed a private reprimand, the lowest possible sanction. As a result, Gentile appealed arguing that [the] Nevada Rule * * * infringed upon his right to free speech and the Supreme Court of the United States reversed, in a complicated decision with two separate majority opinions.

The Supreme Court was split on two different issues. Justice Kennedy wrote an opinion reversing the sanctions and holding [the] Nevada Rule * * * void for vagueness as interpreted and applied by the Nevada Supreme Court. This opinion was joined by Justices Marshall, Blackmun, and Stevens and Justice O'Connor concurred with the judgment. The second issue in the case was whether the "substantial likelihood standard" was constitutional. On this issue, Chief Justice Rehnquist wrote the opinion of the Court, in which Justices White, Scalia, and Souter joined, and Justice O'Connor concurred.

Justice Kennedy's opinion was based on the interpretation of what he considered to be conflicting messages in the text of the rule. He held that [some language within the rule's safe-harbor provision] could mislead an attorney into thinking that he or she could issue comments of the type mentioned in the rule without fear of sanctions. Given that Gentile's comments did fall within the language of the rule and that the Nevada Supreme Court found that he had violated the rule, Kennedy concluded that the application of the rule was invalid for vagueness. As Gentile made an effort to comply with the rule but ultimately could not, Justice Kennedy concluded that the rule created "a trap for the wary as well as the unwary" because it failed to give attorneys enough guidance as to when speech was protected.

On the question of the appropriate constitutional standard, Chief Justice Rehnquist specifically rejected the claim that the state could only discipline an attorney if there was a "clear and present danger" that the attorney's statements would affect the fairness of the proceeding. He concluded that the restraint on attorneys' speech was content neutral and narrowly tailored because it was applied only to speech that was substantially likely to have a prejudicial effect. According to the Chief Justice, the limitations on speech were narrowly aimed at two principal evils: comments that could influence the outcome of a trial and comments that could prejudice the jury venire. Because he thought that voir dire may not be effective in filtering out all the effects of pretrial publicity, he concluded that unless speech is limited under the circumstances, both evils would result in the violation of fundamental rights under the Constitution. Speaking for the Court, therefore, he held that states could impose sanctions on a lawyer for extrajudicial statements that had a "substantial likelihood of materially prejudicing [an adjudicative] proceeding."

Gentile has attracted much criticism over the years. In the end, the Court's opinion does not provide clear guidelines to help courts determine the constitutionality of the ability of a state to regulate in the area of trial publicity. Taken together, the opinions in *Gentile* did not lead the Court to strike down the rule on its face. It only found the rule unconstitutional in its application. In fact, even Justice Kennedy declined to find the "substantial likelihood of material prejudice standard" facially deficient because it could be interpreted in a manner "consistent with the First Amendment." Yet, it is difficult to understand how the rule can be consistent with the First Amendment if it can result in sanctions for protected speech. On the other hand, it has been argued that the disposal of the sanctions on grounds of vagueness should have ended the case, and that, therefore, the discussion of the broader constitutional issue was unnecessary. Finally, it has been said that Chief Justice Rehnquist's opinion may negatively affect criminal defense representation. However, most of the commentary generated by *Gentile* has focused on whether the Court erred in recognizing the use of a "substantial likelihood" standard in a case that implicated First Amendment rights.

C. Gentile's *Aftermath: Amendments to the Rules*

[After *Gentile*], two differing views or approaches to trial publicity rules emerged. Some states chose to use a strict standard along the lines of the "clear and present danger test." Under this standard a lawyer may not be punished unless the challenged statement poses a serious and imminent threat of interference with the administration of justice. In contrast, other states retained a lower threshold for discipline based on "reasonable likelihood of prejudice." Under this approach the state could punish the lawyer for statements that have a reasonable likelihood of interference with the judicial process. * * * The ABA adopted the second [approach].

In response to the holding in *Gentile*, the ABA modified Model Rule 3.6 in several ways. First, subsection (a) was amended to apply only to attorneys who participate or have participated in the litigation. Second, the drafters eliminated the provisions that the Court determined were invalid for vagueness. For example, the words "notwithstanding" and "without elaboration" were eliminated from the text of the rule and the phrase "general nature of the claim or defense" was changed to "the claim, offense or defense involved." Third, the section of the rule that listed the types of statements that could result in discipline was moved from the text of the rule and placed in the comment. Fourth, the rule recognized a new right to reply to prejudicial publicity in certain circumstances. Fifth, a new paragraph was added to extend subsection (a) to lawyers "associated" with a lawyer who is or had been involved in the case. Finally, the comment to the rule was amended to suggest that the nature of the proceeding should be taken into account in determining prejudice. The ABA also modified Model Rule 3.8([f]) to include a specific provision applicable to prosecutors.

NOTES ON RESTRICTING EXTRAJUDICIAL STATEMENTS BY LAWYERS

1. Assume you are involved in a high profile criminal case. The police have named a primary suspect but have not yet made an arrest. Under Model Rule 3.6(b), as an attorney in the prosecutor's office, what specific comments can you make to the media? What can you not say?

Now assume that an arrest has been made and that the suspect is in jail. You have been appointed to represent the suspect. Prior to your client's capture, the media was fascinated with the case and with your client's attempt to flee. Again, under Model Rule 3.6(b), what specific comments can you make to the media? What can you not say?

2. Other commentators have added to the discussion of Model Rule 3.6 following the Court's ruling in *Gentile*. In Ryan Brett Bell & Paula Odysseos, Comment, *Sex, Drugs, and Court TV? How America's Increasing Interest in*

Trial Publicity Impacts Our Lawyers and the Legal System, 15 Geo.J. Legal Ethics 653 (2002), the authors first note the dichotomy produced by *Gentile*'s finding that application of the rule in the case was void for vagueness but that the "substantial likelihood" test was constitutionally permissible. In the authors' view, *Gentile* and the post-*Gentile* version of Model Rule 3.6 also apparently require attorneys to forecast the future whenever they consider making public statements:

MODEL RULE 3.6

Model Rule 3.6 reflects the ABA's best efforts to "strike a balance between protecting the right to a fair trial [while] safeguarding the right of free expression." [Comment [1] to Model Rule 3.6.] Restrictions on attorney speech, most notably through Model Rule 3.6 and its progeny, have been promulgated in an attempt to perpetuate ethical conduct consistent with these ideals. Nonetheless, in practice these rules are arguably unclear and vague. In order to conform to these competing ideals, Model Rule 3.6 states:

> (a) A lawyer who is participating or has participated in the investigation or litigation of a matter shall not make an extrajudicial statement that [the lawyer knows or reasonably should know will] be disseminated by means of public communication [and] will have a substantial likelihood of materially prejudicing an adjudicati[ve] proceeding in the matter.[a]

* * * The wording of Model Rule 3.6 might instill fear in the heart of an attorney faced with his first high-profile case—one can imagine the plethora of hypothetical situations wherein seemingly innocuous or well-intended statements may be transformed into materially prejudicial statements. Despite the apparent lack of guidance provided by this language, Model Rule 3.6 is consistent with *Gentile*'s holding that the substantial likelihood test is constitutionally permissible.

Although critics cite lack of explicit guidance regarding prohibited statements as a general flaw in Model Rule 3.6, Model Rule 3.6(b) attempts to provide some specificity with respect to information that is permissible for dissemination, including:

> (1) the claim, offense or defense involved and, except when prohibited by law, the identity of the persons involved;
>
> (2) information contained in a public record;
>
> (3) that an investigation of a matter is in progress;
>
> (4) the scheduling or result of any step in litigation;
>
> (5) a request for assistance in obtaining evidence and information necessary thereto;

---

a. [When this piece was written, the ABA had not yet adopted the 2002 amendments to Rule 3.6(a). Therefore, the article quotes the pre–2002 version. The bracketed portions reflect the changes adopted in 2002. Eds.]

(6) warning of danger concerning the behavior of a person involved, when there is reason to believe that there exists the likelihood of substantial harm to an individual or to the public interest;

(7) in a criminal case, in addition to subparagraphs (1) through (6):

(i) the identity, residence, occupation and family status of the accused;

(ii) if the accused has not been apprehended, information necessary to aid in the apprehension of that person;

(iii) the fact, time and place of arrest; and

(iv) the identity of investigating and arresting officers or agencies and the length of the investigation.

This is yet another piece of this puzzling rule. [I]t is possible to conceive of situations wherein these delineated exceptions might give rise to potential ethical concerns. For example, if a suspected mass murderer of three-year old children has yet to be apprehended, "a warning of danger" posited by a prosecutor, standing next to weeping parents, arguably might have a prejudicial effect on a potential jury pool. However, [Comment [4]] to Model Rule 3.6 note[s] that paragraph (b), "identifies specific matters about which a lawyer's statements would not ordinarily be considered to present a substantial likelihood of material prejudice, and should not in any event be considered prohibited by the general prohibition of paragraph (a)." Thus, even where Model Rule 3.6 presents specific examples of permissible statements, the discretionary "substantial likelihood" standard might enable a judge, under certain factual scenarios, to impose sanctions on an attorney.

Perhaps the most enigmatic ethical guidance provided by Model Rule 3.6 is its safe-harbor provision, paragraph (c), which notes:

Notwithstanding paragraph (a), a lawyer may make a statement that a reasonable lawyer would believe is required to protect a client from the substantial undue prejudicial effect of recent publicity not initiated by the lawyer or the lawyer's client. A statement made pursuant to this paragraph shall be limited to such information as is necessary to mitigate the recent adverse publicity.

Paragraph (c) effectively makes otherwise unethical publicity valid if "made in response to [statements] made publicly by another party, another party's lawyer, or third persons, where a reasonable lawyer would believe a public response is required in order to avoid prejudice to the lawyer's client." [Rule 3.6, Comment [7].] The behavior permitted by this provision is seemingly unbounded—no case has directly challenged the scope of this provision, or explained how an attorney can limit such speech to "contain only such information as is necessary to mitigate undue prejudice created by the statements made by others." [*Id.*] Again, an attorney is expected to predict the future and impose self-inflicted constraints to ensure conformance with ethical guidelines.

[Comment 5] to Model Rule 3.6 ultimately present[s] a non-exhaustive list of subjects "[that] are more likely than not to have a material prejudicial effect." These aim to serve as additional guidance for attorneys. Examples include:

(1) the character, credibility, reputation or criminal record of a party, suspect in a criminal investigation or witness, or the identity of a witness, or the expected testimony of a party or witness;

(2) in a criminal case or proceeding that could result in incarceration, the possibility of a plea of guilty to the offense or the existence or contents of any confession, admission, or statement given by a defendant or suspect or that person's refusal or failure to make a statement;

(3) the performance or results of any examination or test or the refusal or failure of a person to submit to an examination or test, or the identity or nature of physical evidence expected to be presented;

(4) any opinion as to the guilt or innocence of a defendant or suspect in a criminal case or proceeding that could result in incarceration;

(5) information that the lawyer knows or reasonably should know is likely to be inadmissible as evidence in a trial and that would, if disclosed, create a substantial risk of prejudicing an impartial trial[;

(6) the fact that a defendant has been charged with a crime, unless there is included therein a statement explaining that the charge is merely an accusation and that the defendant is presumed innocent until and unless proven guilty.]

Upon reexamining the safe-harbor provision, however, it might be permissible for an attorney to comment publicly, using the criteria listed above, to respond to damaging media coverage. The safe-harbor provision, in practice, therefore has the potential to generate problems similar to those arising in the *Gentile* case. The text of Model Rule 3.6 thus provides a loophole that allows extrajudicial statements without explicitly delineating the boundaries of this exception.

15 Geo.J. Legal Ethics at 656–60. For reviews of the history of the ABA's rules regarding attorney speech about litigated cases, see *PCG Trading, LLC v. Seyfarth Shaw, LLP*, 951 N.E.2d 315, 318–20 (Mass. 2011) (reviewing evolution of Model Rule 3.6 and finding that an attorney's statements fell "well within" the Model Rule 3.6(b) exceptions allowing attorneys to state the claim and information contained in public records), and Peter A. Joy & Kevin C. McMunigal, *Trial by Media: Arguing Cases in the Court of Public Opinion*, Crim.Just., Summer 2004, at 47.

3. In determining whether to make a public comment, Model Rule 3.6 is not the only provision that a lawyer must consider. In Marjorie P. Slaughter, *Lawyers and the Media: The Right to Speak Versus the Duty to Remain Silent*, 11 Geo.J. Legal Ethics 89, 92–99 (1997), the author reviews other rules that must be considered before a lawyer makes a public comment:

MODEL RULE 1.6: CONFIDENTIALITY OF INFORMATION

Regardless of what information *Model Rule* 3.6 allows a lawyer to divulge to the public, a lawyer's speech always may be restricted by his or her duty of confidentiality pursuant to *Model Rule* 1.6. This rule forever seals the lawyer's lips regarding all matters pertaining to the representation of his or her client. * * *

The lawyer's duty to maintain confidentiality is ironclad. Without the client's consent, only very limited information can be revealed to any other person. * * * A lawyer would be hard pressed to make a case that any conversation with the media was impliedly authorized and necessary [under the exceptions to Rule 1.6]. After all, the media is not the opposition, the court, or a law enforcement authority. A simple "no comment" to the media would best serve the client if the client had given no informed consent * * *.

[T]he duty of confidentiality continues after the client-lawyer relationship has terminated. [Additionally,] the duty of confidentiality exists without regard to whether others share the information or whether it is part of the public record or available from another source. [As a result, only] if the client [gives informed consent] is the lawyer free to divulge any information pertaining to the representation. * * *

Model Rule 1.8: Conflicts of Interest

Regardless of whether she violates *Model Rule* 1.6, a lawyer who engages in extrajudicial, post-trial speech may violate *Model Rule* 1.8(b), which deems it a conflict of interest for a lawyer to use information relating to the representation of a client to the client's disadvantage without the client's consent.

A client could be disadvantaged by his attorney's extrajudicial comments in a number of ways, including * * *: the client's public image or credibility could suffer; the client's opportunity to be brought before an unbiased jury in a separate action could be diminished; the number or quality of client's business opportunities could decrease; or, the value of stock in the client corporation could decrease. Furthermore, suppose the client consents to his attorney's extrajudicial comments only to discover after the consent has been given and the comments have been made that the comments have been to the client's disadvantage. Did the lawyer have the duty to foresee the potential detriment and refrain from placing his client at a disadvantage? * * *

Model Rule 3.5: Impartiality of the Court and the Jurors

If a lawyer wants to speak to the press after her representation of the client has concluded, with her client's consent, not to her client's disadvantage, and without having entered into a literary or media rights contract beforehand, is she free to speak? In other words, if she can do so without violating [other Rules], is the lawyer ethically free to tell all? In this author's opinion, she is not free to speak until she has considered *Model Rule* 3.5, a broad-based rule aimed at maintaining impartiality and decorum in the courtroom.

Much of lawyers' extrajudicial speech is spin control that, depending on its context, may or may not disrupt the impartiality and decorum of the courtroom. While spin control may be in the client's best interest, it nevertheless is designed to influence favorably the public's perception of the client or of the cause which the lawyer or his client is attempting to advance. Clients who may desire extrajudicial publicity include public figures, corporations, and public interest groups, as well as anyone else who is as concerned with the judgment of the public as he is with the judgment of a jury. Specific groups, other than the potential jury, at whom lawyers may aim extrajudicial speech include judges, prosecutors, opposing counsel, politicians, and potential clients.

Lawyers may use the press to make judges aware of particular decisions favorable to their long-term clients or area of practice; they may try to use public pressure to force prosecutors or opposing counsel to proceed with or discontinue a particular course of action; or, they may try to publicly pressure politicians to change laws. The line between being an aggressive advocate for the client and engaging "in conduct intended to disrupt a tribunal" is a fine one in these situations. Thus, the extent to which extrajudicial advocacy violates *Model Rule* 3.5 depends on the intent of the lawyer engaged in the advocacy.

For another outline of the tactical and strategic issues an attorney should consider before engaging in a media campaign, see Peter A. Joy & Kevin C. McMunigal, *Trial by Media: Arguing Cases in the Court of Public Opinion*, Crim.Just., Summer 2004, at 47, 48 (discussing whether the client or attorney should decide whether to engage in a publicity campaign, competence in dealing with the media, possible conflicts of interest between the attorney and client, and potential vicarious Model Rules violations from client statements under instructions from attorneys).

For an example of an attorney who found trouble by violating Model Rule 1.6's confidentiality duty by issuing a press release, see *Sealed Party v. Sealed Party*, No. Civ. A. H–04–2229, 2006 WL 1207732 (S.D.Tex. May 4, 2006). The court held that the attorney breached his confidentiality duty by issuing a press release bragging about his good work for a client specified in the press release, without receiving the client's permission to do so.

4. **2002 Changes to Model Rule 3.6:** Before 2002, Model Rule 3.6(a) prohibited an extrajudicial comment "that a reasonable person would expect to be disseminated by means of public communication if the lawyer knows or reasonably should know that it will have a substantial likelihood of materially prejudicing" the proceedings. After 2002, Model Rule 3.6(a) prohibits an extrajudicial statement "that the lawyer knows or reasonably should know will be disseminated by means of public communication and will have a substantial likelihood of materially prejudicing" the proceedings. Does this change effect the problem, where the prosecutor clumsily requested "off the record" status after making statements to the reporter? For brief reviews of the "off the record" and other unwritten rules of contact with reporters and advice for attorneys in dealing with the press, see Monica Bay, *Dealing with the Media: How to Protect and Enhance Your Clients' Interests*, Law Prac. Mgmt., May/June 2003, at 42; Peter J. Gardner, *Media at the Gates: Panic! Stress! Ethics?*, Vt.B.J., Sept. 2001, at 39.

5. **Prosecutor Statements and Responses by Defense Attorneys:** Prosecutors are subject to the additional restrictions of Model Rule 3.8(f). It

prohibits comments that are likely to increase community condemnation of the defendant, except when they serve a valid law enforcement purpose and are needed to inform the public of the prosecutor's activities. *In re Gansler*, 889 A.2d 285, 287 (D.C. 2005) (disciplining prosecutor who announced at a press conference that a defendant had confessed and that the confession was credible because it " 'provided "incredible details that only the murderer would have known" ' " and announced in a press conference in a different case that " 'we have found the person who committed the crime at this point' and that the case against [him] 'will be a strong case' "). This prohibition is complemented by item (6) on the list of problematic attorney comment subjects in Comment [5] to Model Rule 3.6, *see supra* note 2. This Comment effectively requires a prosecutor who reports a charge to also state that a charge is only an accusation and that the defendant is presumed innocent until proven guilty. *See In re Brizzi*, 962 N.E.2d 1240, 1246 (Ind. 2012) (issuing public reprimand of prosecutor whose office's news release did not include the required statement about the nature of a charge and the presumption of innocence). Under Model Rule 3.8(f), prosecutors are also required to "exercise reasonable care" to keep law enforcement officers and those associated with the prosecutor from making statements that would be prohibited if made by the prosecutor. Advice about press relations for prosecutors can be found in H. Morley Swingle, *Prosecutors Beware: Pretrial Publicity May Be Hazardous to Your Career*, Prosecutor, Sept./Oct. 2001, at 29.

The problems associated with substantial pretrial publicity, generated or at least assisted by prosecutors and law enforcement officers, gained national attention in the first decade of the century. In what was widely known as the "Duke lacrosse case," three members of the Duke lacrosse team were accused of raping an exotic dancer in 2006. The case became a subject of national news attention, with Durham County District Attorney Mike Nifong and law enforcement officers repeatedly appearing in television and print news reports. Despite Model Rule 3.6, District Attorney Nifong called the players " 'a bunch of hooligans' " and proclaimed that " 'he wouldn't allow Durham to become known for "a bunch of lacrosse players from Duke raping a black girl." ' " *See* James R. Devine, *The Duke Lacrosse Matter as a Case Study of the Right to Reply to Prejudicial Pretrial Extrajudicial Publicity Under Rule 3.6(c)*, 15 Vill. Sports & Ent.L.J. 175, 220–21 (2008). The North Carolina Attorney General eventually took over the prosecution, then dismissed the charges and "declared the three indicted lacrosse players to be actually innocent." James E. Coleman, Jr. et al., *The Phases and Faces of the Duke Lacrosse Controversy: A Conversation*, 19 Seton Hall J. Sports & Ent.L. 181, 182 (2009). After Nifong resigned his prosecutorial position and admitted that " 'no credible evidence' existed to tie the Duke lacrosse team to any sexual misconduct," he was disbarred. Devine, *supra,* at 220–21 & n.312.

Among its many lessons, the Duke lacrosse case underscores the importance of prosecutors exercising caution in their pretrial remarks. Some believe it also establishes the importance of allowing defense attorneys to respond to allegations against their clients from prosecutors and law enforcement officers. *See* Devine, *supra.* The attorneys for the Duke lacrosse defendants exercised this right on behalf of their clients, and their comments contributed substantially to stemming the initial publicity favoring the prosecution. *See id.* at 222. Indeed, the potential importance of speaking on behalf of clients has generated articles giving attorneys advice about how to engage in effective media campaigns. *See, e.g.,* Monica Bay, *Dealing with the Media: How to Protect and Enhance Your Clients' Interests,* Law Prac.Mgmt., May/June 2003, at 42; Skyler Bentsen & Daniel Scardino, *Talking to the Press and Making Them Listen,* Litig., Winter 2005, at 40. Even for one who believes defensive speech by attorneys is critical to balance the scales, though, there is difficulty in determining how far a defense attorney can and should go in such comments, and whether the Duke lacrosse defense attorneys went further than necessary to mitigate the damage from the pro-prosecution publicity. *See* Devine, *supra,* at 210–20.

6. **"Gag" Orders:** In *United States v. Salameh,* 992 F.2d 445 (2d Cir. 1993), the trial judge in a criminal case issued an oral, *sua sponte* order at a pretrial hearing prohibiting all parties to the proceeding and their attorneys from all public statements concerning any aspect of the proceeding. When defense attorneys asked the judge to modify the order to permit counsel to discuss evidence already leaked to the press by the government, and to discuss the conditions of the defendant's confinement, the judge said he would do so only if the defense stipulated to refrain from challenging the fairness of jury selection, the jury itself, or the trial. On appeal, the Second Circuit held this was unconstitutional absent notice and an opportunity to be heard, or an inquiry into the adequacy of less stringent measures to preserve the defendants' right to a fair trial before an impartial jury. *See also United States ex rel. Davis v. Prince,* 753 F.Supp.2d 561, 568 (E.D.Va. 2010) (rejecting defendants' request for a blanket gag order "prohibiting the parties from making any extrajudicial statements" because "[b]road gag orders ... raise First Amendment concerns" and should therefore be issued only when there is a reasonable likelihood that extrajudicial statements would prejudice a fair trial); *Rapid City Journal v. Delaney,* 2011 SD 55, ¶ 32, 804 N.W.2d 388, 399–400 (entering a writ of prohibition that rescinded the trial court's "order preventing the parties from discussing the case outside [the courtroom]" because "[w]e are not persuaded that Judge Delaney had [the] statutory or legal authority to issue the gag order under the facts and circumstances of this case"); Kimberley Keyes, *Free Speech, Gag Orders, and the Federal Courts,* Fed.Law., Sept. 2005, at 38 (describing a decision to not issue a gag order and outlining competing tests used in making this decision).

"Gag" orders prohibiting extrajudicial statements by attorneys and other trial participants reflect a controversial balancing of the defendant's right to a fair trial against free speech rights and public access to trials. *See United States v. McGregor,* 838 F.Supp.2d 1256, 1267 (M.D.Ala. 2012) (discussing First Amendment concerns in explanation of rejection of request for gag order and adoption of "the less restrictive alternative of requiring the attorneys and their trial teams to comply with Alabama Rule of Professional Conduct 3.6"); *Mizioch v. Montoya,* No. CV10–01728–PHX–JAT, 2011 WL 4900033, at *6–8 (D.Ariz. Oct. 14, 2011) (similar); *Doe v. Hawaii,* No. 11–00550 DAE–KSC, 2011 WL 4954606, at *4 (D.Haw. Oct. 14, 2011) (denying request for a gag order because "[t]he Supreme Court in *Gentile* was clear [that] a Court [deciding whether to issue a protective order] considers an individual's right to a 'fair trial by impartial jurors,' not potential damage to [an] individual's livelihood"); *State ex rel. Toledo Blade Co. v. Henry Cnty. Ct. Com. Pl.*, 2010–Ohio–1533, 926 N.E.2d 634 (granting writ of prohibition rescinding trial court's gag order and discussing constitutional issues at length).

Nonetheless some believe courts should sometimes adopt this "[im]perfect solution" to "minimize the most damaging pretrial and trial publicity." *See* Eileen A. Minnefor, *Looking for Fair Trials in the Information Age: The Need for More Stringent Gag Orders Against Trial Participants*, 30 U.S.F.L.Rev. 95, 103 (1995). Trial courts occasionally do enter such orders, and appellate courts sometimes affirm them. *See United States v. Hill*, 420 Fed.Appx. 407 (5th Cir. 2011) (affirming trial court's finding that defendants were in contempt of court due to their intentional violation of gag order); *People v. Kelly*, 921 N.E.2d 333, 364 (Ill.App.Ct. 2009) (affirming the "trial court's Decorum Order [because it] tracks closely, in substance if not in language, to Rule 3.6(b) of the Illinois Rules of Professional Conduct").

If you were the judge in a high profile trial in the problem, would you consider entering a gag order? When, if ever, is a gag order appropriate?

7. **Cameras in the Courtroom:** For discussions of the somewhat similar and related issue of cameras in the courtroom, see Stephen D. Easton, *Whose Life Is It Anyway?: A Proposal to Redistribute Some of the Economic Benefits of Cameras in the Courtroom from Broadcasters to Crime Victims*, 49 S.C.L.Rev. 1, 7–27 (1997) (reviewing history of cameras in the courtroom); Clara Tuma, *Open Courts: How Cameras in Courts Help Keep the System Honest*, 49 Clev.St.L.Rev. 417 (2001) (arguing for cameras in the courtroom); Jacob Marvelley, Note, *Lights, Camera, Mistrial: Conflicting Federal Court Local Rules and Conflicting Theories on the Aggregate Effect of Cameras on Courtroom Proceedings*, 16 Suffolk J. Trial & App.Advoc. 30 (2011) (reviewing history of cameras in courtroom, current divergent practices, and policy concerns).

8. **Public Statements by Judges:** On public statements by judges, see, e.g., *United States v. Cooley*, *supra* section 5(F)(2), and Rule 2.10(A) & (C) (formerly Canon 3B(9)) of the Model Code of Judicial Conduct, which requires judges to refrain from making "any public statement that might reasonably be expected to affect the outcome or impair the fairness of a matter pending or impending in any court" and to order subordinates to similarly refrain from comment. *See also Disciplinary Counsel v. Gaul*, 2010–Ohio–4831, ¶ 65, 936 N.E.2d 28, 37 (finding a violation of former Canon 3B(9) when a judge "told the defendant that he would personally see to it that anyone involved in obstruction of justice would be indicted, convicted, and given the maximum sentence"). In the 2007 revision of the Model Code of Judicial Conduct, though, the ABA added a provision allowing the judge to "respond directly or through a third party to allegations in the media or elsewhere concerning the judge's conduct in a matter," as long as this response did not affect the outcome or the fairness of the proceeding. Rule 2.10(E). However, a judge's comments about ongoing proceedings must be constrained. *See Gaul*, 2010–Ohio–4831 at ¶ 66, 936 N.E.2d at 37 (finding that a judge's statement that "he was checking the defendant 'into the boards' and that he would not let the defendant out of jail to go smoke crack again were adversarial in nature, not a description of court procedure").

9. Non–Participant "Legal Commentators" and Model Rule 3.6: As Professor Bernabe–Riefkohl notes, the post-*Gentile* version of Model Rule 3.6 makes the rule's restrictions applicable only to "a lawyer who is participating or has participated in the investigation or litigation of a matter" and that lawyer's firm colleagues. Model Rule 3.6(a) and Comment [3]. The comment explains that the risk of prejudice from other lawyers is small. This presumably precludes discipline of an independent lawyer who responds to a media request for statements about a particular matter.

Not all agree with the idea that the risk of prejudice from non-participants is small. Some cases generate substantial commentary, which could affect the ability of a defendant to receive a fair trial. The 2006 Duke lacrosse case, *see supra* note 5, generated a flurry of comments, in both traditional and electronic media. *See* KC Johnson, *The Duke Lacrosse Case and the Blogosphere*, 71 Law & Contemp.Probs. 155 (2008).

Some have proposed a voluntary code of ethics for legal commentators. *See A Panel Discussion on a Proposed Code of Ethics for Legal Commentators*, 50 Mercer L.Rev. 681 (1999); Erwin Chemerinsky & Laurie Levenson, *Ethical Quandaries Created by the Widespread Use of Legal Pundits Can Only Be Addressed by a Voluntary Code of Ethics*, L.A.Law., Feb. 2000, at 28. The Duke lacrosse case provided impetus to this call, but some believe such a code would have little practical impact in protecting the right to a fair trial and could interfere with free speech rights. *See* Sara K. Fleisch, Comment, *The Ethics of Legal Commentary: A Reconsideration of the Need for an Ethical Code in Light of the Duke Lacrosse Matter*, 20 Geo.J. Legal Ethics 599, 611–12 (2007).

A(4) THE LAWYER IN CRIMINAL LITIGATION

A(4)(a) The Prosecutor

PROBLEM

You are the elected District Attorney for the county that includes your state's largest university. One afternoon, two detectives told you they interviewed Stella Enkoluge, a 20–year–old junior, that morning. Enkoluge told them she was raped at 2:00 a.m. by Hugh Stockton. As you and everyone else knows, Stockton is a university alum who has gone on to great fame as a movie actor.

According to Enkoluge (as reported by the detectives), she attended a fraternity party that Stockton attended after a basketball game the previous night. Stockton, who lived at the fraternity when he was a student, was back in town for the game, so he went to the party. Enkoluge admitted that she drank "about six" beers at the party, even though she was under the legal age to drink alcohol. She said Stockton offered to drive her home as the party wound down after 1:00 a.m., but that he instead drove to a wooded area near the campus and forced her out of the car and onto the ground, saying, "Do what I want or I will get the gun out of the trunk and use it on you." After the sex, he let her run away.

After the detectives left, your best friend from law school, Arnie Benedict, arrived, telling the receptionist he "needed to see his buddy." She admitted him to your office, because she knew him well from his service as the voluntary chair of the fund raising committee for your campaign.

Though Arnie was known as the area's best personal injury plaintiff's attorney, he told you that he wanted to talk about "something that might have an effect on your office." He reported that he had been hired that morning by Stockton in conjunction with "a little misunderstanding." He said that, following consensual sex with a woman he met at the party, the woman stood up, said "how could you do that to me?," and then ran off. According to Benedict, this reaction startled Stockton to the point that he worried the woman "might actually get crazy enough to claim I did something wrong." Benedict then asked you to be sure to "not let a little buyer's remorse turn into something ugly."

As you walked home after work that evening, your neighbor Laura Gallop stopped you and asked if you had heard about the party the previous evening. "From what I heard," Gallop said, "that Enkoluge girl was really throwing herself at Hugh Stockton."

When you meet with her and the detectives, Enkoluge again admitted to drinking, but she denied making any sexual advances toward Stockton. "I hate to admit it now," she said, "but I was just sort of amazed that a guy like that would even talk to me." Then she started sobbing and haltingly choked out, "Everybody at school is mad at me, calling me a 'slut' and a 'whore.' But you have to believe me. I did not consent. That man raped me."

The next day, Benedict called you, threatening to "ruin your career" if you did not "put a stop to this nonsense" by announcing that no charges would be filed. "Even the filing of a charge of rape will ruin his reputation in this town, as well as his career. You don't have enough to charge him, so let this thing drop." Benedict offered to have his client commit to "hundreds" of hours of voluntary community service if no rape charge was filed. He added, "I can even get him to plead guilty to a minor offense like reckless driving, if you want that."

You received calls, faxes, e-mails, and letters from dozens of others who urge you to not charge Stockton, including the governor, the president of the university, the state chair of your political party, and several people who donated money to your campaign. You also heard from a few folks who urge you to "treat Stockton like anybody else," but these calls are considerably fewer in number.

You gather a meeting of the six detectives who have now worked on the case, as well as your two Assistant District Attorneys. After a full review of the evidence, you ask those in attendance "who is telling the truth here?" Two of the detectives and one of the prosecutors vote for Enkoluge. Three of the detectives vote for Stockton. One detective and one prosecutor refuse to vote, with the prosecutor saying, "Who knows?" After the detectives leave the meeting, the abstaining prosecutor says, "Even if he did it, which I doubt, you will never get Stockton convicted on a 'he said, she said' case." The other prosecutor urges you to charge Stockton, saying, "Maybe we will lose at trial, but my gut tells me this guy is lying. Charge him. It's your job."

QUESTIONS

(a) Do you charge Stockton with rape?

(b) If you charge Stockton, do you have an obligation to tell Benedict about your conversation with Gallop?

(c) Assume that you decide to charge Stockton. The jury returns a "not guilty" verdict. You do your best to console Enkoluge in the courtroom while Stockton and Benedict conduct a press conference on the courthouse steps blasting the "lying gold digger and her buddy, the gullible prosecutor." An hour later you are in the bar where you traditionally celebrate wins and try to recuperate from losses. You tell your two assistants, "We gave it our best shot, but the evidence was just not there. One of you warned me about this. We just did not have enough on this guy. Maybe she did consent. I never knew myself, so I thought a jury should decide." Unbeknownst to you, an associate in Benedict's firm, who was in the next booth, recorded your comments on a hand-held tape recorder. Benedict files a complaint with the disciplinary authorities under Model Rule 3.8(a). Will you be disciplined?

RULE REFERENCES

Model Rules 3.8 and 4.2

RESTATEMENT §§ 97 & 110

BERGER v. UNITED STATES

Supreme Court of the United States, 1935.
295 U.S. 78.

MR. JUSTICE SUTHERLAND delivered the opinion of the Court.

Petitioner was * * * charged with having conspired with seven other persons * * * to utter counterfeit notes * * *. Petitioner was convicted upon the conspiracy count only. * * *

That the United States prosecuting attorney overstepped the bounds of that propriety and fairness which should characterize the conduct of such an officer in the prosecution of a criminal offense is clearly shown by the record. He was guilty of misstating the facts in his cross-examination of witnesses; of putting into the mouths of such witnesses things which they had not said; of suggesting by his questions that statements had been made to him personally out of court, in respect of which no proof was offered; of pretending to understand that a witness had said something which he had not said and persistently cross-examining the witness upon that basis; of assuming prejudicial facts not in evidence; of bullying and arguing with witnesses; and, in general, of conducting himself in a thoroughly indecorous and improper manner. * * *

The prosecuting attorney's argument to the jury was undignified and intemperate, containing improper insinuations and assertions calculated to mislead the jury. * * *

The United States Attorney is the representative not of an ordinary party to a controversy, but of a sovereignty whose obligation to govern impartially is as compelling as its obligation to govern at all; and whose interest, therefore, in a criminal prosecution is not that it shall win a case, but that justice shall be done. As such, he is in a peculiar and very definite sense the servant of the law, the twofold aim of which is that guilt shall not escape or innocence suffer. He may prosecute with earnestness and vigor—indeed, he should do so. But, while he may strike hard blows, he is not at liberty to strike foul ones. It is as much his duty to refrain from improper methods calculated to produce a wrongful conviction as it is to use every legitimate means to bring about a just one.

It is fair to say that the average jury, in a greater or less degree, has confidence that these obligations, which so plainly rest upon the prosecuting attorney, will be faithfully observed. Consequently, improper suggestions, insinuations, and, especially, assertions of personal knowledge are apt to carry much weight against the accused when they should properly carry none. * * *

Judgment reversed.

NOTES ON PROSECUTORS

1. Justice Sutherland's musings about the prosecutor occupying a special role and therefore being required to strike hard, but not foul, blows are well known to both prosecutors and criminal defense attorneys. This paragraph can be found on the walls of many prosecutors' offices. At the same time, many a defense brief asserting prosecutorial misconduct quotes the same language.

Prosecutors, like other human beings, are subjected to a myriad of personal and professional pressures. Unlike most other human beings, though, a prosecutor wields tremendous power, due to the ability to decide whether to pursue a case, to decide what crimes to charge, to decide whether to plea bargain, to decide which witnesses to call to the stand, to decide whether to offer immunity or other favorable treatment to a witness in exchange for testimony helpful to the government, to decide how hard to push on sentencing, etc. *See* Fred C. Zacharias & Bruce A. Green, *The Duty to Avoid Wrongful Convictions: A Thought Experiment in the Regulation of Prosecutors*, 89 B.U.L.Rev. 1, 8–9 (2009). Each of these decisions can have substantial impact on other human beings. *See* Patrick J. Fitzgerald, *Thoughts on the Ethical Culture of a Prosecutor's Office*, 84 Wash.L.Rev. 11, 12 (2009) ("Even for people who do not go to jail, their reputations can be tarnished by an indictment or a conviction, or merely by being investigated. Corporations can go out of business, not just by being indicted, but also for the fact that they are being investigated. This can affect * * * employees who had nothing to do with the wrongdoing. In many cases, witnesses who have done nothing wrong have their lives turned upside down merely because they had to testify in court against a friend, a colleague, or a loved one."). Prosecutors must remember that prosecutorial discretion is an aspect of a public office entrusted to them, so they should, as Justice Sutherland noted, seek justice, not simply seek to win or to advance personal interests. They must attempt to overcome such influences as "public familiarity and perception of the crime, career considerations, politics, race, and sheer vindictiveness." Mitchell Stephens, *Ignoring Justice: Prosecutorial Discretion and the Ethics of Charging*, 35 N.Ky.L.Rev. 53, 54 (2008). While all attorneys are held to ethical standards, prosecutors are held to higher standards than those in other roles. *See State v. Gonzalez*, 234 P.3d 1, 11 (Kan. 2010).

2. **Charging a Crime:** Question (a) raises one of the most difficult, and frequent, decisions faced by prosecutors: Should a particular individual be charged? Prosecutors exercise wide discretion in making decisions about such matters as whom to charge, what crimes should be charged, whether to offer a plea agreement with reduced charges or other perceived or actual benefits to a defendant, and whether to dismiss previously filed charges. *See* Ellen S. Podgor, *The Ethics and Professionalism of Prosecutors in Discretionary Decisions*, 68 Fordham L.Rev. 1511, 1513 & n.15 (2000); Abby L. Dennis, Note, *Reining in the Minister of Justice: Prosecutorial Oversight and the Superseder Power*, 57 Duke L.J. 131, 131 (2007) (noting that "prosecutors enjoy limitless, unmonitored, and, for the most part, unreviewable power"). Of course, prosecutorial decision making is constrained by many factors, including, but by no means limited to, the limited availability of prosecutorial, law enforcement, and judicial resources, the seriousness of a particular crime vis-a-vis other crimes, the strength of the evidence, the effect of a trial on victims, political pressure, and the perceived wishes of the community.

Though prosecutors have relatively wide discretion to make charging decisions, subject to these constraints, the Model Rules are not silent on the matter. Under Model Rule 3.8(a), a prosecutor can file only those charges that are "supported by probable cause." Though "probable cause" is a concept that has been difficult for courts and lawyers to precisely define, in the context of Model Rule 3.8(a), it is generally assumed that, at a minimum, a prosecutor cannot file a charge unless that prosecutor believes that the defendant committed the crime charged and that there is evidence to support that conclusion. *See* Bruce A. Green & Fred C. Zacharias, *Regulating Federal Prosecutors' Ethics*, 55 Vand.L.Rev. 381, 471 n.303 (2002) ("[P]rosecutors would agree that they should not charge defendants without probable cause to believe in their guilt."); *see also Iowa Sup. Ct. Attorney Disciplinary Bd. v. Howe*, 706 N.W.2d 360 (Iowa 2005) (suspending a prosecutor for, inter alia, filing and allowing guilty pleas to minor, but factually insupportable, charges as a plea-bargaining mechanism). Indeed, the proposed revisions to the ABA Standards for Criminal Justice would, if adopted, provide that a " 'prosecutor's office should not file or maintain charges if it believes the defendant is innocent, no matter what the state of the evidence.' " Rory K. Little, *The ABA's Project to Revise the Criminal Justice Standards for the Prosecution and Defense Functions*, 62 Hastings L.J. 1111, 1121 (2011) (quoting ABA Standards for Criminal Justice: Prosecution Function § 3–4.4(d) (proposed Revisions 2010)). With regard to evidence, the proposed ABA Standard would set the bar even higher: " 'A prosecutor should file criminal charges only if the prosecutor reasonably believes the charges are supported by probable cause and that the admissible evidence will be sufficient to support the conviction beyond reasonable doubt.' " Little, *supra*, 62 Hastings L.J. at 1120 (quoting ABA Standards for Criminal Justice: Prosecution Function § 3–4.4(a) (proposed Revisions 2010)).

This is a very different standard than the one placed upon civil plaintiff's attorneys and defense attorneys in civil and criminal cases. Those attorneys do not need probable cause, but instead can bring or defend a case as long as there is a non-frivolous basis in fact or law for doing so. Criminal defense attorneys are not even held to this standard when forcing prosecutors to prove every element of the crimes charged. *See* Model Rule 3.1; *supra* section 6(A)(1)(a), note 10. In other words, non-prosecutors are not required to personally believe that the cases they are advancing are factually correct, as long as there is a non-frivolous basis for advancing them.

3. **The Prosecutor's Burdens:** To the ethical prosecutor, then, the only uncertainty at trial is whether she can prove that the defendant committed the crime beyond a reasonable doubt. While this may put the prosecutor in the seemingly comfortable position of never having to pursue a case she does not personally believe, this comes at a price. When a civil attorney or a criminal defense attorney loses a trial, that attorney may be able to comfort herself by concluding that the facts did not support the (non-frivolous) position that she tried to advocate. When a prosecutor loses a trial, she must conclude that she did not perform her duty to prove the defendant committed the crime beyond a reasonable doubt.

The full responsibility, fear, and regret of being a prosecutor who charges a crime that is not proven at trial was neatly summarized by Christopher Darden, the second chair on the unsuccessful O.J. Simpson prosecution team, in Christopher A. Darden, In Contempt 326–28 (1996). It was Darden who made the critical mistake of asking the defendant to try on the infamous "bloody gloves." Darden believes that the gloves were indeed owned by O.J. Simpson, but that he did not adequately consider the possibility of shrinkage or that the defense team might engage in trickery. As a result, when Simpson struggled attempting to try the gloves on in front of the jury, media photos showed a smiling Simpson in front and a disgusted prosecutor Marcia Clark in the background. The look of disgust by his boss was, according to Darden, not for Simpson, but "[f]or me." Following this courtroom disaster, no one in the prosecutor's office wanted to talk to Darden, who knew that he had violated the basic courtroom rule of never asking a question to which he did not know the answer. Darden, who teaches trial practice, has this advice for students:

> [T]o be a prosecutor is to accept the responsibility of being the only thing standing between the defendant and the jailhouse door sometimes. We have the duty to make sure no one else can be victimized by the person we're prosecuting. That pressure, that fear, can choke you, I tell my students, and cause you to become too conservative. That fear has a face: the face of a child molested by someone you couldn't convict, the face of a person killed by a murderer you couldn't put away.

Darden took away from the O.J. Simpson episode not only the notion that the lack of conviction in the case had been his fault, but also some added pressure: "I ached with regret for what I might have done to the case, what I had done to the victims' families."

Political pressure is another burden for prosecutors, especially when they are elected (as is the case for most state chief prosecutors) or appointed (as is the case for U.S. Attorneys and for assistant state and federal prosecutors). Because prosecutors are public officials, it is not realistic to believe they are completely immune from public pressure. Indeed, as public officials, prosecutors should not be completely immune from the desires of the public. At the same time, though, prosecutors must be willing to stand up to public pressure, perhaps even to the point of being forced out of office, rather than engage in an unjustified prosecution or one that is not supported by sufficient evidence. Some believe that the prosecutor in the Duke lacrosse case, *see supra* section 6(A)(3), notes 5 and 9, who was facing an election while the case progressed, gave in too readily to public pressure to move forward with what ultimately was a highly problematic case. Some contend that he might have desired to not be seen as favoring students at an elite college over a local resident who was a member of a minority group that has suffered substantial discrimination over many centuries. *See* Robert P. Mosteller, *The Duke Lacrosse Case, Innocence, and False Identifications: A Fundamental Failure to "Do Justice"*, 76 Fordham L.Rev. 1337, 1352–57 (2007); Jeffrey Rosen, Book Review, Mont. Law., Oct. 2007, at 24 (reviewing Stuart Taylor, Jr. & KC Johnson, Until Proven Innocent: Political Correctness and the Shameful Injustices of the Duke Lacrosse Rape Case (2007)). In a different case, the South Dakota Supreme Court found that a prosecutor "allowed his personal and political views of the golf course project and the mayor's handling of the issue to cloud his independent judgment as a prosecutor." *In re Russell*, 2011 SD 17, ¶ 43; 797 N.W.2d 77, 88–89.

4. **Divulging Information to Defense:** Another important burden on prosecutors is the duty to divulge information harmful to the prosecution's case. In *Brady v. Maryland*, 373 U.S. 83 (1963), which preceded the Model Rules, the Supreme Court held that the right to receive exculpatory information was an element of the defendant's constitutional right to due process. Model Rule 3.8(d) requires the prosecutor to reveal to the defense, in a timely fashion, information known by the prosecutor that "tends to" negate guilt, lessen the offense, or lead to a lower sentence. The Model Rule duty "is separate from disclosure obligations imposed under the Constitution, statutes, procedural rules, court rules, or court orders," ABA Standing Comm. on Ethics and Prof'l Resp., Formal Op. 09–454 (2009), all of which might also produce a responsibility to provide information to the defense, *see* Fed.R.Crim. P., Rule 16(a) (outlining procedural disclosure obligations for prosecutors in federal cases). As one might expect, disputes arise considering what information is exculpatory, known to the prosecutor, and otherwise within the scope of that which must be provided by the prosecutor to the defense. *See* Edward L. Wilkinson, Brady *and Ethics: A Prosecutor's Evidentiary Duties To the Defense Under the Due Process Clause and Their Relation To the State Bar Rules*, 61 Tex.B.J. 435 (1998); David Aaron, Note, *Ethics, Law Enforcement, and Fair Dealing: A Prosecutor's Duty to Disclose Nonevidentiary Information*, 67 Fordham L.Rev. 3005 (1999).

In recent years, there have been high profile cases where prosecutors failed to fulfill their obligation to give defendants information helpful to them. Among other improprieties, the Duke lacrosse case prosecutor "withheld the results of a DNA test, witness statements, and other evidence that cast significant doubt on the guilt of the three accused." Andrew Smith, Note, Brady *Obligations, Criminal Sanctions, and Solutions in a New Era of Scrutiny,* 61 Vand.L.Rev. 1935, 1937 (2008); *see also* Paul Giannelli, *Forensic Science: Scientific Evidence and Prosecutorial Misconduct in the Duke Lacrosse Rape Case,* 45 No. 4 Crim.L.Bull., Art. 7 (Summer 2009). Shortly thereafter, the Department of Justice dismissed its political corruption case against Senator Ted Stevens, after obtaining a guilty verdict, because "prosecutors had withheld crucial evidence supporting the Senator's defense and contradicting the prosecution's key witness." Bruce A. Green, *Beyond Training Prosecutors About Their Disclosure Obligations: Can Prosecutors' Offices Learn from the Lawyers' Mistakes?,* 31 Cardozo L.Rev. 2161, 2161–62 (2010). Several commentators have suggested modifications to disclosure obligations or procedures to lessen the probability of such occurrences. *See, e.g.,* Alafair S. Burke, *Revisiting Prosecutorial Disclosure,* 84 Ind.L.J. 481, 481 (2009) (proposing "a prophylactic open file rule to effectuate defendants' *Brady* rights"); Smith, *supra,* 61 Vand.L.Rev. at 1972 (proposing "[t]he inexpensive and relatively noninvasive practice of open-file discovery policies" and criminal prosecutions of "those ill-willed prosecutors who intentionally and maliciously withhold evidence").

5. **The Prosecutor's Duty to Correct Questionable and Wrongful Convictions:** In 2008, the ABA added subsections (g) and (h) to Model Rule 3.8, along with new comments. *See* Wayne D. Garris, Jr., Comment, *Model Rule of Professional Conduct 3.8: The ABA Takes a Stand Against Wrongful Convictions,* 22 Geo.J. Legal Ethics 829 (2009). Model Rule 3.8(g) requires prosecutors to advise courts and defendants, and also to undertake investigations, when they become aware of new "evidence creating a reasonable likelihood that a convicted defendant did not commit an offense of which the defendant was convicted." *See also Friedman v. Rehal,* 618 F.3d 142, 160 (2d Cir. 2010) (suggesting that a new head prosecutor undertake "a complete review of the underlying case" to determine if it should proceed, due to the possibility that the defendant was wrongfully convicted).

Model Rule 3.8(h) requires a prosecutor to attempt to overturn a wrongful conviction in the prosecutor's jurisdiction when the prosecutor "knows of clear and convincing evidence establishing" that a defendant did not commit the offense. *See also* Bruce A. Green & Ellen Yaroshefsky, *Prosecutorial Discretion and Post–Conviction Evidence of Innocence,* 6 Ohio St.J.Crim.L. 467, 473 (2009) (discussing "the fundamental question of what we affirmatively expect prosecutors to do when new evidence comes their way suggesting that a convicted person may be innocent"). However, comment [9], also added in 2008, provides, "A prosecutor's independent judgment, made in good faith, that the new evidence is not of such nature as to trigger the obligations of sections (g) and (h), though subsequently determined to have been erroneous, does not constitute a violation of" Model Rule 3.8. Therefore, it is difficult for disciplinary authorities to sanction prosecutors under the provisions requiring them to correct questionable and wrongful convictions and, therefore, difficult to gauge the practical impact of these new provisions.

6. **Ex Parte Contact:** Model Rule 4.2's prohibition against a lawyer talking to a person known to be represented by another attorney without

either the presence or permission of that attorney, *see supra* section 6(A)(2)(a), also known as ex parte contact, has been particularly controversial when applied to prosecutors and, through extension, law enforcement officers and others working with prosecutors. *See United States v. Brown*, 595 F.3d 498, 514–16 (3d Cir. 2010) (reviewing Model Rule 4.2 and its history); *United States v. Tapp*, No. CR107–108, 2008 WL 2371422 (S.D.Ga. June 4, 2008) (including extensive discussion of Model Rule 4.2 and its application in criminal cases and against federal prosecutors). As currently constituted, though, there is no doubt that the Model Rules are intended to restrict prosecutors. Model Rule 3.8's outline of the special responsibilities of prosecutors contains a provision that supplements the general prohibition against ex parte contact in Model Rule 4.2. Model Rule 3.8(b) requires prosecutors to make reasonable efforts to assure that the accused is advised of the right to counsel and the procedure for obtaining counsel, and is given an opportunity to obtain counsel. Also, Model Rule 3.8(c) prohibits prosecutors from seeking waivers of "important pretrial rights" from unrepresented defendants. Furthermore, a new paragraph added in 2002 as Comment [6] to Model Rule 3.8 states that prosecutors, like other lawyers, are subject to discipline pursuant to Model Rules 5.1 and 5.3 when they order, ratify, or learn of conduct by their lawyer or nonlawyer subordinates, including those "who work for or are associated with the lawyer's office." Do these provisions require prosecutors to instruct law enforcement officers to refrain from efforts to get suspects to waive the right to remain silent, to waive the right to counsel in investigative interviews, or to consent to warrantless searches? If so, do you believe most prosecutors are actively engaging in efforts to stop these common practices by law enforcement officers? If lawyers in private practice are responsible for the actions of their lawyer and nonlawyer employees, should prosecutors be responsible for the actions of law enforcement officers?

7. **Subpoenas Against Lawyers:** Under Model Rule 3.8(e), a prosecutor cannot subpoena a lawyer to present evidence about a current or former client at a grand jury hearing or other proceeding unless the prosecutor reasonably believes that there is no feasible alternative for acquiring the desired evidence and that the desired evidence is not protected by a privilege, but is essential for an ongoing investigation. The limitations on subpoenas stem from concern about the chilling effect such subpoenas can have on the relationship between a criminal defendant and the defense attorney and from concern about the potential harassment of opposing counsel via subpoenas. *See State v. Gonzalez*, 234 P.3d 1, 13 (Kan. 2010). Perhaps as a result of these concerns, the U.S. Attorneys' Manual, which contains the Department of Justice's policies and procedures, goes even further than Model Rule 3.8(e), by requiring Assistant Attorney General approval of all subpoenas seeking information about an attorney's representation of a client. *See In re Grand Jury Subpoena to [Name of Firm Redacted]*, 533 F.Supp.2d 602, 609 (W.D.N.C. 2007).

8. **Federal Prosecutors and Rules of Professional Conduct:** The Model Rule 4.2 no-contact rule and the Model Rule 3.8(e) restrictions on subpoenas to attorneys have generated substantial controversy when applied to federal prosecutors. For the final two decades of the last century, the Department of Justice battled criminal defense attorneys, disciplinary and

professional responsibility authorities, state and federal judges, and others over the applicability of state professional responsibility rules and disciplinary procedures to federal prosecutors. Federal prosecutors said state rules would impermissibly limit law enforcement efforts if applied to pre-indictment interviews and argued that they sometimes could not possibly comply with all of the versions and interpretations of the professional responsibility restrictions adopted in various states and federal district courts. The Department of Justice's position was articulated in a 1980 opinion by its Office of Legal Counsel, a 1989 memorandum written by Attorney General Richard Thornburgh, and regulations first proposed in 1992 under Attorney General William Barr and finally adopted by Attorney General Janet Reno in 1994. For historical reviews of this dispute, see Ryan E. Mick, Note, *The Federal Prosecutors Ethics Act: Solution or Revolution?*, 86 Iowa L.Rev. 1251, 1255–63 (2001), and Note, *Federal Prosecutors, State Ethics Regulations, and the McDade Amendment*, 113 Harv.L.Rev. 2080, 2083–89 (2000).

One important critic of the Department was Congressman Joseph McDade, who believed he had been improperly investigated by federal authorities in conjunction with his indictment for five counts of bribery-related offenses. *See* Fred C. Zacharias & Bruce A. Green, *The Uniqueness of Federal Prosecutors*, 88 Geo.L.J. 207, 209, 211–14 (2000). He introduced the first version of the "Citizens Protection Act" shortly after his acquittal. *Id.* at 208, 214. Though this bill did not survive the committee process, it became law when it was included in a 1998 federal appropriations bill. *Id.* at 208. The McDade Amendment, as it is often referred to, states, "An attorney for the Government shall be subject to State laws and rules, and local Federal court rules, governing attorneys in **each State** where such **attorney engages** in that attorney's duties, to the same extent and in the same manner as other attorneys in that State." 28 U.S.C. § 530B(a) (2006) (emphasis in original); *see also Brown*, *supra* note 6, 595 F.3d at 514–16 (reviewing history leading to McDade Amendment); *Tapp*, *supra* note 6, 2008 WL 2371422, at *8 (similar). Although the McDade Amendment at least temporarily ended the legal dispute about whether federal prosecutors are subject to state professional responsibility rules and discipline, it may not end up being the last word on the subject. Debate continues about how federal prosecutors' conduct should be regulated, and who should do the regulating. *See, e.g.*, Green & Zacharias, *supra* note 2; Mick, *supra*; Note, 113 Harv.L.Rev. 2080, *supra*.

9. **Closing Argument:** The *Berger* prosecutor gave an improper final argument. In addition to following the final argument restrictions applicable to all lawyers, *see supra* section 6(A)(2)(e), note 4, a prosecutor must refrain from asking jurors to draw improper conclusions from a defendant's exercise of constitutional rights. For example, if the defendant decides not to speak with police or not testify at trial, the prosecutor cannot ask the jury to conclude that these decisions suggest guilt or otherwise comment on them. *See Wainwright v. Greenfield*, 474 U.S. 284, 295 (1986); *Miranda v. Arizona*, 384 U.S. 436, 468 n.37 (1966). Similarly, "the State may not suggest that the defendant has the burden of proof by inquiring in closing argument why the defendant did not call witnesses to testify on his behalf." *Lainhart v. State*, 916 N.E.2d 924, 936 (Ind.Ct.App. 2009); *see State v. Montgomery*, 183 P.3d 267, 277 (Wash. 2008) (reversing conviction despite substantial supporting

evidence where prosecutor's final argument referred to defendant's failure to call witnesses seven times, because a "criminal defendant has no burden to present evidence, and it is error for the State to suggest otherwise"). Also, the prosecution's final argument cannot "cast the defendant's exercise of his constitutional right to counsel in a negative light." *United States v. Farinella*, 558 F.3d 695, 700 (7th Cir. 2009) (chastising prosecutor for arguing " 'don't let the defendant and his high-paid lawyer buy his way out of this' ").

10. **Prosecutors Subject to Rules for All Litigators:** As the litany of prosecutorial misconduct in *Berger* documents, prosecutors are subject to the professional responsibility restrictions applicable to other litigators, *see supra* sections 6(A)(2)–(3), in addition to the Model Rule 3.8 provisions that apply only to them. *See, e.g., In re Howes*, 39 A.3d 1 (D.C. 2012) (disbarring federal prosecutor who violated Model Rules 3.3(a) and 3.4 by giving witness vouchers to individuals who were not eligible to receive them); *In re Zawada*, 92 P.3d 862 (Ariz. 2004) (suspending prosecutor for asking cross-examination questions that were not supported by a good faith basis and making an improper final argument); *In re Peasley*, 90 P.3d 764 (Ariz. 2004) (disbarring prosecutor for inducing perjury by detective); *People v. Pautler*, 35 P.3d 571 (Colo. Office of the Presiding Disciplinary J. 2001) (suspending prosecutor for deceiving murder suspect in a hostage crisis by pretending to be a public defender assigned to represent him); *State v. Gillikin*, 719 S.E.2d 164, 170–71 (N.C.Ct. App. 2011) (criticizing prosecutor who expressed his view that the defendant was a liar in final argument); Peter A. Joy & Kevin C. McMunigal, *Are Prosecutor's Responsibilities "Special"?*, Crim.Just., Spring 2005, at 58, 59 (noting that "many rules of general applicability are of concern to prosecutors because they deal with work that prosecutors routinely do—work that is often indistinguishable from the work other lawyers do").

However, some have argued that disciplinary authorities, judges, and even prosecutors and their supervisors should recognize that prosecutors occupy a somewhat different role than other litigators. As Justice Sutherland's famous passage notes, prosecutors, unlike other attorneys, should recognize a duty to serve justice, in addition to the duty to serve their "client's" interests. In fact, prosecutors do not really have clients in the traditional sense, because they are responsible for deciding the objectives of a particular prosecution and the means by which they will be achieved, including whether to "settle" a case or take it to trial. *See* Jeffrey J. Pokorak, *Rape Victims and Prosecutors: The Inevitable Ethical Conflict of De Facto Client/Attorney Relationships*, 48 S.Tex.L.Rev. 695, 697 (2007) ("Each lawyer, judge and second year law student understands that the prosecution's 'client' is the state."). They also do not have the same type of supervisory relationship over law enforcement officers that law firm members have over their employees. For discussions of the extent to which these differences are, or should be, considered significant and should result in different or extra restrictions on prosecutorial conduct, see Niki Kuckes, *The State of Rule 3.8: Prosecutorial Ethics Reform Since Ethics 2000*, 22 Geo.J. Legal Ethics 427 (2009), Laurie L. Levenson, *Working Outside the Rules: The Undefined Responsibilities of Federal Prosecutors*, 26 Fordham Urb.L.J. 553 (1999), Kevin C. McMunigal, *Are Prosecutorial Ethics Standards Different?*, 68 Fordham L.Rev. 1453

(2000), Pokorak, *supra*, Zacharias & Green, *supra* note 8, and Joy & McMunigal, *supra*. For an empirical report on the issues that are most often the subject of disciplinary proceedings against prosecutors, see Fred C. Zacharias, *The Professional Discipline of Prosecutors*, 79 N.C.L.Rev. 721 (2001). *See also* Monroe H. Freedman, *Professional Discipline of Prosecutors: A Response to Professor Zacharias*, 30 Hofstra L.Rev. 121 (2001).

11. **Absolute Immunity from Tort Suits for State Prosecutors:** In 1976, the U.S. Supreme Court held that "in initiating a prosecution and in presenting the State's case, the prosecutor is immune from a civil suit for damages under [42 U.S.C.] § 1983." *Imbler v. Pachtman*, 424 U.S. 409, 431 (1976). The Supreme Court has recently confirmed the doctrine that prosecutors are absolutely immune while acting in their litigating roles. In 2006, it held that a prosecutor "is absolutely immune from liability for the decision to prosecute," though this immunity does not extend to non-prosecutor law enforcement officials who convince prosecutors to charge a defendant. *Hartman v. Moore*, 547 U.S. 250, 261–62 (2006). In 2009, it held that absolute immunity extends to the prosecution's failure to disclose material that could have been used by defense attorneys to impeach a crucial prosecution witnesses, "due to: (1) a failure properly to train prosecutors, (2) a failure properly to supervise prosecutors, or (3) a failure to establish an information system containing potential impeachment material about informants." *Van de Kamp v. Goldstein*, 555 U.S. 335, 338 (2009).

The Supreme Court's widely applicable absolute immunity for prosecutors has generated many critics, who often point to the power of prosecutors, the need for them to adopt high ethical standards in using that power, and the instances of serious prosecutorial misconduct like the Duke lacrosse and Senator Stevens' cases. *See, e.g.*, Malia N. Brink, *A Pendulum Swung Too Far: Why the Supreme Court Must Place Limits on Prosecutorial Immunity*, 4 Charleston L.Rev. 1 (2009); Margaret Z. Johns, *Unsupportable and Unjustified: A Critique of Absolute Prosecutorial Immunity*, 80 Fordham L.Rev. 509 (2011); Ephraim Unell, Comment, *A Right Not to Be Framed: Preserving Civil Liability of Prosecutors in the Face of Absolute Immunity*, 23 Geo.J. Legal Ethics 955 (2010). To date, though, the Supreme Court has held fast to its position. In *Van de Kamp*, the Court voted unanimously for absolute immunity, even though the state released Goldstein from imprisonment after a federal court found that the key witness against him, a jailhouse informant, had not been truthful and that prosecutors failed to advise Goldstein's attorneys that he had previously received reduced sentences for providing testimony favorable to the state. 555 U.S. at 338. Thus, it appears that Supreme Court is firm in its belief that remedies other than tort suits should be used to sanction prosecutorial misconduct. The Court presumably believes strongly that, as one commentator put it in describing the "primary justification" advanced for prosecutorial immunity, "prosecutors (like other officials that enjoy immunity for official actions) would not be able to properly perform their jobs if they had to protect themselves against civil litigation." Unell, *supra*, at 955.

A(4)(b) The Criminal Defense Attorney

PROBLEM

In the next election after the *Stockton* case described in *supra* section 6(A)(4)(a), you were defeated by the new District Attorney, Arnie Benedict. Because you were no longer welcome in the District Attorney's office, you accepted a job in the Public Defender's Office in Metropolis. Happily, and rather surprisingly, you have discovered that you enjoy the work. Most of the time, anyway.

For three months, though, Metropolis had been gripped by fear. Every Saturday, there was a rape and murder of an elderly resident of an assisted living center. The "Saturday Senior Slasher," as the media has labeled him, struck at a different assisted living senior residence every week. Each week, the police grimly reported the details of the latest attack and again admitted that they had not found the assailant. They described him as "sick, but really smart," because he left no physical evidence and always killed his victims, who were the only potential witnesses against him.

On a Saturday six weeks ago, though, 78–year–old Eldah Lee managed to momentarily thwart the man who entered her assisted living center apartment and tried to tie her up. Upon hearing the alarm she sounded by pulling a cord, the man fled. Lee, the only person in the building who saw him, gave a description to police. She also managed to pick Ray Lebad out of a mug shot book.

Following Lebad's arrest, you were assigned to defend him against charges of false imprisonment, attempted rape, and attempted murder. Lebad wisely did not talk to police, and they have not found evidence tying him to the other Slasher crimes, but they are sure he is their man. Since his arrest and pretrial incarceration, there have been no similar crimes. You, too, have no doubt that Lebad committed each of the charged offenses. In your meetings, he has admitted assaulting Lee and has described her apartment in enough detail to make you certain he was there.

You have decided that the only way for you to win the case is to challenge the identification by Lee. She is the only witness who can tie Lebad to the crime. There is no doubt in your mind that she correctly identified Lebad as her assailant, but you hope you might be able to create some reasonable doubt in the jury's mind about her identification.

One day, you received a letter from the prosecutor enclosing a report from the psychologist who is treating Lee for post traumatic shock syndrome. It indicates that Mrs. Lee is "usually alert, but occasionally delusional." According to the report, Mrs. Lee has, on a few occasions, suggested that the man in her room that Saturday was her husband. Mr. Lee died fifteen years ago.

QUESTIONS

(a) When you meet with Lebad in jail the day after receiving the package, he tells you that he has an idea for you to consider. "I just remembered that my mom once worked with old lady Lee when she was a nurse at another senior facility where Lee lived. In fact, Mom knows her real well. I am sure she would talk to Mom, and I can teach Mom how to use a hand-held recorder." Then Lebad adds, "Just a thought. What do you know? Has anything helpful come up?"

You suspect that, if you tell Lebad about the psychologist's report you received yesterday, he will want to send his mother to try to get Lee to say it was the deceased Mr. Lee in her apartment that Saturday. From your unfortunate experience in the bar after the *Stockton* case, you also know that your state has not outlawed surreptitious recording of conversations by participants in those conversations. Must you tell Lebad about the report you just received from the prosecutor? If you do tell him and he says he wants you to send his Mom to meet with Mrs. Lee, are you required to follow this instruction? Must you tell him about your state's law allowing surreptitious recording? Even if you decide not to tell Lebad about the package from the prosecutor, are you required to independently decide to use his mother to record Mrs. Lee, if you sincerely believe it is your client's best chance for an acquittal?

(b) At trial, can you vigorously cross-examine Mrs. Lee in an attempt to confuse her, even though you have no doubt that she is telling the truth in identifying Lebad as her assailant? Should you do so? Are you required to do so?

(c) When you arrive at your parents' home for Thanksgiving dinner, your father greets you by saying, "Great. The family champion of the scum of the earth is here. How can you defend someone when you know he is guilty? Is that what I get for paying for your law school tuition?" How do you respond?

RULE REFERENCES

Model Rules Preamble ¶ [9] and Model Rules 1.2, 6.2(c), 1.16, 1.4, 1.1, 1.3, 3.1, and 3.3

RESTATEMENT §§ 98, 103, 106, 107 & 110(2)

ROBERT P. LAWRY, CROSS–EXAMINING THE TRUTHFUL WITNESS: THE IDEAL WITHIN THE CENTRAL MORAL TRADITION OF LAWYERING

100 Dickinson Law Review 563 (1996).

When I teach professional responsibility, I tell my students that there are two dominant themes to the course. The first is professionalism. Stripped to its core, professionalism means we serve the client and the public interest above self-interest. Money is always secondary. Always. The second theme is the adversary system and its implications. The adversary system is a system of adjudication with a neutral decision-maker and partisan advocates. We often act in ways that are particularly partisan because the system is set up that way; but our first obligation is to the processes, procedures, and institutions of the law. How we work out the conflicts between client and system is the essence of professional ethics. Oh, and yes, our consciences are our own. Our advocacy can be hired. Not our conscience.

I believe in those themes. * * * However, ideas about the demands of professionalism and the limits of advocacy must be argued for and explored in context. In this essay, I will explore one * * * of the most difficult, especially for criminal defense lawyers: how to cross-examine the truthful witness. Here is a place for practical reason and nuanced judgment. Here is a place where values clash and the lawyer-statesman's public-spiritedness is tested. I conclude that we have gone off-track within the past twenty-five years or so, at least in our rhetoric about this subject and, most likely, with our practice, too. * * *

IV. OFF THE TRACT

So where and when did we get off the track? Oddly, perhaps coincidentally, I think I can document the time and the progression. It occurred within the past twenty-five years. * * * The place to look? The three editions of the prestigious American Bar Association's *Standards for Criminal Justice Prosecution Function and Defense Function.*

In the first edition, adopted in 1971, Standard 7.6(b) for the defense function reads as follows:

> A Lawyer's belief that the witness is telling the truth does not necessarily preclude appropriate cross-examination in all circumstances, but may affect the method and scope of cross-examination. He should not misuse the power of cross-examination or impeachment by employing it to discredit or undermine a witness if he knows the witness is testifying truthfully.

The commentary to this provision was * * * lengthy and replete with ethical concerns * * *. First, it was clearly stated that "the high purpose" of cross-examination and impeachment is to expose "falsehood, not to destroy truth or the reputation of a known truthful witness." There was an awareness that lawyers "may believe that the temperament, personality or inexperience of the witness provide an opportunity, by adroit cross-examination, to confuse the witness and undermine his testimony in the eyes of the jury." However, "it is not proper to use those tools to destroy the truth, or to seek to confuse or embarrass the witness under these circumstances." In short, [using] "methods of impeachment against a witness who had testified truthfully so undermines the administration of justice that it should be avoided." Finally, it was understood that these complex matters are "subjective," and "largely unenforceable." They are, therefore, "addressed essentially to conscience and honor," even though "[e]xperienced advocates and judges can, over a period of time, identify the lawyer who practices in conformity with high standards as distinguished from those who do not."

Less than ten years later, the second edition changed the operative language of what became Standard 4–7.6(b) by removing the second sentence * * *. The language that admonished criminal defense lawyers not to misuse cross-examination "to discredit or undermine" the truthful witness was deleted because "[t]here are some cases where, unless counsel challenges the prosecution's known truthful witnesses, there will be no opposition to the prosecution's evidence, and the defendant will be denied an effective defense." [ABA Standards for Criminal Justice Standard 4–7.6(b) (2d ed. 1980).] The commentary to the standard repeated portions of the first edition [stated] that there is no duty for counsel to "try to impair or destroy the credibility" of a truthful witness. It further admonished the lawyer to avoid this and like tactics, but only if this can be done while still providing "an effective defense for the accused." In fact, the commentary went further, stating:

> [W]here the defendant has admitted guilt to the lawyer and does not plan to testify, and the lawyer simply intends to put the state to its proof and raise a reasonable doubt, skillful cross-examination of the prosecution's witnesses is essential. Indeed, were counsel in this circumstance to forgo vigorous cross-examination of the prosecution's witnesses, counsel would violate the clear duty of zealous representation that is owed to the client.

Thus, there appeared to be a shift from an aspiration not to undermine truthful witnesses, to a duty to do so, at least in some cases. Nevertheless, the black-letter Standard still did not explicitly say that such a duty existed.

In 1991 the third edition of the Defense Standards was passed. Standard 4–7.6(b) is now stark: "Defense counsel's belief or knowledge that the witness is telling the truth does not preclude cross-examination." Though some lip service is paid to ethics, the commentary is written largely in terms of tactics, repeating much of the language quoted above in describing the commentary in the second edition. To compare the language of the third edition to that of the first is to inhabit a vastly different moral universe. The vision in the third edition is extreme role differentiation, focusing on zealous representation, virtually ignoring moral duties to other people or to the truth-seeking function of the adversary system.

What has happened to account for the change in moral vision * * *? What happened in twenty years? What happened is what often happens in law and in life: the minority opinion became the majority opinion. Moreover, it should not be thought that this change really occurred over the period of 1971–1991. The two different moral visions that are caught in the first and the third editions of the ABA Standards have existed side-by-side for a long time * * *.

The dual concerns for truth-finding and for the rights of individual participants in the system have needed adjustment from time to time in Anglo–American legal history, with concerns for the rights of criminal defendants making steady advances over the years. Moreover, a fiercer sort of adversariness has been on the rise in civil matters since the latter part of the nineteenth century, when lawyers began to represent huge corporate interests. Whatever the historical confluence of pressures and arguments, the appropriate moral stance of the lawyer, representing clients in an adversarial system of justice, has been the subject of debate as changes in procedures and substantive rights have occurred. Nevertheless, the current issues are not very different from those that have been argued historically. What has changed is the ideal. The 1971 Standards admit that such matters are "subjective ... largely unenforceable ... addressed essentially to professional conscience and honor." The commentary begins with these words: "The ethic of our legal tradition has long recognized that there are limitations on the manner in which witnesses should be examined beyond those which are contained in the rules of evidence."

The 1991 edition begins with the same words. The sentence that follows, however, states that "[w]itnesses should not be subjected to degrading, demeaning, or otherwise invasive or insulting questioning unless counsel honestly believes that such questioning may prove beneficial to his or her client's case."

Appeals to honor and conscience are gone. In place of the lawyer's discretion and judgment is an admonition to degrade, demean, invade, and insult if there is any tactical advantage to be gained by the client. I suggest there may be tactical advantages in casting the guilt on an innocent. Is that fair game, too?

BARBARA ALLEN BABCOCK, DEFENDING THE GUILTY

32 Cleveland State Law Review 175 (1983–1984).

I. INTRODUCTION

How can you defend a person you know is guilty? I have answered that question hundreds of times, never to my inquirer's satisfaction, and therefore never to my own. In recent years, I have more or less given up, abandoning the high-flown explanations of my youth, and resorting to a rather peevish: "Well, it's not for everybody. Criminal defense work takes a peculiar mind-set, heart-set, soul-set." While I still believe this, the mind-set might at least be more accessible through a better effort at explanation. * * *

II. WHAT IS THE QUESTION?

Most people do not mean to question the defense of those accused of computer crime, embezzlement, or tax evasion. Usually the inquirer is asking how you can defend a robber, a rapist, a murderer. In all its components, the question is: first, how *can* you when you know or suspect that if you are successful, your client will be free to commit other murders, rapes and robberies? Second, how can *you* defend a guilty man— you, with your fancy law degree, your nice clothes, your pleasing manner? Third, how can you *defend*—move to suppress the evidence of clear guilt found on the accused's person, break down on cross-examination an honest but confused witness, subject a rape victim to a psychiatric examination, reveal that an eyewitness to a crime has a history of mental illness?

III.   What are the Answers?

The Garbage Collector's Reason. Yes, it is dirty work, but someone must do it. We cannot have a functioning adversary system without a partisan for both sides. The defense counsel's job is no different from, and the work no more despicable than, that of the lawyer in a civil case who arranges, argues, and even orients the facts with only the client's interests in mind.

This answer may be elegantly augmented by a civil libertarian discussion of the sixth amendment and the ideal of the adversary system as our chosen mode for ascertaining truth. Also, the civil libertarian tells us that the criminally accused are the representatives of us all. When their rights are eroded, the camel's nose is under and the tent may collapse on anyone. In protecting the constitutional rights of criminal defendants, we are only protecting ourselves.

The Legalistic or Positivist's Reason. Truth cannot be known. Facts are indeterminate, contingent, and, in criminal cases, often evanescent. A finding of guilt is not necessarily the truth, but a legal conclusion arrived at after the role of the defense lawyer has been fully played. The sophist would add that it is not the duty of the defense lawyer to act as fact finder. Were she to handle a case according to her own assessment of guilt or innocence, she would be in the role of judge rather than advocate. Finally, there is a difference between legal and moral guilt; the defense lawyer should not let his apprehension of moral guilt interfere with his analysis of legal guilt. The example usually given is that of the person accused of murder who can respond successfully with a claim of self-defense. The accused may feel morally guilty but not be legally culpable. The odds-maker chimes in that it is better that ten guilty people go free than that one innocent be convicted.

The Political Activist's Reason. Most people who commit crimes are themselves the victims of horrible injustice. This statement is true generally because most of those accused of rape, robbery and murder are oppressed minorities. It is also often true in the immediate case because the accused has been battered and mistreated in the process of arrest and investigation. Moreover, the conditions of imprisonment may impose violence far worse than that inflicted on the victim. A lawyer performs good work when he helps to prevent the imprisonment of the poor, the outcast, and minorities in shameful conditions.

The Social Worker's Reason. This reason is closely akin to the political activist's reason but the emphasis is different. Those accused of crime, as the most visible representatives of the disadvantaged underclass in America, will actually be helped by having a defender, notwithstanding the outcome of their cases. Being treated as a real person in our society (almost by definition, one who has a lawyer is a real person) and accorded the full panoply of rights and the measure of concern afforded by a lawyer can promote rehabilitation. Because the accused comes from a community, the beneficial effect of giving him his due will spread to his friends and relatives, decreasing their anger and alienation. To this might be added the humanitarian's reason: the criminally accused are men and women in great need, and it is part of one's duty to one's fellow creatures to come to their aid.

The Egotist's Reason. Defending criminal cases is more interesting than the routine and repetitive work done by most lawyers, even those engaged in what passes for litigation in civil practice. The heated facts of crime provide voyeuristic excitement. Actual court appearances, even jury trials, come earlier and more often in one's career than could be expected in any other area of law. And winning, ah winning has great significance because the cards are stacked for the prosecutor. To win as an underdog, and to win when the victory is clear—there is no appeal from a "Not Guilty" verdict—is sweet.

NOTES ON CRIMINAL DEFENSE ATTORNEYS

1. **"I Just * * * Like My Clients":** In her last paragraph, Professor Babcock discusses the "egotist" rationale for wanting to defend the guilty. Consider another aspect of that same rationale discussed in David Feige, *How to Defend Someone You Know Is Guilty*, The New York Times Magazine, April 8, 2001, at 59. The author defended "Kevin," a crack addict with a thirty page "rap" sheet. Kevin was shot by the police and then accused of the attempted robbery of a police officer. His position was that he had simply purchased some crack and was then shot by the police, while the police alleged that an undercover officer had been threatened during a drug deal gone bad and was forced to fire in self-defense. The author defends such cases for two reasons. First, "trial work is fun, and[,] like most longtime public defenders, I can't imagine incarcerating people for a living." Second, the author does not personalize those in the case on the other side. The "complainant is an abstraction to me. His victimization is an abstraction. My client, on the other hand, is very human and very real. It is his tears I see, his hand I hold and his mother I console." Instead of dehumanizing the defendant, as the author argues much of society does, he dehumanizes the complainants. "Ultimately, the thing that I have so much trouble explaining to people is that when I get to know them, I just really, really like my clients."

2. **Can a Public Defender Refuse Certain Cases?** Even though under Model Rule 1.2(b), a lawyer's representation of a client is not an endorsement of the client or anything the client has done, some cases can be so reprehensible that even a public defender could be tempted to reject the case. If, however, every criminal defendant is entitled to effective assistance of counsel under the Sixth Amendment, can a public defender truly reject cases based on repugnancy? In Abbe Smith, *When Ideology and Duty Conflict, in* Ethical Problems Facing the Criminal Defense Lawyer 18 (Rodney J. Uphoff ed., 1995), the author notes that "[b]ecause poor clients lack the power and resources to choose who represents them, they are forced to rely on the

professionalism and commitment of public defenders." If a public defender rejects cases, this professionalism is compromised. For individual defenders to choose among clients, whatever the reason, undermines that professionalism and commitment. The only time a public defender should reject a case is when continuing the representation would violate Model Rule 6.2(c)'s prohibition against representing clients when the case is so repugnant to the lawyer that the lawyer's ability to adequately represent the client will therefore be compromised. The author uses the example of a "lifelong feminist" who is assigned to a rape case and who finds, upon review of the evidence, that the defendant "is guilty of a brutal sexual assault, and that this is not the first time the defendant has engaged in such conduct." In such cases, the author argues that a public defender's office must have an "opt out" provision allowing attorneys to refuse the case.

3. **Legal But Morally Questionable Tactics:** Questions (a) and (b) raise a fundamental issue: When an unsavory tactic is, in the lawyer's judgment, legal and permissible under the Model Rules and also potentially valuable to the client's case, must the lawyer engage in that tactic to adequately represent the client? To put the issue in the context of the problem, do you, as the defense attorney, have the obligation to help your client arrange his mother's surreptitious recording of Lee, in an effort to document her occasional lapses into senility? Assume that neither your state's criminal law nor the Model Rules prohibit such a recording. *See* ABA Standing Comm. on Ethics and Prof'l Resp., Formal Op. 01–422 (2001) (finding that the Model Rules do not prohibit surreptitious recording by conversation participants in states that do not have statutes outlawing the practice, despite an earlier opinion of same committee concluding that secret recording violated the old Model Code's instruction that lawyers should avoid even the appearance of impropriety). Even if the answer is or could be "no" outside the criminal context, must the criminal defense lawyer engage in the unseemly tactic to provide the client with the assistance of counsel that the Sixth Amendment guarantees? The readings suggest that lay persons and criminal defense attorneys might answer these questions differently, though Professor Lawry might agree with the lay view. Who is right? Is this a constitutional question, a moral one, or one that is answered by the Model Rules?

Consider a New Jersey case, upon which our problem is partially based: Two high school football heroes were accused of sexually assaulting a retarded seventeen-year old young woman. It was alleged that the defendant brothers "invaded" the young woman "with a broomstick, a miniature baseball bat and another, unidentified elongated wooden object." As part of the defense, another young woman, a friend of the defendants, "entrapped" the victim into making statements that were surreptitiously recorded. The defendants' friend pretended to befriend the victim, telling her that she was a sexual novice who needed "advice from someone more mature." The defense lawyers then turned the resulting tapes, two from telephone conversations and one from an automobile conversation, over to prosecutors in support of the defense theory that the retarded woman "was a sexually active, consenting person." A newspaper columnist chided the lawyers for believing that defending the youths was "heaven's work" and then indicated that "lawyers choose to forget from time to time [that] what is legal is not always what is right." "Scummy" practice, according to the author, was not defensible merely because it was done "in the name of the defendant's right to vigorous representation," nor because government prosecutors also use tape recordings. *See* Sydney H. Schanberg, *Just Because It's Legal Doesn't Mean It's Right*, Newsday, May 8, 1990. How do the Model Rules respond to this criticism? Do you believe this is a valid critique of the profession you are about to enter?

4. **Duty to Provide Information to the Criminal Defendant Client:** In the factual circumstances of the problem, Model Rule 1.4 contains at least two provisions that might require you to inform your client about the information about Lee's occasional delusions. First, Model Rule 1.4(a)(4) requires an attorney to promptly provide information about a case when the client reasonably asks for that information. Lebad's question about whether "anything helpful" has come up seems to be a reasonable request for information. Also, Model Rule 1.4(a)(2) requires the attorney to consult with the client about the means of achieving the client's objectives. Model Rule 1.2(a) reiterates this requirement of consultation with the client about the means for achievement of the client's objectives. Given that Lebad's objective is to be found not guilty, these provisions arguably require you to confer with him about how to bring about that goal, including whether to pursue an effort to take advantage of Lee's occasional delusions.

Comment [7] to Model Rule 1.4 allows an attorney to delay transmission of information when a client is likely to respond imprudently to immediate communication of the information. Can you reasonably argue that Lebad's likely request to have his mother tape the desired delusional statement by Lee would be imprudent? In fact, is it not entirely prudent, because it could greatly benefit your defense? Though you may be concerned that causing Lebad to request this taping would be damaging to Lee, Comment [7] provides that information cannot be withheld from a client to serve "the interests or convenience of another person."

5. **Tactical/Legal/Substantive Decision Making Within the Relationship:** Model Rule 1.2(a) explicitly gives the criminal defendant client, not the attorney, authority to decide what plea to enter (and thereby whether to accept a plea agreement offered by the prosecutor), whether to waive the right to a jury trial, and whether to testify. Beyond this clear demarcation of the authority between client and attorney, Model Rule 1.2(a) provides only the general guidance that "a lawyer shall abide by a client's decisions concerning the objectives of representation." Interestingly, the 2002 amendments removed language from the Model Rule 1.2 commentary that postulated that the lawyer was ultimately responsible for "technical and legal tactical issues," but that the lawyer should defer to the client regarding matters like expense and concern for third persons. In its place, Comment [2] now contains more general language that does not attempt to resolve disputes between a lawyer and a client about the means toward achieving the client's objectives. By negative implication, Model Rule 1.2(a) arguably gives responsibility for tactical decisions to the lawyer, because it explicitly requires the lawyer to yield to the client's decisions regarding the objectives of the lawyer's representation and says nothing about the lawyer yielding to the client's desires

concerning the means for achieving these objectives, *see supra* section 3(C), note 3.

Even if you can argue that you, not Lebad, are the one responsible for tactical decisions, there may be little basis for you to refuse to use Lee's delusions to assist in your defense of Lebad. Model Rule 1.1 mandates that you provide Lebad with the "preparation reasonably necessary" for his defense. Does the required preparation for trial include the relatively easy and potentially highly beneficial step of assisting in Lebad's mother's attempt to secure a helpful recording of Lee? Under question (b), could you legitimately argue that you are not required to prepare to cross-examine the key witness on the most helpful impeachment available to you?

If Model Rule 1.2 does not resolve the issue, perhaps Model Rule 1.3's requirement of diligence does. Comment [1] to Model Rule 1.3's diligence requirement requires you to pursue Lebad's defense with "whatever lawful and ethical measures are required." Though Comment [1] later says that you are not required to "press for every advantage that might be realized for a client," is the potential advantage afforded by Lee's delusions one of the advantages that you can afford to refrain from pressing for, when it is almost certainly Lebad's best chance for an acquittal?

Surprisingly, what little basis there may be in the Model Rules and their comments for arguing that you need not pursue Lee's delusions is found in the discussions of zealousness and diligence. The Preamble to the Model Rules states that one of the basic principles underlying the Model Rules is "the lawyer's obligation zealously to protect and pursue a client's legitimate interests, within the bounds of the law, while maintaining a professional, courteous and civil attitude toward all persons involved in the legal system." Model Rules Preamble ¶ [9]. Similarly, Comment [1] to Model Rule 1.3, after the portions quoted above, provides, "The lawyer's duty to act with reasonable diligence does not require the use of offensive tactics or preclude the treating of all persons involved in the legal process with courtesy and respect." The first portion of Preamble language suggests that you have to use the delusions in Lebad's defense. Do the second portion of the Preamble language and the Model Rule 1.3, Comment [1] language give you license to refrain from the potential helpful, but arguably discourteous, uncivil, and offensive taping of an elderly crime victim? Even if this is the case with regard to surreptitiously tricking and taping Lee, can you legitimately maintain that a cross-examination that might reveal her delusions would be discourteous, uncivil, or offensive, when trial attorneys regularly engage in impeaching cross-examinations?

For discussions of other potential conflicts between defense attorneys and their clients, see Margareth Etienne, *The Ethics of Cause Lawyering: An Empirical Examination of Criminal Defense Lawyers as Cause Lawyers*, 95 J.Crim.L. & Criminology 1195 (2005), Monroe H. Freedman, *An Ethical Manifesto for Public Defenders*, 39 Val.U.L.Rev. 911 (2005), and John B. Mitchell, *In (Slightly Uncomfortable) Defense of "Triage" by Public Defenders*, 39 Val.U.L.Rev. 925 (2005).

6. **Withdrawal:** Some might respond to the dilemma in the problem by moving to withdraw from the representation of Lebad. Even Professor

Smith's essay suggests that avoiding some representations may be the best course, at least on occasion. *See supra* note 2. However, does the problem present a circumstance where you can withdraw? Model Rule 1.16(b)(4) permits, but does not require, a lawyer to withdraw from representing a client if the client insists upon "taking action that the lawyer considers repugnant or with which the lawyer has a fundamental disagreement." Perhaps you could reasonably contend that the taping was "repugnant" to you, but could you make the same claim regarding a cross-examination that attempted to demonstrate Lee's delusions? Even if the answer is yes, recall that Model Rule 1.16(c) would require you to seek the court's permission to withdraw. *See supra* section 3(G)(1). It may be difficult for you to convince the court to allow you to withdraw due to a conflict with your client over trial tactics, particularly when Model Rule 1.6 and the attorney-client privilege will limit your ability to make the court fully aware of the circumstances of that conflict.

Even if withdrawal is an option, it is a solution only for a particular defense attorney, not for the criminal justice system or the bar at large. If you withdraw (or if you managed to avoid being assigned to defend Lebad in the first place), won't the next attorney asked to defend Lebad face the same crisis? If she, too, is allowed to withdraw (or avoid the assignment) because taping or cross-examining is too abhorrent, what about the next attorney? Will Lebad eventually end up with an attorney who is willing to pursue the distasteful, but potentially effective, legal tactics? If so, what did you and the other withdrawing attorneys accomplish by withdrawing or avoiding the assignment? Should you derive satisfaction from knowing that "even though some attorneys would do it, and he can therefore get it done for him, at least I know that I did not do it"? Is the system better served by defense (and other) attorneys who are willing to do (almost?) anything or by those who have occasional qualms about legal, but distasteful, tactics?

7. **Applicability of Other Model Rules to Criminal Defense Attorneys:** Not all rules applicable to other litigators apply with equal force to criminal defense attorneys. For example, Model Rule 4.2's prohibition against ex parte contact with a represented person often has little impact on a defense attorney. The victim of a crime, though often a critical witness for the prosecution, is not represented by the prosecutor, so the defense attorney can contact her directly, unless she is one of the relatively rare crime victims who has retained private counsel to represent her. In fact, the prosecutor cannot even ask the victim, who is not the prosecutor's client, to refrain from speaking with the defense attorney, because such a request would violate Model Rule 3.4(f). Of course, Model Rule 4.2 would prohibit a criminal defense attorney from attempting ex parte contact with her client's co-defendant or potential co-defendant, who are ordinarily represented by counsel. Another rule that has less impact on the criminal defense attorney, at least in the trial phase, is Model Rule 3.1. The criminal defense attorney, unlike the civil defense attorney, is allowed to force the prosecution to establish every element of its case, even when there is no non-frivolous basis for disputing the prosecution's claims. *See* Model Rule 3.1; *supra* section 6(A)(1)(a), note 10.

Although a criminal defense attorney is allowed to force the prosecution to prove every element of its case, Model Rule 3.1's prohibition of non-frivolous contentions otherwise applies to her. This restriction, therefore, applies to the attorney who represents a criminal defendant on appeal. At the same time, criminal defendants generally have a right to appeal their convictions to the first appellate court above the trial court. What should the attorney who represents the defendant do if she concludes that there is no valid basis upon which to appeal the conviction? In *Anders v. California*, 386 U.S. 738 (1967), the Supreme Court indicated that the attorney may request withdrawal, but only if she also files a brief noting anything in the trial record that could even arguably be the basis for an appeal. *See* 2 Geoffrey C. Hazard, Jr. & W. William Hodes, The Law of Lawyering § 27.14 (3d ed. 2003). Professors Hazard and Hodes contend that this requirement of what has become known as an *"Anders* brief" is an "anomaly" that "demonstrates the [Supreme] Court's isolation from the realities of practice," because it requires an attorney to simultaneously contend both that an appeal is meritless and that there is some possible merit to the appeal. *See id.* In recognition of the problems with the *Anders* brief procedure, some jurisdictions have developed alternative procedures for the attorney faced with filing an appeal that attorney believes to be wholly or partially meritless, including drafting of a two-part brief that first presents issues the attorney wishes to present and then presents the issues the client wishes to present, *see State v. Korth*, 650 N.W.2d 528 (S.D. 2002) (adopting a procedure created in Oregon), and the filing of a summary of the procedural and factual history of the case that thereby invites the appellate court to identify the best of the defendant's arguments, *see* Hazard & Hodes, *supra*, § 27.14 (describing California procedure).

8. **Closing Arguments:** Is a criminal defense attorney permitted to use closing argument to invite the jury to "nullify" the law by ignoring evidence establishing guilt and returning a not guilty verdict? Classically courts have held that a direct jury nullification argument is improper. *See* District of Columbia Ethics Op. 320 (2003), *discussed in Trial Conduct: In Quest for Jury Nullification, Defense Counsel Must Walk Fine Line*, 19 Laws.Man. on Prof. Conduct (ABA/BNA) 315 (2003) (confirming the prohibition of direct jury nullification appeals, but permitting attorneys to make good faith arguments that could indirectly increase the probability of jury nullification).

9. **Duty to Advise Regarding Collateral Consequences of Conviction:** As noted in *supra* section 3(F)(1), Questions and Notes on Attorney Inadequacy in Criminal Cases, note 3, the U.S. Supreme Court recently held that a criminal defense attorney provided inadequate representation by not informing his client that a guilty plea would result in his automatic deportation. *Padilla v. Kentucky*, 130 S.Ct. 1473 (2010). Thus, after *Padilla*, a criminal defense attorney must "inform her client whether his plea carries a risk of deportation." 130 S.Ct. at 1486. However, the extent to which the defense attorney must advise the client of other collateral consequences is not yet clear.

Sometimes the "collateral consequences" of a felony conviction are more severe than the incarceration, probation, or other direct sentence for the conviction, because the collateral consequences might include "relatively traditional penalties such as disenfranchisement, loss of professional licenses, and deportation in the case of aliens, as well as newer penalties such as felon registration and ineligibility for certain public welfare benefits." Symposium,

ABA Standards for Criminal Justice, Collateral Sanctions and Discretionary Disqualification of Convicted Persons: Black Letter with Commentary, 36 U.Tol.L.Rev. 441, 441 (2005). The criminal defense attorney's duty to advise clients about collateral consequences is likely to expand, if the recent trend of using collateral consequences as "an increasingly significant function of the criminal justice system" continues. Gabriel J. Chin, *Making* Padilla *Practical: Defense Counsel and Collateral Consequences at Guilty Plea,* 54 How.L.J. 675, 676 (2011). Defense attorneys, especially public defenders and others who serve as appointed counsel, will have to manage this element of their duties to their clients while simultaneously dealing with large caseloads, serious budget shortfalls, and limited opportunities to obtain the training that could keep them abreast of developments, including new collateral consequences. *See* Darryl K. Brown, *Why* Padilla *Doesn't Matter (Much),* 58 UCLA L.Rev. 1393, 1396 (2011); Maureen A. Sweeney, *Where Do We Go From* Padilla v. Kentucky? *Thoughts on Implementation and Future Directions,* 45 New Eng. L.Rev. 353, 353 (2011).

To what extent should defense attorneys be required to know about the frequently expanding set of possible collateral consequences to criminal convictions? It is desirable for defense attorneys to know of, and advise their clients about, as many collateral consequences of guilty pleas and resultant convictions as possible. *See* Brown, *supra,* 58 UCLA L.Rev. at 1396 (noting that "[p]rofessional standards urge defense attorneys to advise clients on [collateral] consequences"); Joanne Gottesman, *Avoiding the "Secret Sentence": A Model For Ensuring that New Jersey Criminal Defendants Are Advised About Immigration Consequences Before Entering Guilty Pleas,* 33 Seton Hall Legis.J. 357, 382 & nn.123–24 (citing the ABA Criminal Justice Section Standards, § 19–2.3(b), and the National Legal Aid and Defender Association's Performance Guidelines for Criminal Defense Representation, guideline 6.2(a), as setting high standards regarding the duty to advise of collateral consequences). But it is not realistic to expect every defense attorney to be aware of every possible collateral consequence.

Which collateral consequences are those that the defense attorney must discuss with clients? In *Padilla,* the majority found it relatively easy to require criminal defense attorneys to advise clients about the risk of deportation "because of its close connection to the criminal process." 130 S.Ct. at 1482. Applying this test, Professor Gabriel Chin, who has substantial expertise regarding collateral consequences, has taken a first cut at identifying the collateral consequences that a constitutionally adequate criminal defense attorney might have to advise about:

> *Padilla*'s clear implication is that defense attorneys should warn clients about other serious consequences—the "collateral consequences"—that flow automatically from a criminal conviction, even if they are not technically denominated criminal punishment. Because of their importance and their automatic application after certain criminal convictions, strong candidates for Sixth Amendment coverage include sex offender registration and incarceration, losing the ability to earn a living, and losing the ability to have or gain custody of a relative or foster child. Other collateral consequences may loom large with respect to particular clients based on their particular circumstances.

54 How. L. Rev. at 675–76.

B. ROLES OUTSIDE LITIGATION

PROBLEM

Edward James is a member of a three-person law firm in a small city. He became acquainted with Helen and Richard Trent in a bridge club, and was asked by the Trents to be their lawyer.

Richard inherited some money and decided to establish a small business providing tours in the region. He is negotiating to bring Harold Johnson into the business as a travel expert, in return for a forty percent equity interest in the company. James set up a close corporation for Richard, with fifty shares of outstanding stock, of which twenty shares are to be issued to Johnson and thirty shares to Richard.

The Trents have two grown children. Their son is an accountant with a local firm showing every sign of success. He is married to the daughter of long-time family friends and fellow church members. Their daughter, who did not finish college, is employed as a clerk in a pharmacy. She has fallen in love with a local artist of a different ethnic and religious background who is barely able to keep food on the table, and has taken him into her apartment. Richard is so angry at her rejection of her upbringing that he has stopped providing her with the small monthly checks with which he has supplemented her income. He asks James to draw up a new will that will totally disinherit the daughter. Helen calls James, tells him that she has tried without any success to bring Richard to reason on this issue, and pleads, "Please, Edward, can you talk some sense into him about this?"

QUESTIONS

(a) Johnson asks Richard for a legal opinion concerning the conditions under which the shareholders—and in particular he as the travel expert—might be personally liable to customers for scheduling foul-ups, injuries, etc. Richard asks James to write one, but reminds James of the importance of keeping Johnson committed to the venture. In issuing this opinion, to whom is James responsible? How much of the uncertainty he encounters in researching the legal questions should he include in the opinion letter? Does it matter whether Johnson has his own counsel?

(b) James has no training in philosophy, psychology, or counseling, although he did take a course in psychology while an undergraduate. He personally agrees with Helen that Richard is going overboard about their daughter. How far should he go in talking to Richard about the moral and personal ramifications of changing his will to shut out the daughter?

RULE REFERENCES

Model Rules 1.4, 2.1, 2.3, 1.6, and 1.13

RESTATEMENT §§ 20, 94, 95 & 131

B(1) THE LAWYER AS ADVISOR

OFFICE OF THE UNITED STATES TRUSTEE v. BRESSET (IN RE ENGEL)

United States Bankruptcy Court, Middle District of Pennsylvania, 2000.
246 B.R. 784.

JOHN J. THOMAS, BANKRUPTCY JUDGE:

The United States Trustee has requested the imposition of sanctions against Attorney Stephen Bresset * * *.

The Heinrich Engel bankruptcy was filed as a Chapter Seven [and the] Petition was endorsed by Attorney Stephen Bresset as counsel for the Debtor. * * * The United States Trustee * * * alleges that certain real estate of the Debtor was undervalued at $58,000 despite Bresset's awareness of a $132,000 appraisal. * * * Bresset's scheduling of a market value of Engel's real estate at less than half of the appraised valuation was apparently intended to minimize the possibility of administration by the Trustee.

The root of the problem is not difficult to fathom. After several meetings with the client, the schedules were prepared by an associate who did not review them. * * * Bresset, in fact, disavowed responsibility for their preparation. The schedules were reviewed by Bresset, but apparently not in the presence of the client. * * * They were signed but not read by the client and only in the presence of Bresset's secretary. * * *

Bresset is a busy and capable practitioner whose zealous advocacy and "seat of the pants" representation has pushed the envelope far beyond the ethical limits that can be tolerated by this Court. This raises the ultimate question before me. Just what is the lawyer's responsibility in drafting accurate schedules? * * *

The official bankruptcy schedules and statement of affairs forms provide a well-designed format in a relatively easily understood language geared toward eliciting necessary and relevant information from a bankruptcy filer. While the average layperson should be able to articulate responses to all inquiries, that is not to say that queries within the form cannot pose pitfalls that only an experienced legal practitioner is capable of negotiating. The most obvious example [of a potentially confusing inquiry] may be [the one] at issue before me, i.e. the meaning of the term "market value" used in Schedules A and B (real and personal property listings). * * *

The explanation of debtor counsel's role in assigning a value to a given asset lies in a review of the Model Rules of Professional Conduct which are applicable to cases before this Court. * * * In explaining to a client the nuances of certain terminology, Model [Rule] of Professional Conduct 1.4(b) states, "A lawyer shall explain a matter to the extent reasonably necessary to permit the client to make informed decisions regarding the representation." The obvious rationale for such direction is the concern that a client have sufficient information to participate intelligently in the decisions that the client must make. [*See* Rule 1.4, Comment [5].] The ultimate decisions regarding the matter at hand, including the content of the bankruptcy schedules, remain the clients. This theme is emphasized in [Comment [5] to Model Rule 2.1] indicating, "[i]n general, a lawyer is not expected to give advice until asked by the client." This does not mean, however, that a lawyer can blithely allow a client to casually complete *or review* the official schedules and statements without guidance as to the consequences of such action. "[W]hen a lawyer knows that a client proposes a course of action that is likely to result in substantial adverse legal consequences to the client, [the lawyer's] duty to the client under Rule 1.4 may require that the lawyer [offer advice] if the client's course of action is related to the representation." [Comment [5] to] MRPC Rule 2.1. This is certainly applicable if a client is allowed to execute these critical documents without adequate review, especially because of the rather serious ramifications emanating from erroneous filings. * * *

I assess Mr. Bresset the sum of $2,500 * * *. I am also satisfied that the * * * government should be reimbursed for the time and expense associated with bringing th[is] to my attention.

NOTES ON THE LAWYER AS ADVISOR

1. **Lawyer's Duty to Advise:** Although *Bresset* is a relatively rare instance of court action or discipline against an attorney for violation of the Model Rule 2.1 duty to advise clients, the duty is perhaps the most fundamental and universal of the attorney's duties to the client. Abraham Lincoln is often credited with having declared, "A lawyer's time and advice are his stock in trade." *See Sterling v. Philadelphia*, 106 A.2d 793, 795 n.2, 804 & n.4 (Pa. 1954) (with a dissent asserting the phrase actually originated with a plaque manufacturer). In almost any conceivable attorney-client relationship, the client will or might, at least to some extent, seek, expect, or benefit from the attorney's legal advice. Sometimes advice is the only service the attorney provides to a client. More commonly, legal advice is offered in conjunction with other legal services such as document drafting or advocacy. Advice, however, is just as important as the underlying service.

Model Rule 2.1 explicitly permits the lawyer who is giving advice to refer to matters outside the law, and Comment [2] notes that "[p]urely technical legal advice" may be insufficient in some circumstances. At the same time, Comment [3] notes that some clients request purely legal advice and that attorneys should give some, but not necessarily all, of them purely legal advice. Also, Comment [4] suggests that lawyers should sometimes refer clients to professionals in other fields.

Though a lawyer has a basic obligation to provide advice to clients, the lawyer generally is not required to give advice until and unless the client requests it. Model Rule 2.1, Comment [5]. However, as *Bresset* notes, if the lawyer knows the client will engage in conduct with adverse legal consequences, the lawyer's Model Rule 1.4 duty to communicate with the client may require the presentation of unrequested advice. Model Rule 2.1, Comment [5]. A 2002 addition to this comment says a lawyer sometimes should also volunteer advice regarding alternative dispute resolution mechanisms.

2. **Lawyer's Duty of Candor:** A critical component of the duty to advise clients is the duty to provide candid advice, even when it is unpleasant. *See Hartford Accident & Indem. Co. v. Foster*, 528 So.2d 255, 271 (Miss. 1988) ("The comment under [Rule 2.1] makes it clear that the lawyer must give completely honest and straightforward advice to his client, even though unpalatable, at all stages of his legal representation."). In many situations, this is a difficult task, particularly when combined with the lawyer's Rule 2.1 duty to "exercise independent professional judgment." *See id.* at 273 (observing that a lawyer who must advise both the insurance carrier who pays the lawyer's fees and the insured who is the defendant in a case sometimes faces "a tortuous, perilous path"); *supra* section 5(A)(1)(c) (addressing the conflict of interest aspects of the attorney/insurer/insured relationship). But the duty exists nonetheless, and failure to fulfill it is misconduct. Thus, it was misconduct for a lawyer who had "misgivings" about the actions taken by the lawyer's co-counsel to fail to take steps on behalf of the client. *Ky. Bar Ass'n v. Mills*, 318 S.W.3d 89, 93 (Ky. 2010) (finding that an attorney violated Model Rule 2.1 "by failing to exercise professional judgment independent of his co-counsel regarding the distribution of the settlement funds to the clients").

The duty of candor requires the criminal defense attorney, for example, to inform her client of her conclusion, after three days of prosecution evidence at trial, that there is sufficient risk that the client will be convicted of murder and exposed to the death penalty to make it advisable to plead guilty in order to avoid that risk, where no reduction in the charge is obtainable from the prosecutor. *See Evans v. State*, 477 S.W.2d 94 (Mo. 1972) (holding that the attorney's advice to that effect did not make the client's guilty plea coerced); *see also MacDonald v. State*, 778 A.2d 1064, 1071 (Del. 2001) (in the context of plea negotiations "attorneys are frequently called upon to advise and consult with their clients in order to assist the client in determining how best to proceed"). Attorneys in civil cases also owe their clients candid advice about such matters as settlement. *See Ky. Bar Ass'n v. Helmers*, 353 S.W.3d 599, 601 (Ky. 2011) (disbarring attorney for, inter alia, "failing to render candid advice to his clients ..., including advice relating to their participation in the aggregate settlement"). Like criminal attorneys, civil attorneys must provide candid evaluations of the strengths of their client's cases, even when that means communicating bad news to clients. *See Cambria v. Ass'n of Flight Attendants*, No. Civ.A.03–CV–5605, 2005 WL 1563343, at *15, n.9 (E.D.Pa. June 30, 2005) (finding that a union attorney was obligated to advise a union employee that her grievance case was weak and offer her the option of resigning "because, under Rule 2.1 of the Pennsylvania Rules of Professional Conduct, she owed Plaintiff a duty of candor and honesty").

If the lawyer's duty makes her the bearer of bad tidings, how much concern should she have about whether her advice will be followed? For a discussion of unwelcome or unheeded advice, see Geoffrey C. Hazard, Jr., *Advise and Dissent, in* ETHICS IN THE PRACTICE OF LAW 136–49 (1978).

3. **Advising Juvenile Clients:** In the context of juvenile proceedings, the ABA's Institute of Judicial Administration has declared that counsel for a juvenile should be prepared to counsel the client and even the client's family with respect to nonlegal as well as legal matters. *See* Institute of Judicial Administration, *Juvenile Justice Standards Project: Standards Relating to Counsel for Private Parties* 8–9 (Tent. Draft 1976); David R. Katner, *Revising Legal Ethics in Delinquency Cases by Consulting with Juveniles' Parents*, 79 UMKC L.Rev. 595, 602–03 (2011) (noting that the persons whom a lawyer might consult "would likely include the juvenile's parents," because they generally have the ability to take action to protect the juvenile); Donna Sheen, *Professional Responsibilities Toward Children in Trouble with the Law*, 5 Wyo.L.Rev. 483, 512–13 (2005) (contending that "[p]erhaps the most important rule by which an attorney of a juvenile should abide is the role of advisor in rendering 'candid advice' " and noting that "there are situations where the attorney has an ethical obligation to discuss ... non-legal factors"). Under Model Rule 1.14(a), however, the lawyer representing a juvenile should recognize that the lawyer's primary duty is to maintain a normal attorney-client relationship with the juvenile client, if possible. *See In re Georgette*, 785 N.E.2d 356, 363 (Mass. 2003) (citing Model Rule 1.14(a)).

B(2) THE LAWYER AS EVALUATOR

VANGUARD PRODUCTION, INC. v. MARTIN

United States Court of Appeals, Tenth Circuit, 1990.
894 F.2d 375.

TACHA, CIRCUIT JUDGE.

Plaintiff Vanguard * * * appeals the district court's grant of a motion for summary judgment in favor of defendants, attorneys Billy Martin and David Morgan and the law firm of Ames, Ashabranner, Taylor, Lawrence, Laudick and Morgan ("Ames, Ashabranner") (collectively "defendants"). * * * We hold that the Oklahoma Supreme Court's decision in [*Bradford Securities Processing Services Inc. v. Plaza Bank & Trust*, 653 P.2d 188 (Okla. 1982)] controls this case. An attorney owes a common law duty of ordinary care and workmanlike performance on the underlying contract with his client. When an attorney knows or should know that an opinion he prepares may be exhibited to nonclients, this common law duty extends to those same nonclients that an ordinarily prudent attorney under the circumstances would reasonably foresee could be injured by the attorney's advice contained in and explanatory of the opinion. We further hold that Vanguard has pleaded sufficient facts under *Bradford* to establish a jury question on the element of proximate causation. * * *

Vanguard began negotiations for an assignment of an oil and gas lease covering property in * * * Oklahoma. James Hadsell, an officer and director of Vanguard, represented Vanguard in negotiations with the seller and the lender, Glenfed. Vanguard saw a title opinion on the lease property * * * which was prepared by [attorney] Martin * * * for a third party. This third party opinion on the lease property contained a caveat stating that Texas Rose Petroleum had filed suit against the seller for damages involving the lease. [Thereafter,] Vanguard executed a promissory note for $780,000 in favor of Glenfed, and executed a mortgage, security agreement, financing statement, and assignment in favor of Glenfed as security for the promissory note. Glenfed's loan agreement with Vanguard provided that Glenfed would select the attorneys to do the title and closing work, and that Vanguard would pay for the attorneys' fees. Glenfed selected the law firm of Ames, Ashabranner. Morgan, a partner in Ames, Ashabranner, did the actual legal work and hired Martin, the local attorney in Okmulgee County, to assist him.

Morgan and Martin incorrectly advised Vanguard that the claim on the lease by Texas Rose Petroleum described in Martin's third party title opinion on the lease property would not adversely affect the title because a summons had not been issued. Morgan and Martin told Vanguard that after 120 days Texas Rose Petroleum's case could be dismissed and that the dismissal would cure the defect in the lease title. Morgan and Martin procured dismissal of the suit after 120 days. Morgan and Martin then deleted any mention of the Texas Rose Petroleum claim in the final opinion prepared for Glenfed. The deal was closed [and after it was closed, the] Texas Rose Petroleum suit was refiled, however, about thirty days later. The trial court in the Texas Rose Petroleum litigation eventually ruled that Vanguard and Glenfed had actual knowledge of the adverse Texas Rose Petroleum claim before entering into the lease transaction, and therefore sustained Texas Rose Petroleum's claim to 75% of the lease.

Vanguard sued Martin, Morgan, and Ames, Ashabranner, for malpractice. The district court granted the defendants' motion for summary judgment on the grounds that the defendants owed no duty to Vanguard because there was no attorney/client relationship between the defendants and Vanguard. The district court also noted that even under the *Bradford* rule, liability did not lie because it was not reasonably foreseeable to the defendants that Vanguard would rely solely on the title opinion, prepared by Morgan and Martin, when they were in fact working for Glenfed. * * *

In *Bradford*, a pledgee who had foreclosed and become a forced purchaser of industrial revenue bonds that proved to be of little or no value sued the attorney who prepared the bond opinion for alleged negligence. The pledgee was not a client of the attorney. The pledgee alleged that the bond attorney knew that his bond opinion would appear on the bond certificates and that a purchaser of the bonds foreseeably would rely on his bond opinion. The district court dismissed the pledgee's complaint for failure to state a claim, ruling in part that there could be no liability because the pledgee was not the attorney's client. The pledgee appealed * * *.

The Oklahoma Supreme Court [held] that the pledgee's complaints stated a cause of action under Oklahoma law. Privity of contract does not apply to tort actions under Oklahoma law. * * * The *Bradford* court stated that to determine an attorney's negligence the jury must determine whether the attorney's conduct was *"the conduct of an ordinarily prudent man based upon the dangers he should reasonably foresee* TO THE PLAINTIFF OR ONE IN HIS POSITION *in view of all the circumstances of the case* such as to bring the plaintiff within the orbit of defendant's liability." *Id.* at 191 (emphases in original).

Morgan and Ames, Ashabranner argue, however, that the *Bradford* test applies only when there is a duty running from defendants to the plaintiff, and that in this case the defendants owed no such duty to Vanguard. We agree that *Bradford* applies only when a duty exists and hold that under the facts of this case a duty to Vanguard arose under Oklahoma law. [T]he Oklahoma Supreme Court [has] held that ["a]s a general rule, there is implied in every contract for work or services a duty to perform it skillfully, carefully, diligently, and in a workmanlike manner.[" Thus,] where there is a contract for services a common law duty of workmanlike performance arises and * * * a third party beneficiary is entitled to sue for a breach of that duty.

Bradford extends [this] rule * * * to attorneys and refines the test for determining the class of persons which may sue for breach of the common law duty of workmanlike performance [by stating that a duty arises when] "the circumstances attending a situation are such that an ordinarily prudent person could reasonably apprehend that, as the natural and probable consequences of his act, another person will be in danger of receiving an injury * * *." In our view a contract for legal services is a contract for services giving rise to the duty of workmanlike performance. The record in this case reveals extensive communications between the attorneys, Martin and Morgan, and the purchaser, Vanguard, concerning the title opinion. The record also shows that all parties, including Martin, Morgan, Vanguard, and Glenfed, were concerned about the Texas Rose Petroleum suit. Thus, we find that an ordinarily prudent attorney in the position of the defendants would reasonably have apprehended that Vanguard was among the class of nonclients which, as a natural and probable consequence of the attorneys' actions in preparing the title opinion for Glenfed, could be injured. Thus, we hold that the defendants owed a duty of ordinary care * * * and workmanlike performance * * * to Vanguard in the performance of their contract for legal services with Glenfed. We stress that our holding only addresses the question of the duty of the defendants owed to Vanguard and not the question of whether Martin's, Morgan's, and Ames, Ashabranner's acts were the proximate cause of Vanguard's injuries.

[O]nce a plaintiff is in the class of persons which could foreseeably be injured by the defendants' actions, arguments about remoteness of relation, adversity of interest, etc., go to the element of proximate causation and thus to the *"jury question* whether the *injurious consequences resulting from the negligence could have reasonably been foreseen or anticipated.* * * * " ([E]mphasis added).

NOTES ON THE LAWYER AS EVALUATOR

1. **Model Rules Re Evaluations Used by Third Parties:** Under current Model Rule 2.3(b), a client must give informed consent if a lawyer's evaluation for a third party "is likely to affect the client's interests materially and adversely." *See also* RESTATEMENT, § 95(2) (2000). Disclosure of confidential information is permitted under Model Rule 2.3(c) only when "authorized in connection with a report of an evaluation." *See also FDIC v. White Birch Ctr., Inc.,* 14 Conn.L.Rptr. 166 (Super.Ct. 1995) (citing state equivalent of Model Rule 2.3 and Comment [3] to allow a deposition of an attorney who wrote an opinion letter because the Model Rule and Comment allowing disclosure in connection with a report of an evaluation established "an ethical duty to disclose the basis for his evaluation").

2. **Securities:** The role of lawyer as evaluator has received particular attention, as indicated by the *Bradford* decision relied on in *Vanguard,* in the context of securities law. Opinions of counsel play a large role in that field. The securities lawyer's role often includes finding information that could adversely affect the value of the offered securities. Sometimes these lawyers and their clients disagree about whether these matters must be disclosed in securities offerings. In affirming a finding that a securities lawyer assisted in his client's failure to disclose matters that should have been disclosed, the Ninth Circuit described the inherent conflicts for securities lawyers:

> [E]ffective regulation of the issuance and trading of securities depends, fundamentally, on securities lawyers such as Fehn properly advising their clients of the disclosure requirements and other relevant provisions of the securities regulations. Securities regulation in this country is premised on open disclosure, and it is therefore incumbent upon practitioners like Fehn to be highly familiar with the disclosure requirements and to insist that their clients comply with them.

> We acknowledge the inherent tension between representing a client in criminal or civil litigation—which entails professional obligations such as the duty of confidentiality and the need to advise clients of their privilege against self-incrimination—and counseling a client in connection with regulatory compliance. Commentators have described the tension that arises where a lawyer is called upon to perform a "legal audit" of his own client, such as when a lawyer advises an issuer of securities about the need to disclose certain negative corporate information:

>> What is unusual about such employment, of course, is that the client has in effect hired the lawyer for the very purpose of revealing information that otherwise would be confidential.

Geoffrey C. Hazard, Jr. & W. William Hodes, 1 *The Law of Lawyering: A Handbook on the Model Rules of Professional Conduct* § 2.3, at 101 (Aspen Law & Business 2nd ed. 1990). * * *

> [T]he SEC disclosure requirements mandated disclosure of Wheeler's role as CTI's promoter and of the contingent liabilities stemming from CTI's and Wheeler's earlier securities law violations. In failing to make

the Form 10–Q's comply with these disclosure requirements, Fehn "substantially assist[ed]" in the primary disclosure violations.

U.S. SEC v. Fehn, 97 F.3d 1276, 1294–95 (9th Cir. 1996).

In the early years of this century, significant attention was directed to the conduct of securities attorneys and others who represented organizations, including corporations, following securities scandals concerning Enron and other corporations. Congress responded by passing the Sarbanes–Oxley Act in 2002, the SEC responded by adopting regulations in 2003 requiring an attorney to report misconduct to specified corporate officials and allowing reporting to the SEC in some circumstances, and the ABA responded by modifying Model Rules 1.6 and 1.13 in 2003 to permit reporting of client confidences to rectify or prevent financial losses. *See supra* section 2(B), note 12, and section 4(B), Notes on Corrective Disclosure.

Should securities attorneys, in-house counsel, and others who represent corporations be allowed or required to report otherwise confidential client information to prevent financial harm? Is this, as some bar leaders have argued in opposing Sarbanes–Oxley and the resultant SEC regulations and amendments to Model Rule 1.6 and 1.13, the camel's nose under the tent of attorney-client confidentiality? If securities lawyers can be required to report adverse information about their clients, should criminal defense attorneys similarly be required to report adverse information, such as their client's admissions of criminal activity? Is the practice of securities attorneys substantially different enough from the practice of criminal defense attorneys to require reporting for securities attorneys, but not for defense attorneys? Would some members of the public argue that it is even more important for criminal defense attorneys to report adverse information, to prevent further violent crimes and, therefore, injuries and deaths? How would you respond? Regardless of what type of law you plan to practice, how comfortable will you be if you are required to report adverse information about the people or entities you represent?

For additional guidance about issues facing securities lawyers, see Paula Schaefer, *Harming Business Clients with Zealous Advocacy: Rethinking the Attorney Advisor's Touchstone*, 38 Fla.St.U.L.Rev. 251 (2011), George W. Dent, Jr., Symposium Introduction, *Lawyers in the Crosshairs: The New Legal and Ethical Duties of Corporate Attorneys*, 57 Case W.Res.L.Rev. 337 (2007), William H. Dorton, Note, *Corporate Gatekeepers: An Examination of the Transactional Lawyer's Role*, 99 Ky.L.J. 555 (2010–2011), and James L. Sonne, Note, *Sarbanes–Oxley Section 307: A Progress Report on How Law Firms and Corporate Legal Departments Are Implementing SEC Attorney Conduct Rules*, 23 Geo.J. Legal Ethics 859 (2010).

3. **Other Transactional Practice:** Similar issues arise in other transactional practices. As *Vanguard Production* demonstrates, lenders often rely upon the title opinions paid for and produced on behalf of borrowers. *See also* John C. Murray, *Attorney Malpractice in Real Estate Transactions: Is Title Insurance the Answer?*, 42 Real Prop.Prob. & Tr.J. 221 (2007). Purchasers of municipal bonds rely upon opinions written by the municipality's bond counsel. *See Mehaffy, Rider, Windholz & Wilson v. Century Bank Denver, N.A.*, 892 P.2d 230 (Colo. 1995). Tax experts draft letters outlining their

opinions regarding the likely tax treatment of specified fiscal arrangements. *See* 31 C.F.R. § 10.33 et seq. (outlining the IRS's "[b]est practices for tax advisors"); *Denney v. Deutsche Bank AG*, 443 F.3d 253, 260 (2d Cir. 2006) (noting that an accounting firm allegedly told investors that a law firm "would provide an 'independent' opinion letter confirming the legitimacy of the tax shelters"); *Diaz v. Century Pac. Invest. Corp.*, 21 F.3d 1112 (9th Cir. 1994) (Table), 1994 WL 143949 (noting that the plaintiff alleged that Price Waterhouse "recklessly failed to comply with the [IRS's] standard of care" in drafting tax opinion letters). For further analysis of the issues facing transactional attorneys in presenting opinions, see *Report of the Special Joint Committee on Lawyers' Opinions in Commercial Transactions*, 45 Bus.Law. 705 (1990), John P. Freeman, *Current Trends in Legal Opinion Liability*, 1989 Colum.Bus.L.Rev. 235, and Kelly A. Love, *A Primer on Opinion Letters: Explanations and Analysis*, 9 Transactions: Tenn.J.Bus.L. 67 (2007).

4. **Duties to Third Parties:** As *Vanguard Production* suggests, providing an evaluation for a third party may or may not result in a legal duty to that person. *See* Model Rule 2.3, Comment [3]. *See also Bank IV Wichita, N.A. v. Arn, Mullins, Unruh, Kuhn & Wilson*, 827 P.2d 758, 760 (Kan. 1992) ("Under the facts of the case at bar, no duty is owing from Arn, Mullins to Bank IV, a nonclient."). For a case in which a law firm was held subject to liability to a third person for negligent failure to disclose reasons for doubting the accuracy of the opinion's assertion that the enterprise to which the third person was being asked to loan money constituted a general partnership, see *Roberts v. Ball, Hunt, Hart, Brown & Baerwitz*, 128 Cal.Rptr. 901 (Ct.App. 1976). *See also* RESTATEMENT, § 95, Comment *e* and Reporter's Notes (citing several cases). The lawyer's general duties to third parties are discussed in *supra* section 3(F)(2).

When is an evaluation for a third person not "compatible with other aspects of the lawyer's relationship with the client" per Model Rule 2.3(a)? Presumably when the lawyer's role in relation to the client is that of advocate rather than advisor, since that is inconsistent with the objectivity implicitly required of the evaluator, *see, e.g.*, Model Rule 2.3, Comment [3]; Charles W. Wolfram, Modern Legal Ethics 706 (1986). In *U.S. SEC v. Fehn, supra* note 2, 97 F.3d at 1294, the Ninth Circuit observed:

> This dilemma [between confidentiality and disclosure] is especially pronounced in cases where, as here, a lawyer attempts to represent a client in an SEC investigation of previous disclosure violations and, at the same time, attempts to advise that same client as to ongoing disclosure requirements. We note that ABA Model Rule of Professional Conduct 2.3 makes a special provision for cases where a lawyer is asked by a client to evaluate that client's internal information for the use of an outside party, such as a government agency. * * *

In offering an example of the practical implications that flow from this requirement, [Comment [3]] to Rule 2.3 cautions that

> [I]f the lawyer is acting as advocate in defending the client against charges of fraud, it would normally be incompatible with that responsibility for the lawyer to perform an evaluation for others concerning the same or a related transaction.

Similarly, where the legal situation that the lawyer purports to evaluate is substantially the product of the lawyer's own prior advice to the client, the required objectivity may be impossible to achieve. *See In re John Doe Corp.*, 675 F.2d 482 (2d Cir. 1982) (concluding that the corporation waived attorney-client privilege with respect to a written report of an internal "Business Ethics Review" conducted by a corporation's in-house counsel by disclosing the report to third persons and questioning the appropriateness of house counsel conducting such a review "to allay the concerns of third parties about possible criminal acts").

Another delicate situation arises when an accountant performing an audit of the client's financial records sends an attorney a letter asking the attorney to evaluate the extent of exposure from litigation handled by the attorney for the client. Although at least one court has held that the attorney's letters are covered by the work product doctrine, *see supra* section 4(A)(1)(c), and are therefore outside the scope of discovery, that court's opinion cited cases reaching the opposite conclusion. *See Laguna Beach Cnty. Water Dist. v. Super. Ct.*, 22 Cal.Rptr.3d 387, 391–93 (Ct.App. 2004). Thus, these letters raise concerns about potential disclosure of confidential information and the possibility that evaluative statements by attorneys could be used against the client. *Attorneys Still Doing Balancing Act in Responding to Auditors' Inquiries*, 20 Laws.Man. on Prof. Conduct (ABA/BNA) 598 (2004). The ABA has provided guidance about how an attorney should respond to an audit inquiry letter in a manner that protects the client's interests while still providing auditors with some, though admittedly minimal, information. *See* M. Eric Anderson, *Talkin' 'bout my Litigation—How the Attorney Response to an Audit Inquiry Letter Discloses as Little as Possible*, 7 Transactions: Tenn. J.Bus.L. 143, 150–54 (2005) (reviewing the ABA Statement of Policy Regarding Lawyers' Responses to Auditors' Requests for Information).

One of the significant risks in the process of evaluation for third persons—arguably present in the problem—is that the third person may become a beneficiary of the primary attorney-client relationship, or what Professors Hazard and Hodes have referred to as a "derivative client," *see* 1 Geoffrey C. Hazard & W. William Hodes, The Law of Lawyering § 2.7 (3d ed. Supp. 2003). Such a relationship may entail a duty of candor toward the third person that could be inconsistent with the duty of confidentiality owed to the primary client, rendering proper performance of the evaluation impossible. For this reason, the full implications of the evaluation, and what would have to be disclosed to the third person in conjunction with it, must be clearly explained to the primary client before the lawyer undertakes it. *See* Model Rule 2.3(b) & (c).

Despite the use of the term "derivative client," third-party beneficiaries of an attorney's evaluation are not technically "clients" of the attorney who prepares the evaluation relied upon by the third parties. *See Murray v. Metro. Life Ins. Co.*, 583 F.3d 173, 177 (2d Cir. 2009) ("Not every beneficiary of a lawyer's advice is deemed a client"). Therefore, third parties who rely upon an attorney's evaluation do not create "client" conflicts of interest under Model Rule 1.7 or "former client" conflicts of interest under Model Rule 1.9. *See Hull–Johnson v. Wilmington Trust, C.A.*, No. 96C–03–016, 1996 WL 769457, at *3–5 (Del.Super.Ct. Dec. 9, 1996).

B(3) THE LAWYER IN OTHER ROLES AND CIRCUMSTANCES

RULE REFERENCES

Model Rules 3.9, 1.16(a)(2), and 4.4(b)

RESTATEMENT § 104

NOTES ON THE LAWYER IN OTHER ROLES AND CIRCUMSTANCES

1. The Model Rules contain a few provisions that are not discussed, or are mentioned only tangentially, elsewhere in the text. These notes briefly review these provisions.

2. **Representation Before Administrative or Legislative Body:** Pursuant to Model Rule 3.9, an attorney who represents a client before an administrative agency or a legislative body must disclose the representative nature of the lawyer's appearance. In such a forum, the lawyer must also comply with Model Rules 3.3(a) through (c) regarding candor toward the tribunal, Model Rules 3.4(a) through (c) regarding evidence and the duty to obey the relevant rules, and Model Rule 3.5 regarding ex parte contact and impartiality. *See also* RESTATEMENT, § 104 (2000); *In re Eisenberg*, 2004 WI 14, ¶ 18, 675 N.W.2d 747, 751 (suspending attorney who refused to obey procedural rules and engaged in other "conduct intended to disrupt" an administrative hearing). However, Model Rule 3.7's restrictions on serving as both trial counsel and witness, *see supra* section 6(A)(2)(e), note 6, do not apply to an attorney's appearance before an administrative agency or a legislative body. *Heard v. Foxshire Assocs., LLC*, 806 A.2d 348, 355 (Md.Ct.Spec.App. 2002) ("We conclude . . . that there exists a distinction between a 'trial' and a 'hearing' in the applicability of the Rules of Professional Conduct. We further conclude that the MRPC does not preclude the giving of evidence by an attorney of record for a party before an administrative agency.").

3. **Lawyer's Physical or Mental Condition Affecting Representation:** When a lawyer's mental or physical condition significantly limits the lawyer's ability to represent a client, the lawyer must refrain from taking on a representation or, if representation has already commenced, withdraw. Model Rule 1.16(a)(2). Mental illness can lead to application of this rule. *See, e.g., In re Ricks*, 710 S.E.2d 749, 750 (Ga. 2011) (involving "debilitating depression"); *McClure v. Ky. Bar Ass'n*, 253 S.W.3d 51, 53 (Ky. 2008) (involving an "ongoing struggle with mental illness"); *In re Moise*, 585 S.E.2d 287, 288 (S.C. 2003) (involving "serious depression"). Substance abuse is also another problem that can require attorneys to refrain from representing clients. *See, e.g., In re LeDoux*, 707 S.E.2d 88, 89 (Ga. 2011) (involving "psychiatric treatment due to an acute mental health episode and sedative-hypnotic dependence"); *In re Taylor*, 959 P.2d 901, 902 (Kan. 1998) (involving alcoholism); *Columbus Bar Ass'n v. Williams*, 2011–Ohio–4381, ¶ 14, 955 N.E.2d 354, 357 (involving marijuana use that exacerbated attorney's depression). When the mental or physical impairment is known to a lawyer's partners or

supervisors, they must take steps to prevent violations of the Model Rules. *See* ABA Standing Comm. on Ethics and Prof'l Resp., Formal Op. 03–429 (2003).

4. **Inadvertent Receipt of Confidential Material:** Assume that you are preparing for trial and you receive a twelve page fax with a cover sheet from your opponent's law firm with the scribbling "Ed, this is my latest draft of your direct examination." You know that "Ed" is your opponent's key expert witness. Model Rule 4.4(b) requires you to inform your opponent that you received the fax that was obviously sent to you by mistake, but it does not answer the interesting question: Do you turn the page and start reading, or do you return it to your opponent unread? Your client stands to gain a significant advantage if you are able to read through your opponent's direct of the star witness, right? Even if your opponent switches the order of the questions a bit after becoming aware of your receipt of the direct examination outline, you will know what points and themes your opponent plans to emphasize at trial. Should you deny your client that tactical advantage because you don't feel like "taking advantage" of your opponent's mistake? Do the calls for professionalism and civility, *see supra* section 6(A)(2)(e), note 10, help you answer this question? Has your answer changed from the answer you gave to the problem at the beginning of the book? Why? Why not?

Model Rule 4.4(b) requires an attorney who inadvertently receives a fax or other document to promptly notify the sender, but the Model Rule itself does not place any further obligations on the attorney who inadvertently received the document. *See* ABA Standing Comm. on Ethics and Prof'l Resp., Formal Op. 05–437 (2005) (withdrawing a previous opinion in light of adoption of Model Rule 4.4(b) in 2002 and concluding that a lawyer's only obligation upon receiving inadvertently sent materials is to advise the sender); ABA Standing Comm. on Ethics and Prof'l Resp., Formal Op. 06–440 (2006) (finding that Model Rule 4.4(b) "does not require refraining from reviewing the materials or abiding by instructions of the sender"); *see also* Pa. Comm. on Legal Ethics and Prof'l Resp., Op. 2011–10 (concluding that a plaintiff's attorney who reviewed an e-mail inadvertently copied to him by defense counsel and thereby found out that he named the wrong corporation in the suit must advise his client of the nature, though not necessarily the specific content, of this information to help the client participate in settlement negotiations); *but see Stengart v. Loving Care Agency, Inc.*, 990 A.2d 650, 665 (N.J. 2010) (enforcing New Jersey's Rule 4.4(b), which requires the lawyer who realizes that a document was sent inadvertently to " 'not read the document or, if he or she has begun to do so, . . . stop reading the document' ").

Comment [2] notes that other law outside the Model Rules may place an obligation upon the lawyer to take additional steps, including the return of the original document. If there is a limitation on the receiving attorney's ability to use the inadvertently provided document, it will generally come from the law of attorney-client or other privilege, *see supra* sections 4(A)(1)(a)–(b), or the work product doctrine, *see supra* section 4(A)(1)(c). *See Rico v. Mitsubishi Motors Corp.*, 171 P.3d 1092, 1094 (Cal. 2007) (holding that a previous state supreme court privilege decision established that an attorney who inadvertently receives a privileged document in a state case "may not read [the] document any more closely than is necessary to ascertain that it is privileged" and that "[o]nce it becomes apparent that the content is privileged, counsel must immediately notify opposing counsel and try to resolve the situation").

Since the adoption of Model Rule 4.4(b) in 2002, there have been significant developments in the law of what has come to be known as "inadvertent waiver" of attorney-client privilege and work product protection. In 2006, Rule 26 of the Federal Rules of Civil Procedure was amended to provide potential relief to a party that inadvertently forwarded a document to an opposing party. Under Rule 26(b)(5)(B), a party that inadvertently forwarded a document can later provide notice to the receiving party of its claim of privilege or work product protection. The receiving party must then "return, sequester, or destroy the specified information and any copies it has." If the document is returned to the party that inadvertently produced it in discovery, that party must preserve it until the claim of privilege or work product protection is resolved. The new rule provides a process by which claims of privilege or work product protection can be litigated, while the document in question is isolated and preserved, but it "does not address whether the privilege or protection that is asserted after production was waived by the production." Fed.R.Civ.P. 26(b)(5) advisory committee's note (2006 amendment).

New Rule 502 of the Federal Rules of Evidence, which resulted from a 2008 statute, attempts to provide, or at least guide, the law regarding the extent to which inadvertent production of the document waives attorney-client privilege or work product protection. Rule 502 states:

> The following provisions apply, in the circumstances set out, to disclosure of a communication or information covered by the attorney-client privilege or work-product protection. * * *
>
> **(b) Inadvertent Disclosure.** When made in a federal proceeding or to a federal office or agency, the disclosure does not operate as a waiver in a federal or state proceeding if:
>
> > **(1)** the disclosure is inadvertent;
> >
> > **(2)** the holder of the privilege or protection took reasonable steps to prevent disclosure; and
> >
> > **(3)** the holder promptly took reasonable steps to rectify the error, including (if applicable) following Federal Rule of Civil Procedure 26(b)(5)(B).
>
> **(c) Disclosure Made in a State Proceeding.** When the disclosure is made in a state proceeding and is not the subject of a state-court order concerning waiver, the disclosure does not operate as a waiver in a federal proceeding if the disclosure:
>
> > **(1)** would not be a waiver under this rule if it had been made in a federal proceeding; or
> >
> > **(2)** is not a waiver under the law of the state where the disclosure occurred.

The new rule requires the party claiming that production of a document was inadvertent to make an interesting argument. Pursuant to Rule

502(b)(2), the party must establish that it took "reasonable steps" to prevent the inadvertent disclosure of the document to the opposing party. By definition, though, the disclosing party will be making this argument in a circumstance when the "reasonable steps" that it took were not successful, because they failed to prevent the inadvertent disclosure. When Rule 502 of the Federal Rules of Evidence is combined with Rule 26(b)(5)(B) of the Federal Rules of Civil Procedure, though, there is now a means by which a party can assert work product protection after inadvertent disclosure. *See Coburn Grp., LLC v. Whitecap Advisors, LLC,* 640 F.Supp.2d 1032, 1043 (N.D.Ill. 2009) (granting inadvertently producing party's motion for return of e-mail and holding that the receiving party could not use it).

The rather unusual step of Congress passing a statute writing Rule 502 into the Federal Rules of Evidence suggests that there is substantial support for the idea that inadvertent production of a document, particularly in the modern reality where many "documents" are actually electronically stored information, should not always constitute a waiver of attorney-client privilege or work product protection. The uneasiness that at least some attorneys feel about using a document that was inadvertently disclosed is also reflected in the comments adopted with Model Rule 4.4(b) in the Ethics 2000 process. Comment [3] to Model Rule 4.4 indicates that some lawyers might choose to return an inadvertently disclosed document without reading it and that deciding to do so is ordinarily a decision the lawyer is permitted to make under Model Rules 1.2 and 1.4. *See* Andrew M. Perlman, *Untangling Ethics Theory from Attorney Conduct Rules: The Case of Inadvertent Disclosures,* 13 Geo. Mason L.Rev. 767, 768–69 (2005) (noting the "unsettled" law of inadvertent e-mails, faxes, electronic discovery, and other disclosures, and the "conflicting advice about what receiving lawyers must do under these circumstances" from court opinions, rules, and ethics committee opinions); Adam Pierson, *What's Yours Is Ours: Making Sense of Inadvertent Disclosure,* 22 Geo.J. Legal Ethics 1095, 1096 (2009) (discussing "the lack of clear guidance regarding ethical obligations for attorneys receiving inadvertently sent documents").

C. THE LAWYER AS A PARTICIPANT IN ALTERNATIVE DISPUTE RESOLUTION

Very few cases go to trial. *See* Robert P. Burns, *What Will We Lose if the Trial Vanishes?,* 37 Ohio N.U.L.Rev. 575, 577 (2011) (noting that only 1.7% of federal civil cases went to trial in 2009). In our system, the vast majority of disputes are resolved before trial, and sometimes before the initiation of any formal litigation processes. With the recent growth of alternative dispute resolution, many alternatives to trial have been developed and used to facilitate the resolution of disputes. These include, but are not limited to: negotiation between parties, usually conducted through their attorneys (which may or may not be considered an "alternative" dispute resolution mechanism, depending upon one's definition, because it has been the primary means of resolving civil disputes for decades);

mediation, where a mediator attempts to facilitate negotiation and settlement; binding arbitration, where an arbitrator or panel of arbitrators issues a final decision after a hearing in which each party presents evidence and legal arguments, usually through attorneys; non-binding arbitration, where parties retain the right to reject the decision of the arbitrator or arbitrators; early neutral evaluation, where a neutral professional evaluates a case based upon presentations by the parties or their attorneys; and mini trials and summary jury trials, where a set of lay persons evaluates a case based upon presentations by the parties or their attorneys.

For the sake of simplicity, this section primarily will discuss three of these alternatives to trial—negotiation, mediation, and binding arbitration (hereinafter "arbitration"). Most of the other mechanisms function primarily as complements to either negotiation or mediation. Interestingly, though, these other mechanisms have some similarity to trials, because they usually involve competing evidence presentations or summaries, as well as legal arguments by attorneys. In this sense, they perhaps approximate arbitration in operation, though they serve as an aid to negotiation or mediation.

C(1) THE LAWYER AS ADVOCATE IN ALTERNATIVE DISPUTE RESOLUTION

PROBLEM

You represent Rhea Llewellyn, who was blinded in her left eye when it was struck by a twig thrown into the air when she was using her new Chopper lawn trimmer. You contact the Chopper's manufacturer, Shopper Corp., threatening to bring a products liability lawsuit unless a settlement or other resolution can be reached. As your letter explains, your primary claim will be that the Chopper (referred to by your fellow plaintiffs' attorneys as "the Shopper Chopper") was defective due to the absence of a warning to users to always wear safety glasses while using it.

A plaintiffs' lawyer magazine reported that Shopper had a problem with Chopper warnings. Some of the large hang tags placed on the trimmers were coming loose during shipping or being removed by retail sales personnel or customers, so they were often absent when customers purchased Choppers. The Chopper hang tags contained the warning that you allege was needed. Because you know that almost all civil suits are resolved without trial, you do not expect this one to go to trial. If it does, though, one of the key issues will be whether the hang tag was on the Chopper when Llewellyn purchased it. Llewellyn told you that she "is not sure, but I kind of think the hang tag might have been there, because I sort of remember reading something somewhere about safety glasses." Because she knows this weakens her case, she told you that she would settle her claim for $100,000, even though you told her that a claim for blindness in one eye ordinarily is worth "about $250,000."

QUESTIONS

(a) You receive a call from Patty Fogren, an in house attorney with Shopper Corp., suggesting that you may be able to settle the suit, and inviting you to enter into negotiations with her. In your negotiations with her, can you make the following statements?

> (1) "It will cost Shopper $500,000 to settle this case."

> (2) "This is a 'blind in one eye' case, so it is worth at least $500,000."

> (3) "My client's testimony will indicate that the hang tag was not on the Chopper."

> (4) "The hang tag was not on the Chopper."

> (5) "Shopper's hang tags were notorious for not being on in the store, and there is no evidence that the hang tag was on this Chopper, so it is logical to conclude there was no hang tag on this Chopper."

(b) When you and Ms. Fogren are unable to negotiate a settlement, she suggests referring the matter to a mediator. In this mediation, are you allowed to make statements (1) through (5)?

(c) Now assume that you never heard from anyone at Shopper, so you filed suit in federal court. Under the standard practice for civil suits in this district, the federal magistrate judge is assigned to mediate the case. In this mediation, are you allowed to make statements (1) through (5)?

(d) Now assume, instead, that Ms. Fogren and you agreed to refer this matter to binding arbitration. In your "opening statement" in this arbitration, can you make statements (2) through (5)?

RULE REFERENCES

Model Rules Preamble ¶ [2] and Model Rules 8.4(c), 3.3(a), 1.0(m), and 4.1

RESTATEMENT § 98

FORMAL OPINION 06–439

American Bar Association Standing Committee on
Ethics and Professional Responsibility, 2006.

Lawyer's Obligation of Truthfulness When Representing a Client in Negotiation: Application to Caucused Mediation

In this opinion, we discuss the obligation of a lawyer to be truthful when making statements on behalf of clients in negotiations, including the specialized form of negotiation known as caucused mediation.

It is not unusual in a negotiation for a party, directly or through counsel, to make a statement in the course of communicating its position that is less than entirely forthcoming. For example, parties to a settlement negotiation often understate their willingness to make concessions to resolve the dispute. A plaintiff might insist that it will not agree to resolve a dispute for less than $200, when, in reality, it is willing to accept as little as $150 to put an end to the matter. * * * In the criminal law context, a prosecutor might not reveal an ultimate willingness to grant immunity as part of a cooperation agreement in order to retain influence over the witness.

A party in a negotiation also might exaggerate or emphasize the strengths, and minimize or deemphasize the weaknesses, of its factual or legal position. A buyer of products or services, for example, might over-state its confidence in the availability of alternate sources of supply to reduce the appearance of dependence upon the supplier with which it is negotiating. Such remarks, often characterized as "posturing" or "puffing," are statements upon which parties to a negotiation ordinarily would not be expected justifiably to rely, and must be distinguished from false statements of material fact. An example of a false statement of material fact would be a lawyer representing an employer in labor negotiations stating to union lawyers that adding a particular employee benefit will cost the company an additional $100 per employee, when the lawyer knows that it actually will cost only $20 per employee. Similarly, it cannot be considered "posturing" for a lawyer representing a defendant to declare that documentary evidence will be submitted at trial in support of a defense when the lawyer knows that such documents do not exist or will be inadmissible. In the same vein, neither a prosecutor nor a criminal defense lawyer can tell the other party during a plea negotiation that they are aware of an eyewitness to the alleged crime when that is not the case.

APPLICABLE PROVISION OF THE MODEL RULES

The issues addressed herein are governed by Rule 4.1(a).[2] That rule prohibits a lawyer, "[i]n the course of representing a client," from knowingly making "a false statement of material fact or law to a third person." As to what constitutes a "statement of fact," Comment [2] to Rule 4.1 provides additional explanation:

2. Although Model Rule 3.3 also prohibits lawyers from knowingly making untrue statements of fact, it is not applicable in the context of a mediation or a negotiation among parties. Rule 3.3 applies only to statements made to a "tribunal." It does not apply in mediation because a mediator is not a "tribunal" as defined in Model Rule 1.0(m). Comment [5] to Model Rule 2.4 confirms the inapplicability of Rule 3.3 to mediation:

Lawyers who represent clients in alternative dispute-resolution processes are governed by the Rules of Professional Conduct. When the dispute-resolution process takes place before a tribunal, as in binding arbitration (see Rule 1.0(m)), the lawyer's duty of candor is governed by Rule 3.3. Otherwise, the lawyer's duty of candor toward both the third-party neutral and other parties is governed by Rule 4.1.

Rule 3.3 does apply, however, to statements made to a tribunal when the tribunal itself is participating in settlement negotiations, including court-sponsored mediation in which a judge participates. See ABA Comm. on Ethics and Prof'l Responsibility, Formal Op. 93–370 (1993) (Judicial Participation in Pretrial Settlement Negotiations), in Formal and Informal Ethics Opinions 1983–1998 at 157, 161 (ABA 2000).

Rule 8.4(c), which on its face broadly proscribes "conduct involving dishonesty, fraud, deceit or misrepresentation," does not require a greater degree of truthfulness on the part of lawyers representing parties to a negotiation than does Rule 4.1. * * *

This Rule refers to statements of fact. Whether a particular statement should be regarded as one of fact can depend on the circumstances. Under generally accepted conventions in negotiation, certain types of statements ordinarily are not taken as statements of material fact. Estimates of price or value placed on the subject of a transaction and a party's intentions as to an acceptable settlement of a claim are ordinarily in this category, and so is the existence of an undisclosed principal except where nondisclosure of the principal would constitute fraud. Lawyers should be mindful of their obligations under applicable law to avoid criminal and tortious misrepresentation.

TRUTHFULNESS IN NEGOTIATION * * *

Although this Committee has not addressed the precise question posed herein, we previously have opined on issues relating to lawyer candor in negotiations. For example, we stated in Formal Opinion 93–370 that, although a lawyer may in some circumstances ethically decline to answer a judge's questions concerning the limits of the lawyer's settlement authority in a civil matter, the lawyer is not justified in lying or engaging in misrepresentations in response to such an inquiry. We observed that:

> [w]hile ... a certain amount of posturing or puffery in settlement negotiations may be an acceptable convention between opposing counsel, a party's actual bottom line or the settlement authority given to a lawyer is a material fact. A deliberate misrepresentation or lie to a judge in pretrial negotiations would be improper under Rule 4.1. Model Rule 8.4(c) also prohibits a lawyer from engaging in conduct involving dishonesty, fraud, deceit, or misrepresentation, and Rule 3.3 provides that a lawyer shall not knowingly make a false statement of material fact or law to a tribunal. The proper response by a lawyer to improper questions from a judge is to decline to answer, not to lie or misrepresent.

Similarly, in Formal Opinion 94–387, we expressed the view that a lawyer representing a claimant in a negotiation has no obligation to inform the other party that the statute of limitations has run on the client's claim, but cannot make any affirmative misrepresentations about the facts. In contrast, we stated in Formal Opinion 95–397 that a lawyer engaged in settlement negotiations of a pending personal injury lawsuit in which the client was the plaintiff cannot conceal the client's death, and must promptly notify opposing counsel and the court of that fact. Underlying this conclusion was the concept that the death of the client was a material fact, and that any continued communication with opposing counsel or the court would constitute an implicit misrepresentation that the client still was alive. Such a misrepresentation would be prohibited under Rule 4.1 and, with respect to the court, Rule 3.3. Opinions of the few state and local ethics committees that have addressed these issues are to the same effect.

False statements of material fact by lawyers in negotiation, as well as implicit misrepresentations created by a lawyer's failure to make truthful statements, have in some cases also led to professional discipline. * * * Affirmative misrepresentations by lawyers in negotiation also have been the basis for the imposition of litigation sanctions, and the setting aside of settlement agreements, as well as civil lawsuits against the lawyers themselves.

In contrast, statements regarding negotiating goals or willingness to compromise, whether in the civil or criminal context, ordinarily are not considered statements of material fact within the meaning of the Rules. Thus, a lawyer may downplay a client's willingness to compromise, or present a client's bargaining position without disclosing the client's "bottom line" position, in an effort to reach a more favorable resolution. Of the same nature are overstatements or understatements of the strengths or weaknesses of a client's position in litigation or otherwise, or expressions of opinion as to the value or worth of the subject matter of the negotiation. Such statements generally are not considered material facts subject to Rule 4.1.

APPLICATION OF THE GOVERNING PRINCIPLES TO CAUCUSED MEDIATION

Having delineated the requisite standard of truthfulness for a lawyer engaged in the negotiation process, we proceed to consider whether a different standard should apply to a lawyer representing a client in a caucused mediation.

Mediation is a consensual process in which a neutral third party, without any power to impose a resolution, works with the disputants to help them reach agreement as to some or all of the issues in controversy. Mediators assist the parties by attempting to fashion creative and integrative solutions to their problems. In the most basic form of mediation, a neutral individual meets with all of the parties simultaneously and attempts to moderate and direct their discussions and negotiations. Whatever is communicated to the mediator by a party or its counsel is heard by all other participants in the mediation. In contrast, the mediator in a caucused mediation meets privately with the parties, either individually or in aligned groups. These caucuses are confidential, and the flow of information among the parties and their counsel is controlled by the mediator subject to the agreement of the respective parties.

It has been argued that lawyers involved in caucused mediation should be held to a more exacting standard of truthfulness because a neutral is involved. The theory underlying this position is that, as in a game of "telephone," the accuracy of communication deteriorates on successive transmissions between individuals, and those distortions tend to become magnified on continued retransmission. * * * It has also been asserted that, to the contrary, less attention need be paid to the accuracy of information being communicated in a mediation—particularly in a caucused mediation—precisely because consensual deception is intrinsic to the process. Information is imparted in confidence to the mediator, who controls the flow of information between the parties in terms of the content of the communications as well as how and when in the process it is conveyed. * * *

Whatever the validity may be of these competing viewpoints, the ethical principles governing lawyer truthfulness do not permit a distinction to be drawn between the caucused mediation context and other negotiation settings. The Model Rules do not require a higher standard of truthfulness in any particular negotiation contexts. Except for Rule 3.3, which is applicable only to statements before a "tribunal," the ethical prohibitions against lawyer misrepresentations apply equally in all environments. Nor is a lower standard of truthfulness warranted because of the consensual nature of mediation. Parties otherwise protected against lawyer misrepresentation by Rule 4.1 are not permitted to waive that protection, whether explicitly through informed consent, or implicitly by agreeing to engage in a process in which it is somehow "understood" that false statements will be made. Thus, the same standards that apply to lawyers engaged in negotiations must apply to them in the context of caucused mediation.

We emphasize that, whether in a direct negotiation or in a caucused mediation, care must be taken by the lawyer to ensure that communications regarding the client's position, which otherwise would not be considered statements "of fact," are not conveyed in language that converts them, even inadvertently, into false factual representations. For example, even though a client's Board of Directors has authorized a higher settlement figure, a lawyer may state in a negotiation that the client does not wish to settle for more than $50. However, it would not be permissible for the lawyer to state that the Board of Directors had formally disapproved any settlement in excess of $50, when authority had in fact been granted to settle for a higher sum.

CONCLUSION

Under Model Rule 4.1, in the context of a negotiation, including a caucused mediation, a lawyer representing a party may not make a false statement of material fact to a third person. However, statements regarding a party's negotiating goals or its willingness to compromise, as well as statements that can fairly be characterized as negotiation "puffing," are ordinarily not considered "false statements of material fact" within the meaning of the Model Rules.

NOTES ON TRUTHFULNESS AND PUFFERY BY ADVOCATES IN NEGOTIATION, MEDIATION, AND ARBITRATION

1. **The Model Rules and Advocacy in ADR:** There are no Model Rules provisions designed specifically to govern the actions of attorneys who act as advocates for their clients in ADR proceedings. As a result, an attorney's conduct while representing a client in these processes is governed by the Model Rules that generally apply to attorney conduct. Model Rule

8.4(c)'s broad language prohibiting attorney conduct "involving dishonesty, fraud, deceit or misrepresentation" provides little guidance. Therefore, with regard to the restrictions on untruthful statements by attorneys, the two possibly applicable rules are Model Rule 4.1, which governs statements to "[o]thers," and Model Rule 3.3(a), which governs statements to "[t]ribunal[s]." After 2002, Model Rule 3.3(a) prohibits all knowing misstatements, while the black letter of Model Rule 4.1 still prohibits only "material" misstatements. Even before this change in 2002, Model Rule 4.1, as applied and interpreted, was considered substantially more permissive than Model Rule 3.3 regarding the extent to which an attorney can make statements that are not "true." Therefore, as Formal Opinion 06–439 reflects, the critical question with regard to a lawyer's statements while advocating on behalf of a client in an ADR context is whether the more permissive Model Rule 4.1 or the more restrictive Model Rule 3.3(a) governs these statements.

2. **"Puffery" in Negotiation:** As Formal Opinion 06–439 suggests, Model Rule 4.1 leaves plenty of room for puffery and gamesmanship in negotiation. One court's decision reflects the common view:

> Patently, certain aspects of the [negotiation] process unavoidably involve statements that are less than completely accurate, such as posturing or puffery, intentional vagueness regarding a negotiating party's "bottom line," estimates of price or value, and the party's ultimate intentions regarding what an acceptable settlement would be—all of which are thought to encompass representations that are not "material."

Ausherman v. Bank of Am. Corp., 212 F.Supp.2d 435, 446 (D.Md. 2002); *see also In re Trans Union Corp. Privacy Litig.*, No. 00 C 4729, 2009 WL 4799954, at *41 (N.D.Ill. Dec. 9, 2009) (observing that, "while an attorney can be disciplined for lying in a negotiation about an objective material fact, such as the amount of available insurance coverage or the death of the client ..., a threat to take particular legal action is a statement about the future and is not generally received as a hard promise, but rather as something the speaker 'might' do").

This does not mean that absolutely "anything goes" in negotiation. As Formal Opinion 06–439 notes, statements about material facts, as distinguished from puffery about matters like settlement position, can be misconduct if the attorney who makes them knows that they are false. Thus, it is possible to violate Model Rule 4.1's relatively permissive standard by making "knowing, material misrepresentations * * * during settlement negotiations." *Ausherman, supra,* 212 F.Supp.2d at 446–48 (citing other cases involving misstatements of material fact and referring attorney's misrepresentations of fact during negotiation to disciplinary committee); *see also In re Rosen*, 198 P.3d 116, 118 (Colo. 2008) (disciplining attorney who falsely told defendant's insurer that "his client needed additional medical treatment," when the client had died); *Statewide Grievance Comm. v. Kennelly*, 38 Conn.L.Rptr. 798 (Super.Ct. 2005) (reprimanding attorney who misrepresented the amount of available insurance coverage during settlement discussions); *In re Scanio*, 919 A.2d 1137 (D.C. 2007) (suspending attorney who made several false statements about lost income to defendant's insurer during settlement negotiations).

Because Model Rule 4.1(a) only prohibits false statements, it usually allows an attorney to remain silent and not disclose facts harmful to the attorney's case, even if an adversary might be unaware of, or mistaken about, those facts. *See* N.Y. Cnty. Lawyers' Ass'n Comm. on Prof'l Ethics, Op. 731 (2003) (finding that a defense attorney, while negotiating with a plaintiff's attorney who had offered to accept fifteen cents on the dollar because of the defendant's pending insolvency, had no duty to advise the plaintiff's attorney that the defendant was fully insured, unless the plaintiff's attorney was relying on false information about insurance coverage provided by the defendant or its agents). However, Model Rule 4.1(b) requires an attorney to disclose "a material fact to a third person when disclosure is necessary to avoid assisting a criminal or fraudulent act by a client, unless disclosure is prohibited by [Model] Rule 1.6." The Montana Supreme Court drew the line as follows:

> [Model] Rule 4.1 ... prohibits [an attorney] from knowingly making a false statement of fact to a third party. Comment 1, Rule 4.1, ABA Model R. Prof. Conduct, provides that a lawyer, while having no affirmative duty to inform an opposing party of relevant facts, must be truthful when dealing with others on a client's behalf. Comment 1 also warns that "a misrepresentation can occur if the lawyer incorporates or affirms a statement of another person that the lawyer knows is false ... or by omissions that are the equivalent of affirmative false statements."

In re Potts, 2007 MT 81, ¶ 53, 158 P.3d 418, 427. In Formal Opinion 06–439, *supra*, the ABA Committee discussed an instance where an attorney would have to reveal a material fact—the death of a personal injury plaintiff. The death of a client before negotiations have been completed is often a material fact, because many plaintiffs' cases are worth less after plaintiffs' deaths than they were worth while they are alive. Therefore, others have also found that plaintiffs' attorneys must disclose their clients' deaths during negotiations. *See Rosen, supra*, 198 P.3d at 117–18; *Harris v. Jackson*, 192 S.W.3d 297, 305–07 (Ky. 2006). Aside from the situation of a death of a plaintiff unknown to the defendant, which seems to occur with some frequency, there are relatively few instances where Model Rule 4.1 requires an attorney to correct an adversary's factual misperceptions during negotiations.

Is the standard for negotiation too permissive? Are you comfortable with a system that seems to expect "posturing or puffery" from attorneys? *See* Russell Korobkin & Chris Guthrie, *Opening Offers and Out-of-Court Settlement: A Little Moderation May Not Go a Long Way*, 10 Ohio St.J. on Disp.Resol. 1 (1994) (reporting the results of an empirical study suggesting that, because posturing is assumed, those who make reasonable settlement offers at the start of negotiation are nonetheless assumed to be posturing by their opponents, so they ultimately are faced with the prospect of less favorable settlement terms). If failing to "puff" harms your clients, do you have a duty to puff, to adequately represent them? Consider the following oft-quoted statement of an attorney's conflicting responsibilities in negotiations:

> On the one hand the negotiator must be fair and truthful; on the other he must mislead his opponent. Like the poker player, a negotiator hopes that his opponent will overestimate the value of his hand. Like the poker

player, in a variety of ways he must facilitate his opponent's inaccurate assessment.

James J. White, *Machiavelli and the Bar: Ethical Limitations on Lying in Negotiation*, 1980 Am.B.Found.Res.J. 926, 927; *see also* Douglas R. Richmond, *Lawyers' Professional Responsibilities and Liabilities in Negotiations*, 22 Geo.J. Legal Ethics 249, 249 (2009) (quoting White in discussing the "inherently paradoxical nature of negotiation" that simultaneously requires an attorney to be truthful, while also somewhat misleading); *see also* Alain Burrese, *The Ethics of Negotiating*, Mont.Law., June/July 2007, at 28, 28 (quoting White, contending that "we must negotiate honestly and ethically," and admitting "there are strategies and tactics that incorporate 'puffing' as part of the negotiation game").

Some believe attorneys should be held to a higher standard in negotiation than one that only prohibits affirmative misstatements of material fact. *See, e.g.*, James J. Alfini, *Settlement Ethics and Lawyering in ADR Proceedings: A Proposal to Revise Rule 4.1*, 19 N.Ill.U.L.Rev. 255, 270 (1999) (proposing changes to Model Rule 4.1 to prevent all knowingly false statements by lawyers, settlements based upon false statements of fact by the client, and failure to disclose material facts when necessary to avoid assisting criminal or fraudulent acts by the client); Van M. Pounds, *Promoting Truthfulness in Negotiation: A Mindful Approach*, 40 Willamette L.Rev. 181, 183 (2004) (advocating the practice of mindfulness as a way to "contribute to greater truthfulness in negotiation"). On the other hand, one commentator believes "an attorney should have no duty to make any affirmative factual representations in the course of settlement negotiations." Barry R. Temkin, *Misrepresentation by Omission in Settlement Negotiations: Should There Be a Silent Safe Harbor?*, 18 Geo.J. Legal Ethics 179, 182 (2004).

3. **"Puffery" in Mediation:** Mediation is essentially assisted negotiation, but it does involve the presence of a non-party, the mediator. However, a mediator, unlike an arbitrator, *see infra* note 4, does not make a binding legal judgment, so Model Rule 1.0(m)'s definition of tribunal does not fit. Therefore, attorneys are free to make statements in mediation under the more permissive standard of Model Rule 4.1, which generally outlaws only knowing misstatement of material fact. *See also* Model Rule 2.4, Comment [5]; Alfini, *supra* note 3, at 269. In other words, as Formal Opinion 06–439, *supra*, concludes, the relatively open-ended rules of negotiation apply equally to mediation.

Should attorneys be subject to a more restrictive standard when advocating in mediation? *See* Don Peters, *When Lawyers Move Their Lips: Attorney Truthfulness in Mediation and a Modest Proposal*, 2007 J.Disp.Resol. 119, 120 (advocating "regulatory reform ... to encourage more truth-telling" in mediation). In both mediation and negotiation?

4. **"Puffery" in Arbitration:** Arbitration is the ADR mechanism that is most dissimilar to negotiation between the parties and most similar to trial. In recognition of the similarity of arbitration to trial, the Model Rules explicitly define "tribunal" to include "an arbitrator in a binding arbitration." Model Rule 1.0(m). Therefore, attorneys are bound by the more restrictive provisions of Model Rule 3.3 when making statements to arbitra-

tors. *See* Model Rule 3.3, Comment [1] (referencing the Model Rule 1.0(m) definition of "tribunal," which includes an arbitrator); *Zurich Am. Ins. Co. v. St. Paul Surplus Lines, Inc.*, No. 4095–VCP, 2009 WL 4895120, at *2, n.3 (Del.Ch. Apr. 14, 2010) (noting that Model Rule 3.3 applies to arbitration).

As discussed in *supra* section 6(A)(2)(d), Model Rule 3.3(a)(1) prohibits a lawyer from knowingly making a false statement of fact or law to a tribunal. Model Rule 3.3 also prevents a lawyer from assisting or counseling another to make false statements or present false evidence. It also requires the lawyer to take remedial action if she learns that previously presented statements or evidence were false. While these standards are more restrictive than the Model Rule 4.1 standard applicable to negotiation and mediation, do they eliminate all opportunities for "puffery" in arbitration?

5. **Court–Ordered ADR Activities:** What if the court forced the parties to mediate and appointed the mediator, as in Question (c)? Comment [1] to Model Rule 3.3(a) provides some basis for arguing that Model Rule 3.3 applies, though this may be a weak argument. After stating that Model Rule 3.3 applies to proceedings of a tribunal and referring the reader to Model Rule 1.0(m)'s definition of "tribunal," Comment [1] states, "[This Rule] also applies when the lawyer is representing a client in an ancillary proceeding conducted pursuant to the tribunal's adjudicative authority, such as a deposition." If a deposition involves statements to a tribunal, should statements to a court-appointed mediator be considered statements to a tribunal? Is a court-mandated mediation ancillary to the court's "adjudicative authority"? Model Rule 1.0(m) suggests that "adjudicative capacity" involves a process where a decision-maker will eventually make a binding determination. In theory, a deposition might lead to such a decision, if the case is tried, but a court-mandated mediation will not lead to such a determination, because a mediator facilitates negotiation among the parties, but does not decide unresolved disputes. Is this distinction critical? *See* Model Rule 2.4, Comment [5].

If the judge is conducting the mediation herself, there is a more direct argument that Model Rule 3.3 applies. If mediation does not settle the case, the judge will eventually act in an adjudicative capacity to resolve it, perhaps with the assistance of a jury. Note that footnote 2 to Formal Opinion 06–439, *supra*, cites a previous Formal Opinion and concludes that "Rule 3.3 does apply . . . to statements made to a tribunal when the tribunal itself is participating in settlement negotiations, including court-sponsored mediation in which a judge participates."

6. **ABA Ethics-in-Settlement Guidelines:** In 2002, the ABA's Section of Litigation issued its "Ethical Guidelines for Settlement Negotiations." These non-binding standards discuss a variety of matters arising in the settlement context, including the party's control over the settlement decision, statements and omissions in settlement negotiations, discouraged and improper settlement terms, and fairness issues. *See In re Hager*, 812 A.2d 904, 919 n.18 (D.C. 2002) (noting that an attorney's conduct "touched upon several of the" Settlement Guidelines and listing these Guidelines). For an extensive review and critique of the Settlement Guidelines, see Brian C. Haussman, Note, *The ABA Ethical Guidelines for Settlement Negotiations: Exceeding the Limits of the Adversarial Ethic*, 89 Cornell L.Rev. 1218 (2004).

7. **Collaborative Law:** One relatively recent development in the practice of law is the emergence of "Collaborative Law," which is sometimes referred to as "Collaborative Practice." The key component of Collaborative Law, which to date is "a practice almost entirely limited to the area of family law, typically divorces," Christopher M. Fairman, *Growing Pains: Changes in Collaborative Law and the Challenge of Legal Ethics*, 30 Campbell L.Rev. 237, 242 (2008), is the signing of a "participation agreement" whereby key participants agree to modify the traditional arrangement between opposing parties and their attorneys:

> In CL, lawyers and clients sign a four-way "participation agreement" promising to use an interest-based approach to negotiation and fully disclose all relevant information. A key element of the participation agreement is the "disqualification agreement," which provides that both parties' CL lawyers would be disqualified from representing the clients if the case is litigated. The disqualification agreement is intended to motivate parties and lawyers to negotiate constructively because termination of a CL process would require both parties to hire new lawyers if they want legal representation.

John Lande & Forrest S. Mosten, *Before You Take a Collaborative Law Case: What the Ethical Rules Say About Conflicts of Interest, Client Screening, and Informed Consent*, Fam.Advoc., Fall 2010, at 31, 31. This alternative form of practice raises several ethical questions.

Under Model Rule 1.7(a)(2), a lawyer cannot represent a client if there is a significant risk that the representation will be "materially limited" by the lawyer's responsibility to "a third person or by a personal interest of the lawyer." *See supra* sections 5(A)(1)(b) and 5(A)(2). The Colorado Bar Ethics Committee opined that the Collaborative Law participation agreement improperly creates a conflict of interest, because an attorney's duty to the opposing client to withdraw rather than represent the lawyer's client in litigation interferes with her duty to fully represent the client. Colo.B.Ass'n, Op. 115 (2007); *see also* Rebecca A. Koford, Comment, *Conflicted Collaborating: The Ethics of Limited Representation in Collaborative Law*, 21 Geo.J. Legal Ethics 827 (2008) (discussing Colorado opinion). This is a minority opinion, however. The ABA Ethics Committee disagreed with the Colorado Ethics Committee, concluding instead that a Collaborative Law participation agreement can be an acceptable limited scope engagement under Model Rule 1.2(c). ABA Standing Comm. on Ethics and Prof'l Resp., Op. 07–447 (2007). Several state bar ethics committees have agreed with the ABA committee's conclusion that the Model Rules allow Collaborative Law. *See American Bar Association Section of Dispute Resolution Collaborative Law Committee Ethics Subcommittee Summary of Ethics Rules Governing Collaborative Practice*, 15 Tex. Wesleyan L.Rev. 555, 557 (2009) ("Ethics opinions in Minnesota (1997), North Carolina (2002), Maryland (2004), Pennsylvania (2004), Kentucky (2005), New Jersey (2005), and Missouri (2008), have approved the use of Collaborative Practice. Only one state, Colorado (2007), has said otherwise. . . .").

Pursuant to Model Rule 1.2(c), the Collaborative Law client would have to give informed consent to the participation agreement. One commentator described the approach envisioned by the ABA Ethics Committee:

[The ABA Committee's] analysis turns on the assumption that *in addition* to the four-way agreement, there is a separate limited retention or limited scope agreement in place between each lawyer and his or her client. As understood by the ABA, in other words, collaborative lawyers get informed consent from their clients to limit the scope of their representation to settlement, and *then* sign a four-way document that simply reaffirms that preexisting commitment. It thus found no ethical problem.

Scott R. Peppet, *The (New) Ethics of Collaborative Law*, Disp.Resol.Mag., Winter 2008, at 23, 25. To obtain the informed consent required by Model Rule 1.2(c), an attorney seeking a client's informed consent must communicate "adequate information and explanation about the material risks of and reasonably available alternatives to" the participation agreement. Model Rule 1.0(e). One of the obvious alternatives to a Collaborative Law representation is a traditional representation where an attorney would attempt to reach a settlement with the opposition, but would represent the client in litigation if settlement was not reached. Thus, Model Rules 1.0(e) and 1.2 presumably require an attorney to explain this traditional alternative to the Collaborative Law approach.

Thus, although Collaborative Law practice differs in significant ways from traditional practice, lawyers engaging in this form of practice must comply with the version of the Model Rules adopted in their state. *See* Robert F. Cochran, Jr., *Legal Ethics and Collaborative Practice Ethics*, 38 Hofstra L.Rev. 537, 537 (2009). In addition, the International Association of Collaborative Professionals has adopted a set of "Ethical Standards for Collaborative Practitioners." *See id.* at 538; *see also infra* section 6(C)(2), note 6 (discussing ethical codes adopted by specialty bars).

C(2) THE LAWYER AS NEUTRAL

RULE REFERENCES

Model Rules Preamble ¶ [3] and Model Rules 2.2 (deleted in 2002), 2.4, and 1.12

RESTATEMENT § 130

NOTES ON MEDIATOR AND ARBITRATOR PROFESSIONAL RESPONSIBILITY

1. **Lawyer as Intermediary:** Before the current version of the Model Rules, Model Rule 2.2 governed an attorney who served as an "intermediary" between multiple clients. Model Rule 2.2 was the first attempt to recognize that attorneys sometimes facilitate legal affairs for multiple clients with potentially adverse interests, such as those wishing to formalize business transactions, spouses seeking amicable divorces, or the donor and donee in a charitable contribution. Former Model Rule 2.2(a) permitted representation by a single attorney if the lawyer advised each party of the problems with joint representation and if the lawyer reasonably concluded that each client's interests could be protected, that each client could make informed decisions,

and that the joint representation could be undertaken impartially. Former Model Rule 2.2(b) required the lawyer to confer with each client about decisions and their implications. It also required the lawyer to withdraw from the joint representation if any client requested, or if the conditions required for joint representation ceased to exist. It prohibited the lawyer from representing any of the former clients regarding matters within the former joint representation.

Model Rule 2.2 was written several years before the widespread growth of ADR, which often involves an attorney acting as a third-party neutral in attempting to resolve a dispute between two or more parties who are separately represented by other attorneys. As the language of former Model Rule 2.2 indicates, it was designed for a different dynamic—the lawyer who represented two or more parties who were not separately represented by other attorneys. Though it was considered rather innovative when first included in the Model Rules and was widely adopted, Model Rule 2.2 was largely ignored and, later, criticized. According to Professor Carl Pierce, "Rule 2.2 has been criticized for its failure to clearly indicate what is meant by intermediation, its failure to clarify its relationship to [the conflict interest provisions of] Rule 1.7, its incomplete specification of the lawyer's duties when serving as an intermediary, and its unduly restrictive prohibition against a lawyer's continued representation of intermediation clients if any one of the clients withdraws from the intermediation." Carl A. Pierce, *ABA Model Rule 2.2: Once Applauded and Widely Adopted, Then Criticized, Ignored or Evaded, Now Sentenced to Death with Few Mourners, But Not In Tennessee*, 2 Transactions: Tenn.J.Bus.L. 9, 11 (2000).

This dissatisfaction led to an unusual step by the Ethics 2000 Commission. Model Rule 2.2 was the only rule deleted in its entirety by the 2002 revisions. A portion of the comments to the former rule were moved to the Model Rule 1.7 commentary. *See* Model Rule 1.7, Comments [29]–[33]. Though Model Rule 2.2 is no longer a part of the ABA's Model Rules, several states have retained versions of rules based on the former Model Rule 2.2. *See* Ala.R.Prof'l Conduct, R. 2.2; Haw.R.Prof'l Conduct, R. 2.2; Ind.R.Prof'l Conduct, R. 2.2; Mich.R.Prof'l Conduct, R. 2.2; Miss.R.Prof'l Conduct, R. 2.2 (containing several changes from original Model Rule 2.2 provisions); Nev. R.Prof'l Conduct, R. 2.2; Tenn.R.Prof'l Conduct, R. 2.2 (containing several changes from original Model Rule 2.2 provisions); W.Va.R.Prof'l Conduct, R. 2.2; Wyo.R.Prof'l Conduct, R. 2.2. Therefore, the rule has not yet become merely a historic relic.

2. **Lawyer as Dispute Resolution Neutral:** The current Model Rules give increased recognition to the role of attorneys as ADR neutrals. The Preamble's list of the common attorney roles of advocate, negotiator, and evaluator was supplemented with a separate paragraph, the Preamble's third, which noted the "nonrepresentational" attorney role of "third-party neutral" and briefly discussed this role. Professors Douglas Yarn and Wayne Thorpe, experts in ADR ethics, heralded this as "perhaps the most significant revision" of the Model Rules for those involved in ADR, because it signaled recognition of a new role for attorneys and also clarified that this role will be governed by the Model Rules, rather than the ABA's Model Code of Judicial Conduct. Douglas Yarn & Wayne Thorpe, *Ethics 2000: The ABA Proposes New*

Ethics Rules for Lawyer–Neutrals and Attorneys in ADR, Disp.Resol.Mag., Spring 2001, at 3, 4.

3. **Model Rule 2.4:** As Professors Yarn and Thorpe note, the black-letter rules governing lawyers who serve as mediators, arbitrators, or other neutrals take "a 'minimalist' approach, tackling only those ADR ethics issues specific to lawyers and creating or modifying existing Model Rules as little as possible." Yarn & Thorpe, *supra* note 2, at 3–4. Most of what the Model Rules say to lawyer neutrals is contained in Model Rule 2.4, "Lawyer Serving as Third–Party Neutral." This indisputably minimalist rule first explicitly permits a lawyer to serve as a third-party neutral, then requires the lawyer serving in this capacity to inform the parties that the lawyer is not representing them and, when necessary, to explain the difference between service as a third-party neutral and typical attorney representation. *See Griswold v. Griswold*, 942 N.E.2d 208 (Mass.App.Ct. 2011) (noting that an attorney who acted as a neutral in preparation of marital separation agreement, "consistent with the requirements of [Model Rule 2.4, had] informed them that he did not, would not, and could not represent either one of them"). Comment [3] suggests that the explanation of the difference in roles might be necessary when the parties are not represented by attorneys or when they are not veterans of ADR processes. Several courts already have cited Model Rule 2.4 or its Comments. *See, e.g., Papdopoulos v. Dhillon (In re Dhillon)*, No. 10–41700, 2011 WL 3651308, at *2 (Bankr.S.D.Ill. Aug. 13, 2011); *La Serena Props. v. Weisbach*, 112 Cal.Rptr.3d 597, 607, n.7 (Ct.App. 2010); *Matlock v. Rourk*, No. M2009–01109–COA–R3–CV, 2010 WL 2836638, at *3, n.5 (Tenn. Ct.App. July 20, 2010).

4. **ADR Roles and Conflicts of Interest:** If a lawyer serves as a mediator, arbitrator, or other neutral, can she later represent one of the parties in the same matter? Comment [4] to Model Rule 2.4 refers those contemplating this question to Model Rule 1.12. Model Rule 1.12 applies not only to former judges and arbitrators, but also to mediators, *see In re W.R.*, 966 N.E.2d 1139 (Ill.App.Ct. 2012); Va. State Bar Standing Comm. on Legal Ethics, Op. 1826 (2006), and other third-party neutrals. Model Rule 1.12(a) prohibits a lawyer who served in any of these roles from representing any party, *see Papdopoulos, supra* note 3, 2011 WL 3651308, at *3, except for an arbitrator who was selected as a partisan arbitrator by the party she later represents, *see* Model Rule 1.12(d). Model Rule 1.12(b) prohibits judges, arbitrators, mediators, and other third-party neutrals from negotiating for employment with a party or attorney appearing before her. For a somewhat lengthier discussion of these issues, see *supra* section 5(E), Notes on the Former Government Attorney's Current Firm, note 2.

5. **Imputing Third Party Neutral's Conflicts to Members of Firm:** If an attorney who served as a third-party neutral (or, for that matter, judge) is or becomes a member of a law firm, should other members of the firm also be prohibited from representing parties in the matters handled by the attorney as a neutral or judge? The Ethics 2000 Commission originally considered disqualifying all members of an ADR neutral's firm pursuant to the conflict of interest provisions of Model Rule 1.9, but later withdrew this proposal in favor of expanding Model Rule 1.12(c)'s less restrictive imputed disqualification provisions to mediators and other ADR neutrals, in addition

to arbitrators and judges. *See* Margaret Colgate Love, *The Revised ABA* Model Rules of Professional Conduct*: Summary of the Work of Ethics 2000*, 15 Geo.J. Legal Ethics 441, 462–63 (2002); Yarn & Thorpe, *supra* note 2, at 5.

Under current Model Rule 1.12(c), lawyers in the former neutral's or judge's firm may represent a party in the matter when the former neutral or judge is screened from any participation in the matter and receives no fees, if prompt written notice is provided to all parties. Consent of the unrepresented party is not required. The Ethics 2000 Commission allowed the screening and notice process after determining that ADR neutrals typically do not share confidential information with other lawyers and that not allowing representation by other lawyers in the disqualified lawyer's firm would "discourage arbitration and mediation practice by lawyers in firms, including participation in voluntary court-sponsored ADR programs." Love, *supra*, at 463. Is this the correct resolution of this issue? If you represented a client in an ADR proceeding and then faced a partner of the ADR neutral in further proceedings, how would you react? Would you be less likely to agree to an ADR proceeding in a future case?

6. **ADR Roles and Other Professional Codes:** Perhaps in recognition of the rather minimal restrictions placed on lawyers who serve as ADR neutrals by Model Rules 2.4 and 1.12, Comment [2] to Model Rule 2.4 notes that ADR neutrals may also be subject to the more expansive regulations in assorted industry, association, and voluntary codes of ethics. The most well-established of these codes is the Code of Ethics for Arbitrators in Commercial Disputes, written by the ABA and the American Arbitration Association ("AAA"), which was originally adopted in 1977 and updated by the AAA and ABA in 2004. *See* John D. Feerick, *The 1977 Code of Ethics for Arbitrators: An Outside Perspective*, 18 Ga.St.U.L.Rev. 907 (2002); Robert A. Holtzman, *The Role of Arbitrator Ethics*, 7 DePaul Bus. & Com.L.J. 481, 483 (2009). Its predecessor, the Rules of the American Arbitration Association, was quoted by the Supreme Court. *See Commw. Coatings Corp. v. Cont'l Cas. Co.*, 393 U.S. 145 (1968) (with Justice Black's opinion announcing the decision noting that the AAA Rules, though not controlling in the case, required an arbitrator to disclose possible bias and Justice White's concurring opinion noting that an arbitrator should only be required to disclose "a substantial interest in a firm which has done more than trivial business with a party"). As Comment [2] notes, another prominent code is the Model Standards of Conduct for Mediators drafted by the ABA, the AAA, and the Society of Professionals in Dispute Resolution. *See* Paula M. Young, *Rejoice! Rejoice! Rejoice, Give Thanks, and Sing: ABA, ACR, and AAA Adopt Revised Model Standards of Conduct for Mediators*, 5 Appalachian J.L. 195 (2006); Laura E. Weidner, Comment, *Model Standards of Conduct for Mediators (2005)*, 21 Ohio St.J. on Disp.Resol. 547 (2006). Other ethics codes include the National Academy of Arbitrator's Code of Professional Responsibility and the ABA's Standards of Practice for Lawyer Mediators in Family Disputes.

In some respects, these largely voluntary codes harken back to the aspirational canons adopted for all lawyers shortly after the turn of the last century. *See supra* section 1(A). Because these ADR codes have not been incorporated into the Model Rules, they do not carry the same coercive force as a particular state's versions of the Model Rules, which can be enforced through a state's disciplinary system. How are these codes "enforced"? Because many mediators and arbitrators are chosen and hired by parties, does the market for their services provide a means for enforcing ethical standards? Should parties who suffer from a violation of these codes be allowed to sue mediators and arbitrators for malpractice and offer the codes into evidence? If these codes conflict with a state's version of the Model Rules, which should be followed by a lawyer who is serving as a mediator or arbitrator? Should the ADR codes evolve into mandatory rules that can be enforced through the attorney discipline system? Will they? At least one state, Florida, has adopted an enforcement mechanism. *See* Sharon Press, *Standards ... and Results: Florida Provides Forum for Grievances Against Mediators*, Disp.Resol.Mag., Spring 2001, at 8; *see also Judicial Council of California Adopts Ethics Standards for Private Arbitrators*, 13 World Arb. & Med.Rep. 176 (2002).

Arbitration and mediation also have been the subject of uniform statutes containing some provisions covering a few of the topics discussed in this text outside of ADR. Almost every state based its arbitration statute on the 1955 Uniform Arbitration Act drafted by the National Conference of Commissioners on Uniform State Laws (NCCUSL). *See* Timothy J. Heinsz, *The Revised Uniform Arbitration Act: Modernizing, Revising, and Clarifying Arbitration Law*, 2001 J.Disp.Resol. 1. NCCUSL revised this uniform statute in 2000. It prohibits a person with a direct material interest in the outcome of a proceeding from serving as a neutral arbitrator, requires an arbitrator to disclose financial or personal interests that could affect her impartiality, and protects an arbitrator from testifying in court in most circumstances. *See* Revised Uniform Arbitration Act §§ 11(b), 12(a)(1) & 14 (2000). Its much younger cousin, the Uniform Mediation Act, was adopted by NCCUSL in 2001 and by the ABA in 2002. It provides a privilege against disclosure of information by a mediator, requires confidentiality to the extent agreed upon by the parties, requires prospective mediators to disclose conflicts of interest, and mandates mediator neutrality in most circumstances. *See* Uniform Mediation Act §§ 4, 8 & 9 (2001). In the absence of a statute creating a privilege against testimony or other disclosure by a mediator of matters revealed in mediation, can a mediator promise non-disclosure? If the parties agree that they will not call the mediator as a witness before the mediation begins, should this agreement be enforceable against them, or does the general doctrine that a jury is entitled to every person's evidence trump the contract claim? What if the party calling the mediator as a witness at a later trial was not a party to the mediation or the mediation contract?

7. **Non–Lawyers as ADR Neutrals:** As Comment [2] to Model Rule 2.4 notes, non-lawyers also serve as mediators, arbitrators, evaluators, conciliators, or other neutrals in ADR procedures. Should such service be considered the "practice of law," *see supra* section 2(D)(1), at least in some contexts? *See Bowater Inc. v. Zager*, 901 So.2d 658, 670–71 (Ala. 2004) (holding that non-lawyers could serve as arbitrators in Alabama); Or. Judicial Dep't Ct.–Connected Mediator Qualifications Rules, § 2.2 (providing that those with qualifying bachelor's, master's, doctoral, and law degrees are eligible to become mediators).

D. LAWYER AS JUDGE

PROBLEM

Tom Calvin, Ben Bigsby, and Steve Sargent have been friends since grade school. Their annual fishing trips, which even survived Tom's three rough years in law school, have become so popular that they now involve not only themselves, but their brothers and dozens of friends that they have met over the thirty years since high school. They facetiously call their loose knit group the "Fishing Forever Club." The "club" and its annual week long fishing and camping trips involve only men, supposedly because most of the "members" are married and they do not wish to upset their wives.

On a boat one summer, Ben asked Tom about the latest area scandal, which involved a high school teacher who allegedly engaged in sexual relationships with her students. "If you were a judge a year from now and she came up for sentencing," Ben asked, "what would you do?" Tom replied, "That is easy. She would get the max. So would almost every criminal who came before me."

Enthused by this response, Ben turned to Steve and said, "That settles it. You and I are going to start up the 'Tom Calvin for Judge' Committee right now." In the next few days, Ben and Steve secured large contributions to the Committee from each of the other twenty men on the trip. They also secured promises from their fellow fisherman to "write letters to the editor and letters to the people who count" on behalf of Tom, and the men followed through on these promises by writing letters describing how tough on crime Tom would be, and how weak his opponent would be.

QUESTIONS

(a) Assume that Tom was a practicing lawyer, but that he announced his candidacy for election to a state judgeship the week before the trip. Has he engaged in misconduct?

(b) Now assume that Tom was hoping to be named to the federal judgeship that opened up when the sitting judge died a month before the trip. Has he engaged in misconduct?

(c) Now assume that Tom was a sitting state court judge at the time of the trip, that he was assigned to the teacher's case, and that he was seeking re-election. Has he engaged in misconduct?

(d) Now assume Ben and another fishermen are lawyers. Have they engaged in misconduct?

RULE REFERENCES

Model Rules 8.2, 3.5, 8.4, 7.6, 1.12, and 8.3(b)

Model Code of Judicial Conduct (all except Rules 2.9 and 2.11 (formerly Canons 3B(7), 3E, and 3F))

RESTATEMENT §§ 113 & 114

D(1) THE LAWYER AS CANDIDATE FOR A JUDGESHIP

NOTES ON JUDICIAL ELECTION AND SELECTION

1. **Applicability of Code of Judicial Conduct to Candidates:** Model Rule 8.2(b) requires lawyers who are candidates for judgeships to follow the portions of the Model Code of Judicial Conduct applicable to candidates for judgeships. The Code of Judicial Conduct's Terminology section defines "judicial candidate" to include those who have publicly announced their intention to seek a judgeship, have declared or filed a certification of candidacy, have been nominated for election or appointment, or have authorized or participated in campaign fundraising.

2. **Judicial Candidate Statements About Issues:** When it was originally drafted in 1972, the Code of Judicial Conduct included an "announce clause," which prohibited a judicial candidate from announcing her views on political and legal issues. Concerns over the perhaps limited prospects for this clause withstanding scrutiny under the First Amendment led the ABA to replace the announce clause with a "commitment clause" when it revised the Code in 1990. In its 1990 iteration, Canon 5A(3)(d)(ii), the commitment clause, prohibited judicial candidates from "mak[ing] statements that commit or appear to commit the candidate with respect to cases, controversies or issues that are likely to come before the court." This provision was accompanied by the "pledges or promises clause," Canon 5A(3)(d)(i), which prohibited a judicial candidate from making a promise or pledge regarding her conduct in office, other than a commitment to faithfully and impartially perform the duties of the office.

Concerns about the constitutionality of the announce clause proved to be well-founded. In a 5–4 vote in *Republican Party of Minn. v. White*, 536 U.S. 765 (2002), the Supreme Court held that Minnesota's announce clause impermissibly restrained First Amendment free speech rights. In an opinion joined by three justices, Justice Scalia rejected the bar's argument that the announce clause was needed to protect judicial impartiality. *See* 536 U.S. at 774–84. Justice Scalia's opinion announcing the decision of the court also contended that Justice Ginsburg's dissent supporting the announce clause, which was written for four justices, "greatly exaggerate[d] the difference between judicial and legislative elections." *Id.* at 784.

The full impact of *White* is not yet known, because only nine states still had announce clauses at the time of the decision. *See* Cynthia Gray, *The States' Response to* Republican Party of Minnesota v. White, Judicature, Nov./Dec. 2002, at 163, 163. The Supreme Court said it was making no decision regarding the pledges and promises clause. *See White*, 536 U.S. at 770. The status of the commitment clause is unclear, because the *White* respondents argued that, as interpreted and applied by the courts, the announce clause was no broader than the commitment clause. *Id.* at 773 n.5. Justice Scalia's opinion stated, "We do not know whether the announce clause (as interpreted by state authorities) and the [commitment clause] are one and the same. No aspect of our constitutional analysis turns on this question." *Id.*;

cf. Bauer v. Shepard, 620 F.3d 704 (7th Cir. 2010) (upholding Indiana's commitment clause).

Although the impact of *White* on the 1990 "commitment" and "pledges and promises" clauses was unknown at the time, the ABA revised these clauses in 2003. *See* 1990 Version of the ABA Model Code of Judicial Conduct, Canon 5A(3)(d) n.*, in John S. Dzienkowski, Professional Responsibility Standards, Rules & Statutes 629 (abridged ed. 2010–2011). The ABA's latest iteration of the Model Code, adopted in 2007, includes what could be described as an "affect the outcome or impair fairness of pending or impending matter" clause and a "pledges, promises, or commitments in issues likely to come before the court" clause. Rule 4.1(A) of the 2007 Model Code of Judicial Conduct states (subject to some exceptions) that judicial candidates shall not:

(12) make any statement that would reasonably be expected to affect the outcome or impair the fairness of a matter pending or impending in any court; or

(13) in connection with cases, controversies, or issues that are likely to come before the court, make pledges, promises, or commitments that are inconsistent with the impartial performance of the adjudicative duties of judicial office.

Rules 4.1(A)(12) and (13) ban substantially less judicial candidate speech than the original "announce" clause, and at least a bit less judicial candidate speech than the 1990 "commitment" and "pledges and promises" clauses. Are these new provisions reasonable resolutions of the tension between judicial impartiality and free speech, which generally warrants significant protection in the campaign and election context? *See* David K. Stott, Comment, *Zero–Sum Judicial Elections: Balancing Free Speech and Impartiality Through Recusal Reform*, 2009 BYU L.Rev. 481. Would you allow less speech by judicial candidates than Rules 4.1(A)(12) and (13)? More? Are judicial elections different than other elections? Can you have an election without a campaign where candidates announce how they intend to act in office? Is the problem, as Justice O'Connor's *White* concurrence suggests, the state's decision to hold judicial elections instead of appointing judges? *See also* Charles Gardner Geyh, *Why Judicial Elections Stink*, 64 Ohio St.L.J. 43 (2003). Is it significant that this suggestion came from the only member of the *White* Court who was ever elected to judicial office?

3. **Misstatements by or About Judicial Candidates:** Rule 4.1(A)(11) (formerly Canon 5A(3)(d)(ii)) prohibits a candidate from making a knowingly or recklessly false or misleading statement in an attempt to secure a judgeship. Model Rule 8.2(a) prohibits a lawyer from knowingly or recklessly making a false statement about the integrity or qualifications of a candidate for judge, a judge, or another "adjudicatory officer or public legal officer." *See Disciplinary Counsel v. Gallo*, 2012–Ohio–758, 964 N.E.2d 1024 (publicly reprimanding attorney under Model Rule 8.2 for filing affidavit accusing judge of abuse of office without first adequately investigating, despite attorney's immediate motion to withdraw affidavit upon realizing he was mistaken); *State ex rel. Okla. Bar Ass'n v. Wilcox*, 2009 OK 81, ¶ 65, 227 P.3d 642, 663 (publicly reprimanding an attorney for "recklessly making a false statement about a judicial candidate"); *Moseley v. Va. State Bar*, 694 S.E.2d 586, 588

(Va. 2010) (suspending attorney who, inter alia, wrote a letter with false accusations that the judge " 'was bribed' "); *see also* RESTATEMENT, § 114. Some have argued that attorneys should have the right to question a judge's integrity. *See* Margaret Tarkington, *A Free Speech Right to Impugn Judicial Integrity in Court Proceedings*, 51 B.C.L.Rev. 363 (2010). Some courts have rejected First Amendment challenges to Model Rule 8.2(a). *See Statewide Grievance Comm. v. Burton*, 10 A.3d 507, 513 (Conn. 2011); *Ky. Bar Ass'n v. Deters*, 360 S.W.3d 224, 230 (Ky. 2012). Others have attempted to balance First Amendment concerns and the need for respect for the judiciary, thereby indicating that the First Amendment does indeed limit the reach of Model Rule 8.2(a). *See In re Pyle*, 156 P.3d 1231, 1242–44 (Kan. 2007); *Bd. of Prof'l Resp. v. Davidson*, 2009 WY 48, ¶ 21, 205 P.3d 1008, 1017.

4. **Additional Restrictions on All Judicial Candidates:** The Code of Judicial Conduct contains some restrictions, in addition to those already discussed, *see supra* notes 1–3, that apply to all judicial candidates, including sitting judges. Judicial candidates cannot serve as officers or leaders of, or speak for, political organizations, Rule 4.1(A)(1)–(2) (formerly Canon 5A(1)(a) & (c)), raise funds for candidates or political organizations, Rule 4.1(A)(4) (formerly Canon 5A(1)(e)), publicly identify themselves as candidates of political organizations (except in partisan elections), Rule 4.1(A)(6), seek or accept political organization endorsements (except in partisan elections), Rule 4.1(A)(7), or personally solicit or accept campaign contributions, Rule 4.1(A)(8) (formerly Canon 5C(2)). A judicial candidate cannot use, or allow others to use, campaign contributions for private benefit. Rule 4.1(A)(9) (formerly Canon 5C(2)). A sitting judge cannot use court staff, facilities, or resources to support her candidacy. Rule 4.1(A)(10). Also, a judicial candidate must "take reasonable measures to ensure" that their supporters do not engage in conduct that Rule 4.1(A) bans for the judicial candidate. Rule 4.1(B) (formerly Canon 5A(3)(b)).

5. **Candidates for Judicial Election:** The Code contains additional restrictions that apply to candidates for election to judgeships, in either multi-candidate or retention elections. Rule 4.2(A)(1) (formerly Canon 5A(3)(a)) requires a candidate for judicial election to act "in a manner consistent with the independence, integrity, and impartiality of the judiciary." The Code also requires candidates for judicial election to comply with all election laws, Rule 4.2(A)(2), to review and approve all campaign statements, Rule 4.2(A)(3), and to work to ensure that campaign supporters do not engage in prohibited activities, Rule 4.2(A)(4) (formerly Canon 5A(3)(c)). In addition, candidates for judicial election cannot publicly oppose or endorse candidates for office other than the one they seek. Rule 4.1(A)(3) (formerly Canon 5A(1)(b)) & Rule 4.2(B)(3)).

The Code of Judicial Conduct allows judicial election candidates to engage in several activities that are usually prohibited for candidates for appointive judicial office, *see infra* note 8, including forming campaign committees, Rule 4.2(B)(1) (formerly Canon 5C(2)), *see infra* note 6, speaking and advertising in support of their candidacy, Rule 4.2(B)(2) (formerly Canon 5C(1)(b)(i)–(iii)), endorsing others for the same judicial office, Rule 4.2(B)(3) (formerly Canon 5C(1)(b)(iv)), purchasing tickets for and attending political events, Rule 4.2(B)(4) (formerly Canon 5C(1)(a)(i)), seeking endorsements from nonpartisan organizations, Rule 4.2(B)(5), and contributing, up to specified amounts, to political organizations and candidates, Rule 4.2(B)(6) (formerly 5C(1)(a)(iii)). If the judicial election is partisan, the Code of Judicial Conduct also allows a candidate to identify herself as a candidate of, Rule 4.2(C)(1) (formerly Canon 5C(1)(a)(ii)), and seek and use the endorsement of, Rule 4.2(C)(2), a political organization.

6. **Judicial Election Campaign Contributions and Other Support:** The Code allows candidates in judicial elections to form campaign committees for the receipt and spending of campaign contributions. Rules 4.2(B)(1) & 4.4(A) (formerly Canon 5C(2)); *see also* Rule 4.1(A)(8) (allowing solicitation of and acceptance of campaign contributions through a campaign committee in a judicial election).

Rule 4.4 regulates campaign committees in judicial elections. Pursuant to Rule 4.4(A), the judicial candidate is responsible for ensuring that her committee complies with the Code and other law. Rule 4.4(B)(1) (formerly Canon 5C(2)–(3)) allows the campaign committee to seek and accept contributions, but only in "reasonable" amounts, with the possibility of a jurisdiction setting maximum contribution levels for individual or organizational donors. Rule 4.4(B)(2) (formerly Canon 5C(2)) allows jurisdictions to set starting and ending dates for judicial campaign fundraising. Rule 4.4(B)(3) (formerly Canon 5C(4)) requires the campaign committee to report all contributions above a designated level to the jurisdiction's designated election authorities and to comply with other election laws.

Can a judicial election candidate personally ask for campaign contributions or other support? Historically, the answer was "no," due to concerns about interference with judicial integrity and independence, but parts of that prohibition may be softening. After *White, supra* note 2, the Eleventh Circuit held that a rule prohibiting judicial candidates from personally requesting or accepting contributions or statements of support, like the one in former Canon 5C(2), was unconstitutional. *See Weaver v. Bonner*, 309 F.3d 1312 (11th Cir. 2002). The Eighth Circuit, sitting en banc, disagreed, *see Wersal v. Sexton*, 674 F.3d 1010, 1028–31 (8th Cir. 2012 (en banc)), as did a federal district court, *see Wolfson v. Brammer*, 822 F.Supp.2d 925, 929–30 (D.Ariz. 2011) (upholding Arizona's prohibition of personal solicitation of campaign contributions by judicial candidates). Rule 4.1(A)(8) still states that a judicial candidate may not "personally solicit or accept campaign contributions other than through a campaign committee." Comment [1] to Rule 4.4 cites this provision when reiterating that "[j]udicial candidates are prohibited from personally soliciting campaign contributions or personally accepting campaign contributions." However, the ban in former Canon 5C(2) on judicial candidates "personally solicit[ing] publicly stated support" did not find its way into the 2007 revision of the Model Code of Judicial Conduct.

7. **Campaign Contributions by Lawyers and Litigants:** Comment [3] to Rule 4.4 (in language somewhat akin to that in Comment [1] to former Canon 5C(2)) states:

> Although lawyers and others who might appear before a successful candidate for judicial office are permitted to make campaign contributions, the candidate should instruct his or her campaign committee to be

especially cautious in connection with such contributions, so they do not create grounds for disqualification if the candidate is elected to judicial office. See Rule 2.11.

An attempt by a lawyer to use campaign contributions to influence or bribe a judge regarding a particular case would presumably violate Model Rule 3.5(a)'s prohibition of illegal efforts to influence a judge and Model Rule 8.4's prohibitions of committing dishonest criminal acts, engaging in dishonest, fraudulent, or deceitful conduct, prejudicing the administration of justice, and knowingly assisting a judge in a judicial misconduct. *See In re Bolton*, 2002–0257 (La. 6/21/02); 820 So.2d 548 (affirming, over vigorous dissents, a hearing committee's factual conclusion that an attorney did not intentionally attempt to influence the judge with proposed campaign contributions, thereby confirming that such conduct would violate Model Rule 8.4 if proven); *see also* RESTATEMENT, § 113(2) (2000). Such an effort usually would also violate Model Rule 3.5(b)'s prohibition of ex parte contact with a judge, *see Bolton, supra; see also* RESTATEMENT, § 113(1), as well as Model Rule 8.4(e)'s ban on statements or implications by a lawyer of an ability to improperly influence a government official. Also, Model Rule 7.6 prevents a lawyer from accepting employment or a legal engagement by a judge or other government official after soliciting or making campaign contributions in exchange for being considered for the appointment or legal engagement.

The legal, political, and ethical issues surrounding judicial elections make for an unsettling and volatile mix. Concerns about judicial integrity and independence, as well as public confidence in the judicial system, lead to rules limiting contributions by lawyers and litigants and rules banning personal campaign fundraising by judicial candidates. In an infamous instance where state rules were not sufficient to stop a huge campaign contribution to a judicial candidate who became the judge casting the key vote on an appellate case of importance to the contributor, the U.S. Supreme Court found that the sordid affair constituted a due process violation in *Caperton v. A.T. Massey Coal Co., Inc.*, 556 U.S. 868 (2009), *see supra* section 5F(1), note 1. Pushing in the other direction, First Amendment and other constitutional principles sometimes cause courts and others to reject limitations on political activity. After holding that announce clause unconstitutionally restrained judicial candidates free speech rights in *White, see supra* note 2, the same U.S. Supreme Court that decided *Caperton* also struck down non-judicial campaign restrictions on political activity in *Citizens United v. Federal Election Commission*, 130 S.Ct. 876 (2010).

In a mix this dynamic, involving multiple sources of law that include, but are not limited to, the Model Code of Judicial Conduct, its state counterparts, the Model Rules, their state counterparts, federal statutes regulating judicial conduct, state and federal election law, the First Amendment, and the Due Process Clause, it is not wise to predict the future law regulating judicial elections, except to predict continued volatility. At press time for this text, the ABA was expected to consider proposed amendments to the Model Code of Judicial Conduct that would require judicial candidates to do more to track campaign contributions and their possible influence on litigated cases. *See* John Gibeaut, *Show Me the Money: States and the ABA Try to Figure Out When Campaign Cash Adds Up to a Judge's Recusal*, ABA J., Mar. 2012, at

48, 50. It is perhaps understandable that the provisions of the Code of Judicial Conduct regulating judicial campaigns seem to be in a state of continual revision.

8. **Candidates for Appointed Judgeships:** Those seeking appointment to judgeships are subject to all of the restrictions that apply to all judicial candidates, as described *supra* in notes 1–4. In addition, they are subject to several restrictions that do not generally apply to candidates for judicial election. They cannot publicly oppose or endorse other candidates for any office, Rule 4.1(A)(3) (formerly Canon 5A(1)(b)), make contributions to political organizations or candidates, Rule 4.1(A)(4) (formerly Canon 5A(1)(e)), or buy tickets for or attend political gatherings, Rule 4.1(A)(5) (formerly Canon 5A(1)(e)). They cannot seek or accept contributions supporting their judicial candidacy, either personally or through a committee. Rule 4.1(A)(8) (formerly Canon 5B(1)).

The Code also contains two explicit statements about permitted activity by candidates for judicial appointment. Rule 4.3(A) (formerly Canon 5B(2)(a)(i)) allows such a candidate to communicate with those who will nominate or select the judge. Rule 4.3(B) (formerly Canon 5B(2)(a)(ii)) allows appointment candidates to seek non-partisan endorsements from individual or group supporters.

9. **Judges as Candidates for Non–Judicial Office:** Rule 4.5(A) (formerly Canon 5A(2)) requires a judges to resign from judicial office upon becoming a candidate for a non-judicial elective office. *See In re Dunleavy*, 2003 ME 124, ¶¶ 7–24, 838 A.2d 338, 345–48 (enforcing predecessor provision against probate judge who ran for state senate). Rule 4.5(B) does not require a judge to resign upon becoming a candidate for a non-judicial appointive office.

D(2) THE LAWYER'S JUDICIAL CONDUCT

IN RE SCHAPIRO

Supreme Court of Florida, 2003.
845 So.2d 170.

PER CURIAM.

We review the recommendation of the Judicial Qualifications Commission (JQC) that Judge Sheldon Schapiro be disciplined. * * * In a stipulation with the JQC, Judge Schapiro admits engaging in inappropriate behavior in court that is unbecoming a member of the judiciary, brings the judiciary into disrepute, and impairs the citizens' confidence both in the integrity of the judicial system and in Judge Schapiro as a judge.

The stipulation, which quotes the notice of formal charges directed to Judge Schapiro, sets forth the facts as follows:

> **Charge No. 1**—In violation of Canon 1,[a] Canon 2A, and Canon 3B(4), * * * you chastised an attorney, Joseph Dawson, for allegedly speaking in your courtroom by stating, "Why do I always have to treat you

---

a. [This decision predates the 2007 revision of the Model Code of Judicial Conduct. As a result, the references in the decision use the pre–2007 numbering. Eds.]

like a school child?" or words to that effect. When Mr. Dawson responded that you routinely treat everyone in your courtroom like a school child, you ordered him out of the courtroom. Since that time, Mr. Dawson has routinely sought your recusal and you have granted those requests.

Charg[es Nos. 2 and 3]—In violation of Canon 1, Canon 2A, and Canon 3B(4), [you refused reasonable requests for continuances and screamed at an attorney.]

Charge No. 4—In violation of Canon 1, Canon 2A, and Canon 3B(4), you have routinely berated and unnecessarily embarrassed attorneys for allegedly talking in your courtroom when those attorneys were either not talking at all or speaking in appropriately low tones of voice concerning legitimate business of the court (e.g. state attorneys and defense counsel conferring with one another concerning plea negotiations). * * *

Charge No. 6—In violation of Canon 1, Canon 2A, and Canon 3B(4), several years ago, as a criminal defense attorney was making an argument in a sexual battery case, you cut him off and said, "Do you know what I think of your argument?" or words to that effect, at which time you pushed a button on a device that simulated the sound of a commode flushing.

Charge No. 7—In violation of Canon 1, Canon 2A, and Canon 3B(4), in a case involving a defendant driving with a suspended driver's license approximately four years ago, Louis Pironti, an assistant public defender at the time, advised you during a sidebar conference that he might need a continuance in order to secure an expert witness. The sidebar was held in a small room behind the bench commonly known as the woodshed among attorneys familiar with your courtroom (hereinafter "backroom"). Instead of simply denying the motion, you became agitated and responded by saying to Mr. Pironti, "You're going to try this mother fu_ing case." You then returned to the bench and threw the docket down on a desk.

Charge No. 8—In violation of Canon 1, Canon 2A, Canon 3B(4), and Canon 3B(5), * * * as Shari Tate, a female assistant state attorney, was arguing a motion to revoke bond, you summoned Ms. Tate to the backroom behind your bench and told her that she needed to emulate the style of male attorneys when addressing the court because male attorneys did not get as emotional about their cases as the female attorneys did. As a result of this experience, Ms. Tate advised you that she would never go to the backroom with you again without a court reporter being present.

Charge No. 9—In violation of Canon 1, Canon 2A, and Canon 3B(4), in another incident involving Ms. Tate when she was eight months pregnant, she was hospitalized because of pregnancy complications on the third day of a trial over which you presided. As a result of her hospitalization, Ms. Tate requested a continuance of the trial. You denied the continuance and further advised Ms. Tate that she should get another prosecutor from her office to complete the trial. When Ms. Tate advised your chambers that "substituting" counsel was not feasible in that no other assistant state attorney was familiar enough with the case to step in her place, you, or your chambers, advised Ms. Tate that if she were not in court the following morning, you would dismiss the case. As a result, Ms. Tate left the hospital against her doctor's orders in order to complete the trial before you.

Charge No. 10—In violation of Canon 1, Canon 2A, and Canon 3B(4), * * * you presided over a bond hearing where a motorcyclist had killed a child and left the scene. The child's mother and neighbor came to the bond hearing, which was approximately two days after the incident and before the child was buried. After you made a preliminary determination that the defendant was entitled to bond, the assistant state attorney advised you that the mother of the victim was present and wanted to address the court. You responded by saying, "What do I need to hear from the mother of a [deceased][1] kid for? All she will tell me is to keep the guy in custody and never let him out" or words to that effect. The victim's mother heard your sarcastic remarks and was then afraid to address the court.

Charge No. 11—In violation of Canon 1, Canon 2A, and Canon 3B(4), you have fallen into a general pattern of rude and intemperate behavior by needlessly interjecting yourself into counsel's examinations of witnesses; embarrassing and belittling counsel in court; and questioning the competence of counsel by making remarks such as, "What, are you stupid?" * * *

We agree with the JQC's determination that Judge Sheldon Schapiro has violated the Code of Judicial Conduct. We conclude that Judge Schapiro has clearly undermined the public's confidence in and respect for both the integrity of the judicial system and Judge Schapiro as a judge. These violations are extreme in their seriousness, in their number, and in the length of time over which they occurred. To undermine public confidence and respect by such serious violations strikes at the very roots of an effective judiciary, for those who are served by the courts will not have confidence in and respect for the courts' judgments if judges engage in this egregious conduct. Were it not for Judge Schapiro's efforts to participate in behavioral therapy, this Court would have sanctioned Judge Schapiro in a substantially more severe manner. Judge Schapiro is expressly notified that if his efforts do not consistently continue as agreed to in the stipulation, this Court will severely sanction Judge Schapiro's misconduct.

In view of the stipulation and the [judge's] ongoing treatment program, we approve the [JQC's] recommendation of a public reprimand and a continual treatment program but also order Judge Schapiro to, within

---

1. The original Notice of Formal Charges alleged that Judge Schapiro used the word "dead" instead of "deceased." Judge Schapiro denies that he used the word "dead;" rather, he contends he used the word "deceased." Regardless of the actual verbiage used, however, Judge Schapiro admits that his statement was inappropriate under the circumstances.

thirty days of the filing of this opinion, write and mail personal letters of apology to those individuals identified in the above-quoted portion of the stipulation.

NOTES ON JUDICIAL CONDUCT

1. **Promotion of Respect for the Office of Judge:** As *Schapiro* demonstrates, many of the Code of Judicial Conduct's restrictions on judges are designed to protect and enhance respect for the judiciary and judicial impartiality. *See* Stephanie Cotilla & Amanda Suzanne Veal, *Judicial Balancing Act: The Appearance of Impartiality and the First Amendment*, 15 Geo.J. Legal Ethics 741 (2002). Canon 1 admonishes judges to "uphold and promote the independence, integrity, and impartiality of the judiciary" and to "avoid impropriety and the appearance of impropriety." Canon 2 commands judges to "perform the duties of judicial office impartially, competently, and diligently." Pursuant to Canon 3, a judge "shall conduct the judge's personal and extrajudicial activities to minimize the risk of conflict with the obligations of judicial office." Many of the more specific restrictions in the Codes' Rules are also designed to augment judicial reputation and impartiality.

2. **Avoiding Bias or Prejudice:** Rules 2.3(A) and 2.3(B) (formerly Canon 3B(5)) require judges to act without prejudice or bias and to refrain from words or conduct manifesting bias, prejudice, or harassment based upon "race, sex, gender, religion, national origin, ethnicity, disability, age, sexual orientation, marital status, socioeconomic status, or political affiliation." *See also In re Govendo*, No. 2008–SLD–0001–JDA, 2010 WL 4955947 (N.Mar.I. Dec. 1, 2010) (disciplining judge who made disparaging remarks about Filipinos). Rule 2.3(C) (formerly Canon 3B(6)) instructs judges to require lawyers appearing before them to refrain from such bias, prejudice, and harassment, but Rule 2.3(D) (formerly Canon 3B(6)) allows legitimate advocacy based on the listed factors.

Rule 2.4(B) (formerly Canon 2B) tells judges not to be influenced by concerns like their relationships with family and friends or political and financial interests. Rule 3.3 (formerly Canon 2B) prevents a judge from voluntarily testifying as a character witness. *But see Sansone v. Garvey, Schubert & Barer*, 71 P.3d 124 (Or.Ct.App. 2003) (allowing judge to testify in attorney malpractice trial regarding defendant law firm's handling of underlying trial). Rule 3.6 forbids judges from belonging to, or benefitting from, organizations that practice "invidious discrimination on the basis of race, sex, gender, religion, national origin, ethnicity, or sexual orientation."

3. **Public Comments by Judges:** A judge's public comments can run afoul of the Code's prohibitions. As noted in *supra* section 6(A)(3), note 8, Rule 2.10(A) (formerly Canon 3B(9)) restricts public comments by a judge about pending or impending litigation. These rules prohibit a judge from making "any public statement that might reasonably be expected to affect the outcome or impair the fairness of a matter pending or impending in any court." Rule 2.10(C) (formerly Canon 3B(9)) extends the practical reach of this provision by mandating that judges require their subordinates refrain from such comments. However, the 2007 version of the Code includes a new

provision permitting the judge to "respond directly or through a third party to allegations in the media or elsewhere concerning the judge's conduct in a matter," unless the response would affect the outcome or impair the fairness of the trial or hearing. Rule 2.10(E).

Rule 2.10(B) (previously Canon 3B(10)) prevents judges from making "pledges, promises or commitments" about pending or likely litigation that are inconsistent with "the impartial performance of the adjudicative duties of judicial office." Rule 3.5 (formerly Canon 3B(12)) forbids a judge from disclosing or using nonpublic information she acquires as a judge for purposes outside judicial duties. Rule 2.8(C) (formerly Canon 3B(11)) prohibits the judge from complimenting or criticizing the jury for its verdict, except in an opinion or court order.

4. **Requiring Order in the Courtroom:** Pursuant to Rule 2.8(A) (formerly Canon 3B(3)), judges must require order and decorum in court. As *Schapiro* makes clear, Rule 2.8(B) (formerly Canon 3B(4), as repeatedly cited in *Shapiro*) orders judges to "be patient, dignified, and courteous" to parties, jurors, witnesses, attorneys, and others, and to require attorneys, judicial staff members, and court personnel to behave in a similar fashion. Judges must also give all who have a legal interest at stake a chance to be heard. Rule 2.6(A) (formerly Canon 3B(7)). Although judges can encourage settlement, they cannot coerce any party to settle. Rule 2.6(B) (formerly Comment [1] to Canon 3B(8)).

5. **Timeliness:** Rule 2.1 (formerly Canon 3A) requires a judge to give her judicial duties precedence over all of her personal and other "extrajudicial" activities. Rule 2.7 (formerly Canon 3B(1)) compels a judge to hear and decide all matters assigned to her, absent recusal. Similarly, Rule 2.2 (formerly Canons 3B(2) and 3B(8)) requires a judge to apply and uphold the law and to perform duties "fairly and impartially." Inattention to cases, including those taken under advisement, is a not infrequent basis for complaints and discipline against judges. *See Disciplinary Counsel v. Squire,* 2007–Ohio–5588, ¶ 95, 876 N.E.2d 933, 950 (finding that a judge's "misconduct personifies the expression 'justice delayed is justice denied,' " because "her failure to make rulings in pending cases demeaned attorneys and litigants in her court, causing them to seek justice in the courtrooms of other judges").

6. **Limitations on Non–Judicial Activities of Judges:** Several Code provisions limit a judge's non-judicial activities. Rule 3.11(C) (formerly Canon 4D(1)) outlaws business or financial activities that interfere with judicial duties, lead to frequent recusal, or involve repeated business interaction with lawyers or others who are likely to be in the judge's court. Rule 3.11(B) (formerly Canon 4D(3)) precludes a judge from serving as an employee, manager, general partner, officer, or director of a business, unless it is owned by the judge's family or it primarily manages investments for the judge or her family. Subject to these and other restrictions in the Code, a judge is allowed to manage her investments and those of her family. Rule 3.11(A) (formerly Canon 4D(2)). Rule 3.8(A) (formerly Canon 4E) applies similar restrictions to a judge's service as a fiduciary.

A judge cannot consult with an executive or legislative body or appear at a public hearing, except regarding matters concerning the administration of justice, the legal system, the law, the expertise she gained as a judge, or the judge's own interests. Rule 3.2 (formerly Canon 4C(1)). She cannot take an appointment to a government commission or committee unless it concerns the law, the legal system, or the administration of justice. Rule 3.4 (formerly Canon 4C(2)). She can be a director, officer, trustee, or "nonlegal advisor" for a governmental agency or organization dedicated to improvement of the administration of justice or the legal system or a nonprofit religious, educational, fraternal, charitable, or civic group, except where such activities would violate the Code. Rule 3.7(A) (formerly Canon 4C(3)). She cannot serve in such a capacity if the organization is likely to be involved in litigation before the judge or her court. Rule 3.7(A)(6) (formerly Canon 4C(3)(a)). Rule 3.7 (formerly Canon 4C) contains other limitations on a judge's activities for educational, religious, charitable, fraternal, or civic organizations.

A judge cannot practice law, but she can provide free legal assistance to family members, if it does not include representation in a forum. Rule 3.10 (formerly Canon 4G). She also cannot act as a mediator or arbitrator, aside from doing so in her official capacity. Rule 3.9 (formerly Canon 4F). She can be reasonably compensated, and be reimbursed her expenses, for permissible extrajudicial activities and reimbursed for related expenses, as long as such compensation does not interfere with her "independence, integrity, or impartiality." Rule 3.12 & 3.14 (formerly Canon 4H(1)). She might have to file a report regarding some, but not all, benefits she receives. Rule 3.13(B) & (C) (formerly Canon 4H).

Finally, except when expressly authorized by the Code, a judge cannot accept a gift, favor, bequest, or loan, if doing so violates the law or "would appear to a reasonable person to undermine the judge's independence, integrity, or impartiality." Rule 3.13(A) (formerly Canon 4D(5)). Rule 3.13(B) lists benefits a judge can receive without reporting, while Rule 3.13(C) lists items that the judge must report upon receipt. (*See also* former Canons 4D and 4H.)

7. **Duty to Report Professional Misconduct by Other Judges and Lawyers:** When a judge knows that a fellow judge or an attorney has engaged in misconduct raising a substantial question regarding the judge's fitness for office or the attorney's trustworthiness, honesty, or fitness to serve as an attorney, she must inform the appropriate disciplinary authority. Rule 2.15(A) & (B) (formerly Canons 3D(1) & (2)). When the judge receives information suggesting a substantial likelihood of misconduct, she "shall take appropriate action." Rule 2.15(C) & (D) (formerly Canons 3D(1) & (2)). For a more detailed discussion of judicial reporting responsibilities, see *supra* section 2(E), note 6.

8. **Other Provisions of the Code of Judicial Conduct:** The Code also requires a judge to competently and diligently conduct administrative responsibilities assigned to her, Rule 2.5(A) (formerly Canon 3C(1)), to require subordinates to comply with the standards applicable to the judge, Rule 2.12 (formerly Canon 3C(2)–(3)), and to act impartially and appropriately in making appointments, Rule 2.13 (formerly Canon 3C(4)–(5)).

Several of the Code's most important provisions have been discussed elsewhere in the text. For example, *supra* section 5F discusses the judicial disqualification provisions of Rule 2.11 (formerly Canons 3E and 3F). These provisions are supplemented by the Code's requirements that judges conduct extrajudicial activities to minimize their effect on judicial impartiality and responsibilities, Rules 3.1 and 3.11 (formerly Canons 4A and 4D(4)), and keep reasonably advised of circumstances that would require disqualification or other action, Rule 2.11(B) (formerly Canon 3E(2)), and by the requirement added to the Federal Rules of Civil Procedure in 2002 of a statement of corporate ownership by attorneys representing corporations. *See* Fed.R.Civ.P. 7.1. *Supra* section 6(A)(2)(b) discusses the Rule 2.9 (formerly Canon 3B(7)) prohibition against ex parte contact by judges. In addition, *supra* section 5(E), Notes on the Former Government Attorney's Current Firm, note 2, and *supra* section 6(C)(2) discuss Model Rule 1.12's restrictions on former judges and their firms representing parties that appeared before the judge.

9. **Application of the Code of Judicial Conduct:** The Code applies to all (including non-lawyers) serving as officers executing judicial system duties, including full- and part-time judges, referees, special masters, magistrates, court commissioners, and administrative law judges. *See* Model Code of Judicial Conduct, Application, § I (formerly Application of the Code of Judicial Conduct § A (following Canon 5)). Retired judges, periodic part-time judges, and pro tempore part-time judges are explicitly exempted from some of the Code's provisions, mostly to facilitate their nonjudicial activities, including the practice of law. *See* Model Code of Judicial Conduct, Application, §§ II–V (formerly Application of the Code of Judicial Conduct §§ B–E); *Howard v. Wilkes & McHugh, P.A.*, No. 06–2833–JPM, 2007 WL 4370584, at *14–15 (W.D.Tenn. Dec. 3, 2007) (rejecting argument for application of the state version of the Code due to an attorneys "prior temporary appointments as a Special Probate Judge"). The Code is enhanced by Model Rule 8.4(f), which makes it impermissible for a lawyer to knowingly assist a judge in violating it.

10. **A Final Note on Lawyer Trial Conduct and Judicial Discipline:** Consider again the "bookend" cases in this Chapter. In *Giangrasso v. Kittatinny Regional High School Board of Education*, a lawyer filed consistently frivolous lawsuits in what the court found was a vendetta against the school and school officials. In *In re Schapiro*, the judge repeatedly treated lawyers badly. As with attorneys, see *supra* section 6(A)(2)(e), note 5, instances of judicial misbehavior cannot be classified as extraordinary. For chronicles of several instances of judicial misbehavior, see Bruce A. Green & Rebecca Roiphe, *Regulating Discourtesy on the Bench: A Study in the Evolution of Judicial Independence*, 64 N.Y.U.Ann.Surv.Am.L. 497 (2009), David Pimentel, *The Reluctant Tattletale: Closing the Gap in Federal Judicial Discipline*, 76 Tenn.L.Rev. 909, 910 (2009) (observing that "it is difficult to find an attorney who practices in federal court who cannot relate at least one story about a judge's outrageous conduct"), Douglas R. Richmond, *Bullies on the Bench*, 72 La.L.Rev. 325 (2012), and Justin A. Barkley, Comment, *Judges Behaving Badly: The Disciplining of Judges by the Alabama Court of the Judiciary, from Richard Emmet to Roy Moore*, 29 J. Legal Prof. 191 (2004–2005).

These cases, along with the cataloguing of repeated misbehavior by the trial attorney in *In re Vincenti*, see *supra* section 6(A)(2)(e), are different from many of the cases you have read in this course, where attorneys faced close ethical questions. They should have left you asking the question: Why did it take so long for these lawyers and judges to be disciplined? Under Model

Rules 8.3(a) and 8.3(b) and Rule 2.15 (formerly Canon 3D) of the Model Code of Judicial Conduct, other lawyers and judges who observed previous instances of misconduct by these lawyers and judges had a duty to report misconduct that raised a substantial question as to fitness. As an attorney, when would you have reported either of the two lawyers or the judge? Does your answer reflect both the inherent competitiveness that is trial practice as well as the automatic respect that we prefer to extend to members of the judiciary? Does fear of repercussions from another lawyer or, perhaps worse yet, a judge, affect your answer? Does consideration of these realities help you understand why, in dealing with misconduct of lawyers and judges in the trial venue, rarely is discipline imposed for a single act of misconduct?

E.   THE LAWYER AS PROFESSIONAL AND HUMAN BEING

PROBLEM

After working hard as an undergraduate and doing well on the LSAT, you were accepted into law school. The day the official acceptance letter arrived was a happy one, because it meant you were well on your way to accomplishing your dream of becoming a lawyer.

That first year of law school was tough. For quite a while, it seemed like your professors were speaking a different language. A few of your new friends from your first year even got discouraged enough to leave. But you hung tough. Eventually things started to make sense. Almost without realizing it, you started to "think like a lawyer."

Now you are at least half way through law school, so you are starting to think about life after law school. The job market is tight. Your debt load continues to grow. Those things are not complete surprises, but they are still discouraging. The real problem, though, is that you are hearing things about lawyers that are starting to concern you. Some members of your family, and even some of your non-law school friends, seem less than pleased with your decision to enter the practice of law. The lawyer jokes they tell have a bite to them. The jokes are not that significant, of course, except for the message they send. You are starting to realize that there are some folks—maybe even a lot of them—who simply do not like lawyers.

You are also starting to notice that even some lawyers—maybe even a lot of them—who do not seem to be enjoying the practice of law. They complain about the long hours they spend at work instead of with their families. They are tired of fighting with other lawyers about things that seem trivial. They do not even like all of their clients.

To top it off, you have just spent a semester in a class called "Professional Responsibility." During that semester, you learned about a slew of rules that you will have to comply with when you practice law. Some of those rules seem to place inconsistent demands and expectations on you. Some require you to do unpleasant things. Some seem to go even further, possibly requiring you do things you would not do if you were not a lawyer—i.e., things that seem immoral to non-lawyers, but are required of lawyers.

QUESTIONS

(a) What should you do now? Is practicing law as tough a career as it sometimes seems?

(b) Are there steps you can take to enjoy practicing law, maybe not every hour of every day, but at least some of the time?

STEPHEN D. EASTON, MY LAST LECTURE: UNSOLICITED ADVICE FOR FUTURE AND CURRENT ATTORNEYS

56 South Carolina Law Review 229 (2004)a

INTRODUCTION

This is my last lecture, so it is the last chance I will have to exert any influence on you. * * * I have given serious thought to what I should talk to you about in this short time. I have [decided] to pass on a few suggestions about how to live the life of a lawyer. My suggestions are based largely upon my own efforts, both successful and unsuccessful, in the same endeavor.

Please note that this lecture's topic is not "How to Achieve Constant Happiness with a Law License." If there is a way to guarantee only happiness in your life as a lawyer, it has eluded my efforts to find it. This does not mean that life as a lawyer is without happiness: That has not been the case for me, and I certainly hope that it will not be the case for you. Indeed, my years as a lawyer have included several moments of not just happiness, but sheer, unmitigated ecstasy. Few experiences surpass successfully cross-examining a dishonest witness or hearing the clerk read the "right" verdict after years of hard work that included several days or weeks of sleepless nights and almost round-the-clock effort.

But no life in the law is filled only with glorious moments. If there is nothing quite as wonderful as getting that verdict you so desperately hoped and worked for, there is nothing quite as awful as getting the "wrong" verdict after you invested just as much hope and work. Along with the obvious downfalls, there are other, less notorious, but still difficult times ahead for you. You will: have clients, crime victims, or witnesses sobbing in your office; face agonizing decisions about how to handle thorny ethical dilemmas and other difficult issues; see the wee hours of many mornings inside your office; and make mistakes that directly hurt your clients.

My aim, then, is considerably more modest than trying to outline a guarantee of unending happiness. In addition to as much happiness as you can garner, my hope for you is that you achieve contentment and perhaps

---

a. In the "Last Lecture" series presented ... at the University of Missouri–Columbia, professors [we]re asked to assume that they are giving the last lecture that they will ever present to a group of students. The following Article ... is based upon this same premise: If you knew that this was your last chance to communicate with students, what would you say?

pride in knowing that, armed with your law license, you have helped your clients and your community far more often than you have hurt them, have conducted your practice with dignity and honor, and have enjoyed the ride. * * *

I. DETERMINE WHAT IS WORTH FIGHTING ABOUT, AND CONCEDE EVERYTHING ELSE

The first suggestion ought to be the one thing that attorneys could do that would most increase their satisfaction with their careers. In that spirit, I offer this advice: When you encounter a potential dispute with one of your opponents, be it large or small, do not fight with your opponent over that issue until you first determine whether it is important to fight about it. If it is, fight hard, fight smart, fight with conviction, passion, and perseverance, and fight to win. If it is not worth fighting about, concede that issue to your opponent, or find a compromise that is acceptable to you, your client, your opponent, and your opponent's client.

A. IDENTIFYING MATTERS THAT ARE NOT WORTH FIGHTING ABOUT

The key to determining whether to fight is this: Most issues that you could fight about are not worth fighting about. Once you discover this principle, your life as a lawyer will become far more enjoyable.

Generally, those of us who are attracted to this profession are fighters by instinct. In addition, we quickly learn that our primary loyalty in most instances is to our clients, and we are proud of how hard we are willing to fight for them. Nothing I say here should diminish your willingness to fight for your clients about important matters.

Instead, I am suggesting that many matters of potential conflict between attorneys are simply not matters of importance. The daily interactions between attorneys who represent opposing parties involve numerous potential matters for disagreement * * *. It is certainly possible to practice law by turning every interaction with opposing counsel into a chance to demonstrate your zeal, by barking at opposing counsel in telephone calls, face-to-face meetings, and letters, and by refusing to cooperate on any matter, regardless of how unimportant. If you adopt this strategy, you will not be alone. In fact, you might convince yourself that this approach to opposing counsel is required because any time you acquiesce to the other side on anything, you are somehow compromising your client's interests and therefore failing in your duty to zealously represent your client.

That, ladies and gentlemen, is hogwash. The Preamble to the Model Rules of Professional Conduct cautions lawyers to "zealously ... protect and pursue a client's legitimate interests, within the bounds of the law, *while maintaining a professional, courteous and civil attitude toward all persons involved in the legal system.*" In other words, though it might be easier to act like a jerk, whenever the possibility arises, on the grounds that you are somehow required to do so, the Model Rules hold you to a more nuanced and more difficult standard. * * *

B. FIGHTING THE GOOD FIGHT OVER MATTERS WORTH FIGHTING ABOUT

* * * Please note that my first suggestion is not "do not fight." In suggesting that *most* fights are not worth fighting, I do not mean that *no* fight is worth fighting. If no fight was worth fighting, there would be no need for lawyers.

Lawyers are called into action when there is a conflict. A seller wants to sell a piece of property for the highest possible price and a buyer wants to pay the lowest possible price. Business *A* wants a contract on terms favorable to Business *A* and Business *B* wants the contract on terms favorable to Business *B*. A plaintiff wants to receive money to compensate her for damages she suffered, and the defendant does not want to pay. Police officers and the victims of a crime want the defendant to be convicted and imprisoned, and the defendant wants to avoid conviction and prison.

Although it is perhaps understandable that the people involved in these conflicts do not relish them and therefore tend not to see the lawyers who manage these disputes in a favorable light, nothing is shameful about this work. Indeed, it is we lawyers who create the mechanism for people involved in serious conflicts to peacefully resolve their conflicts in a system that places a search for the truth as a centerpiece of dispute resolution. That is important and noble work.

Negotiating a settlement between conflicting parties is often the best way to resolve their conflict. But this is not always the case. Settlement, after all, is a resolution that requires compromise, and sometimes the parties should not compromise. In the criminal context, if a defendant has not committed a crime, the criminal justice system should not expect the defendant to plead guilty to *any* crime, even a lesser offense. Alternatively, if the prosecutor is capable of proving that the defendant has committed a serious felony, there should be some concern over the prosecutor allowing the defendant to plead guilty to a lesser charge merely as a matter of judicial economy. In the civil context, if the plaintiff's injuries were not caused by the defendant, the civil justice system should not expect the defendant to settle the case. Alternatively, if the defendant has caused the plaintiff's injuries, there should be some concern over the expectation that the plaintiff should forfeit some portion of the damages to which he or she is entitled merely as a matter of judicial economy.

In other words, although I applaud the growth of the alternative dispute resolution system and efforts to improve the mechanisms for settling cases where settlement is appropriate, I part company with those who suggest that trials are an inappropriate or overly costly means for resolving disputes. Some issues are worth fighting about, and lawyers serve both their clients and the justice system as a whole when they focus their fights on those matters. Therefore, I urge you to resist the considerable pressures that will be placed upon you to settle all cases. Some of the proudest moments for our profession have come when lawyers have refused to compromise their clients' rights and have instead defended those rights at trial. When the time comes, be prepared to fight the good fight.

II. Have the Courage to Win and to Lose

Once you have resolved yourself to fight, be prepared and willing to chance winning and losing, because both are valuable experiences that you can use to build your career. * * * Whenever you have the choice between winning and losing, I highly recommend winning. In the first place, victory is a lot more fun. In many offices, your coworkers will even throw you a party after the trial. In addition, winning helps you gain confidence, the trust of your bosses, and perhaps even new clients. Do everything you can do ethically to win.

Surprisingly, losing can also benefit your career. Defeat is, of course, no fun. But it has one huge advantage that winning will never have—it is far more educational. When you win, remembering all of the mistakes you made during the trial is almost impossible. When you lose, you remember every mistake.

I remember the details of my first criminal trial, which lasted a week. The jury got the case on Friday around 10:30 a.m. * * * Sometime around 1:30 a.m. Saturday morning, the clerk's office called. I dutifully drove back to the courthouse. After more than fifteen hours, I was almost certain the news would be bad. I was right.

For the rest of that night and the next, I slept like a baby. You know how a baby sleeps, of course. Every two or three hours, I would wake up screaming, then cry myself back to sleep. * * * After those two restless nights, I snuck into my office to put the file away so that it would be gone before the start of the next workweek. As I did so, I took out a yellow legal pad and started writing down all of the mistakes I made during the trial. I quickly filled page after page with my rantings about my performance. * * * Five years later, those notes became the basic outline for my trial practice book.

To this day, I wish I had won that trial. To this day, the mistakes I made in that trial gnaw at me. I have no doubt, however, that I learned more in that one unsuccessful and horrible trial than I have in the many happier trials before and after it.

Surprisingly, there is yet another unexpected benefit to your first loss. Once you have lost, you no longer fear that the next trial will result in your first loss. After the first loss, the worst thing that can happen in any future trial is simply another loss. Though losing can paralyze you if you let it, losing can also liberate you if you let it. * * * For what it is worth, I am happy to report that my second criminal trial, a case significantly tougher than the first, resulted in a win.

Eventually you will come to understand that the difference between winning and losing can be somewhat haphazard and is often controlled by factors other than your skills and effort. After all, we do not ask jurors to decide which lawyer did a better job of trying the case. We ask them to determine disputed issues of historical fact. If the system is working properly and the evidence is against you, you generally should lose, despite your best efforts. Therefore, in many cases, you cannot control whether you win or lose, but you can control your effort. Ultimately, you will come to realize that your satisfaction must come not from winning, but from giving your all.

Thus, the key is not winning or losing per se, but the willingness to do either. As Theodore Roosevelt said:

> The credit belongs to the man who is actually in the arena; whose face is marred by dust and sweat and blood; who strives valiantly; who errs and comes short again and again; who knows the great devotions, and spends himself in a worthy cause, who at the best knows in the end the triumph of high achievement; and who at the worst, if he fails, at least fails while daring greatly; so that his place shall never be with those cold and timid souls who know neither victory nor defeat.

The courtroom is a place of high achievement and excruciating loss. May you have the courage to encounter both.

III. BUILD AND GUARD A STRONG REPUTATION

A lawyer's single most important asset is his or her reputation. If judges and jurors trust you, they will believe your arguments and will be more likely to find in your favor. If opposing lawyers trust you, you will be able to secure more favorable settlements in negotiations. If your bosses— your potential partners—trust you, they will give you more responsibility and more desirable assignments. If your subordinates trust you, they will work harder for you. If your clients trust you, they will bring you additional cases and send you other clients.

You cannot demand trust. It is something you must earn. How do you earn trust as a lawyer? Two things are essential: honesty and hard work.

A. HONESTY * * *

You will encounter situations in which someone will ask a question that, if answered honestly, will hurt your position in the short run. A potential client with a big case, who is also interviewing other lawyers, will ask for your assessment of her chances of success. An opposing attorney will ask if you have located any witnesses to support your potential claim. A judge will ask you whether the cases from a particular circuit favor your position. If the answer to any of these questions is going to hurt you or your client, and you cannot avoid answering the question, what should you do?

The answer is simple to state, yet painful to implement: Answer the question honestly. These are, after all, the precise circumstances in which your reputation is formed—more so than the situations when it is easy to give an honest answer. Even a dishonest person has no trouble giving an honest answer when that answer helps him or her. When you tell a judge that "the cases from Circuit X go the other way, Your Honor, but let me explain why we should still win," you are establishing a reputation that will help you the next time when you say the cases support your position. Likewise, when you give your potential client, opposing counsel, or office colleagues an honest, but painful, answer, you are increasing the credibility of your other statements.

Although you are building your long-term reputation among the legal profession, this does not mean that the answer will not hurt you in the short run. When the judge hears that the cases from the controlling circuit are against you, you may lose your motion even though you presented your best argument for why you should still win. Similarly, the potential client may take her business elsewhere, the opposing attorney may take a tougher negotiating stance, and your colleagues may be upset with you. But that is the point. You build your reputation by being honest when it hurts.

B. HARD WORK

Honesty alone is not enough to build the reputation you need as an attorney, because honesty alone does not lead to credibility and trust. To be believable, you must be both honest and knowledgeable.

In the practice of law, knowledge comes from hard work. Your goal, though not always obtainable, should be to know more about your case than anyone else, especially opposing counsel. I do not mean to say that you should claim to have a superior level of knowledge. Instead, you should establish this authority by the accuracy of your statements and the precision of your questions during direct and cross-examination.

Unless you are one of the unusual individuals who is blessed with a photographic or other extraordinary memory, you can acquire that superior level of knowledge only through hard work. Real estate agents are fond of saying that the three most important things are location, location, and location. For a lawyer, the three most important things are preparation, preparation, and preparation. * * *

IV. TO THINE OWN SELF BE TRUE (AT LEAST EVERY ONCE IN A WHILE) * * *

A legal career will occasionally require you to do things that you would not do in your life outside the law. Most of the time, you should accept this requirement as the duty of serving as your clients' agent.

That having been said, I offer this admittedly controversial advice: Maintain, nurture, and develop your own sense of morality, even when it is sometimes inconsistent with your duties as an attorney. Though you should usually allow your duties under the law of professional responsibility to trump your personal conscience when acting as an attorney, be prepared to say you will not do things you find deplorable.

A. RESIST IMMORAL DEMANDS

Before you begin the practice of law, know how far you are willing to go in your duties as a lawyer, and mark well the line that you will not cross on a client's or an employer's behalf. Although your client has the power to force you to implement her wishes through the threat of firing you, you should retain the authority to say you are unwilling to be the lawyer who follows the client's orders to engage in activity you consider immoral, even if she can find another lawyer who is willing to engage in this activity.

To put this concept in context, * * * permit me to recommend the role model that my law school professors recommended to me as a student: Thomas More. As portrayed in the Robert Bolt play, *A Man for All Seasons*, a literary masterpiece that should be read or seen by all attorneys, More was an accomplished attorney who worked his way up to become Lord Chancellor, the highest attorney position in the English government. He certainly did not attain this position without performing exemplary service for his client, King Henry VIII. Presumably, he did not relish everything he did while climbing the career ladder to the exalted position of Lord Chancellor, but like other lawyers before and after him, he did those things for his client nonetheless. But More had his breaking point—his line beyond which he would not go. His line, perhaps like yours, was based in his faith. As a Catholic, More refused to break from his church and sanction King Henry VIII's divorce and remarriage. His client did not take kindly to his attorney's refusal to abide by his wishes. When More persisted in his refusal to sanction the divorce, King Henry VIII, acting through his government, stripped him of his office, imprisoned him, and eventually executed him.

For current purposes, ignore your view on the legitimacy of Thomas More's position on divorce, because that is not the point here. The point is that this man—this attorney—who had spent his life building his legal career through hard work and zealous representation of clients, would go only so far for a client, even when that client was the most powerful man on earth. For all his political and legal climbing, Thomas More was ultimately true to himself and his core beliefs. Though it is unlikely that you will be called upon to make the sacrifices demanded of Thomas More, I urge you to be prepared to draw the line, if necessary, and make the sacrifices that result from that stand.

B. ACT ETHICALLY WHEN NOBODY IS LOOKING

For most lawyers, dramatic instances of the conflict between personal morality and attorney amorality are rare. On the other hand, almost all lawyers will have to decide whether to be true to themselves in other more commonplace situations that often occur outside the view of anyone else. While judges, your opponents, your office colleagues, or your clients will review much of what you will do as a lawyer, you will also face numerous situations in which only you will know whether you are engaging in unethical conduct.

[Consider one example] that almost everyone destined to join a law firm will face. As a young associate, or even a partner, you will be expected to bill a certain number of hours every year. The billing requirement is rather high, so you must work extremely hard to meet it. At the end of the day, you realize that you have only worked 6.5 hours researching a particular case, instead of the 7.5 hours you need to bill that day. You realize, though, that the well-heeled client will never miss the money it pays for the extra hour and that nobody but you will ever know if you massage that 6.5 hours into 7.5 hours.

My friends, that is a very real dilemma. How you resolve billing requirement shortfalls will determine what kind of person you will be in the practice of law. While you can never be absolutely sure that "nobody" will know, you will not be an ethical lawyer if you follow the rules only because you could be caught. Sometimes you can be almost certain that "nobody" will know. But you will know. Ultimately, that is what matters.

As hard as it sometimes is to stay on the right side of the ethics line, you must stay on that side. Once you cross that line, you have started down a dangerous path that tends to have a snowball effect. Since you probably will not get "caught" by anyone the first time you cross the line, it will be that much easier to cross the line the next time, the time after that, and the time after that time.

V. CHOOSE YOUR FRIENDS CAREFULLY

Withdrawing from representing a client is the most common way out of the unusual situation when you refuse to perform an act demanded of you by the client. But withdrawal will not always be an available option. Even when you are allowed, or otherwise required, to withdraw, a judge can deny your request to withdraw, thereby forcing you to continue to represent a client and to use your resources and skills to further that client's interests.

Even when withdrawal is allowed, it is an unpleasant experience. Refusing to continue client representation on the basis of principle is no simple matter, especially if that client is treasured by your firm for its long-standing relationship with the firm. Your refusal to represent your firm's client may result in you looking not only for new clients, but for a new job. If your firm does not demand that you leave, your conscience might.

Even though attorneys cannot avoid all serious ethical dilemmas through good planning, foresight is important. Choose your employer and, to the extent possible, your clients carefully. Your life as a lawyer will be considerably less stressful if you work in an office with other ethical lawyers who value adherence to ethical principles, along with financial and other successes of the office. Also, your life as a lawyer will be less stressful if you represent clients who want to win through ethical means, not by cheating. * * *

VI. FIND WORK YOU ENJOY, THEN ENJOY YOUR WORK

The fact that staggering numbers of lawyers are unhappy in their jobs is one sad reality of modern practice. Why are so many lawyers dissatisfied with their jobs? Although a multitude of reasons come to mind, I am willing to suggest an important one: Too many lawyers take jobs that they do not want. With the many different types of work that an individual can do with a Juris Doctor degree and a law license, this is unfortunate and unnecessary.

With the wide variety of jobs available to lawyers, why do so many accept jobs they hate? One of the primary reasons is money. Too many lawyers try to maximize their incomes, instead of their happiness. This is understandable, to a degree, considering the circumstances a new lawyer now faces when looking for a first law job. Many of you have acquired staggering student loan debt, so the jobs that provide the most compensation seem the most attractive, regardless of whether you think you will enjoy the work required to earn that pay. But I am not willing to let you off the hook that easily. Although it may be difficult to handle your student loan debt on the salary of a public defender, a prosecutor, or a legal aid attorney, it is not impossible. Thousands of lawyers manage to make ends meet on these salaries.

Too often, students use student loan debt as an excuse to cover up the reality that we human beings, particularly in our country, keep score with money. Sometimes without realizing it, we seem to believe that those with higher incomes are automatically doing more important work. * * *

Not necessarily. I am not saying that there is anything wrong with pursuing a job with a firm that interviews on campus, if you have determined that working for this type of firm is what will make you happiest. I have worked at a large law firm and have twice been a partner in a smaller firm. During most of my time at those firms, I enjoyed the work I was doing. Therefore, I do not subscribe to the view that law firm life is necessarily a drudgery to be endured and not enjoyed.

But work can be a drudgery for those whose passions lie elsewhere. Before you take a job with a law firm, large or small, or any other type of law office, I urge you to ask yourself this question: Six months from now, when I am driving, riding, walking, or biking to work in the morning, will I look forward to getting there, or dread it? Of course, regardless of what job you accept, there will be occasional days when you dread going to work. If you expect those days to become the norm, though, do not take that job.

Too many students come to law school with dreams about what they will do with a law license, then toss those dreams aside to chase the highest paying job available. I am not suggesting that you should be inflexible and closed to new possibilities. Replacing one dream for another is perfectly acceptable. But do not drop a dream for a paycheck, regardless of its size. If you came to law school to become a trial attorney and that is still your dream, find a job that will lead you into the courtroom. If you dream of pursuing justice for the poor, pursue it. If you dream of prosecuting, take that assistant district attorney offer. If you want to represent criminal defendants, go to work in the public defender's office.

Many people, including loved ones, will tell you that you would be crazy to turn down higher paying work to chase a dream. Fine. Be a little crazy. But do not let someone else tell you what should be important to you, and never forget to pursue happiness.

[B]e prepared for the difficult task of getting out of a job that you thought you would enjoy, if it turns into a nightmare. Of course, I am not suggesting that you expect every day to be wonderful. Every lawyer's life has its share of tough moments, days, weeks, and months. Therefore, when these tough times arise, you should attempt to endure them, at least for a while. On the other hand, if the job turns out to be something that regularly makes you unhappy, look for a new job, even if it pays less. * * *

Once you find yourself in a job you enjoy, remember that you enjoy it. This task is just as important, but far easier, than getting the job. Every job, legal or not, has unpleasant aspects. The key to continuing to enjoy a good legal job is to recognize that those unpleasant aspects are simply the price you pay for the pleasure of having that good job. Concentrate on why you like your job. If you let yourself focus on the negative aspects of the job, you will no longer be able to remember why you liked your job in the first place.

VII.   RETURN PHONE CALLS

Although this suggestion does not merit equal billing with something like, "To thine own self be true," you would be astonished to know how many lawyers cannot follow this simple piece of advice. Furthermore, I am hoping to provide you not only with thoughts about how to handle the major ethical dilemmas that will only invade your career occasionally, but also with some practical advice that you can use on a daily basis.

Within that context, regular communication with your client is one of the most important obligations you have as a lawyer. In fact, the most common complaint filed with attorney disciplinary authorities is not that a lawyer has abused a client trust fund, or even that a lawyer has missed the statute of limitations deadline. The most common client complaint alleges that an attorney has failed to communicate with a client and, more specifically, that an attorney has not returned a client's telephone calls. * * *

More importantly, rifts between clients and attorneys are highly unpleasant affairs, even if they do not result in disciplinary complaints and inquiries. To avoid these unpleasant encounters, develop the habit of promptly returning phone calls, e-mails, and letters from clients. * * * Be sure to make a record of your call-back attempts, even if it is simply a note on a phone message sheet that you toss into the matter's correspondence file. This should offer some protection in case your client later complains, to you or to the disciplinary authorities, about your failure to return phone calls. * * *

While on the topic of practical tips that can help you avoid trouble, I will give you two more rules to follow. First, do not miss statutes of limitations or other deadlines. The best method to avoid deadline trouble is to have two separate and independent tickler systems. Different persons must run each system, and only one, by definition, can be you. If possible, only one of those systems should be computerized. Give the other person running a tickler system the right and duty to demand that you meet the tickler system deadlines.

Second, never steal from, "borrow" from, or otherwise mess with the client trust fund. Never means *never*, even if you or your children are starving. No circumstance justifies your use or misuse of your clients' funds. Doing so is the quickest way out of the legal profession.

VIII.   KNOW THE RULES

As you practice law, it may be helpful to remember how the contemporary social commentator, Jerry Seinfeld, described your job, in the opening monologue for a 1993 episode of the sitcom *Seinfeld*. He said:

> What are lawyers, really? To me a lawyer is basically the person that knows the rules of the country. We're all throwing the dice, playing the game, moving our pieces around the board, but if there's a problem, the lawyer is the only person that has read the inside of the top of the box.

Amazingly, despite that reputation, a substantial number of lawyers forget to peruse the inside of the box-top which, of course, is actually a series of books containing the rules that govern the practice of law.

Regardless of what type of practice you enter, you should be generally familiar with the locally adopted version of the ABA's Model Rules of Professional Conduct. After all, violations of these rules can result in disbarment or other unpleasant sanctions. * * * This does not mean that you must memorize the local professional responsibility rules. * * * Nonetheless, you should recognize when you are facing a problem that the rules may discuss. In other words, you need to know when to reach for the rule book. * * *

In addition to the professional responsibility rules, most lawyers should be familiar with the procedural or other rules that control their practices. For civil litigators, the Federal Rules of Civil Procedure and the equivalent state rules or statutes are critical. For prosecutors and criminal defense attorneys, the Federal Rules of Criminal Procedure and state analogs occupy a similarly important role. For both civil and criminal trial attorneys, the Federal Rules of Evidence and similar state rules or statutes are fundamental. For tax attorneys, certain provisions of the Internal Revenue Code are cornerstones of practice. For some transactional attorneys, the Uniform Commercial Code is the primary road map.

Over time, certain portions of the rules should become familiar to you, but others will remain in the "know-when-to-reach-for-the-book" category. What is critical to remember is that our profession is rule and statute based. Case law and appeals to a judge's sense of justice have their place in the practice of law, but a good lawyer also refers to the applicable rules or statutes. Grab the rules book or the code on occasion and spend some time perusing the rules or statutes. Because rules and statutes change, and because human memory is quite imperfect, the language of the rules might surprise you.

IX.   MAKE TIME FOR LIFE AND FOR LOVE * * *

Do not let the practice of law completely take over your life. It is perhaps true in all professions that no one looks back from his or her deathbed and says "I wish I had spent more time at the office," but we lawyers are particularly prone to spending too much time working and later regretting this failure to balance work and family.

Why do lawyers have this propensity? First, for an attorney, there is always more that can be done. For example, I have told you that preparation and hard work are critical to success. No matter how much you prepare, it is always possible to prepare more.

Second, on top of the constant pressure to work harder, which is certainly not unique to our profession, many lawyers must manage the particular pressure of the billable hour. In any practice where income is largely or wholly built upon billable hours, pressure to work more will always exist. * * * Based upon your salary and bonus rates, you will know how much you can earn in a given time period by working and billing that work. * * * You will be savvy enough to figure out your effective earning rate per hour in relatively short order. This is a good piece of information for you to have, but it is also dangerous. Once you know what you earn per hour, you will start to see that the old saying "time is money" is more valid in the law firm environment than in almost any other employment context. After you calculate your effective earning rate per hour, as long as there is billable work waiting to be done, you will find it impossible to ignore the "cost" of not doing that work.

Assume you are considering taking one of your children to a baseball game or a concert. The alternative is to stay at the office and complete some billable work that evening. "I sure would like to spend the evening with Tracy," you say to yourself, "but I could get in at least five billable hours if I just stay at work. Five times [a take home rate of] $50 is $250. Can I really afford to give up $250 with all the bills that are piling up at home?"

This question plagues every attorney whose compensation is tied to billings. My plea to you is that, when faced with the choice between family and work, at least a significant number of the times, you say, "I am spending the evening with Tracy."

I am not suggesting that you can always expect to answer the question that way. If you expect to always answer the question in favor of your family, you should try to find a career outside the law, because lawyers work extremely long hours.

What I am saying instead is that sometimes you must be willing to turn down income, and perhaps even career advancement, in favor of spending time with the people you love. Although this may seem obvious, it is not easy to accomplish. The economic and other pressures of the practice of law have caused far too many lawyers to decide against spending time with family too many times. * * *

Although these pressures are most extreme and direct for those whose compensation is tied to billings, other lawyers are not exempt from similar pressures. Prosecutors, public defenders, and other government attorneys earn promotions by putting in extra time. Even law professors feel the pressure to write more law review articles and spend more time preparing for class. In almost any legal career, there will be pressure to spend more time at the office. Sometimes you must give in to that pressure, but sometimes you must resist it.

Finally, in the interest of full disclosure, I feel compelled to point out that, perhaps more so than in other areas I have outlined here, I have failed at this balancing process. As I look back on my own career, my primary regret is that I have too often resolved the tension between work and home in favor of work. Sadly, I am quite confident that I am not alone in this assessment. The practice of law—any practice of law—can be a black hole that will swallow up all of your time and energy if you let it. One of your biggest challenges as a lawyer will be finding time to not be a lawyer.

X. GIVE BACK

We lawyers are given many gifts. As is often the case for beneficiaries of largess, we sometimes forget how much we have been given. Allow me to quickly list just a few of the things others have given you. First, though you have certainly sacrificed a lot for the law license you will soon obtain, so have your parents and other loved ones. Second, by the time you have graduated from law school, you will have been the beneficiary of at least twenty years of education, much, if not all, of it subsidized by taxpayers. Third, when you get that law license, you will become a member of the only profession to which an entire branch of government is devoted. Think of it: courthouses, judges, clerks, bailiffs, jurors, and many other resources, all taxpayer-funded. Although taxpayers may hate us, they have provided us with the infrastructure that makes our jobs possible.

So give something back. Not because you have to. Because you should. It is undignified to take without giving in return. Moreover, give because you can. You have skills that can be very valuable to the community. Finally, give because it feels good.

Perhaps the best place to start is to provide pro bono legal services to the poor, but this, at least in my view, is not the only valuable way to give back to the community. Aside from providing services to the poor, attorneys serve their communities by: sitting on boards of charitable organizations and offering their legal skills and advice without compensation; sacrificing income to run for office because they have unique skills for drafting legislation, advocating on behalf of constituencies, and resolving disputes; accepting low-paying legal jobs that help those who would otherwise go without legal services; and volunteering to assist public interest groups. There are countless ways for attorneys to offer their valuable combination of intellect, education, advocacy, conflict resolution, and logic skills. Find one or, better yet, several.

While service is on your mind, let me offer one specific suggestion. Before the end of your legal career, make sure you have been someone's Atticus Finch. At least once in your career, represent an unpopular client even though you will not make a dime (and may, in fact, lose income); even though your partners will complain about it; even though your other clients will be concerned that you are not paying adequate attention to them; and even though the judge will be irate that you are wasting her time.

Of course, the case need not be for a "client" in the traditional sense, and you do not have to be a private practitioner, but the idea is the same. I am talking about the kind of case that hurts you because it keeps you from other pressing concerns. At least one time, throw yourself into a case just because it is the right thing to do. At least one time, do what you came to law school to do—seek justice.

When you have represented your last client, that one case will mean more to you than any of the others, regardless of whether you "win" or simply spend every ounce of energy you can muster trying to win and nevertheless fail. There is no higher use for a law license than for the person who holds it to fight against all odds, and perhaps even against all common sense, for justice.

CONCLUSION

As you strive for the law license that will become the cornerstone of your career, there is much that you simply cannot know about how that law license will change your life. Although a time existed when most lawyers ended their careers practicing law in the same firm that they entered immediately after law school, that is no longer the case. These days, most careers, including most legal careers, include several job changes.

You do know this, however. The day will come, perhaps a lot sooner than you expect, when you will no longer practice law. When that day comes, if you are fortunate enough to be able to look back on your legal career, the two questions you should ask yourself in order to measure your career are:

First, did that law license you worked so hard to obtain make your life a richer experience?

Second, did you use your law license to make your corner of the world a better place?

My hope for you is as simple, and as complex, as this: When the time comes to ask yourself those two questions, I hope you can answer both of them "yes." For each question, "yes" is neither automatic nor easy, but for each, "yes" is achievable.

Different attorneys define success differently, but I believe any lawyer who can honestly answer "yes" to both questions is a success, while a lawyer who must answer "no" to either is not. As you pursue your "yes" answers, wherever and however you pursue them, I wish you the best your life can offer, in the practice of law and outside that practice. May your journey to those two "yes" answers be full of challenge, adventure, joy, and love, with just enough heartache to remind you that, like all significant accomplishments, those two "yes" answers do not come without sacrifice.

INDEX

References are to Pages

†